INTRODUCTION TO

THE STUDY OF THE

LAW OF THE CONSTITUTION

INTRODUCTION

TO THE STUDY OF THE

LAW OF THE CONSTITUTION

BY

A. V. DICEY, K.C., Hon. D.C.L.

OF THE INNER TEMPLE; FORMERLY VINERIAN PROFESSOR OF ENGLISH LAW,
FELLOW OF ALL SOULS COLLEGE, OXFORD,
HON. LL.D. CAMBRIDGE, GLASGOW, AND EDINBURGH

TENTH EDITION

WITH INTRODUCTION BY

E. C. S. WADE, Q.C., M.A., LL.D., F.B.A.

DOWNING PROFESSOR EMERITUS OF THE LAWS OF ENGLAND IN THE UNIVERSITY OF CAMBRIDGE; FELLOW OF GONVILLE AND CAIUS COLLEGE, CAMBRIDGE; HONORARY BENCHER OF INNER TEMPLE; HON. D.C.L. DURHAM

LONDON
MACMILLAN & CO LTD
NEW YORK · ST MARTIN'S PRESS
1965

First Edition 1885. *Second Edition* 1886.
Third Edition 1889. *Fourth Edition* 1893.
Fifth Edition 1897. *Sixth Edition* 1902.
Seventh Edition 1908. *Eighth Edition* 1915.
Reprinted 1920 (*twice*). *Reprinted* 1923, 1924, 1926, 1927, 1931.
Ninth Edition 1939. *Reprinted* 1941, 1945, 1948, 1950, 1952, 1956.
Tenth Edition 1959. *Reprinted* 1960, 1961, 1962, 1964 1965.

MACMILLAN AND COMPANY LIMITED
St Martin's Street London WC 2
also Bombay Calcutta Madras Melbourne

THE MACMILLAN COMPANY OF CANADA LIMITED
70 Bond Street Toronto 2

ST MARTIN'S PRESS INC
175 Fifth Avenue New York 10 NY

PRINTED IN GREAT BRITAIN

PREFACE TO THE FIRST EDITION

THIS book is (as its title imports) an introduction to the study of the law of the constitution; it does not pretend to be even a summary, much less a complete account of constitutional law. It deals only with two or three guiding principles which pervade the modern constitution of England. My object in publishing the work is to provide students with a manual which may impress these leading principles on their minds, and thus may enable them to study with benefit in Blackstone's *Commentaries* and other treatises of the like nature those legal topics which, taken together, make up the constitutional law of England. In furtherance of this design I have not only emphasised the doctrines (such, for example, as the sovereignty of Parliament) which are the foundation of the existing constitution, but have also constantly illustrated English constitutionalism by comparisons between it and the constitutionalism on the one hand of the United States, and on the other of the French Republic. Whether I have in any measure attained my object must be left to the judgment of my readers. It may perhaps be allowable to remind them that a book consisting of actually delivered lectures must, even though revised for publication, exhibit the characteristics inseparable from oral exposition, and that a treatise on the principles of the law of the constitution differs in its scope and purpose, as well from a constitutional history of England as from works like Bagehot's incomparable *English Constitution*, which analyse the practical working of our complicated system of modern Parliamentary government.

If, however, I insist on the fact that my book has a special aim of its own, nothing is further from my intention than to underrate the debt which I owe to the labours of the lawyers and historians who have composed works on the English constitution. Not a page of my lectures could have been written without constant reference to writers such as Blackstone, Hallam, Hearn, Gardiner, or Freeman, whose books are in the hands of every student. To three of these authors in particular I am so deeply indebted that it is a duty no less than a pleasure to make special acknowledgment of the extent of my obligations. Professor Hearn's *Government of England* has taught me more than any other single work of the way in which the labours of lawyers established in early times the elementary principles which form the basis of the constitution. Mr. Gardiner's *History of England* has suggested to me the conclusion on which, confirmed as I found it to be by all the information I could collect about French administrative law, stress is frequently laid in the course of the following pages, that the views of the prerogative maintained by Crown lawyers under the Tudors and the Stuarts bear a marked resemblance to the legal and administrative ideas which at the present day under the

Third Republic still support the *droit administratif* of France. To my friend and colleague Mr. Freeman I owe a debt of a somewhat different nature. His *Growth of the English Constitution* has been to me a model (far easier to admire than to imitate) of the mode in which dry and even abstruse topics may be made the subject of effective and popular exposition. The clear statement which that work contains of the difference between our so-called "written law" and "our conventional constitution," originally led me to seek for an answer to the inquiry, what may be the true source whence constitutional understandings, which are not laws, derive their binding power, whilst the equally vigorous statements contained in the same book of the aspect in which the growth of the constitution presents itself to an historian forced upon my attention the essential difference between the historical and the legal way of regarding our institutions, and compelled me to consider whether the habit of looking too exclusively at the steps by which the constitution has been developed does not prevent students from paying sufficient attention to the law of the constitution as it now actually exists. The possible weakness at any rate of the historical method as applied to the growth of institutions, is that it may induce men to think so much of the way in which an institution has come to be what it is, that they cease to consider with sufficient care what it is that an institution has become.

A. V. DICEY.

All Souls College,
Oxford, 1885.

PREFACE TO THE TENTH EDITION

Professor Dicey amended the text up to and including the Seventh Edition 1908, so as to "embody any change in or affecting the Constitution" which had occurred since 1885, for it was the main features of the constitution in that year which Dicey set out to describe. When the time came in 1914 for preparing what proved to be the last edition by the author, he adopted a different course. Instead of making further changes in the text he wrote a long Introduction which served two purposes.

(1) To trace and comment on the effect upon the main principles of the constitution of changes of law or of the working of the constitution during the period between 1885 and 1914, as the author had expounded it; and (2) to study and analyse the main constitutional ideas which could in 1914 fairly be called new, either because they had come into existence or had begun to exert a new influence during that period.

As on the occasion of the Ninth Edition in 1939, I have tried to follow this method. The influence of Dicey lies in the principles stated in the body of the book rather than in matters of contemporary controversy, such as figured in his Introduction in 1914. In this way it is possible to preserve the text of a book which is a classic and at the same time to review in the light of the present day those aspects of the constitution which Dicey used to illustrate his principles. Dicey never claimed that the constitutional ideas which he expounded were axiomatic principles which must abide for all time. Indeed as far back as 1885 he felt himself compelled "to consider whether the habit of looking too exclusively at the steps by which the constitution has been developed does not prevent students from paying sufficient attention to the law of the constitution as it now actually exists."[1] He was conscious of the danger of the historical method as applied to the growth of institutions, lest it might induce men to consider with insufficient care what it is that an institution has become.

It is idle to speculate as to the extent to which Dicey might have changed his views had he been writing of the modern constitution. My task has been to summarise some of the modifications which he himself suggested, in particular his ultimate acceptance of administrative law, and to discuss the application of his three principles under modern conditions. It is worth attention that Dicey's critics seldom suggest any addition to his three principles. They are concerned to determine whether his principles are right or wrong rather than to suggest there may be others. The last twenty years have seen a revival in the interest roused by the conception of the rule of law. There is little doubt that his conception of the rule of law has influenced the development of public law in this country more than his exposition of the sovereignty of Parliament and conventions of

[1] Preface, 1st ed., p. vii, *ante*.

the constitution. Nor has the interest in the rule of law been limited to the common law world.[1] Nowadays it is the principle of the sovereignty of Parliament which has come under attack with the emergence of independent States within the Commonwealth, all with their written constitutions. Even so, the critics have not succeeded in shaking the fundamental principle of the constitution of the United Kingdom, that in the eyes of the law Parliament is supreme. No one who is familiar with Dicey's book can read the Report of the Committee on Administrative Tribunals and Public Inquiries without recognising the unacknowledged influence which his exposition of the rule of law must have had upon the evidence given to the Committee and, we may assume, upon its deliberations.

Professor F. H. Lawson kindly allowed me to read in proof his essay *Dicey Revisited.* This essay is due for publication during 1959 in *Political Studies*, the Journal of the Political Studies Association. The author pleads that Dicey should be read with reference to the conditions existing when he wrote. He is convinced that to place the rule of law in its historical setting will lead to a better understanding. Although Dicey has often been criticised for his failure to understand *droit administratif*, Professor Lawson argues convincingly that Dicey had a greater awareness of the subject as it developed between 1885 and 1908 than is commonly credited to him. He makes the important point that even as late as 1908 wrongs committed by public officials were mainly of the type which involved interference with personal liberty or property rather than cases where damage was caused

[1] Introduction, pp. cvi-cx, *post*.

negligently by doing something which was otherwise lawful. There is an interesting explanation of why Dicey overlooked the writ of certiorari; it is thought that he was over-insistent in his search for deterring the official who was a wrong-doer and so overlooked the main instrument for obtaining the annulment of illegal acts where no question of an award of damages against the responsible official could arise. These are only two highlights in a closely reasoned analysis of Dicey's explanation of the rule of law. Professor Lawson, as a comparative lawyer, has done a great deal to explain Dicey's method, and in particular the contents of Chapter XII, "Rule of Law compared with *Droit Administratif.*"

E. C. S. WADE.

GONVILLE AND CAIUS COLLEGE,
CAMBRIDGE, *October*, 1958.

CONTENTS

OUTLINE OF SUBJECT

PART I

THE SOVEREIGNTY OF PARLIAMENT

CHAPTER I

CHAPTER II

CHAPTER III

PART II

THE RULE OF LAW

CHAPTER IV

CHAPTER V

CHAPTER VI

CHAPTER VII

CHAPTER VIII

CHAPTER IX

CHAPTER X

CHAPTER XI

CHAPTER XII

CHAPTER XIII

PART III

THE CONNECTION BETWEEN THE LAW OF THE CONSTITUTION AND THE CONVENTIONS OF THE CONSTITUTION

CHAPTER XIV

CHAPTER XV

APPENDICES

TABLE OF ABBREVIATIONS

C.B.R.	= Canadian Bar Review.
C.L.C.	= *Constitutional Laws of the Commonwealth*, Vol. I, by Sir Ivor Jennings (Clarendon Press).
C.L.J.	= Cambridge Law Journal.
H.L. or H.C. Deb.	= House of Lords (or Commons) Debates (Hansard).
K. & L.	= *Cases in Constitutional Law*, by Sir David Keir and Professor F. H. Lawson, 4th edition (Clarendon Press).
L.Q.R.	= Law Quarterly Review.
M.L.R.	= Modern Law Review.
S.I.	= Statutory Instrument.
S.R. & O.	= Statutory Rule and Order.

INTRODUCTION

CONTENTS OF INTRODUCTION

INTRODUCTION

(1) GENERAL

DICEY'S warning of the danger of not paying "sufficient attention to the law of the constitution as it now actually exists "[1] is of even greater importance to-day. The constitution of 1958 is not the constitution of 1885. The historical method as applied to the growth both of Government and Parliament of the United Kingdom could indeed, in the words of the author, induce men to think so much of the way in which those institutions have come to be what they are that they would cease to consider with sufficient care what they have become in the second half of the twentieth century with all the impact of two World Wars behind them. None the less the impression made by *The Law of the Constitution* upon the study of public law throughout the Commonwealth, and to some extent even abroad, has remained such that there has been an even greater danger of " looking too exclusively at the steps by which the constitution has been developed "[1] since the author's lifetime, with the result that insufficient attention may be paid to the present state of the law and practice of the constitution. It is the purpose

[1] 1st ed. (1885), Preface, p. vii, *ante*.

of this introduction in some measure to equate the three principles, as Dicey understood them, to modern conditions. The method of depicting the constitution in terms of principles rather than by description of its details is one which naturally attracts the political scientist, but it is for the lawyer to ensure that the existing rules of constitutional law are not lost in the generalisations which necessarily accompany an exposition of principles. The constitution of the United Kingdom offers little material to students of constitutional theory for an examination of the limits of legal authority. But constitutional developments in the Commonwealth, based as they invariably are on parliamentary systems of government, sometimes in a different political background, have ensured that parliamentary sovereignty is no longer confined to the legislature of the United Kingdom. In its overseas setting, the expression has both political and legal implications which cannot be entirely explained by reference to the historical evolution of the Parliament at Westminster. These implications have lately been examined by a student of politics and the result is contained in Dr. Geoffrey Marshall's *Parliamentary Sovereignty and the Commonwealth.*[1]

It may be said of Dicey that his continuing influence on the study of the constitution would have been less enduring if he had not written primarily as a lawyer. Like Dicey we must never lose sight of what are the rules of the constitution in any endeavour to bring up to date the application of the sovereignty of Parliament and the rule of law to modern conditions. In the sphere of conventions a

[1] Clarendon Press, 1957.

lawyer naturally treads more warily, though he has to-day the advantage which was denied to the author of having seen several important constitutional conventions enacted as law in the course of a lifetime.

There is another aspect of this book which no editor can hope to reproduce in an introduction. Dicey was a master of exposition by the written word. There is little doubt that generations of readers have been convinced of the truth of his assertions and so his views at one time were in some danger of being regarded as axiomatic. It can be the experience of few writers to find in the terms of reference to a Royal Commission or important Departmental Committee a direction that the inquiry should be into the very principles which the writer had propounded. Yet it was in 1929, within a few years after Dicey's death, that the Lord Chancellor of the day required the Committee on Ministers' Powers to report what safeguards were desirable or necessary to secure the constitutional principles of the sovereignty of Parliament and the supremacy of the law. The report of the Committee [1] showed that the authority of the *Law of the Constitution* was accepted fifty years after its first appearance.

It has, however, for some years now been apparent to those who study the working of modern government that both the sovereignty of Parliament and the principle of the rule of law can only with some difficulty be reconciled with a state of affairs in which Governments dictate legislation to Parliament and administer public services which demand sacrifices of individual liberty of action, whether those services

[1] Cmd. 4060, 1932.

are part of the modern welfare State or are the result of external political or economic pressure. The very functions of Governments and Parliaments were different in the heyday of the Whig tradition of *laissez faire* which coincided with the first edition of this book. By 1914, when Dicey published the second edition of his *Law and Opinion in England during the Nineteenth Century*, he recorded in the preface that "by 1900 the doctrine of *laissez faire*, in spite of the large element of truth which it contains, had more or less lost its hold upon the English people." He later saw with some misgivings the advent of national health insurance and legislation to regulate wages and conditions of employment in certain important industries. His latest published views on what is nowadays accepted to be administrative law are contained in an article in the *Law Quarterly Review* in 1915 which is reproduced in the appendix.[1] It is tempting to speculate more than forty years later what view a writer of an earlier generation would take of the modern welfare State. It is more profitable to try and explain how well-established principles such as the sovereignty of Parliament and the rule of law can be reconciled with changing social and economic conditions.

It is undeniable that Parliament has suffered in the eyes of the general public a loss of prestige over the last seventy years. This is not the place to discuss what changes are needed for modernising antiquated procedure. The exercise of sovereignty cannot, however, be entirely divorced from procedural rules. There is, too, little doubt that the

[1] 31 L.Q.R. 148; App. 2, *post*.

attractions of a career in Parliament, and more particularly in the House of Commons, are less obvious under modern conditions. The working of the party system, particularly when the difference in numbers between Government and Opposition is small, has tended to destroy the part-time nature of membership and so to introduce the professional politician who, in the past, could seldom be found, at all events on the back benches. But the body which exercises sovereignty may well be more dangerous to stability than in the days when Parliament commanded universal respect. It must not be forgotten that the inevitable consequence of the supremacy of Parliament in the legislative field is that there can be no check upon the unscrupulous use of power by a Government which finds itself in command of a majority in the House of Commons. It is less than thirty years ago that a leader of one of the major political parties then in opposition suggested that parliamentary sovereignty should be used to abolish the Second Chamber and to introduce government by decree for the purpose of effecting an economic revolution as soon as his party obtained power. We are so accustomed to constitutional evolution as opposed to revolution that we are apt to forget the dangers which may arise should there be a further decline in the prestige which attaches to membership of Parliament. The character of the body affects its authority with the general public as well as its capacity for working good or ill. But the changing nature of the prestige of Parliament has not been accompanied by any change in the attitude of the courts to the legislation which Parliament enacts.

It is here that the lawyer must resist any temptation to probe too deeply into the nature of sovereignty. Rather must he emphasise that it is still for Parliament and for Parliament alone finally to determine what shall be the law of the land, no matter the changing characteristics of the law makers and those influences which determine what law they shall make.

The House of Commons once performed the function of resisting the demands of the Crown for supply until its grievances had been redressed. Lip service is still paid to this historic function when, at the beginning of each session, there is introduced into each House of Parliament a Bill with an antiquated title so that a measure of their own choice can be considered in priority to government business. This picturesque survival must not obscure the fact that the modern House of Commons is a forum in which both parties put forward incessant demands for the remedying of some social or economic ill of the body politic. The remedy necessarily increases the demands of the Government for supply, *i.e.* for the money necessary to administer the control or service which is demanded. The changing conditions have all been brought about by the action of Parliament. Whether the change in the law is fundamental or trivial, Parliament, and only Parliament, can alter the law, and whatever Parliament declares to be the law, the courts must accept. But other countries have introduced similar measures of social and economic improvements comparable with those which have been enacted by Parliament. It is clear that the doctrine of the sovereignty of Parliament does not prevail in most, if not all of those countries, because they are governed under written constitutions which limit the capacity of the legislature in respect of certain classes of legislation. One may admit that this country could have achieved all that it has without the doctrine of the sovereignty of Parliament being a feature of the constitution. That, however, does not alter the proposition so emphatically propounded by Dicey that in the United Kingdom there is no law which Parliament cannot change. It may be that the changes of the law have operated more smoothly here than elsewhere because there can be no challenge to the validity of any enactment.

On the other hand, if one seeks to reconcile what the author understood by the rule of law with the sovereignty of Parliament, it cannot be denied that legislation has shifted the emphasis on individual liberty to the provision of services for the public good. It was Dicey's purpose to reconcile the two principles. This he did by stressing the independent position which the courts enjoyed under the constitution. It was the preservation of the rule of law which rested upon the independence of the judges. Parliament guaranteed that independence ; the judges in their turn accepted that Parliament had the last word in declaring what law was to prevail. In 1958 it may be more difficult to attempt such a reconciliation, if only because the sphere of operation of the common law has been repeatedly circumscribed by statute. If we accept, as we must, that the administration of the modern statutory services gives a wide discretion to the administrator, it follows that he is in a position to encroach upon individual liberty of action. Even so it remains important to ensure that all administration is conducted in accordance with the law. No longer do we look to the common law as the protector of individual liberty in certain spheres. But in some fields it remains as important as ever, particularly with regard to freedom of the person and freedom of speech. Even where in other directions statute law, whether directly enacted by Parliament or by statutory instrument made under authority of Parliament by the Executive, provides that the course of action of the individual is less a matter of his own choice than that of a governmental authority, the independence of the Judiciary guarantees that there shall be no excess or abuse of the power which has been entrusted to that agency by Parliament. It is no longer merely a question of the State regulating public expenditure. Nowadays it seeks also to control the use of property and through the incidence of taxation and compulsory insurance to legislate for the general standard of living. The wider administrative activities extend, the more important it is that all administration should be in accordance with law. It is of course possible for Parliament using its sovereignty to decree that administration should be at the absolute discretion of the administrator. The fact that it seldom, if ever, grants so wide a discretion is due not least to the influence of the concept of the rule of law which in its historical setting grew up to arm first Parliament and later the judges with the power to resist the tyranny of Kings and Queens.

Nowadays there is a tendency for political scientists to discuss problems which, to the lawyer at all events, seem more legal than political. This is particularly true with regard to the doctrine of the sovereignty of Parliament. In defence of the political scientist it must be admitted that the lawyer cannot explain those parts of the constitution which are laws in the strict sense without explaining their political background. The author said in relation to constitutional conventions or understandings that the subject was "not one of law but of politics, and need trouble no lawyer or the class of any professor of law."[1] But this did not prevent him from considering the internal and external limitations which are placed upon the exercise of parliamentary supremacy and thus to distinguish between the legal and the political sovereign. Moreover he included the political code of conventions in his exposition of the constitution. Constitutional law and political science are divided by a line which it is hard to distinguish. It does not help much if the lawyer accuses the political scientist of invading his territory, but it behoves each to be acquainted with the technique of the other's studies. This point hardly needs illustrating; how can such measures as the Parliament Acts, 1911, and 1949, or the Statute of Westminster, 1931, be understood without reference to their political background? The latter measure, as will be seen, affords the best illustration of the difficulty of distinguishing between convention and law. Acknowledgment of the lawyer's debt to political science must not, however, conceal the fact that constitutional arrangements in the United Kingdom are not very readily susceptible to theoretical treatment. The analysis of a written constitution which endeavours to put into practical working scientific theories may seem natural,

[1] P. 31.

particularly to foreign readers. But this method is denied to the student of the constitution of the United Kingdom.

How should a study of the text of *The Law of the Constitution* be approached at the present day? Three methods are possible:

(i) to accept Dicey's principles, and more particularly the sovereignty of Parliament and the rule of law, as portraying only the period of which he wrote;

(ii) to regard these principles critically and in the light of future events to admit that they were only partially true of the nineteenth century and certainly inapplicable to-day;

(iii) to accept these principles, supplemented if need be by later developments, and to show how they can be fitted into modern public law.

The first is, of course, the easiest method, for it avoids the need to reconcile the past with the present. The critics have naturally concentrated on the second method of approach. The third method has perhaps found—despite the weight of criticism—the most favour. Certainly no one will deny that many generations of lawyers and politicians have had their interest in public law and government first aroused by studying *The Law of the Constitution.* Reference has already been made to the terms of reference given to the Committee on Ministers' Powers which could only have been drawn by one trained in the traditions of Dicey. If the critics have been many, there have been not a few defenders; among the latter was Sir William Holdsworth, and lately a notable contribution has come from the pen of the Professor of Comparative Law of the University of Oxford, Dr. F. H. Lawson, who, in his *Dicey Revisited*,[1] has sought to place the book in what he describes as "the shifting contemporary settings of its various editions." So far at all events as this article is limited to the rule of law and Dicey's views on *droit administratif*, he has succeeded in showing that the author was well aware of the developments which took place in *droit administratif* at the turn of the century.

Much attention has lately been directed to the challenge to liberty which has been discussed in the Report of the Committee on Administrative Tribunals and Public Inquiries, presided over by Sir Oliver Franks.[2] It was no part of the task of this Committee to examine the principle of the rule of law—their terms of reference required them to investigate, one by one, a limited range of processes for settling disputes by resort to tribunals or public inquiries where subject and authority come into conflict. The test which this Committee decided to apply was not the rule of law by that title but the simpler conceptions of openness, fairness and impartiality. No one can read the general parts of this report, which seeks to extend the impartiality of the judges to newer judicial processes, without recognising that the processes of the law which Dicey found as the safeguard of freedom of the person, of discussion and of association in public meeting, were in the view of the Committee applicable to that field of contest which nowadays attracts so much criticism, namely, the

[1] To be published during 1959 in *Political Studies*, the Journal of the Political Studies Association.

[2] Cmnd. 218, 1957.

controlled use of property where the public interest competes with the wishes of the private owner. This revival of interest in the rule of law can be traced back to the Second World War and is a new challenge to Dicey's critics. The bulk of the recommendations of the Committee have been accepted and put into force by the Tribunals and Inquiries Act, 1958, or by administrative action.

(2) OUTLINE OF THE SUBJECT

It is important to emphasise the limits which the author stated in his Outline of the Subject[1] as being imposed upon the functions of a professor of constitutional law. He did not regard himself as called upon to perform the part either of a critic or of an apologist or of a eulogist, but simply as an expounder. He was keenly aware of the special difficulties imposed on teachers who sought to expound the provisions of an unwritten constitution. For him there was no definite assignable part of the law of his country which could be recorded as the constitution of the United Kingdom. In order to appreciate Dicey's choice of the three guiding principles on which he concentrated his attention, one must stress that rules recognised by the courts were his only direct concern. Nevertheless we do not find that he illustrates the doctrine of the supremacy of Parliament by reference to its source in decided cases brought before the courts. The contention that conventions of the constitution depended in the last resort upon the courts is, on his own admission,

[1] Pp. 1-35, *post*.

doubtful and speculative.[1] But the reader is left in no doubt in the exposition of the rule of law that it is to the courts and to the courts alone that the principles of the English Constitution are due.

Two things strike the reader who has some acquaintance with modern governmental organisation in reading the author's outline:

(i) Dicey was only concerned with the organs which had attracted the exclusive attention of most writers on the constitution up to his time: Parliament; the Crown, with special regard to the prerogative in relation to cabinet government; the High Court and its duty to recognise the supremacy of Parliament and to administer common law. With administration as such he was only concerned in a purely negative way to point out how the courts can control excesses of administrative power in relation to such matters as personal liberty, freedom of speech and police action in dealing with public meetings.

(ii) No attempt is made to examine the actual working of the machinery of administrative government.

In the Introduction to the last edition, these points were stated to account in part for the almost complete disregard by the author of modern statute law, which some critics have considered to be a weakness in the book. In view, however, of his later *Law and Opinion during the 19th Century*, in which he examined the trend of current legislation, the omission must have been a deliberate one. No doubt he regarded administration as concerned too much with

[1] See note 4 to p. 26.

detailed function and was therefore unwilling to include it as part of constitutional law. This is borne out by his treatment of the Army and the Revenue. He dwells upon these branches of the public services only in order to show how they are subordinated to the law. All this was entirely in accordance with tradition. Even to-day it is customary to take a narrow view of constitutional law, postponing to a subsequent course on administrative law the examination of the operation of the public services. It was Maitland who was one of the first to plead for a wider view of the subject.[1] This plea came in Maitland's lectures two or three years after the first edition of *The Law of the Constitution*.[2] But Dicey himself said the field had not been fully mapped out. Austin had limited the subject to a consideration of the organs exercising the sovereign power.

It has long been admitted that no branch of law has extended so widely as constitutional law. To-day, even if the student accepts Dicey's own limitation of only being concerned with rules recognised by the courts in their applications to the constitution, he will necessarily include some of the law administered by, at all events, the major Government Departments and local authorities as well as the services which Parliament has entrusted to statutory bodies, such as the Transport Commission, the National Health Service Hospital Boards and Executive Councils and the Assistance Board. In the sphere of legal remedies he must study prohibition, certiorari and mandamus, and not merely habeas

[1] *Constitutional History of England* (1920), pp. 526-539.

[2] Pp. 33-34, *post*.

corpus; actions for declarations and injunctions and relator actions, together with the machinery of some of the more important administrative tribunals. He must be in a position at least to appreciate the constitutional relationship of the United Kingdom with the other member States of the Commonwealth and with Colonial Territories. Clearly the fuller the examination of the working of the government machine extends, in contrast to what Maitland called "its showy parts," the more difficult it becomes to accept unchallenged axiomatic principles. If Dicey had wished to discuss the positive aspect of administration, he would have had to explain even in 1885 that much of it was based upon Acts of Parliament which determined the position of the Crown and its servants and had already established a number of statutory authorities which, though part of government, were not under the Crown. He would not have regarded this development as establishing that the law of the constitution proceeded from the rights of individuals as defined and enforced by the courts.[1] Nor would he have regarded as arbitrary power, in contrast to regular law, the statutory powers of public servants in relation to the various services.

These are some of the considerations which must be borne in mind if we are to understand the background in which Dicey wrote. They admittedly make the book more valuable to the study of the history of the nineteenth century than to the study of modern public law. But Dicey was writing for his own age; it was not at the outset his intention to be definitive. Moreover, he expressly warned his readers against

[1] P. 203, *post*.

"ceasing to consider with sufficient care what it is that an institution has become."[1]

In considering the three guiding principles formulated in the text, we are not so much concerned in explaining how they came to be enunciated as to review them in the light of nearly seventy-five years. This was the method which the author adopted in later editions. In 1914, in preparing the eighth edition, he left unaltered the text of the seventh (1908) edition and embodied his views on recent developments in a long Introduction which to some extent concentrated on then current issues. The present Introduction, while it is not intended to pass over without comment important constitutional changes, is more concerned with noting the influence which *The Law of the Constitution* has to-day. In particular, in the last few years there has been a new challenge to the doctrine of the sovereignty of Parliament, while the rule of law, which came under fire from many quarters in the years between the two World Wars, is nowadays accepted, with full recognition of the appropriate adjustments, as at least a desirable end to be attained by a democratic legal system.

(3) THE SOVEREIGNTY OF PARLIAMENT

The Principle and its Application.—The principle of parliamentary sovereignty was repeated by the author in each edition of this book up to 1914 when he emphasised that the truth of the doctrines had never been denied. They were :

(1) Parliament has the right to make or unmake any law whatever.

[1] Preface to 1st ed., p. vii, *ante*.

(2) No person or body is recognised by the law of England as having a right to override or set aside the legislation of Parliament.

(3) The right or power of Parliament extends to every part of the Queen's dominions.

Despite recent criticism,[1] it is still true to-day as a proposition of the law of the United Kingdom to say that Parliament has the right to make or unmake any law whatever. Nor can any court within the United Kingdom set aside the provisions of an Act of Parliament. All that a court of law can do with such an Act is to apply it, *i.e.* to interpret the meaning of the enactment.[2] This is enough to satisfy the lawyer, but it must be admitted that the conception is purely a legal one. The examples which the author gives in the text [3] can be multiplied by reference to recent enactments, the Parliament Act, 1911, the Government of Ireland Act, 1920, the Irish Free State (Agreement) Act, 1922, and His Majesty's Declaration of Abdication Act, 1936. It is probably also safe to include the Statute of Westminster, 1931, and more certainly the Acts giving independent status to other member States of the Commonwealth, such as the Indian Independence Act, 1947.

The fact that a court of law cannot question the exercise of legislative power is not conclusive of the extent of that power.[4] An excess of legislative power may be a matter between the legislature and the electors. As Dicey pointed out, neither in France

[1] Pp. lvii-lxvi, *post.*

[2] Pp. xliii-xliv, *post.*

[3] Pp. 64-70, *post.*

[4] See Jennings, *The Law and the Constitution*, 4th ed., pp. 139-140.

nor in Belgium do the judges pronounce upon the constitutionality of enactments, despite the fact that those States possess formal constitutions of the rigid type. Indeed it is unusual in a unitary State, as opposed to a State governed under a federal constitution, to find that the courts can pass judgment on the validity of legislation; but within the Commonwealth this is not the case with South Africa and Ceylon.

The question whether or not the sovereign can bind himself cannot be answered by a mere assertion of supremacy. Naturally the issue is more complex when, as in a modern democratic society, sovereignty is vested in a legislative body of two chambers containing some hundreds of members. With a federal State where powers are divided between the central Government and Parliament and the corresponding organs in the member States which go to make up the federation, the sole source of ultimate authority will not be vested in a single legislature acting by itself. Otherwise it would be within the power of the federal legislature to tip the balance in favour of the federation and against the member States, and so destroy the agreement upon which the federal solution itself rested. In particular, the process of legislation on constitutional matters will inevitably be subject to special rules of procedure for ensuring the concurrence of at least a majority of the member States in any change proposed by the federation. There are within the Commonwealth already six examples of federal States, only one of which existed at the time of the first edition of this book. Even in the case of the unitary States within the Commonwealth, since each has its separate written constitution, there may be doubts as to the application of the sovereignty of the legislature, as understood by the author, particularly where the written constitution seeks to entrench, *i.e.* to subject to special legislative procedure certain important constitutional topics. If we accept, as did Dicey, the doctrine of unqualified legal supremacy in its application to the Queen in Parliament of the United Kingdom, we must face the difficulties which the application of the doctrine has caused in Commonwealth States. The Statute of Westminster, 1931, is a case in point. Section 4 of this Statute enacts that the Parliament of the United Kingdom shall not for the future legislate for a Dominion without the request and consent of that Dominion. If the right and power of Parliament extends, as the author claimed, to all realms and territories under the Crown, it must follow that it is within the power of Parliament to repeal Section 4 at a future date. Everybody knows that even the suggestion that such a power could be exercised would disrupt the Commonwealth and that the sovereignty which it was the purpose of the Statute of Westminster to confer on members of the Commonwealth where it was so desired, having once been granted, cannot be revoked as a matter of practical politics. To this matter we shall return hereafter.[1]

Federal government is a system of government which embodies a division of powers between a central and a number of regional authorities. Each of these "in its own sphere is co-ordinate with the others and independent of them." [2] This involves a

[1] Pp. xlix-lii, *post*.

[2] K. C. Wheare, *Federal Government*, 3rd ed., pp. 32-33.

division of plenary powers and such a division is a negation of sovereignty. Yet somewhere lies the power to change this division. Wherever that power rests, there is to be found legal sovereignty. In the nature of things it will seldom be invoked, though as the cases show, the federal constitution may be strained.

The law reports abound with decisions of the Judicial Committee of the Privy Council which seek to determine where lies legislative power within the Dominion of Canada and the Commonwealth of Australia. In the case of Canada the source of authoritative decisions is nowadays confined to those of the Canadian Supreme Court, but Australia still allows reference of its constitutional battles to the Board room in Downing Street.[1]

To return to Dicey's exposition of the sovereignty of the Parliament of the United Kingdom, the method of argument was to show that certain alleged limitations on the powers of Parliament did not exist. His account covers the subordination to Parliament of the Queen in Council which dates from *The Case of Proclamations*, 1610;[2] he shows how resolutions of one House of Parliament cannot alter the law; that sovereignty as a matter of law does not lie in the electorate, whose right is restricted to choosing members of Parliament; nor yet in the law courts, where even if a decision is equivalent to judicial legislation it nevertheless remains subject to repeal by Parliament. He argues that there are no legal limitations which

[1] For an authoritative work on Federalism, see K. C. Wheare, *Federal Government*, 3rd ed., 1953.

[2] 12 Co. Rep. 74; K. & L. 78.

can be explained by reference to moral law; in fact the plea that an Act of Parliament was contrary to natural justice failed as far back as the seventeenth century. Whatever may have been the powers of the Crown to legislate under the prerogative by ordinance or proclamation in earlier centuries, no doubt can now be cast upon the control over the prerogative power which is frequently exercised by Parliament. Nor does sovereignty mean that any one Parliament can prevent the repeal of its enactments by a succeeding Parliament.

Purely as a legal doctrine it is too late to question the supremacy of Parliament.

> The question, who is legal sovereign? stands quite apart from the questions, why is he sovereign? and who made him sovereign? The historical facts which have vested power in any given sovereign, as well as the moral grounds on which he is entitled to obedience, lie outside the questions with which the law is concerned, and belong to historical or to political philosophy or to ethics; and nothing but confusion is caused by introducing them into purely legal questions of the determination of the sovereign and the definition of his powers.[1]

With this citation in mind and with due regard to the volume of current literature which relates to the political philosophy of the doctrine of the sovereignty of Parliament, it is necessary to emphasise that Dicey was concerned first and foremost with the doctrine as a characteristic of the body which is now the Parliament of Great Britain and Northern Ireland. As a matter of history, the doctrine is comparatively

[1] Bryce, *Studies in History and Jurisprudence* (1901), vol. ii, p. 57, cited by D. V. Cowen in *Legislature and Judiciary*, 15 M.L.R. at pp. 295-296.

recent; in its present form it can be traced to the alliance effected in the seventeenth century between Parliament and the common lawyers. It is not derived from statute or any formal constitutional enactment. It was essential if royal power was to be subordinated to the law as declared by Parliament. In order to achieve this, the lawyers had to abandon, however reluctantly, the claim that Parliament could not legislate in derogation of the principles of the common law. Since Parliament had at last established that the King as head of the Executive could no longer challenge the validity of what was enacted by the King in Parliament, it had to follow that his subjects were equally so bound. No one any longer could ask a court to annul or otherwise challenge an Act of Parliament. But it was established earlier that the court could not inquire into the legislative process. In the famous *Case of Shipmoney—Hampden's Case*, 1637,[1] the court accepted the so-called Statutum de Tallagio non concedendo as an Act of Parliament because it appeared on the Parliamentary Roll; it would seem, however, that it had never been passed by a Parliament. This early precedent shows that an Act which appears on the Roll of Parliament is good law, whatever the method adopted for its passage.

The reluctance, if not the inability, of the courts to inquire into what takes place in Parliament was recently emphasised in the litigation which resulted from an attempt to challenge the validity of reports of the Parliamentary Boundary Commissioners in 1954.[2] Where the purported sovereign is anyone

[1] 3 St. Tr. 825.

[2] *Harper* v. *Home Secretary* [1955] Ch. 238, discussed at p. xlv, *post*.

but a single individual, rules are necessary to ascertain the will of the sovereign; the view was expressed in the last edition that such rules must be observed as a condition of the validity of legislation and that the rules are therefore logically superior to the sovereign; thus the Queen, Lords and Commons meeting as a single joint assembly could not, even by unanimous resolution, enact a single statute to which the courts would be bound to give effect.[1] But if the courts cannot inquire into what takes place in Parliament, it may be asked, what is there to prevent each House of Parliament changing its procedure so that, in place of the customary stages through which a Bill passes before it receives the Royal assent, there were substituted a simple resolution by each House as the procedure for enacting a statute? It would seem that no court could inquire into the change of procedural rules by each House of the Legislature, and that there is no known judicial control over the legislative procedure of Parliament at Westminster.[2]

So long as the rules of parliamentary procedure as laid down by each House require these customary stages, the courts will refuse to allow any attempt to alter the law by mere resolution to be treated as the equivalent to an alteration by a statute enacted through the regular process. This was shown in the great case relating to parliamentary privilege decided more than one hundred and twenty years ago. But this attitude of the courts in declining to recognise as legislation a mere resolution of one or other House is

[1] This view was based on R. T. E. Latham, *The Law and the Commonwealth*, in *Survey of the British Commonwealth Affairs* (1937), vol. i, pp. 523-524; see 9th ed., p. xxxviii.

[2] See p. lxxi, *post*, for Non-Sovereign Legislatures.

in itself an acceptance that the law of Parliament requires that all legislation should go through the proper stages of enactment. Nothing that was decided by the Queen's Bench in *Stockdale* v. *Hansard*[1] would stand in the way of a change in procedure being made by Parliament itself. Indeed there have been several such changes over the years and no court has ever challenged their validity. Thus, for example, various devices for closure in debate have all been developed since the 1880s and there have been variations introduced from time to time in the rules relating to the various readings and the committee and report stage of Bills.

It is worth remembering that the idea that a court of law can determine the legality of legislation does not come from any English or Scotch court. It is otherwise in States with a federal type of constitution where the function is assumed by, or, more often in modern times, given to, the courts. It is the case that in most countries with a unitary constitution the powers of the legislature are limited, but it does not follow that it is the prerogative of the court to override legislation. Dicey was concerned to show that there were no restrictions on the powers of Parliament whether on the part of the courts or any other authority, so far as the Parliament at Westminster was concerned. He has been criticised because he failed to support his assertion of principle by authority. That criticism can be met if one is content to view the issue, as Dicey himself did, from the legal angle by showing the authority of the court in support of certain propositions. These are :

(1) That a court will not take any note of the

[1] (1839) 9 A. & E. 1 ; K. & L. 127.

procedure in Parliament whereby a Bill comes to be enacted.

(2) That a court will not allow a judicial process to be used in the sphere where Parliament, and not the courts, has jurisdiction;

(3) That Parliament cannot bind itself as to the form of subsequent legislation, and therefore the provisions of a later Act, so far as they are inconsistent with an earlier Act, must prevail.

(1) For the first proposition it is necessary to go for an example to the field of Private Bill legislation. In *Lee* v. *Bude and Torrington Junction Railway Company*[1] it was held that the control of the procedure for enactment rests with the two Houses of Parliament as a matter of privilege which each House asserts separately to the exclusion of the courts. Thus the court refused to take any notice of the procedure in Parliament whereby the Bill came to be enacted. The case arose out of an allegation that the Bill had only been passed by Parliament through fraud. While there appears to be no authority for this proposition which arises from consideration of a Public Bill, it is to be noted that there has never been any difference in the legal effect of an enactment once passed whether it was promoted by a Minister or Private Member as a Public Bill or by a private promoter as a Private or Local Bill. There is, however, further authority in *Edinburgh and Dalkeith Railway Company* v. *Wauchope.*[2] Here an unsuccessful attempt was made to impugn the validity of a Private Act on the ground that the quasi-judicial

[1] (1871) L.R. 6 C.P. 576 at p. 582; K. & L. 1.

[2] (1842) 8 Cl. and F. 710 at p. 725; K. & L. 3.

nature of the procedure, which is prescribed by Standing Orders of both Houses of Parliament, equated a Private Act to a judgment of a court of law, and if the judgment of the latter can be set aside when obtained by fraud, so the former. This was a decision of the House of Lords and it would seem that any attempt to challenge in the courts the procedure which either House of Parliament has so prescribed for itself in Standing Orders for the enactment of a Bill, must be unsuccessful. At all events no successful attempt has ever been made in the history of the Parliament of the United Kingdom.

(2) That the judicial process does not lie where Parliament has exclusive jurisdiction has been recognised by decisions of the courts both in the field of privilege and in Private Bill legislation. It is more than seventy years since Mr. Justice Stephen in *Bradlaugh* v. *Gossett*,[1] examining the area of judicial control over matters relating to the internal procedure of the House of Commons, recognised that its privilege of regulating its own internal proceedings invested it with a judicial character. No court to-day would seriously challenge that matters concerning the proceedings within either House are to be discussed and adjudged in that House and not elsewhere. This is not, of course, to say the courts have ever receded from the position which the Queen's Bench took up in *Stockdale* v. *Hansard*[2] that one House of the Legislature could not change the law of the land by its resolution, unless an Act of Parliament should so provide.

The relationship between Parliament and the High Court was the subject of an important decision

[1] (1884) 12 Q.B.D. 271; K. & L. 144. [2] (1839) 9 A. & E. 1; K. & L. 127.

at the end of 1954 when in *Harper* v. *Home Secretary*[1] the Court of Appeal declined to restrain a Minister of the Crown from presenting a draft Order in Council to the Privy Council. This was an Order which had been approved by resolutions in both Houses of Parliament and on receiving the approval of Her Majesty in Council would have had statutory effect as provided in the House of Commons (Redistribution of Seats) Act, 1949. The court was being asked by the Lord Mayor of Manchester, in his capacity of an ordinary elector in that city, to say that a report of the Boundary Commission for England, which proposed the revision of constituencies in the Manchester area, was *ultra vires*; that accordingly the Home Secretary was not required by the Act to submit to the Privy Council the draft Order which embodied the recommendations of the report even if it had been approved, as it had been in this case, by the resolution of each House. The Court of Appeal took the view that the report was not a departure from the rules, but the Master of the Rolls went on to say that in the view of the court it was exclusively for Parliament and not for a court of law to determine whether any matter was or was not within the discretion of the Commission. "If it were competent for the courts to pass judgment of that kind on the reports, I am at a loss to see where the process would end and what the function of Parliament would then turn out to be."[2]

In resisting the application to the court, the Attorney-General put forward the view that once a

[1] [1955] Ch. 238.

[2] Cf. *The Table*, vol. 23, pp. 73 *et seq.*, for the contrary view.

draft Order has been approved by resolution of both Houses of Parliament, the position is the same as where a Bill has been passed by both Houses through the ordinary stages of three readings. It was, however, unnecessary to agree with this submission in order to determine the case in point. But at all events the Court of Appeal implicitly accepted his argument that there was no power to grant an injunction to prevent a Minister from taking to the Sovereign for royal assent a Bill which had already passed its third reading in each of the two Houses. The question is not simply that there is no procedure to coerce a Minister in this respect, but the courts have clearly recognised that this is one of the several matters which the Sovereign Parliament has determined for itself. There is thus a sphere of supremacy or sovereignty where the Queen in Parliament rules.

In *Bilston Corporation* v. *Wolverhampton Corporation*[1] the High Court refused to allow its process to be used to stifle opposition to a local Bill which had been presented to Parliament by one of the corporations. An agreement not to offer such opposition had actually been incorporated into an earlier local Act which had provided that a certain course should not be taken in any future parliamentary proceedings by the parties who were bound by the provisions of that earlier Act. The court declined to enforce by injunction an existing statutory obligation under a local Act of 1893 not to oppose a later Bill, which, if enacted, would have changed the rights of the promoting corporation to the disadvantage of the opposing corporation. The ground for this refusal

[1] [1942] Ch. 391; K. & L. 13.

was that the function of Parliament was wholly different from that of a court. To have granted the injunction would have prevented the normal operation of the Standing Orders for Private Bill procedure, since those Orders provided for opponents of a Bill to be heard. In effect the court said that it would not enforce even an existing statutory right, because that right related to a sphere where Parliament, and not the courts, had jurisdiction. It may thus be argued that it would be an infringement of the jurisdiction of Parliament for the courts to make an order which relates directly to proceedings in Parliament; that so exclusive is the jurisdiction of Parliament in matters relating to its own procedure that the court will leave it to Parliament to determine whether an existing statutory obligation should or should not be enforced.

When in 1911 the Parliament Act sought to draw a distinction between the procedure for the enactment of Money Bills as defined in the Act and that for other Public Bills so far as their passage through the House of Lords was concerned, the Act placed upon the Speaker of the House of Commons the duty of certifying a Bill to be a Money Bill and provided that the Speaker's certificate was to be conclusive and not to be questioned in any court. This is a further example of the exclusion of judicial procedure where Parliament has decided to retain exclusive jurisdiction. This can, however, be explained by saying that if a court were asked to upset the ruling of the Speaker on a Bill duly certified by him and refused, it would only be applying the express will of Parliament and would not, as in the previous examples, be asserting its inherent incapacity to adjudicate in the parliamentary field.

(3) Dicey, citing Coke and Blackstone, never had any doubt that the legislative authority of an existing Parliament could not be limited by the enactments of its predecessors, but he did not cite any authority from a court in support of his proposition. Nor is it easy before the twentieth century to find direct authority which is now forthcoming in three decisions in the space of as many years. The first two cases dealt with the interpretation of the provisions of two Acts under which compensation for the compulsory acquisition of land was assessable. The earlier of the two Acts attempted to provide a permanent code and in so doing Parliament enacted that the provisions of any Act authorising the acquisition of land which might be inconsistent with that Act should cease to have or should not have effect. Within six years Parliament enacted inconsistent provisions and the court was invited to say whether or not the provisions of the earlier Act should prevail. The cases are *Vauxhall Estates Ltd.* v. *Liverpool Corporation* [1] and *Ellen Street Estates Ltd.* v. *Minister of Health.*[2] In the latter case it was said by Maugham L.J.: [3]

> The legislature cannot according to our constitution bind itself as to the form of subsequent legislation, and it is impossible for Parliament to enact that in a subsequent statute dealing with the same subject matter there can be no implied repeal. If in a subsequent Act Parliament chooses to make it plain that the earlier Statute is being to some extent

[1] [1932] 1 K.B. 733.

[2] [1934] 1 K.B. 590; K. & L. 5. For discussion on this point see H. W. R. Wade, *The Basis of Legal Sovereignty* [1955] C.L.J. 172.

[3] [1934] 1 K.B. 590 at p. 597.

repealed, effect must be given to that intention just because it is the will of the legislature.

The case is thus direct authority for the repeal by implication by a later Act of the provisions of an earlier Act. Of particular interest is the opening sentence of this extract from the judgment because it gives the direct authority of the Court of Appeal for the proposition that it is not only the substance but the form of subsequent legislation which no Parliament can bind its successor not to alter.

The third case—*British Coal Corporation* v. *The King*[1]—raises a number of difficult questions, though it is cited here simply for the proposition that any succeeding Parliament can repeal the legislation of its predecessors. The appellants had been fined for a customs offence in a court of the Province of Quebec. The conviction had been upheld on appeal. A petition for special leave to appeal from the Quebec Court of Appeal to the Judicial Committee of the Privy Council was refused. Before the Statute of Westminster, 1931, appeal by leave in criminal cases lay to the Judicial Committee. A Canadian Statute[2] which was enacted in 1933 by the Dominion Parliament had provided that, notwithstanding any royal prerogative, no appeal should be brought in any criminal case from any judgment or order of any court in Canada to any Court of Appeal or authority in which in the United Kingdom, appeals or petitions to His Majesty might be heard. If the statute was valid, it was clear that the petition was barred. But the question was raised in argument

[1] [1935] A.C. 500; C.L.C. 160.

[2] Criminal Code Amendment Act, 1933, 23 and 24 Geo. V c. 53 s. 17 (Canada).

that the power of the United Kingdom Parliament to pass any legislation that it thought fit extending to Canada remained unimpaired ; that thus as a matter of strict law Section 4 of the Statute of Westminster, which declared that no Act of Parliament of the United Kingdom passed after the commencement of the Statute should extend to a Dominion as part of the law of that Dominion, unless it was expressly declared that that Dominion had requested and consented to the enactment, could in theory be itself repealed by Parliament. The Judicial Committee accepted the view that as a matter of abstract law the repeal or disregard of the section was within the powers of Parliament but declared that this was theory and had no relation to realities. Here then is an example of the sovereignty of Parliament being restricted by political considerations, unless one can accept the view that Section 4 of the Statute of Westminster operated as a legal restriction upon the capacity of the United Kingdom Parliament to legislate hereafter in this field. This latter view has been expressed by writers from the Commonwealth, including the present Chief Justice of Australia,[1] and also by the Appellate Division of the South African High Court.[2]

It is tempting to suggest that this decision does no more than give judicial recognition to the author's view that the existence of actual limitations of power

[1] Mr. Justice Owen Dixon, *The Law and the Constitution*, 51 L.Q.R. 611 ; but cf. his doubts on this in *Hughes* and *Vale Pty. Ltd.* v. *Gair* (1954) 90 C.L.R. 203.

[2] *Ndlwana* v. *Hofmeyer* N.O. (1937) A.D. 229 at p. 237 ; K. & L. 484. Although this case was overruled by the same court in *Harris* v. *Minister of the Interior* 1952 (2) S.A. 428 ; (1952) 1 T.L.R. 1245 ; K. & L. 506 ; the latter case expressly upheld the sovereignty of the Parliament of the Union ; see pp. lvii *et seq.*, *post*.

were not inconsistent with the sovereign power of Parliament. The external limitation to the real power of the Sovereign was the possibility or certainty that some laws would be disobeyed or resisted even if made under the most despotic monarchies. Long before the enactment of the Statute of Westminster it had become the conventional practice of the United Kingdom Parliament not to pass legislation extending to a Dominion except at the request of the Dominion concerned. This operated in particular in relation to the Dominion of Canada where, ever since the coming into force of the Federal Constitution in 1867, the power to amend the Constitution remained with the Parliament at Westminster. The convention secured the passage without controversy, criticism or indeed even debate, of measures for amending the British North American Act of 1867 which were introduced into Parliament by a Secretary of State of the United Kingdom Government in exactly the form proposed by the Government of the Dominion of Canada and duly enacted without alteration. All that the Statute of Westminster did then was to give statutory effect to a long-standing political practice. Whatever view lawyers may form as to the nature or basis of parliamentary sovereignty, the ultimate sanction must lie in the possibility of resistance to the exercise of power by those who are subject to it. This certainly suggests that supremacy in law-making is to be distinguished from ultimate political sovereignty. If for any reason it should ever happen that Parliament at Westminster attempted to legislate for the Dominion of Canada otherwise than under Section 4 of the Statute of Westminster at the express request of the Dominion, it is as certain as anything could be that the Courts of Canada would refuse to recognise the legislation so enacted. It is, however, less certain that the Courts in this country, if called upon to interpret an Act of the United Kingdom Parliament purporting to make law for Canada, would not give effect to the legislation. The question is hypothetical; it would seldom, if ever, be the case that the courts of this country would be called upon to interpret the law of Canada however enacted. Now that appeals from Canada to the Judicial Committee of the Privy Council have been abolished, the issue of validity would fall to be determined by the Supreme Court of Canada and its decision disregarding legislation of the United Kingdom Parliament repealing Canadian law would be final. It would not, however, be a decision of a court of the United Kingdom denying the sovereignty of the Parliament of the United Kingdom.

Perhaps it is the fact that one is driven to seek examples in the realm of the improbable or the ridiculous that reassures lawyers of the validity of Dicey's thesis that only political restrictions can restrain the omnipotence of Parliament.[1] The recent controversies have shown that attempts to extend Dicey's interpretation of sovereignty to other constitutions, all of the written type, have raised considerable doubts and disputations. There is validity in the criticism that the results of interpreting constitutions by judges who have been trained in the traditional view of the sovereignty of Parliament

[1] "Adventures in metaphysics" is the description coined by Sir Ivor Jennings.

have not been altogether satisfactory. But this is a plea that judges should enlarge the ambit of their traditional approach to give effect to considerations other than those of strict law when called upon to interpret constitutional enactments.

The sovereignty of Parliament is not limited by the rules of public international law though Parliament normally gives effect to these rules since they are accepted by the Executive. The courts, however, will not accept a plea that the legislature has violated such rules.[1] No Act of Parliament can be held *ultra vires* on any ground of contravention of generally accepted principles of morality or of law. It is not obligatory for the municipal law of any State to correspond with public international law unless it is so provided in the constitution,[2] and therefore it cannot be said that the capacity of Parliament to override public international law is a consequence of the sovereignty of Parliament. Nevertheless this capacity of Parliament is an illustration of its omnipotence.

Parliament normally restricts the operation of legislation to its own territories, British ships wherever they may be being included in the ambit of territory. This is itself in accordance with international law. Parliament does on occasions, however, pass legislation controlling the activities of its own citizens when they are abroad. In this respect the territorial conception of law is stronger than that of most other countries; in practice only a few of the more serious criminal offences are punishable in the courts of the

[1] *Mortensen* v. *Peters* (1906), 8 F. 93.

[2] Thus under the constitution of the United States of America a treaty duly concluded becomes part of the law of the land.

United Kingdom no matter where they may be committed by a British national. Here the question is not so much the omnipotence of Parliament but the practical difficulty of law enforcement. Thus one may say that the supremacy of Parliament is limited not only by the possibility of disobedience or resistance on the part of subjects, but also by the impossibility of enforcement. Even in the case of an offence committed abroad and therefore beyond the jurisdiction of the English courts, there is nothing to prevent the enforcement of the statute if and when the offender comes within the jurisdiction.

If the rule of parliamentary sovereignty simply expresses the relationship of the courts to Parliament as a legal conception, it may be objected that legal sovereignty is not sovereignty as such but merely a rule for lawyers which is accepted and acted upon because it suits political conditions that the unrestricted power of law-making should rest in Parliament alone. Dicey himself appreciated the difficulty which Austin felt in finding the sovereign in the Queen, Lords and Commons. But he rejected the explanation of Austin that members of the House of Commons are trustees for the electors in the sense that the latter are able in the long run to impose their will on Parliament. No such trusteeship has ever been recognised by the courts and it is difficult to see how it could be established as a matter of law.

Events have shown that the political limitations of the legal rule go even further than Dicey would have admitted. His examples of the possibility of resistance to laws are chiefly concerned with the possibility or certainty that there will be disobedience or resistance to actions of despots and that this constituted the external limit to the real power of the Sovereign. He did, however, envisage political resistance to Parliament in relation to the constitutional affairs of Ireland in particular, as well as on the issue of women's suffrage which was current towards the end of his active life. In these predictions he was unfortunate. Moreover subsequent events have shown that Parliament has, without such resistance, changed the succession of the throne as it did on the abdication of Edward VIII in 1936, and prolonged its own life without consulting the electorate, as it did on several occasions in each of the two World Wars. Nevertheless it would not be difficult to think of topics upon which modern Parliaments would decline to legislate for political reasons.

While it can readily be admitted that political expediency operates to limit the working of the legal rule, the question "Where lies sovereignty ?" as a political concept remains unanswered, except that in the last resort the power of government and with it the power to control Parliament depends on the result of a general election. But this question need not be answered by a lawyer.

But the lawyer does seek to explain why it is a rule that the courts enforce without question all Acts of Parliament. There is admittedly no Act of Parliament which says that they must. The source then of this rule must lie in the common law. Why cannot Parliament change that rule, since all other rules of the common law are subject to its sovereignty? One answer is that Parliament has done so in creating constitutions for certain States of the Commonwealth where in the courts of these States challenge can be made to the validity of Acts of the local legislature. But it has admittedly never attempted either to define or to restrict, much less to repeal the rule of judicial obedience in the United Kingdom to Acts of Parliament. This question has been examined by H. W. R. Wade in his article *The Basis of Legal Sovereignty*.[1] He finds that the rule enjoining judicial obedience to statutes is one of the fundamental rules upon which the legal system depends. The sacrosanctity of the rule is, he argues, an inevitable corollary of Parliament's continuing sovereignty. He cites Salmond, *Jurisprudence*,[2] for the proposition that the rule that Acts of Parliament have the force of law is legally ultimate and that its source is historical only, not legal.

> It is the law because it is the law, and for no other reason that it is possible for the law itself to take notice of. No Statute can confer this power upon Parliament, for this would be to assume and act on the very power that is to be conferred.

Once, says Professor Wade, this truth is grasped, the dilemma is solved. For if no statute can establish the rule that the courts obey Acts of Parliament, similarly no statute can abolish or alter that rule.

> The rule of judicial obedience is in one sense a rule of common law, but in another sense—which applies to no other rule of common law—it is the ultimate political fact upon which the whole system of legislation hangs.

Political facts call for historical justification; of this there is no lack of material. In the seventeenth century when one King was executed, when a Com-

[1] [1955] C.L.J. 172. [2] 11th ed., p. 137.

monwealth was established, when another King abdicated, the courts, Professor Wade points out, without any authority from the previous sovereign legislature, transferred their allegiance from the King in Parliament to the King-less Parliament. The courts were prepared to recognise the change in the seat of sovereignty as a political fact from which legal consequences flowed. Equally of their own authority the courts resumed their allegiance to the King in Parliament at the termination of the Commonwealth, and at a later date transferred their obedience from the departed James II to William and Mary. This part of the exposition concludes as follows:

> What Salmond calls the "ultimate legal principle" is therefore a rule which is unique in being unchangeable by Parliament—it is changed by revolution, not by legislation; it lies in the keeping of the courts, and no Act of Parliament can take it from them. This is only another way of saying that it is always for the courts, in the last resort, to say what is a valid Act of Parliament; and that the decision of this question is not determined by any rule of law which can be laid down or altered by any authority outside the courts. It is simply a political fact.[1]

The above examination of the basis of legal sovereignty was inspired by the decisions of the South African Courts which arose out of the constitutional crisis over the coloured vote. The three leading cases to which the crisis gave rise have been fully examined elsewhere.[2] Professor Cowen has

[1] [1955] C.L.J. 139; the same point is well put by K. C. Wheare, *The Statute of Westminster and Dominion Status* (5th ed.), pp. 155-156.

[2] Reference may be made in particular to D. V. Cowen, *Legislature and Judiciary*, (1952) 15 M.L.R. 282, (1953) 16 M.L.R. 273; *The Entrenched Sections of the South Africa Act* (1953) 70 S.A. L.J. 238. B. Beinart, *Parliament and the Courts*, Butterworth (1954) S.A. Law Rev.

carried the examination of parliamentary sovereignty beyond the confines of the Union and raised doubts even as to the conclusiveness of the Parliament Roll and other aspects of sovereignty in relation to the Parliament of the United Kingdom. So far as the Union Parliament is concerned, the South African Court found that Parliament to be different in kind from the Parliament at Westminster since it began its career with certain limitations which were contained in an Act of the Parliament of the United Kingdom—the South Africa Act, 1909. In the Union Parliament the three elements, the Queen, the Senate and the House of Assembly, are required to combine for legislative action in different ways according to whether the purpose is ordinary legislation, entrenched business or the solution of a deadlock between the two Houses. The constitutional elements of the Union Parliament include the entrenched sections which accordingly are not a limitation on its powers. So far as sovereignty is concerned the Union Parliament has always had complete power to amend the South African Constitution. The Statute of Westminster did nothing to change the definition and mode of legislating, though it did terminate the legal supremacy in South Africa of the Parliament of the

134; *The South African Senate*, (1957) 20 M.L.R. 549. H. R. Gray, *The Sovereignty of Parliament Today*, (1953) 10 University of Toronto Law Journal 54. E. N. Griswold, *The Coloured Vote Case in South Africa*, (1952) 65 H.L.R. 1361; *The Demise of the High Court of Parliament in South Africa*, (1953) 66 H.L.R. 864. E. McWhinney, *The Union Parliament, the Supreme Court and the "Entrenched Clauses" of the South Africa Act*, (1952), 30 C.B.R. 692. G. Marshall, *Parliamentary Sovereignty and the Commonwealth* (1957), ch. xi, South Africa; The Courts and the Constitution, and app. i and ii. H. W. R. Wade, *The Senate Act Case and the Entrenched Sections of the South Africa Act*, (1957) 74 S.A.L.J. 160.

United Kingdom which had enacted the South Africa Act, 1909. So the conclusion of the court amounts to this. For reasons which are basically political, the court was bound in *Harris* v. *Minister of the Interior* [1] to recognise the sovereignty of the Union Parliament. That Parliament was created by the South Africa Act, which gave it its powers and defined how they must be exercised. Since the court took the view that the Statute of Westminster had not changed the definition and mode of legislation in the Union, it was also bound to accept the entrenched provisions, observance of which, prior to the Statute of Westminster, was required under the South Africa Act for certain amendments of the constitution, including the retention of the coloured franchise.

Leaving the South African field, Professor Cowen has raised doubts on the conclusiveness of the Parliament Roll. But he is forced to rely on *Pylkington's Case*,[2] which produced no final decision that a special Act which was not to be found on the Parliament Roll was void. It was, therefore, necessary, as so often in a discussion of sovereignty, to consider hypothetical and unusual applications of the principle. Suppose, says Professor Cowen, that the House of Commons alone passed an enactment to which the Sovereign gave her assent for the prolongation of the life of Parliament, notwithstanding that under the Parliament Act, 1911, any such enactment requires the assent also of the House of Lords. Could the validity of that Act be successfully challenged in the High Court? The court is bound, it will be

[1] 1952 (2) S.A. 428; (1952) 1 T.L.R. 1245; K. & L. 506.

[2] Year Book 33 Hen. VI fo. 17, p. 8.

remembered, to accept the conclusiveness of a certificate by the Speaker that the Bill was presented to Her Majesty for assent in accordance with the provisions of the Parliament Act. Surely the answer to this is that the court could not question the validity of such an enactment because the Parliament Act makes the Speaker's certificate conclusive for all purposes and it cannot be challenged in any court of law? Here is a case where Parliament itself has provided in advance against judicial review. It might be safer to pose hypothetical statutes in a different sphere, but any attempt to challenge the conclusiveness of the Parliament Roll is as yet unsupported by any formal precedent from the Law Reports. One way of circumventing this difficulty is to argue that conclusiveness has nothing to do with parliamentary sovereignty and to say that it is merely a rule of evidence for determining how far the courts may pursue the enquiry into the observance of legal rules. If Parliament speaks according to fixed rules, the courts are only concerned with the question "Has Parliament spoken?" To this it is submitted there can be only one answer if the evidence is found on the Parliament Roll.

Under the heading of parliamentary privilege, Professor Cowen admits the elementary proposition "that the Houses of the British Parliament are privileged to be exclusive arbiters of the legality of their own proceedings." Any other view is scarcely tenable in view of the decision of the High Court in the line of cases which culminated with *Bradlaugh* v. *Gossett*.[1] But in the South African constitution

[1] (1884) 12 Q.B.D. 271; K. & L. 144.

the entrenched sections protect substantive rights and therefore their observance can be investigated by the courts without being met with the answer that the privilege of the Union Parliament is being infringed if the courts seek to examine the rules of procedure for legislating in that Parliament. In any case in South Africa the whole subject of parliamentary privilege is of statutory origin, whereas in the United Kingdom the law and custom of Parliament, so far as they relate to the origins of privilege, are enshrined in the traditions of the institution and only exceptionally have been defined by statute.

Of that aspect of the sovereignty of Parliament, which gives it unlimited legislative authority, there is little material for discussion which can be found in the annals of the Parliament at Westminster. But Professor Cowen suggests that in the light of the existence of the entrenched sections of the South African constitution, the unlimited power of Parliament to legislate can be examined under three heads :

(i) The power to make any law whatsoever.
(ii) One manner of law-making.
(iii) The absence of power to bind succeeding Parliaments.

The South African Parliament can change the entrenched sections and therefore their existence does not conflict with Parliament's power to make or unmake any law whatever, but there can be more than one manner of law-making. Thus in South Africa the legal sovereignty is divisible, being entrusted for ordinary purposes to each element of the legislature acting singly, but for the purpose of changing the entrenched sections requiring a special majority at a joint sitting of the Senate and House of Assembly. This raises a doubt whether Dicey was correct in equating flexibility with sovereignty. For if the conclusion that the Parliament of the Union of South Africa is sovereign be right, then the constitution is less flexible so far as it is contained in entrenched sections than are those parts of it (they form the majority) which can be changed by the ordinary process of bi-cameral legislation.

And what of the power of Parliament to bind successors ? Certainly the South African Parliament has been held to be bound by the South Africa Act, 1909, in the three cases arising out of the coloured vote crisis. This followed of necessity on the view taken by the court that the Statute of Westminster did not expressly or by implication repeal or modify the South Africa Act. But it is only this Act which is binding on the Union Parliament unless and until it amends or repeals it in the manner enacted in the Act itself. The explanation must be that in South Africa Parliament is based on the constitution, and that constitution in its turn is based on a fundamental statute. The sovereignty of the Union Parliament carries with it the power of each succeeding Parliament to repeal or alter the Acts of its predecessors. The only limitation is in the manner of legislating, which must comply with the constitution.

Considered apart from the South African constitution, the rule that a sovereign Parliament cannot bind its successors calls for careful analysis. Professor Cowen argues that it must be examined in relation to a total abdication of power, to a partial divesting and to the grant of power without divesting. Dicey considered why Parliament has failed to enact unchangeable enactments in the long footnote at pages 68-70, *post*. He found that the impossibility of placing a limit on the exercise of sovereignty did not in any way prohibit either logically or in matter of fact the abdication of sovereignty. "Parliament can put an end to its own existence by legally dissolving itself and leaving no means whereby a subsequent Parliament could be legally summoned." At the time of the Union this action was taken by the Parliaments both of England and of Scotland.[1] A new sovereign body resulted from this joint action, namely, the Parliament of Great Britain. But abdication of power is at least as much a political as a legal event, and it is only by accepting the political change that the courts can recognise the legality of the new situation.

If total abdication of sovereignty is possible, partial divesting, of which Section 4 of the Statute of Westminster is a conspicuous example, raises less difficulty. As we have seen,[2] whatever be the legal position, the question is unlikely to arise because of the force of the convention which prohibits interference with the legislative powers of other Commonwealth States on the part of the Parliament at Westminster. It is not altogether easy to separate partial divesting of sovereignty from the grant of sovereign power without divesting, and there are many who would regard Section 4 of the Statute of Westminster as an example of the latter. Perhaps reconciliation is possible in this way. Since the Parliament at

[1] See especially T. B. Smith, *The Union of 1707*, [1957] Public Law 99, "the British Parliament is the creation of the terms of the Union—by what was in effect a revolution by consent."

[2] Intro. p. li, *ante*.

Westminster has provided that it will not enact laws for the Dominions without their consent or request, it is purporting to divest itself of power in a field where it was previously competent, but at the same time it has not expressly divested itself of power to legislate in that field in so far as it has retained the power to repeal the Section. Section 4 is not unrepealable. Yet it seeks to implement an existing well-established convention which would be violated by a repeal.

The English doctrine of parliamentary sovereignty, as the Lord President called it, was criticised in the Court of Session in *MacCormick* v. *Lord Advocate.*[1] In this case the Rector of Glasgow University together with a law student sought a declaratory order, as sanctioned by the Crown Proceedings Act, 1947, s. 21, that the use of the numeral " II " in the Royal title was not only inconsistent with historical fact and political reality but involved a contravention of Article I of the Act of Union, 1706. This was the article which declared that the Kingdoms of England and Scotland should for ever be united into one Kingdom. The issue of the sovereignty of Parliament arose in this way. The title adopted by Queen Elizabeth on her accession was determined by her and her advisers under the royal prerogative. Parliament subsequently passed the Royal Titles Act, 1953, in order to sanction certain changes which had been made in the title at the time of the accession, consequent upon further discussion at a meeting of the Prime Ministers of the Commonwealth held late in 1952. The Act did not mention the matter of the numeral attached to the royal name, but was con-

[1] 1953 S.L.T. 255.

cerned solely with changes of Commonwealth status and, in the case of Ireland, of territory. Lord Cooper himself was not satisfied that the Act had any proper bearing on the issue of the numeral which was before the court and in fact the proclamation made under the Act had not altered the numeral II which the Queen adopted at her accession. Nevertheless, Lord Cooper, alone among the judges who took part in the decision, stated that he did not understand why the new Parliament of Great Britain must have inherited in 1706 all the characteristics of the old English Parliament including the attribute of sovereignty, but none of those of the old Scottish Parliament. He pointed out that the Act of Union was a treaty which contained some clauses expressly reserving to Parliament the right of amendment, but that Article I was not such a clause. The argument was therefore that it would be a violation of the treaty provision for union of the two Kingdoms for a Sovereign who was the first of her name since the Union to adopt any numeral but I in the royal title. Of course, if the sovereignty of Parliament was recognised it could not be seriously argued that a statutory alteration of the royal title could be invalid. Lord Cooper was disposed to draw a distinction between academic logic, which required Scots law to accept the sovereignty of Parliament, and political reality. He relied too on the undoubted fact that there was no provision in the Act of Union, or, for that matter, elsewhere, that the Parliament of the United Kingdom should be absolutely sovereign. In answer to this argument may not the explanation be that the English Parliament could not be taken to have given up in 1706 what it already had, namely, the attribute of sovereignty? Lord Russell, who sat with Lord Cooper in the Inner House, doubted whether any Parliament of Scotland in the two hundred years preceding the Union did enjoy unchallengeable sovereignty. There would thus appear to have been every reason why the first Parliament of the newly united Kingdoms should inherit the admitted attribute of the English partner and so the sovereignty of the English Parliament became the sovereignty of the United Kingdom. Even Lord Cooper went on to say: [1]

> This at least is plain: that there is neither precedent nor authority of any kind for the view that the domestic courts of either Scotland or England have jurisdiction to determine whether a governmental act of the type here in controversy is, or is not, in conformity with the provisions of a Treaty, least of all when that Treaty is one under which both Scotland and England ceased to be independent States and merged their identity in an incorporating Union.

All this only means that Lord Cooper regarded the Act of Union as a fundamental part of constitutional law and that he regretted that the state of the law was such that even a fundamental provision was subject to alteration by Act of Parliament which the courts were bound to accept. It is indeed somewhat surprising that an understandable expression of patriotism on the part of a great Scottish judge should have been erected into a serious challenge to the doctrine of parliamentary sovereignty within the United Kingdom.[2]

[1] 1953 S.L.T., at p. 263.

[2] See especially T. B. Smith, *The Union of 1707*, in (1957) *Public Law* at p. 108, but cf. G. Marshall, *Parliamentary Sovereignty and the Commonwealth*, ch. 5; Hood Phillips, *Constitutional Law*, 2nd ed., pp. 52-53.

Internal Limitations upon Legal Sovereignty.— There are in the sphere of internal government, and to a less extent of external government, limitations upon the exercise by Parliament of its sovereignty which could hardly have been foreseen in 1885. Dealing first with external government, the obligations of any State which has adhered as a Great Power to the United Nations restrict freedom of action in relation to foreign affairs. It is quite true that in this sphere prerogative powers are more important than the statute book; nevertheless no member State of the United Nations could promote legislation in its Parliament in direct and open violation of its international obligations. In the internal sphere the limitation is mainly the result of the rapid growth of the practice of consultation between government departments and associations reflecting organised interests outside government circles. Nowadays it is seldom the case that even a minor Bill is presented by a Minister until he has taken the views of organised interests whose members are most concerned with the contents of the proposed legislation. This does not, of course, apply to a major matter of government policy or in relation to taxation, but in practically every other form of legislation prior consultation is the rule. Indeed in some cases the obligation to consult beforehand is imposed upon a Minister by statute; a notable example of this is to be found in the National Insurance Advisory Committee before which must be laid in draft every proposal relating to national insurance to which effect is given by statutory instrument. The result is that the Government comes to Parliament with a request for the enactment of what is more or less an agreed measure. As far back as 1929 some striking evidence of the effect of this prior consultation was given by the Ministry of Health, which then included local government in its responsibilities, to the Committee on Ministers' Powers.[1] This mainly related to the contents of subordinate legislation, but since subordinate legislation is normally directed to implementing the general provisions of an Act of Parliament, the evidence supports the view that neither Governments nor Parliaments can disregard organised public opinion in promoting legislation. Lately there have been striking illustrations of the force of public opinion in restraining the exercise of the law-making power by Parliament. Such power is controlled nowadays by the Government of the day, sure in the knowledge that its proposals will be passed through the Commons without alteration of principle. Nevertheless it does not follow that even when the Government has procured authoritative advice from outside sources on controversial topics, particularly those with moral implications, it will ask Parliament to give legislative effect to that advice. The failure to bring before Parliament the measures based upon the major recommendations of recent Royal Commissions, such as those dealing with the Marriage and Divorce Laws, Betting and Gaming Laws, and of the Committee on Homosexual Offences and Prostitution, shows that Parliament will not necessarily impose legislation simply because an impartial body has spoken in an authoritative way. What is certain now that rule by

[1] See Ministers' Powers Report (Cmd. 4060, 1932), vol. ii, Minutes of Evidence, p. 120.

advisory committees is in such favour is that there will be consultation beforehand with the result that what is ultimately passed into law, if it comes before Parliament at all, will be more or less an agreed measure. Indeed in the case of the Royal Commission on Marriage and Divorce Laws, it was really the failure of the members of the Commission to speak with a single voice which wrecked the prospect of legislation on any but minor points resulting from their recommendations.[1] The latest example of prior consultation with a view to legislation is to be found in the Report of the Committee on Sexual Offences.[2] This committee, with a single dissentient, reported in favour of taking out of the criminal law homosexual practices between consenting adults. So far the Government has refused to introduce legislation on this subject of the recommendations, offering as the excuse that public opinion is not in favour. There would thus seem to be limitations upon the exercise of the law-making power which go further than the requirements of prior consultation, and suggest that at all events in the case of certain topics of legislation, even the recommendations of a well-informed inquiry may not be heeded.

All this does not destroy the validity of the assertion that rule by advisory committee is a device which has found much favour since the end of the First World War without giving the force of law to the obligation to consult beforehand. This limitation is without legal sanction, but, as has been seen, it is now quite common to make the seeking of advice an express condition precedent to action by legislation;[3]

[1] Cmd. 9678, 1956. [2] Cmnd. 247, 1957. [3] P. lxvii, *ante*.

the result is that before the sovereignty of Parliament can be invoked to make or unmake laws the normal process, at all events as regards the administration of internal public services, is for the Minister to seek advice from the appropriate advisory committee. He may also take into consultation as many other bodies of a representative character as he chooses to consult. When the Bill which is the result of these consultations comes before Parliament, where alone it can be given the force of law, it will usually prove to be, except perhaps in some details, an agreed measure which those most affected by its operations are prepared, however reluctantly, to accept. This is equally true of much delegated legislation. The effect of this type of legislation, without which the sovereign Parliament could never have enlarged the sphere of administration, has been to weaken the control of Parliament as is generally the case when power is devolved. Here, however, the courts can intervene to ensure that the delegate of legislative power keeps within the limitations prescribed by the Act which has created the regulation-making power.

Thus the political supremacy of Parliament, as distinct from its legal omni-competence as a law-making organ, has become more and more unreal. All legislation is a compromise of conflicting interests. Truly representative government can but imperfectly be achieved by the legislature acting alone. But a convention which secures consultation before the framing of legislation does not mean that the Government must accept dictation upon major matters of policy. It would be dangerous doctrine to admit, for example, that the foreign policy of the State could be controlled by the refusal of a small but powerful trade organisation to make, say, munitions of war to the orders of the Government. The consultation of private interests by Ministers in advance of legislation is in practice directed to matters of detail rather than to the determination of fundamental issues of policy. As has been seen from the failure of Governments to heed the recommendations of Royal Commissions, Parliament will not necessarily be invoked because authoritative outside opinion has spoken.

Non-Sovereign Legislatures.—At the time when Dicey wrote, he likened the constitutions of territories which were then colonies to what he called municipal bodies such as railway companies, school boards and town councils which possessed a limited power of making laws. Nowadays no student of the Commonwealth would think of comparing the constitution of New Zealand, a colony in 1885, with the by-laws of the City of Cambridge, though Dicey thought a comparison valid with the by-laws of the old Great Western Railway Company. Nevertheless there are, within the Commonwealth, non-sovereign legislatures, though the comparison with statutory corporations under English municipal law is no more valid now than it was then. Legislatures of Colonial Territories, and such exist in all such territories as have made any progress towards self-governing status, are given power to legislate for the "peace, order and good government" of the territory. These words give full power of legislation to a local legislature and no colonial court could declare a statute invalid as being unnecessary or as containing, for example, provisions which a court might regard as contrary to order and good government. The power to legislate is subject only to any limitations contained in the constitution itself. Such constitutions are normally derived from the exercise by the Crown of its prerogative powers, but exceptionally they are contained in an Act of the United Kingdom Parliament where the prerogative power has already been surrendered, showing that the prerogative has been superseded by the sovereign legislature. It is thus competent for a colonial legislature to enact whatever laws it chooses, including the delegation of its law-making powers to other authorities in the colony. Provided that it does not attempt to abdicate its functions or, though this is doubtful, to give extra-territorial effect to its enactments, the courts of a colony will not declare the Acts of a colonial legislature *ultra vires*.

There is, however, one important restriction on the powers of colonial legislatures. This is contained in Section 5 of the Colonial Laws Validity Act, 1865, which provides that every colonial representative legislature shall have power to make laws respecting the constitution, powers and procedure of its own body, provided that such laws are passed in such manner and form as may from time to time be required by any Act of Parliament, letters patent, Order in Council or colonial laws for the time being in force in the colony. The statutory definition of a representative legislature is one in which there is a majority of elected members in the legislature, or, if there are two houses, of the lower house. This means in practice that it is only in the more advanced colonial territories that the legislature can alter the constitution and that in so doing it must observe the procedure laid down in the constitution for that type of enactment. This will normally be contained either in an Act of the Parliament at Westminster or, more usually, in letters patent issued by Her Majesty on the advice of her Government in the United Kingdom. If an attempt is made by a colonial legislature to change its constitution without observing the prescribed manner and form, then the enactment can be set aside as *ultra vires* by the courts of the colony.

In *Attorney-General for New South Wales* v. *Trethowan* [1] the Judicial Committee of the Privy Council, affirming a decision of the High Court of Australia, held to be invalid a Bill which proposed to abolish the Legislative Council of New South Wales. This Bill had not been enacted in the New South Wales Parliament in accordance with the provisions of an earlier Act which required the approval of the electorate, in addition to the assent of Parliament, to be given to such a Bill. The Privy Council rejected the argument that the earlier Act which required the approval of the electorate for its repeal was invalid as fettering the freedom of a future Parliament. This argument was, of course, an attempt to apply Dicey's proposition that the sovereignty of Parliament involved the right of each succeeding Parliament to make or unmake any law whatsoever. But Dicey never suggested that this doctrine applied to subordinate legislatures. To the extent that it is fettered by Section 5 of the Colonial Laws Validity Act, the New South Wales legislature is thus non-sovereign. This case has been cited by some of the author's critics as illustrating the proposition that a "legal

[1] [1932] A.C. 526; C.L.C. 78.

sovereign " is able to impose legal limitations on itself.[1] We can agree, however, with the view of the judges who decided the *Trethowan Case* that it is simply an application of the principle of *ultra vires* which has no relevance to any Act of the United Kingdom Parliament.[2]

In this connection it is necessary to recall the relationship between Parliament and the High Court which was discussed in *Harper* v. *Home Secretary* [3] where the Court of Appeal refused to issue an injunction restraining the Home Secretary from presenting a draft Order in Council to the Queen in Council. In the *Trethowan Case* the Supreme Court of New South Wales had granted an injunction to restrain the officers of the State Parliament from presenting the Bill for the assent of the Governor. The Privy Council was not called upon to decide whether this injunction had been rightly granted because it found that the Bill was itself invalid.

It is sometimes suggested that since the Parliament Act, 1911, the Parliament of the United Kingdom has itself provided an alternative manner and form for its legislation. Another suggestion is that the procedure under the Parliament Act is a form of delegation of legislative power to the Queen and the House of Commons. The Parliament Act itself can only be amended by the ordinary process of legislation and therefore no question arises as to the manner and

[1] Jennings, *The Law and the Constitution*, 4th ed., p. 148; W. Friedmann in (1950), 24, *Australian L.J.* 103.

[2] H. W. R. Wade, *The Basis of Legal Sovereignty* [1955], C.L.J. 172, at pp. 177-183. This article shows that the *Trethowan Case* has been wrongly used by the critics to support the argument that the United Kingdom Parliament could bind its successors.

[3] [1955], Ch. 238; p. xlv, *ante*.

form of such amendment. But if, as Sir Ivor Jennings has argued,[1] Parliament enacted that the House of Lords should not be abolished except after a majority of electors had expressly agreed to it and that no Act repealing that Act should be passed except after a similar referendum, there is nothing to prevent Parliament passing the repealing Act without obtaining the approval of a majority of electors. All that the Act requiring the referendum establishes is that it was the intention of the Parliament which passed the Act that there should be no repeal without a referendum. It cannot be seriously argued that the Colonial Laws Validity Act applies to the United Kingdom Parliament, and as we have seen [2] there are no means whereby a skilful draughtsman could entrench an Act of Parliament. The *Trethowan Case* cannot be used to refute the ancient theory of parliamentary sovereignty or to dismiss it as a misconception of the author. An English judge has the support of older professional opinions, of which that of Bacon is set out in the text.[3] It is otherwise with statutory corporations under English law. Dicey compared the legislatures of colonies with representative and responsible government to such bodies as the railway companies, which even in the days when they operated under private management had limited powers to enact by-laws, as also have local authorities such as county councils. Such bodies, however, could not, and may not, enact by-laws which are unreasonable and oppressive nor delegate their law-making powers without express

[1] *Op. cit.*, 4th ed., at p. 149.

[2] Pp. xlviii-xlix, *ante*.

[3] See p. 64, note 2, and see Coke 4. Inst. 42, Blackstone, *Commentaries*, vol. i, 90.

statutory authority. In other words, whereas the powers of colonial legislatures may be described as sovereign within their own sphere and limited only by the constitution itself, the validity of the enactments of local authorities, and still more of trading corporations such as have by-law making powers is open to review by the courts. The former are plenary powers, the latter are strictly limited by the form of the grant.

Thus in *Hodge* v. *The Queen* [1] the question arose whether the legislature of Ontario had or had not the power of entrusting to a board of commissioners the enactment of regulations with respect to the local Liquor Licence Act, 1877, of creating offences for breach of those regulations and of annexing penalties thereto. It was held by the Judicial Committee of the Privy Council that there was such a power. Provincial legislatures are in no sense delegates of, or acting under any mandate from, the Imperial Parliament under the British North America Act, 1867. That Act created a legislative assembly for Ontario with exclusive authority to make laws for the Province in relation to certain enumerated topics. It conferred powers not in any sense to be exercised by delegation from, or as agents of, the Imperial Parliament, but gave authority as plenary and as ample, within the limits prescribed for provincial as opposed to federal legislation, as the Imperial Parliament in the plenitude of its power possessed or could bestow.[2] There is thus no comparison as a matter of law between the powers of such a legislature and those of, say, a

[1] (1883) 9 App. Cas. 117 C.L.C.

[2] See also *The Queen* v. *Burah* (1878) 3 A.C. 889; C.L.C. 65; *Powell* v. *Apollo Candle Company Ltd.* (1885) 10 A.C. 282; C.L.C. 67.

borough council to enact by-laws on special topics; the council has not in law any authority to act as a legislature for the good government generally of its property, but is strictly a delegate exercising its power of making by-laws by delegation from Parliament. Still less can a trading corporation so act.

Parliamentary Sovereignty and Federalism.[1]—The essential characteristic of federalism is "the distribution of limited executive, legislative and judicial authority among bodies which are co-ordinate with and independent of each other." The supremacy of the constitution is fundamental to the existence of a federal State in order to prevent either the legislature of the federal unit or those of the member States from destroying or impairing that delicate balance of power which satisfies the particular requirements of States which are desirous of union, but not prepared to merge their individuality in a unity. This supremacy of the constitution is protected by the authority of an independent judicial body to act as the interpreter of a scheme of distribution of powers. Nor is any change possible in the constitution by the ordinary process of federal or State legislation.

It follows that the assumption of additional power by a federal Government in the interests of national unity can only lawfully be achieved by constitutional amendment. This is in practice difficult, whatever be the form which is prescribed for securing it. For it raises inevitably the question of surrender of power by the federating States to the central Government. Experience has shown that, when the need for a radical change in the relations between federal and

[1] See also pp. 138-139, *post*.

member States is felt by the former, its Cabinet will proceed, not by direct constitutional amendment, but by way of legislation framed to achieve the purpose of national unity without directly infringing the express or implied terms of the constitution. Illustrations of this may be found in the New Deal legislation presented to Congress by the Administration of the United States in the 1930s. Action by the Federal Government was deemed necessary to mitigate the rigours of an economic blizzard. Legislation provided for regulations of varying character to control trade and industry, for relief of poverty on a national scale, for governmental works to reduce unemployment. The validity of the legislation, which attempted to keep within the constitution, was contested in the Federal Supreme Court. The court was asked to decide whether the legislation encroached upon State rights which the founders of the constitution had sought rigidly to preserve. The answer to such a question cannot be easy. How is a document of comparative brevity which was framed in a different age to be read in the light of modern conditions which could not have been foreseen at the time of federation ? Several ways of approach to the task of interpretation are possible. The choice lies with individual judges so that the court may sometimes favour one method, sometimes another. The vagueness of the language may invite the judges to become legislators. Nor does their position of independence necessarily secure their decisions from the influence of political prejudice. Being composed, as is the United States Supreme Court, of nine judges it is not always unanimous in its decision of constitutional issues, though the cases show that unanimity, at all events until recently, has usually been achieved. In the event of dissenting opinions the courts are likely to prevent fundamental changes being achieved by legislation, though they may ultimately provoke changes by more violent methods, or at least force an amendment of the constitution.

The judges can hamper a New Deal, whether in the United States or in Canada, by a single judgment on a point of law. No such function can fall to the House of Lords sitting in its appellate capacity.[1] Legislation far more drastic in the inroads which it makes upon the property and civil rights of the individual than anything hitherto suggested in the United States or Canada is unchallengeable in the courts of this country, because no court can declare invalid the provisions of an Act of Parliament on any ground. There is no such doctrine as the unconstitutionality of legislation by Parliament. The Canadian programme of social legislation prior to the Second World War was extremely moderate compared with the development of social services which had been attained in the United Kingdom. Yet it was destroyed as encroaching upon the spheres reserved to the federating Provinces by the British North America Act, 1867, in a series of judgments. Canada also as an independent member of the family of nations was denied a power which she could enjoy as a unit of the Commonwealth. This result followed because Section 132 of the British North America Act, 1867, gave the Parliament of Canada power to legislate in order to implement treaties concluded by the Crown

[1] Except to a limited extent in appeals from Northern Ireland.

for Canada as a part of the British Empire on the advice of the Cabinet of the United Kingdom. The Act did not provide for a similar power to legislate in cases where the King was advised seventy years later as to the exercise of the treaty-making power by his Canadian Ministers to ratify an international convention for Canada in her new status as an international juristic person. The delegation of the treaty-making power to a colonial Government was not in contemplation in 1867. It was an accomplished fact of some ten years' standing when the Judicial Committee of the Privy Council was called upon to decide upon the constitutionality of the Weekly Rest in Industrial Undertakings Act, 1935, and the Minimum Wages Act, 1935, in the *Attorney-General for Canada* v. *Attorney-General for Ontario*.[1] The distribution of legislative power between the Dominion and the Provinces is based upon classes of subjects. " Property and civil rights " in a Province are assigned by the constitution to the Provincial legislatures. Save by the method of constitutional amendment, no further legislative competence could be obtained by the Dominion from its accession to international status despite the consequential increase in its executive functions. Canada is fully equipped to legislate upon every topic, including the performance of treaty obligations, but the legislative powers remain distributed. It is only by co-operation between the Dominion and the Provinces that real progress can be made in any topic of legislation, which though falling within the ambit of the Provinces is considered ripe for action by the Dominion as a whole.

[1] [1937] A.C. 326; C.L.C. 256.

This example, taken from a series of cases which with two exceptions were decided against the validity of the New Deal legislation in the Dominion of Canada,[1] suffices to show that in a federal constitution (1) it is difficult to adapt the constitution to changing political conditions: (2) the federal administration is not free to adopt a policy of centralisation, no matter how urgent may be the demand for national, as opposed to provincial, action, save only within the boundaries of a constitution which in practice is apt to be unalterable: (3) unless the member States are willing to abandon their sphere of legislative competence, no federal State in the enjoyment of a parliamentary form of government can by constitutional means achieve that concentration of power which is essential to the totalitarian State. That it can be achieved in other circumstances is evident from the evolution of the Union of Soviet Socialist Republics, which remains after forty years definitely a dictatorship.

It may then be argued that the federal State constitutes a bulwark against dictatorship. In every federal State there exists a dual bureaucracy, but it is a bureaucracy which is controlled by the constitution. One part cannot enlarge its powers at the expense of the other. Judicial interpretation may swing the balance in favour of federal or State government, but a drastic increase of power one way or the other is unattainable. On the other hand, it may be difficult in such circumstances to achieve that new conception of liberty which is

[1] See 15 *Canadian Bar Review*, (1937), 393-507, for a series of critical articles upon these decisions.

regarded as essential in modern civilisation. For liberty to-day involves the ordering of social and economic conditions by governmental authority, even in those countries where political, if not economic, equality of its citizens has been attained. Without expansion of that authority, which federal States must find more difficult to achieve than a unitary State like the United Kingdom, there is inevitably a risk that the constitution may break down before a force which is not limited by considerations of constitutional niceties.

Dicey was concerned to show that under a federal, as under a unitarian, system there existed a legal sovereign power, difficult though that sovereign was to discover and still more difficult to rouse to action. The comparison which he sought to make was between the Parliament of the United Kingdom and the sovereign power in the United States with its complicated machinery for constitutional amendment. But the rigidity of a constitution may equally be a feature of a unitary State. The real ground of contrast is between a State where the constitution may be altered by simple enactment of the legislature and one where special machinery has to be evoked to effect such a change. In the former case the political sovereign is more powerful. For it can, by determining the political character of the Administration for the time being, ensure that radical changes are brought about by a simple act of the legislature. Under the latter type of constitution, particularly in a federation of States, any amendment is difficult to secure and may raise the issue of constitutionality in the courts.

Sovereignty and the Statute of Westminster.—Apart from problems of federation the legal rule of parliamentary sovereignty raises more difficult issues both of inter-Commonwealth relations and of constitutional law within the member States of the Commonwealth. Dicey's statement that the rule of the Queen in Parliament at Westminster extended everywhere in the Queen's dominions has ceased to be the law. Long before 1931 the independence of the older members of the Commonwealth had received recognition. Independence from the United Kingdom became a political reality in the years which immediately followed the First World War. This culminated in the famous pronouncement from the Imperial Conference, 1926, which acknowledged independence of status. It was left to the Statute of Westminster, 1931, to give legal effect to an independence which in the sphere of legislation had been achieved by the customary abstention by the United Kingdom Parliament from passing legislation for the Dominions (as they were then called) unless a Bill was expressly requested by a particular Dominion. Canada thus continued to seek legal effect for its changing constitution in the form of legislation passed at Westminster but shaped in Ottawa. The initiative for legislation for a Dominion had long ceased to come from Westminster. But this did not represent the law. It was a legal requirement that the British North America Act, 1867, could only be amended at Westminster. Moreover the Colonial Laws Validity Act, 1865, extended to every colony, and therefore despite the change from colonial to self-governing status of such former colonies as the Provinces of

Canada and the States of Australia, all were bound by the provisions of the Act which forbade the enactment by the local legislature of any Bill which conflicted with the statute law of the United Kingdom which extended to such colony. Despite the convention of non-interference in the legislative field, there were even as late as 1930 a number of Acts of the Westminster Parliament which operated throughout the territories of the Crown, irrespective of their constitutional status. For example, the Judicial Committee Acts, 1833 and 1844, placed restrictions on the competence of all the Parliaments of the Dominions to legislate upon judicial appeals. The Merchant Shipping Act, 1894, applied to all British ships, though colonial legislatures were empowered to modify its local application.

Accordingly, the first main provision of the Statute of Westminster was to repeal the Colonial Laws Validity Act in its application to the Dominions—at that time limited to Canada, Australia, New Zealand, South Africa, the Irish Free State [1] and Newfoundland.[2] This Act provided that the enactments of a colonial legislature must not be repugnant to any statute law of the United Kingdom Parliament which extended to such colony, but authorised repugnancy to English common law. The Act never applied to Ireland under the Union and therefore had no application to the Irish Free State (as it then was). The repeal of the Act necessitated provision being made

[1] By the Ireland Act, 1949, the republican status of Ireland outside the Commonwealth was recognised.

[2] Subsequently, by agreement with the Dominion of Canada, Newfoundland became a province of the Dominion.

to avoid a restoration of the doubtful position which existed in colonies with representative legislatures prior to 1865. Accordingly the repealing section goes on to provide:

> No law and no provision of any law made after the commencement of this Act by the Parliament of a Dominion shall be void or inoperative on the ground that it is repugnant to the law of England [*sc.* the common law] or to the provisions of any existing or future Act of Parliament of the United Kingdom, or to any order, rule or regulation made under any such Act, and the powers of the Parliament of a Dominion shall include the power to repeal or amend any such Act, order, rule or regulation in so far as the same is part of the law of the Dominion. (S. 2 (2).)

The subsection thus ensured that the doctrine of repugnancy should have no application to a Dominion and that the Parliament of any Dominion shall have power to repeal or amend any existing or future Act of the Parliament at Westminster which is or might in the future be part of the law of that Dominion. There is no provision as to the manner in which the Parliament of a Dominion should exercise this power. We have seen above how the South African Courts have interpreted the section as not changing the definition or mode of legislation in the Union.[1] The Statute of Westminster itself provided in Sections 7, 8 and 9 that the law relating to constitutional amendment in Canada, Australia and New Zealand before its enactment should remain in force for the time being. There has been much discussion as to the intention of Parliament in enacting Section 2 (2) and its bearing on the nature of legislative authority to

[1] Pp. lvii *et seq.*, *ante*.

be exercised in the Commonwealth after 1931.[1] Prior to the decision in *Harris* v. *Minister of the Interior* legal opinion in the Commonwealth was practically unanimous in regarding Section 2 as freeing a Dominion to which the section applied without qualification from any existing restrictions on constitutional amendment.[2] The South African decision is of binding effect only within its own jurisdiction.

But the exercise of sovereign authority to-day is based upon the Statute of Westminster not only in those Dominions which were parties to the Statute, but also in the Asian members of the Commonwealth and Ghana by reason of specific statutory enactment similar to that in Section 2 (2) of the Statute of Westminster. Thus the intention in each case has been to limit the area of legislative authority of the sovereign Parliament at Westminster. As to this, as we have seen, Dicey had no doubt that the abdication of sovereignty, whether total or partial, was consistent with his conception of parliamentary sovereignty. He argued that a sovereign power could divest itself of authority in two ways only, by putting an end to its own existence and leaving no means whereby a subsequent Parliament could be legally summoned or by transferring sovereign power wholly or in part to a new sovereign body.

[1] See especially G. Marshall, *Parliamentary Sovereignty and the Commonwealth*, ch. xi, where recourse is had to the history of the enactment which shows that South Africa objected to the insertion of any restrictive provisions to limit the apparently unqualified powers afforded by s. 2.

[2] This view was expressed in the introduction to the 9th ed., pp. li, *et seq*. Professor D. V. Cowen in his essay, *Parliamentary Sovereignty and the Entrenched Sections of the South Africa Act* (1951), challenged this opinion.

It remained to guarantee independent status in the legislative field for the future. This was achieved by Section 4 of the Statute,

> no Act of Parliament of the United Kingdom passed after the enactment of this Act shall extend, or be deemed to extend, to a Dominion as part of the law of that Dominion, unless it is expressly declared in that Act that that Dominion has requested and consented to the enactment thereof.

This provision is a challenge to the rule of legal sovereignty of the United Kingdom Parliament because it raises the question, what would be the effect of an Act of the Parliament at Westminster repealing or amending Section 4 of the Statute? It may be accepted that the question is an academic one and that Dicey's external limitation upon the exercise of parliamentary supremacy would prevent any such repeal or amendment on the initiative of the United Kingdom alone; for it is certain that the existence of the Commonwealth would be shattered by such an action.

It has been seen above [1] that this point was the subject of a judicial pronouncement in the case of *British Coal Corporation* v. *The King*.[2] The Judicial Committee accepted the view put forward by Dicey that the power of a succeeding Parliament to repeal the enactment of its predecessors would prevail as a matter of abstract law, though it was recognised that this power could not in practice be exercised. What Parliament was seeking to do by Section 4 of the Statute of Westminster was to give legal effect to an existing convention which indeed was recited, along with other conventions, in the preamble to the

[1] Pp. xlix-l, *ante*. [2] [1935] A.C. 500; C.L.C. 160.

Statute itself in language identical with that enacted in Section 4.

As a matter of political expediency Parliament is unlikely to repeal or amend the section. It is, however, to be noticed that when the Dominion Governments were confronted with the need for legislation on the abdication of King Edward VIII in 1936 in only one case, that of Canada, was the request and assent accorded to His Majesty's Declaration of Abdication Act which was enacted by the United Kingdom Parliament in accordance with the provisions of this section. Strictly as a matter of law it cannot be denied that the Statute of Westminster, so far as the courts of the United Kingdom including the Judicial Committee of the Privy Council are concerned, has the same effect as any other Act of Parliament. Parliament, therefore, could repeal or amend. But there would be nothing remarkable in the continued observance of a long-established constitutional convention such as that which restrains the Parliament at Westminster from legislating for other States of the Commonwealth. It is moreover a feature of constitutions of the enacted type, particularly those in force in the British Commonwealth, that there are implicit a number of conventions. More particularly the doctrine of ministerial responsibility had not been enacted in the constitution of any such State until Eire enacted a constitution in 1937. Cabinet government thus rests as much upon convention in Canada and Australia, notwithstanding their federal constitutions, as it does in the United Kingdom, except that the actual institution which performs cabinet functions, *e.g.* Federal

Executive Council in Australia, is provided in the Constitution Act. If then the Statute of Westminster is regarded as a document equivalent to a constitutional charter so far as the grant of legislative autonomy to the States of the Commonwealth is concerned, there must be read into Section 4 the established convention of non-interference in order to make permanent the legislative autonomy given by the section. This is implicit in the recital of the preamble to the Statute which declares that it would be in accordance with the established constitutional position that the Parliament of each member should assent to alterations in the Succession to the Throne or the Royal Style and Titles, and that the position with regard to legislation by the Parliament at Westminster is already as enacted by Section 4.

It is to be observed that the Statute of Westminster did not say that Parliament should not legislate for other States of the Commonwealth. Indeed, such legislation was to continue. Section 7, at the request of Canada, saved the power of amendment of the British North America Acts, and to a limited extent amendments to the constitution of the Dominion of Canada are still enacted at Westminster.[1] Neither the Parliament nor the Government of the Commonwealth of Australia is given competence under Section 9 (2) to encroach upon that field of the authority of the States of Australia where before 1931 the Parliament of the United Kingdom could still

[1] British North America (No. 2) Act, 1949, which gave legislative authority to enact constitutional amendments to the Dominion Parliament, excluded certain topics in order to safeguard provincial powers.

enact law without the concurrence of the Commonwealth. In this subsection there is express reference to the existing constitutional practice in relation to legislation by the Parliament of the United Kingdom with respect to matters within the authority of the Australian States; the subsection, therefore, gives recognition as a matter of strict law to an existing convention. It is thus possible to argue that in so far as the constitutions of the States of Australia are contained in Acts of the United Kingdom Parliament which were enacted before federation in 1900, the legal sovereignty remains with the United Kingdom Parliament, subject to the observance of the constitutional convention of non-interference; this means that no change will be made except at the request of a particular State.

In 1934 the Parliament of the Union of South Africa enacted the Status of the Union Act, by Section 2:

> The Parliament of the Union shall be the sovereign legislative power in and over the Union; and notwithstanding anything in any other law contained, no Act of the Parliament of the United Kingdom and Northern Ireland passed after the eleventh day of December 1931 shall extend, or be deemed to extend, to the Union as part of the law of the Union, unless extended thereto by an Act of the Parliament of the Union.

By this Act South Africa has incorporated the Sections of the Statute of Westminster of general application into the law of the Union, but the last words of Section 2 go further than Section 4 of the Statute of Westminster, which only stipulates for the declaration in a United Kingdom Act of the request and consent of the Dominion. There is no reason why as a matter of South African law the request and consent should not be given by the prior or simultaneous enactment in South Africa of the contents of a proposed Act of the United Kingdom Parliament, though this would be awkward in practice and can scarcely have been intended by those who framed the Statute of Westminster. On another view, Section 2 of the Union Act has amended Section 4 of the Statute of Westminster. This view conflicts directly with the legal sovereignty of the Parliament of the United Kingdom, for it cannot be assumed that that Parliament has limited its legal rights under Section 4 of the Statute through the agency of the Union Parliament. That Parliament has power to amend since 1931 existing and future Acts of the United Kingdom Parliament so far as they may be part of the law of South Africa; Statute of Westminster, s. 2. Upon this would seem to rest the claim to modify the Act which gave it this power. On the other hand, the courts of South Africa have accepted the view that the Union Parliament is sovereign in its own sphere and that its power to amend the South Africa Act, 1909, which gave it this constitution, is derived from that Act and not from Section 2 of the Statute of Westminster.[1] No one can doubt that the claim of the Union of South Africa to autonomy must prevail and it is easier to accept this view if the question of a future amendment or repeal of Section 4 of the Statute of Westminster is regarded as limited by the constitutional convention of non-interference.

[1] For recent developments in South Africa in relation to the sovereignty of Parliament, see pp. lvii *et seq.*, *ante*.

Although the Statute of Westminster applied only to four of the existing States of the Commonwealth, namely, Canada, Australia, New Zealand and South Africa, provisions reproducing the effect of Section 4 of that Statute are to be found in the legislation which gives independent status within the Commonwealth to India, Pakistan, Ceylon, Ghana and the Federation of Malaya. Similarly, except in the case of India, Pakistan and Malaya, which were never colonies in the legal sense, the Colonial Laws Validity Act was repealed in its application to these countries before they assumed independence.

The Statute of Westminster also changed a rule of the common law which detracted from the full sovereign status of colonial territories. This rule, which purported to limit the application of colonial legislation to the territory of the colony, has itself always been the subject of disputation since the colonies obtained self-governing status. The Statute of Westminster by Section 3 declared that the rule no longer had any application to the Parliaments of the Dominions, which henceforth had full power to make laws having extra-territorial operation. The section does not apply to the Provinces of Canada or the States of Australia, nor to existing colonial territories. It does, however, apply by express enactment to all Commonwealth States created since 1931.

Dicey's Views on the Parliament Act, 1911.—In the Introduction to the eighth edition in 1914, which was the last from the pen of the author, he discussed the effect of the Parliament Act, 1911, on the sovereign power of Parliament. His conclusion was that sovereignty still rested in the King and the two Houses of Parliament, but that the Act had greatly increased the share of sovereignty possessed by the House of Commons. Since 1914 we have seen a further increase in the powers of the House of Commons in relation to legislation which is rejected by the House of Lords: the Parliament Act, 1949, has reduced the suspensive veto of the House of Lords, in the case of Bills other than Money Bills, to a period of not more than twelve months provided that identical Bills have passed the Commons in two successive sessions, but made no change in relation to Money Bills, which continue as under the Act of 1911 to be capable of receiving the Royal assent without the assent of the House of Lords. It is also to be noted that no more than three measures, all of them non-Money Bills, have become law under the provisions of the Parliament Acts over the long period of forty-seven years since the enactment of the Act of 1911. It is particularly to be remarked that during the six years of the Labour Administration of 1945–1951 only one measure, namely that which became the Parliament Act, 1949, had to be enacted without the assent of the House of Lords. This means that the large Opposition majority in the House were persuaded that the convention that at some point the Lords ought to give way to the Commons was to be interpreted in the light of the Parliament Acts as an obligation to yield without first rejecting.

The debates in Parliament and elsewhere which preceded the enactment of the Life Peerages Act, 1958, show that there is no clear policy in any party to dispense altogether with the Second Chamber.[1] There is a clear view in the Labour Party that the hereditary principle ought to be abolished and the opposition to the Act was largely based on the objection that to change the composition of the Upper House by the addition of life peers without altering in any way the hereditary character of the majority of the members was not justified. An argument used by the Government in introducing the measure was that the power to nominate to life peerages would enable the Labour Party more adequately to be represented in the Lords. This curious concern of a Government for its opponents is to be explained by the recognition that the House of Lords has an important task to perform as a revising chamber. Revision is more effective if arguments on both sides can be weighed. The relevance of this to the sovereignty of Parliament is that so important a task as an alteration of law which cannot be challenged in the courts ought to be preceded by as careful a scrutiny in the Second Chamber as is provided by the committee procedure of the House of Commons. Once the sovereign Parliament has acted, nothing but a repealing or amending Act can alter the law. It is thus important to ensure that all legislation receives adequate scrutiny in both Houses of Parliament prior to its enactment. This is particularly necessary when on account of the guillotine or other forms of closure, debate in the House of Commons is liable to curtailment. This is not, of

[1] In most continental countries the House of Lords as the Upper House, in England invariably referred to as the Second Chamber, would be described as the First Chamber.

course, the only argument in favour of a strong Second Chamber. In federal States the Upper House is usually constituted with a view to preserving absolute equality of voices among the member States whereas the Lower House reflects the varying population of each State. In such a federal State the central legislature is never sovereign, since to give it plenary powers would enable it to reduce the powers of the legislature of the member States without their consent.

The two Parliament Acts have reduced the capacity of the House of Lords to reject legislation to a suspensive veto which can operate only for a few months. It was the policy adopted by the House of Lords during the rule of the Labour Government, 1945–1951, which made it unnecessary for the House of Commons to assert its superiority.[1] In all the years which have elapsed since 1914, when the First World War stilled any further conflicts between the Liberal majority in the House of Commons and the Lords, there have really only been six years when the Lords and the Government were likely to conflict. It may be that the fear of rejection by the Lords weighed with Mr. Attlee (as he then was) and his colleagues in presenting measures to Parliament. There is, however, little direct evidence that this was so. The Opposition Peers, despite their overwhelming numerical superiority, were ready to acknowledge that the Government had the authority of the electorate for the legislative programme which was presented to Parliament after the Second World War. It seems to be a fact that until the unforeseen introduction of the Parliament Bill, 1947, there was

[1] P. clxx, *post.*

never any question of rejection of any Bill promoted by the Labour Government. So long as the House of Lords of its own accord accepts the rule that it is not entitled to reject legislation which has been passed by the Commons, it is difficult to assess the validity of Dicey's conclusion that the Parliament Act had greatly increased the share of sovereignty possessed by the House of Commons. But it is possible to agree that the relationship between the two Houses has changed. The House of Lords has shown itself unwilling to risk conflict with the Commons and, reluctant to invoke the procedure of the Parliament Act, it has accepted the right of the majority of the House of Commons to impose its legislative will rather than to emphasise its own impotence by using its delaying powers. The value of these powers is perhaps increased by their non-use. If a future Government using its majority in the House of Commons insisted on legislation which was clearly opposed to the wishes of the vast majority of the electorate, even the present very short period during which the suspensive veto can operate might suffice to prevent the operation of the unpopular enactment. When one sees the ease with which revolutionary changes have been introduced on the continent of Europe, it would be rash indeed to acknowledge the absolute right of the Commons to legislate without reference to the Upper House.

(4) THE RULE OF LAW

The Principle ; what it means.—The supremacy of the law of the land was not a novel doctrine in the nineteenth century. Let no one suppose that Dicey invented the rule of law. He did of course put his own interpretations upon the meaning of that rule. The rule itself, Holdsworth has shown, may be traced back to the mediaeval notion that law, whether it be attributed to a supernatural or human source, ought to rule the world.[1] It is within memory that a principal war aim of the Allies in the Second World War was the restoration of the rule of law in Europe. By this was meant that the rule of the occupying State which had invaded another State by an act of war should be replaced by the restoration to the invaded country of its own system. This did not mean a system identical with that prevailing in the United Kingdom or any other Allied State, but only that the occupied State should be free to adopt whatever system of law it chose in place of the existing rule of the occupying State by force of arms. In another sense the rule of law means the recognition of certain fundamental obligations as binding upon States in their dealings with one another. These are the rules of public international law. To-day in the United Nations we have an organisation which claims to give effect to the rule of law, however imperfectly it may function in practice. The progress which has been made towards the recognition of the human rights of individual citizens within their own States approaches more closely to Dicey's conception of equality before the law. The fact that any reign of law may be reduced to anarchy by a lawless minority or gravely obstructed by diplomatic finesse does not detract from the recognition that the rule of law in

[1] See Holdsworth, *History of English Law*, vol. ii (1923), pp. 121, 133, 195, 196, and vol. x (1938), pp. 647-650.

this sense should be observed throughout the civilised world.

Sometimes the term is synonymous with the maintenance of law and order. In this sense, no State would deny its recognition. Law and order can be preserved by a dictatorship as well as by a parliamentary or other liberal form of government. Had the Stuart claim to rule by prerogative prevailed, England would have achieved a rule of law, more primitive in its conception, but none the less efficacious for the maintenance of law and order. Nor need tyranny necessarily have ensued. For the absolutism of the monarch is a feature practically unknown to English history. Even Henry VIII was a rigid adherent to constitutional niceties, if the phrase may be permitted of an era which did not yet know the term, constitution. The famous *Lex Regia*, 1539 (Statute of Proclamations), did not give the King and the Council power to do anything they pleased by royal ordinance. It was in fact a genuine attempt by the King and Parliament to deal finally with the obscure problem of the authority possessed by proclamations. It safeguarded the common law, existing Acts of Parliament, rights of property, and prohibited the infliction of the death penalty for breach of a proclamation.[1]

Although this Statute was repealed six years later on the accession of Edward VI, the Crown under Mary and Elizabeth I continued to use proclamations for purposes of legislation. With the coming of the

[1] Holdsworth, *History of English Law*, vol. iv (1924), pp. 102, 103; Adair, *English Historical Review*, vol. xxxii (1917), p. 35; and cf. Dicey's view on p. 51, *post*, which finds little support among modern authorities.

Stuarts, James I could appeal to the law and invoke precedents from an earlier period with at least as much conviction as his opponents.

The Case of Proclamations[1] is nowadays rightly regarded as denying to the Crown the power to legislate by prerogative. Even though the decision may have been disregarded by Charles I, there is no doubt that it paved the way for modern constitutional developments which have brought the Crown under the law.

The notion of the rule of law in the narrower sense of the predominance of the law of the State usually takes the form of the supremacy of certain fundamental laws. Modern constitutions which are based upon the continental rather than the British model stress the value of certain primary rights. The presence of such in a constitution is some guarantee of permanence; in theory they are intended to be unchangeable, unless the safety of the State demands temporary suspension. Even with us the idea of unchangeable rules of law finds some support, partly in the presence of Magna Carta in the forefront of the statute-book, more directly in those provisions of the Bill of Rights and Act of Settlement which are accepted as the basis of the modern constitution.

When it is claimed for the Bill of Rights that it is the starting point of modern parliamentary government, it is important to note that nothing in the Bill denied the existence of the royal prerogative to the Crown. The Bill enumerated specific acts hitherto performed under the authority of the prerogative

[1] (1610) 12 Co. Rep. 74; K. & L. 73.

and either brought them under parliamentary control or alternatively denied the existence of the particular power in the Crown. Thus there has always remained a residue of discretionary power in the Crown. It is the fact that this discretion is circumscribed by rules both of the common law and of statute law which enables the claim to be made that in England the Executive no longer is endowed with wide absolute discretionary powers. In other words the Crown, *i.e.* the Executive, is under the law.

In England the doctrine of the supremacy of the common law had to be reconciled with the claims of Parliament to supremacy. The recognition of the legislative powers of Parliament precluded insistence on the part of the lawyers that in the common law there existed a system of fundamental laws which Parliament could not alter, but only the judges could interpret. The price paid by Coke and his followers for their alliance with Parliament, which ensured the defeat of the Crown's claim to rule by prerogative, was that the common law could be changed by Parliament, but by Parliament alone. Moreover, the judges evolved a technique of interpretation which created a presumption against any but express alteration of the common law in interpreting statute law.[1] But the common law could never have

[1] Abandoning the mediaeval idea that there was a fundamental and immutable law, the common law recognised the legislative supremacy of Parliament. But to the words of the Parliament whose literal authority it thus recognised it accorded none of that aura of respect and generosity of interpretation with which it surrounded its own doctrines. The courts never entered into the spirit of the Benthamite game, but treated the statute throughout as an interloper upon the rounded majesty of the common law. The tendency still persists; the courts show a ripe appreciation of institutions of long standing,

achieved those radical changes in the State which were overdue even in the seventeenth century. These could, however, have been effected as well by the prerogative as by Parliament. But the alliance of Parliament and the common lawyers made it certain that in the long run the supremacy of the law would come to mean the supremacy of Parliament. "The supremacy of the existing law, so long as Parliament saw fit to leave it unaltered, was guaranteed by the powers of Parliament; and to Parliament they (the common lawyers) could safely leave the task of maintaining this position."[1] Sir William Holdsworth wrote these words of the sixteenth century, of a period before issue was joined with the Crown. But they were justified by the results of the revolution of 1689, which laid the foundation of the modern constitution. Much of Dicey's analysis of the rule of law rests upon this foundation, as a comparison between some of the principal provisions of the Bill of Rights and the contents of Chapters V-X of this book will show. He discusses what Holdsworth calls the common law of the constitution, with special reference to personal liberty, liberty of discussion and freedom of assembly.

whether founded by statute or in the common law, but they inhibit themselves from seizing the spirit of institutions and situations which are in substance the creation of modern legislation. By repercussion draftsmen tend to concern themselves with minutiae, so that their intention may be manifest in every particular instance to upset the hydra-headed presumptions of the courts in favour of the common law. R. T. E. Latham, *The Law and the Commonwealth* in *Survey of British Commonwealth Affairs*, vol. i (1937), pp. 510-511. It is fair to add that in the opinion of Lord Wright, this principle of construction is now discredited: *Liberty in the Common Law*, 9 C.L.J. 3.

[1] Holdsworth, *History of English Law*, vol. iv (1924), pp. 187-188.

To-day the common lawyer is faced with a position in which Parliament has enacted a complex body of administrative law particularly for the maintenance of public services which formed no part of the functions of government in the past. Apart from these services the State has assumed control over the use of land and in a number of cases is able compulsorily to acquire land for public purposes. None of this has made any great change in the traditional protection which the common law affords to liberty of the person and freedom of discussion. Even when Parliament in each of the two World Wars authorised the Executive in wide terms to invade these fields of individual liberty, relatively small use was made of the powers of detention and censorship by the Executive and they were revoked within a short period after the end of active hostilities. While they were in force, they were kept under constant criticism in Parliament.[1] The growth of new functions of the State has made Dicey's analysis far from comprehensive, but in so far as "the principles of 1689 have become part of the accepted theory of democracy" it is still relevant to the modern constitution. As Jennings puts it,[2] there is much in the Whig philosophy with which any democrat will agree, and the Whig philosophy was derived from those principles of 1689. It is indeed the principal ground of criticism of Dicey's interpretation of the rule of law that it reflects the author's attachment to the Whig tradition. Thus the supremacy of the legislature, which by 1885 had become a representative legislature

[1] Wade and Phillips, *Constitutional Law*, 6th ed., 1960, pp. 674-676.

[2] *The Law and the Constitution*, 4th ed., pp. 299-300.

in fact as well as in name, the control by Parliament of the armed forces, the protection afforded by an independent judiciary against the excesses of administrative officials, and the remedies of the common law against illegal acts as being the means whereby the political doctrines of free discussion and free association are secured, are all in keeping with this tradition and therefore find their place in the analysis.

It was the attainment of independence by the judges of the higher courts which gave emphasis to Dicey's conception of the rule of law,[1] which rests upon the power of the courts to punish individual wrong-doers. There are, of course, two aspects of judicial independence—freedom from dictation by the Administration and freedom from control by Parliament. It is an accepted constitutional doctrine that the Ministers of the Crown do not tamper with the administration of justice, but Parliament indirectly has reduced the sphere of influence of judicial independence by the character of modern legislation. The abandonment of the principle of *laissez faire* has altered the nature of much of our law. A system of law, which like the common law is based on the protection of individual rights, is not readily comparable with legislation which has for its object the welfare of the public, or a large section of it, as a whole. The common law rests upon an individualistic conception of society and lacks the means of enforcing public rights as such. The socialisation of the activities of the people has meant restriction of individual rights by the conferment of powers of a novel character upon governmental organs. But these

[1] Cf. Holdsworth, *History of English Law*, vol. x (1938), pp. 644-650.

powers are exercised by an authority which is unquestionably as lawful as that by which the courts impose control in their own sphere. So far as the provision of State social services and the regulation of economic conditions have become part of the accepted philosophy of government, the rule of law rests upon the supremacy of Parliament. It is only, where constitutional law is concerned, in that small but vital sphere where liberty of person and of speech are guarded that it means the rule of the common law. For here alone has Parliament seen fit to leave the law substantially unaltered and to leave the protection of the freedom of individuals to the operation of the common law. Even so there are many examples to-day of control of individual liberty by statutes. The National Service Act, 1948, and the Official Secrets Acts, 1911 and 1920, are outstanding examples.

It is true that the supremacy of Parliament means that as a matter of law the authority of administrative agencies may be still further enlarged. But the difference between judicial and administrative agencies is not fundamental. Both apply the law to individual cases and thereby exercise a discretion. History has shown that in the absolutist State rule by the administration is arbitrary. But if the safeguards which protect the exercise of the judicial function are applied to administrative bodies this result need not follow.[1] It is not the case that Dicey failed to realise that all lawful authority within the State is legal authority, but he relied upon the one organ, the courts, to restrain the illegal excesses of the other,

[1] Cf. Lauterpacht, *Function of Law in the International Community* (1933), ch. xix, sec. 2.

the administration, and did not examine the full extent of the latter's lawful powers. It is upon this limited view of administration that his interpretation of the rule of law rests. But the change of emphasis in the functions of the State has not destroyed the older principles which are protected by the rule of law as Dicey interpreted it in the field of personal liberty.

For behind the elaborate organisation of governmental machinery there rests a fundamental assumption of faith in a democratic form of government. This assumption gives rise to a belief, sentiment, principle or prejudice (it may be named according to taste), which is firmly rooted in public opinion, that there must be no interference by Governments and Parliaments with freedom of speech and freedom of political association to ensure free elections. The appeal to reason must not be restricted by law ; for it is the basis of the democratic form of government. By limiting the restrictions upon liberty of person and speech to offences against the common law determined by impartial judges, by emphasising the personal liability of officials for their unlawful acts, Dicey was giving expression in terms of law to what is still regarded as a principle of democracy. The value of this is more evident in 1958 than it ever was in the author's lifetime.

The Committee on Administrative Tribunals and Inquiries [1] stated that the rule of law stands for the view that decisions should be made by the application of known principles or laws ; in general such decisions will be predictable, and the citizen will

[1] Cmnd. 218 (1957), Para. 29.

know where he is. A decision may be without principle, without any rules; it is therefore unpredictable, the antithesis of a decision taken in accordance with the rule of law. The Committee went on to say that this antithesis, like that between what is judicial and what is administrative, fails to yield a valid principle on which to determine whether the duty of making certain decisions should be laid upon a tribunal or upon a Minister. Without disregarding such principle they prefer an empirical approach. Since they were asked to examine each institution, be it tribunal or public inquiry, or, exceptionally, the Minister as judge, example by example, their deliberations did not at first sight make any notable contribution to establishing the validity of the rule of law. But good adjudication in the view of the Committee calls for the characteristics of openness, fairness and impartiality. These same characteristics are the attributes by which the judges of the higher courts have maintained their independence. We have already seen[1] that it was the attainment of independence by these judges which gave emphasis to Dicey's conception of the rule of law as meaning the capacity of the courts to punish wrong-doers, notwithstanding their official status. The Report of this Committee can thus be regarded as having made a substantial contribution to that revival of the rule of law which has been noticeable in the past fourteen years.

It is when one turns to the international field that there is to be found the most striking evidence of universal interest which this subject has lately

[1] P. ciii, *ante*.

invoked, even in some Communist States, *e.g.* in Poland. Without detailing fully the various activities which have resulted from this interest, the International Commission of Jurists in particular and other organisations of comparative law have concentrated on examining the rule of law. The Commission has sought to formulate the basic elements of that rule. It is encouraging to those who find it difficult to justify all the meanings which seemed so clear to Dicey seventy-five years ago, to find the Commission appreciating that the conception is a complex one which cannot be expressed in a dogmatic formula. If it is to have practical effect in the legal systems of the world, it cannot naturally be confined to the common law jurisdictions with which Dicey was alone concerned. Indeed, the whole approach to formulating the basic elements of the rule negatives the unfavourable comparison which Dicey sought to establish between the common law of England and the jurisprudence of continental countries and in particular of France.

The International Commission of Jurists considers that the basic idea uniting lawyers in many different legal systems is a conception of the rule of law: this is expressed as:

> The institutions and procedures, not always identical, but broadly similar, which experience and tradition in different countries of the world, often having themselves varying political structures and economic backgrounds, have shown to be essential to protect the individual from arbitrary government and to enable him to enjoy the dignity of man.

With this conception in view the Commission has prepared a questionnaire on the nature and working of certain legal procedures and institutions which are widely felt to be an essential protection of the individual within the framework of an organised society. The general report which has been prepared on the information contained in the answers to the questionnaire is not, at the time of writing, available. That such a project should be undertaken in at least twenty-six countries is sufficient evidence that the rule of law is at the present time a realistic conception.

In 1957 there was held in the University of Chicago a conference which devoted the whole of the five days of the meeting to a colloquium on *The Rule of Law as understood in the West*. The conference was attended by thirty-four participants from the United States, including five Deans of Law Schools. The other participants, twenty-four in number, represented the United Kingdom, Western Germany, Italy, Canada, Sweden, Turkey, Brazil, Mexico, Israel, and a representative from both the U.S.S.R. and from Poland. The meeting was held within the general framework of U.N.E.S.C.O. A similar colloquium was arranged to be held in Eastern Europe in Warsaw in September, 1958. It emerged at Chicago that the rule of law as it exists in the Western World is a high achievement, not limited to those countries whose systems of law are based on the common law; that it is the instrument of organised society whose objective is the creation of a community in which a person is enabled to fulfil himself by the full development of his capacities. In short, the conclusion seems to have been that the rule of law is a phenomenon of a free society and the mark of it.

The discussion may be summarised under two

main titles: (1) The presentation of particular national ideas. For example, the methods of controlling executive power, as in the United Kingdom and France, or the control by the courts of the legislatures as in the federal communities of the United States and Western Germany. (2) The impact of the Welfare State upon the rule of law and the relationship of discretionary powers in administrative law to the rule of law.

The discussion was broadly based. The more important of the general statements have been summarised by the Secretary of the Colloquium as follows: [1]

(1) The rule of law is an expression of an endeavour to give reality to something which is not readily expressible; this difficulty is due primarily to identification of the rule of law with the concept of the rights of man . . . all countries of the West recognise that the rule of law has a positive content, though that content is different in different countries; it is real and must be secured principally, but not exclusively, by the ordinary courts.

(2) The rule of law is based upon the liberty of the individual and has as its object the harmonising of the opposing notions of individual liberty and public order. The notion of justice maintains a balance between these notions. Justice has a variable content and cannot be strictly defined, but at a given time and place there is an appropriate standard by which the balance between private interest and the common good can be maintained.

(3) There is an important difference between the concept of the rule of law as the supremacy of law over the Govern-

[1] J. A. Jolowicz, Fellow of Trinity College, Cambridge. The Report and the Digest of Discussion at the Colloquium have not yet been published, but some reference to them may be found in Professor Goodhart's *The Rule of Law and Absolute Sovereignty* (*Pennsylvania Law Review*, vol. 106, pp. 943-963).

ment and the concept of the rule of law as the supremacy of law in society generally. The first concept is the only feature common to the West, connoting as it does the protection of the individual against arbitrary government . . . different techniques can be adopted to achieve the same ends and the rule of law must not be conceived of as being linked to any particular technique. But it is fundamental that there must exist some technique for forcing the Government to submit to the law; if such a technique does not exist, the Government itself becomes the means whereby the law is achieved. This is the antithesis of the rule of law.

(4) Although much emphasis is placed upon the supremacy of the legislature in some countries of the West, the rule of law does not depend only upon contemporary positive law . . . it may be expressed in positive law but essentially it consists of values and not of institutions; it connotes a climate of legality and of legal order in which the nations of the West live and in which they wish to continue to live.

There is no doubt that arbitrary power is to-day resented and feared to an even greater extent than in the late nineteenth century in those States which retain their faith in a democratic form of government. It is needless to emphasise that the main cause for this lies in the menace of communism. Thus the criticisms which in the past were concentrated with some force upon this aspect of the author's work have been superseded by a revival of interest in the conception of the rule of law as being the antithesis to the arbitrary and despotic forms of government which have since come into being in the Soviet Union and its satellite States as well as in China and in other parts of Asia.

The rule of law presupposes the absence of arbitrary power and so gives the assurance that the individual can ascertain with reasonable certainty what legal powers are available to government if there is a proposal to affect his private rights. A person who takes the trouble to consult his lawyer ought to be able to ascertain the legal consequences of his own acts and what are the powers of others to interfere with those acts. The reason why lawyers are apt to be critical of powers of delegated legislation and of the exercise by bodies other than the regular courts of powers of judicial decision lies in the uncertainty which these powers are alleged to produce. It is true enough that on many matters the law as administered in the ordinary courts is difficult to ascertain with any assurance. But in public law this uncertainty is accentuated by the bulk and detail of statutory instruments which are enacted by the departmental Ministers as well as by the impossibility of predicting how in the event of a dispute discretion will be exercised whether the last word rests with a tribunal or with a Minister.

In recent years a good deal has been done to reduce this uncertainty, notably by the enactment of the Statutory Instruments Act, 1946, and the acceptance by the Government of the bulk of the recommendations of the Franks Committee with regard to procedure of administrative tribunals and public inquiries. *Droit administratif* has enriched the law of France because it is administered by a regular tribunal which has all the attributes of a judicial body. It is more difficult to assess the value of the contribution made by the great variety of administrative tribunals which have been set up piecemeal by Parliament in this country. Their types are so various, their decisions promulgated in so many different ways, that hitherto there has been little certainty of the state of the law. A main defect has been the absence of any assurance of a consistent technique of interpretation which alone could make the decisions of administrative tribunals reasonably foreseeable. Now that there is the assurance of an appeal on points of law to the High Court as well as, in some cases, an appeal to a higher administrative tribunal it should be easier to ascertain the limits of administrative discretion.[1] The requirement of reasoned decisions will do much to convince the citizen that administrative tribunals exhibit the characteristics of fairness and impartiality.

Delegated legislation, which was fully reviewed by the Committee on Ministers' Powers more than twenty-five years ago, did not come under examination by the Franks Committee. The terms of reference of the later Committee were strictly limited to the constitution and working of statutory tribunals other than the ordinary courts and to the working of such administrative procedures as included the holding of inquiries. There is in this system an element which may explain some of the criticism which is directed to this aspect of administrative law. Delegated legislation is not, except in form, considered or controlled in a democratically elected legislature. Obedience to an Act of Parliament is more readily obtained because the law is regarded as representing the general will of the people. The passage of a Bill through Parliament can be followed in the press; its provisions not infrequently are modified to meet popular criticism. A government department authorised to

[1] Tribunals and Inquiries Act, 1958, ss. 9, 10, 11.

implement by statutory instrument the provisions of an Act may be at pains to consult those organised interests which are likely to be affected by the regulations which it proposes to promulgate. But statutory instruments do not normally require the approval of Parliament. Nor can they be amended by either House before they come into operation. Since 1944 they have all been subject to scrutiny by a Sessional Select Committee of the House of Commons. In theory either House can reject an instrument—in practice this does not happen. In spite of the better publicity for this type of legislation which has resulted from the Statutory Instruments Act, 1946, there remains a feeling that ministerial legislation is uncontrolled and therefore does not represent the general will of the community. Such a belief engenders disrespect for the law which may on occasion ripen into active disobedience. By way of illustration of the foregoing, the law relating to the use and construction of motor vehicles affords abundant evidence of general disregard on the part of the motoring public of much of the law which is contained in the regulations, though few would be found to assert that the main offences which are contained in the Road Traffic Acts are either unnecessary or unknown.

Application of the Rule of Law to-day.—It is difficult to compare the operation of the rule of law as Dicey understood it in 1885 or even in 1914 with its operation to-day. The difficulty lies principally in the denial by the author that there was a system of administrative law in England; moreover he reacted unfavourably to what he originally regarded as the tyranny of administrative law—*droit administratif* in France—though later he modified his views.[1] He was concerned not with the whole body of the law relating to administration, but with a single aspect of it, namely, administrative jurisdiction (in France, *contentieux administratif*). His comparison was between the favourable position of the English citizen when in conflict with the State in contrast to that of the French citizen. He was at pains to emphasise that powers of government must be exercised in accordance with ordinary common law principles, whereas in France administrative law was contained in a separate system. There is no doubt that Dicey was historically correct up to a point, but originally he failed to interpret the true nature of the *Conseil d'Etat*. As time went on it is possible to detect a fuller appreciation of merit in the French system. But it was not until 1915 that Dicey recognised administrative law as a branch of English public law.[2] These limitations, however, did not seriously diminish the value of his interpretation of the right to personal freedom, the right to freedom of discussion and the right of public meeting. For it is in these subjects that the common law then, as now, plays its most important part in securing the liberty of the individual to criticise government without fear of imprisonment or other forms of suppression. It may be necessary for the State to supplement the common law on these topics by statutory provisions, but so long as the law relating to arrest and the law

[1] See especially an analysis of the contents of ch. xii in successive editions by Professor F. H. Lawson in his article, *Dicey Revisited*, in *Political Studies* (to be published in 1959).

[2] See pp. cxlviii *et seq.*, *post*, and Appendix 2.

of defamation rest on the common law, so long it will be true, as Dicey asserted, that " no man can be made to suffer restraint on his physical freedom or to pay damages for expressions of opinion not forbidden by law " ; so long too will his rights and liabilities be determined by the ordinary courts ; and, provided one recognises the above limitations, an individual's rights, as Dicey asserted, are far less the result of our constitution than the basis on which constitutional liberty (rather than the constitution itself) is founded.

It is instructive to look at the contents of Part II, the Rule of Law. The chapter titles reveal that the Army and the Revenue are the only branches of central administration which come under consideration. With local government Dicey is not concerned at all. The police forces figure prominently in the chapters which deal with the liberties of the subject because their powers are mainly governed by the common law. The emphasis is upon the limitations placed by the law on the exercise of power. In a society which desired to limit the functions of the State to the maintenance of order and did not envisage taxation as a means of redistributing the wealth of the nation or of providing public social services, the Army, the Revenue and the Police in their relation to the individual subject are clearly the most important topics for discussion. This is admittedly only one aspect of public administration. The activities of Governments can be controlled by the law and by ministerial responsibility to Parliament. Dicey's emphasis is largely upon control through the law. Chapter XI (Responsibility of Ministers) occupies but three pages of the text and dismisses the responsibility of Ministers to Parliament as a matter depending on the conventions of the constitution with which law has no direct concern. For the rest he only discusses the legal responsibility of Ministers for the prerogative acts of the Sovereign. Individual liberty of action and how it is guarded by the courts is his theme. The argument is that the courts afford remedies for all illegalities by whomsoever committed and that these are at least as effective as the guarantees contained in a formal constitution.

In one respect Dicey paints a picture more favourable to individual liberty than was at that time the case in point of actual law, for he does not discuss the immunities enjoyed by the Crown prior to the enactment of the Crown Proceedings Act, 1947, which first brought the Crown within the ordinary rules of vicarious liability for the acts of its servants or agents. His interest is in the wrongful interference with personal liberty or property rather than in the damage caused negligently by doing something which is otherwise lawful.[1] Had Dicey examined the full range of administrative law in the sense of the organisation, method, powers and control of public authorities, he would have been forced, even in 1885, to enumerate a long list of statutes permitting the exercise of discretionary powers which could not be called in question by the courts. Abuse and excess could be checked then

[1] This is the view expressed by Professor Lawson in his *Dicey Revisited* in connection with Dicey's understanding of the French treatment of wrongful acts committed by officials. He makes the point that at the time Dicey first wrote, and even as late as 1908, wrongs committed by public officials were mainly of the former type; hence Dicey's emphasis that no action could be brought in an ordinary French court against a public official.

as now by certiorari, prohibition and, to some extent, mandamus. For example, the Public Health Act, 1875, afforded many examples of such powers. Administration rests not upon the illegal use of power but on the exercise of discretion by the administrator. But Dicey's interest in discretions is not in their control by the courts whether they could be challenged, in particular by certiorari, but in denying their existence. Yet discretions are the most important of all topics for the modern constitutional lawyer.[1] It is not then surprising that an exposition of the rule of law which denied the existence of " the exercise by persons in authority of wide arbitrary or discretionary powers of constraint " has served as a text for those who are opposed to the collectivist activities of the modern State. The administrator to-day is fully equipped with statutory powers and therefore has in law the discretionary power wherewith to perform his branch of administrative activity in the public interest. But the reader can still turn to Dicey's chapters on the rule of law with profit if his interest lies in what may be called the political rather than the economic field of liberty, that of person and of opinion in its various manifestations. It is, therefore, more profitable to discuss the application of the rule of law as Dicey understood it rather than to try to apply it to the complicated modern administrative system with which even if it had its beginnings in his time, he could never have had close acquaintance.

His three meanings may be paraphrased as follows:

(i) Liberty of action by the individual in England is conditioned by the regular rules of law which the

[1] K. & L. 256.

courts apply. This excludes arbitrary interference by the Government. Like private individuals, the officers and servants of public authorities are liable not only for their criminal acts, but civilly in respect of breaches of contract and tort at the suit of an injured person according to law. He was contrasting the rule of law with those systems of government which are based on the exercise of arbitrary power by the rulers.

(ii) The courts of law are alone able to determine what is a breach of the law. They apply the law equally to all men. The official position in the State of a particular defendant will not protect him. He will be judged as an individual in the civil courts and not by a special tribunal.

(iii) Foreign constitutions contain statements of guaranteed rights. Such rights with us proceed from the enforcement of private rights by the courts which are able to punish all illegalities. Therefore the constitution, so far as it is concerned with the protection of private rights, comes from the common law. Such private rights are protected by the law relating to arrest, civil defamation and criminal libel, unlawful assembly, the common law prohibition on martial law, and the control by Parliament of taxation and public expenditure.

Nowadays the trend of legislation has narrowed the meaning of liberty of action of the individual, particularly with regard to the disposition and the user of his property. The frequent occurrence of the compulsory acquisition of land for a particular public purpose is one example of this. The owner is obliged to sell against his free judgment. He regards as inadequate the rate of compensation which Parliament allows the public authority to give him, while his neighbour remains free to realise the market value of similar land. No matter how carefully the rules for compulsory acquisition may be revised to ensure fairness of dealing with an objector, ultimately the decision to acquire or not to acquire must lie with a member of the Executive, normally a Minister. This is a negation of that freedom of disposition of land which the common law guarantees. Moreover, the inquiry which considers his objections is a statutory body which Parliament has set up not to administer the common law or indeed, at all events until lately, to follow the procedure of a court of law. Even Dicey towards the end of his life[1] doubted whether official law, "*i.e.* administrative law," could be as effectively enforced by the High Court as by "a body of men who combine official experience with legal knowledge" provided, he stipulated, that they are entirely independent of the Government of the day. Since administrative law is of equal validity with the common law, the latter has grown less significant in its application to certain fields, especially the law of property.

Administrative Law; Substantive Rules.—The chief function of the courts nowadays in relation to the control of public authorities is to prevent an excess or abuse of statutory power. It is in this connection that the topic of discretions is all important. But it is also the function of the courts to enforce the contracts

[1] 8th ed. (1915), pp. xlviii and cxlv, *post*.

and redress the tortious injuries and, if need be, to punish the crimes of public authorities and their servants. In the absence of statutory immunity, every individual is personally liable for wrongful acts whether of commission or omission. Actions in tort lie both at common law and for breach of statutory duty. Obedience to orders does not normally constitute a defence. This is so whether the orders are those of the Crown and its Ministers or of a local authority or other governmental body. The police constable who is sued for false arrest cannot plead that he was acting under the orders of his Chief Constable any more than can the servant of an individual employer or firm. It is, however, comparatively rare for the servants of public authorities to be sued in respect of acts done in the course of duty without the employing authority being joined as defendant. This is so mainly because the authority, like a private employer who can be held vicariously liable, is a more substantial defendant; there are also a number of statutes which grant exemption to servants of a local authority in respect of acts done bona fide in the course of duty.[1] On the other hand, before the Crown Proceedings Act, 1947, it was not possible to sue the Crown in tort and accordingly liability could only be enforced against the individual servant concerned. Where the wrongful act is not done in the course of duty, action will only lie against the individual wrong-doer.

All public authorities are now liable for the wrongful acts of their servants or agents committed in the

[1] Public Health Act, 1875, s. 265; Public Health Act, 1936, s. 305; Food & Drugs Act, 1938, s. 94; National Health Service Act, 1946, s. 72.

course of their employment. The principal exceptions concern the Post Office in relation to the carriage of inland letters and parcels, unless registered, and the Service Departments for injuries sustained by one member of the Forces at the hands of another in the course of duty.[1] This liability was established in the leading case of *Mersey Docks and Harbour Board Trustees* v. *Gibbs*.[2] Accordingly, a public body is in the same position as a private trading company or individual with regard to liability for the negligent execution of their duties by servants or agents.

Where Parliament has expressly authorised something to be done, the doing of it cannot be wrongful. Compensation for resulting damage is usually provided by Parliament. Certain presumptions are, however, observed in the interpretation of statutory authority. When discretionary power is given to a public body, it is assumed that there is no intention to interfere with private rights unless the power is expressed in such a way as to make interference inevitable. Thus, statutory powers which authorised the building of a smallpox hospital in a London suburb were held not to have sanctioned the erection of the building in such a way as to constitute a nuisance at common law.[3] If, however, the exercise of a statutory power, and *a fortiori* of a statutory duty, inevitably involves injury to private rights, or if express powers are given to do something in a particular way which must involve injury, *e.g.* to

[1] Provision is, however, made for disability payment under Royal Warrant.

[2] (1866), L.R. 1 H.L. 93; K. & L. 240.

[3] *Metropolitan Asylum District* v. *Hill* (1881), 6 App. Cas. 193; K. & L. 19.

construct a building upon a particular site for a particular purpose, there is no remedy unless the statute makes provision for compensation.[1] The negligent performance of a statutory duty or exercise of a statutory power may, however, be tortious; and where the exercise of a statutory power necessarily involves injury, care must none the less be taken to avoid aggravating the injury by negligent execution.[2] Where a statutory power can be exercised in a manner either hurtful to an individual or in a manner innocuous to an individual

that man or body will be held to be guilty of negligence if he chooses, or they choose, the former mode of exercising his power or their power, and not the latter, both being available to him or them.[3]

Thus in *Fisher* v. *Ruislip-Northwood Urban District Council*,[4] where a motorist had been injured through colliding with an unlit shelter, it was held that a statutory power to erect air-raid shelters on the highway could only be exercised subject to a duty to take reasonable care to safeguard the public user of the highway by such special lighting as was permissible, even though ordinary street lighting was at that time prohibited.

The omission to perform a statutory duty sometimes gives rise to tortious liability. But this is only if it can be shown that the duty is owed to members of the public as such. It may be that the duty is only to a higher public authority. Thus a farmer who

[1] *Hammersmith and City Railway Co.* v. *Brand* (1869), L.R. 4 H.L. 171.

[2] *Geddis* v. *Proprietors of Bann Reservoir* (1878), 3 App. Cas. 430 at pp. 455-456.

[3] *Lagan Navigation Co.* v. *Lambeg Bleaching, Dyeing and Finishing Co.*, [1927] A.C. 226 per Lord Atkinson at p. 243.

[4] [1945] K.B. 504.

complained of the omission to repair sea defences which had been breached by a storm and resulted in his land being waterlogged for many months, failed to recover from the appropriate public authority damages for the loss suffered by him through the failure of the authority efficiently to execute the necessary repairs. The statute made the authority responsible to a central government department, but not to individual landowners in its area.[1] If a statutory duty coincides with a common law duty, the right to claim damages for its breach remains, unless it is taken away by the statute, as may be the case if the statute imposes a money penalty for failure to perform the duty. It then becomes a question of interpretation whether the remedy for breach of duty is limited to the penalty or whether an action in tort also lies. Usually where a statutory authority owes a duty only to the general public, an action in tort is not available. Thus failure to maintain pressure in water mains, as required of a water undertaking by statute, does not give rise to liability in tort to a plaintiff whose house is burnt down because of the failure of the water pressure. Some statutory duties are absolute. In particular the obligation to fence dangerous machinery is imposed by the Factories Act, 1937, which binds the Crown and all other public authorities, so that an injured workman can recover damages in civil proceedings from a public authority.[2]

So far this short account of the legal liability in

[1] *East Suffolk Catchment Board* v. *Kent*, [1941] A.C. 74; K. & L. 332.

[2] The Crown Proceedings Act, 1947, does not impose criminal liability on the Crown.

tort of public authorities is in accord with the first two meanings attributed by Dicey to the rule of law.[1] It is, however, in the judicial control of the exercise of discretions by administrative agencies that the interpretation of the rule causes most difficulty. If in the exercise of its discretion it can be shown that the authority has acted in excess of its powers, the act can be declared invalid. This does not necessarily, or indeed usually, involve a claim for damages. The remedy can only be sought from the courts by a person who is deemed in law to have an interest in the performance of its duties by the authority. The simplest illustration of this is to be found in the interest which a ratepayer has in the exercise by his local council of its powers *intra vires*. In the nature of things the deliberate commission of an act *ultra vires* is exceptional; moreover the validity of an Act of Parliament cannot be challenged on the grounds that it is *ultra vires*. Accordingly the intervention of the courts is more often sought to prevent a power being abused rather than being exceeded. In particular the exercise of a discretion without taking into account all relevant considerations may be equivalent to a failure to exercise it. Nor will the exercise of a power for an improper purpose be held by the courts to be the exercise of a power within the statute which confers it. Again, acts which are prima facie lawful may be invalidated if they are performed by a wrong procedure. Where a power is deemed to be of a judicial character, its exercise in abuse of natural justice will be treated as a failure to exercise it at all and accordingly the decision reached

[1] Pp. cxvii-cxviii, *ante*.

by the authority may be set aside. This does not mean that where a discretion is given to an administrator an appeal based solely on the merits of his decision lies to the courts. In such a case the appeal is normally to a higher administrative authority or by raising the matter in Parliament. It is not the function of the courts to substitute their own discretion for that of an administrator in the legitimate exercise of his powers.

It is here perhaps that it is most difficult to accept Dicey's interpretation of the rule of law as meaning that no one can lawfully be made to suffer in body or goods through the exercise by persons in authority of discretionary powers of constraint, at all events if by goods he meant also property in general, including land; for it is very largely in relation to the use and ownership of land that restraint can lawfully be imposed by the modern administrative machine. There are spheres of administrative activity where special tribunals are provided for the decision of disputes. In addition to those concerned with land, there are tribunals in relation to national insurance, national assistance, the national health service, military service, the regulation of transport, the imposition of taxation and some other matters where a direct clash between public and private interests may be involved. In most cases, as has been seen, a right of appeal has been provided to a higher administrative tribunal as well as to the ordinary courts on points of law. So far, provided that the tribunals operate in accordance with established judicial impartiality, there is nothing in their existence which conflicts with the rule of law, but it must be remembered that varied and numerous though such tribunals are, their jurisdiction covers a relatively small part of the whole field of administrative activity. Thus it can be argued that all modern governments have that wide arbitrary power of constraint, the existence of which Dicey would deny. This conflict can only be satisfactorily reconciled if it is accepted that Dicey was concerned with a relatively narrow field of administration and more particularly with the attitude of the State to freedom of the person and freedom of speech.

From time to time proposals have been put forward for the establishment of a general administrative appeal tribunal. Two sets of proposals were put before the Franks Committee. The first, that of Professor W. A. Robson,[1] advocated the establishment of a general tribunal with jurisdiction to hear not only appeals from the tribunals or from decisions of Ministers consequent upon the holding of public inquiries, but also appeals against harsh or unfair decisions in that sphere of administration—and it is a wide one—in which no special tribunal or inquiry procedure is provided. Professor Robson has long been an advocate of appellate machinery outside the framework of the ordinary courts which would provide for redress in cases of alleged maladministration. The second proposal, which was first put forward in the pamphlet, *The Rule of Law*, published by the Inns of Court Conservative and Unionist Society in 1955,[2] suggested the establishment of an

[1] Cmnd. 218, para. 120; Minutes of Evidence, days 13-14, pp. 491-495, 506-512.

[2] *Op. cit.*, para. 124; Minutes of Evidence, days 9-10, p. 306.

Administrative Division of the High Court. The new Division, it was proposed, should have general appellate jurisdiction over administrative decisions. Administrators and experts of high standing could either sit as assessors with a High Court Judge, as at present in Admiralty cases, or they could actually form part of the court, as was the case with the old Railway and Canal Commission. The Franks Committee, while expressing their sympathy with the desire to provide machinery for hearing appeals against administrative decisions generally, sheltered behind their terms of reference, which were limited to special statutory procedures involving an inquiry or hearing. They found little merit in a general tribunal to which appeals would lie from an expert tribunal. They also expressed the view on Professor Robson's proposal that the establishment of a general appellate body would involve a departure from the principle whereby all adjudicating bodies are in matters of jurisdiction subject to the control of the High Court. They also felt that final determinations on points of law by an administrative appeal court in relation to tribunals, but by the High Court in relation to matters decided by the inferior courts, would re-create two systems of law. This would be comparable with the former division between law and equity and ultimately no doubt call for a twentieth-century Judicature Act. These last two objections did not apply to *The Rule of Law* proposal, the main purpose of which was to provide a forum of appeal against administrative decisions in general without special reference to decisions by the types of tribunal which were envisaged by the Committee.

There is a substantial body of opinion, not restricted to the legal profession, which would like to see the administrative machine brought under judicial control for remedying acts of maladministration as distinct from excess or abuse of legal powers. Such a proposal would constitute a revolutionary departure from the traditions of our legal system and would, it would seem, inevitably confuse the exercise of jurisdiction with the decision of policy issues. It would also be difficult to preserve the judicial independence of members of the tribunal who would be drawn into the arena of policy-making. If it be right that administrative tribunals should not be regarded as part of the machinery of administration but as separate organs of adjudication, it would be a reactionary step to divorce the ultimate appeal court from the ordinary judiciary. Maladministration involves the misconduct of officials and is quite a separate problem from the control of decisions by administrative tribunals, which are normally staffed by members of the public and not by members of the civil service or local government services.

There are important restrictions on the exercise of discretion where the courts can intervene at the insistence of a person affected. An authority to which the exercise of discretion has been entrusted cannot delegate that exercise to another, unless it is clear that responsibility remains with the delegating authority. In the war-time control of agriculture it was held that an agricultural executive committee could not delegate to one of its officers its discretion regarding the issue of cropping orders given to farmers.[1] This meant in practice that a farmer was entitled to receive his instructions from an expert committee representative of local farming interests. This does not mean that subordinate officers may not be used to give advice, but it does require that the authority to which a discretion is committed must take responsibility for its exercise. It has also been held that an administrative discretion cannot be surrendered if the surrender takes the form of agreeing in advance to exercise it in a particular way or of prejudging the way in which it shall be exercised. Thus in licensing matters, although the licensing committees of the justices have full discretion, they must hear each application and give their minds to each case presented to them whatever general policy they may have decided upon. This is perhaps the strongest example of the courts requiring an all-extensive discretion to be exercised in a judicial manner.[2] Nor can orders of a superior take away the power to exercise a discretion, as where a subordinate official of the Ministry of Labour and National Service who had been given statutory power to reinstate dismissed employees at his discretion failed to exercise it, but applied instead a general instruction given to him by his Minister to order reinstatement in all cases of a particular type.[3] These three examples of the power of the court to enforce the proper exercise of a discretion, without in any of the cases imposing its own discretion for that of the authority, support the

[1] *Allingham* v. *Minister of Agriculture and Fisheries*, [1948] 1 All E.R. 780; K. & L. 336.

[2] *Sharp* v. *Wakefield* [1891] A.C. 173.

[3] *Simms Motor Units Ltd.* v. *Minister of Labour*, [1946] 2 All E.R. 201.

view that even in this field administration must be according to law. Certainly these are cases which in other jurisdictions it would be natural to find the dispute referred to an administrative court rather than to the ordinary courts of the land.

It is through the judicial control of administrative discretions that the observance of the rules of natural justice is secured. These rules apply in particular to the procedure of administrative courts and other statutory tribunals whose powers have been interpreted by the ordinary courts as involving functions of a judicial or quasi-judicial character. This is not the place to discuss the niceties of the distinction between a power to adjudicate which is judicial and one which is quasi-judicial. But it is easy to explain the principle that the proceedings of any tribunal should be conducted in a manner which will ensure that justice shall not only be done, but shall also be seen to be done. The idea of natural justice is one which the ordinary courts have long recognised. So far as this idea is satisfied by giving both sides to a dispute an opportunity of being heard, there should be no difficulty in ensuring observance of the rules. But bias may hamper and even prevent an impartial decision, and it is one of the principles of natural justice that a man ought not to be judge in his own cause. Where it is a dispute between a private individual and a public authority, provision is normally made for the dispute to be heard in public either before an administrative tribunal, or before a public inquiry to be held before a decision is taken. If the decision is one upon which the public authority must ultimately make up its own mind, there is always the danger from the point of view of the opposing individual that the authority may arrive at a decision with a definite bias in favour of the public as distinct from the private viewpoint. A dispute arising as an incident in the administration of a public service cannot, by reason solely of prejudice to private rights, be isolated from the general administrative responsibility of the department responsible for that service. It is for this reason that Parliament has provided in so many cases an independent tribunal to adjudicate the dispute. But where a Minister is required to take the decision it is important that he should explain the reasons by which he seeks to justify it. Only so can he satisfy the private citizen concerned that he has listened to his arguments. Even if he seeks to justify his decision solely by an appeal to the public interest, it is all-important that he should say so. Explanations may not satisfy; they can at least prevent abuses of power which might result from an absence of any obligation to justify their exercise.

If it is difficult to give precise definition to the rule of natural justice which seeks to exclude bias in an adjudication, there are other rules, the scope of which is even less clear. How far does it accord with natural justice that one side knows nothing of the intentions of the other, as may in the past have been the case, before objections are heard at public inquiries? These matters formed the subject of recommendations by the Franks Committee. They favoured a much fuller disclosure of the internal processes by which government departments in particular arrive at decisions. The recommendations have been accepted and have been put into force by the departments concerned, but they are limited to the types of procedure with which the Committee alone was concerned.

Much of the difficulty of the courts in exercising control over acts of the administration has arisen from their own interpretation of what is a judicial power, as will be seen when the procedure of the courts in these matters is discussed.[1] There has never been any doubt that at common law the older principles of natural justice applied to judicial acts in all the ordinary courts, and in particular to the administration of the criminal law in magistrates' courts, where cases most commonly arise for review by the High Court. As first local government and then central government received administrative powers from Parliament, the courts were invited to apply the principles of natural justice in order to ensure that in cases where the right of the individual was in question the decision was not taken without proper investigation into both sides of the question. This was achieved by invoking the rule that both sides should be heard before the administrative decision was reached. Accordingly, judicial procedure has come to be applied as a condition precedent to a certain class of administrative acts.[2] *Cooper* v. *Wandsworth Board of Works*[3] is an early illustration of the reluctance of the court to allow a man to be deprived of his property, even where the deprivation

[1] See p. cxxxiv, *post*.

[2] See H. W. R. Wade, *Quasi-judicial and its Background*, 10 C.L.J. 216, and the same author's *The Twilight of Natural Justice ?* 67 L.Q.R. 103 at p. 106.

[3] (1863) 14 C.B.B. (N.S.) 180 ; K. & L. 366.

is expressly authorised by Parliament, unless he has been given due notice and thus given an opportunity of showing any reason against the deprivation. The district board had power to demolish the plaintiff's partially built house because he had failed to give the statutory notice to the board of his intention to build it. The court nevertheless held that the board ought to have given notice to the plaintiff and to have allowed him to be heard before they exercised their power of demolition of what was in fact an uncompleted structure. This position that no man should be condemned unheard, even when the action taken against him could not be described as of a judicial character, was maintained by the courts until relatively recently. The leading case on the topic is *Local Government Board* v. *Arlidge*,[1] which shows that, although the administrator need not conduct himself as in a court of law or in accordance with strict rules of evidence, the courts will see that justice shall not only be done but also be seen to be done. This means that officials must deal with a question referred to them without bias and give the parties an opportunity of presenting their case in adequate form, but otherwise the administrator can follow his own particular methods of procedure, even though it does not follow meticulously that of a court of law. In this connection it should be remembered that even in a court of law evidence need not in some circumstances be given by way of an oral hearing. In the years which succeeded the Second World War the courts in a number of cases seemed reluctant to intervene in disputes between citizens and public

[1] [1915] A.C. 120 ; K. & L. 369.

authorities.[1] There are, however, signs that this phase is passing and that the meaning of the duty to act judicially is again being extended by the courts.

The true view, as it seems to us, is that the duty to act judicially may arise in widely different circumstances which it would be impossible, and, indeed, inadvisable, to attempt to define exhaustively. Where the decision is that of a court, then, unless, as in the case, for instance, of justices granting excise licences, it is acting in a purely ministerial capacity, it is clearly under a duty to act judicially. When, on the other hand, the decision is that of an administrative body and is actuated in whole or in part by questions of policy, the duty to act judicially may arise in the course of arriving at that decision. Thus, if, in order to arrive at the decision, the body concerned had to consider proposals and consider evidence, then there is the duty to act judicially in the course of that inquiry.

The case from which this citation [2] is taken shows that the courts are unwilling to give up their controlling power over an administrative body whenever the power which is challenged is one that can be decided solely on the evidence and apart from extraneous questions of policy. A legal aid committee is not concerned with questions of policy; it must therefore act judicially in deciding an application solely on the facts of the particular case. On the

[1] In particular *Franklin* v. *Minister of Town and Country Planning* [1948] A.C. 87 ; K. & L. 360, where the selection of a site for a new town was treated as a purely executive decision, and *Nakkudi Ali* v. *Jayaratne* [1951] A.C. 66 ; K. & L. 378, where a government controller was held to be under no duty to act judicially before revoking a war-time licence to trade in textiles.

[2] *The Queen* v. *Manchester Legal Aid Committee*, [1952] 2 Q.B. 413 ; K. & L. 323, where a legal aid committee which had issued a certificate for assistance was held to be under a duty to act judicially although there was no dispute before the committee to be settled. Especially per Parker J. (as he then was) at pp. 428-429.

other hand, many matters which an administrator is called upon to decide are concerned with questions of policy. With these it is not the function of a court of law to reach a decision either in conflict or in agreement with the administrative agency. Parliament has placed the duty of reaching a decision on the administrator. Only in the event of his exceeding or abusing his power can the court be asked to intervene ; even then it cannot substitute its own decision, but can only declare the administrator's action to be illegal and disallow it.

The general public is little interested in nice distinctions between what is administrative and what is judicial. A citizen may feel as much aggrieved when a local authority invades his house or deprives him of his land as if he had been arbitrarily fined by the authority for alleged misconduct. The insistence by the courts of observance of the rules of natural justice can, however, do much to lessen the feeling of grievance on the part of the citizen if he is afforded a judicial hearing before the administrative act becomes final.

Administrative Law ; Methods of Judicial Control.— Without describing in detail procedural remedies by which the courts can control administrative action which is not authorised by law, some explanation of the highly technical processes of the courts is necessary if only in order to understand why so much importance has been attached to the meaning of " judicial " in construing governmental power. Dicey's opinion was that the writ of habeas corpus invested the judges " in truth though not in name with the means of hampering or supervising the whole administrative action of the government and at once putting a veto upon any proceeding not authorised by the letter of the law."[1] He naturally was primarily concerned with this remedy because it is the ultimate guarantee of personal liberty. It is at first sight strange that he did not discuss the other prerogative writs, as they were in his day, which enabled the courts to review, to restrain and even to compel administrative action in the exercise of statutory powers. Had he been concerned to discuss administration as such he would inevitably have dealt with the judicial orders (as they are now termed) of prohibition, certiorari and mandamus.

The primary purpose of the order of prohibition is prevention by a higher court (the Queen's Bench Division of the High Court of Justice) of excess or abuse of jurisdiction or an abuse of legal process by violation of the rules of natural justice on the part of a lower court; the term, lower court, includes not only magistrates' courts and the county courts but also administrative tribunals. Similarly an order of certiorari will issue to remove a case from a lower court into the High Court either to secure a fair trial or to remedy an excess or abuse of jurisdiction or to challenge an error of law disclosed by the record of the lower court. Mandamus is an order issued by the High Court to compel performance of a public duty. Like the other orders it is entirely a matter for the discretion of the court. It lies to enforce the performance of a public duty which has been imposed by statute upon a public authority, but it is necessary for the applicant to show that the duty is one which is owed to him personally and not merely to the

[1] P. 222, *post*.

Crown or the public at large. Moreover it does not lie if there is an alternative remedy. On account of these limitations, the operation of mandamus in comparison with the other orders is confined to a more limited class of cases affecting the administration of public affairs.

So far as the protection of personal liberty is concerned, certiorari and prohibition are seldom invoked. The reason for this is that the writ of habeas corpus raises the general issue of the legality of detention, whereas certiorari is limited to reviewing particular judicial proceedings, and prohibition similarly lies to restrain excess or abuse of jurisdiction by a body which is required to act judicially. In any case, modern administrative methods seldom result in unlawful interference with physical liberty of the person.[1] Even if the police occasionally make a false arrest, government departments, except in relation to the lawful detention of aliens, and local councils do not resort to arbitrary detention. The writ of habeas corpus is a way of challenging peremptorily any action which leads to detention of the person and there is no need, as with certiorari and prohibition, to bring the action within the category of a judicial act in order to secure the remedy. Thus habeas corpus lies to the governor of a prison, who by no stretch of imagination can be said to be acting judicially when he detains a person on a committal warrant issued by the sentencing court. Against such a one neither certiorari nor prohibition could lie. The writ enables investigation of the legality of the detention of the

[1] But cf. *The Queen* v. *Board of Control, ex parte Rutty*, [1956] 2 Q.B. 109.

insane or mentally deficient. In *Rutty's Case* a young woman who had been brought up, on account of abandonment by her parents, in the care of the local authority was made the subject of a judicial order for detention in an institution for the mentally deficient on attaining the age of 17. Up to that age she had remained in the custody of the authority by virtue of its powers in relation to children neglected by their parents. The medical officer concerned with the case regarded the girl as a high grade mental defective, and there was no question of the honesty of his belief. He made, however, the error of securing her detention under an order which only applied to a person who was neglected at the time of its being made. So far from being neglected at that time, she was being looked after by the same public authority as applied for the order. The girl, therefore, had remained in the institution under an order which was illegal. Some years later, with the assistance of a near-relative, the girl, who by that time had been released on licence and was earning her own living, successfully applied to the High Court for revocation of the order. The sequel to the case is interesting since it resulted in an examination of the orders under which a large number of similar "patients" were detained. As a result, a considerable proportion were released from hospital care. Whether or not there was medical justification for the decision in *Rutty's Case*, the requirement that no one can be deprived of their liberty except by due process of law was vindicated.

On the other hand, the orders of prohibition and certiorari fit the need for the protection of proprietary private interests which are so much affected by modern administrative controls. So long as it is the policy of the State to control the use of land, the administration of these controls must conflict with the common law which has always protected the individual proprietor in the enjoyment and disposition of his land and goods. These orders have been used by the courts to ensure the strictest interpretation of the statutes which conflict with common law principles. So much has this been so that it is not uncommon to find that certain statutes have purported to exclude the controlling jurisdiction of the courts by various formulae including one which purports to deprive the citizen of these remedies. But it is doubtful whether any statutory formula has yet been evolved which has the effect of excluding certiorari in the matter of jurisdiction. By Section 11 of the Tribunals and Inquiries Act, 1958, any existing statutory provision that an order or determination shall not be called into question in any court or any provision which by similar words excludes any of the powers of the High Court is not to prevent the removal of the proceedings into the High Court by order of certiorari, or to prejudice the powers of that Court to make orders of mandamus. The effect of this provision is to remove any existing doubt that it was ever the intention of Parliament to exclude certiorari in relation to jurisdiction. Under it the availability of certiorari is not limited solely to matters of jurisdiction. The commonest type of case where certiorari and prohibition have been excluded aimed at the provision of a more summary method of challenge in order to finalise the administrative act, if upheld, more speedily than if it were subject to the longer time limit during which the exercise of jurisdiction could be challenged by these orders.

A more serious limitation on the operation of the orders is to be found in the requirement that they only lie when the body challenged is deemed to be under a duty to act judicially. In the previous section there has been some discussion of what constitutes a duty so to act. It is plain that there are many decisions which any Government may be called upon to take which by no straining of language can be deemed to be judicial. At the other end of the scale no one would dispute that the functions of a High Court judge in determining an action for civil injuries are exclusively judicial. The trouble is that in between these extremes there are widely different circumstances in which it is possible to argue that there is such a duty. In the extract from the case of the Manchester Legal Aid Committee which has been given above,[1] the example of justices granting liquor licences is given as one of the exercise of a purely ministerial power. But this example is doubtful. Certainly justices responsible for administration of the licensing laws are under a duty to hear and determine each individual application and cannot grant or dismiss an application without hearing the parties. To this extent they are under a procedural duty to act judicially. The decisions of the courts, despite the general tendencies which have been discussed above, range over such a wide variety of administrative acts that it is sometimes tempting to conclude that the answer to the question " What is a judicial function ? " depends as much upon the composition of a particu-

[1] P. cxxxiv, *ante*.

lar court as upon the doctrine of precedent. But from the point of view of the application of the rule of law, the conclusion is surely clear. The courts follow the tradition of the rule of law unless their intervention is excluded either by Act of Parliament or by their own interpretation of a power as being beyond their control because of its purely discretionary character.[1]

There are two other methods of judicial control, namely, an injunction and a declaration. The former is a remedy in the strict sense, but the latter, as the name implies, is a mere declaration of the legal position which cannot be directly enforced. Since a public body is unlikely to disregard a decision of the High Court that it is acting or is proposing to act unlawfully, this remedy is one which is obviously capable of affording wide relief. An action for a declaration, however, must be based on a concrete case; the courts will not answer hypothetical questions, lest they should prejudge an actual case which may subsequently come before them.

The High Court may grant an injunction to restrain a person from acting in an office to which he is not entitled.[2] A local government elector may challenge the right of a person to act as an elected member of a local authority.[3] But the commonest

[1] For details of the methods of judicial control see Wade and Phillips, *Constitutional Law*, 6th ed., pt. iii, especially chs. 44 and 45; Hood Phillips, *Constitutional Law*, 2nd ed., pt. iv, especially ch. 25; Griffiths and Street, *Principles of Administrative Law*, 2nd ed., ch. 30 Griffiths and Street, *Principles of Administrative Law*, 2nd ed., ch. 5.

[2] Administration of Justice (Miscellaneous Provisions Act, 1938, s. 9). This procedure replaces the old information in the nature of a writ of quo warranto.

[3] Local Government Act, 1933, s. 84.

use of the injunction is when a citizen who can show that he will suffer special damage as a result of contemplated illegal action or that he has suffered such damage as a result of action which it is not too late to restrain claims that the authority be restrained by this remedy. It can be used to prevent improper expenditure of borough funds. The Attorney-General, either at his own instance or at the request of a relator (one who informs), can seek an injunction if a public body is doing an act which tends to injure the public. The relator need have no personal interest in the claim apart from his interest as a member of the general public. It is at the discretion of the Attorney-General whether or not to proceed. This type of action may be brought even though the validity of the act could be tested by certiorari, and even though the infringement of public rights could be visited with other penalties. An instance of this arose before the modern statutes for the regulation of public service vehicles, when a bus proprietor was restrained from operating his services in breach of a local Act. He had frequently been successfully prosecuted under the Act by the Manchester Corporation, but still found it profitable to operate his buses. The court granted the injunction since the rights of the public were involved by his action, and the remedies provided by the Act had proved to be ineffective.[1]

Relief by a declaratory judgment may be granted under Order xxv r 5 of the Rules of the Supreme Court, which provides that:

> No action or proceedings shall be open to objection on the ground that a merely declaratory judgment or order is sought

[1] *Attorney-General* v. *Sharp*, [1931] 1 Ch. 121.

thereby, and the court may make binding declarations of right whether any consequential relief is, or could be, claimed or not.

This "remedy" is often used in the Commonwealth and in the United States to elucidate the validity of statutes. It is particularly appropriate for the type of dispute which arises under a federal constitution between the Federal and State Governments. In England it has had a more restricted scope. It provides a convenient way of settling a dispute between a ratepayer and his local authority or, more particularly, between two local authorities who are able to have the law determined without seeking a coercive remedy. It is not normally available where there is an alternative remedy, and, as has already been said, the question propounded must not be hypothetical. It can, however, be sought when an alternative remedy is barred by lapse of time. Although a court will only use this discretionary relief sparingly, the Court of Appeal, without laying down the bounds of its jurisdiction, has expressed itself competent and willing to declare any injustice unlawful in the absence of an alternative remedy and further to restrain that injustice by an injunction. The relief has been obtained not only against administrative courts but also against a domestic tribunal.[1]

There is another check which plays an important part in the exercise of discretionary power by a local government authority. This is the power of disallowance of expenditure and surcharge upon the individual members of a council for excessive or

[1] *Barnard* v. *National Dock Labour Board,* [1953] 2 Q.B. 18; K. & L. 523; *Lee* v. *Showmen's Guild,* [1952] 2 Q.B. 329.

illegal expenditure.[1] There is a right of appeal from the surcharge ordered by a district auditor. This lies to the High Court but there is an alternative appeal to the Minister of Housing and Local Government if the amount of the surcharge does not exceed £500. Both the Court and the Minister have power to remit the surcharge at their discretion. Thus a local authority must not, since it is handling public money, use it even for a legal purpose to an extent so excessive as to be unreasonable.

Dicey's Later Views on the Rule of Law.—In the last edition to which he penned an introduction, Dicey made little change with regard to the principle of the rule of law, although he had in an earlier edition somewhat modified his attitude to the nature of *droit administratif*. His principal motif in the Introduction to the eighth edition was the marked decline, as he saw it, in the modern Englishman's respect or reverence for the rule of law. The causes which at that time the author regarded as making for lawlessness have now lost much of their interest. He was concerned with the growing distrust of the judges as shown by trades unionists; with the increasing lawlessness among the clergy with regard to the law of the church; with the passive resistance by dissenters to the payment of local rates; with the conscientious objection to the vaccination law and with the lawlessness of the militant suffragettes. Of more current interest was his view of lawlessness as suggested by the mis-development of party government. "The rule of a party cannot be permanently identified with the authority of the nation or with the dictates of

[1] Wade and Phillips, *op. cit.*, p. 639.

patriotism." A Liberal Government had been in power for eight years when these words were written. Events in Ulster in 1914 had led the author to admit that armed rebellion might occasionally, though very rarely, be morally justifiable. He had been prominent among those who advocated resistance to the Government's Home Rule Bill which passed into law in 1914 under the provisions of the Parliament Act, 1911.[1]

With regard to *droit administratif*, he had by then acknowledged the judicial character of the *Conseil d'Etat* and the work of the *Tribunal des Conflits*. With regard to English public law he showed a change of heart in that he questioned the effectiveness of the High Court to enforce public law. "Nor is it quite certain that the ordinary law courts are in all cases the best body for adjudicating upon the offences or the errors of civil servants. It may require consideration whether some body of men who combined official experience with legal knowledge and who were entirely independent of the Government of the day might not enforce official law with more effectiveness than any Division of the High Court."[2] It could be argued from this that Dicey envisaged ultimately the advent of a final administrative appeal tribunal.

At this point it may be interesting to compare the views expressed in the author's "Outline of Subject"[3] in words which remained unaltered in substance throughout the eight editions, with what he wrote in 1914 in the Introduction to *Law and Opinion*,[4] and

[1] 8th ed. (1915), pp. xxxvii-xlviii.

[2] 8th ed., p. xlviii.

[3] Pp. 1-35, *post*.

[4] 2nd ed. (1914).

again early in 1915 in his article, *The Development of Administrative Law in England.*[1] It may be noted that Dicey used the term, administrative law, as early as 1915. It was not until somewhat later that the subject came to be regarded as academically respectable.

It will be seen [2] that the view was expressed that constitutional law was a province of law, the field of which had not been fully mapped out. The footnote acknowledged the contribution to this task made by Sir William Anson's later work. This work, however, even in its present form, practically excludes consideration of the substance of administrative law, fully though it deals with the organisation of many of the Departments of State.

In formulating the well-known division with its savour of Austinian dogma between rules which are true law—the law of the constitution—and rules which are not laws—conventions of the constitution—the examples given make it clear that Dicey was concerned only with the Sovereign, especially in his relations with the Cabinet, the Central Legislature and the Superior Courts of Record. The administration of public social services hardly entered into his purview.[3]

In 1914 Dicey wrote [4] that "by 1900 the doctrine "of *laissez faire*, in spite of the large element of "truth which it contains, had more or less lost its "hold upon the English people." He pointed to

[1] This is reproduced in Appendix 2, from *Law Quarterly Review*, vol. xxxi (1915), pp. 148 *et seq.*

[2] Pp. 33, 34, *post*.

[3] But cf. pp. 388-390, *post*.

[4] *Law and Opinion* (2nd ed.), pp. xxix, xxxi.

the progress of collectivism in the years 1906–13,[1] citing such important sources of administrative law as the Old Age Pensions Act, 1908, the National Insurance Act, 1911, the Coal Mines (Regulation) Act, 1908, and the Coal Mines (Minimum Wage) Act, 1912, together with the Finance (1909–10) Act, 1910, and other examples. He noted [2] that the National Insurance Act had greatly increased the legislative and judicial authority of the Government or of officials closely connected with the Government of the day and admitted [3] that the Act had created in England a system bearing a marked resemblance to the administrative law of France; and further that such law had some distinct merits. He went on [4] to discuss the causes of the main current of legislative opinion from the beginning of the twentieth century being vehemently towards collectivism. The interdependence of public and private interests, as with the railway companies and their individual shareholders, made it difficult to maintain the antithesis between the individual and the State. He noted a decline in the passion for nationalism and the disappointment at what it had achieved in Germany and Italy. This, he considered, and the declining influence of other movements, made socialism attractive. He expressed some astonishment at the general acquiescence in proposals tending towards collectivism, especially on the part of rich men towards proposals affecting property interests. He recognised the advent of a parliamentary democracy with the growing strength of a Labour minority.

[1] *Op. cit.*, p. xxxiii.
[2] *Op. cit.*, p. xxxix.
[3] *Op. cit.*, p. xliii.
[4] *Op. cit.*, pp. liii *et seq.*

He recorded the spread of collectivism in other countries, and finally referred to the existence of industrial discontent. He saw, however, certain cross-currents.[1] The distrust of State interference was still entertained by the mass of English citizens. Collectivism was inconsistent, in his view, with true democracy. "The ideal of democracy is government "for the good of the people, by the people and in "accordance with the wish of the people; the ideal "of collectivism is government for the good of the "people by experts or officials who know or think "they know what is good for the people better than "any non-official person or than the mass of the "people themselves." [2] Opposition to the financial burdens of collectivism was natural in one whose political faith deplored the use of taxation for the promotion of political or social ends. Finally, Dicey confirmed his belief in individualism in no uncertain terms.[3] But the book leaves little doubt that its author realised the fundamental assumption of collectivism—faith in the benefit to be derived from State intervention—as the explanation of the opinion current in England at the opening of the present century.

The article, *The Development of Administrative Law in England*, was inspired by the decision of the House of Lords in *Local Government Board* v. *Arlidge*,[4] to be read together with *Board of Education* v. *Rice*.[5] The latter case had determined conclusively that an administrative department had power to

[1] *Op. cit.*, pp. lxxi *et seq.*
[2] *Op. cit.*, p. lxxiii.
[3] *Op. cit.*, p. lxxxvii.
[4] [1915] A.C. 120; K. & L. 369.
[5] [1911] A.C. 179.

determine finally a question of law. *Arlidge's Case* showed that such a department in the exercise of statutory functions of a judicial character need not follow the procedure of a court of law, but could employ any rules which appeared reasonable and fair for the conduct of its business. Dicey's deductions from the cases were as follows:

(1) Any power conferred upon a government department must be exercised in strict conformity with the terms of the statute.

(2) A statutory judicial or quasi-judicial authority is not bound to follow the rules of procedure applied in a court of law, but must act with judicial fairness and equity.

He then proceeded to inquire whether these deductions answered the following question: "Has recent legislation, as now (1915) interpreted by English courts, introduced, or tended to introduce, into the law of England a body of administrative law resembling in spirit, though certainly by no means identical with the administrative law (*droit administratif*) which has for centuries been known to, and during the last hundred years been carefully developed by, the jurists and legislators of France?"

He gave several considerations which suggested to him the right reply:

1. New governmental obligations of the past fifty years (1865–1915) almost implied, and certainly had promoted, the transference to departments of the central Government of judicial or quasi-judicial functions. These functions might, as with the procedure under the Workmen's Compensation Acts,

have been left to the courts, but the obvious convenience of the transfer was conceded. Nevertheless "such transference of authority saps the foundation of that rule of law which has been for generations a leading feature of the English Constitution."[1] But, he continued, the Government, like an individual, cannot run a business as a court would conduct a trial. The two things must in many respects be governed by totally different rules.

2. He suggested that it was in harmony with the dominant legislative opinion of 1915 that the House of Lords should have held that the President of the Local Government Board ought to follow the rules which were found fair and convenient for the business of the department rather than exercise the procedure of a court of law.

3. There remained two legal checks upon abuse of judicial or quasi-judicial power, (*a*) the *ultra vires* doctrine, (*b*) natural justice.

Dicey considered the check upon administrative irregularities afforded by ministerial responsibility, which was suggested by Lord Haldane in the *Arlidge Case*, to be a poor guarantee as compared with review by the courts, since it really meant responsibility to the majority for the time being in Parliament. He preferred to recall that legal action by the High Court of Parliament, impeachment, still remained part of the law of England. His hesitant answer to his own question was:

"Modern legislation and that dominant legisla-"tive opinion which in reality controls the action of "Parliament has undoubtedly conferred upon the

[1] 31 L.Q.R. at p. 150.

"Cabinet, or upon servants of the Crown who may "be influenced or guided by the Cabinet, a considerable amount of judicial or quasi-judicial authority. "This is a considerable step towards the introduction among us of something like the *droit administratif* of France, but the fact that the ordinary law "courts can deal with any actual and provable "breach of the law committed by any servant of "the Crown still preserves that rule of law which is "fatal to the existence of true *droit administratif*."[1]

Thus there is evidence that the developments in the early part of the twentieth century had not escaped Dicey's notice and that he had indeed come to recognise the existence of administrative law in England. With regard to the French system equally he had come to modify the critical views which he originally held with regard to *droit administratif*. Chapter XII, The Rule of Law compared with *Droit Administratif*, in the course of the several editions underwent substantial changes. It would now seem that Dicey kept more abreast of developments across the Channel than his earlier critics would have us suppose. But in any case his original criticisms of the French system have been adequately answered by subsequent writers.[2]

(5) CONVENTIONS OF THE CONSTITUTION

The Widened Sphere of Constitutional Conventions.—It is largely through the influence of Dicey that the term, convention, has been accepted to describe a

[1] *Law and Opinion* (2nd ed.), p. 152.

[2] For short Bibliography see pp. 500-502, *post*.

constitutional obligation, obedience to which is secured despite the absence of the ordinary means of enforcing the obligation in a court of law. Dicey defined conventions as "rules for determining the mode in which the discretionary powers of the Crown (or of the Ministers as servants of the Crown) ought to be exercised."[1] He was concerned to establish that conventions were "intended to secure the ultimate supremacy of the electorate as the true political sovereign of the State."

In discussing conventions as a source of constitutional law it must be noted that the obligation does not necessarily, or indeed usually, derive from express agreement. It is more likely to take its origin from custom or from practice arising out of sheer expediency. But international lawyers use the term to describe the results arrived at by express agreement at conferences between individual States as, for example, the Geneva Conventions governing such matters as the use of the Red Cross and the treatment of prisoners of war. Thus the Geneva Conventions Act, 1957, gives effect in English law to the express obligations undertaken by the Government of the United Kingdom as a party to the Geneva Conventions, 1949.

Dicey discusses mainly the rules governing the exercise of the royal prerogative by Ministers of the Crown and that part of the "law and custom" of Parliament which rests upon custom alone. In both these cases the rules are based on custom or expediency rather than as a result of formal agreement. Conventions, however, have a wider application and

[1] P. 423, note 1, *post*.

have, during the present century, played an important part in building up the political relationship between the various member States of the British Commonwealth. Some of these conventions, in particular the rules governing the full competence of Commonwealth Parliaments to legislate, were made statutory by the Statute of Westminster, 1931, and later enactments. But much of the relationship is still conventional and has been based on agreement reached by Prime Ministers at Imperial Conferences. Constitutional matters no longer figure prominently on the agenda of the periodic meetings of Prime Ministers or other Ministers of Commonwealth Governments which are less formal than the earlier Imperial Conferences. But this is because constitutional issues have now been settled and in no way minimises the important part which conventions have in the past played in this sphere of constitutional development. With this recognition it is unnecessary here to refer further to that association of constitutional conventions with law which has long been familiar in the history of the British Commonwealth. As was recognised by the Conference held in 1929 before the enactment of the Statute of Westminster, this association has been characteristic of political development both in the domestic government of Commonwealth communities as well as in their relations with each other. The Conference was in effect saying in a different context what Dicey expounds in Chapter XIV when he states that the association of conventions with law provided a means of harmonising relations where a purely legal solution of practical problems was impossible or would have impaired free development or would have failed to catch the spirit which gives life to institutions.[1]

Dicey concentrated attention upon the conventional rules which precedent showed were fundamental to the working of the Cabinet; that he also included some of the customary relationships between the hereditary House of Lords and the elected Commons reinforces the similarity between the prerogatives of the Crown and the privileges of Parliament. On one view neither are laws proper in the narrow sense that their exercise can be reviewed by the courts, though the courts have always asserted the right to restrain their abuse or excess.

It is the prerogative of the Sovereign to appoint the Prime Minister. Convention limits the range of choice to that of a party leader who can command a majority in the House of Commons. This convention to some extent lacks the binding force which conventions in other fields possess. This does not mean that the rules can normally be disregarded, but that unforeseen circumstances may deprive them of their force on a particular occasion; any departure from the normal would have to conform to recognising the supremacy of the electorate and not to serve autocratic ends. Some writers would not include a practice or usage which is not regarded as obligatory, though none the less usually followed, in the category of constitutional conventions.[2] It is, however, very difficult to draw the line between an obligatory and a non-obligatory practice. The

[1] Cmd. 3479 (1929), p. 20. See generally K. C. Wheare, *The Statute of Westminster and Dominion Status* (5th ed., 1953), and Sir Ivor Jennings, *Constitutional Laws of the Commonwealth*, vol. i (1957).

[2] See Hood Phillips, *Constitutional Law*, 2nd ed., p. 61.

characteristic of conventions, namely, that they supplement the laws which are enforced by the courts, would seem to preclude their precise definition. On the whole it seems preferable to regard the political practices of Sovereigns in choice of Prime Ministers as within the category of conventional rules, even though those rules are still somewhat inconclusive and therefore sufficiently flexible to meet unforeseen circumstances. For they are clearly rules of conduct referable to the requirements of constitutional government and are aimed at reflecting the supremacy of the electorate. The same is true of the practices and precepts which surround the prerogative of dissolution of Parliament. But in this case there is the fundamental understanding that the power may only be exercised on the advice of Ministers. That advice may not be available to the Sovereign in the choice of a Prime Minister, where his predecessor has been removed by death or his own resignation.

Perhaps the relationship between law and convention is best illustrated by contrasting the legal and conventional position of Ministers. They, like civil servants and members of the armed forces, are in law the servants of the Crown. By convention they, unlike all other servants of the Crown, are responsible directly to Parliament both for their own activities and those of civil servants, their subordinates, who by custom are never referred to by name in Parliament. This responsibility of Ministers is designed to make them answerable through Parliament to the electorate. To rely solely on their legal responsibility to their master, the Sovereign, would entirely fail to secure their responsibility to the public in general and indeed might make them the agents of a Sovereign who disregarded the public will, as in the days before the prerogative powers were restricted by Parliament.

Conventions relating to internal government go much further than the examples which were chosen by Dicey from the exercise of the royal prerogative and the relationship between the two Houses of Parliament. They nowadays provide for the working of the whole complicated governmental machine. A Cabinet in deciding upon policy will require to know whether it already has the power in law to take the action which it proposes. It is certainly not limited to exercising those prerogative powers of the Sovereign which are entrusted to it by convention. Through its command of a majority in the House of Commons it is normally in a position to take legal powers if they do not already exist. Moreover it is the responsibility of the Cabinet to ensure unity in the constitutional system and in particular to avoid or, if need be, to settle conflicts of policy and of action by the various departments. In all these activities rules and practices develop in order to secure the desired end. The growth of the committee system within the Cabinet organisation is an extra-legal development which has introduced important changes in Cabinet government since Dicey formulated his views on the place of conventions in the working of the constitution. One can properly describe this development as conventional. It is in no sense an obligation imposed by law upon Ministers that they should consult an elaborate system of committees. Yet no one supposes that a modern government could be conducted without some such machinery. So we have the position that the Cabinet itself is to all intents and purposes the creation of convention designed to secure political harmony between the Crown and its subjects. From this conventional institution there have grown up in the present century such devices as formal committees, like the Defence Committee, and *ad hoc* committees, appointed for a particular purpose but often remaining in being after their original purpose has been fulfilled. Outside the Cabinet itself there are bodies with ministerial chairmen like the former Committee of Imperial Defence and advisory bodies such as the current controversial committee known as the Council on Prices, Productivity and Income. In addition there are royal commissions, select committees of either House of Parliament, committees appointed by departmental Ministers, all of which play an important part in the formulation of policy. For none of these is there any legal requirement. But no appreciation of the working of the governmental machine would be complete without their inclusion. And since their purpose is to focus public opinion on a particular problem, they are designed to secure that harmony between the Ministers of the Crown and the public which is the principal justification for supplementing the law of the constitution with conventions.

Conventions and the Increase of Governmental Power.—As long ago as 1914 Dicey saw in the conventions which he then noted as new, a general tendency to increase the power of any party which possessed a parliamentary majority.[1] " Party warfare

[1] See 8th ed. (1915), pp. lv-lvii.

in England is in short, conducted by leading parliamentarians who constitute the actual Cabinet or the expected Cabinet. . . . It may be maintained with much plausibility that under the quinquennial Parliament created by the Parliament Act the British electorate will each five years do little else than elect the party or the Premier by whom the country shall be governed for five years." He noted the decline in the influence of the private member of Parliament and that legislation had become in effect the business exclusively of the Cabinet. "The plain truth is that the power which has fallen into the hands of the Cabinet may be all but necessary for the conduct of popular government in England under our existing constitution."

At the present time no one would deny the truth of these assertions. Nowadays we have the shadow Cabinet which is formed by leading members of the Opposition in the early days of each new Parliament. General Elections have become contests for power between two parties; the Liberal party no longer has any expectation of taking office; the independent member has been extinguished with the abolition of the university constituencies and the total failure of independent candidates elsewhere to secure support. The influence of the private member has further declined. His opportunities for taking the initiative are fewer than they were forty-five years ago. The power of the Cabinet has further increased, partly as a result of war-time administrations, but mainly on account of the complexity of modern government. This is not the place to discuss the organisation of the Cabinet in time of war, but experience has shown that the normal type of Cabinet must be superseded and control vested in a smaller body. There is, however, a permanent legacy from the war-time administrations which has contributed to increasing the power of the Cabinet and in particular of the Prime Minister. The size of the Cabinet seems to have become fairly constant and after each of the wars of this century has rapidly returned to the peace-time type and size, varying in number between fifteen and twenty. What primarily increased the power of the Cabinet was the institution of the Cabinet Secretariat which was first introduced by Mr. Lloyd George in 1917. Until that date the Cabinet had no formal machinery and indeed kept no records save the traditional letter from the Prime Minister to the Sovereign informing him of the business transacted at each meeting. All this has been changed and the Cabinet is now a body whose decisions, which are called conclusions, give an authentic record of the business transacted. The form of conclusions gives a summary of the information and the general nature of the arguments upon which decisions are based. Conclusions are communicated to departmental Ministers whose task it is to ensure that the necessary action is taken. In contrast, in the past it rested with each member of the Cabinet to interpret in his own terms its deliberations so far as they affected his departmental responsibilities. Nor is this the only contribution which the establishment of the Cabinet Secretariat has made to the effectiveness of the Cabinet itself. It has developed to a high degree the collection and distribution of relevant material in advance of meetings both for the Cabinet and its numerous committees, and gone a long way to securing co-ordination of inter-departmental business. The Secretariat has no executive functions like those of a department, but it has become a highly efficient instrument both for the collection of information and for the reporting, distributing and following-up of decisions taken in the Cabinet and Cabinet committees.

The position of the Prime Minister has undergone change in recent years. Despite his not infrequent protestations to the contrary, few would regard Sir Winston Churchill as an equal among equals, inside or outside the Cabinet. No doubt the extent to which any particular Prime Minister influences the Cabinet depends as much upon personality as any conventional practice. He is, however, no longer simply the chairman of a body whose decisions are not formally recorded but are left for their execution to the fallibility of each departmental Minister. As chairman of an executive body whose decisions are nowadays communicated to departmental Ministers for the necessary action to be taken, he, as presiding in Cabinet, is in a stronger position to influence action than was the case in the days before the establishment of the Cabinet Secretariat started the practice of formally transmitting Cabinet conclusions to Ministers.

There is one department with which every Prime Minister nowadays must be in continuous touch. The perpetual complexity of foreign relations demands that Prime Ministers shall be closely associated with the work of Foreign Secretaries. Prior to the First World War, foreign affairs seem seldom to have occupied the time of the Cabinet. It is clear that of late both Prime Minister and Cabinet must largely concern themselves with the work of the Foreign Office.

Any technique which increases the efficiency of Cabinet government necessarily places greater power in the hands of a Ministry. Up to the outbreak of the Second World War a feature of the political scene was the strength of Ministries in the House of Commons, *e.g.* from 1905 to 1910, 1915 to 1922, 1924 to 1929 and 1931 to 1939. This feature suggested a weakening in the powers of Oppositions and that the assumption of office by Coalition or National Governments had cut at the basis of party government. There was a tendency to claim that party and national interests were identical and to put the Opposition in a false position of being regarded as anti-national if they performed effectively the traditional function of an Opposition, to criticise and, if need be, to oppose. But it is an essential condition of parliamentary government that the Government should govern by agreement with the Opposition. Whatever differences there are should be settled after reasoned argument, for one side of which the Opposition is principally responsible. If a Government successfully identifies its policy with the honour and safety of the nation, the task of the Opposition becomes invidious and correspondingly the partisan authority of the party in power increases in extent. Throughout the Second World War, party warfare was in suspense from the accession to office of the Churchill Government in 1940 until the early part of 1945. From 1945 to 1950 the Labour Government held office with the command of a very large majority in the House of

Commons. Thus far the tendencies already noted would seem to have continued. Since 1950 successive Governments have held office with majorities which have fluctuated between six and sixty. A narrow margin between Government and Opposition in the past would have prevented effective power being exercised for any length of time. But notwithstanding the power which Governments derive from their control of the machinery of State and the sources of information, Oppositions, even though in a position to bring about the defeat of the Government in the House of Commons, have been content to let the life of Governments dependent on slender majorities run their course. For this there are many reasons, among them the dislike of disrupting the life of the community by forcing frequent elections, but perhaps the chief cause for Governments remaining in power, however hard pressed by an Opposition, has been the narrowing margin between their respective policies. To this can be attributed the rapid decline of the third great party in the State, the Liberals. For when the differences between two outwardly contrasting parties such as the Conservative and the Labour Parties are reviewed, experience seems to show that there is difficulty in devising a distinctive policy for yet another party. All parties accept the obligations of the Welfare State, the rule of law in national and international affairs, a defence policy in agreement as far as practicable with our Allies. There is little room for vital differences except in the economic sphere. Even here, to secure the balance of payments is the overriding necessity which any Government must sustain.

Dicey's Later Views upon Conventions.—Dicey's analysis of constitutional conventions has been rightly described by his most formidable critic as a magnificent contribution to English public law.[1] He used the term, conventions, to describe the various customs, practices, maxims and precepts of which constitutional or political ethics consist. He then sought to explain—after a brilliant analysis of their content—the connection between the legal and the conventional elements in the constitution. If to-day the reasons he gave for obedience to conventions are generally rejected, we can be grateful that they afforded him this opportunity for discussing political theory.

A survey of the field of conventions in 1958 must necessarily cover a wider field than was open to examination in 1885. Since that date there have developed most of the conventions upon which depend the constitutional relations between the members of the Commonwealth. The author, in the Introduction to the eighth edition, asked himself whether there had been any notable changes between 1885 and 1914. He found the answer twofold because (A) new conventions had arisen and (B) old ones had been converted into enacted law, or alternatively their operation closely affected by changes in the law. If under the latter head Dicey found his best example in the then recent Parliament Act, 1911, to-day it is in the Statute of Westminster, 1931, and the subsequent enactments affecting Asiatic and African members of the Commonwealth that we find

[1] Sir Ivor Jennings, *In Praise of Dicey*, 13 *Public Administration*, 2.

the legal form brought into line with the conventions which formerly governed the exercise of legislative power in relation to the Dominions. Among the new conventions Dicey discussed the one which he considered virtually compelled a Minister to resign office after defeat at a general election. On four occasions between 1860 and 1886 a Prime Minister had resigned in these circumstances without waiting to meet Parliament; this was contrary to the precedent which had been set by Peel in 1834. This new convention he considered to be an acknowledgment that the electorate constituted politically the true sovereign; that a general election tended to decide that a particular party should hold office for the duration of a new Parliament, and in some cases to elect a particular Prime Minister for that period.

His other examples of conventions which had been developing in the preceding thirty years were: (1) the habit of the reigning monarch to share in and to give expression to the moral feelings of British subjects; (2) the procedure adopted by the House of Commons to prevent obstruction, *i.e.* the various special devices for closure in order to expedite legislation.

What have subsequent developments shown to support these observations?

A. (1) *Resignation of a Ministry following upon defeat at a general election.* In 1923 Mr. Baldwin advised a dissolution in order to secure approval for introducing a system of tariffs as a remedy for unemployment. His party remained the strongest numerically after the election, but had no absolute majority over the Labour and Liberal Oppositions. The Conservative Government met Parliament, was defeated and resigned. The next year Mr. Ramsay MacDonald's Labour Ministry, which commanded only one-third of the votes in the House, except when supported by the Liberals, was defeated on the Campbell case (withdrawal of a political prosecution). The Prime Minister advised a dissolution. The Conservatives were returned with a clear majority and the Ministry resigned without meeting Parliament. At the General Election, 1929, the Conservative majority was lost and the Government resigned. A Labour Ministry took office, though also without a majority, before Parliament met. Similarly in 1945 Mr. Winston Churchill and in 1951 Mr. Attlee tendered their resignations immediately the result of the General Election became clear.

It may be agreed that Mr. Baldwin was not bound by Dicey's new convention in 1923; indeed the situation created by the electorate returning three opposing parties to the Commons in approximately equal numbers makes it even more difficult to accept the electorate as the "true political sovereign"; for that "sovereign" in 1923 had, in Austin's language,[1] failed to impose upon any party the trust "to be imported by the correlative expressions 'delegation' and 'representation.'" In 1924 and again in 1945 and 1951 the General Election decided that a new party should hold office with its acknowledged leader as Prime Minister. In 1929 the decision was less certain; the election showed a decided preference in favour of a change of party, though the Labour

[1] Pp. 74, 75, *post*.

Ministry took office without a clear majority over the other two parties.[1]

(2) *The habit of the reigning Monarch to share and give expression to the moral feelings of British subjects.* It is permissible to say that—(*a*) King George V as witnessed by his actions during 1914–18, by the sympathy shown during his illness in 1928–29, by the acclamation which greeted him and Queen Mary in 1935 on the occasion of his Jubilee (despite the attempt to make political capital out of the proposed celebration) showed to the full his appreciation of the ethical code which is expected of the Sovereign; (*b*) King Edward VIII, who had long sought to develop the code by his closer contacts with the lives of the more humble and the more distant of his father's subjects, recognised, as did those who advised him, that the new convention must be extended into his domestic affairs. Incidentally, if Dicey be right in including this "political habit or convention," it is clearly outside the sanction of law proper, however indirectly enforced.[2] It can scarcely be argued that the breach of this convention could have led to any action being taken in the courts against the King or his advisers who might have accepted responsibility for his marriage, had he chosen to remain on the Throne. The rapidity with which action was taken by King George VI to restore the court régime of his father is evidence that his Ministers feared the pace at

[1] See Emden, *The People and the Constitution*, 2nd ed., for a full discussion of the People as a deciding factor in the choice of Ministries, esp. pp. 159-166. For the mandate principle, cf. Jennings, *The Law and the Constitution*, 4th ed., pp. 162-165; Jennings, *Cabinet Government*, 3rd ed., pp. 503-509.

[2] See discussion on why conventions are observed, pp. clxxix *et seq.*, *post*, and ch. xv.

which the convention had been allowed to develop. There have been several signs in the present reign that this convention is accepted by Her Majesty.

(3) *House of Commons procedure to prevent obstruction.* It was in the lifetime of the author that the House of Commons was driven to adopt devices for the prevention of obstruction to public business, and in particular to the passage of Bills. The obstruction originated with the attitude of the Irish Members in the early days of the Home Rule controversy. Home Rule was very much in the author's mind when he penned the Introduction to the eighth edition. Subsequent developments came with the congested state of parliamentary business, particularly in the years immediately succeeding each of the two World Wars. The problem is not merely how to curtail contumacious obstruction on the part of the Opposition. Where a measure is sufficiently controversial the ordinary procedure of examination of a Bill at the committee stage is such that little, if any, progress can be made, except by agreement between the Government and Opposition, unless something like a time-table for each part or maybe each group of clauses is imposed in advance.

The following is a very brief account of closure and similar devices:

The complicated stages through which a Bill must go and the amount of time involved have led, with the increase of the amount of business to which Parliament must attend and of the number of members who wish to speak, to the adoption of various methods of curtailing debates. The simplest method is that known as the "closure," first introduced to check obstruction by the Opposition.

Any member may, either in the House or in Committee, move "that the question be now put." The chairman may refuse to put the motion on the ground that it is an infringement of the rights of the minority, but, if the motion is put and carried, it brings to an end the debate which is in progress. The motion "that the question be now put" is voted upon without debate. It can only be carried in the House itself if the number voting is not less than 100. Another method is known as the "kangaroo" closure. The Speaker has the power, when a Bill is being discussed on the report stage, to select from among the various amendments proposed those which shall be discussed. The chairman of a Committee of the whole House may exercise similar power, as since 1934 may the Chairman of Standing Committees. More drastic still is the "guillotine." By resolution of the House, various periods of time are allotted to each stage of a Bill. At the end of each period the portion of the Bill in question is voted upon without further discussion. The guillotine can also be employed in Standing Committees by a Time Order passed by the House; this empowers a Business Sub-Committee of the relevant Standing Committee to allocate a time-table for the Bill within the period allowed and fixes the date on which the Bill has to be reported back to the House.[1] An allocation of time by agreement was substituted for the guillotine to deal with the Government of India Bill in

[1] This procedure, first authorised in 1945, was applied to the Transport and Town and Country Planning Bills in 1947 and resulted in a large part of each Bill not being considered at all in committee. The result was that the Government, as well as the Opposition, tabled a very large number of amendments in the Lords.

1935, and may be followed in other cases.

B. *Enacted Conventions as illustrated by the Parliament Act*, 1911. Dicey saw in the enactment of rules governing the relations between the two Houses in legislative matters: (1) some progress towards the establishment of an enacted constitution; (2) a great restraint upon, if not the abolition of, the royal prerogative to create peers to swamp the House of Lords; (3) the likelihood of each Parliament enduring for the full span of five years (which replaced the seven years of the Septennial Act, 1715)—a matter also affected by the payment of salaries to members from 1911 onwards; (4) power for the Commons' majority to resist or overrule the will of the electors; (5) peril to the Speaker's independent position.[1]

The Parliament Act, despite the statements in the preamble that it was a temporary measure, remained the law until 1949 when it was amended by reducing the period of delay from two years to one. Although the enactment in 1958 of the Life Peerages Act enabled the Crown to create life peers and peeresses without restriction as to number, there are few signs of agreement about changes in the powers of the House of Lords. Only two measures have reached the Statute Book and come into operation through the provisions of the Parliament Act, namely, the Welsh Church Act, 1914, and the Parliament Act, 1949; another was enacted, suspended and subsequently repealed (Government of Ireland Act, 1914). The positive effect of the Act has thus been very small. For this there have been two main causes.

[1] 8th ed. (1915), pp. li-lviii.

From 1915 until 1945 Coalition or National Governments held office for the greater part of the time. The causes which produced this type of government were unlikely to produce conditions which would lead to a conflict between the House of Commons and the House of Lords. The first two Labour Governments, not being in command of a majority over the other parties in the House of Commons, similarly avoided such conflict. Different conditions prevailed from 1945 to 1951 when the Government were heavily outnumbered in the House of Lords, but apart from the conflict over the Parliament Bill, 1947, and the difference of opinion over the abolition of capital punishment in 1948 when the House of Lords, unlike the House of Commons, took the view acceptable to the Government, no clash resulted despite the traditional hostility of the House of Lords to a progressive Government.

(1) *Progress towards an enacted constitution.* Just as the Statute of Westminster gave legal form to the convention of non-interference in matters of Dominion legislation, so the Parliament Act in more certain terms made law the conventional rule of some two and a half centuries that the Lords may not reject a Bill dealing exclusively with national finance. Until the rejection of the Finance Bill, 1909, this rule had been unbroken, with the exception of the rejection of the Paper Duties Bill, 1860, which led to the practice of Governments embodying their complete programme of new or amended taxes in a single Finance Bill. But the Parliament Act did more; for it destroyed the power to reject measures other than those relating exclusively to finance and

substituted therefor a short suspensive veto. This power of total rejection had frequently been used and was subject only to the convention that at some point or other the Lords ought to give way to the Commons. An enacted constitution will normally provide for the solution of deadlocks between the two Houses of the Legislature; cf. British North America Act, 1867, s. 26, and Commonwealth of Australia Constitution Act, 1900, s. 57. It may then be agreed that the enactment of constitutional practices which were ambiguous to some extent has at least reduced the risk of conflict between the Lords and the Government, should the former adopt an antagonistic attitude to the latter's legislative programme. It is not, however, easy to state how some of the rules prescribed by the Parliament Acts, though undoubtedly laws proper, could be enforced in a court.[1] It is unlikely that such a question could arise over the Speaker's duties of certification of Money Bills. The difficulty, moreover, applies with equal force to other constitutional enactments, which prescribe no sanction, *e.g.* the provision in the Bill of Rights that the election of members of Parliament ought to be free—a provision which goes to the root of the democratic principle in the constitution, however imperfectly it was fulfilled in the eighteenth century.

(2) *Creation of peers.* Dicey's opinion was that the Parliament Act operated as a great restraint upon, if not as the abolition of, the royal prerogative to create peers to swamp the House of Lords. We can see now that the Parliament Act in its amended form has not prevented a Conservative Government from taking

[1] P. xlvii, *ante*.

statutory powers in the Life Peerages Act, 1958, to create life peers partly for the purpose of securing an adequate representation of the Opposition in the Upper House. There is little likelihood that this new power will be used indiscriminately to create a sufficient number of peers so as to reverse the overwhelming Conservative majority. But clearly the Act has removed one of the principal difficulties of reconstituting the House of Lords by providing an alternative to hereditary peerages. There is a view held by a small minority of those who are impatient of progress under a parliamentary form of government. Those who hold this view seek to bring about the changes they desire by administrative decrees issued under an emergency Act. For the enactment of such an Act, the suspensive veto of the House of Lords must be destroyed, so it is argued, immediately upon accession to power of a Government possessing a majority in favour of drastic economic and social changes. There is less force in this argument now that the suspensive period has been halved. There is, moreover, a precedent in the emergency legislation of the Second World War which contained Defence Regulation 55. This regulation authorised the Government to control the whole of the means of production and distribution by Order in Council.

The establishment of a Second Chamber constituted upon a democratic basis with greater rather than less power than the present House of Lords would be more in harmony with the process of evolution which has always characterised the history of our constitution, than the drastic use of the royal prerogative to force the hand of the Lords to assent to their own destruction. But at present, as could be seen from the debates in Parliament on the Life Peerages Bill, any further change in the composition of the House of Lords seems improbable, while no agreement is in prospect between the Government and the Opposition which could result in an increase in the powers of that House. But even supposing that drastic amendment was proposed, it could be enacted under the machinery of the Parliament Acts and therefore could not be suspended by the Lords for a longer period than two sessions—a period which need not exceed one year. It is therefore improbable that the Sovereign would ever again be asked to assent to the creation of a large number of peers in order to give a Government a majority in the Upper House. The Acts provide a substitute process for securing that the Lords do not reject a measure which is supported by a majority opinion outside. Though the prerogative power to coerce the Lords by new creations has not been abolished, it is unlikely to be exercised.

(3) *Duration of Parliament for the full five years.* The Parliament elected in December, 1910, was dissolved eight years later, its life having been prolonged by statute four times beyond the five-year limit in order to avoid a general election in war-time. Four subsequent Parliaments have had their duration influenced by considerations of the time limit. The Parliament elected in October, 1924, was dissolved in May, 1929, on the advice of Mr. Baldwin, who was Prime Minister throughout its duration. The "National" Parliament elected in 1931 (October) sat for four years before its dissolution in the autumn

of 1935. The Parliament elected in 1935 remained in office until after the end of the Second World War in 1945, having on several occasions used statutory powers to prolong its existence. The general election in the spring of 1950 could at most have been delayed by a few months before Parliament's automatic dissolution under the Parliament Acts. In 1955 a new Prime Minister chose his own time, some eighteen months before the statutory life of Parliament was due to end, for successfully inviting a renewal of support. From these precedents it may be said that a Prime Minister will choose the occasion which he deems most favourable to the Government party for a dissolution within a period of anything up to two years before the statutory life of Parliament comes to an end. Indeed Mr Baldwin, who in the 1931–35 Parliament was the leader of by far the largest number of the supporters of the National Government. stated that he regarded the life of Parliament as limited to less than the full five years for this rather naïve reason.

Payment of salaries to members has made the back bench member more reluctant to face a dissolution This factor increases the authority of the Whips over their supporters, particularly on the Government side. Even the Opposition may be less anxious again to face the electors at an early stage of a Parliament's life. There are other factors than the payment of salaries which operate to this end. The inevitable upheaval in the life of a nation which is involved in a general election; the huge expense to the parties and the instability of even a large constituency majority under conditions of universal franchise. Provided that a Government has a small working majority, which recent experience would put at as low as twenty, it seems unlikely that Parliament will in future endure for much less than the statutory period.

(4) *The Commons and the Electorate.* The power of a majority in the House of Commons to resist or overrule the will of the electors is not an obvious result of the Parliament Act, so far as regards legislation other than Money Bills. There is a remote danger lest the absence of an effective veto by a Second Chamber might tempt a Government to force through under cover of the provisions of a Money Bill a new proposal opposed by a large section of the electorate. This risk is minimised, if not eliminated, by the provisions relating to certification of such Bills by the Speaker. Proposals for legislation other than Money Bills are now subject to a suspensive veto for two successive sessions with a minimum interval of one year between the second reading of the Bill in the House of Commons in the first session and the date of the third reading in that House in the second session. This period under the Parliament Act, 1911, was for three successive sessions. The reason for reducing the period under the provisions of the Parliament Act, 1949, to one year was the wish of the Labour Government of the day to dispel the idea that the House of Lords should stand between the House of Commons and the electorate except for the minimum possible time. The Government was still prepared to use the House of Lords as a revising chamber, despite the objection felt by most of its supporters to the retention of the hereditary principle

in its composition. In the absence of any agreement about the composition of a reformed House of Lords the easier course was to diminish the powers of the existing House in such a way as to ensure that any Government Bill which had been rejected by that House could be passed into law in the lifetime of a Parliament, provided always that the Bill was not introduced at the end of the five-year period. When under the 1911 Act the delay could extend over three sessions with a minimum interval of two years between the second reading on the first occasion and the third reading on the third occasion in the Commons, the House of Lords was obviously in a stronger position to exercise a suspensive veto, especially during the last three years of a Parliament's life. No Government would have risked taking advantage of the Parliament Act in face of an early appeal to the electorate if a measure after three sessions still aroused substantial opposition in the country.

(5) *The Speaker's position.* Lastly, the powers of certification conferred by the Act upon the Speaker led Dicey to see peril to his independent position. He feared lest the majority party would secure for that office a partisan rather than a judge. Events since 1914 have shown that the Labour party has on occasions shared Dicey's fears. In 1935, in face of some disapproval from their parliamentary leaders, the local organisation of the Labour party decided to oppose the sitting Speaker in his constituency. For many years the return of successive Speakers to Parliament had been unopposed. The motive was largely to protest against the constituency being deprived of active representation in the House; for

by convention the Speaker is above party. The Speaker contested the election and was returned by an overwhelming majority. Since that date the Speaker has been unsuccessfully opposed on several occasions, as has the re-election of a sitting Speaker by the House of Commons itself. There is a tendency for the Deputy Speakership also to be filled from the ranks of the party in power. It is of interest to note that certification of Money Bills, which is a duty entrusted to the Speaker by the Parliament Act, 1911, has raised no difficulties of definition or partiality.

One final observation on the Parliament Act must suffice. There is some evidence that the prestige of the House of Lords has been increased by the curtailment of its legal powers of rejection. The voice of reason is more readily heard when it can persuade, but no longer coerce. Those of the members, albeit a small minority, who are assiduous in their attendance to parliamentary duties, constitute an assembly of elder statesmen and pro-consuls of Commonwealth as well as of industry and commerce. The principle of the hereditary legislator may be indefensible (notwithstanding the survival of the houses of Cecil and Stanley), but the practice of conferring peerages upon leaders of public life does ensure in the House of Lords a body of experienced opinion which might otherwise be lost to politics. The arrival of life peers and peeresses will assist in this. In order to secure that only those peers who are interested in the work of Parliament shall in practice attend and record their votes, if need be, the House of Lords adopted in June, 1958, a new Standing Order relating to leave of absence.[1] This order emphasises the obligation on Lords of Parliament to attend the sittings of the House in accordance with the writ of summons, but provides for a Lord to apply for leave of absence at any time during a Parliament for a session or part of one. A Lord who has been granted leave of absence is then expected not to attend the sittings of the House during the period of his leave. In this way it is presumably expected to eliminate the influence of the so-called "backwoodsman" as provision is made for a Lord who wishes to terminate his leave of absence to give a month's notice.

It is a function of the Lords to debate policy where the enactment of legislation is not required. Foreign affairs in particular benefit from discussion away from the more controversial atmosphere of the Commons. Non-controversial subjects of legislation, *e.g.* measures of technicality such as law reform which are not affected by the usual cleavage between the Government and the Opposition, can conveniently be introduced in the Second Chamber with an assurance that they will receive fuller consideration by a small body of experienced opinion than is probable or possible in the Commons. There have been occasions of late years when the Lords have risen to far greater heights than the Commons. The debates in 1927 and 1928 on the Measures of the Church Assembly proposing the use of the reformed book of common prayer furnished an illustration of the superiority of the Lords over the popular assembly. Again it was the Lords (and not the Commons) who in 1937 secured the ear of the Government in regard

[1] Standing Order 21.

to "massacre by motor." But if there has been an increase in prestige accompanying the loss of power, there also remains the threat to democratic government in an assembly where the members of one party are in a permanent minority, while in the background lies the menace of the legion of Conservative peers who might once again emerge as in 1909 from the "backwoods" to defeat a progressive Government and so hasten their own political annihilation.

Why Conventions are observed.—Dicey's conclusion was that conventions are supported and enforced by something beyond and in addition to, public approval. His "something" was that it is nothing else than the force of law. By this he did not mean fear of the obsolescent process of impeachment. He regarded the sanction which constrained the boldest political adventurer to obey the fundamental principles of the constitution as expressed in the form of conventions as the fact that any breach would bring the offender into conflict with the courts and the law of the land.[1] It is easy to support Dicey's reasoning from certain examples of conventions governing the use of the royal prerogative, but even here there is the difficulty of drawing a clear distinction between a rule which at one time is based on convention and later is passed by statute into the law of the land. The absence of a written constitution is responsible for the difficulty of dividing law and convention by a clear line, but it is equally true of States with written constitutions that conventions, though not written into the constitution, play an essential part in the working of government. It is, however, possible to

[1] Pp. 445-446, *post*.

enact a convention as law and yet exclude it from enforcement by an action in the courts, thus the Ceylon Constitution enacts certain conventions which relate to the exercise of the powers of the Crown on ministerial advice, but expressly excludes them from enforcement by legal action.[1]

Dicey himself was mindful of political sanctions as shown by his discussion of the external limitations upon the sovereignty of Parliament, as well as by his examination of the power of public opinion in securing obedience to conventions. Even if legal action is possible, it is far more likely in practice that political action will be taken rather than proceedings in court. Dicey argued that the refusal of a defeated Ministry to resign would ultimately lead to administrative action which Parliament had not sanctioned and so to illegal acts for which the courts would give redress. It is surely safe to assume that long before such a state of affairs was reached, the Ministry would be compelled by public pressure to surrender office. Ministers do not shrink from responsibility for fear of proceedings in court. Their conduct is conditioned by force of public opinion as shown by an adverse vote at the polls or by the estrangement of some of their supporters in the House of Commons. They are influenced in their political conduct by the desire to govern in accordance with the traditions of representative government. In short, whether it be the Sovereign in the exercise of the personal prerogatives, or Ministers in all their public conduct, there is a standard of political authority which commands obedience. Those who govern cannot ultimately

[1] Section 4 (ii).

control the judgment of public opinion; they can only seek to influence it in their political activities. In the sphere of inter-Commonwealth relations it is even more difficult to see how Dicey's argument that a breach of convention ultimately leads to illegal conduct can be upheld. Here, what secures equilibrium is the knowledge that there are economic and political issues which depend upon moderation in the use to which independence can safely be asserted by each member State. No one nowadays supposes that the United Kingdom in particular can impose any legal sanction against any other member State. But in this sphere the importance of conventions lies not so much in inter-Commonwealth relations as in the absorption of the rules and practices of parliamentary government into the written constitution of a new State. Here the choice lies between the constitution remaining silent leaving the customary rules to the choice of Ministers who are new to responsible government, and giving the rigidity of law to a rule which may well prove unacceptable or even unworkable in a new setting. It cannot be argued that because of its conventional origin a convention which has been made part of the law of the land is not enforceable in the courts, unless, as in the case of the Ceylon constitution which has been given above, enforcement by the courts is expressly excluded.

The conclusion which Dicey reached that obedience was ultimately secured by their connection with a legal sanction may well have resulted from his initial decision to exclude conventions from the province of the constitutional lawyer.[1] Certainly no constitu-

[1] Pp. 30-31 and cf. pp. 417-418, *post*.

tional lawyer can ever assert with confidence the exact line of distinction between what is constitutional law and what is convention. There are statutes which assume conventions as the basis of the law which they contain and cases where the judges have treated conventions as having legal effect.[1] The example of the Statute of Westminster, where a convention recited in the preamble (among several other conventions) is explicitly enacted as an operative section (4), established beyond any doubt the place of conventions in constitutional law. If it could be agreed that there was a clear division between those rules of the constitution which are obligatory because they are enforced in the courts and those which are observed merely as a matter of convenient practice, it would be easier to accept the necessity for explaining obedience to the latter through their connection with the former, but no such clear line of distinction exists once it is accepted that the range of conventions extends beyond the rules for securing ministerial responsibility to Parliament for the exercise of the royal prerogative. Ministerial responsibility is a conventional obligation which has in practice superseded the legal responsibility which was formerly enforced by impeachment.[2] It was a natural line of reasoning for a lawyer to show that legal consequences might ensue from disregard of the usages by which ministerial responsibility had been established.

Dicey took as one illustration of the ultimate legal sanction to conventions the rule which compels annual meetings of Parliament in order to pass the Appropria-

[1] Jennings, *The Law of the Constitution*, 4th ed., pp. 116-120.

[2] Pp. 326-327, *post*.

tion and Finance Bills. There is no express rule of law requiring an annual meeting of Parliament. The Triennial Act, 1694, requires Parliament to meet every three years, but in practice legislation relating to the expenditure of public funds and an important part of taxation is only passed for one year and must be renewed annually. This ensures that there is a session of Parliament at least once a year in order to secure continuity in the legal authority for expenditure and the collection of (*inter alia*) the income tax. It is interesting to recall that the author was for many years Counsel to the Commissioners of Inland Revenue. This may explain this example. It was, however, in his lifetime that the practice of collecting a tax in advance of its authorisation by Parliament was held to be illegal. The law was promptly adjusted by Parliament so as to make a legal practice of the illegal custom of collecting taxes in advance of their authorisation by Parliament.[1] The only result of the Commissioners having broken the law was to secure an alteration of the law. Governments can go further since their majority in the House of Commons normally can secure the passage of an Indemnity Bill to excuse, if need be, the penal consequences of a past illegality.

We have already said something of the wider field of conventions, of their extension over the whole range of governmental activity, of the all-important part which they have played in the attainment of independent status by the several States of the Commonwealth, which in the case of the older

[1] See *Bowles* v. *Bank of England* [1913] 1 Ch. 57; K. & L. 162 and the sequel to the case, Provisional Collection of Taxes Act, 1913.

members was achieved with little assistance from the actual law as it was until the enactment of the Statute of Westminster in 1931. Conventions which embodied the measure of agreement reached at Imperial Conferences between Heads of Governments were normally implemented on their return home and thereafter were regarded as binding. Such conventions rested only upon acceptance by the Governments concerned of the commitments undertaken by their Prime Ministers. Resolutions of such conferences had no legal force. On one occasion a change of Government prevented their being implemented. There has never been a tribunal to decide such disputes as may arise about their meaning and application. Proposals for an Inter-Commonwealth Tribunal have made little progress, though a dispute on a matter of international law between member States within the Commonwealth is not submitted to the International Court of Justice at The Hague.

Examples of the mingling of law and convention abound in the law and custom of Parliament. Some part of the law of Parliament is statutory; the law relating to representation in the House of Commons, *i.e.* the distribution of seats, the franchise, the secrecy of the ballot, is clearly part of the law of the constitution which may be enforced in the courts. But is it clear that the statutory limitation by the Parliament Act, 1911, on the powers of the House of Lords could ever be so enforced?[1] Or are these limitations any less a matter of law than others which are purely conventional, such as the rule which enables the Commons as a matter of

[1] P. clxxi, *ante*.

privilege to resist amendment of financial Bills by the Lords, a rule which is not included in the Parliament Act? Such a rule is as binding upon the Lords as the statutory restriction of their power.

The Standing Orders of each House closely resemble law proper. They are definite rules enforced by the House and not, it is true, by an independent outside tribunal, but they are for the greater part treated as obligatory. They are in no sense rules which call for enforcement by the ordinary courts. One fundamental principle of British constitutional law which is enacted in the constitution of most Commonwealth States is to be found in these Orders. The Standing Orders of the House of Commons relating to public money, among which are to be found the earliest and, for more than a century, the only orders made for the Commons for their self-government,[1] require that every motion which in any way creates a charge upon the public revenue must receive the recommendation of the Crown, *i.e.* be recommended by a Minister of the Crown, before it can be sanctioned by the House, and upon receipt of such recommendation from a Minister the matter must be adjourned to a future day and be referred to the consideration of a Committee of the Whole House before any resolution or vote of the House is passed.

The fact that in the United Kingdom this principle is conventional, while in other States it is contained in the Constitution Act, does not mean that it is regarded as less fundamental here than it is in other

[1] May, *Parliamentary Practice*, 16th ed., pp. 687-692. Standing Orders Nos. 66-71B. Nos. 66, 67 and 68 date from 1713, 1707 and 1715 respectively.

parts of the British Commonwealth. It is a rule of constitutional law, not because it is part of the law of the land enforceable by the courts, but because it has proved its value over a long period and so become established by custom. It may be conceded that it would be easier to change the rule by amendment of Standing Orders than by amendment of the constitution. But since no Government could conceivably wish to wreck this corner-stone of its responsibility for the conduct of affairs, the principle is in fact as safely secured in the United Kingdom as it is as a rule of law in the Constitution Acts of the Dominions.

Lastly the positions of the Prime Minister and of his potential successor, the Leader of the Opposition, illustrate that conventions are part and parcel of constitutional law. It is true, as Jennings points out,[1] that the Prime Minister is not mentioned in the statute book before 1917 and that by this test he receives an emolument of £10,000 a year, the right to a pension, and the occupation of a country seat in return for performing the task of nominating members to sit on two councils for physical training; and that the Leader of the Opposition is legally non-existent except for the provision of his salary.[2] But the legislation is based upon the assumption that there is a Prime Minister and a Leader of the Opposition. It is merely pedantic to deny legal entity to

[1] Jennings, *The Law and the Constitution*, 4th ed., p. 117.

[2] In particular, the Ministers of the Crown Act, 1937, which provides for payment of salaries for Ministers and the Leader of the Opposition, implies the existence of the Cabinet, a purely conventional body. Similarly the Schedule of the Chequers' Estate Act, 1917, assumes the existence of the office of Prime Minister whose functions in law are dependent upon his holding another office, usually First Lord of the Treasury.

the most important office in the Administration and to the Cabinet as such, when they have been in existence for over two hundred years.

Recognition of the impossibility of separating law and convention by any hard and fast line suggests that the distinction depends upon the meaning to be attached to the word "court,"[1] and that there is no necessary difference in their nature beyond the fact that there are institutions for the application of law and that there may be none for the application of conventions—or, at all events, none of a judicial character. Some conventions are indeed more precise in their terms than rules of law. This is true of some of the conventions which were the result of agreement reached at Imperial Conferences. Many others are of a vague character, which suggests a distinction between usages and conventions proper. There is, too, a borderline between law and convention where it is not clear to which category a rule belongs. It has already been asked on the one hand, what court can enforce the statutory duties of the Speaker under the Parliament Act with regard to Money Bills? On the other hand, could a court refuse to recognise the validity of a State document because the sealing thereof departed from the traditional practice, which is regarded as legally necessary, though it is sanctioned by no statute or judge-made law?

The recognition that the dividing line is not clear suggests that Dicey may have been influenced too much by the Austinian view of law—the command

[1] Cf. Jennings, *op. cit.* (1st ed., 1933), p. 98. The passage does not appear in later editions, but the reasoning which supports it remains; cf. 4th ed., pp. 102-105.

of the Sovereign to be enforced as such. If it is clear that Dicey was following in the steps of Austin in being the first to apply the method of analysis to constitutional law, it is not difficult to appreciate why he deemed it necessary to explain obedience to conventions upon the same ground, namely, enforcement. But much law, perhaps all law, is obeyed because of the general acquiescence of the community in its content. It is questionable whether it is fear of the consequences which impels the observance of law on the part of the bulk of the community. Indeed, if a law is regarded as unreasonable, it is often disregarded to such an extent that its enforcement by the ordinary methods becomes impossible. Why, then, need it be said that Cabinet Ministers obey conventions because disregard of them might bring them into conflict with the law ? The Prime Minister to-day stands in no fear of impeachment, much less of an appearance at the Old Bailey or in the High Court, on account of his obligations to observe the rules of ministerial responsibility.

There are other dominant motives which secure obedience to those conventions which were examined by Dicey: (1) the desire to carry on the traditions of constitutional government; (2) the wish to keep the intricate machinery of the ship of State in working order; and (3) the anxiety to retain the confidence of the public, and with it office and power. These influences secure that the conventions of Cabinet government, which are based on binding precedents and convenient usage, are observed by successive generations of Ministers. The exact content of a convention may change, or even be reversed, but each departure from the previous practice is defended by those responsible as not violating the older precedents. Objections are only silenced when time has proved that the departure from precedent has created a new convention, or has shown itself to be a bad precedent and, therefore, constituted in itself a breach of convention. An illustration may make this clear. The Cabinet, when it formulated in 1932 the "agreement to differ" over the tariff issue (Import Duties Bill), while remaining united on all other matters of national policy, broke with precedent which demanded that the Cabinet should speak with a unanimous voice, as being collectively responsible to the House of Commons.

The decision was made public in the following terms:

> The Cabinet has had before it the Report of its Committee on the Balance of Trade, and after prolonged discussion it has been found impossible to reach a unanimous conclusion on the Committee's recommendations.
>
> The Cabinet, however, is deeply impressed with the paramount importance of maintaining national unity in the presence of the grave problems now confronting this country and the whole world.
>
> It has accordingly determined that some modification of usual Ministerial practice is required, and has decided that Ministers who find themselves unable to support the conclusions arrived at by the majority of their colleagues on the subject of import duties and cognate matters are to be at liberty to express their views by speech and vote.
>
> The Cabinet being essentially united in all other matters of policy believe that by this special provision it is best interpreting the will of the nation and the needs of the time.

It is to be observed that the justification purported to be the belief that the Cabinet was best interpreting the will of the nation and the needs of the time. This is the ultimate justification for all conventions modifying or regulating the use of the prerogatives of government. The dissenting Ministers resigned after a few months on the cognate issue of imperial preference. In the result the convention of Cabinet unanimity was reinforced. Had the experiment succeeded the convention might have been modified if it had been followed by a series of similar decisions.

A second illustration is afforded by the convention which Dicey noted as new in his last Introduction—that which all but compels a Ministry to resign on defeat at a general election without waiting to meet Parliament. Four precedents occurring between 1868 and 1886 constituted a sufficient departure from the precedent set by Peel, who found himself in a minority after the general election in 1834, but resisted in Parliament the attempt to force him from office.[1] In this example a new usage emerged after several breaches of the old convention, and in due course the new precedents were treated as binding.

It should be pointed out that the argument that breaches of law would follow failure to observe conventions applies only to those conventions, or to most of them, which determine the relations between the Cabinet and the House of Commons. No breach of the law would ensue from the failure of the House of Commons to enforce its Standing Orders. Some of these are by agreement disregarded. Nor could such a result follow from the failure of a Government Department to consult organised interests in the

[1] P. clxiv, *ante*.

framing of legislation; nor from the neglect of the Government of the United Kingdom to consult the Canadian Government upon a topic of common interest; nor from the Queen inviting a peer to take office as Prime Minister and First Lord of the Treasury in breach of a recent usage. Consequences of greater or less moment would doubtless follow departure from established practice in most cases. But in none could there result any consequence which could come before the courts for decision.

Dicey was absolutely right to include his analysis of constitutional conventions, perhaps the most valuable part of the book. But he had imposed upon himself the limitation to exclude politics. Conventions are political expedients; therefore he had to connect them with law as enforced in the courts. Since he belonged to the school of thought which regarded obedience to an enforcing authority as of the essence of law, he solved his difficulty in the way he did. That this conception of obedience no longer explains the observance of the intricate mass of precepts, which furnish the key to an understanding of parliamentary government and the status of the British Commonwealth, does not lessen the debt which is owed to the author for his brilliant exposition of the nature of conventions.

(6) CONCLUSION

The merit of this book lies in the author's application of the analytic method to constitutional law. An analysis leads to conclusions. Dicey deduced certain guiding principles which seemed to him to underlie our constitutional machinery. His exposition of these principles was expressed in terms which seemed at the time to admit of little doubt. The clarity of his diction assisted to make the book a classic. His method has certain disadvantages as compared with descriptive writings on legal institutions. Bagehot in *The English Constitution* described Cabinet government as he saw it in operation in the middle of the nineteenth century in a way that has been of abiding value to the historian as well as making clear the relations of the Cabinet to the Crown and Parliament at that particular time. Dicey's task was more ambitious. He was searching for principles in an unwritten constitution which offers little stimulus to theorists. He sought to frame an explanation for such of the laws and customs of the constitution as might be regarded as fundamental. He was not in a position to compare the unwritten constitution of the United Kingdom with what has been called by a recent author " controlled experiments " in other parts of the Commonwealth.[1] It is easy to-day to attack his view of parliamentary sovereignty by showing that it can be no longer examined solely by reference to the legislature of the United Kingdom. Once reduce a constitution to enacted form, the question arises, how much of the constitution can be changed by the ordinary process of legislation ? If the answer is that Parliament by itself cannot enact a change, then we must seek an explanation different from Dicey's for the legal sovereignty in that constitution. But it must be em-

[1] G. Marshall, *Parliamentary Sovereignty and the Commonwealth*, p. 1.

phasised that Dicey was expounding the sovereignty of Parliament as the dominant characteristic of the political institutions of the United Kingdom alone.

Some criticism has been directed to the limited field of government which was covered. Such text-books as there were on constitutional law in 1885, the date of the first edition, concentrated on the Crown, Parliament and the Courts. Local government found no place; the widening field of administrative activity of the central government was passed over in silence until Maitland drew attention to it a few years later. The growth of conventions in the colonial sphere passed unheeded even by such writers as Sir William Anson. Dicey was later to appreciate how much the conception of the function of government was altering. When his *Law and Opinion during the Nineteenth Century* made its appearance his appreciation of the changing functions of government was made known, though still with some natural reluctance.

There is no need then to apologise for the limitations of *The Law of the Constitution* if one remembers the background in which the book was written. This does not, however, explain the remarkable influence which the book has had over a period of nearly seventy-five years. Yet no modern writer on the constitution, however critical of the author's work, fails to include some detailed comment on his principles. Twenty years ago his concept of the rule of law was challenged more vigorously than the principle of parliamentary sovereignty. To-day we find that the position has been reversed. There is more disputation about sovereignty of Parliament and a greater readiness to accept the conception of the rule of law.

There is thus no need to close this Introduction by apologising for the limitations of the book. It may, however, be helpful to attempt a short summary of the application of the principles to-day.

Sovereignty of Parliament.—The legal rule that Parliament is supreme is unquestioned by the courts and is accepted by the Administration. The political supremacy of the electorate is still acknowledged as a limitation upon the exercise of legislative power, though a lawyer can claim no special qualification to say precisely how political power is exercised. The power of the electorate is qualified by the recognition of the increased power of the Cabinet, which is able to utilise the power entrusted to it by the electorate to change the law at its will. But every Government is disposed to keep its ear to the ground to detect electoral rumblings. In other words, there is a change of emphasis. It is the Cabinet system which is fundamental to parliamentary government. That system depends for its efficiency as an instrument of government upon being able to use the legal supremacy of Parliament (or rather of the Commons) to serve its ends ; it is saved from being an autocratic instrument by the knowledge that at intervals the electorate may alter the composition of the Commons and so place the supremacy of Parliament in other hands. But it is the political supremacy rather than the legal doctrine which saves the democratic principle. Indeed the legal instrument of parliamentary supremacy stands in some risk of actually facilitating the creation of an extreme form of government at the present time, since any change, however fundamental, can be accomplished in law by an ordinary enactment of Parliament. In all the States of the Commonwealth which have attained independence and a written constitution, independence has meant that the Parliament of the United Kingdom no longer exercises sovereignty. Yet these constitutions, modelled as most of them are on that of the United Kingdom, are based on the idea that sovereignty lies within the State.[1] But a State which owes its existence to a written constitution is not necessarily prepared to allow the legislature to have supreme control over the fundamental basis of authority. If the constitution provides that the power of change shall be shared between the legislature and the electorate then at once there is the difficulty of reconciling Dicey's conception of parliamentary sovereignty with sovereignty in that State.

Rule of Law.—The changed conception of liberty narrows the field for the application of the rule of law in the sense of affording the protection of the common law against the Crown, its Ministers and the other organs of administrative government, central, local or independent. The courts still restrict excesses of the prerogative so far as illegal arbitrary action against the individual subject is concerned. But it is the political control exercised through the House of Commons which grows more important as the enacted law extends the legal powers of government. The courts may not declare illegal what Parliament has said is law, however much it may

[1] To a limited extent this is still not the case with the Dominion of Canada, see p. lxxxix, *ante*.

restrict the freedom of individuals. But there is a sphere where so far Parliament has tampered but little in the direction of restriction. Freedom of speech and freedom of association are as essential to democracy as freedom of person. For without them criticism of political institutions and social conditions is impossible. It is clear that Parliament could impose restrictions on freedom of speech, just as it has regulated the liberty of the individual to deal with his property as he chooses. But freedom of person still finds its bulwark in the common law, buttressed by the writ of habeas corpus against the Administration. It is in this connection that Dicey's conception of the rule of law operates to-day. It has played, and still plays, its part in strengthening the tradition of political liberty which is the foundation of our parliamentary government. Public opinion is as ready as ever to resist encroachments proposed to Parliament by Governments who are embarrassed by their critics.

That public opinion to-day is influenced by Dicey's exposition of the opposition of the common law to inroads upon individual liberty may be evidenced by the storm of criticism which greets every extension of governmental power. This is not entirely due to distrust of the official, for the unbiassed must admit that the standard of the higher ranks of the Civil Service is above reproach. There is still a strong affection for the emphasis upon individual liberty which cannot be attributed to purely selfish motives. Proposals, far milder than the existing law, for checking the dissemination of political propaganda among the armed forces, were greeted by arguments founded upon the rule of law as well by those of the left who feared the growth of fascism as by lifelong supporters of the right, when the Incitement to Disaffection Bill was before Parliament in 1934. Effective action against shirted organisations was long delayed, despite the grievous inconveniences caused by their activities to the peaceful inhabitants of populous districts. For public opinion was loath to admit the need for increasing the powers of the police. The Public Order Bill received a scrutiny from all quarters of the House of Commons in 1936, which contrasted favourably with the attention given to Bills of greater importance. Even in war-time powers of detention and censorship were jealously watched by the House of Commons and revoked immediately after the end of hostilities in Europe. It is to Dicey that the politician as well as the lawyer turns whenever a threat to individual liberty is proposed. Largely to him is owed the insistence upon careful safeguards which make government regulation much more tolerable than it is in other States where the individual is subordinated to national ends.

Conventions of the Constitution.—The reason why conventions are obeyed may be obscure, just as their actual operation is a mystery too deep to be fathomed by the lawyer. But the fact that Cabinet government and indeed the whole administrative machine only function effectively by these means must be acknowledged. In their application to Cabinet government Dicey was the first constitutional lawyer to analyse their nature. His was, indeed, a magnificent contribution to our public law, if only because it led to the recognition that conventions are indispensable to an understanding of our legal institutions. Conventions are indeed part and parcel of constitutional law. With the widening of the scope of conventions there has come the realisation that the dividing line between law and convention is by no means clear. Nor can the observance of rules of a conventional character be always, or even usually, explained by reference to the ultimate sanction of law enforced in courts of justice.

OUTLINE OF SUBJECT

NOTE BY THE EDITOR

The text remains in the form in which it appeared in the seventh edition published in 1908. This was the edition in which the Author finally settled the text.

The footnote references which show the authorities upon which the Author relied are also preserved. But a few additions to the notes have been made, particularly where there has been a change in the law, in order to avoid giving the impression that the statements in the text refer to the present day. The citation of modern authorities has been restricted by reason of space. Instead a short Bibliography is printed in the Appendix.

No attempt has been made to remove certain typographical inconsistencies, as it has been thought preferable to reproduce as closely as possible the actual text printed as it last passed the scrutiny of Professor Dicey.

OUTLINE OF SUBJECT

THE TRUE NATURE OF CONSTITUTIONAL LAW

Optimistic view of English constitution.

"GREAT critics," writes Burke in 1791, "have taught us "one essential rule. . . . It is this, that if ever we should "find ourselves disposed not to admire those writers "or artists, Livy and Virgil for instance, Raphael or "Michael Angelo, whom all the learned had admired, "not to follow our own fancies, but to study them until "we know how and what we ought to admire; and if "we cannot arrive at this combination of admiration "with knowledge, rather to believe that we are dull, "than that the rest of the world has been imposed "on. It is as good a rule, at least, with regard to "this admired constitution (of England). We ought "to understand it according to our measure; and "to venerate where we are not able presently to "comprehend."[1]

"No unbiassed observer," writes Hallam in 1818, "who derives pleasure from the welfare of his species, "can fail to consider the long and uninterruptedly in-"creasing prosperity of England as the most beautiful "phænomenon in the history of mankind. Climates "more propitious may impart more largely the mere

[1] *The Works of Edmund Burke* (1872 ed.), vol. iii, p. 114.

"enjoyments of existence; but in no other region have "the benefits that political institutions can confer been "diffused over so extended a population; nor have any "people so well reconciled the discordant elements of "wealth, order, and liberty. These advantages are "surely not owing to the soil of this island, nor to the "latitude in which it is placed; but to the spirit of its "laws, from which, through various means, the char-"acteristic independence and industriousness of our "nation have been derived. The constitution, there-"fore, of England must be to inquisitive men of all "countries, far more to ourselves, an object of superior "interest; distinguished, especially, as it is from all "free governments of powerful nations, which history "has recorded, by its manifesting, after the lapse of "several centuries, not merely no symptom of irre-"trievable decay, but a more expansive energy."[1]

These two quotations from authors of equal though of utterly different celebrity, recall with singular fidelity the spirit with which our grandfathers and our fathers looked upon the institutions of their country. The constitution was to them, in the quaint language of George the Third, "the most perfect of human formations";[2] it was to them not a mere polity to be compared with the government of any other state, but so to speak a sacred mystery of states-manship; it "had (as we have all heard from our youth up) not been made but had grown"; it was

[1] Hallam, *Middle Ages* (12th ed., 1860), vol. ii, p. 267. Nothing gives a more vivid idea of English sentiment with regard to the constitution towards the end of the eighteenth century than the satirical picture of national pride to be found in Goldsmith, *The Citizen of the World*, Letter iv.

[2] Stanhope, *Life of Pitt* (2nd ed., 1862), vol. i, App. p. x.

the fruit not of abstract theory but of that instinct which (it is supposed) has enabled Englishmen, and especially uncivilised Englishmen, to build up sound and lasting institutions, much as bees construct a honeycomb, without undergoing the degradation of understanding the principles on which they raise a fabric more subtly wrought than any work of conscious art. The constitution was marked by more than one transcendent quality which in the eyes of our fathers raised it far above the imitations, counterfeits, or parodies, which have been set up during the last hundred years throughout the civilised world; no precise date could be named as the day of its birth; no definite body of persons could claim to be its creators, no one could point to the document which contained its clauses; it was in short a thing by itself, which Englishmen and foreigners alike should "venerate, where they are not able presently to comprehend."

Modern view of constitution.

The present generation must of necessity look on the constitution in a spirit different from the sentiment either of 1791 or of 1818. We cannot share the religious enthusiasm of Burke, raised, as it was, to the temper of fanatical adoration by just hatred of those "doctors of the modern school," who, when he wrote, were renewing the rule of barbarism in the form of the reign of terror; we cannot exactly echo the fervent self-complacency of Hallam, natural as it was to an Englishman who saw the institutions of England standing and flourishing, at a time when the attempts of foreign reformers to combine freedom with order had ended in ruin. At the present day students of the constitution wish neither to criticise, nor to venerate, but to understand; and a professor whose duty it is to lecture on constitutional law, must feel that he is called upon to perform the part neither of a critic nor of an apologist, nor of an eulogist, but simply of an expounder; his duty is neither to attack nor to defend the constitution, but simply to explain its laws. He must also feel that, however attractive be the mysteries of the constitution, he has good reason to envy professors who belong to countries, such as France, Belgium, or the United States, endowed with constitutions of which the terms are to be found in printed documents, known to all citizens and accessible to every man who is able to read. Whatever may be the advantages of a so-called "unwritten" constitution, its existence imposes special difficulties on teachers bound to expound its provisions. Any one will see that this is so who compares for a moment the position of writers, such as Kent or Story, who commented on the constitution of America, with the situation of any person who undertakes to give instruction in the constitutional law of England.

Special difficulty of commenting on English constitution.

When these distinguished jurists delivered, in the form of lectures, commentaries upon the constitution of the United States, they knew precisely what was the subject of their teaching and what was the proper mode of dealing with it. The theme of their teaching was a definite assignable part of the law of their country; it was recorded in a given document to which all the world had access, namely, "the constitution of the United States established and ordained by the People of the United States." The articles of this constitution fall indeed far short of perfect logical arrangement, and lack absolute lucidity of expression; but they contain, in a clear and intelligible form, the fundamental law of the Union. This law (be it noted) is made and can only be altered or repealed in a way different from the method by which other enactments are made or altered; it stands forth, therefore, as a separate subject for study; it deals with the legislature, the executive, and the judiciary, and, by its provisions for its own amendment, indirectly defines the body in which resides the legislative sovereignty of the United States. Story and Kent therefore knew with precision the nature and limits of the department of law on which they intended to comment; they knew also what was the method required for the treatment of their topic. Their task as commentators on the constitution was in kind exactly similar to the task of commenting on any other branch of American jurisprudence. The American lawyer has to ascertain the meaning of the articles of the constitution in the same way in which he tries to elicit the meaning of any other enactment. He must be guided by the rules of grammar, by his knowledge of the common law, by the light (occasionally) thrown on American legislation by American history, and by the conclusions to be deduced from a careful study of judicial decisions. The task, in short, which lay before the great American commentators was the explanation of a definite legal document in accordance with the received canons of legal interpretation. Their work, difficult as it might prove, was work of the kind to which lawyers are accustomed, and could be achieved by the use of ordinary legal methods. Story and Kent indeed were men of extraordinary capacity; so, however, were our own Blackstone, and at least one of Blackstone's editors. If, as is undoubtedly the case, the American jurists have produced commentaries on the constitution of the United States utterly unlike, and, one must in truth add, vastly superior to, any commentaries on the constitutional law of England, their success is partly due to the possession of advantages denied to the English commentator or lecturer. His position is entirely different from that of his American rivals. He may search the statute-book from beginning to end, but he will find no enactment which purports to contain the articles of the constitution; he will not possess any test by which to discriminate laws which are constitutional or fundamental from ordinary enactments; he will discover that the very term "constitutional law," which is not (unless my memory deceives me) ever employed by Blackstone, is of comparatively modern origin; and in short, that before commenting on the law of the constitution he must make up his mind what is the nature and the extent of English constitutional law.[1, 2]

Commentator seeks help from constitutional lawyers, constitutional historians and constitutional theorists.

His natural, his inevitable resource is to recur to writers of authority on the law, the history, or the practice of the constitution. He will find (it must

[1] See this point brought out with great clearness by Monsieur Boutmy, *Etudes de Droit constitutionnel* (2nd ed., 1888), p. 8, English translation by E. M. Dicey (1891), p. 8. Monsieur Boutmy well points out that the sources of English constitutional law may be considered fourfold, namely—(1) Treaties or Quasi-Treaties, *i.e.* the Acts of Union; (2) The Common Law; (3) Solemn Agreements (pacts), *e.g.* the Bill of Rights; (4) Statutes. This mode of division is not exactly that which would be naturally adopted by an English writer, but it calls attention to distinctions often overlooked between the different sources of English constitutional law.

[2] To-day conventions would certainly be included as a source of constitutional law and emphasis would be placed upon the fact that administrative law as part of constitutional law is almost exclusively derived from statute law.—Ed.

be admitted) no lack of distinguished guides; he may avail himself of the works of lawyers, such as Blackstone, of the investigations of historians, such as Hallam or Freeman, and of the speculations of philosophical theorists, such as Bagehot or Hearn. From each class he may learn much, but for reasons which I am about to lay before you for consideration, he is liable to be led by each class of authors somewhat astray in his attempt to ascertain the field of his labours and the mode of working it; he will find, unless he can obtain some clue to guide his steps, that the whole province of so-called "constitutional law" is a sort of maze in which the wanderer is perplexed by unreality, by antiquarianism, and by conventionalism.

I. Lawyer's view of constitution. Its unreality. Blackstone.

Let us turn first to the lawyers, and as in duty bound to Blackstone.

Of constitutional law as such there is not a word to be found in his *Commentaries*. The matters which appear to belong to it are dealt with by him in the main under the head Rights of Persons. The Book which is thus entitled treats (*inter alia*) of the Parliament, of the King and his title, of master and servant, of husband and wife, of parent and child. The arrangement is curious and certainly does not bring into view the true scope or character of constitutional law. This, however, is a trifle. The Book contains much real learning about our system of government. Its true defect is the hopeless confusion, both of language and of thought, introduced into the whole subject of constitutional law by Blackstone's habit—common to all the lawyers of his time—of applying old and inapplicable terms to new institutions, and especially of ascribing in words to a modern and constitutional King the whole, and perhaps more than the whole, of the powers actually possessed and exercised by William the Conqueror.

"We are next," writes Blackstone, "to consider "those branches of the royal prerogative, which invest "thus our sovereign lord, thus all-perfect and immortal "in his kingly capacity, with a number of authorities "and powers; in the exertion whereof consists "the executive part of government. This is wisely "placed in a single hand by the British constitution, "for the sake of unanimity, strength, and dispatch. "Were it placed in many hands, it would be subject "to many wills: many wills, if disunited and drawing "different ways, create weakness in a government; and "to unite those several wills, and reduce them to one, is "a work of more time and delay than the exigencies of "state will afford. The King of England is, therefore, "not only the chief, but properly the sole, magistrate "of the nation; all others acting by commission from, "and in due subordination to him; in like manner as, "upon the great revolution of the Roman state, all the "powers of the ancient magistracy of the common-"wealth were concentrated in the new Emperor: so "that, as Gravina expresses it, *in ejus unius persona* "*veteris reipublicae vis atque majestas per cumulatas* "*magistratuum potestates exprimebatur*."[1]

The language of this passage is impressive; it stands curtailed but in substance unaltered in Stephen's *Commentaries*.[2] It has but one fault; the statements

[1] 1 Bl., *Comm.* p. 250.

[2] 14th ed., 1903, vol. ii, p. 490. This work has since been re-written and is now in its twenty-first edition.—Ed.

it contains are the direct opposite of the truth. The Executive of England is in fact placed in the hands of a committee called the Cabinet. If there be any one person in whose single hand the power of the State is placed, that one person is not the Sovereign, but the chairman of the committee, known as the Prime Minister. Nor can it be urged that Blackstone's description of the royal authority was a true account of the powers of the Sovereign at the time when Blackstone wrote. George the Third enjoyed far more real authority than has fallen to the share of any of his descendants. But it would be absurd to maintain that the language I have cited painted his true position. The terms used by the commentator were, when he used them, unreal, and known[1] to be so. They have become only a little more unreal during the cen-

[1] Paley, *Moral Philosophy* (1785), Book vi, ch. vii. "In the British, "and possibly in all other constitutions, there exists a wide difference "between the actual state of the government and the theory. The "one results from the other; but still they are different. When we "contemplate the *theory* of the British government, we see the King "invested with the most absolute personal impunity; with a power of "rejecting laws, which have been resolved upon by both Houses of "Parliament; of conferring by his charter, upon any set or succession "of men he pleases, the privilege of sending representatives into one "House of Parliament, as by his immediate appointment he can place "whom he will in the other. What is this, a foreigner might ask, but "a more circuitous despotism? Yet, when we turn our attention from "the legal existence to the actual exercise of royal authority in England, "we see these formidable prerogatives dwindled into mere ceremonies; "and in their stead, a sure and commanding influence, of which the "constitution, it seems, is totally ignorant, growing out of that enormous "patronage, which the increased extent and opulence of the Empire "has placed in the disposal of the executive magistrate." Paley sees far more clearly into the true nature of the then existing constitution than did Blackstone. It is further noticeable that in 1785 the power to create Parliamentary boroughs was still looked upon as in theory an existing prerogative of the Crown. The power of the Crown was still large, and rested in fact upon the possession of enormous patronage.

tury and more which has since elapsed. "The King," he writes again, "is considered in domestic affairs . . . "as the fountain of justice, and general conservator "of the peace of the kingdom. . . . He therefore "has alone the right of erecting courts of judicature: "for, though the constitution of the kingdom hath en-"trusted him with the whole executive power of the "laws, it is impossible, as well as improper, that he "should personally carry into execution this great and "extensive trust: it is consequently necessary, that "courts should be erected to assist him in executing this "power; and equally necessary, that if erected, they "should be erected by his authority. And hence it is, "that all jurisdictions of courts are either mediately "or immediately derived from the Crown, their pro-"ceedings run generally in the King's name, they pass "under his seal, and are executed by his officers."[1] Here we are in the midst of unrealities or fictions. Neither the King nor the Executive has anything to do with erecting courts of justice. We should rightly conclude that the whole Cabinet had gone mad if to-morrow's Gazette contained an order in council not authorised by statute erecting a new Court of Appeal. It is worth while here to note what is the true injury to the study of law produced by the tendency of Blackstone, and other less famous constitutionalists, to adhere to unreal expressions. The evil is not merely or mainly that these expressions exaggerate the power of the Crown. For such conventional exaggeration a reader could make allowance, as easily as we do for ceremonious terms of respect or of social

[1] 1 Bl., *Comm.* pp. 266, 267.

courtesy. The harm wrought is, that unreal language obscures or conceals the true extent of the powers, both of the Queen and of the Government. No one, indeed, but a child, fancies that the Queen sits crowned on her throne at Westminster, and in her own person administers justice to her subjects. But the idea entertained by many educated men that an English King or Queen reigns without taking any part in the government of the country, is not less far from the truth than the notion that the Sovereign ever exercises judicial powers in what are called her courts. The oddity of the thing is that to most Englishmen the extent of the authority actually exercised by the Crown—and the same remark applies (in a great measure) to the authority exercised by the Prime Minister and other high officials—is a matter of conjecture. We have all learnt from Blackstone, and writers of the same class, to make such constant use of expressions which we know not to be strictly true to fact, that we cannot say for certain what is the exact relation between the facts of constitutional government and the more or less artificial phraseology under which they are concealed. Thus to say that the Queen appoints the Ministry is untrue; it is also, of course, untrue to say that she creates courts of justice; but these two untrue statements each bear a very different relation to actual facts. Moreover, of the powers ascribed to the Crown, some are in reality exercised by the Government, whilst others do not in truth belong either to the Queen or to the Ministry. The general result is that the true position of the Crown as also the true powers of the Government are concealed under the fictitious ascription to the Sovereign of political omnipotence, and the reader of, say, the first Book of Blackstone, can hardly discern the facts of law with which it is filled under the unrealities of the language in which these facts find expression.

II. Historian's view of constitution. Its antiquarianism.

Let us turn from the formalism of lawyers to the truthfulness of our constitutional historians.

Here a student or professor troubled about the nature of constitutional law finds himself surrounded by a crowd of eminent instructors. He may avail himself of the impartiality of Hallam: he may dive into the exhaustless erudition of the Bishop of Oxford:[1] he will discover infinite parliamentary experience in the pages of Sir Thomas May,[2] and vigorous common sense, combined with polemical research, in Mr. Freeman's *Growth of the English Constitution*. Let us take this book as an excellent type of historical constitutionalism. The *Growth of the English Constitution* is known to every one. Of its recognised merits, of its clearness, of its accuracy, of its force, it were useless and impertinent to say much to students who know, or ought to know, every line of the book from beginning to end. One point, however, deserves especial notice. Mr. Freeman's highest merit is his unrivalled faculty for bringing every matter under discussion to a clear issue. He challenges his readers to assent or deny. If you deny, you must show good cause for your denial, and hence may learn fully as much from rational disagreement with our author as from unhesitating assent to his views. Take, then, the *Growth of the English Constitution* as a first-rate

[1] Dr. William Stubbs, author of *Constitutional History of England*, *Select Charters*, and numerous other works.

[2] Sir Thomas Erskine May (later Lord Farnborough), author of *Constitutional History of England*, 1760–1860, and *Parliamentary Practice*.

specimen of the mode in which an historian looks at the constitution. What is it that a lawyer, whose object is to acquire the knowledge of law, will learn from its pages? A few citations from the ample and excellent head notes to the first two chapters of the work answer the inquiry.

They run thus:—

The Landesgemeinden of Uri and Appenzell; their bearing on English Constitutional History; political elements common to the whole Teutonic race; monarchic, aristocratic, and democratic elements to be found from the beginning; the three classes of men, the noble, the common freeman, and the slave; universal prevalence of slavery; the Teutonic institutions common to the whole Aryan family; witness of Homer; description of the German Assemblies by Tacitus; continuity of English institutions; English nationality assumed; Teutonic institutions brought into Britain by the English conquerors; effects of the settlement on the conquerors; probable increase of slavery; Earls and Churls; growth of the kingly power; nature of kingship; special sanctity of the King; immemorial distinction between Kings and Ealdormen. . . . Gradual growth of the English constitution; new laws seldom called for; importance of precedent; return to early principles in modern legislation; shrinking up of the ancient national Assemblies; constitution of the Witenagemót; the Witenagemót continued in the House of Lords; Gemóts after the Norman Conquest; the King's right of summons; Life Peerages; origin of the House of Commons; comparison of English and French national Assemblies; of English and French history generally; course of events influenced by particular men; Simon of Montfort . . . Edward the First; the constitution finally completed under him; nature of later changes; difference between English and continental legislatures.

All this is interesting, erudite, full of historical importance, and thoroughly in its place in a book concerned solely with the "growth" of the constitution; but in regard to English law and the law of the constitution, the *Landesgemeinden* of Uri, the witness of Homer, the ealdormen, the constitution of the Witenagemót, and a lot more of fascinating matter are mere antiquarianism. Let no one suppose that to say this is to deny the relation between history and law. It were far better, as things now stand, to be charged with heresy, than to fall under the suspicion of lacking historical-mindedness, or of questioning the universal validity of the historical method. What one may assert without incurring the risk of such crushing imputations is, that the kind of constitutional history which consists in researches into the antiquities of English institutions, has no direct bearing on the rules of constitutional law in the sense in which these rules can become the subject of legal comment. Let us eagerly learn all that is known, and still more eagerly all that is not known, about the Witenagemót. But let us remember that antiquarianism is not law, and that the function of a trained lawyer is not to know what the law of England was yesterday, still less what it was centuries ago, or what it ought to be to-morrow, but to know and be able to state what are the principles of law which actually and at the present day exist in

England. For this purpose it boots nothing to know the nature of the Landesgemeinden of Uri, or to understand, if it be understandable, the constitution of the Witenagemót. All this is for a lawyer's purposes simple antiquarianism. It throws as much light on the constitution of the United States as upon the constitution of England; that is, it throws from a legal point of view no light upon either the one or the other.

Contrast between legal and historical view of constitution.

The name of the United States serves well to remind us of the true relation between constitutional historians and legal constitutionalists. They are each concerned with the constitution, but from a different aspect. An historian is primarily occupied with ascertaining the steps by which a constitution has grown to be what it is. He is deeply, sometimes excessively, concerned with the question of "origins." He is but indirectly concerned in ascertaining what are the rules of the constitution in the year 1908. To a lawyer, on the other hand, the primary object of study is the law as it now stands; he is only secondarily occupied with ascertaining how it came into existence. This is absolutely clear if we compare the position of an American historian with the position of an American jurist. The historian of the American Union would not commence his researches at the year 1789; he would have a good deal to say about Colonial history and about the institutions of England; he might, for aught I know, find himself impelled to go back to the Witenagemót; he would, one may suspect, pause in his researches considerably short of Uri. A lawyer lecturing on the constitution of the United States would, on the other hand, necessarily start from the constitution itself. But he would soon see that the articles of the constitution required a knowledge of the Articles of Confederation ; that the opinions of Washington, of Hamilton, and generally of the "Fathers," as one sometimes hears them called in America, threw light on the meaning of various constitutional articles ; and further, that the meaning of the constitution could not be adequately understood by any one who did not take into account the situation of the colonies before the separation from England and the rules of common law, as well as the general conceptions of law and justice inherited by English colonists from their English forefathers. As it is with the American lawyer compared with the American historian, so it is with the English lawyer as compared with the English historian. Hence, even where lawyers are concerned, as they frequently must be, with the development of our institutions, arises a further difference between the historical and the legal view of the constitution. Historians in their devotion to the earliest phases of ascertainable history are infected with a love which, in the eyes of a lawyer, appears inordinate, for the germs of our institutions, and seem to care little about their later developments. Mr. Freeman gives but one-third of his book to anything as modern as the days of the Stuarts. The period of now more than two centuries which has elapsed since what used to be called the "Glorious Revolution," filled as those two centuries are with change and with growth, seems hardly to have attracted the attention of a writer whom lack, not of knowledge, but of will has alone prevented from sketching out the annals of our modern constitution. A lawyer must look at the matter differently. It is from the later annals of England he derives most help in the study of existing law. What we might have obtained from Dr. Stubbs, had he not surrendered to the Episcopate gifts which we hoped were dedicated to the University alone, is now left to conjecture. But, things being as they are, the historian who most nearly meets the wants of lawyers is Mr. Gardiner. The struggles of the seventeenth century, the conflict between James and Coke, Bacon's theory of the prerogative, Charles's effort to substitute the personal will of Charles Stuart for the legal will of the King of England, are all matters which touch not remotely upon the problems of actual law. A knowledge of these things guards us, at any rate, from the illusion, for illusion it must be termed, that modern constitutional freedom has been established by an astounding method of retrogressive progress; that every step towards civilisation has been a step backwards towards the simple wisdom of our uncultured ancestors. The assumption which underlies this view, namely, that there existed among our Saxon forefathers a more or less perfect polity, conceals the truth both of law and of history. To ask how a mass of legal subtleties "would have looked ". . . in the eyes of a man who had borne his part "in the elections of Eadward and of Harold, and "who had raised his voice and clashed his arms in "the great Assembly which restored Godwine to his "lands,"[1] is to put an inquiry which involves an untenable assumption; it is like asking what a Cherokee Indian would have thought of the claim of George the Third to separate taxation from representation. In

[1] See Freeman, *Growth of the English Constitution* (1st ed., 1872), p. 125.

each case the question implies that the simplicity of a savage enables him to solve with fairness a problem of which he cannot understand the terms. Civilisation may rise above, but barbarism sinks below the level of legal fictions, and our respectable Saxon ancestors were, as compared, not with ourselves only, but with men so like ourselves as Coke and Hale, respectable barbarians. The supposition, moreover, that the cunning of lawyers has by the invention of legal fictions corrupted the fair simplicity of our original constitution, underrates the statesmanship of lawyers as much as it overrates the merits of early society. The fictions of the courts have in the hands of lawyers such as Coke served the cause both of justice and of freedom, and served it when it could have been defended by no other weapons. For there are social conditions under which legal fictions or subtleties afford the sole means of establishing that rule of equal and settled law which is the true basis of English civilisation. Nothing can be more pedantic, nothing more artificial, nothing more unhistorical, than the reasoning by which Coke induced or compelled James to forego the attempt to withdraw cases from the courts for his Majesty's personal determination.[1] But no achievement of sound argument, or stroke of enlightened statesmanship, ever established a rule more essential to the very existence of the constitution than the principle enforced by the obstinacy and the fallacies of the great Chief Justice. Oddly enough, the notion of an ideal constitution corrupted by the technicalities of lawyers is at bottom a delusion of the legal imagination. The idea of

[1] *Prohibitions del Roy* (1607) 12 Co. Rep. 63; K. & L. 76; Hearn, *Government of England* (2nd ed., 1887), ch. iii.

retrogressive progress is merely one form of the appeal to precedent. This appeal has made its appearance at every crisis in the history of England, and indeed no one has stated so forcibly as my friend Mr. Freeman himself the peculiarity of all English efforts to extend the liberties of the country, namely, that these attempts at innovation have always assumed the form of an appeal to pre-existing rights. But the appeal to precedent is in the law courts merely a useful fiction by which judicial decision conceals its transformation into judicial legislation; and a fiction is none the less a fiction because it has emerged from the courts into the field of politics or of history. Here, then, the astuteness of lawyers has imposed upon the simplicity of historians. Formalism and antiquarianism have, so to speak, joined hands; they have united to mislead students in search for the law of the constitution.

Let us turn now to the political theorists.

III. View of political theorists. Its defect that it deals solely with conventions of constitution.

No better types of such thinkers can be taken than Bagehot and Professor Hearn. No author of modern times (it may be confidently asserted) has done so much to elucidate the intricate workings of English government as Bagehot. His *English Constitution* is so full of brightness, originality, and wit, that few students notice how full it is also of knowledge, of wisdom, and of insight. The slight touches, for example, by which Bagehot paints the reality of Cabinet government, are so amusing as to make a reader forget that Bagehot was the first author who explained in accordance with actual fact the true nature of the Cabinet and its real relation to the Crown and to Parliament. He is, in short, one of those rare teachers who have explained intricate matters with such complete clearness, as to make the public forget that what is now so clear ever needed explanation. Professor Hearn may perhaps be counted an anticipator of Bagehot. In any case he too has approached English institutions from a new point of view, and has looked at them in a fresh light; he would be universally recognised among us as one of the most distinguished and ingenious exponents of the mysteries of the English constitution, had it not been for the fact that he made his fame as a professor, not in any of the seats of learning in the United Kingdom, but in the University of Melbourne. From both these writers we expect to learn, and do learn much, but, as in the case of Mr. Freeman, though we learn much from our teacher which is of value, we do not learn precisely what as lawyers we are in search of. The truth is that both Bagehot and Professor Hearn deal and mean to deal mainly with political understandings or conventions and not with rules of law. What is the precise moral influence which might be exerted by a wise constitutional monarch; what are the circumstances under which a Minister is entitled to dissolve Parliament; whether the simultaneous creation of a large number of Peers for a special purpose is constitutionally justifiable; what is the principle on which a Cabinet may allow of open questions;—these and the like are the kind of inquiries raised and solved by writers whom, as being occupied with the conventional understandings of the constitution, we may term conventionalists. These inquiries are, many of them, great and weighty; but they are not inquiries which will ever be debated in the law courts. If the Premier should advise the creation of five hundred Peers, the Chancery Division would not, we may be sure, grant an injunction to restrain their creation. If he should on a vote of censure decline to resign office, the Queen's Bench Division would certainly not issue a *quo warranto* calling upon him to show cause why he continues to be Prime Minister. As a lawyer, I find these matters too high for me. Their practical solution must be left to the profound wisdom of Members of Parliament; their speculative solution belongs to the province of political theorists.

And conventional view does not explain how conventions enforced.

One suggestion a mere legist may be allowed to make, namely, that the authors who insist upon and explain the conventional character of the understandings which make up a great part of the constitution, leave unexplained the one matter which needs explanation. They give no satisfactory answer to the inquiry how it happens that the understandings of politics are sometimes at least obeyed as rigorously as the commands of law.[1] To refer to public opinion and to considerations of expediency is to offer but a very inadequate solution of a really curious problem. Public opinion approves and public expediency requires the observance of contracts, yet contracts are not always observed, and would (presumably) be broken more often than they are did not the law punish their breach, or compel their performance. Meanwhile it is certain that understandings are not laws, and that no system of conventionalism will explain the whole nature of constitutional law, if indeed "constitutional law" be in strictness law at all.

[1] See further on this point, Part iii, ch. xv, *post*.

Is constitutional law really "law" at all?

For at this point a doubt occurs to one's mind which must more than once have haunted students of the constitution. Is it possible that so-called "constitutional law" is in reality a cross between history and custom which does not properly deserve the name of law at all, and certainly does not belong to the province of a professor called upon to learn or to teach nothing but the true indubitable law of England? Can it be that a dark saying of de Tocqueville's, "the English constitution has no real existence" (*elle n'existe point* [1]), contains the truth of the whole matter? In this case lawyers would gladly surrender a domain to which they can establish no valid title. The one half of it should, as belonging to history, go over to our historical professors. The other half should, as belonging to conventions which illustrate the growth of law, be transferred either to my friend the Corpus Professor of Jurisprudence, because it is his vocation to deal with the oddities or the outlying portions of legal science, or to my friend the Chichele Professor of International Law, because he being a teacher of law which is not law, and being accustomed to expound those rules of public ethics which are miscalled international law, will find himself at home in expounding political ethics which, on the hypothesis under consideration, are miscalled constitutional law.

Before, however, admitting the truth of the supposition that "constitutional law" is in no sense law at all, it will be well to examine a little further into the precise meaning which we attach to the term con-

[1] de Tocqueville, *Œuvres complètes* (14th ed., 1864), vol. i (Démocratie en Amérique), pp. 166, 167.

stitutional law, and then consider how far it is a fit subject for legal exposition.

It consists of two different kinds of rules.

Constitutional law, as the term is used in England, appears to include all rules which directly or indirectly affect the distribution or the exercise of the sovereign power in the state.[1] Hence it includes (among other things) all rules which define the members of the sovereign power, all rules which regulate the relation of such members to each other, or which determine the mode in which the sovereign power, or the members thereof, exercise their authority. Its rules prescribe the order of succession to the throne, regulate the prerogatives of the chief magistrate, determine the form of the legislature and its mode of election. These rules also deal with Ministers, with their responsibility, with their spheres of action, define the territory over which the sovereignty of the state extends and settle who are to be deemed subjects or citizens. Observe the use of the word "rules," not "laws." This employment of terms is intentional. Its object is to call attention to the fact that the rules which make up constitutional law, as the term is used in England, include two sets of principles or maxims of a totally distinct character.

(i.) Rules which are true laws—law of the constitution.

The one set of rules are in the strictest sense "laws," since they are rules which (whether written or unwritten, whether enacted by statute or derived from the

[1] Cf. Holland, *Jurisprudence* (10th ed., 1906), pp. 138, 139, and 359-363. "By the constitution of a country is meant so much of its law as "relates to the designation and form of the legislature; the rights and "functions of the several parts of the legislative body; the construction, "office, and jurisdiction of courts of justice. The constitution is one "principal division, section, or title of the code of public laws, dis-"tinguished from the rest only by the superior importance of the subject "of which it treats."—Paley, *Moral Philosophy* (1785), Book vi, ch. vii.

mass of custom, tradition, or judge-made maxims known as the common law) are enforced by the courts; these rules constitute "constitutional law" in the proper sense of that term, and may for the sake of distinction be called collectively "the law of the constitution."

(ii) Rules which are not laws—conventions of the constitution.

The other set of rules consist of conventions, understandings, habits, or practices which, though they may regulate the conduct of the several members of the sovereign power, of the Ministry, or of other officials, are not in reality laws at all since they are not enforced by the courts. This portion of constitutional law may, for the sake of distinction, be termed the "conventions of the constitution," or constitutional morality.

To put the same thing in a somewhat different shape, "constitutional law," as the expression is used in England, both by the public and by authoritative writers, consists of two elements. The one element, here called the "law of the constitution," is a body of undoubted law; the other element, here called the "conventions of the constitution," consists of maxims or practices which, though they regulate the ordinary conduct of the Crown, of Ministers, and of other persons under the constitution, are not in strictness laws at all. The contrast between the law of the constitution and the conventions of the constitution may be most easily seen from examples.[1]

Examples of rules belonging to law of constitution.

To the law of the constitution belong the following rules:—

"The Queen can do no wrong." This maxim, as now interpreted by the courts, means, in the first place, that by no proceeding known to the law can

[1] See, however, Jennings, *The Law and the Constitution* (4th ed., 1952), pp. 102-105, and Intro. p. clv, *ante*.

the Queen be made personally responsible for any act done by her; if (to give an absurd example) the Queen were herself to shoot the Premier through the head, no court in England could take cognisance of the act. The maxim means, in the second place, that no one can plead the orders of the Crown or indeed of any superior officer in defence of any act not otherwise justifiable by law; this principle in both its applications is (be it noted) a law and a law of the constitution, but it is not a written law. "There is no power in the Crown to dispense with the obligation to obey a law;" this negation or abolition of the dispensing power now depends upon the Bill of Rights; it is a law of the constitution and a written law. "Some person is legally responsible for every act done by the Crown." This responsibility of Ministers appears in foreign countries as a formal part of the constitution; in England it results from the combined action of several legal principles, namely, first, the maxim that the Queen can do no wrong; secondly, the refusal of the courts to recognise any act as done by the Crown, which is not done in a particular form, a form in general involving the affixing of a particular seal by a Minister, or the counter-signature or something equivalent to the counter-signature of a Minister; thirdly, the principle that the Minister who affixes a particular seal, or countersigns his signature, is responsible for the act which he, so to speak, endorses;[1] this again is part of the constitution and a law, but it is not a written law. So again the right to personal liberty, the right of public meeting, and many other rights, are part of the law of

[1] Cf. Hearn, *Government of England* (2nd ed., 1887), ch. iv.

the constitution, though most of these rights are consequences of the more general law or principle that no man can be punished except for direct breaches of law (*i.e.* crimes) proved in the way provided by law (*i.e.* before the courts of the realm).[1]

To the conventions of the constitution belong the following maxims :[2]—

Examples of rules which belong to conventions of the constitution.

"The Sovereign must assent to, or (as it is inaccurately expressed) cannot 'veto'[3] any bill passed by the two Houses of Parliament ;"—"the House of Lords does not originate any money bill ;"—"when the House of Lords acts as a Court of Appeal, no peer who is not a law lord takes part in the decisions of the House ;"—"Ministers resign office when they have ceased to command the confidence of the House of Commons ;"—"a bill must be read a certain number of times before passing through the House of Commons." These maxims are distinguished from each other by many differences ;[4] under a new or written constitu-

[1] With one exception these examples are taken from the common law. Statutes as a source of constitutional law are generally disregarded throughout the text, especially in the chapters on the rule of law.—Ed.

[2] See Jennings, *Cabinet Government* (3rd ed., 1959), ch. i.

[3] As to the meaning of veto, see Hearn, *op. cit.*, pp. 51, 60, 61, 63, and Jennings, *op. cit.*, pp. 395-400, 539-542.

[4] Some of these maxims are never violated, and are universally admitted to be inviolable. Others, on the other hand, have nothing but a slight amount of custom in their favour, and are of disputable validity. The main distinction between different classes of conventional rules may, it is conceived, be thus stated : Some of these rules could not be violated without bringing to a stop the course of orderly and pacific government ; others might be violated without any other consequence than that of exposing the Minister or other person by whom they were broken to blame or unpopularity.

In the opinion of the author this difference will at bottom be found to depend upon the degree of directness with which the violation of a given constitutional maxim brings the wrongdoer into conflict with the

tion some of them probably would and some of them would not take the form of actual laws. Under the English constitution they have one point in common: they are none of them "laws" in the true sense of that word, for if any or all of them were broken, no court would take notice of their violation.

It is to be regretted that these maxims must be called "conventional," for the word suggests a notion of insignificance or unreality.[1] This, however, is the last idea which any teacher would wish to convey to his hearers. Of constitutional conventions or practices some are as important as any laws, though some may be trivial, as may also be the case with a genuine law. My object, however, is to contrast, not shams with realities, but the legal element with the conventional element of so-called "constitutional law."

This distinction differs essentially, it should be

law of the land. Thus a Ministry under whose advice Parliament were not summoned to meet for more than a year would, owing to the lapse of the Army (Annual) Act, become through their agents engaged in a conflict with the Courts. The violation of a convention of the constitution would in this case lead to revolutionary or reactionary violence. The rule, on the other hand, that a Bill must be read a given number of times before it is passed is, though a well-established constitutional principle, a convention which might be disregarded without bringing the Government into conflict with the ordinary law. A Ministry who induced the House of Commons to pass an Act, *e.g.* suspending the Habeas Corpus Act, after one reading, or who induced the House to alter their rules as to the number of times a Bill should be read, would in no way be exposed to a contest with the ordinary tribunals. Ministers who, after Supplies were voted and the Army (Annual) Act passed, should prorogue the House and keep office for months after the Government had ceased to retain the confidence of the Commons, might or might not incur grave unpopularity, but would not necessarily commit a breach of law. See further Part iii, *post*, and cf. Intro. pp. clxxx *et seq.*, *ante*.

[1] Cf. Jennings, *The Law and the Constitution* (4th ed., 1952), p. 80, for further criticism of the term.

Distinction between laws and conventions not the same as difference between written and unwritten law.

noted, from the distinction between "written law" (or statute law) and "unwritten law" (or common law). There are laws of the constitution, as, for example, the Bill of Rights, the Act of Settlement, the Habeas Corpus Acts, which are "written law," found in the statute-books—in other words, are statutory enactments. There are other most important laws of the constitution (several of which have already been mentioned) which are "unwritten" laws, that is, not statutory enactments. Some further of the laws of the constitution, such, for example, as the law regulating the descent of the Crown, which were at one time unwritten or common law, have now become written or statute law. The conventions of the constitution, on the other hand, cannot be recorded in the statute-book, though they may be formally reduced to writing. Thus the whole of our parliamentary procedure is nothing but a mass of conventional law; it is, however, recorded in written or printed rules. The distinction, in short, between written and unwritten law does not in any sense square with the distinction between the law of the constitution (constitutional law properly so called) and the conventions of the constitution. This latter is the distinction on which we should fix our whole attention, for it is of vital importance, and elucidates the whole subject of constitutional law. It is further a difference which may exist in countries which have a written or statutory constitution.[1] In the United States the legal

[1] The conventional element in the constitution of the United States is far larger than most Englishmen suppose. See Woodrow Wilson, *Congressional Government* (1925 ed.); Bryce, *American Commonwealth* (1910 ed.), vol. i, ch. xxxiv and xxxv; Horwill, *The Usages of the American Constitution* (1925). It may be asserted without much exag-

powers of the President, the Senate, the mode of electing the President, and the like, are, as far as the law is concerned, regulated wholly by the law of the constitution. But side by side with the law have grown up certain stringent conventional rules, which, though they would not be noticed by any court, have in practice nearly the force of law. No President has ever been re-elected more than once: the popular approval of this conventional limit (of which the constitution knows nothing) on a President's re-eligibility proved a fatal bar to General Grant's third candidature. Constitutional understandings have entirely changed the position of the Presidential electors. They were by the founders of the constitution intended to be what their name denotes, the persons who chose or selected the President; the chief officer, in short, of the Republic was, according to the law, to be appointed under a system of double election. This intention has failed; the "electors" have become a mere means of voting for a particular candidate; they are no more than so many ballots cast for the Republican or for the Democratic nominee. The understanding that an elector is not really to elect, has now become so firmly established, that for him to exercise his legal power of choice is considered a breach of political honour too gross to be committed

geration that the conventional element in the constitution of the United States is as large as in the English constitution. Under the American system, however, the line between "conventional rules" and "laws" is drawn with a precision hardly possible in England.

Under the constitution of the existing French Republic, constitutional conventions or understandings exert a considerable amount of influence. They considerably limit, for instance, the actual exercise of the large powers conferred by the letter of the constitution on the President. See Chardon, *L'Administration de la France—Les fonctionnaires* (1908), pp. 79-105.

by the most unscrupulous of politicians. Public difficulties, not to say dangers, might have been averted if, in the contest between Mr. Hayes and Mr. Tilden, a few Republican electors had felt themselves at liberty to vote for the Democratic candidate. Not a single man among them changed his side. The power of an elector to elect is as completely abolished by constitutional understandings in America as is the royal right of dissent from bills passed by both Houses by the same force in England. Under a written, therefore, as under an unwritten constitution, we find in full existence the distinction between the law and the conventions of the constitution.

Constitutional law as subject of legal study means solely law of constitution.

Upon this difference I have insisted at possibly needless length, because it lies at the very root of the matter under discussion. Once grasp the ambiguity latent in the expression "constitutional law," and everything connected with the subject falls so completely into its right place that a lawyer, called upon to teach or to study constitutional law as a branch of the law of England, can hardly fail to see clearly the character and scope of his subject.

With conventions or understandings he has no direct concern. They vary from generation to generation, almost from year to year. Whether a Ministry defeated at the polling booths ought to retire on the day when the result of the election is known, or may more properly retain office until after a defeat in Parliament, is or may be a question of practical importance. The opinions on this point which prevail to-day differ (it is said) from the opinions or understandings which prevailed thirty years back, and are possibly different from the opinions or understandings which may prevail ten years hence. Weighty precedents and high authority are cited on either side of this knotty question; the dicta or practice of Russell and Peel may be balanced off against the dicta or practice of Beaconsfield and Gladstone. The subject, however, is not one of law but of politics, and need trouble no lawyer or the class of any professor of law. If he is concerned with it at all, he is so only in so far as he may be called upon to show what is the connection (if any there be) between the conventions of the constitution and the law of the constitution.[1]

This the true constitutional law is his only real concern. His proper function is to show what are the legal rules (*i.e.* rules recognised by the courts) which are to be found in the several parts of the constitution. Of such rules or laws he will easily discover more than enough. The rules determining the legal position of the Crown, the legal rights of the Crown's Ministers, the constitution of the House of Lords, the constitution of the House of Commons, the laws which govern the established Church, the laws which determine the position of the non-established Churches, the laws which regulate the army,—these and a hundred other laws form part of the law of the constitution, and are as truly part of the law of the land as the articles of the constitution of the United States form part of the law of the Union.[2]

[1] See Jennings, *Cabinet Government* (3rd ed., 1959), ch. i.

[2] Cf. Jennings, *The Law and the Constitution* (4th ed., 1952), pp. 69-70. Many of these rules are statutory. The argument excludes cabinet government which is the outcome of conventions. Part iii of the text, however, shows that the author intended to include those conventions which he regarded as dependent upon rules of law.—ED.

Law of constitution can be expounded like any other branch of English law.

The duty, in short, of an English professor of law is to state what are the laws which form part of the constitution, to arrange them in their order, to explain their meaning, and to exhibit where possible their logical connection. He ought to expound the unwritten or partly unwritten constitution of England, in the same manner in which Story and Kent have expounded the written law of the American constitution. The task has its special perplexities, but the difficulties which beset the topic are the same in kind, though not in degree, as those which are to be found in every branch of the law of England. You are called upon to deal partly with statute law, partly with judge-made law; you are forced to rely on Parliamentary enactments and also on judicial decisions, on authoritative dicta, and in many cases on mere inferences drawn from judicial doctrines; it is often difficult to discriminate between prevalent custom and acknowledged right. This is true of the endeavour to expound the law of the constitution; all this is true also in a measure of any attempt to explain our law of contract, our law of torts, or our law of real property.

Moreover, teachers of constitutional law enjoy at this moment one invaluable advantage. Their topic has, of recent years,[1] become of immediate interest and of pressing importance. These years have brought into the foreground new constitutional questions, and have afforded in many instances the answers thereto. The series of actions connected with the name of

[1] This treatise was originally published in 1885. Between that date and 1914 legal decisions and public discussion threw light upon several matters of constitutional law, such, for example, as the limits to the right of public meeting and the nature of martial law.

Mr. Bradlaugh [1] has done as much to clear away the obscurity which envelops many parts of our public law as was done in the eighteenth century by the series of actions connected with the name of John Wilkes. The law of maintenance has been rediscovered; the law of blasphemy has received new elucidation. Everybody now knows the character of a penal action. It is now possible to define with precision the relation between the House of Commons and the courts of the land; the legal character and solemnity of an oath has been made patent to all the world, or at any rate to all those persons who choose to read the *Law Reports.* Meanwhile circumstances with which Mr. Bradlaugh had no connection have forced upon public attention all the various problems connected with the right of public meeting. Is such a right known to the law? What are the limits within which it may be exercised? What is the true definition of an "unlawful assembly"? How far may citizens lawfully assembled assert their right of meeting by the use of force? What are the limits within which the English constitution recognises the right of self-defence? These are questions some of which have been raised and all of which may any day be raised before the courts. They are inquiries which touch the very root of our public law. To find the true reply to them is a matter of importance to every citizen. While these inquiries require an answer the study of the law of the constitution must remain a matter of pressing interest. The fact, however, that

[1] See for Bradlaugh's political career, *Dictionary of National Biography,* vol. xxii (Supplement), Reissue, 1908–9, p. 248.

the provisions of this law are often embodied in cases which have gained notoriety and excite keen feelings of political partisanship may foster a serious misconception. Unintelligent students may infer that the law of the constitution is to be gathered only from famous judgments which embalm the results of grand constitutional or political conflicts. This is not so. Scores of unnoticed cases, such as the *Parlement Belge*,[1] or *Thomas* v. *The Queen*,[2] touch upon or decide principles of constitutional law. Indeed every action against a constable or collector of revenue enforces the greatest of all such principles, namely, that obedience to administrative orders is no defence to an action or prosecution for acts done in excess of legal authority. The true law of the constitution is in short to be gathered from the sources whence we collect the law of England in respect to any other topic, and forms as interesting and as distinct, though not as well explored, a field for legal study or legal exposition as any which can be found. The subject is one which has not yet been fully mapped out. Teachers and pupils alike therefore suffer from the inconvenience as they enjoy the interest of exploring a province of law which has not yet been entirely reduced to order.[3]

This inconvenience has one great compensation. We are compelled to search for the guidance of first

[1] (1879) 4 P.D. 129; on appeal (1880) 5 P.D. 197. Cf. *Walker* v. *Baird* [1892] A.C. 491, at p. 497; K. & L. 115.

[2] (1874) L.R. 10 Q.B. 31.

[3] Since these words were written in 1885, Sir William Anson's admirable *Law and Custom of the Constitution* has gone far to provide a complete scheme of English constitutional law. The latest editions of this work are: vol. i (5th ed., 1922), ed. Gwyer; vol. ii (4th ed., 1935), ed. Keith. It does not deal in detail with administrative powers.

principles, and as we look for a clue through the mazes of a perplexed topic, three such guiding principles gradually become apparent. They are, *first*, the legislative sovereignty of Parliament;[1] *secondly*, the universal rule or supremacy throughout the constitution of ordinary law;[2] and *thirdly* (though here we tread on more doubtful and speculative ground), the dependence in the last resort of the conventions upon the law of the constitution.[3] To examine, to elucidate, to test these three principles, forms, at any rate (whatever be the result of the investigation), a suitable introduction to the study of the law of the constitution.

[1] See Part i, *post*.

[2] See Part ii, *post*.

[3] See Part iii, *post*.

PART I

THE SOVEREIGNTY OF PARLIAMENT

CHAPTER I

THE NATURE OF PARLIAMENTARY SOVEREIGNTY[1]

Chapter I

THE sovereignty of Parliament is (from a legal point of view) the dominant characteristic of our political institutions.

Aim of chapter.

My aim in this chapter is, in the first place, to explain the nature of Parliamentary sovereignty and to show that its existence is a legal fact, fully recognised by the law of England; in the next place, to prove that none of the alleged legal limitations on the sovereignty of Parliament have any existence; and, lastly, to state and meet certain speculative difficulties which hinder the ready admission of the doctrine that Parliament is, under the British constitution, an absolutely sovereign legislature.

Nature of Parliamentary Sovereignty.

A. *Nature of Parliamentary Sovereignty.*—Parliament means, in the mouth of a lawyer (though the word has often a different sense in ordinary conversation), the Queen, the House of Lords, and the House of Commons; these three bodies acting together may be aptly described as the "Queen in Parliament," and constitute Parliament.[2]

The principle of Parliamentary sovereignty means neither more nor less than this, namely, that Parliament thus defined has, under the English constitu-

[1] Cf. Intro. pp. xxxiv *et seq.*, *ante*. [2] Cf. 1 Bl., *Comm.* p. 153.

Part I.

tion, the right to make or unmake any law whatever; and, further, that no person or body is recognised by the law of England as having a right to override or set aside the legislation of Parliament.[1]

A law may, for our present purpose, be defined as "any rule which will be enforced by the courts." The principle then of Parliamentary sovereignty may, looked at from its positive side, be thus described: Any Act of Parliament, or any part of an Act of Parliament, which makes a new law, or repeals or modifies an existing law, will be obeyed by the courts. The same principle, looked at from its negative side, may be thus stated: There is no person or body of persons who can, under the English constitution, make rules which override or derogate from an Act of Parliament, or which (to express the same thing in other words) will be enforced by the courts in contravention of an Act of Parliament. Some apparent exceptions to this rule no doubt suggest themselves. But these apparent exceptions, as where, for example, the Judges of the High Court of Justice make rules of court repealing Parliamentary enactments, are resolvable into cases in which Parliament either directly or indirectly sanctions subordinate legislation.[2] This is not the place for entering into any details as to the nature of judicial legislation; the matter is mentioned here only in order to remove an obvious difficulty which might present itself to some students.

[1] This is not a distinctive characteristic. In France and Belgium the courts do not in practice question the validity of acts of the legislature, notwithstanding that in each case the powers of the legislature are limited by the constitution.—ED.

[2] Rules of court are made by a statutory committee of judges, barristers, and solicitors.—ED.

It will be necessary in the course of these lectures to say a good deal more about Parliamentary sovereignty, but for the present the above rough description of its nature may suffice. The important thing is to make clear that the doctrine of Parliamentary sovereignty is, both on its positive and on its negative side, fully recognised by the law of England.

Unlimited legislative authority of Parliament.

I. *Unlimited legislative authority of Parliament.* —The classical passage on this subject is the following extract from Blackstone's *Commentaries* :—

"The power and jurisdiction of Parliament, says "Sir Edward Coke,[1] is so transcendent and absolute, "that it cannot be confined, either for causes or per-"sons, within any bounds. And of this high court, he "adds, it may be truly said, '*Si antiquitatem spectes,* "*est vetustissima ; si dignitatem, est honoratissima ; si* "*jurisdictionem, est capacissima.*' It hath sovereign "and uncontrollable authority in the making, confirm-"ing, enlarging, restraining, abrogating, repealing, re-"viving, and expounding of laws, concerning matters "of all possible denominations, ecclesiastical or tem-"poral, civil, military, maritime, or criminal : this "being the place where that absolute despotic power, "which must in all governments reside somewhere, is "entrusted by the constitution of these kingdoms. All "mischiefs and grievances, operations and remedies, "that transcend the ordinary course of the laws, are "within the reach of this extraordinary tribunal. It "can regulate or new-model the succession to the "Crown ; as was done in the reign of Henry VIII. and "William III. It can alter the established religion

[1] *Fourth Institute*, p. 36.

Part I.

"of the land; as was done in a variety of instances, "in the reigns of king Henry VIII. and his three "children. It can change and create afresh even the "constitution of the kingdom and of parliaments them-"selves; as was done by the act of union, and the "several statutes for triennial and septennial elections. "It can, in short, do everything that is not naturally "impossible; and therefore some have not scrupled "to call its power, by a figure rather too bold, the "omnipotence of Parliament. True it is, that what the "Parliament doth, no authority upon earth can undo. "So that it is a matter most essential to the liberties of "this kingdom, that such members be delegated to this "important trust, as are most eminent for their probity, "their fortitude, and their knowledge; for it was a "known apophthegm of the great lord treasurer Bur-"leigh, 'that England could never be ruined but by "a Parliament': and, as Sir Matthew Hale observes, "this being the highest and greatest court over which "none other can have jurisdiction in the kingdom, if "by any means a misgovernment should any way fall "upon it, the subjects of this kingdom are left without "all manner of remedy. To the same purpose the "president Montesquieu, though I trust too hastily, "presages; that as Rome, Sparta, and Carthage have "lost their liberty and perished, so the constitution of "England will in time lose its liberty, will perish: "it will perish whenever the legislative power shall "become more corrupt than the executive."[1]

[1] 1 Bl., *Comm.* pp. 160, 161; cf. as to the sovereignty of Parliament, *De Republica Anglorum; A Discourse on the Commonwealth of England*, by Sir Thomas Smith, edited by L. Alston (1906), Book ii, ch. i, p. 148. This book was originally published in 1583.

Chapter I.

De Lolme has summed up the matter in a grotesque expression which has become almost proverbial. "It is a fundamental principle with English lawyers, "that Parliament can do everything but make a "woman a man, and a man a woman."

Historical examples of Parliamentary sovereignty. Act of Settlement.

This supreme legislative authority of Parliament is shown historically in a large number of instances.

The descent of the Crown was varied and finally fixed under the provisions of the Act of Settlement, whereby the Sovereign occupies the throne under a Parliamentary title; his claim to reign depends upon and is the result of a statute. This is a proposition which, at the present day, no one is inclined either to maintain or to dispute; but a glance at the statute-book shows that not much more than two hundred years ago Parliament had to insist strenuously upon the principle of its own lawful supremacy. The first section of 6 Anne, c. 7, enacts (*inter alia*), "That if any person or "persons shall maliciously, advisedly and directly, by "writing or printing, maintain and affirm, that our "sovereign lady the Queen that now is, is not the "lawful and rightful Queen of these realms, or that the "pretended Prince of Wales, who now styles himself "King of Great Britain, or King of England, by the "name of James the Third, or King of Scotland, by the "name of James the Eighth, hath any right or title to "the Crown of these realms, or that any other person "or persons hath or have any right or title to the same, "otherwise than according to an Act of Parliament "made in England in the first year of the reign of their "late Majesties King William and Queen Mary, of "ever blessed and glorious memory, intituled, An Act "declaring the rights and liberties of the subject, and

Part I.

"settling the succession of the Crown; and one other "Act made in England in the twelfth year of the reign "of his said late Majesty King William the Third, "intituled, An Act for the further limitation of the "Crown, and better securing the rights and liberties of "the subject; and the Acts lately made in England "and Scotland mutually for the union of the two "kingdoms; or that the Kings or Queens of this realm, "with and by the authority of Parliament, are not able "to make laws and statutes of sufficient force and "validity to limit and bind the Crown, and the descent, "limitation, inheritance and government thereof; "every such person or persons shall be guilty of high "treason, and being thereof lawfully convicted, shall "be adjudged traitors, and shall suffer pains of death, "and all losses and forfeitures as in cases of high "treason."[1]

Acts of Union.

The Acts of Union (to one of which Blackstone calls attention) afford a remarkable example of the exertion of Parliamentary authority. But there is no single statute which is more significant either as to the theory or as to the practical working of the constitution than the Septennial Act. The circumstances of its enactment and the nature of the Act itself merit therefore special attention.

Septennial Act.

In 1716 the duration of Parliament was under an Act of 1694 limited to three years, and a general election could not be deferred beyond 1717. The King and the Ministry were convinced (and with reason) that an appeal to the electors, many of whom were Jacobites, might be perilous not only to the Ministry but to the tranquillity of the state. The

[1] This enactment is still in force; 6 Anne, c. 41, in the Statutes Revised (3rd ed.).

Parliament then sitting, therefore, was induced by the Ministry to pass the Septennial Act by which the legal duration of Parliament was extended from three to seven years, and the powers of the then existing House of Commons were in effect prolonged for four years beyond the time for which the House was elected.[1] This was a much stronger proceeding than passing say an Act which enabled future Parliaments to continue in existence without the necessity for a general election during seven instead of during three years. The statute was justified by considerations of statesmanship and expediency. This justification of the Septennial Act must seem to every sensible man so ample that it is with some surprise that one reads in writers so fair and judicious as Hallam or Lord Stanhope attempts to minimise the importance of this supreme display of legislative authority. "Nothing," writes Hallam, "can be more extravagant "than what is sometimes confidently pretended by "the ignorant, that the legislature exceeded its rights "by this enactment; or, if that cannot legally be "advanced, that it at least violated the trust of the "people, and broke in upon the ancient constitution;" and this remark he bases on the ground that "the "law for triennial Parliaments was of little more than "twenty years' continuance. It was an experiment, "which, as was argued, had proved unsuccessful; it "was subject, like every other law, to be repealed "entirely, or to be modified at discretion."[2]

[1] Similarly the Parliament elected in December, 1910, was extended by its own Acts until November, 1918; this Parliament by the Parliament Act, 1911, had reduced the legal duration to five years; see also the series of Prolongation of Parliament Acts, 1940–1944.—Ed.

[2] Hallam, *Constitutional History of England* (1884 ed.), vol. iii, p. 236.

Part I.

"We may," says Lord Stanhope, ". . . cast aside "the foolish idea that the Parliament overstepped its "legitimate authority in prolonging its existence; an "idea which was indeed urged by party-spirit at the "time, and which may still sometimes pass current in "harangues to heated multitudes, but which has been "treated with utter contempt by the best constitu- "tional writers."[1]

Constitutional importance of Septennial Act.

These remarks miss the real point of the attack on the Septennial Act, and also conceal the constitutional importance of the statute. The thirty-one peers who protested against the Bill because (among other grounds) "it is agreed, that the House of Commons "must be chosen by the people, and when so chosen, "they are truly the representatives of the people, "which they cannot be so properly said to be, when "continued for a longer time than that for which they "were chosen; for after that time they are chosen by "the Parliament, and not the people, who are thereby "deprived of the only remedy which they have against "those, who either do not understand, or through "corruption, do wilfully betray the trust reposed in "them; which remedy is, to choose better men in their "places,"[2] hit exactly the theoretical objection to it. The peculiarity of the Act was not that it changed the legal duration of Parliament or repealed the Triennial Act; the mere passing of a Septennial Act in 1716 was not and would never have been thought to be anything more startling or open to graver censure than the passing of a Triennial Act in 1694. What was startling was that an existing Parliament

[1] Lord Mahon, *History of England* (2nd ed., 1839), vol. i, p. 301.

[2] Thorold Rogers, *Protests of the Lords* (1875), vol. i, p. 218.

of its own authority prolonged its own legal existence. Nor can the argument used by Priestley,[1] and in effect by the protesting Peers, "that Septennial Parliaments "were at first a direct usurpation of the rights of the "people; for by the same authority that one Parlia- "ment prolonged their own power to seven years, they "might have continued it to twice seven, or like the "Parliament of 1641 have made it perpetual," be treated as a blunder grounded simply on the "ignorant assumption" that the Septennial Act prolonged the original duration of Parliament.[2] The contention of Priestley and others was in substance that members elected to serve for three years were constitutionally so far at least the delegates or agents of their constituents that they could not, without an inroad on the constitution, extend their own authority beyond the period for which it was conferred upon them by their principals, *i.e.* the electors. There are countries, and notably the United States, where an Act like the Septennial Act would be held legally invalid; no modern English Parliament would for the sake of keeping a government or party in office venture to pass say a Decennial Act and thus prolong its own duration; the contention therefore that Walpole and his followers in passing the Septennial Act violated the understandings of the constitution has on the face of it nothing absurd. Parliament made a legal though unprecedented use of its powers. To underrate this exertion of authority is to deprive the Septennial Act of its true constitutional importance. That Act proves to demonstration that in a legal point

[1] See Priestley, *Essay on Government* (1771), p. 20.

[2] Hallam, *op. cit.*, vol. iii, p. 236 (note).

Part I.

of view Parliament is neither the agent of the electors nor in any sense a trustee for its constituents. It is legally the sovereign legislative power in the state, and the Septennial Act is at once the result and the standing proof of such Parliamentary sovereignty.

Interference of Parliament with private rights.

Hitherto we have looked at Parliament as legally omnipotent in regard to public rights. Let us now consider the position of Parliament in regard to those private rights which are in civilised states justly held specially secure or sacred. Coke (it should be noted) particularly chooses interference with private rights as specimens of Parliamentary authority.

"Yet some examples are desired. Daughters and "heirs apparent of a man or woman, may by Act of "Parliament inherit during the life of the ancestor.

"It may adjudge an infant, or minor, of full age.

"To attaint a man of treason after his death.

"To naturalise a mere alien, and make him a "subject born. It may bastard a child that by law "is legitimate, viz. begotten by an adulterer, the "husband being within the four seas.

"To legitimate one that is illegitimate, and born "before marriage absolutely. And to legitimate "*secundum quid*, but not *simpliciter*."[1]

Coke is judicious in his choice of instances. Interference with public rights is at bottom a less striking exhibition of absolute power than is the interference with the far more important rights of individuals; a ruler who might think nothing of overthrowing the constitution of his country, would in all probability hesitate a long time before he touched the property or interfered with the contracts

[1] Coke, *Fourth Institute*, p. 36. See Intro. p. xxxv, *ante*, for later examples in regard to public law.

of private persons. Parliament, however, habitually interferes, for the public advantage, with private rights. Indeed such interference has now (greatly to the benefit of the community) become so much a matter of course as hardly to excite remark, and few persons reflect what a sign this interference is of the supremacy of Parliament. The statute-book teems with Acts under which Parliament gives privileges or rights to particular persons or imposes particular duties or liabilities upon other persons. This is of course the case with every railway Act, but no one will realise the full action, generally the very beneficial action of Parliamentary sovereignty, who does not look through a volume or two of what are called *Local and Private Acts*. These Acts are just as much Acts of Parliament as any Statute of the Realm. They deal with every kind of topic, as with railways, harbours, docks, the settlement of private estates, and the like. To these you should add Acts such as those which declare valid marriages which, owing to some mistake of form or otherwise, have not been properly celebrated, and Acts, common enough at one time but now rarely passed, for the divorce of married persons.

Chapter I.

One further class of statutes deserve in this connection more notice than they have received—these are Acts of Indemnity.

Acts of Indemnity.

An Act of Indemnity is a statute, the object of which is to make legal transactions which when they took place were illegal, or to free individuals to whom the statute applies from liability for having broken the law; enactments of this kind were annually passed with almost unbroken regularity for more than

Part I.

a century (1727–1828) to free Dissenters from penalties, for having accepted municipal offices without duly qualifying themselves by taking the sacrament according to the rites of the Church of England. To the subject of Acts of Indemnity, however, we shall return in a later chapter.[1] The point to be now noted is that such enactments being as it were the legalisation of illegality are the highest exertion and crowning proof of sovereign power.

So far of the sovereignty of Parliament from its positive side: let us now look at the same doctrine from its negative aspect.

No other competing legislative authority.

II. *The absence of any competing legislative power.*—The Queen, each House of Parliament, the Constituencies, and the Law Courts, either have at one time claimed, or might appear to claim, independent legislative power. It will be found, however, on examination that the claim can in none of these cases be made good.

The Queen.

(i.) *The Queen.*—Legislative authority originally resided in the King in Council,[2] and even after the commencement of Parliamentary legislation there existed side by side with it a system of royal legislation under the form of Ordinances,[3] and (at a later period) of Proclamations.

Statute of Proclamations.

These had much the force of law, and in the year 1539 the Act 31 Henry VIII., c. 8, formally empowered the Crown to legislate by means of proclamations.

[1] See ch. v, *post.*

[2] See Stubbs, *Constitutional History of England*, vol. i (1874), pp. 126-128, and vol. ii (1875), pp. 245-247.

[3] Stubbs, *op. cit.*, vol. ii, ch. xv.

This statute is so short and so noteworthy that it may well be quoted *in extenso.* "The King," it runs, "for "the time being, with the advice of his Council, or the "more part of them, may set forth proclamations under "such penalties and pains as to him and them shall "seem necessary, which shall be observed as though "they were made by Act of Parliament; but this shall "not be prejudicial to any person's inheritance, offices, "liberties, goods, chattels, or life; and whosoever shall "willingly offend any article contained in the said pro-"clamations, shall pay such forfeitures, or be so long "imprisoned, as shall be expressed in the said pro-"clamations; and if any offending will depart the "realm, to the intent he will not answer his said "offence, he shall be adjudged a traitor."

This enactment marks the highest point of legal authority ever reached by the Crown, and, probably because of its inconsistency with the whole tenor of English law, was repealed in the reign of Edward the Sixth.[1] It is curious to notice how revolutionary would have been the results of the statute had it remained in force. It must have been followed by two consequences. An English king would have become nearly as despotic as a French monarch. The statute would further have established a distinction between "laws" properly so called as being made by the legislature and "ordinances" having the force of law, though not in strictness laws as being rather decrees of the executive power than Acts of the legislature. This distinction exists in one form or another in most continental states, and is not without great

[1] Cf. Holdsworth, *History of English Law*, vol. iv (1924), pp. 102, 103, and Intro. p. xcviii, *ante*. This view now finds little support.—Ed.

Part I. practical utility. In foreign countries the legislature generally confines itself to laying down general principles of legislation, and leaves them with great advantage to the public to be supplemented by decrees or regulations which are the work of the executive. The cumbersomeness and prolixity of English statute law is due in no small measure to futile endeavours of Parliament to work out the details of large legislative changes. This evil has become so apparent that in modern times Acts of Parliament constantly contain provisions empowering the Privy Council, the judges, or some other body,[1] to make rules under the Act for the determination of details which cannot be settled by Parliament. But this is only an awkward mitigation[2] of an acknowledged evil, and the substance no less than the form of the law would, it is probable, be a good deal improved if the executive government of England could, like that of France, by means of decrees, ordinances, or proclamations having the force of law,

[1] Commonly Departmental Ministers.

[2] One of the author's critics objected to the words "awkward mitigation of an acknowledged evil" on the ground that they condemned in England a system which as it existed abroad was referred to as being not without great practical utility. The expression objected to was, however, justifiable, in the author's view. "Under the English system elaborate and detailed statutes are passed, and the power to make rules under the statute, *e.g.* by Order in Council or otherwise, is introduced only in cases where it is obvious that to embody the rules in the statute is either highly inexpedient or practically impossible. Under the foreign, and especially the French system, the form of laws, or in other words, of statutes, is permanently affected by the knowledge of legislators and draftsmen that any law will be supplemented by decrees. English statutes attempt, and with very little success, to provide for the detailed execution of the laws enacted therein. Foreign laws are, what every law ought to be, statements of general principles" (8th ed., p. 50, n. 1). For a review of the tendencies of legislation by regulation in the United Kingdom, see *Report of the Committee on Ministers' Powers* (Cmd. 4060, 1932), s. ii, and Willis, *The Parliamentary Powers of the English Government Departments* (1933).—Ed.

work out the detailed application of the general principles embodied in the Acts of the legislature.[1] In this, as in some other instances, restrictions wisely placed by our forefathers on the growth of royal power, are at the present day the cause of unnecessary restraints on the action of the executive government. For the repeal of 31 Henry VIII, c. 8, rendered governmental legislation, with all its defects and merits, impossible, and left to proclamations only such weight as they might possess at common law. The exact extent of this authority was indeed for some time doubtful. In 1610, however, a solemn opinion or protest of the judges[2] established the modern doctrine that royal proclamations have in no sense the force of law; they serve to call the attention of the public to the law, but they cannot of themselves impose upon any man any legal obligation or duty not imposed by common law or by Act of Parliament. In 1766 Lord Chatham attempted to prohibit by force of proclamation the exportation of wheat, and the Act of Indemnity, passed in consequence of this attempt, may be considered the final legislative disposal of any claim on the part of the Crown to make law by force of proclamation.

The main instances[3] where, in modern times,

[1] See Duguit, *Manuel de Droit Public français*; *Droit Constitutionnel* (1907), paras. 140 and 141, pp. 1013-1038.

[2] See *Case of Proclamations* (1610) 12 Co. Rep. 74; K. & L. 78; and Gardiner, *History of England*, vol. ii (1883), pp. 104, 105.

[3] In rare instances, which are survivals from the time when the King of England was the true "sovereign" in the technical sense of that term, the Crown exercises legislative functions in virtue of the prerogative. Thus the Crown can legislate, by proclamations or Orders in Council, for a newly conquered country (*Campbell* v. *Hall* (1774) Lofft. 655; K. & L. 487), and has claimed the right, though the validity thereof is doubtful, to legislate for the Channel Islands by

Part I. proclamations or orders in council are of any effect are cases either where, at common law, a proclamation is the regular mode, not of legislation, but of announcing the executive will of the Sovereign, as when Parliament is summoned by proclamation, or else where orders in council have authority given to them by Act of Parliament.

Houses of Parliament. (ii.) *Resolutions of either House of Parliament.*—The House of Commons, at any rate, has from time to time appeared to claim for resolutions of the House, something like legal authority. That this pretension cannot be supported is certain, but there exists some difficulty in defining with precision the exact effect which the courts concede to a resolution of either House.

Two points are, however, well established.

Orders in Council. *In the Matter of the States of Jersey* (1853) 9 Moo. P.C.C. 185, 262. "The Channel Islands indeed claim to have conquered England, and are the sole fragments of the dukedom of Normandy which still continue attached to the British Crown. For this reason, in these islands alone of all British possessions does any doubt arise as to whether an Act of the Imperial Parliament is of its own force binding law. In practice, when an Act is intended to apply to them, a section is inserted authorising the King in Council to issue an Order for the application of the Act to these islands, and requiring the registration of that Order in the islands, and the Order in Council is made by the King and registered by the States accordingly." Sir H. Jenkyns, *British Rule and Jurisdiction beyond the Seas* (1902), p. 37. But whatever doubt may arise in the Channel Islands, every English lawyer knows that any English court will hold that an Act of Parliament clearly intended to apply to the Channel Islands is in force there *proprio vigore*, whether registered by the States or not. See also *Renouf* v. *Attorney-General for Jersey* [1936] A.C. 445 for an interesting account of legislation in the Channel Islands.

As to the legislative power of the Crown in Colonies which are not self-governing, see further Jenkyns, *op. cit.*, p. 95, and Jennings, *Constitutional Laws of the Commonwealth* (1957), vol. i, pp. 48-55.

Chapter I.

Resolutions of either House.

First, The resolution of neither House is a law.

This is the substantial result of the case of *Stockdale* v. *Hansard*.[1] The gist of the decision in that case is that a libellous document did not cease to be a libel because it was published by the order of the House of Commons, or because the House subsequently resolved that the power of publishing the report which contained it, was an essential incident to the constitutional functions of Parliament.

Secondly, Each House of Parliament has complete control over its own proceedings, and also has the right to protect itself by committing for contempt any person who commits any injury against, or offers any affront to the House, and no court of law will inquire into the mode in which either House exercises the powers which it by law possesses.

The practical difficulty lies in the reconciliation of the first with the second of these propositions, and is best met by following out the analogy suggested by Mr. Justice Stephen, between a resolution of the House of Commons, and the decision of a court from which there is no appeal.

"I do not say," runs his judgment, "that the "resolution of the House is the judgment of a court "not subject to our revision; but it has much in "common with such a judgment. The House of "Commons is not a court of justice; but the effect "of its privilege to regulate its own internal concerns, "practically invests it with a judicial character when "it has to apply to particular cases the provisions of

[1] See *Stockdale* v. *Hansard* (1839) 9 A. & E. 1; K. & L. 127; *Case of the Sheriff of Middlesex* (1840) 11 A. & E. 273; K. & L. 140; *Bradlaugh* v. *Gossett* (1884) 12 Q.B.D. 271; K. & L. 144; *Burdett* v. *Abbot* (1811) 14 East 1.

Part I.

"Acts of Parliament. We must presume that it discharges this function properly, and with due regard "to the laws, in the making of which it has so great "a share. If its determination is not in accordance "with law, this resembles the case of an error by a "judge whose decision is not subject to appeal. There "is nothing startling in the recognition of the fact "that such an error is possible. If, for instance, a "jury in a criminal case give a perverse verdict, the "law has provided no remedy. The maxim that there "is no wrong without a remedy, does not mean, as it "is sometimes supposed, that there is a legal remedy "for every moral or political wrong. If this were its "meaning, it would be manifestly untrue. There is "no legal remedy for the breach of a solemn promise "not under seal, and made without consideration; "nor for many kinds of verbal slander, though each "may involve utter ruin; nor for oppressive legislation, though it may reduce men practically to "slavery; nor for the worst damage to person and "property inflicted by the most unjust and cruel war. "The maxim means only that legal wrong and legal "remedy are correlative terms; and it would be more "intelligibly and correctly stated, if it were reversed, "so as to stand, 'Where there is no legal remedy, "there is no legal wrong.'"[1]

Law as to effect of resolutions of either House.

The law therefore stands thus. Either House of Parliament has the fullest power over its own proceedings, and can, like a court, commit for contempt any person who, in the judgment of the House, is guilty of insult or affront to the House. The *Case of the Sheriff of Middlesex* [2] carries this right to the very

[1] *Bradlaugh* v. *Gossett, ante.*

[2] (1840) 11 A. & E. 273; K. & L. 140.

farthest point. The Sheriff was imprisoned for contempt under a warrant issued by the Speaker. Every one knew that the alleged contempt was nothing else than obedience by the Sheriff to the judgment of the Court of Queen's Bench in the case of *Stockdale* v. *Hansard,* and that the Sheriff was imprisoned by the House because under such judgment he took the goods of the defendant Hansard in execution. Yet when the Sheriff was brought by habeas corpus before the Queen's Bench the Judges held that they could not inquire what were the contempts for which the Sheriff was committed by the House. The courts, in other words, do not claim any right to protect their own officials from being imprisoned by the House of Commons for alleged contempt of the House, even though the so-called contempt is nothing else than an act of obedience to the courts. A declaration or resolution of either House, on the other hand, is not in any sense a law. Suppose that *X* were by order of the House of Commons to assault *A* out of the House, irrespective of any act done in the House, and not under a warrant committing *A* for contempt; or suppose that *X* were to commit some offence by which he incurred a fine under some Act of Parliament, and that such fine were recoverable by *A* as a common informer. No resolution of the House of Commons ordering or approving of *X's* act could be pleaded by *X* as a legal defence to proceedings, either civil or criminal, against him.[1] If proof of this were wanted it would be afforded by the Parliamentary Papers Act, 1840. The object of this Act, passed in consequence of the controversy connected with the

[1] Cf. *Attorney-General* v. *Bradlaugh* (1885) 14 Q.B.D. 667.

Part I. case of *Stockdale* v. *Hansard*, is to give summary protection to persons employed in the publication of Parliamentary papers, which are, it should be noted, papers published by the order of one or other of the Houses of Parliament. The necessity for such an Act is the clearest proof that an order of the House is not of itself a legal defence for the publication of matters which would otherwise be libellous. The House of Commons, "by invoking the authority of the whole "Legislature to give validity to the plea they had "vainly set up in the action [of *Stockdale* v. *Hansard*], "and by not appealing against the judgment of the "Court of Queen's Bench, had, in effect, admitted the "correctness of that judgment and affirmed the great "principle on which it was founded, viz. that no single "branch of the Legislature can, by any assertion of its "alleged privileges, alter, suspend, or supersede any "known law of the land, or bar the resort of any "Englishman to any remedy, or his exercise and "enjoyment of any right, by that law established."[1]

[1] Arnould, *Memoir of Thomas, first Lord Denman* (1873), vol. ii, p. 70. Nothing is harder to define than the extent of the indefinite powers or rights possessed by either House of Parliament under the head of privilege or law and custom of Parliament. The powers exercised by the Houses, and especially in practice by the House of Commons, make a near approach to an authority above that of the ordinary law of the land. Parliamentary privilege has from the nature of things never been the subject of precise legal definition. One or two points are worth notice as being clearly established.

(1.) Either House of Parliament may commit for contempt, and the courts will not go behind the committal and inquire into the facts constituting the alleged contempt provided that the cause of the contempt is not stated; May, *Parliamentary Practice* (16th ed., 1957), pp. 94-98. Hence either House may commit to prison for contempt any person whom the House think guilty of contempt; *Burdett* v. *Abbot* (1811) 14 East 1; *Case of the Sheriff of Middlesex, ante*. If the cause of committal stated in the writ is insufficient in law, a writ of habeas corpus will "lie" to secure the release of the person committed; *Paty's Case* (1704) 2 Ld. Raym. 1105, per Holt, C.J.

Chapter I.

The Constituencies.

(iii.) *The Vote of the Parliamentary Electors.*[1]— Expressions are constantly used in the course of political discussions which imply that the body of persons entitled to choose members of Parliament possess under the English constitution some kind of legislative authority. Such language is, as we shall see, not without a real meaning;[2] it points to the important consideration that the wishes of the constituencies influence the action of Parliament. But any expressions which attribute to Parliamentary electors a legal part in the process of law-making are quite inconsistent with the view taken by the law of the position of an elector. The sole legal right of electors under the English constitution is to elect members of Parliament. Electors have no legal means of initiating, of sanctioning, or of repealing the legislation of Parliament. No court will consider for a moment the argument that a law is invalid as being opposed to the opinion of the electorate; their opinion can be legally expressed through Parliament, and through Parliament alone. This is not a necessary incident of representative government. In Switzer-

(2.) The House of Lords have power to commit an offender to prison for a specified term, even beyond the duration of the session (May, *Parliamentary Practice* (16th ed., 1957), pp. 100, 101). But the House of Commons cannot commit for a definite period, and prisoners committed by the House are, if not sooner discharged, released from their confinement on a prorogation.

(3.) A libel upon either House of Parliament or upon a member thereof, in his character of a member, has been often treated as a contempt. (*Ibid.*)

(4.) The Houses and all the members thereof have all the privileges necessary for the performance of their duties. (See generally May, *op. cit.*, ch. iii.)

[1] For an account of the development of the people's part in English government, see Emden, *The People and the Constitution* (2nd ed., 1956). —Ed.

[2] See pp. 72-76, *post*.

Part I.

land no change can be introduced in the constitution[1] which has not been submitted for approval or disapproval to all male citizens who have attained their majority; and even an ordinary law which does not involve a change in the constitution may, after it has been passed by the Federal Assembly, be submitted on the demand of a certain number of citizens to a popular vote, and is annulled if a vote is not obtained in its favour.[2]

The Courts.

(iv.) *The Law Courts.*—A large proportion of English law is in reality made by the judges, and whoever wishes to understand the nature and the extent of judicial legislation in England, should read Pollock's admirable essay on the *Science of Case Law.*[3] The topic is too wide a one to be considered at any length in these lectures. All that we need note is that the adhesion by our judges to precedent, that is, their habit of deciding one case in accordance with the principle, or supposed principle, which governed a former case, leads inevitably to the gradual formation by the courts of fixed rules for decision, which are in effect laws. This judicial legislation might appear, at first sight, inconsistent with the supremacy of Parliament. But this is not so. English judges do not claim or exercise any power to repeal a Statute, whilst Acts of Parliament may override and constantly do override the law of the judges. Judicial legislation is, in short, subordinate legislation,

[1] *Constitution Fédérale de la Confédération Suisse*, Arts. 118-121; see Adams and Cunningham, *The Swiss Confederation* (1889), ch. vi.

[2] *Constitution Fédérale de la Confédération Suisse*, Art. 89.

[3] Pollock, *Essays in Jurisprudence and Ethics* (1882), p. 237 (The Science of Case Law), and see Dicey, *Law and Opinion in England* (2nd ed., 1914), Lecture xi (p. 361), and Note iv (p. 483).

Chapter I.

carried on with the assent and subject to the supervision of Parliament.

Alleged limitations.

B. *Alleged legal limitations on the legislative sovereignty of Parliament.*—All that can be urged as to the speculative difficulties of placing any limits whatever on sovereignty has been admirably stated by Austin and by Professor Holland.[1] With these difficulties we have, at this moment, no concern. Nor is it necessary to examine whether it be or be not true, that there must necessarily be found in every state some person, or combination of persons, which, according to the constitution, whatever be its form, can legally change every law, and therefore constitutes the legally supreme power in the state. Our whole business is now to carry a step further the proof that, under the English constitution, Parliament does constitute such a supreme legislative authority or sovereign power as, according to Austin and other jurists, must exist in every civilised state, and for that purpose to examine into the validity of the various suggestions, which have from time to time been made, as to the possible limitations on Parliamentary authority, and to show that none of them are countenanced by English law.

The suggested limitations are three in number.[2]

[1] See Austin, *Jurisprudence* (4th ed., 1879), pp. 270-274, and Holland, *Jurisprudence* (10th ed., 1906), pp. 47-52 and 359-363. The nature of sovereignty is also stated with brevity and clearness in Lewis, *Remarks on the Use and Abuse of some Political Terms* (1832), pp. 37-53; cf. Bryce, *Studies in History and Jurisprudence* (1901), vol. ii, Essay ix, Obedience, and Essay x, The Nature of Sovereignty.

[2] Another limitation has been suggested more or less distinctly by judges such as Coke (*Bonham's Case* (1610) 8 Co. Rep. 118, and *Case of Proclamations* (1610) 12 Co. Rep. 74, at p. 76; K. & L. 78, and see Hearn, *Government of England* (2nd ed., 1887), pp. 48, 49); an Act of Parliament cannot (it has been intimated) overrule the principles of

Part I.

Moral law.

First, Acts of Parliament, it has been asserted, are invalid if they are opposed to the principles of morality or to the doctrines of international law. Parliament, it is in effect asserted, cannot make a law opposed to the dictates of private or public morality. Thus Blackstone lays down in so many words that the "law of nature being coeval with mankind, and "dictated by God himself, is of course superior in "obligation to any other. It is binding over all the "globe, in all countries, and at all times: no human "laws are of any validity if contrary to this; and such "of them as are valid derive all their force and all "their authority, mediately or immediately, from this "original;"[1] and expressions are sometimes used by modern judges which imply that the courts might refuse to enforce statutes going beyond the proper limits (internationally speaking) of Parliamentary authority.[2] But to words such as those of Blackstone, and to the *obiter dicta* of the Bench, we must give a very qualified interpretation. There is no legal basis for the theory that judges, as exponents of morality, may overrule Acts of Parliament. Language which might seem to imply this amounts in reality to nothing more than the assertion that the judges, when attempting to ascertain what is the meaning to be affixed to an Act of Parliament, will presume that Parliament did not intend to violate[3]

the common law. This doctrine once had a real meaning (see Maine, *Early History of Institutions* (7th ed., 1905), pp. 381, 382), but it has never received systematic judicial sanction and is now obsolete.

[1] 1 Bl., *Comm.* 41, and see Hearn, *Government of England* (2nd ed., 1887), pp. 48, 49.

[2] See *Ex parte Blain* (1879) 12 Ch. D. 522, at p. 531.

[3] See *Colquhoun* v. *Brooks* (1888) 21 Q.B.D. 52; and compare Lord Esher, at pp. 57, 58, with Fry, L.J., at pp. 61, 62. See K. & L. 8-12 for an account of the presumptions which regulate in some measure the applications of statutes.

the ordinary rules of morality, or the principles of international law, and will therefore, whenever possible, give such an interpretation to a statutory enactment as may be consistent with the doctrines both of private and of international morality. A modern judge would never listen to a barrister who argued that an Act of Parliament was invalid because it was immoral, or because it went beyond the limits of Parliamentary authority. The plain truth is that our tribunals uniformly act on the principle that a law alleged to be a bad law is *ex hypothesi* a law, and therefore entitled to obedience by the courts.

Prerogative.

Secondly, Doctrines have at times been maintained which went very near to denying the right of Parliament to touch the Prerogative.[1]

In the time of the Stuarts[2] the doctrine was maintained, not only by the King, but by lawyers and statesmen who, like Bacon, favoured the increase of royal authority, that the Crown possessed under the name of the "prerogative" a reserve, so to speak, of wide and indefinite rights and powers, and that this prerogative or residue of sovereign power was superior to the ordinary law of the land. This doctrine combined with the deduction from it that the Crown could suspend the operation of statutes, or at any rate grant dispensation from obedience to them, certainly suggested the notion that the high powers of the prerogative were to a certain extent beyond the reach of Parliamentary enactment. We need not, however,

[1] See Stubbs, *Constitutional History of England*, vol. ii (1875), pp. 239, 486, 513-515.

[2] Gardiner, *History of England*, vol. iii (1883), pp. 1-5; cf. as to Bacon's view of the prerogative, Abbott, *Francis Bacon* (1885), pp. 140, 260, 279.

Part I.

now enter into the political controversies of another age. All that need be noticed is that though certain powers—as, for example, the right of making treaties—are now left by law in the hands of the Crown, and are exercised in fact by the executive government, no modern lawyer would maintain that these powers or any other branch of royal authority could not be regulated or abolished by Act of Parliament, or, what is the same thing, that the judges might legally treat as invalid a statute, say, regulating the mode in which treaties are to be made, or making the assent of the Houses of Parliament necessary to the validity of a treaty.[1]

Preceding Acts of Parliament.

Thirdly, Language has occasionally been used in Acts of Parliament which implies that one Parliament can make laws which cannot be touched by any subsequent Parliament, and that therefore the legislative authority of an existing Parliament may be limited by the enactments of its predecessors.[2]

[1] The recommendation of the Crown is required before the House of Commons considers a motion for a charge upon the public revenue. The Queen places at the disposal of the House her prerogative powers when it is proposed to change these by legislation.

[2] This doctrine was known to be erroneous by Bacon. "The "principal law that was made this Parliament was a law of a strange "nature, rather just than legal, and more magnanimous than provident. "This law did ordain, That no person that did assist in arms or "otherwise the King for the time being, should after be impeached "therefor, or attainted either by the course of law or by Act of "Parliament; for if any such act of attainder did hap to be made, it "should be void and of none effect. . . . But the force and obligation "of this law was in itself illusory, as to the latter part of it; (by a "precedent Act of Parliament to bind or frustrate a future). For a "supreme and absolute power cannot conclude itself, neither can that "which is in nature revocable be made fixed; no more than if a man "should appoint or declare by his will that if he made any later will "it should be void. And for the case of the Act of Parliament, there "is a notable precedent of it in King Henry the Eighth's time, who "doubting he might die in the minority of his son, provided an Act to

Chapter I.

The Acts of Union.

That Parliaments have more than once intended and endeavoured to pass Acts which should tie the hands of their successors is certain, but the endeavour has always ended in failure. Of statutes intended to arrest the possible course of future legislation, the most noteworthy are the Acts which embody the treaties of Union with Scotland[1] and Ireland.[2] The legislators who passed these Acts assuredly intended to give to certain portions of them more than the ordinary effect of statutes. Yet the history of legislation in respect of these very Acts affords the strongest proof of the futility inherent in every attempt of one sovereign legislature to restrain the action of another equally sovereign body. Thus the Act of Union with Scotland enacts in effect that every professor of a Scotch University shall acknowledge and profess and subscribe the Confession of Faith as his profession of faith, and in substance enacts that this provision shall be a fundamental and essential condition of the treaty of union in all time coming.[3] But this very provision has been in its main part repealed by the Universities (Scotland) Act, 1853, which relieves most professors in the Scotch universities from the necessity of subscribing the Confession of Faith. Nor is this by any means the only inroad made upon the terms of the

"pass, That no statute made during the minority of a King should "bind him or his successors, except it were confirmed by the King "under his great seal at his full age. But the first Act that passed in "King Edward the Sixth's time was an Act of repeal of that former "Act; at which time nevertheless the King was minor. But things "that do not bind may satisfy for the time."—*The Works of Francis Bacon*, ed. by Spedding, Ellis and Heath, vol. vi (1858 ed.), pp. 159, 160.

[1] Act of Union with Scotland, 1706.

[2] Act of Union with Ireland, 1800.

[3] See Act of Union with Scotland, 1706, art. 25.

Part I.

Act of Union; from one point of view at any rate the Act 10 Anne, c. 21,[1] restoring the exercise of lay patronage, was a direct infringement upon the Treaty of Union. The intended unchangeableness, and the real liability of these Acts or treaties to be changed by Parliament, comes out even more strikingly in the history of the Act of Union with Ireland. The fifth Article of that Act runs as follows:—"That it be the "fifth article of Union, that the Churches of England "and Ireland as now by law established, be united into "one Protestant Episcopal Church, to be called the "United Church of England and Ireland; and that "the doctrine, worship, discipline, and government of "the said United Church shall be and shall remain "in full force for ever, as the same are now by law "established for the Church of England; and that "the continuance and preservation of the said United "Church, as the established Church of England and "Ireland, shall be deemed and be taken to be an "essential and fundamental part of the Union."

That the statesmen who drew and passed this Article meant to bind the action of future Parliaments is apparent from its language. That the attempt has failed of success is apparent to every one who knows the contents of the Irish Church Act, 1869.

Act limiting right of Parliament to tax colonies.

One Act, indeed, of the British Parliament might, looked at in the light of history, claim a peculiar sanctity. It is certainly an enactment of which the terms, we may safely predict, will never be repealed and the spirit will never be violated. This Act is the Taxation of Colonies Act, 1778. Section one provides that Parliament "will not impose any duty, tax, or "assessment whatever, payable in any of his Majesty's

[1] Cf. Innes, *Law of Creeds in Scotland* (1867), pp. 118-121.

"colonies, provinces, and plantations in North America "or the West Indies; except only such duties as it "may be expedient to impose for the regulation of "commerce; the net produce of such duties to be "always paid and applied to and for the use of the "colony, province, or plantation, in which the same "shall be respectively levied, in such manner as other "duties collected by the authority of the respective "general courts, or general assemblies, of such "colonies, provinces, or plantations, are ordinarily "paid and applied."

This language becomes the more impressive when contrasted with the American Colonies Act, 1776, which, being passed in that year to repeal the Acts imposing the Stamp Duties, carefully avoids any surrender of Parliament's right to tax the colonies. There is no need to dwell on the course of events of which these two Acts are a statutory record. The point calling for attention is that though policy and prudence condemn the repeal of the Taxation of Colonies Act, 1778, or the enactment of any law inconsistent with its spirit, there is under our constitution no legal difficulty in the way of repealing or overriding this Act. If Parliament were tomorrow to impose a tax, say on New Zealand or on the Canadian Dominion, the statute imposing it would be a legally valid enactment.[1] As stated in short by a very judicious writer—"It equally is certain that a "Parliament cannot so bind its successors by the "terms of any statute, as to limit the discretion of a "future Parliament, and thereby disable the Legis- "lature from entire freedom of action at any future

[1] Cf. Statute of Westminster, 1931, s. 4, and Intro. pp. xlix *et seq.*, *ante*.

Part I. "time when it might be needful to invoke the "interposition of Parliament to legislate for the "public welfare."[1]

Parliamentary sovereignty is therefore an undoubted legal fact.

It is complete both on its positive and on its

[1] Todd, *Parliamentary Government in the British Colonies* (1st ed., 1880), p. 192; cf. Jennings, *The Law and the Constitution* (4th ed., 1952), pp. 146 *et seq.* It is a matter of curious, though not uninstructive, speculation to consider why it is that Parliament, though on several occasions passing Acts which were intended to be immutable, has never in reality succeeded in restricting its own legislative authority.

This question may be considered either logically or historically.

The logical reason why Parliament has failed in its endeavours to enact unchangeable enactments is that a sovereign power cannot, while retaining its sovereign character, restrict its own powers by any particular enactment. An Act, whatever its terms, passed by Parliament might be repealed in a subsequent, or indeed in the same, session, and there would be nothing to make the authority of the repealing Parliament less than the authority of the Parliament by which the statute, intended to be immutable, was enacted. "Limited Sovereignty," in short, is in the case of a Parliamentary as of every other sovereign, a contradiction in terms. Its frequent and convenient use arises from its in reality signifying, and being by any one who uses words with any accuracy understood to signify, that some person, *e.g.* a king, who was at one time a real sovereign or despot, and who is in name treated as an actual sovereign, has become only a part of the power which is legally supreme or sovereign in a particular state. This, it may be added, is the true position of the king in most constitutional monarchies.

Let the reader, however, note that the impossibility of placing a limit on the exercise of sovereignty does not in any way prohibit either logically, or in matter of fact, the abdication of sovereignty. This is worth observation, because a strange dogma is sometimes put forward that a sovereign power, such as the Parliament of the United Kingdom, can never by its own act divest itself of sovereignty. This position is, however, clearly untenable. An autocrat, such as the Russian Czar, can undoubtedly abdicate; but sovereignty or the possession of supreme power in a state, whether it be in the hands of a Czar or of a Parliament, is always one and the same quality. If the Czar can abdicate, so can a Parliament. To argue or imply that because sovereignty is not limitable (which is true) it cannot be surrendered (which is palpably untrue) involves the confusion of two distinct ideas. It is like arguing that because no man can, while he lives, give up, do what he will, his freedom of volition, so no man

negative side. Parliament can legally legislate on any topic whatever which, in the judgment of Parlia-

can commit suicide. A sovereign power can divest itself of authority in two ways, and (it is submitted) in two ways only. It may simply put an end to its own existence. Parliament could extinguish itself by legally dissolving itself and leaving no means whereby a subsequent Parliament could be legally summoned. (See Bryce, *American Commonwealth* (1910 ed.), p. 243, note 1). A step nearly approaching to this was taken by the Barebones Parliament when, in 1653, it resigned its power into the hands of Cromwell. A sovereign again may transfer sovereign authority to another person or body of persons. The Parliament of England went very near doing this when, in 1539, the Crown was empowered to legislate by proclamation; and though the fact is often overlooked, the Parliaments both of England and of Scotland did, at the time of the Union, each transfer sovereign power to a new sovereign body, namely, the Parliament of Great Britain. This Parliament, however, just because it acquired the full authority of the two legislatures by which it was constituted, became in its turn a legally supreme or sovereign legislature, authorised therefore, though contrary perhaps to the intention of its creators, to modify or abrogate the Act of Union by which it was constituted. If indeed the Act of Union had left alive the Parliaments of England and of Scotland, though for one purpose only, namely, to modify when necessary the Act of Union, and had conferred upon the Parliament of Great Britain authority to pass any law whatever which did not infringe upon or repeal the Act of Union, then the Act of Union would have been a fundamental law unchangeable legally by the British Parliament: but in this case the Parliament of Great Britain would have been, not a sovereign, but a subordinate, legislature, and the ultimate sovereign body, in the technical sense of that term, would have been the two Parliaments of England and of Scotland respectively. The statesmen of these two countries saw fit to constitute a new sovereign Parliament, and every attempt to tie the hands of such a body necessarily breaks down, on the logical and practical impossibility of combining absolute legislative authority with restrictions on that authority which, if valid, would make it cease to be absolute.

The historical reason why Parliament has never succeeded in passing immutable laws, or in other words, has always retained its character of a supreme legislature, lies deep in the history of the English people and in the peculiar development of the English constitution. England has, at any rate since the Norman Conquest, been always governed by an absolute legislator. This lawgiver was originally the Crown, and the peculiarity of the process by which the English constitution has been developed lies in the fact that the legislative authority of the Crown has never been curtailed, but has been transferred from

Part I.

ment, is a fit subject for legislation. There is no power which, under the English constitution, can come into rivalry with the legislative sovereignty of Parliament.

No one of the limitations alleged to be imposed by law on the absolute authority of Parliament has any real existence, or receives any countenance, either from the statute-book or from the practice of the courts.

This doctrine of the legislative supremacy of Parliament is the very keystone of the law of the constitution. But it is, we must admit, a dogma which does not always find ready acceptance, and it is well worth while to note and examine the difficulties which impede the admission of its truth.

Difficulties as to Parliamentary sovereignty.

C. *Difficulties as to the doctrine of Parliamentary Sovereignty.*—The reasons why many persons find

the Crown acting alone (or rather in Council) to the Crown acting first together with, and then in subordination to, the Houses of Parliament. Hence Parliament, or in technical terms the Queen in Parliament, has become—it would perhaps be better to say has always remained—a supreme legislature. It is well worth notice that on the one occasion when English reformers broke from the regular course of English historical development, they framed a written constitution, anticipating in many respects the constitutionalism of the United States, and placed the constitution beyond the control of the ordinary legislature. It is quite clear that, under the Instrument of Government of 1653, Cromwell intended certain fundamentals to be beyond the reach of Parliament. It may be worth observing that the constitution of 1653 placed the Executive beyond the control of the legislature. The protector under it occupied a position which may well be compared either with that of the American President or of the German Emperor. See Harrison, *Oliver Cromwell* (1888), pp. 194-203. For a view of sovereignty which, though differing to a certain extent from the view put forward in this work, is full of interest and instruction, see Sidgwick, *Elements of Politics* (1897), ch. xxi (Sovereignty and Order).

it hard to accept the doctrine of Parliamentary sovereignty are twofold.

Chapter I.

Difficulty from Austin's theory.

The dogma sounds like a mere application to the British constitution of Austin's theory of sovereignty, and yet intelligent students of Austin must have noticed that Austin's own conclusion as to the persons invested with sovereign power under the British constitution does not agree with the view put forward, on the authority of English lawyers, in these lectures. For while lawyers maintain that sovereignty resides in "Parliament," *i.e.* in the body constituted by the Queen, the House of Lords, and the House of Commons, Austin holds[1] that the sovereign power is vested in the Queen, the House of Lords, and the Commons or the electors.

Difficulty from actual limitation on power of Parliament.

Every one, again, knows as a matter of common sense that, whatever lawyers may say, the sovereign power of Parliament is not unlimited, and that King, Lords, and Commons united do not possess anything like that "restricted omnipotence"—if the term may be excused—which is the utmost authority ascribable to any human institution. There are many enactments, and these laws not in themselves obviously unwise or tyrannical, which Parliament never would and (to speak plainly) never could pass. If the doctrine of Parliamentary sovereignty involves the attribution of unrestricted power to Parliament, the dogma is no better than a legal fiction, and certainly is not worth the stress here laid upon it.[2]

[1] See Austin, *Jurisprudence* (4th ed., 1879), vol. i, pp. 251-255. Compare Austin's language as to the sovereign body under the constitution of the United States (*ibid.*, p. 268).

[2] Cf. Jennings, *The Law and the Constitution* (4th ed., 1952), pp. 144-145.

Part I.

Both these difficulties are real and reasonable difficulties. They are, it will be found, to a certain extent connected together, and well repay careful consideration.

Criticism on Austin's theory.

As to Austin's theory of sovereignty in relation to the British constitution.—Sovereignty, like many of Austin's conceptions, is a generalisation drawn in the main from English law, just as the ideas of the economists of Austin's generation are (to a great extent) generalisations suggested by the circumstances of English commerce. In England we are accustomed to the existence of a supreme legislative body, *i.e.* a body which can make or unmake every law; and which, therefore, cannot be bound by any law. This is, from a legal point of view, the true conception of a sovereign, and the ease with which the theory of absolute sovereignty has been accepted by English jurists is due to the peculiar history of English constitutional law. So far, therefore, from its being true that the sovereignty of Parliament is a deduction from abstract theories of jurisprudence, a critic would come nearer the truth who asserted that Austin's theory of sovereignty is suggested by the position of the English Parliament, just as Austin's analysis of the term "law" is at bottom an analysis of a typical law, namely, an English criminal statute.

It should, however, be carefully noted that the term "sovereignty," as long as it is accurately employed in the sense in which Austin sometimes[1] uses it, is a merely legal conception, and means simply the power of law-making unrestricted by any legal limit.

[1] Cf. Austin, *op. cit.*, vol. i, p. 268.

If the term "sovereignty" be thus used, the sovereign power under the English constitution is clearly "Parliament." But the word "sovereignty" is sometimes employed in a political rather than in a strictly legal sense. That body is "politically" sovereign or supreme in a state the will of which is ultimately obeyed by the citizens of the state. In this sense of the word the electors of Great Britain may be said to be, together with the Crown and the Lords, or perhaps, in strict accuracy, independently of the King and the Peers, the body in which sovereign power is vested. For, as things now stand, the will of the electorate, and certainly of the electorate in combination with the Lords and the Crown, is sure ultimately to prevail on all subjects to be determined by the British government. The matter indeed may be carried a little further, and we may assert that the arrangements of the constitution are now such as to ensure that the will of the electors shall by regular and constitutional means always in the end assert itself as the predominant influence in the country. But this is a political, not a legal fact. The electors can in the long run[1] always enforce their will. But the courts will take no notice of the will

[1] The working of a constitution is greatly affected by the rate at which the will of the political sovereign can make itself felt. In this matter we may compare the constitutions of the United States, of the Swiss Confederacy, and of the United Kingdom respectively. In each case the people of the country, or to speak more accurately the electorate, are politically sovereign. The action of the people of the United States in changing the Federal Constitution is impeded by many difficulties, and is practically slow; the Federal Constitution has, except after the civil war, not been materially changed during the century which has elapsed since its formation. The Articles of the Swiss Confederation admit of more easy change than the Articles of the United States Constitution, and since 1848 have undergone considerable modification. But though in one point of view the constitution,

Part I.

of the electors. The judges know nothing about any will of the people except in so far as that will is expressed by an Act of Parliament, and would never suffer the validity of a statute to be questioned on the ground of its having been passed or being kept alive in opposition to the wishes of the electors. The political sense of the word "sovereignty" is, it is true, fully as important as the legal sense or more so. But the two significations, though intimately connected together, are essentially different, and in some part of his work Austin has apparently confused the one sense with the other.

"Adopting the language," he writes, "of most of "the writers who have treated of the British constitu-"tion, I commonly suppose that the present parlia-"ment, or the parliament for the time being, is possessed "of the sovereignty: or I commonly suppose that the "King and the Lords, with the members of the Com-"mons' house, form a tripartite body which is sove-"reign or supreme. But, speaking accurately, the "members of the Commons' house are merely trustees

which was revised in 1874, may be considered a new constitution, it does not differ fundamentally from that of 1848. As things now stand, the people of England can change any part of the law of the constitution with extreme rapidity. Theoretically there is no check on the action of Parliament whatever, and it may be conjectured that in practice any change however fundamental would be at once carried through, which was approved of by one House of Commons, and, after a dissolution of Parliament, was supported by the newly elected House. But it is to be noted that by means of the *initiative constitutionnelle* the Swiss electorate can change the constitution itself. If a change proposed by 50,000 electors receives the approval of a majority of the electors and a majority of the Cantons, it becomes part of the constitution. Thus the Swiss Constitution can be changed by the people without waiting, as in the United Kingdom, for a change of Government, *e.g.* a right to poor relief could by means of the *initiative constitutionnelle* be added to the constitution without a change of Government.

"for the body by which they are elected and "appointed: and, consequently, the sovereignty "always resides in the King and the Peers, with the "electoral body of the Commons. That a trust is "imposed by the party delegating, and that the party "representing engages to discharge the trust, seems "to be imported by the correlative expressions *delega-"tion* and *representation.* It were absurd to suppose "that the delegating empowers the representative "party to defeat or abandon any of the purposes for "which the latter is appointed: to suppose, for "example, that the Commons empower their repre-"sentatives in parliament to relinquish their share in "the sovereignty to the King and the Lords."[1]

Austin owns that the doctrine here laid down by him is inconsistent with the language used by writers who have treated of the British constitution. It is further absolutely inconsistent with the validity of the Septennial Act. Nothing is more certain than that no English judge ever conceded, or, under the present constitution, can concede, that Parliament is in any legal sense a "trustee"[2] for the electors. Of such a feigned "trust" the courts know nothing. The plain truth is that as a matter of law Parliament is the sovereign power in the state, and that the "supposition" treated by Austin as inaccurate is the correct statement of a legal fact which forms the basis of our whole legislative and judicial system. It is, however, equally true that in a political sense the electors are

[1] Austin, *Jurisprudence* (4th ed., 1879), vol. i, p. 253.

[2] This Austin concedes, but the admission is fatal to the contention that Parliament is not in strictness a sovereign. (See *ibid.*, pp. 252, 253.)

Part I.

the most important part of, we may even say are actually, the sovereign power, since their will is under the present constitution sure to obtain ultimate obedience. The language therefore of Austin is as correct in regard to "political" sovereignty as it is erroneous in regard to what we may term "legal" sovereignty. The electors are a part of and the predominant part of the politically sovereign power. But the legally sovereign power is assuredly, as maintained by all the best writers on the constitution, nothing but Parliament.

It may be conjectured that the error of which (from a lawyer's point of view) Austin has been guilty arises from his feeling, as every person must feel who is not the slave to mere words, that Parliament is (as already pointed out[1]) nothing like an omnipotent body, but that its powers are practically limited in more ways than one. And this limitation Austin expresses, not very happily, by saying that the members of the House of Commons are subject to a trust imposed upon them by the electors. This, however, leads us to our second difficulty, namely, the coexistence of parliamentary sovereignty with the fact of actual limitations on the power of Parliament.

Existence of actual limitations to power not inconsistent with sovereignty

As to the actual limitations on the sovereign power of Parliament.—The actual exercise of authority by any sovereign whatever, and notably by Parliament, is bounded or controlled by two limitations. Of these the one is an external, the other is an internal limitation.

External limit.

The external limit to the real power of a sovereign consists in the possibility or certainty that his subjects,

[1] See p. 71, *ante*.

or a large number of them, will disobey or resist his laws.

This limitation exists even under the most despotic monarchies. A Roman Emperor, or a French King during the middle of the eighteenth century, was (as is the Russian Czar at the present day) in strictness a "sovereign" in the legal sense of that term. He had absolute legislative authority. Any law made by him was binding, and there was no power in the empire or kingdom which could annul such law. It may also be true,—though here we are passing from the legal to the political sense of sovereignty,—that the will of an absolute monarch is in general obeyed by the bulk of his subjects. But it would be an error to suppose that the most absolute ruler who ever existed could in reality make or change every law at his pleasure. That this must be so results from considerations which were long ago pointed out by Hume. Force, he teaches, is in one sense always on the side of the governed, and government therefore in a sense always depends upon opinion. "Nothing," he writes, "appears "more surprising to those, who consider human affairs "with a philosophical eye, than the easiness with which "the many are governed by the few; and the implicit "submission, with which men resign their own senti-"ments and passions to those of their rulers. When "we inquire by what means this wonder is effected, we "shall find, that, as force is always on the side of the "governed, the governors have nothing to support "them but opinion. It is, therefore, on opinion only "that government is founded; and this maxim extends "to the most despotic and most military governments, "as well as to the most free and most popular. The

Part I.

"Soldan of Egypt, or the Emperor of Rome, might "drive his harmless subjects, like brute beasts, against "their sentiments and inclination: But he must, at "least, have led his *mamalukes* or *prætorian bands*, "like men, by their opinion."[1]

Illustrations of external limit on exercise of sovereign power.

The authority, that is to say, even of a despot, depends upon the readiness of his subjects or of some portion of his subjects to obey his behests; and this readiness to obey must always be in reality limited. This is shown by the most notorious facts of history. None of the early Cæsars could at their pleasure have subverted the worship or fundamental institutions of the Roman world, and when Constantine carried through a religious revolution his success was due to the sympathy of a large part of his subjects. The Sultan could not abolish Mahommedanism. Louis the Fourteenth at the height of his power could revoke the Edict of Nantes, but he would have found it impossible to establish the supremacy of Protestantism, and for the same reason which prevented James the Second from establishing the supremacy of Roman Catholicism. The one king was in the strict sense despotic; the other was as powerful as any English monarch. But the might of each was limited by the certainty of popular disobedience or opposition. The unwillingness of subjects to obey may have reference not only to great changes, but even to small matters. The French National Assembly of 1871 was emphatically the sovereign power in France. The majority of its members were (it is said) prepared for a monarchical restoration, but they were not prepared to restore the white flag: the army which would have acquiesced in

[1] Hume, *Essays, Moral, Political and Literary* (1875 ed.), vol. i, pp. 109, 110.

the return of the Bourbons, would not (it was anticipated) tolerate the sight of an anti-revolutionary symbol: "the *chassepots* would go off of themselves." Here we see the precise limit to the exercise of legal sovereignty; and what is true of the power of a despot or of the authority of a constituent assembly is specially true of the sovereignty of Parliament; it is limited on every side by the possibility of popular resistance. Parliament might legally establish an Episcopal Church in Scotland; Parliament might legally tax the Colonies; Parliament might without any breach of law change the succession to the throne or abolish the monarchy; but every one knows that in the present state of the world the British Parliament will do none of these things. In each case widespread resistance would result from legislation which, though legally valid, is in fact beyond the stretch of Parliamentary power. Nay, more than this, there are things which Parliament has done in other times, and done successfully, which a modern Parliament would not venture to repeat. Parliament would not at the present day prolong by law the duration of an existing House of Commons. Parliament would not without great hesitation deprive of their votes large classes of Parliamentary electors; and, speaking generally, Parliament would not embark on a course of reactionary legislation; persons who honestly blame Catholic Emancipation and lament the disestablishment of the Irish Church do not dream that Parliament could repeal the statutes of 1829 or of 1869. These examples from among a score are enough to show the extent to which the theoretically boundless sovereignty of Parliament is curtailed by the external limit to its exercise.

Part I.

Internal limit. Illustrations.

The internal limit to the exercise of sovereignty arises from the nature of the sovereign power itself. Even a despot exercises his powers in accordance with his character, which is itself moulded by the circumstances under which he lives, including under that head the moral feelings of the time and the society to which he belongs. The Sultan could not if he would change the religion of the Mahommedan world, but if he could do so it is in the very highest degree improbable that the head of Mahommedanism should wish to overthrow the religion of Mahomet; the internal check on the exercise of the Sultan's power is at least as strong as the external limitation. People sometimes ask the idle question why the Pope does not introduce this or that reform? The true answer is that a revolutionist is not the kind of man who becomes a Pope, and that the man who becomes a Pope has no wish to be a revolutionist. Louis the Fourteenth could not in all probability have established Protestantism as the national religion of France; but to imagine Louis the Fourteenth as wishing to carry out a Protestant reformation is nothing short of imagining him to have been a being quite unlike the *Grand Monarque*. Here again the internal check works together with the external check, and the influence of the internal limitation is as great in the case of a Parliamentary sovereign as of any other; perhaps it is greater. Parliament could not prudently tax the Colonies; but it is hardly conceivable that a modern Parliament, with the history of the eighteenth century before its eyes, should wish to tax the Colonies. The combined influence both of the external and of the internal limitation on legislative

Chapter I.

sovereignty is admirably stated in Leslie Stephen's *Science of Ethics*, whose chapter on "Law and Custom" contains one of the best statements to be met with of the limits placed by the nature of things on the theoretical omnipotence of sovereign legislatures.

"Lawyers are apt to speak as though the legisla-"ture were omnipotent, as they do not require to go "beyond its decisions. It is, of course, omnipotent "in the sense that it can make whatever laws it pleases, "inasmuch as a law means any rule which has been "made by the legislature. But from the scientific "point of view, the power of the legislature is of course "strictly limited. It is limited, so to speak, both from "within and from without; from within, because the "legislature is the product of a certain social condition, "and determined by whatever determines the society; "and from without, because the power of imposing "laws is dependent upon the instinct of subordination, "which is itself limited. If a legislature decided that "all blue-eyed babies should be murdered, the preserva-"tion of blue-eyed babies would be illegal; but legis-"lators must go mad before they could pass such a "law, and subjects be idiotic before they could submit "to it."[1]

Limits may not coincide.

Though sovereign power is bounded by an external and an internal limit, neither boundary is very definitely marked, nor need the two precisely coincide. A sovereign may wish to do many things which he either cannot do at all or can do only at great risk of serious resistance, and it is on many accounts worth

[1] Stephen, *Science of Ethics* (1882), p. 143; cf. Jennings, *op. cit.*, p. 143. "Parliament passes many laws which many people do not want. But it never passes any laws which any substantial section of the population violently dislikes."

Part I.

observation that the exact point at which the external limitation begins to operate, that is, the point at which subjects will offer serious or insuperable resistance to the commands of a ruler whom they generally obey, is never fixed with precision. It would be rash of the Imperial Parliament to abolish the Scotch law courts, and assimilate the law of Scotland to that of England. But no one can feel sure at what point Scotch resistance to such a change would become serious. Before the War of Secession the sovereign power of the United States could not have abolished slavery without provoking a civil war; after the War of Secession the sovereign power abolished slavery and conferred the electoral franchise upon the Blacks without exciting actual resistance.

Representative government produces coincidence between external and internal limit.

In reference to the relation between the external and the internal limit to sovereignty, representative government presents a noteworthy peculiarity. It is this. The aim and effect of such government is to produce a coincidence, or at any rate diminish the divergence, between the external and the internal limitations on the exercise of sovereign power. Frederick the Great may have wished to introduce, and may in fact have introduced, changes or reforms opposed to the wishes of his subjects. Louis Napoleon certainly began a policy of free trade which would not be tolerated by an assembly which truly represented French opinion. In these instances neither monarch reached the external limit to his sovereign power, but it might very well have happened that he might have reached it, and have thereby provoked serious resistance on the part of his subjects. There might, in short, have arisen a divergence between the internal and the external check.

The existence of such a divergence, or (in other words) of a difference between the permanent wishes of the sovereign, or rather of the King who then constituted a predominant part of the sovereign power, and the permanent wishes of the nation, is traceable in England throughout the whole period beginning with the accession of James the First and ending with the Revolution of 1688. The remedy for this divergence was found in a transference of power from the Crown to the Houses of Parliament; and in placing on the throne rulers who from their position were induced to make their wishes coincide with the will of the nation expressed through the House of Commons; the difference between the will of the sovereign and the will of the nation was terminated by the foundation of a system of real representative government. Where a Parliament truly represents the people, the divergence between the external and the internal limit to the exercise of sovereign power can hardly arise, or if it arises, must soon disappear. Speaking roughly, the permanent wishes of the representative portion of Parliament can hardly in the long run differ from the wishes of the English people, or at any rate of the electors; that which the majority of the House of Commons command, the majority of the English people usually desire. To prevent the divergence between the wishes of the sovereign and the wishes of subjects is in short the effect, and the only certain effect, of bonâ fide representative government. For our present purpose there is no need to determine whether this result be good or bad. An enlightened sovereign has more than once carried out reforms in advance of the wishes of his subjects. This is true

Part I.

both of sovereign kings and, though more rarely, of sovereign Parliaments. But the sovereign who has done this, whether King or Parliament, does not in reality represent his subjects.[1] All that it is here necessary to insist upon is that the essential property of representative government is to produce coincidence between the wishes of the sovereign and the wishes of the subjects; to make, in short, the two limitations on the exercise of sovereignty absolutely coincident. This, which is true in its measure of all real representative government, applies with special truth to the English House of Commons.

"The House of Commons," writes Burke, "was sup-"posed originally to be *no part of the standing govern-"ment of this country*. It was considered as a *control*, "issuing *immediately* from the people, and speedily to "be resolved into the mass from whence it arose. In "this respect it was in the higher part of government "what juries are in the lower. The capacity of a magis-"trate being transitory, and that of a citizen permanent, "the latter capacity it was hoped would of course pre-"ponderate in all discussions, not only between the "people and the standing authority of the Crown, but "between the people and the fleeting authority of the "House of Commons itself. It was hoped that, being of a "middle nature between subject and government, they "would feel with a more tender and a nearer interest "everything that concerned the people, than the other "remoter and more permanent parts of legislature.

"Whatever alterations time and the necessary ac-"commodation of business may have introduced, this "character can never be sustained, unless the House of

[1] Cf. Dicey, *Law and Opinion in England* (2nd ed., 1914), pp. 4, 5.

"Commons shall be made to bear some stamp of the "actual disposition of the people at large. It would "(among public misfortunes) be an evil more natural and "tolerable, that the House of Commons should be in-"fected with every epidemical phrensy of the people, "as this would indicate some consanguinity, some sym-"pathy of nature with their constituents, than that they "should in all cases be wholly untouched by the opinions "and feelings of the people out of doors. By this "want of sympathy they would cease to be a House "of Commons." [1]

[1] *The Works of Edmund Burke* (1808 ed.), vol. ii, pp. 287, 288.

THE reader will not be misled by the examples of non-sovereign law-making bodies which the author uses by way of contrast with a Sovereign Parliament. What he wrote originally in 1885 of the Legislative Council of British India was, of course, obsolete long before India attained independent statehood in 1947. He chose New Zealand as an example of an English colony with representative and responsible government. What follows on pp. 102-121 is only true to-day of one or two colonies on their way to independence. Paradoxically, New Zealand is the best example within the Commonwealth of a State which has reproduced the purely Dicey doctrine in its entirety, for she has a Parliament which can change any and every law, albeit a uni-cameral legislature. It is perhaps unnecessary to add that Dicey was not writing about the constitution of the Fifth Republic when he takes France as an illustration of a foreign non-sovereign legislature, any more than in the succeeding chapter, Parliamentary Sovereignty and Federalism, could he have envisaged in place of the German Empire, whose constitution he examined, the Federal constitution of Western Germany to-day.

CHAPTER II

PARLIAMENT AND NON-SOVEREIGN LAW-MAKING BODIES

In my last chapter I dwelt upon the nature of Parliamentary sovereignty; my object in this chapter is to illustrate the characteristics of such sovereignty by comparing the essential features of a sovereign Parliament like that of England with the traits which mark non-sovereign law-making bodies. Chapter II. Aim of chapter.

A. *Characteristics of Sovereign Parliament.*— The characteristics of Parliamentary sovereignty may be deduced from the term itself. But these traits are apt to escape the attention of Englishmen, who have been so accustomed to live under the rule of a supreme legislature, that they almost, without knowing it, assume that all legislative bodies are supreme, and hardly therefore keep clear before their minds the properties of a supreme as contrasted with a non-sovereign law-making body. In this matter foreign observers are, as is natural, clearer-sighted than Englishmen. De Lolme, Gneist, and de Tocqueville seize at once upon the sovereignty of Parliament as a salient feature of the English constitution, and recognise the far-reaching effects of this marked peculiarity in our institutions. Parliamentary sovereignty.

Part I.

"In England," writes de Tocqueville, "the Parliament has an acknowledged right to modify the constitution; as, therefore, the constitution may undergo perpetual changes, it does not in reality exist; the Parliament is at once a legislative and a constituent assembly."[1]

His expressions are wanting in accuracy, and might provoke some criticism, but the description of the English Parliament as at once "a legislative and a constituent assembly" supplies a convenient formula for summing up the fact that Parliament can change any law whatever. Being a "legislative" assembly it can make ordinary laws, being a "constituent" assembly it can make laws which shift the basis of the constitution. The results which ensue from this fact may be brought under three heads.

No law Parliament cannot change.

First, There is no law which Parliament cannot change, or (to put the same thing somewhat differently), fundamental or so-called constitutional laws are under our constitution changed by the same body and in the same manner as other laws, namely, by Parliament acting in its ordinary legislative character.

A Bill for reforming the House of Commons, a Bill for abolishing the House of Lords, a Bill to give London a municipality, a Bill to make valid marriages celebrated by a pretended clergyman, who is found after their celebration not to be in orders, are each equally within the competence of Parliament, they each may be passed in substantially the same manner, they none of them when passed will be, legally

[1] de Tocqueville, *Œuvres complètes* (14th ed., 1864), vol. i (Démocratie en Amérique), pp. 166, 167.

Chapter II.

speaking, a whit more sacred or immutable than the others, for they each will be neither more nor less than an Act of Parliament, which can be repealed as it has been passed by Parliament, and cannot be annulled by any other power.

No distinction between constitutional and ordinary laws.

Secondly, There is under the English constitution no marked or clear distinction between laws which are not fundamental or constitutional and laws which are fundamental or constitutional. The very language therefore, expressing the difference between a "legislative" assembly which can change ordinary laws and a "constituent" assembly which can change not only ordinary but also constitutional and fundamental laws, has to be borrowed from the political phraseology of foreign countries.

Relation between Parliamentary sovereignty and an unwritten constitution.

This absence of any distinction between constitutional and ordinary laws has a close connection with the non-existence in England of any written or enacted constitutional statute or charter. de Tocqueville indeed, in common with other writers, apparently holds the unwritten character of the British constitution to be of its essence: "L'Angleterre n'ayant point de constitution écrite, qui peut dire qu'on change sa constitution?"[1] But here de Tocqueville falls into an error, characteristic both of his nation and of the weaker side of his own rare genius. He has treated the form of the constitution as the cause of its substantial qualities, and has inverted the relation of cause and effect. The constitution, he seems to have thought, was changeable because it was not reduced to a written or statutory form. It is far nearer the truth to assert that the constitution has never

[1] de Tocqueville, *op. cit.*, p. 312.

been reduced to a written or statutory form because each and every part of it is changeable at the will of Parliament. When a country is governed under a constitution which is intended either to be unchangeable or at any rate to be changeable only with special difficulty, the constitution, which is nothing else than the laws which are intended to have a character of permanence or immutability, is necessarily expressed in writing, or, to use English phraseology, is enacted as a statute. Where, on the other hand, every law can be legally changed with equal ease or with equal difficulty, there arises no absolute need for reducing the constitution to a written form, or even for looking upon a definite set of laws as specially making up the constitution. One main reason then why constitutional laws have not in England been recognised under that name, and in many cases have not been reduced to the form of a statutory enactment, is that one law, whatever its importance, can be passed and changed by exactly the same method as every other law. But it is a mistake to think that the whole law of the English constitution might not be reduced to writing and be enacted in the form of a constitutional code. The Belgian constitution indeed comes very near to a written reproduction of the English constitution, and the constitution of England might easily be turned into an Act of Parliament without suffering any material transformation of character, provided only that the English Parliament retained—what the Belgian Parliament, by the way, does not possess—the unrestricted power of repealing or amending the constitutional code.

Thirdly, There does not exist in any part of the

British Empire any person or body of persons, executive, legislative or judicial, which can pronounce void any enactment passed by the British Parliament on the ground of such enactment being opposed to the constitution, or on any ground whatever, except, of course, its being repealed by Parliament.

No person entitled to pronounce Act of Parliament void.

These then are the three traits of Parliamentary sovereignty as it exists in England: first, the power of the legislature to alter any law, fundamental or otherwise, as freely and in the same manner as other laws; secondly, the absence of any legal distinction between constitutional and other laws; thirdly, the non-existence of any judicial or other authority having the right to nullify an Act of Parliament, or to treat it as void or unconstitutional.

Flexibility of the constitution.

These traits are all exemplifications of the quality which my friend Mr. Bryce has happily denominated the "flexibility"[1] of the British constitution. Every part of it can be expanded, curtailed, amended, or abolished, with equal ease. It is the most flexible polity in existence, and is therefore utterly different in character from the "rigid" constitutions (to use another expression of Mr. Bryce's) the whole or some part of which can be changed only by some extraordinary method of legislation.

Characteristics of non-sovereign law-making bodies.

B. *Characteristics of non-sovereign law-making bodies.*—From the attributes of a sovereign legislature it is possible to infer negatively what are the characteristics all (or some) of which are the marks of a non-sovereign law-making body, and which therefore

[1] See Bryce, *Studies in History and Jurisprudence* (1901), vol. i, Essay iii, Flexible and Rigid Constitutions.

Part I.

may be called the marks or notes of legislative subordination.

These signs by which you may recognise the subordination of a law-making body are, first, the existence of laws affecting its constitution which such body must obey and cannot change; hence, secondly, the formation of a marked distinction between ordinary laws and fundamental laws; and lastly, the existence of some person or persons, judicial or otherwise, having authority to pronounce upon the validity or constitutionality of laws passed by such law-making body.

Wherever any of these marks of subordination exist with regard to a given law-making body, they prove that it is not a sovereign legislature.

Meaning of term "law-making body."

Observe the use of the words "law-making body." This term is here employed as an expression which may include under one head[1] both municipal bodies,

[1] This inclusion has been made the subject of criticism, and see also Intro. pp. lxxi *et seq.*, *ante*.

The author said: "The objections taken to it are apparently threefold.

"*First*, There is, it is said, a certain absurdity in bringing into one class things so different in importance and in dignity as, for example, the Belgian Parliament and an English School-board. This objection rests on a misconception. It would be ridiculous to overlook the profound differences between a powerful legislature and a petty corporation. But there is nothing ridiculous in calling attention to the points which they have in common. The sole matter for consideration is whether the alleged similarity be real. No doubt when features of likeness between things which differ from one another both in appearance and in dignity are pointed out, the immediate result is to produce a sense of amusement, but the apparent absurdity is no proof that the likeness is unreal or undeserving of notice. A man differs from a rat. But this does not make it the less true or the less worth noting that they are both vertebrate animals.

"*Secondly*, The powers of an English corporation, it is urged, can in generally only be exercised reasonably, and any exercise of them is invalid which is not reasonable, and this is not true of the laws made, *e.g.*, by the Parliament of a British colony.

such as railway companies, school-boards, town councils, and the like, which possess a limited power of making laws, but are not ordinarily called legislatures, and bodies such as the Parliaments of the British Colonies, of Belgium, or of France, which are ordinarily called "legislatures," but are not in reality sovereign bodies.

Chapter II.

The reason for grouping together under one name

"This objection admits of more than one reply. It is not universally true that the by-laws made by a corporation are invalid unless they are reasonable. But let it be assumed for the sake of argument that this restriction is always, as it certainly is often, imposed on the making of by-laws. This concession does not involve the consequence that by-laws do not partake of the nature of laws. All that follows from it is a conclusion which nobody questions, namely, that the powers of a non-sovereign law-making body may be restricted in very different degrees.

"*Thirdly*, The by-laws of a corporation are, it is urged, not laws, because they affect only certain persons, *e.g.* in the case of a railway company the passengers on the railway, and do not, like the laws of a colonial legislature, affect all persons coming under the jurisdiction of the legislature; or to put the same objection in another shape, the by-laws of a railway company apply, it is urged, only to persons using the railway, in addition to the general law of the land by which such persons are also bound, whereas the laws, *e.g.*, of the New Zealand Parliament constitute the general law of the colony.

"The objection is plausible, but does not really show that the similarity insisted upon between the position of a corporation and, *e.g.*, a colonial legislature is unreal. In either case the laws made, whether by the corporation or by the legislature, apply only to a limited class of persons, and are liable to be overridden by the laws of a superior legislature. Even in the case of a colony so nearly independent as New Zealand, the inhabitants are bound first by the statutes of the Imperial Parliament, and in addition thereto by the Acts of the New Zealand Parliament. The very rules which are by-laws when made by a corporation would admittedly be laws if made directly by Parliament. Their character cannot be changed by the fact that they are made by the permission of Parliament through a subordinate legislative body. The Council of a borough, which for the present purpose is a better example of my meaning than a railway company, passes in accordance with the powers conferred upon it by Parliament a by-law prohibiting processions with music on Sunday. The same prohibition if contained in an Act of Parliament would be admittedly a law. It is none the less a law because made by a body which is permitted by Parliament to legislate."

Part I.

such very different kinds of "law-making" bodies is, that by far the best way of clearing up our ideas as to the nature of assemblies which, to use the foreign formula,[1] are "legislative" without being "constituent," and which therefore are not sovereign legislatures, is to analyse the characteristics of societies, such as English railway companies, which possess a certain legislative authority, though the authority is clearly delegated and subject to the obvious control of a superior legislature.

It will conduce to clearness of thought if we divide non-sovereign law-making bodies into the two great classes of obviously subordinate bodies such as corporations, the Council of India, etc., and such legislatures of independent countries as are legislative without being constituent, *i.e.* are non-sovereign legislative bodies.

The consideration of the position of the non-sovereign legislatures which exist under the complicated form of constitution known as a federal government is best reserved for a separate chapter.[2]

I. *Subordinate Law-making Bodies*.[3]

Subordinate bodies.

Corporations.

(i.) *Corporations*.—An English railway company is as good an example as can be found of a subordinate law-making body. Such a company is in the strictest sense a law-making society, for it can under the powers of its Act make laws (called by-laws) for the regulation (*inter alia*) of travelling upon the railway,[4]

[1] See p. 88, *ante*. [2] See ch. iii, *post*.

[3] Cf. Jennings, *Constitutional Laws of the Commonwealth*, vol. i, ch. ii.

[4] See especially the Railways Clauses Consolidation Act, 1845. This

and can impose a penalty for the breach of such laws, which can be enforced by proceedings in the courts. The rules therefore or by-laws made by a company within the powers of its Act are "laws" in the strictest sense of the term, as any person will discover to his own cost who, when he travels by rail from Oxford to Paddington, deliberately violates a by-law duly made by the Great Western Railway Company.

But though an English railway company is clearly a law-making body, it is clearly a non-sovereign law-making body. Its legislative power bears all the marks of subordination.

First, The company is bound to obey laws and (amongst others) the Act of Parliament creating the company, which it cannot change. This is obvious, and need not be insisted upon.

Secondly, There is the most marked distinction between the Act constituting the company, not a line of which can be changed by the company, and the by-laws which, within the powers of its Act, the company can both make and change. Here we have on a very small scale the exact difference between constitutional laws which cannot, and ordinary laws which can, be changed by a subordinate legislature, *i.e.* by the company. The company, if we may apply to it the terms of constitutional law, is not a constituent, but is within certain limits a legislative assembly; and these limits are fixed by the constitution of the company.

Thirdly, The courts have the right to pronounce, and indeed are bound to pronounce, on the validity

Act was incorporated in the special Act constituting the company. Its provisions therefore formed part of the constitution of a railway company.

Part I. of the company's by-laws; that is, upon the validity, or to use political terms, on the constitutionality of the laws made by the company as a law-making body. Note particularly that it is not the function of any court or judge to declare void or directly annul a by-law made by a railway company. The function of the court is simply, upon any particular case coming before it which depends upon a by-law made by a railway company, to decide for the purposes of that particular case whether the by-law is or is not within the powers conferred by Act of Parliament upon the company; that is to say, whether the by-law is or is not valid, and to give judgment in the particular case according to the court's view of the validity of the by-law. It is worth while to examine with some care the mode in which English judges deal with the inquiry whether a particular by-law is or is not within the powers given to the company by Act of Parliament, for to understand this point goes a good way towards understanding the exact way in which English or American courts determine the constitutionality of Acts passed by a non-sovereign legislature.

The London and North-Western Railway Company made a by-law by which "any person travelling with-"out the special permission of some duly authorised "servant of the company in a carriage or by a train of "a superior class to that for which his ticket was issued "is hereby subject to a penalty not exceeding forty "shillings, and shall, in addition, be liable to pay his "fare according to the class of carriage in which he is "travelling from the station where the train originally "started, unless he shows that he had no intention to "defraud." *X*, with the intention of defrauding the company, travelled in a first-class carriage instead of a second-class carriage for which his ticket was issued, and having been charged under the by-law was convicted in the penalty of ten shillings, and costs. On appeal by *X*, the court determined that the by-law which attempted to shift the burden of proof on to the accused was illegal and void as being repugnant to 8 Vict. c. 20, s. 103, which made proof of fraudulent intent the gist of the offence, or in effect to the terms of the Act incorporating the company,[1] and that therefore *X* could not be convicted of the offence charged against him.

A by-law of the South-Eastern Railway Company required that a passenger should deliver up his ticket to a servant of the company when required to do so, and that any person travelling without a ticket or failing or refusing to deliver up his ticket should be required to pay the fare from the station whence the train originally started to the end of his journey. *X* had a railway ticket enabling him to travel on the South-Eastern Railway. Having to change trains and pass out of the company's station he was asked to show his ticket, and refused to do so, but without any fraudulent intention. He was summoned for a breach of the by-law, and convicted in the amount of the fare from the station whence the train started. The Queen's Bench Division held the conviction wrong on the ground that the by-law was for several reasons invalid, as not being authorised by the Act under which it purported to be made.[2]

[1] *Dyson* v. *L. & N.W. Ry. Co.* (1881) 7 Q.B.D. 32.

[2] *Saunders* v. *S.E. Ry. Co.* (1880) 5 Q.B.D. 456. Cf. *Bentham* v. *Hoyle* (1878) 3 Q.B.D. 289 and *The London and Brighton Ry. Co.* v. *Watson* (1878) 3 C.P.D. 429; on appeal (1879) 4 C.P.D. 118.

Now in these instances, and in other cases where the courts pronounce upon the validity of a by-law made by a body (*e.g.* a railway company or a school-board) having powers to make by-laws enforceable by penalties, it is natural to say that the courts pronounce the by-laws valid or invalid. But this is not strictly the case. What the judges determine is not that a particular by-law is invalid, for it is not the function of the courts to repeal or annul the by-laws made by railway companies, but that in a proceeding to recover a penalty from *X* for the breach of a by-law judgment must be given on the basis of the particular by-law being beyond the powers of the company, and therefore invalid. It may indeed be thought that the distinction between annulling a by-law and determining a case upon the assumption of such by-law being void is a distinction without a difference. But this is not so. The distinction is not without importance even when dealing with the question whether *X*, who is alleged to have broken a by-law made by a railway company, is liable to pay a fine; it is of first rate importance when the question before the courts is one involving considerations of constitutional law, as for example when the Privy Council is called upon, as constantly happens, to determine cases which involve the validity or constitutionality of laws made by the Dominion Parliament or by one of the provincial Parliaments of Canada. The significance, however, of the distinction will become more apparent as we proceed with our subject; the matter of consequence now is to notice the nature of the distinction, and to realise that when a court in deciding a given case considers whether a by-law is, or is not, valid, the court does a different thing from affirming or annulling the by-law itself. Chapter II.

Council of British India.

(ii.) *Legislative Council of British India.*[1]—Laws are made for British India by a Legislative Council having very wide powers of legislation. This Council, or, as it is technically expressed, the "Governor-General in Council," can pass laws as important as any Acts passed by the British Parliament. But the authority of the Council in the way of law-making is as completely subordinate to, and as much dependent upon, Acts of Parliament as is the power of the London and North-Western Railway Company to make by-laws.

The legislative powers of the Governor-General and his Council arise from definite Parliamentary enactments.[2] These Acts constitute what may be termed as regards the Legislative Council the constitution of India. Now observe, that under these Acts the Indian Council is in the strictest sense a non-sovereign legislative body, and this independently of the fact that the laws or regulations made by the Governor-General in Council can be annulled or disallowed by the Crown; and note that the position of the Council exhibits all the marks or notes of legislative subordination.

[1] See Ilbert, *Government of India* (3rd ed., 1915), pp. 224-240, Digest of Statutory Enactments, secs. 60-69.

The paragraphs which follow were based upon Indian constitutional law which was repealed in the early part of the twentieth century. Immediately before the grant of independence in 1947 to India and to Pakistan the government of the Provinces of British India was regulated by the Government of India Act, 1935, which introduced cabinet government.—Ed.

[2] Government of India Act, 1833, ss. 45-48, 51, 52; Indian Councils Act, 1861, ss. 16-25; Government of India Act, 1865.

Part I.

First, The Council is bound by a large number of rules which cannot be changed by the Indian legislative body itself, and which can be changed by the superior power of the Imperial Parliament.

Secondly, The Acts themselves from which the Council derives its authority cannot be changed by the Council, and hence in regard to the Indian legislative body form a set of constitutional or fundamental laws, which, since they cannot be changed by the Council, stand in marked contrast with the laws or regulations which the Council is empowered to make. These fundamental rules contain, it must be added, a number of specific restrictions on the subjects with regard to which the Council may legislate. Thus the Governor-General in Council has no power of making laws which may affect the authority of Parliament, or any part of the unwritten laws or constitution of the United Kingdom, whereon may depend in any degree the allegiance of any person to the Crown of the United Kingdom, or the sovereignty or dominion of the Crown over any part of India.[1]

Thirdly, The courts in India (or in any other part of the British Empire) may, when the occasion arises, pronounce upon the validity or constitutionality of laws made by the Indian Council.

The courts treat Acts passed by the Indian Council precisely in the same way in which the King's Bench Division treats the by-laws of a railway company. No judge in India or elsewhere ever issues a decree which declares invalid, annuls, or makes void a law or regulation made by the Governor-General in Council. But when any particular case comes before

[1] Indian Councils Act, 1861, s. 22.

the courts, whether civil or criminal, in which the rights or liabilities of any party are affected by the legislation of the Indian Council, the court may have to consider and determine with a view to the particular case whether such legislation was or was not within the legal powers of the Council, which is of course the same thing as adjudicating as regards the particular case in hand upon the validity or constitutionality of the legislation in question. Thus suppose that *X* is prosecuted for the breach of a law or regulation passed by the Council, and suppose the fact to be established past a doubt that *X* has broken this law. The court before which the proceedings take place, which must obviously in the ordinary course of things be an Indian court, may be called upon to consider whether the regulation which *X* has broken is within the powers given to the Indian Council by the Acts of Parliament making up the Indian constitution. If the law is within such powers, or, in other words, is constitutional, the court will by giving judgment against *X* give full effect to the law, just as effect is given to the by-law of a railway company by the tribunal before whom an offender is sued pronouncing judgment against him for the penalty. If, on the other hand, the Indian Court deem that the regulation is *ultra vires* or unconstitutional, they will refuse to give effect to it, and treat it as void by giving judgment for the defendant on the basis of the regulation being invalid or having no legal existence. On this point the *Empress* v. *Burah and Book Singh*[1] is most instructive. The details of the case are immaterial; the noticeable thing is that the High

[1] (1877) 3 Ind. L.R. (Calcutta Series) 63.

Part I.

court held a particular legislative enactment of the Governor-General in Council to be in excess of the authority given to him by the Imperial Parliament and therefore invalid, and on this ground entertained an appeal from two prisoners which, if the enactment had been valid, the court would admittedly have been incompetent to entertain. The Privy Council, it is true, held on appeal[1] that the particular enactment was within the legal powers of the Council and therefore valid, but the duty of the High Court of Calcutta to consider whether the legislation of the Governor-General was or was not constitutional, was not questioned by the Privy Council. To look at the same thing from another point of view, the courts in India treat the legislation of the Governor-General in Council in a way utterly different from that in which any English court can treat the Acts of the Imperial Parliament. An Indian tribunal may be called upon to say that an Act passed by the Governor-General need not be obeyed because it is unconstitutional or void. No British court can give judgment, or ever does give judgment, that an Act of Parliament need not be obeyed because it is unconstitutional. Here, in short, we have the essential difference between subordinate and sovereign legislative power.[2]

English colonies.

(iii.) *English Colonies with Representative and Responsible Governments.*—Many English colonies, and notably the Dominion of New Zealand (to which country our attention had best for the sake of

[1] *The Queen* v. *Burah* (1878) 3 App. Cas. 889.

[2] See especially *The Empress* v. *Burah and Book Singh* (1877) 3 Ind. L.R. (Calcutta Series) 63, at pp. 86-89, *per* Markby, J.

Chapter II.

clearness be specially directed), possess representative assemblies which occupy a somewhat peculiar position.

Powers exercised by colonial Parliaments.

The Parliament of the Dominion of New Zealand exercises throughout that country many of the ordinary powers of a sovereign assembly, such as the Parliament of the United Kingdom.[1] It makes and repeals laws, it puts Ministries in power and dismisses them from office, it controls the general policy of the New Zealand Government, and generally makes its will felt in the transaction of affairs after the manner of the Parliament at Westminster. An ordinary observer would, if he looked merely at the everyday proceedings of the New Zealand legislature, find no

[1] New Zealand is now one of the States of the Commonwealth to which the Statute of Westminster, 1931, gave legislative autonomy by the repeal of the Colonial Laws Validity Act, 1865, in its application to the (then) Dominions and by the conferment of power to enact legislation with extra-territorial operation. To find a parallel with the position of New Zealand as a Colonial Parliament, the reader should substitute at the present time colonial territory with a representative legislature such as Mauritius.

The author stated at this point that "no colonial legislature has as such any authority beyond the territorial limits of the colony." This has never been formally decided by the Judicial Committee, though there is persuasive authority in the case of *Macleod* v. *Attorney-General of New South Wales* [1891] A.C. 455; C.L.C. 99; see generally C.L.C. 53-54. In various cases it has been held that the scope of a colonial enactment could operate beyond the limits of the Colony or Dominion so far as it purported to enact provisions ancillary to the maintenance of peace, order and good government. For example in *Croft* v. *Dunphy* [1933] A.C. 156; C.L.C. 106; the validity of a Canadian statute which authorised the seizure of vessels outside the territorial waters of Canada was held valid. Such seizure was necessarily ancillary to the enforcement of the customs laws of the Dominion. The author correctly pointed out that in various instances Imperial Acts have expressly given extended powers of legislation to colonial legislatures to enable the enactment of laws on a specified topic to operate beyond the limits of the colony, *e.g.* the Merchant Shipping Act, 1894, ss. 478, 735, 736. As to the last two sections, see now section 5 of the Statute of Westminster.—Ed.

Part I.

reason to pronounce it a whit less powerful within its sphere than the Parliament of the United Kingdom. No doubt the assent of the Governor is needed in order to turn colonial Bills into laws: and further investigation would show our inquirer that for the validity of any colonial Act there is required, in addition to the assent of the Governor, the sanction, either express or implied, of the Crown. But these assents are constantly given almost as a matter of course, and may be compared (though not with absolute correctness) to the Crown's so-called "veto" or right of refusing assent to Bills which have passed through the Houses of Parliament.

Limit to powers.

Yet for all this, when the matter is further looked into, the Dominion Parliament (together with other colonial legislatures) will be found to be a non-sovereign legislative body, and bears decisive marks of legislative subordination. The action of the Dominion Parliament is restrained by laws which it cannot change, and are changeable only by the Imperial Parliament; and further, New Zealand Acts, even when assented to by the Crown, are liable to be treated by the courts in New Zealand and elsewhere throughout the British dominions as void or unconstitutional, on the ground of their coming into conflict with laws of the Imperial Parliament, which the colonial legislature has no authority to touch.[1]

[1] As also upon the ground of their being in strictness *ultra vires*, *i.e.* beyond the powers conferred upon the Dominion legislature. This is the ground why a colonial Act is in general void, in so far as it is intended to operate beyond the territory of the colony. "In 1879, the Supreme Court of New Zealand held that the Foreign Offenders Apprehension Act, 1863, of that colony, which authorises the deportation of persons charged with indictable misdemeanours in other

That this is so becomes apparent the moment we realise the exact relation between colonial and Imperial laws. The matter is worth some little examination, both for its own sake and for the sake of the light it throws on the sovereignty of Parliament.

The charter of colonial legislative independence is the Colonial Laws Validity Act, 1865.[1]

Colonial Laws Validity Act, 1865.

This statute seems (oddly enough) to have passed through Parliament without discussion; but it permanently defines and extends the authority of colonial legislatures, and its main provisions are of such importance as to deserve verbal citation:—

"Sec. 2. Any colonial law which is or shall be in "any respect repugnant to the provisions of any Act "of Parliament extending to the colony to which "such law may relate, or repugnant to any order or "regulation made under authority of such Act of "Parliament, or having in the colony the force and "effect of such Act, shall be read subject to such "Act, order, or regulation, and shall, to the extent of "such repugnancy, but not otherwise, be and remain "absolutely void and inoperative.

"3. No colonial law shall be or be deemed to "have been void or inoperative on the ground of

colonies, was beyond the competence of the New Zealand legislature, for it involved detention on the high seas, which the legislature could not authorise, as it could legislate only for peace, order, and good government within the limits of the colony." Jenkyns, *British Rule and Jurisdiction beyond the Seas* (1902), p. 70, citing *In re Gleich* (1879) Ollivier, Bell and Fitzgerald's N.Z. Reports, S.C. 39; cf. Keith, *Responsible Government in the Dominions* (2nd ed., 1928), vol. i, p. 329. This case is in conflict with *Attorney-General for Canada* v. *Cain* [1906] A.C. 542; C.L.C. 103.

[1] See on this enactment, Jenkyns, *op. cit.*, pp. 71, 72; and C.L.C. 51-53, 97.

"repugnancy to the law of England, unless the same "shall be repugnant to the provisions of some such "Act of Parliament, order, or regulation as afore- "said.

"4. No colonial law, passed with the concurrence "of or assented to by the Governor of any colony, or "to be hereafter so passed or assented to, shall be or "be deemed to have been void or inoperative, by "reason only of any instructions with reference to "such law or the subject thereof which may have "been given to such Governor by or on behalf of "Her Majesty, by any instrument other than the "letters - patent or instrument authorising such "Governor to concur in passing or to assent to "laws for the peace, order, and good government "of such colony, even though such instructions "may be referred to in such letters-patent or last- "mentioned instrument.

"5. Every colonial legislature shall have, and be "deemed at all times to have had, full power within "its jurisdiction to establish courts of judicature, and "to abolish and reconstitute the same, and to alter the "constitution thereof, and to make provision for the "administration of justice therein; and every repre- "sentative legislature[1] shall, in respect to the colony "under its jurisdiction, have, and be deemed at all "times to have had, full power to make laws re- "specting the constitution, powers, and procedure "of such legislature; provided that such laws shall "have been passed in such manner and form[2] as may

[1] *I.e.* a colonial legislature of which at least one half of the members of one house are elected by the inhabitants of the colony.

[2] See *Attorney-General for New South Wales* v. *Trethowan* [1932] A.C. 526; C.L.C. 78; and Intro. p. lxxvi, *ante*.

"from time to time be required by any Act of "Parliament, letters-patent, order in council, or "colonial law for the time being in force in the "said colony."

The importance, it is true, of the Colonial Laws Validity Act, 1865, may well be either exaggerated or quite possibly underrated. The statute is in one sense less important than it at first sight appears, because the principles laid down therein were, before its passing, more or less assumed, though with some hesitation, to be good law and to govern the validity of colonial legislation. From another point of view the Act is of the highest importance, because it determines, and gives legislative authority to, principles which had never before been accurately defined, and were liable to be treated as open to doubt.[1] In any case the terms of the enactment make it now possible to state with precision the limits which bound the legislative authority of a colonial Parliament.

The Dominion Parliament may make laws opposed to the English common law, and such laws (on receiving the required assents) are perfectly valid.

Thus a New Zealand Act which changed the common law rules as to the descent of property, which gave the Governor authority to forbid public meetings, or which abolished trial by jury, might be inexpedient or unjust, but would be a perfectly valid law, and would be recognised as such by every

[1] Up to 1865 the prevalent opinion in England seems to have been that any law seriously opposed to the principles of English law was repugnant to the law of England, and colonial laws were from time to time disallowed solely on the ground of such supposed repugnancy and invalidity. See *Report of Conference on Operation of Dominion Legislation*, 1929 (Cmd. 3479, 1930), pp. 17, 18; Keith, *The Sovereignty of the British Dominions* (1929), pp. 45, 46.

tribunal throughout the British Empire.[1]

The Dominion Parliament, on the other hand, cannot make any laws inconsistent with any Act of Parliament, or with any part of an Act of Parliament, intended by the Imperial Parliament to apply to New Zealand.

Suppose, for example, that the Imperial Parliament were to pass an Act providing a special mode of trial in New Zealand for particular classes of offences committed there, no enactment of the colonial Parliament, which provided that such offences should be tried otherwise than as directed by the imperial statute, would be of any legal effect. So again, no New Zealand Act would be valid that legalised the slave trade in the face of the provisions of the Slave Trade Act, 1824, which prohibit slave trading throughout the British dominions; nor would Acts passed by the Dominion Parliament be valid which repealed, or invalidated, several provisions of the Merchant Shipping Act, 1894, meant to apply to the colonies, or which deprived a discharge under the English Bankruptcy Act of the effect which, in virtue of the imperial statute, it has as a release from debts contracted in any part whatever of the British dominions. No colonial legislature, in short, can override imperial legislation which is intended to apply to the colonies. Whether the intention be expressed in so many words, or be apparent only from the general scope and nature of the enactment, is immaterial. Once establish that an imperial law

[1] Assuming, of course, that such Acts are not inconsistent with any imperial statute applying to the colony. Cf. *Robinson* v. *Reynolds* (1867) Macassey's N.Z. Reports 562.

Chapter II.

is intended to apply to a given colony, and the consequence follows that any colonial enactment which contravenes that law is invalid and unconstitutional.[1]

Acts of colonial legislature may be pronounced void by courts.

Hence the courts in the Dominion of New Zealand, as also in the rest of the British Empire, may be called upon to adjudicate upon the validity or constitutionality of any Act of the Dominion Parliament. For if a New Zealand law really contradicts the provisions of an Act of Parliament extending to New Zealand, no court throughout the British dominions could legally, it is clear, give effect to the enactment of the Dominion Parliament. This is an inevitable result of the legislative sovereignty exercised by the Imperial Parliament. In the supposed case the Dominion Parliament commands the judges to act in a particular manner, and the Imperial Parliament commands them to act in another manner. Of these two commands the order of the Imperial Parliament is the one which must be obeyed. This is the very meaning of Parliamentary sovereignty. Whenever, therefore, it is alleged that any enactment of the Dominion Parliament is repugnant to the provisions of any Act of the Imperial Parliament extending to the colony, the tribunal before which the objection is raised must pronounce upon the validity or constitutionally of the colonial law.[2]

The constitution of New Zealand is created by and

[1] See Tarring, *Law relating to the Colonies* (4th ed., 1913), pp. 209-221, for a list of imperial statutes which relate to the colonies in general, and which therefore no colonial legislation can, except under powers given by some Act of the Imperial Parliament, contravene. For the legislative competence of the Dominions, see Intro. pp. lxxxiv *et seq.*, *ante.*

[2] See *Powell* v. *Apollo Candle Co.* (1885) 10 App. Cas. 282, C.L.C. 67; *Hodge* v. *The Queen* (1883) 9 App. Cas. 117 ; cf. Intro. pp. lxxvi, *ante.*

Part I.

Colonial Parliament may be a "constituent" as well as legislative body.

depends upon the New Zealand Constitution Act, 1852, and the Acts amending the same. One might therefore expect that the Parliament of the Dominion of New Zealand, which may conveniently be called the New Zealand Parliament, would exhibit that "mark of subordination" which consists in the inability of a legislative body to change fundamental or constitutional laws, or (what is the same thing) in the clearly drawn distinction between ordinary laws which the legislature can change and laws of the constitution which it cannot change, at any rate when acting in its ordinary legislative character. But this anticipation is hardly borne out by an examination into the Acts creating the constitution of New Zealand. A comparison of the Colonial Laws Validity Act, 1865, s. 5, with the New Zealand Constitution Act, as subsequently amended, shows that the New Zealand Parliament can change the articles of the constitution. This power, derived from imperial statutes, is of course in no way inconsistent with the legal sovereignty of the Imperial Parliament.[1] One may fairly therefore assert that the New Zealand Parliament, in common with many other colonial legislative assemblies, is, though a "subordinate," at once a legislative and a constituent assembly. It is a "subordinate" assembly[2] because its powers are limited by the

[1] The constitutions of some self-governing States of the British Commonwealth, *e.g.* Victoria, certainly show that a Victorian law altering the constitution must in some instances be passed in a manner different from the mode in which other laws are passed. This is a faint recognition of the difference between fundamental and other laws. Compare 18 & 19 Vict. c. 55, Sched. I. s. 60 ; but there appears to have been considerable laxity in regard to observing these constitutional provisions. See Jenks, *Government of Victoria* (1891), pp. 247-249, and Intro. pp. lxii *et seq.*, *ante.*

[2] It is now the law that a member State of the Commonwealth

legislation of the Imperial Parliament; it is a constituent assembly since it can change the articles of the constitution of New Zealand. The authority of the New Zealand Parliament to change the articles of the constitution of New Zealand is from several points of view worth notice.

Chapter II.

Reason of this.

We have here a decisive proof that there is no necessary connection between the written character and the immutability of a constitution. The New Zealand constitution is to be found in a written document; it is a statutory enactment. Yet the articles of this constitutional statute can be changed by the Parliament which it creates, and changed in the same manner as any other law.[1] This may seem an

such as New Zealand has plenary powers to change its constitution. The exact extent of this power and the mode in which it can be exercised depend upon the terms of the statute which in the case of the older members is contained in an Act of the United Kingdom Parliament. Thus the Parliament of New Zealand, which now consists of a single House, has unrestricted power of constitutional amendment. This power was conferred upon New Zealand by the enactment at Westminster of the New Zealand Constitution (Amendment) Act, 1947. The Federal Parliament of the Dominion of Canada received legislative authority to amend the constitution by the British North America (No. 2) Act, 1949, which was enacted at Westminster at the request of Canada, but there are still excluded from the power a few matters; in particular, matters which are by the constitution exclusively assigned to the provincial legislatures can only be amended by the Parliament of the United Kingdom. The Parliament of the Commonwealth of Australia, on the other hand, occupies a peculiar position. It can by virtue of the terms of the constitution itself alter, by way of ordinary legislation, certain of the articles of the constitution (see, *e.g.*, Constitution of Commonwealth, ss. 65, 67), whilst it cannot, by way of ordinary legislation, change other articles of the constitution. All the articles, however, of the constitution which cannot be changed by ordinary parliamentary legislation can—subject, of course, to the sanction of the Crown—be altered or abrogated by the Houses of the Parliament, and a vote of the people of the Commonwealth, as provided by the Constitution of the Commonwealth, s. 128.

[1] For powers of constitutional amendment in New Zealand, see Wheare, *The Statute of Westminster and Dominion Status* (5th ed., 1953), pp. 227-235.

Part I.

obvious matter enough, but writers of eminence so often use language which implies or suggests that the character of a law is changed by its being expressed in the form of a statute as to make it worth while noting that a statutory constitution need not be in any sense an immutable constitution. The readiness again with which the English Parliament has conceded constituent powers to colonial legislatures shows how little hold is exercised over Englishmen by that distinction between fundamental and non-fundamental laws which runs through almost all the constitutions not only of the Continent but also of America. The explanation appears to be that in England we have long been accustomed to consider Parliament as capable of changing one kind of law with as much ease as another. Hence when English statesmen gave Parliamentary government to the colonies, they almost as a matter of course bestowed upon colonial legislatures authority to deal with every law, whether constitutional or not, which affected the colony, subject of course to the proviso, rather implied than expressed, that this power should not be used in a way inconsistent with the supremacy of the British Parliament. The colonial legislatures, in short, are within their own sphere copies of the Imperial Parliament. They are within their own sphere sovereign bodies; but their freedom of action is controlled by their subordination to the Parliament of the United Kingdom.

How conflicts between imperial and colonial legislation avoided.

The question may naturally be asked how the large amount of colonial liberty conceded to countries like New Zealand has been legally reconciled with Imperial sovereignty?

The inquiry lies a little outside our subject, but is not really foreign to it, and well deserves an answer. Nor is the reply hard to find if we keep in mind the true nature of the difficulty which needs explanation.

The problem is not to determine what are the means by which the English Government keeps the colonies in subjection, or maintains the political sovereignty of the United Kingdom. This is a matter of politics with which this book has no concern.

The question to be answered is how (assuming the law to be obeyed throughout the whole of the British Empire) colonial legislative freedom is made compatible with the legislative sovereignty of Parliament? How are the Imperial Parliament and the colonial legislatures prevented from encroaching on each other's spheres?

No one will think this inquiry needless who remarks that in confederations, such as the United States, or the Canadian Dominion, the courts are constantly occupied in determining the boundaries which divide the legislative authority of the Central Government from that of the State Legislatures.

Conflicts averted by (i.) supremacy of British Parliament;

The assertion may sound paradoxical, but is nevertheless strictly true, that the acknowledged legal supremacy of Parliament is one main cause of the wide power of legislation allowed to colonial assemblies.

The constitutions of the colonies depend directly or indirectly upon imperial statutes. No lawyer questions that Parliament could legally abolish any colonial constitution, or that Parliament can at any

Part I.

moment legislate for the colonies and repeal or override any colonial law whatever. Parliament moreover does from time to time pass Acts affecting the colonies, and the colonial,[1] no less than the English, courts completely admit the principle that a statute of the Imperial Parliament binds any part of the British dominions to which the statute is meant to apply. But when once this is admitted, it becomes obvious that there is little necessity for defining or limiting the sphere of colonial legislation. If an Act of the New Zealand Parliament contravenes an imperial statute, it is for legal purposes void; and if an Act of the New Zealand Parliament, though not infringing upon any statute, is so opposed to the interests of the Empire that it ought not to be passed, the British Parliament may render the Act of no effect by means of an imperial statute.

(ii.) right of veto.

This course, however, is rarely, if ever, necessary; for Parliament exerts authority over colonial legislation by in effect regulating the use of the Crown's "veto" in regard to colonial Acts. This is a matter which itself needs a little explanation.

The Crown's right to refuse assent to bills which have passed through the Houses of Parliament is practically obsolete.[2] The power of the Crown to

[1] See Todd, *Parliamentary Government in the British Colonies* (2nd ed., 1894), ch. v.

[2] This statement has been questioned—see Hearn, *Government of England* (2nd ed., 1887), p. 63—but is, it is submitted, correct. The so-called "veto" has never been employed as regards any public bill since the accession of the House of Hanover. When George the Third wished to stop the passing of Fox's India Bill, he abstained from using the Crown's right to dissent from proposed legislation, but availed himself of his influence in the House of Lords to procure the rejection of the measure. No stronger proof could be given that the right of veto was more than a century ago already obsolete. But the statement that a power is practically obsolete does not involve the assertion that

negative or veto the bills of colonial legislatures stands on a different footing. It is virtually, though not in name, the right of the Imperial Parliament to limit colonial legislative independence, and is frequently exercised.

This check on colonial legislation is exerted in two different manners.[1]

How right of "veto" exercised.

The Governor of a colony, say New Zealand, may directly refuse his assent to a bill, passed by both

it could under no conceivable circumstances be revived. On the whole subject of the veto, and the different senses in which the expression is used, the reader should consult an excellent article by Professor Orelli of Zurich, to be found under the word "Veto" in *Encyclopædia Britannica* (9th ed., 1888), vol. xxiv, p. 206.

The history of the Royal Veto curiously illustrates the advantage which sometimes arises from keeping alive in theory prerogatives which may seem to be practically obsolete. The Crown's legislative "veto" has certainly long been unused in England, but it has turned out a convenient method of regulating the relations between the United Kingdom and the Colonies. If the right of the King to refuse his assent to a bill which had passed the two Houses of Parliament had been abolished by statute, it would have been difficult, if not impossible, for the King to veto, or disallow, Acts passed by a legislature of a Crown Colony. It would, in other words, have been hard to create a parliamentary veto of colonial legislation.

[1] The mode in which power to veto colonial legislation is exercised may be best understood from the following extract from the *Rules and Regulations for Her Majesty's Colonial Service* (Colonial Office, 1867), ch. iii, pp. 13, 14 :—

§ 1. *Legislative Councils and Assemblies*

48. In every Colony the Governor has authority, either to give or to withhold his assent to Laws passed by the other branches or members of the Legislature, and until that assent is given no such Law is valid or binding.

49. Laws are in some cases passed with Suspending Clauses ; that is, although assented to by the Governor they do not come into operation or take effect in the Colony until they shall have been specially confirmed by Her Majesty, and in other cases Parliament has for the same purpose empowered the Governor to reserve laws for the Crown's assent, instead of himself assenting or refusing his assent to them.

50. Every Law which has received the Governor's assent (unless it contains a Suspending Clause) comes into operation immediately, or at the time specified in the Law itself. But the Crown retains power to disallow the Law ; and if such power be exercised . . . the Law ceases to have operation from the date at which such disallowance is published in the Colony.

51. In Colonies having Representative Assemblies the disallowance of any Law, or the Crown's assent to a Reserved Bill, is signified by Order in Council. The confirmation of an Act passed with a Suspending Clause, is not signified by Order in

Part I.

Houses of the New Zealand Parliament. In this case the bill is finally lost, just as would be a bill which had been rejected by the colonial council, or as would be a bill passed by the English Houses of Parliament if the Crown were to exert the obsolete prerogative of refusing the royal assent. The Governor, again, may, without refusing his assent, reserve the bill for the consideration of the Crown. In such case the bill does not come into force until it has received the royal assent, which is in effect the assent of the English Ministry, and therefore indirectly of the Imperial Parliament.

The Governor, on the other hand, may, as representing the Crown, give his assent to a New Zealand bill. The bill thereupon comes into force throughout New Zealand. But such a bill, though for a time a valid Act, is not finally made law even in New Zealand, since the Crown may, after the Governor's assent has been given, disallow the colonial Act. The case is thus put by Mr. Todd: "Although a governor as repre-

Council unless this mode of confirmation is required by the terms of the Suspending Clause itself, or by some special provision in the Constitution of the Colony.

52. In Crown Colonies the allowance or disallowance of any Law is generally signified by despatch.

53. In some cases a period is limited, after the expiration of which Local Enactments, though not actually disallowed, cease to have the authority of Law in the Colony, unless before the lapse of that time Her Majesty's confirmation of them shall have been signified there; but the general rule is otherwise.

54. In Colonies possessing Representative Assemblies, Laws purport to be made by the Queen or by the Governor on Her Majesty's behalf or sometimes by the Governor alone, omitting any express reference to Her Majesty, with the advice and consent of the Council and Assembly. They are almost invariably designated as Acts. In Colonies not having such Assemblies, Laws are designated as Ordinances, and purport to be made by the Governor, with the advice and consent of the Legislative Council (or in British Guiana of the Court of Policy).

The "veto," it will be perceived, may be exercised by one of two essentially different methods: first, by the refusal of the Governor's assent; secondly, by the exercise of the royal power to disallow laws, even when assented to by the Governor. As further the Governor may reserve bills for the royal consideration, and as colonial laws are sometimes passed containing a clause which suspends their operation until the signification of the royal assent, the check on colonial legislation may be exercised in four different forms—

"senting the Crown is empowered to give the royal "assent to bills, this act is not final and conclusive; "the Crown itself having, in point of fact, a second "veto. All statutes assented to by the governor of "a colony go into force immediately, unless they "contain a clause suspending their operation until the "issue of a proclamation of approval by the queen "in council, or some other specific provision to the "contrary; but the governor is required to trans- "mit a copy thereof to the secretary of state for the "colonies; and the queen in council may, within "two years after the receipt of the same, disallow "any such Act."[1]

(1) The refusal of the Governor's assent to a bill.

(2) Reservation of a bill for the consideration of the Crown, and the subsequent lapse of the bill owing to the royal assent being refused, or not being given within the statutory time.

(3) The insertion in a bill of a clause preventing it from coming into operation until the signification of the royal assent thereto, and the want of such royal assent.

(4) The disallowance by the Crown of a law passed by the Colonial Parliament with the assent of the Governor.

The reader should note, however, the essential difference between the three first modes and the fourth mode of checking colonial legislation. Under the three first a proposed law passed by the colonial legislature never comes into operation in the colony. Under the fourth a colonial law which has come into operation in the colony is annulled or disallowed by the Crown from the date of such disallowance. In the case of more than one colony, such disallowance must, under the Constitution, be signified within two years. See the British North America Act, 1867, s. 56. Compare the Australian Constitutions Act, 1842, ss. 32, 33; the Australian Constitutions Act, 1850, and the Victoria Constitution Act, 1855, s. 3. In the case of the Dominions the exercise of the powers of reservation and disallowance have long since been allowed to lapse and in some cases have been abolished by legislation.

[1] Todd, *Parliamentary Government in the British Colonies* (2nd ed., 1894), p. 171. See Conference on Operation of Dominion Legislation, 1929 (Cmd. 3479, 1930), pp. 11-17. The Governor-General of Canada on the advice of the Dominion Cabinet disallowed certain Acts of the Legislature of Alberta in 1938.

Part I. The result therefore of this state of things is, that colonial legislation is subject to a real veto on the part of the imperial government, and no bill which the English Ministry think ought for the sake of imperial interests to be negatived can, though passed by the New Zealand or other colonial legislature, come finally into force. The home government is certain to negative or disallow any colonial law which, either in letter or in spirit, is repugnant to Parliamentary legislation, and a large number of Acts can be given which on one ground or another have been either not assented to or disallowed by the Crown. In 1868 the Crown refused assent to a Canadian Act reducing the salary of the Governor-General.[1] In 1872 the Crown refused assent to a Canadian Copyright Act because certain parts of it conflicted with imperial legislation. In 1873 a Canadian Act was disallowed as being contrary to the express terms of the British North America Act, 1867; and on similar grounds in 1878 a Canadian Shipping Act was disallowed.[2] So again the Crown has at times in effect passed a veto upon Australian Acts for checking Chinese immigration.[3] And Acts passed by a colonial legislature, allowing divorce on the ground solely of the husband's adultery or (before the passing of the Deceased Wife's Sister's Marriage Act, 1907) legalising marriage with a deceased wife's sister or with a deceased husband's brother, have (though not consistently with the general tenor of our colonial policy)

[1] Todd, *op. cit.*, pp. 177, 178.

[2] *Ibid.*, pp. 180, 183.

[3] As regards the Australian Colonies prior to 1900 such legislation had, the author was informed, been checked in the following manner. Immigration Bills were reserved by the Governors for the consideration of the Crown, and if the assent of the Crown were not given, the Bills never came into force.

been sometimes disallowed by the Crown, that is, in effect by the home government.

The general answer therefore to the inquiry, how colonial liberty of legislation is made legally reconcilable with imperial sovereignty, is that the complete recognition of the supremacy of Parliament obviates the necessity for carefully limiting the authority of colonial legislatures, and that the home government, who in effect represent Parliament, retain by the use of the Crown's veto the power of preventing the occurrence of conflicts between colonial and imperial laws. To this it must be added that imperial treaties legally bind the colonies, and that the "treaty-making power," to use an American expression, resides in the Crown, and is therefore exercised by the home government in accordance with the wishes of the Houses of Parliament, or more strictly of the House of Commons; whilst the authority to make treaties is, except where expressly allowed by Act of Parliament, not possessed by any colonial government.[1]

It should, however, be observed that the legislature of a self-governing colony is free to determine whether or not to pass laws necessary for giving effect to a treaty entered into between the imperial government and a foreign power; and further, that there might in practice be great difficulty in enforcing within the limits of a colony the terms of a treaty, *e.g.* as to the extradition of criminals, to which colonial sentiment was opposed. But this does not affect the principle of law that a colony is bound by treaties made by the imperial government, and does not, unless under some special provision of an Act of

[1] See Todd, *op. cit.*, pp. 268 *et seq.*

Part I.

Parliament, possess authority to make treaties with any foreign power.

Policy of imperial government not to interfere with action of colonies.

Any one who wishes justly to appreciate the nature and the extent of the control exerted by Great Britain over colonial legislation should keep two points carefully in mind. The tendency, in the first place, of the imperial government is as a matter of policy to interfere less and less with the action of the colonies, whether in the way of law-making [1] or otherwise.[2] Colonial Acts, in the second place, even when finally assented to by the Crown, are, as already pointed out, invalid if repugnant to an Act of Parliament applying to the colony. The imperial policy therefore of non-intervention in the local affairs of

[1] Thus the New Zealand Deceased Husband's Brother Marriage Act, 1900, legalising marriage with a deceased husband's brother, the Immigration Restriction Act, 1901, passed by the Commonwealth Parliament, the Immigrant Restriction Act, 1907, passed by the Transvaal Legislature, all received the sanction of the Crown. The last enactment illustrated the immensely wide legislative authority which the home government would under some circumstances concede to a colonial Parliament. The Secretary of State for India (Mr. John Morley) "regrets that he cannot "agree that the Act in question can be regarded as similar to the "legislation already sanctioned in other self-governing Colonies. . . . "Section 2 (4) of the Transvaal Act introduces a principle to which no "parallel can be found in previous legislation. This clause . . . will "debar from entry into the Transvaal British subjects who would be "free to enter into any other Colony by proving themselves capable of "passing the educational tests laid down for immigrants. It will, for "instance, permanently exclude from the Transvaal members of "learned professions and graduates of European Universities of Asiatic "origin who may in future wish to enter the Colony." See *Correspondence relating to Legislation affecting Asiatics in the Transvaal* (1908, Cd. 3887), pp. 52, 53, and cf. pp. 31, 32.

[2] Except in the case of political treaties, such as the Hague Conventions, the Government of the United Kingdom did not even in 1914 bind the Dominions by treaties, but secured the insertion in treaties of clauses allowing colonies to adhere to a treaty if they desired to do so. Since 1923 the Crown has exercised its treaty-making powers on the advice of the Ministers of whichever State of the Commonwealth is

Chapter II.

British dependencies combines with the supreme legislative authority of the Imperial Parliament to render encroachments by the Parliament of the United Kingdom on the sphere of colonial legislation, or by colonial Parliaments on the domain of imperial legislation, of comparatively rare occurrence.[1]

II. *Foreign Non-sovereign Legislatures.*

Non-sovereign legislatures of independent nations.

We perceive without difficulty that the Parliaments of even those colonies, such as the Dominion of Canada, or the Australian Commonwealth, which are most nearly independent states, are not in reality sovereign legislatures. This is easily seen, because the sovereign Parliament of the United Kingdom, which legislates for the whole British Empire, is visible in the background, and because the colonies, however large their practical freedom of action, do not act as independent powers in relation to foreign states; the Parliament of a dependency cannot itself be a sovereign body. It is harder for Englishmen to realise that the legislative assembly of an independent nation may not be a sovereign assembly. Our political habits of thought indeed are so based upon the assumption of Parliamentary omnipotence, that the position of a Parliament which represents an independent nation and yet is not itself a sovereign power is apt to appear to us exceptional or anomalous. Yet whoever examines the constitutions of civilised

entering into treaty obligations. In the case of multi-lateral treaties separate plenipotentiaries sign in the name of the Crown for each member State.

[1] There were, prior to 1914, a number of conflicts between imperial and local legislation as to matters affecting merchant shipping.

Part I.

countries will find that the legislative assemblies of great nations are, or have been, in many cases legislative without being constituent bodies. To determine in any given case whether a foreign legislature be a sovereign power or not we must examine the constitution of the state to which it belongs, and ascertain whether the legislature whose position is in question bears any of the marks of subordination. Such an investigation will in many or in most instances show that an apparently sovereign assembly is in reality a non-sovereign law-making body.

France.

France has within the last hundred and thirty years made trial of at least twelve constitutions.[1]

These various forms of government have, amidst all their differences, possessed in general one common feature. They have most of them been based upon the recognition of an essential distinction between constitutional or "fundamental" laws intended to be either immutable or changeable only with great difficulty, and "ordinary" laws which could be changed by the ordinary legislature in the common course of legislation. Hence under the constitutions which France has from time to time adopted the common Parliament or legislative body has not been a sovereign legislature.

Constitutional monarchy of Louis Philippe.

The constitutional monarchy of Louis Philippe, in outward appearance at least, was modelled on the constitutional monarchy of England. In the Charter not a word could be found which expressly limits the legislative authority possessed by the Crown and the two Chambers, and to an Englishman it

[1] Demombynes, *Les Constitutions européennes* (2nd ed., 1883), vol. ii, pp. 1-5.

would seem certainly arguable that under the Orleans dynasty the Parliament was possessed of sovereignty. This, however, was not the view accepted among French lawyers. The "immutability of the constitution of "France," writes de Tocqueville, "is a necessary con-"sequence of the laws of that country. . . . As the "King, the Peers, and the Deputies all derive their "authority from the constitution, these three powers "united cannot alter a law by virtue of which alone "they govern. Out of the pale of the constitution "they are nothing; where, then, could they take their "stand to effect a change in its provisions? The alter-"native is clear: either their efforts are powerless "against the Charter, which continues to exist in spite "of them, in which case they only reign in the name "of the Charter; or they succeed in changing the "Charter, and then the law by which they existed "being annulled, they themselves cease to exist. By "destroying the Charter, they destroy themselves. "This is much more evident in the laws of 1830 than "in those of 1814. In 1814 the royal prerogative "took its stand above and beyond the constitution; "but in 1830 it was avowedly created by, and de-"pendent on, the constitution. A part, therefore, of "the French constitution is immutable, because it is "united to the destiny of a family; and the body of "the constitution is equally immutable, because there "appear to be no legal means of changing it. These "remarks are not applicable to England. That country "having no written constitution, who can assert when "its constitution is changed?"[1]

[1] de Tocqueville, *Democracy in America* (translation by H. Reeve, 1875), vol. ii, App. pp. 322, 323. *Œuvres complètes* (14th ed., 1864), vol. i (Démocratie en Amérique), p. 311.

Part I.

de Tocqueville's reasoning[1] may not carry conviction to an Englishman, but the weakness of his argument is of itself strong evidence of the influence of the hold on French opinion of the doctrine which it is intended to support, namely, that Parliamentary sovereignty was not a recognised part of French constitutionalism. The dogma which is so naturally assented to by Englishmen contradicts that idea of the essential difference between constitutional and other laws which appears to have a firm hold on most foreign statesmen and legislators.

Republic of 1848.

The Republic of 1848 expressly recognised this distinction; no single article of the constitution proclaimed on 4th November 1848 could be changed in the same way as an ordinary law. The legislative assembly sat for three years. In the last year of its existence, and then only, it could by a majority of three-fourths, and not otherwise, convoke a constituent body with authority to modify the constitution. This constituent and sovereign assembly differed in numbers, and otherwise, from the ordinary non-sovereign legislature.

Present Republic.

The National Assembly of the French Republic exerts at least as much direct authority as the English Houses of Parliament. The French Chamber of Deputies exercises at least as much influence on the appointment of Ministers, and controls the action of the government, at least as strictly as does our House

[1] His view was certainly paradoxical. (See Duguit, *Manuel de Droit Public français*; *Droit Constitutionnel* (1907), para. 149, pp. 1090-1098. As a matter of fact one provision of the Charter, namely, art. 23, regulating the appointment of Peers, was changed by the ordinary process of legislation. See Law of 29th December, 1831, Hélie, *Les Constitutions de la France* (1879), ch. vi. p. 1006 (Loi du 29 Decembre, 1831).

Chapter II.

of Commons. The President, moreover, does not possess even a theoretical right of veto. For all this, however, the French Parliament is not a sovereign assembly, but is bound by the laws of the constitution in a way in which no law binds our Parliament. The articles of the constitution, or "fundamental laws," stand in a totally different position from the ordinary law of the land. Under article 8 of the constitution, no one of these fundamental enactments can be legally changed otherwise than subject to the following provisions :—

"8. *Les Chambres auront le droit, par délibéra-*
"*tions séparées, prises dans chacune à la majorité*
"*absolue des voix, soit spontanément, soit sur la*
"*demande du Président de la République, de déclarer*
"*qu'il y a lieu de réviser les lois constitutionnelles.*
"*Après que chacune des deux Chambres aura pris*
"*cette résolution, elles se réuniront en Assemblée*
"*nationale pour procéder à la révision.—Les dé-*
"*libérations portant révision des lois constitution-*
"*nelles, en tout ou en partie, devront être prises*
"*à la majorité absolue des membres composant*
"*l'Assemblée nationale.*"[1]

[1] Duguit et Monnier, *Les Constitutions et les principales lois politiques de la France depuis 1789* (1898), Loi du 25 Fév. 1875, art. viii, p. 320. A striking example of the difference between English and French constitutionalism is to be found in the division of opinion which exists between French writers of authority on the answer to the inquiry whether the French Chambers, when sitting together, have constitutionally the right to change the constitution. To an Englishman the question seems hardly to admit of discussion, for Art. 8 of the constitutional laws enacts in so many words that these laws may be revised, in the manner therein set forth, by the Chambers when sitting together as a National Assembly. Many French constitutionalists therefore lay down, as would any English lawyer, that the Assembly is a constituent as well as a legislative body, and is endowed with the right to change the constitution (Duguit, *Manuel de Droit Public français*; *Droit Con-*

Part I.

Supreme legislative power is therefore under the Republic vested not in the ordinary Parliament of two Chambers, but in a "national assembly," or congress, composed of the Chamber of Deputies and the Senate sitting together.

Distinction between flexible and rigid constitutions.

The various constitutions, in short, of France, which are in this respect fair types of continental polities,[1] exhibit, as compared with the expansiveness or "flexibility" of English institutions, that characteristic which may be conveniently described as "rigidity."

And here it is worth while, with a view to understanding the constitution of our own country, to make perfectly clear to ourselves the distinction already referred to between a "flexible" and a "rigid" constitution.

stitutionnel (1907), para. 151, pp. 1100-1107 ; Moreau, *Précis élémentaire de Droit Constitutionnel* (10th ed., 1928), pp. 395-413). But some eminent authorities maintain that this view is erroneous, and that in spite of the words of the constitution the ultimate right of constitutional amendment must be exercised directly by the French people, and that therefore any alteration in the constitutional laws by the Assembly lacks, at any rate, moral validity unless it is ratified by the direct vote of the electors. (See, on the one side, Duguit, *op. cit.*, para. 151 ; Bard et Robiquet, *La Constitution française de 1875* (2nd ed., 1878), pp. 374-390, and on the other side, Esmein, *Eléments de Droit constitutionnel français et comparé* (7th ed., 1921), vol. ii, ch. vii, pp. 495-511; Borgeaud, *Etablissement et révision des Constitutions en Amérique et en Europe* (1893), part iii, bk. ii, ch. viii, pp. 303-307.) [The above refers to the Third Republic.—Ed.]

[1] No constitution better merits study in this as in other respects than the constitution of Belgium. Though formed after the English model, it rejects or omits the principle of parliamentary sovereignty. The ordinary Parliament cannot change anything in the constitution ; it is a legislative, not a constituent body ; it can declare that there is reason for changing a particular constitutional provision, and having done so is *ipso facto* dissolved (*après cette déclaration les deux chambres sont dissoutes de plein droit*). The new Parliament thereupon elected has a right to change the constitutional article which has been declared subject to change (*Constitution de La Belgique*, arts. 131, 71).

Flexible constitutions.

A "flexible" constitution is one under which every law of every description can legally be changed with the same ease and in the same manner by one and the same body. The "flexibility" of our constitution consists in the right of the Crown and the two Houses to modify or repeal any law whatever; they can alter the succession to the Crown or repeal the Acts of Union in the same manner in which they can pass an Act enabling a company to make a new railway from Oxford to London. With us, laws therefore are called constitutional, because they refer to subjects supposed to affect the fundamental institutions of the state, and not because they are legally more sacred or difficult to change than other laws. And as a matter of fact, the meaning of the word "constitutional" is in England so vague that the term "a constitutional law or enactment" is rarely applied to any English statute as giving a definite description of its character.

Rigid constitutions.

A "rigid" constitution is one under which certain laws generally known as constitutional or fundamental laws cannot be changed in the same manner as ordinary laws. The "rigidity" of the constitution, say of Belgium or of France, consists in the absence of any right on the part of the Belgian or French Parliament, when acting in its ordinary capacity, to modify or repeal certain definite laws termed constitutional or fundamental. Under a rigid constitution the term "constitutional" as applied to a law has a perfectly definite sense. It means that a particular enactment belongs to the articles of the constitution, and cannot be legally changed with the same ease and in the same manner as ordinary laws. The articles of

Part I.

the constitution will no doubt generally, though by no means invariably, be found to include all the most important and fundamental laws of the state. But it certainly cannot be asserted that where a constitution is rigid all its articles refer to matters of supreme importance. The rule that the French Parliament must meet at Versailles was at one time one of the constitutional laws of the French Republic. Such an enactment, however practically important, would never in virtue of its own character have been termed constitutional; it was constitutional simply because it was included in the articles of the constitution.[1]

The contrast between the flexibility of the English and the rigidity of almost every foreign constitution suggests two interesting inquiries.

Whether rigidity of constitution secures permanence?

First, Does the rigidity of a constitution secure its permanence and invest the fundamental institutions of the state with practical immutability?

To this inquiry historical experience gives an indecisive answer.

In some instances the fact that certain laws or institutions of a state have been marked off as placed beyond the sphere of political controversy, has, apparently, prevented that process of gradual innovation

[1] The terms "flexible" and "rigid" (originally suggested by the author's friend, Lord Bryce) are used throughout this work without any connotation either of praise or of blame. The flexibility and expansiveness of the English constitution, or the rigidity and immutability of, *e.g.*, the constitution of the United States, may each be qualities which according to the judgment of different critics deserve either admiration or censure. With such judgments this treatise has no concern. The author's whole aim was to make clear the exact difference between a flexible and a rigid constitution. It was not his object to pronounce any opinion on the question whether the flexibility or rigidity of a given polity be a merit or a defect.

which in England has, within not much more than sixty years, transformed our polity. The constitution of Belgium stood for more than half a century without undergoing, in form at least, any material change whatever. The constitution of the United States has lasted for more than a hundred years, but has not undergone anything like the amount of change which has been experienced by the constitution of England since the death of George the Third.[1] But if the inflexibility of constitutional laws has in certain instances checked the gradual and unconscious process of innovation by which the foundations of a commonwealth are undermined, the rigidity of constitutional forms has in other cases provoked revolution. The twelve unchangeable constitutions of France have each lasted on an average for less than ten years, and have frequently perished by violence. Louis Philippe's monarchy was destroyed within seven years of the time when de Tocqueville pointed out that no power existed legally capable of altering the articles of the Charter. In one notorious instance at least —and other examples of the same phenomenon might be produced from the annals of revolutionary France—the immutability of the constitution was the ground or excuse for its violent subversion. The best plea for the *Coup d'état* of 1851 was, that while the French people wished for the re-election of the President, the article of the constitution requiring a majority of three-fourths of

[1] No doubt the constitution of the United States had in reality, though not in form, changed a good deal since the beginning of last century; but the change had been effected far less by formally enacted constitutional amendments than by the growth of customs or institutions which have modified the working without altering the articles of the constitution. See Horwill, *The Usages of the American Constitution* (1925).

Part I. the legislative assembly in order to alter the law which made the President's re-election impossible, thwarted the will of the sovereign people. Had the Republican Assembly been a sovereign Parliament, Louis Napoleon would have lacked the plea, which seemed to justify, as well as some of the motives which tempted him to commit, the crime of the 2nd of December.

Nor ought the perils in which France was involved by the immutability with which the statesmen of 1848 invested the constitution to be looked upon as exceptional; they arose from a defect which is inherent in every rigid constitution. The endeavour to create laws which cannot be changed is an attempt to hamper the exercise of sovereign power; it therefore tends to bring the letter of the law into conflict with the will of the really supreme power in the state. The majority of French electors were under the constitution the true sovereign of France; but the rule which prevented the legal re-election of the President in effect brought the law of the land into conflict with the will of the majority of the electors, and produced, therefore, as a rigid constitution has a natural tendency to produce, an opposition between the letter of the law and the wishes of the sovereign. If the inflexibility of French constitutions has provoked revolution, the flexibility of English institutions has, once at least, saved them from violent overthrow. To a student, who at this distance of time calmly studies the history of the first Reform Bill, it is apparent, that in 1832 the supreme legislative authority of Parliament enabled the nation to carry through a political revolution under the guise of a legal reform.

The rigidity, in short, of a constitution tends to check gradual innovation; but, just because it impedes change, may, under unfavourable circumstances, occasion or provoke revolution.

What are the safeguards against unconstitutional legislation?

Secondly, What are the safeguards which under a rigid constitution can be taken against unconstitutional legislation?

The general answer to our inquiry (which of course can have no application to a country like England, ruled by a sovereign Parliament) is that two methods may be, and have been, adopted by the makers of constitutions, with a view to rendering unconstitutional legislation, either impossible, or inoperative.

Reliance may be placed upon the force of public opinion and upon the ingenious balancing of political powers for restraining the legislature from passing unconstitutional enactments. This system opposes unconstitutional legislation by means of moral sanctions, which resolve themselves into the influence of public sentiment.

Authority, again, may be given to some person or body of persons, and preferably to the courts, to adjudicate upon the constitutionality of legislative acts, and treat them as void if they are inconsistent with the letter or the spirit of the constitution. This system attempts not so much to prevent unconstitutional legislation as to render it harmless through the intervention of the tribunals, and rests at bottom on the authority of the judges.

This general account of the two methods by which it may be attempted to secure the rigidity of a constitution is hardly intelligible without further

Part I. — II.

illustration. Its meaning may be best understood by a comparison between the different policies in regard to the legislature pursued by two different classes of constitutionalists.

Safeguards provided by continental constitutionalists.

French constitution-makers and their continental followers have, as we have seen, always attached vital importance to the distinction between fundamental and other laws, and therefore have constantly created legislative assemblies which possessed "legislative" without possessing "constituent" powers. French statesmen have therefore been forced to devise means for keeping the ordinary legislature within its appropriate sphere. Their mode of procedure has been marked by a certain uniformity; they have declared on the face of the constitution the exact limits imposed upon the authority of the legislature; they have laid down as articles of the constitution whole bodies of maxims intended to guide and control the course of legislation; they have provided for the creation, by special methods and under special conditions, of a constituent body which alone should be entitled to revise the constitution. They have, in short, directed their attention to restraining the ordinary legislature from attempting any inroad upon the fundamental laws of the state; but they have in general trusted to public sentiment,[1] or at any rate to political con-

[1] "Aucun des pouvoirs institués par la constitution n'a le droit "de la changer dans son ensemble ni dans ses parties, sauf les réformes "qui pourront y être faites par la voie de la révision, conformément "aux dispositions du titre VII. ci-dessus.

"L'Assemblée nationale constituante en remet le dépôt à la "fidélité du Corps législatif, du Roi et des juges, à la vigilance des "pères de famille, aux épouses et aux méres, à l'affection des jeunes "citoyens, au courage de tous les Français."—Constitution de 1791,

siderations, for inducing the legislature to respect the restraints imposed on its authority, and have usually omitted to provide machinery for annulling unconstitutional enactments, or for rendering them of no effect.

Chapter II.

French Revolutionary constitutions.

These traits of French constitutionalism are specially noticeable in the three earliest of French political experiments. The Monarchical constitution of 1791, the Democratic constitution of 1793, the Directorial constitution of 1795 exhibit, under all their diversities, two features in common. They each, on the one hand, confine the power of the legislature within very narrow limits indeed; under the Directory, for instance, the legislative body could not itself change any one of the 377 articles of the constitution, and the provisions for creating a constituent assembly were so framed that not the very least alteration in any of these articles could have been carried out within a period of less than nine years.[1] None of these constitutions, on the other hand,

Tit. vii, Art. 8; Duguit et Monnier, *Les Constitutions et les principales lois politiques de la France depuis 1789* (1898), Constitution du 3 Sept. 1791, p. 34.

These are the terms in which the National Assembly entrusts the Constitution of 1791 to the guardianship of the nation. It is just possible, though not likely, that the reference to the judges is intended to contain a hint that the courts should annul or treat as void unconstitutional laws. Under the Constitution of the Year VIII. the senate had authority to annul unconstitutional laws. But this was rather a veto on what in England we should call Bills than a power to make void laws duly enacted. See Constitution of Year VIII., Tit. ii. Arts. 26, 28, Hélie, *Les Constitutions de la France* (1879), ch. iv, p. 579 (Constitution du 22 Frimaire, An viii, Tit. 2, arts. 26-28).

[1] See Constitution of 1795, Tit. xiii. Art. 338, Hélie, *Les Constitutions de la France* (1879), ch. iv, p. 463 (Constitution du 5 Fructidor, An iii. art. 338).

Part I.

contain a hint as to the mode in which a law is to be treated which is alleged to violate the constitution. Their framers indeed hardly seem to have recognised the fact that enactments of the legislature might, without being in so many words opposed to the constitution, yet be of dubious constitutionality, and that some means would be needed for determining whether a given law was or was not in opposition to the principles of the constitution.

Existing Republican constitution.

These characteristics of the revolutionary constitutions have been repeated in the works of later French constitutionalists. Under the present French Republic there exist a certain number of laws (not it is true a very large number), which the Parliament cannot change; and what is perhaps of more consequence, the so-called Congress [1] could at any time increase the number of fundamental laws, and thereby greatly decrease the authority of future Parliaments. The constitution, however, contains no article providing against the possibility of an ordinary Parliament carrying through legislation greatly in excess of its constitutional powers. Any one in fact who bears in mind the respect paid in France from the time of the Revolution onwards to the legislation of *de facto* governments and the traditions of the French judicature, will assume with confidence that an enactment passed through the Chambers, promulgated by the President, and published in the *Bulletin des Lois*, will

[1] The proper title for a so-called Congress was *L'Assemblée Nationale.* The Assembly consisted of the members of each chamber (Deputies and Senators) sitting as one body at Versailles. Each chamber must previously have declared separately for revision and the subject for revision must have been specified.—Ed.

be held valid by every tribunal throughout the Republic.

Are the articles of continental constitutions "laws"?

This curious result therefore ensues. The restrictions placed on the action of the legislature under the French constitution are not in reality laws, since they are not rules which in the last resort will be enforced by the courts. Their true character is that of maxims of political morality, which derive whatever strength they possess from being formally inscribed in the constitution and from the resulting support of public opinion. What is true of the constitution of France applies with more or less force to other polities which have been formed under the influence of French ideas. The Belgian constitution, for example, restricts the action of the Parliament no less than does the Republican constitution of France. But it is at least doubtful whether Belgian constitutionalists have provided any means whatever for invalidating laws which diminish or do away with the rights (*e.g.* the right of freedom of speech) "guaranteed" to Belgian citizens. The jurists of Belgium maintain, in theory at least, that an Act of Parliament opposed to any article of the constitution ought to be treated by the courts as void. But during the whole period of Belgian independence, no tribunal, it is said, has ever pronounced judgment upon the constitutionality of an Act of Parliament. This shows, it may be said, that the Parliament has respected the constitution, and certainly affords some evidence that, under favourable circumstances, formal declarations of rights may, from their influence on popular feeling, possess greater weight than is generally attributed to them in England; but it also

Part I.

suggests the notion that in Belgium, as in France, the restrictions on Parliamentary authority are supported mainly by moral or political sentiment, and are at bottom rather constitutional understandings than laws.

To an English critic, indeed, the attitude of continental and especially of revolutionary statesmen towards the ordinary legislature bears an air of paradox. They seem to be almost equally afraid of leaving the authority of the ordinary legislature unfettered, and of taking the steps by which the legislature may be prevented from breaking through the bonds imposed upon its power. The explanation of this apparent inconsistency is to be found in two sentiments which have influenced French constitution-makers from the very outbreak of the Revolution —an over-estimate of the effect to be produced by general declarations of rights, and a settled jealousy of any intervention by the judges in the sphere of politics.[1] We shall see, in a later chapter, that the public law of France is still radically influenced by the belief, even now almost universal among Frenchmen, that the law courts must not be allowed to interfere in any way whatever with matters of state, or indeed with anything affecting the machinery of government.[2]

Safeguards provided by founders of United States.

The authors of the American constitution have, for reasons that will appear in my next chapter, been even more anxious than French statesmen to limit the authority of every legislative body throughout the Republic. They have further shared the faith

[1] de Tocqueville, *Œuvres complètes* (14th ed., 1864), vol. i (Démocratie en Amérique), pp. 167, 168.

[2] See ch. xii, *post*.

of continental politicians in the value possessed by general declarations of rights. But they have, unlike French constitution-makers, directed their attention, not so much to preventing Congress and other legislatures from making laws in excess of their powers, as to the invention of means by which the effect of unconstitutional laws may be nullified; and this result they have achieved by making it the duty of every judge throughout the Union to treat as void any enactment which violates the constitution, and thus have given to the restrictions contained in the constitution on the legislative authority either of Congress or the State legislatures the character of real laws, that is, of rules enforced by the courts. This system, which makes the judges the guardians of the constitution, provides the only adequate safeguard which has hitherto been invented against unconstitutional legislation.

CHAPTER III

PARLIAMENTARY SOVEREIGNTY AND FEDERALISM

Part I.

Subject.

My present aim is to illustrate the nature of Parliamentary sovereignty as it exists in England, by a comparison with the system of government known as Federalism as it exists in several parts of the civilised world, and especially in the United States of America.[1]

Federalism best understood by studying constitution of United States.

There are indeed to be found at the present time three other noteworthy examples of federal government—the Swiss Confederation, the Dominion of Canada, and the German Empire.[2] But while from a study of the institutions of each of these states one may draw illustrations which throw light on our subject, it will be best to keep our attention throughout this chapter fixed mainly on the institutions of the great American Republic. And this for two reasons. The Union, in the first place, presents the most completely developed type of federalism.

[1] On the subject of American Federalism see Bryce, *American Commonwealth*, 1910 edition, especially vol. i, pt. i; see also Amos, *The American Constitution*, 1938, for a short account by an English lawyer. A useful, up-to-date account is contained in Bernard Schwartz, *American Constitutional Law*, 1955.

[2] To these should be added the Commonwealth of Australia (1900), the Federal Union of India (1950), Pakistan (1957) and the Central African Federation (1953), Federation of Malaya (1957), and the British Caribbean Federation (1958). Western Germany is a Federal Republic.

Chapter III.

All the features which mark that scheme of government, and above all the control of the legislature by the courts, are there exhibited in their most salient and perfect form; the Swiss Confederation,[1] moreover, and the Dominion of Canada, are more or less copied from the American model, whilst the constitution of the German Empire is too full of anomalies, springing both from historical and from temporary causes, to be taken as a fair representative of any known form of government. The constitution of the United States, in the second place, holds a very peculiar relation towards the institutions of England. In the principle of the distribution of powers which determines its form, the constitution of the United States is the exact opposite of the English constitution, the very essence of which is, as I hope I have now made clear, the unlimited authority of Parliament. But while the formal differences between the constitution of the American Republic and the constitution of the English monarchy are, looked at from one point of view, immense, the institutions of America are in their spirit little else than a gigantic development of the ideas which lie at the basis of the political and legal institutions of England. The principle, in short, which gives its form to our system of government is (to use a foreign but convenient expression) "unitarianism," or the habitual exercise of supreme legis-

[1] The essential feature of the Swiss Commonwealth is that it is a genuine and natural democracy, but a democracy based on Continental, and not on Anglo-Saxon, ideas of freedom and of government.

The constitution of the Commonwealth of Australia contains at least one feature apparently suggested by Swiss federalism, namely, the referendum or general vote of the electorate on amendments of the constitution.

Part I.

lative authority by one central power, which in the particular case is the British Parliament. The principle which, on the other hand, shapes every part of the American polity, is that distribution of limited, executive, legislative, and judicial authority among bodies each co-ordinate with and independent of the other which, we shall in a moment see, is essential to the federal form of government. The contrast therefore between the two polities is seen in its most salient form, and the results of this difference are made all the more visible because in every other respect the institutions of the English people on each side the Atlantic rest upon the same notions of law, of justice, and of the relation between the rights of individuals and the rights of the government, or the state.

We shall best understand the nature of federalism and the points in which a federal constitution stands in contrast with the Parliamentary constitution of England if we note, first, the conditions essential to the existence of a federal state and the aim with which such a state is formed; secondly, the essential features of a federal union; and lastly, certain characteristics of federalism which result from its very nature, and form points of comparison, or contrast, between a federal polity and a system of Parliamentary sovereignty.

Conditions of federalism.

A federal state requires for its formation two conditions.[1]

[1] The author referred to the following authorities: Story, *Commentaries on the Constitution of the United States* (4th ed., 1873); Bryce, *American Commonwealth* (1910 ed.); British North America Act, 1867; Bourinot, *Parliamentary Procedure and Practice in the Dominion of Canada* (1st ed., 1884); *Constitution Fédérale de la Confédération Suisse du* 29 *Mai*, 1874; Blumer, *Handbuch des Schweizerischen Bundes-*

There must exist, in the first place, a body of countries such as the Cantons of Switzerland, the Colonies of America, or the Provinces of Canada, so closely connected by locality, by history, by race, or the like, as to be capable of bearing, in the eyes of their inhabitants, an impress of common nationality. It will also be generally found (if we appeal to experience) that lands which now form part of a federal state were at some stage of their existence bound together by close alliance or by subjection to a common sovereign. It were going further than facts warrant to assert that this earlier connection is essential to the formation of a federal state. But it is certain that where federalism flourishes it is in general the slowly-matured fruit of some earlier and looser connection.

Chapter III.

Countries capable of union.

Existence of federal sentiment

A second condition absolutely essential to the founding of a federal system is the existence of a very peculiar state of sentiment among the inhabitants of the countries which it is proposed to unite. They must desire union, and must not desire unity. If there be no desire to unite, there is clearly no basis for federalism; the wild scheme entertained (it is said) under the Commonwealth of forming a union between the English Republic and the United Provinces was one of those dreams which may haunt the imagination of politicians but can never be trans-

staatsrechtes; Lowell, *Governments and Parties in Continental Europe* (1896), vol. ii, ch. xi-xiii; Adams and Cunningham, *Swiss Confederation* (1889); and see App. sec. iv, *post*; Quick and Garran, *Annotated Constitution of the Australian Commonwealth* (1901); Moore, *The Commonwealth of Australia* (2nd ed., 1910); and Bryce, *Studies in History and Jurisprudence* (1901), vol. i, Essay viii (The Constitution of the Commonwealth of Australia).

formed into fact. If, on the other hand, there be a desire for unity, the wish will naturally find its satisfaction, not under a federal, but under a unitarian constitution; the experience of England and Scotland in the eighteenth and of the states of Italy in the nineteenth century shows that the sense of common interests, or common national feeling, may be too strong to allow of that combination of union and separation which is the foundation of federalism. The phase of sentiment, in short, which forms a necessary condition for the formation of a federal state is that the people of the proposed state should wish to form for many purposes a single nation, yet should not wish to surrender the individual existence of each man's State or Canton. We may perhaps go a little farther, and say, that a federal government will hardly be formed unless many of the inhabitants of the separate States feel stronger allegiance to their own State than to the federal state represented by the common government. This was certainly the case in America towards the end of the eighteenth century, and in Switzerland at the middle of the nineteenth century. In 1787 a Virginian or a citizen of Massachusetts felt a far stronger attachment to Virginia or to Massachusetts than to the body of the confederated States. In 1848 the citizens of Lucerne felt far keener loyalty to their Canton than to the confederacy, and the same thing, no doubt, held true in a less degree of the men of Berne or of Zurich. The sentiment therefore which creates a federal state is the prevalence throughout the citizens of more or less allied countries of two feelings which are to a certain extent inconsistent—

the desire for national unity and the determination to maintain the independence of each man's separate State. The aim of federalism is to give effect as far as possible to both these sentiments.

The aim of federalism.

A federal state is a political contrivance intended to reconcile national unity and power with the maintenance of "state rights." The end aimed at fixes the essential character of federalism. For the method by which Federalism attempts to reconcile the apparently inconsistent claims of national sovereignty and of state sovereignty consists of the formation of a constitution under which the ordinary powers of sovereignty are elaborately divided between the common or national government and the separate states. The details of this division vary under every different federal constitution, but the general principle on which it should rest is obvious. Whatever concerns the nation as a whole should be placed under the control of the national government. All matters which are not primarily of common interest should remain in the hands of the several States. The preamble to the constitution of the United States recites that "We, the people of the United States, in order "to form a more perfect union, establish justice, "ensure domestic tranquillity, provide for the common "defence, promote the general welfare, and secure the "blessings of liberty to ourselves and our posterity, "do ordain and establish this constitution for the "United States of America." The tenth amendment enacts that "the powers not delegated to the United "States by the constitution nor prohibited by it to "the States are reserved to the States respectively or "to the people." These two statements, which are

Part I.

reproduced with slight alteration in the constitution of the Swiss Confederation,[1] point out the aim and lay down the fundamental idea of federalism.

Essential characteristics of federalism. United States.

From the notion that national unity can be reconciled with state independence by a division of powers under a common constitution between the nation on the one hand and the individual States on the other, flow the three leading characteristics of completely developed federalism,—the supremacy of the constitution—the distribution among bodies with limited and co-ordinate authority of the different powers of government—the authority of the courts to act as interpreters of the constitution.

Supremacy of constitution.

A federal state derives its existence from the constitution, just as a corporation derives its existence from the grant by which it is created. Hence, every power, executive, legislative, or judicial, whether it belong to the nation or to the individual States, is subordinate to and controlled by the constitution. Neither the President of the United States nor the Houses of Congress, nor the Governor of Massachusetts, nor the Legislature or General Court of Massachusetts, can legally exercise a single power which is inconsistent with the articles of the constitution. This doctrine of the supremacy of the constitution is familiar to every American, but in England even trained lawyers find a difficulty in following it out to its legitimate consequences. The difficulty arises from the fact that under the English constitution no principle is recognised which bears any real resemblance to the doctrine (essential to federalism) that the Constitution constitutes the "supreme law of the land."[2]

[1] *Constitution Fédérale,* Preamble, and art. 3.
[2] See Constitution of the United States, art. 6 (s. 2).

In England we have laws which may be called fundamental[1] or constitutional because they deal with important principles (as, for example, the descent of the Crown or the terms of union with Scotland) lying at the basis of our institutions, but with us there is no such thing as a supreme law, or law which tests the validity of other laws. There are indeed important statutes, such as the Act embodying the Treaty of Union with Scotland, with which it would be political madness to tamper gratuitously; there are utterly unimportant statutes, such, for example, as the Dentists Act, 1878, which may be repealed or modified at the pleasure or caprice of Parliament; but neither the Act of Union with Scotland nor the Dentists Act, 1878, has more claim than the other to be considered a supreme law. Each embodies the will of the sovereign legislative power; each can be legally altered or repealed by Parliament; neither tests the validity of the other. Should the Dentists Act, 1878, unfortunately contravene the terms of the Act of Union, the Act of Union would be *pro tanto* repealed, but no judge would dream of maintaining that the Dentists Act, 1878, was thereby rendered invalid or unconstitutional. The one fundamental dogma of English constitutional law is the absolute legislative sovereignty or despotism of the King in Parliament. But this dogma is incompatible with the existence of a fundamental compact, the provisions of which control every authority existing under the constitution.[2]

[1] The expression "fundamental laws of England" became current during the controversy as to the payment of ship-money (1635). See Gardiner, *History of England*, vol. viii (1884), pp. 84, 85.

[2] Cf. especially Kent, *Commentaries* (12th ed., 1873). para. 447-449.

Part I.

Consequences. Written constitution.

In the supremacy of the constitution are involved three consequences:—

The constitution must almost necessarily be a "written" constitution.

The foundations of a federal state are a complicated contract. This compact contains a variety of terms which have been agreed to, and generally after mature deliberation, by the States which make up the confederacy. To base an arrangement of this kind upon understandings or conventions would be certain to generate misunderstandings and disagreements. The articles of the treaty, or in other words of the constitution, must therefore be reduced to writing. The constitution must be a written document, and, if possible, a written document of which the terms are open to no misapprehension. The founders of the American Union left at least one great question unsettled. This gap in the constitution gave an opening to the dispute which was the plea, if not the justification, for the War of Secession.[1]

Rigid constitution.

The constitution must be what I have termed a "rigid"[2] or "inexpansive" constitution.

The law of the constitution must be either legally immutable, or else capable of being changed only by

[1] No doubt it is conceivable that a federation might grow up by the force of custom, and under agreements between different States which were not reduced into writing, and it appears to be questionable how far the Achæan League was bound together by anything equivalent to a written constitution. It is, however, in the highest degree improbable, even if it be not practically impossible, that in modern times a federal state could be formed without the framing of some document which, whatever the name by which it is called, would be in reality a written constitution, regulating the rights and duties of the federal government and the States composing the Federation.

[2] See pp. 91. 126 *et seq.*, *ante*.

some authority above and beyond the ordinary legislative bodies, whether federal or state legislatures, existing under the constitution.

In spite of the doctrine enunciated by some jurists that in every country there must be found some person or body legally capable of changing every institution thereof, it is hard to see why it should be held inconceivable[1] that the founders of a polity should have deliberately omitted to provide any means for lawfully changing its bases. Such an omission would not be unnatural on the part of the authors of a federal union, since one main object of the States entering into the compact is to prevent further encroachments upon their several state rights; and in the fifth article of the United States constitution may still be read the record of an attempt to give to some of its provisions temporary immutability. The question, however, whether a federal constitution necessarily involves the existence of some ultimate sovereign power authorised to amend or alter its terms is of merely speculative interest, for under existing federal governments the constitution will be found to provide the means for its own improvement. It is, at any rate, certain that whenever the founders of a federal government hold the maintenance of a federal system to be of primary importance, supreme

[1] Eminent American lawyers maintain that under the constitution there exists no person, or body of persons, possessed of legal sovereignty, in the sense given by Austin to that term, and it is difficult to see that this opinion involves any absurdity. Cf. Constitution of United States, art. 5. The truth is that a federal constitution partakes of the nature of a treaty, and it is quite conceivable that the authors of the constitution may intend to provide no constitutional means of changing its terms except the assent of all the parties to the treaty.

legislative power cannot be safely vested in any ordinary legislature acting under the constitution.[1] For so to vest legislative sovereignty would be inconsistent with the aim of federalism, namely, the permanent division between the spheres of the national government and of the several States. If Congress could legally change the constitution, New York and Massachusetts would have no legal guarantee for the amount of independence reserved to them under the constitution, and would be as subject to the sovereign power of Congress as is Scotland to the sovereignty of Parliament; the Union would cease to be a federal state, and would become a unitarian republic. If, on the other hand, the legislature of South Carolina could of its own will amend the constitution, the authority of the central government would (from a legal point of view) be illusory; the United States would sink from a nation into a collection of independent countries united by the bond of a more or less permanent alliance. Hence the power of amending the constitution has been placed, so to speak, outside the constitution, and one may say, with sufficient accuracy for our present purpose, that the legal sovereignty of the United States resides in the States' governments as forming one aggregate body

[1] Under the constitution of the German Empire the Imperial legislative body could amend the constitution. But the character of the Federal Council (*Bundesrath*) gave ample security for the protection of State rights. No change in the constitution could be effected which was opposed by fourteen votes in the Federal Council. This gave a veto on change to Prussia and to various combinations of some among the other States. The extent to which national sentiment and State patriotism respectively predominated under a federal system may be conjectured from the nature of the authority which had the right to modify the constitution.

represented by three-fourths of the several States at any time belonging to the Union.[1] Now from the necessity for placing ultimate legislative authority in some body outside the constitution a remarkable consequence ensues. Under a federal as under a unitarian system there exists a sovereign power, but the sovereign is in a federal state a despot hard to rouse. He is not, like the English Parliament, an ever-wakeful legislator, but a monarch who slumbers and sleeps. The sovereign of the United States has been roused to serious action but once during the course of more than a century. It needed the thunder of the Civil War to break his repose, and it may be doubted whether anything short of impending revolution will ever again arouse him to activity. But a monarch who slumbers for years is like a monarch who does not exist. A federal constitution is capable of change, but for all that a federal constitution is apt to be unchangeable.[2]

Every legislative assembly existing under a federal

[1] "The Congress, whenever two-thirds of both houses shall deem "it necessary, shall propose amendments to this constitution, or, on the "application of the legislatures of two-thirds of the several States, shall "call a convention for proposing amendments, which, in either case, "shall be valid to all intents and purposes, as part of this constitution, "when ratified by the legislatures of three-fourths of the several States, "or by conventions in three-fourths thereof, as the one or the other "mode of ratification may be proposed by the Congress; provided that "no amendments which may be made prior to the year one thousand "eight hundred and eight shall in any manner affect the first and fourth "clauses in the ninth section of the first article; and that no State, "without its consent, shall be deprived of its equal suffrage in the "Senate."—*Constitution of the United States*, art. 5. Cf. Austin, *Jurisprudence* (4th ed., 1879), vol. i, p. 278; and see Bryce, *American Commonwealth* (1910 ed.), vol. i, ch. xxxii (The Amendment of the Constitution).

[2] Note, however, the ease with which the provisions of the constitution of the United States with regard to the election of Senators by the Legislature and the transference of such election to the people of each State, were carried through by Amendment xvii, passed in 1913.

Part I.

Every legislature under federal constitution is a subordinate law-making body.

constitution is merely[1] a subordinate law-making body, whose laws are of the nature of by-laws, valid whilst within the authority conferred upon it by the constitution, but invalid or unconstitutional if they go beyond the limits of such authority.

There is an apparent absurdity[2] in comparing the legislature of the United States to an English railway company or a municipal corporation, but the comparison is just.[3] Congress can, within the limits of its legal powers, pass laws which bind every man throughout the United States. The Great Eastern Railway Company can, in like manner, pass laws which bind every man throughout the British dominions. A law passed by Congress which is in excess of its legal powers, as contravening the Constitution, is invalid; a law passed by the Great Eastern Railway Company in excess of the powers given by Act of Parliament, or, in other words, by the legal constitution of the company, is also invalid; a law passed by Congress is called an Act of Congress, and if *ultra vires* is described as unconstitutional; a law passed by the Great Eastern Railway Company is called a by-law, and if *ultra vires* is called, not unconstitutional, but invalid. Differences, however, of words must not conceal from us essential similarity in things. Acts of Congress, or of the Legislative Assembly of New York or of Massachusetts, are at bottom simply by-laws, depending for their validity

[1] This is so in the United States, but it need not necessarily be so. The Federal Legislature may be a sovereign power, but may be so constituted that the rights of the States under the constitution are practically protected. This condition of things existed in the German Empire. [2] See p. 92, note 1, *ante*.

[3] See Intro. pp. lxxi, *et seq.*, *ante*, and Jennings, *The Law and the Constitution* (4th ed., 1952), pp. 145-146.

upon their being within the powers given to Congress or to the state legislatures by the constitution. The by-laws of the Great Eastern Railway Company, imposing fines upon passengers who travel over their line without a ticket, are laws, but they are laws depending for their validity upon their being within the powers conferred upon the Company by Act of Parliament, *i.e.* by the Company's constitution. Congress and the Great Eastern Railway Company are in truth each of them nothing more than subordinate law-making bodies. Their power differs not in degree, but in kind, from the authority of the sovereign Parliament of the United Kingdom.[1]

Distribution of powers.

The distribution of powers is an essential feature of federalism. The object for which a federal state is formed involves a division of authority between the national government and the separate States. The powers given to the nation form in effect so many limitations upon the authority of the separate States, and as it is not intended that the central government should have the opportunity of encroaching upon the rights retained by the States, its sphere of action necessarily becomes the object of rigorous definition. The constitution, for instance, of the United States delegates special and closely defined powers to the executive, to the legislature, and to the judiciary of the Union, or in effect to the Union itself, whilst it

[1] See as to by-laws made by municipal corporations, and the dependence of their validity upon the powers conferred upon the corporation: *Johnson* v. *The Mayor, etc. of Croydon* (1886) 16 Q.B.D. 708; *The Queen* v. *Powell* (1884) 51 L.T. 92; *Munro* v. *Watson* (1887) 57 L.T. 366; *Kruse* v. *Johnson* [1898] 2 Q.B. 91; K. & L. 38. *Powell* v. *May* [1946] K.B. 330.

Part II.

provides that the powers "not delegated to the United States by the constitution nor prohibited by it to the States are reserved to the States respectively or to the people."[1]

Division of powers carried in fact beyond necessary limit.

This is all the amount of division which is essential to a federal constitution. But the principle of definition and limitation of powers harmonises so well with the federal spirit that it is generally carried much farther than is dictated by the mere logic of the constitution. Thus the authority assigned to the United States under the constitution is not concentrated in any single official or body of officials. The President has definite rights, upon which neither Congress nor the judicial department can encroach. Congress has but a limited, indeed a very limited, power of legislation, for it can make laws upon eighteen topics only; yet within its own sphere it is independent both of the President and of the Federal Courts. So, lastly, the judiciary have their own powers. They stand on a level both with the Presi-

[1] Constitution of the United States, Amendments, art. 10. See provisions of a similar character in the Swiss constitution, *Constitution Fédérale,* art. 3; cf. the constitution of the Dominion of Canada, British North America Act, 1867, ss. 91, 92.

There exists, however, one marked distinction in principle between the constitution of the United States and the constitution of the Dominion of Canada. The constitution of the United States in substance reserves to the separate States all powers not expressly conferred upon the national Government. The Canadian constitution in substance confers upon the Dominion Government all powers not assigned exclusively to the Provinces. In this matter the Swiss constitution follows that of the United States.

The constitution of the Australian Commonwealth follows in effect the example of the constitution of the United States. The powers conferred upon the Commonwealth Parliament are, though very large, definite; the powers reserved to the Parliaments of the States are indefinite. See Commonwealth Constitution, ss. 51, 52, and 107.

dent and with Congress, and their authority (being directly derived from the constitution) cannot, without a distinct violation of law, be trenched upon either by the executive or by the legislature. Where, further, States are federally united, certain principles of policy or of justice must be enforced upon the whole confederated body as well as upon the separate parts thereof, and the very inflexibility of the constitution tempts legislators to place among constitutional articles maxims which (though not in their nature constitutional) have special claims upon respect and observance. Hence spring additional restrictions on the power both of the federation and of the separate states. The United States constitution prohibits both to Congress[1] and to the separate States[2] the passing of a bill of attainder or an *ex post facto* law, the granting of any title of nobility, or in effect the laying of any tax on articles exported from any State,[3] enjoins that full faith shall be given to the public acts and judicial proceedings of every other State, hinders any State from passing any law impairing the obligation of contracts,[4] and prevents every State from entering into any treaty, alliance, or confederation; thus it provides that the elementary principles of justice, freedom of trade, and the rights of individual property shall be absolutely respected throughout the length and breadth of the Union. It further ensures that the right of the people to keep and bear arms shall not be infringed, while it also provides that no member can be expelled from either House of Con-

[1] Constitution of the United States, art. 1, s. 9.

[2] *Ibid.*, art. 1, s. 10.

[3] *Ibid.*, art. 1, s. 9; cf. art. 1, s. 10.

[4] *Ibid.*, art. 1, s. 10.

gress without the concurrence of two-thirds of the House. Other federal constitutions go far beyond that of the United States in ascribing among constitutional articles either principles or petty rules which are supposed to have a claim of legal sanctity; the Swiss constitution is full of "guaranteed" rights.

Nothing, however, would appear to an English critic to afford so striking an example of the connection between federalism and the "limitation of powers" as the way in which the principles of the federal constitution pervade in America the constitutions of the separate States. In no case does the legislature of any one State possess all the powers of "state sovereignty" left to the States by the Constitution of the Republic, and every state legislature is subordinated to the constitution of the State.[1] The ordinary legislature of New York or Massachusetts can no more change the state constitution than it can alter the Constitution of the United States itself; and, though the topic cannot be worked out here in detail, it may safely be asserted that state government throughout the Union is formed upon the federal model, and (what is noteworthy) that state constitutions have carried much further than the Constitution of the Republic the tendency to clothe with constitutional immutability any rules which strike the people as important. Illinois has em-

[1] Contrast with this the indefinite powers left to State Parliaments under the Commonwealth of Australia Constitution, ss. 106, 107, which did not repeal the constitutions of the States. The Constitutionalists of Australia who created the Commonwealth were as much influenced by the traditions of English parliamentary sovereignty as American legislators had in their dealings with the State constitutions been influenced by the spirit of federalism.

bodied, among fundamental laws, regulations as to elevators.[1]

But here, as in other cases, there is great difficulty in distinguishing cause and effect. If a federal form of government has affected, as it probably has, the constitutions of the separate States, it is certain that features originally existing in the State constitutions have been reproduced in the constitution of the Union; and, as we shall see in a moment, the most characteristic institution of the United States, the Federal Court, appears to have been suggested at least to the founders of the Republic, by the relation which before 1789 already existed between the state tribunals and the state legislatures.[2]

Division of powers distinguishes federal from unitarian system of government.

The tendency of federalism to limit on every side the action of government and to split up the strength of the state among co-ordinate and independent authorities is specially noticeable, because it forms the essential distinction between a federal system such as that of America or Switzerland, and a unitarian system of government, such as that which

[1] See *Munn* v. *Illinois* (1887) 4 Otto, 113.

[2] European critics of American federalism have paid in general too little attention to the working and effect of the State constitutions, and have overlooked the great importance of the action of the State legislatures. See Boutmy, *Etudes de Droit constitutionnel* (2nd ed., 1888), pp. 103-111.

"It has been truly said that nearly every provision of the Federal "constitution that has worked well is one borrowed from or suggested "by some State constitution; nearly every provision that has worked "badly is one which the Convention, for want of a precedent, was "obliged to devise for itself."—Bryce, *American Commonwealth* (1910 ed.), vol. i, p. 35. One capital merit of Bryce's book was that it for the first time revealed, even to those who had already studied American institutions, the extent to which the main features of the constitution of the United States were suggested to its authors by the characteristics of the State Governments.

exists in England or Russia. We talk indeed of the English constitution as resting on a balance of powers, and as maintaining a division between the executive, the legislative, and the judicial bodies. These expressions have a real meaning. But they have quite a different significance as applied to England from the sense which they bear as applied to the United States. All the power of the English state is concentrated in the Imperial Parliament, and all departments of government are legally subject to Parliamentary despotism. Our judges are independent, in the sense of holding their office by a permanent tenure, and of being raised above the direct influence of the Crown or the Ministry; but the judicial department does not pretend to stand on a level with Parliament; its functions might be modified at any time by an Act of Parliament; and such a statute would be no violation of the law. The Federal Judiciary, on the other hand, are co-ordinate with the President and with Congress, and cannot without a revolution be deprived of a single right by President or Congress. So, again, the executive and the legislature are with us distinct bodies, but they are not distinct in the sense in which the President is distinct from and independent of the Houses of Congress. The House of Commons interferes with administrative matters, and the Ministry are in truth placed and kept in office by the House. A modern Cabinet would not hold power for a week if censured by a newly elected House of Commons. An American President may retain his post and exercise his very important functions even though his bitterest opponents command majorities both in the Senate and in the House of Representatives. Unitarianism, in short, means the concentration of the strength of the state in the hands of one visible sovereign power, be that power Parliament or Czar. Federalism means the distribution of the force of the state among a number of co-ordinate bodies each originating in and controlled by the constitution.

Authority of Courts.

Whenever there exists, as in Belgium or in France, a more or less rigid constitution, the articles of which cannot be amended by the ordinary legislature, the difficulty has to be met of guarding against legislation inconsistent with the constitution. As Belgian and French statesmen have created no machinery for the attainment of this object, we may conclude that they considered respect for the constitution to be sufficiently secured by moral or political sanctions, and treated the limitations placed on the power of Parliament rather as maxims of policy than as true laws. During a period, at any rate of more than sixty years, no Belgian judge has (it is said) ever pronounced a Parliamentary enactment unconstitutional. No French tribunal, as has been already pointed out, would hold itself at liberty to disregard an enactment, however unconstitutional, passed by the National Assembly, inserted in the *Bulletin des Lois*, and supported by the force of the government; and French statesmen may well have thought, as de Tocqueville certainly did think, that in France possible Parliamentary invasions of the constitution were a less evil than the participation of the judges in political conflicts. France, in short, and Belgium being governed under unitarian constitutions, the non-sovereign character of the legislature is in each

Part I.

case an accident, not an essential property of their polity. Under a federal system it is otherwise. The legal supremacy of the constitution is essential to the existence of the state; the glory of the founders of the United States is to have devised or adopted arrangements under which the constitution became in reality as well as name the supreme law of the land. This end they attained by adherence to a very obvious principle, and by the invention of appropriate machinery for carrying this principle into effect.

How authority of the Courts is exerted.

The principle is clearly expressed in the Constitution of the United States. "This constitution," runs article 6, "and the laws of the United States which "shall be made in pursuance thereof . . . shall be "the supreme law of the land, and the judges in "every State shall be bound thereby, anything in "the constitution or laws of any State to the con-"trary notwithstanding."[1] The import of these expressions is unmistakable. "Every Act of Con-"gress," writes Chancellor Kent, "and every Act of "the legislatures of the States, and every part of the "constitution of any State, which are repugnant to "the Constitution of the United States, are neces-"sarily void. This is a clear and settled principle "of [our] constitutional jurisprudence."[2] The legal duty therefore of every judge, whether he act as a judge of the State of New York or as a judge of the Supreme Court of the United States, is clear. He is bound to treat as void every legislative act, whether proceeding from Congress or from the state legis-

[1] Constitution of the United States, art. 6 (s. 2).

[2] Kent, *Commentaries* (12th ed., 1873), vol. i, para. 314; cf. *ibid.*, para. 449.

latures, which is inconsistent with the Constitution of the United States. His duty is as clear as that of an English judge called upon to determine the validity of a by-law made by the Great Eastern or any other Railway Company. The American judge must in giving judgment obey the terms of the constitution, just as his English brother must in giving judgment obey every Act of Parliament bearing on the case.

Supremacy of constitution secured by creation of Supreme Court.

To have laid down the principle with distinctness is much, but the great problem was how to ensure that the principle should be obeyed; for there existed a danger that judges depending on the federal government should wrest the constitution in favour of the central power, and that judges created by the States should wrest it in favour of State rights or interests. This problem has been solved by the creation of the Supreme Court and of the Federal Judiciary.

Nature and action of Supreme Court.

Of the nature and position of the Supreme Court itself thus much alone need for our present purpose be noted. The court derives its existence from the constitution, and stands therefore on an equality with the President and with Congress; the members thereof (in common with every judge of the Federal Judiciary) hold their places during good behaviour, at salaries which cannot be diminished during a judge's tenure of office.[1] The Supreme Court stands at the head of the whole federal judicial department, which, extending by its subordinate courts throughout the Union, can execute its judgments through its own officers without requiring the aid of state officials.

[1] Constitution of the United States, art. 3, ss. 1, 2.

The Supreme Court, though it has a certain amount of original jurisdiction, derives its importance from its appellate character; it is on every matter which concerns the interpretation of the constitution a supreme and final court of appeal from the decision of every court (whether a Federal court or a State court) throughout the Union. It is in fact the final interpreter of the constitution and therefore has authority to pronounce finally as a court of appeal whether a law passed either by Congress or by the legislature of a State, *e.g.* New York, is or is not constitutional. To understand the position of the Supreme Court we must bear in mind that there exist throughout the Union two classes of courts in which proceedings can be commenced, namely, the subordinate federal courts deriving their authority from the constitution, and the state courts, *e.g.* of New York or Massachusetts, created by and existing under the state constitutions; and that the jurisdiction of the federal judiciary and the state judiciary is in many cases concurrent, for though the jurisdiction of the federal courts is mainly confined to cases arising under the constitution and laws of the United States, it is also frequently dependent upon the character of the parties, and though there are cases with which no state court can deal, such a court may often entertain cases which might be brought in a federal court, and constantly has to consider the effect of the constitution on the validity either of a law passed by Congress or of state legislation. That the Supreme Court should be a court of appeal from the decision of the subordinate federal tribunals is a matter which excites no surprise. The point to be noted is that it is also a court of appeal from decisions of the Supreme Court of any State, *e.g.* New York, which turn upon or interpret the articles of the constitution or Acts of Congress. The particular cases in which a party aggrieved by the decision of a state court has a right of appeal to the Supreme Court of the United States are regulated by an Act of Congress of 24th September 1789, the twenty-fifth section of which provides that "a final "judgment or decree, in any suit in the highest court "of law or equity of a State, may be brought up on "error in point of law, to the Supreme Court of the "United States, provided the validity of a treaty, or "statute of, or authority exercised under the United "States, was drawn in question in the state court, and "the decision was against that validity; or provided "the validity of any state authority was drawn in "question, on the ground of its being repugnant to the "constitution, treaties, or laws of the United States, "and the decision was in favour of its validity; or pro-"vided the construction of any clause of the constitu-"tion or of a treaty, or statute of, or commission held "under the United States, was drawn in question, and "the decision was against the title, right, privilege, "or exemption, specially claimed under the authority "of the Union."[1] Strip this enactment of its technicalities and it comes to this. A party to a case in the highest court, say of New York, who bases his claim or defence upon an article in the constitution or law made under it, stands in this position: If judgment be in his favour there is no further appeal; if judgment goes against him, he has a right of appeal to the Supreme Court of the United States. Any

[1] Kent, *Commentaries* (12th ed., 1873), vol. i, paras. 299, 300.

Part I. lawyer can see at a glance how well devised is the arrangement to encourage state courts in the performance of their duty as guardians of the constitution, and further that the Supreme Court thereby becomes the ultimate arbiter of all matters affecting the constitution.

Let no one for a moment fancy that the right of every court, and ultimately of the Supreme Court, to pronounce on the constitutionality of legislation and on the rights possessed by different authorities under the constitution is one rarely exercised, for it is in fact a right which is constantly exerted without exciting any more surprise on the part of the citizens of the Union than does in England a judgment of the Queen's Bench Division treating as invalid the by-law of a railway company. The American tribunals have dealt with matters of supreme consequence; they have determined that Congress has the right to give priority to debts due to the United States,[1] can lawfully incorporate a bank,[2] has a general power to levy or collect taxes without any restraint, but subject to definite principles of uniformity prescribed by the constitution; the tribunals have settled what is the power of Congress over the militia, who is the person who has a right to command it,[3] and that the power exercised by Congress during the War of Secession of issuing paper money was valid.[4] The courts again have controlled the power of the separate States fully as

[1] Kent, *op. cit.*, vol. i, paras. 244-248.

[2] *Ibid.*, paras. 248-254. [3] *Ibid.*, paras. 262-266.

[4] Story, *Commentaries on the Constitution* (4th ed., 1873), vol. ii, secs. 1116, 1117.

See *Hepburn* v. *Griswold* (1870) 8 Wallace 603, and *Knox* v. *Lee* (1871) 12 Wallace 457.

vigorously as they have defined the authority of the United States. The judiciary have pronounced unconstitutional every *ex post facto* law, every law taxing even in the slightest degree articles exported from any State, and have again deprived of effect state laws impairing the obligation of contracts. To the judiciary in short are due the maintenance of justice, the existence of internal free trade, and the general respect for the rights of property; whilst a recent decision shows that the courts are prepared to uphold as consistent with the Constitution any laws which prohibit modes of using private property, which seem to the judges inconsistent with public interest.[1] The power moreover of the courts which maintains the articles of the constitution as the law of the land, and thereby keeps each authority within its proper sphere, is exerted with an ease and regularity which has astounded and perplexed continental critics. The explanation is that while the judges of the United States control the action of the constitution, they nevertheless perform purely judicial functions, since they never decide anything but the cases before them. It is natural to say that the Supreme Court pronounces Acts of Congress invalid, but in fact this is not so. The court never directly pronounces any opinion whatever upon an Act of Congress. What the court does do is simply to determine that in a given case *A* is or is not entitled to recover judgment against *X*; but in determining that case the court may decide that an Act of

[1] *Munn* v. *Illinois* (1877) 4 Otto 113. See especially the Judgments of Marshall, C.J., collected in *The Writings of John Marshall upon the Federal Constitution* (1839).

Congress is not to be taken into account, since it is an Act beyond the constitutional powers of Congress.[1]

The true merit of the founders of the United States.

If any one thinks this is a distinction without a difference he shows some ignorance of politics, and does not understand how much the authority of a court is increased by confining its action to purely judicial business. But persons who, like de Tocqueville, have fully appreciated the wisdom of the statesmen who created the Union, have formed perhaps an exaggerated estimate of their originality. Their true merit was that they applied with extraordinary skill the notions which they had inherited from English law to the novel circumstances of the new republic. To any one imbued with the traditions of English procedure it must have seemed impossible to let a court decide upon anything but the case before it. To any one who had inhabited a colony governed under a charter the effect of which on the validity of a colonial law was certainly liable to be considered by the Privy Council, there was nothing startling in empowering the judiciary to pronounce in given cases upon the constitutionality of Acts passed by assemblies whose powers were limited by the constitution, just as the authority of the colonial legislatures was limited by charter or by Act of Parliament. To a French jurist, indeed, filled with the traditions of the French Parliaments, all this might well be incomprehensible, but an English lawyer can easily see that the fathers of the republic treated Acts of Congress as English Courts treat by-laws, and in forming the Supreme Court may probably have had in mind the functions of the Privy

[1] See chap. ii, pp. 94-99, *ante*.

Chapter III.

Council. It is still more certain that they had before their eyes cases in which the tribunals of particular States had treated as unconstitutional, and therefore pronounced void, Acts of the state legislature which contravened the state constitution. The earliest case of declaring a law unconstitutional dates (it is said) from 1786, and took place in Rhode Island, which was then, and continued till 1842, to be governed under the charter of Charles II. An Act of the legislature was declared unconstitutional by the Courts of North Carolina in 1787[1] and by the Courts of Virginia in 1788,[2] whilst the constitution of the United States was not adopted till 1789, and *Marbury* v. *Madison*, the first case in which the Supreme Court dealt with the question of constitutionality, was decided in 1803.[3]

But if their notions were conceptions derived from English law, the great statesmen of America gave to old ideas a perfectly new expansion, and for the first time in the history of the world formed a constitution which should in strictness be "the law of the land," and in so doing created modern federalism. For the essential characteristics of federalism—the supremacy of the constitution—the distribution of powers—the authority of the judiciary—reappear, though no doubt with modifications, in every true federal state.

The Canadian Dominion.

Turn for a moment to the Canadian Dominion. The preamble to the British North America Act, 1867, asserts with diplomatic inaccuracy that the Provinces

[1] Martin 421. [2] 1 Virginia Cases 198.

[3] 1 Cranch 137. For the facts as to the early action of the State Courts in declaring legislative enactments unconstitutional the author was indebted, as for much other useful criticism, to his friend Professor Thayer of Harvard.

Part I. of the present Dominion have expressed their desire to be united into one Dominion "with a constitution similar in principle to that of the United *Kingdom*." If preambles were intended to express anything like the whole truth, for the word "*Kingdom*" ought to have been substituted "*States*": since it is clear that the Constitution of the Dominion is in its essential features modelled on that of the Union. This is indeed denied, but in my judgment without adequate grounds, by competent Canadian critics.[1] The differences between the institutions of the United States and of the Dominion are of course both considerable and noteworthy. But no one can study the provisions of the British North America Act, 1867, without seeing that its authors had the American Constitution constantly before their eyes, and that if Canada were an independent country it would be a Confederacy governed under a constitution very similar to that of the United States. The constitution is the law of

[1] The difference between the judgment as to the character of the Canadian constitution formed by the author and the judgment of competent and friendly Canadian critics, was summarised and explained as follows: "If we look at the federal character of the constitution of the Dominion, we must inevitably regard it as a copy, though by no means a servile copy, of the constitution of the United States. Now in the present work the Canadian constitution is regarded exclusively as a federal government. Hence my assertion, which I still hold to be correct, that the government of the Dominion is modelled on that of the Union. If, on the other hand, we compare the Canadian Executive with the American Executive, we perceive at once that Canadian government is modelled on the system of Parliamentary cabinet government as it exists in England, and does not in any wise imitate the Presidential government of America. This, it has been suggested to me by a friend well acquainted with Canadian institutions, is the point of view from which they are looked upon by my Canadian critics, and is the justification for the description of the Constitution of the Dominion given in the preamble to the British North America Act, 1867. The suggestion is a just and valuable one; in deference to it some of the expressions used in the earlier editions of this book have undergone a slight modification."

the land; it cannot be changed (except within narrow limits allowed by the British North America Act, 1867) either by the Dominion Parliament[1] or by the Provincial Parliaments;[2] it can be altered only by the sovereign power of the British Parliament. Nor does this arise from the Canadian Dominion being a dependency. New Zealand is, like Canada, a colony, but the New Zealand Parliament can with the assent of the Crown do what the Canadian Parliament cannot do—change the colonial constitution. Throughout the Dominion, therefore, the constitution is in the strictest sense the immutable law of the land. Under this law again, you have, as you would expect, the distribution of powers among bodies of co-ordinate authority;[3] though undoubtedly the powers bestowed on the Dominion Government and Parliament are greater when compared with the powers reserved to the Provinces than are the powers which the Constitution of the United States gives to the federal government. In nothing is this more noticeable than in the authority given to[4] the Dominion Government to disallow Provincial Acts.[5]

[1] See now British North America Act (No. 2), 1949, which gives the Parliament of the Dominion authority to amend the constitution. There are excluded from the new power matters which by s. 92 of the British North America Act, 1867, are within the exclusive authority of the provincial legislature, the statutory rights and privileges of provincial governments, certain matters affecting schools and the use of the English or the French languages and the requirement of annual sessions and the maximum duration of the life of the Dominion Parliament. These matters still can only be changed by an Act enacted at Westminster.

[2] The legislatures of each Province have, nevertheless, authority to make laws for "the amendment from time to time, notwithstanding "anything" [in the British North America Act, 1867] "of the "Constitution of the Province, except as regards the office of Lieutenant "Governor." See British North America Act, 1867, s. 92.

[3] British North America Act, 1867, ss. 91, 92. [4] *Ibid.*, ss. 56, 90.

[5] Bourinot, *Parliamentary Procedure and Practice in the Dominion of Canada* (1st ed., 1884), p. 76.

Part I.

This right was possibly given with a view to obviate altogether the necessity for invoking the law courts as interpreters of the constitution; the founders of the Confederation appear in fact to have believed that "the care taken to define the respective "powers of the several legislative bodies in the "Dominion would prevent any troublesome or danger-"ous conflict of authority arising between the central "and local governments."[1] The futility, however, of a hope grounded on a misconception of the nature of federalism is proved by the existence of two thick volumes of reports filled with cases on the constitutionality of legislative enactments, and by a long list of decisions as to the respective powers possessed by the Dominion and by the Provincial Parliaments—judgments given by the true Supreme Court of the Dominion, namely, the Judicial Committee of the Privy Council. In Canada, as in the United States, the courts inevitably become the interpreters of the constitution.[2]

The Swiss Confederation.

Swiss federalism repeats, though with noteworthy variations, the essential traits of the federal polity as it exists across the Atlantic.[3] The constitution is the law of the land, and cannot be changed either by the federal or by the cantonal legislative bodies;[4] the constitution enforces a distribution of the powers be-

[1] Bourinot, *op. cit.*, p. 694.

[2] For the Canadian Constitution, see W. P. M. Kennedy, *The Constitution of Canada*, 1534–1937 (1938); R. M. Dawson, *The Government of Canada* (2nd ed., 1956).—Ed.

[3] For the Swiss Constitution, see C. Hughes, *The Federal Constitution of Switzerland*, 1954.

[4] This needs qualification. The Federal Assembly has power to change the constitution, subject to the approval of the electors and a majority of the Cantons (*Constitution Fédérale*, Arts. 85 (14), and 123). In practice the Federal Legislative Assembly plays an important part.—Ed.

tween the national government and the Cantons, and directly or indirectly defines and limits the power of every authority existing under it. The Common Government has in Switzerland, as in America, three organs—a Federal Legislature, a Federal Executive (*Bundesrath*), and a Federal Court (*Bundesgericht*).

Of the many interesting and instructive peculiarities which give to Swiss federalism an individual character, this is not the occasion to write in detail. It lies, however, within the scope of this chapter to note that the Constitution of the Confederation differs in two most important respects from that of the United States. It does not, in the first place, establish anything like the accurate division between the executive and the judicial departments of government which exists both in America and in Canada; the Executive exercises, under the head of "administrative law," some functions[1] of a judicial character, and thus, for example, till 1893 dealt in effect with questions[2] having reference to the rights of religious bodies. The Federal Assembly is the final arbiter on all questions as to the respective jurisdiction of the Executive and of the Federal Court. The judges of that court are elected by the Federal Assembly, they are occupied greatly with questions of public law (*Staatsrecht*), and so experienced a statesman as Dr. Dubs laments that the Federal Court should possess jurisdiction in matters of private law.[3] When to this it is added that the judgments of

[1] See for example, p. 610, note, *post*.

[2] The decision thereof belonged till 1893 to the Assembly, guided by the Federal Council; it now belongs to the Federal Court. See Dubs, *Das öffentliche Recht*, ii (2nd ed.), pp. 92-95; Lowell, *Governments and Parties in Continental Europe* (1896), vol. ii, pp. 217, 218.

[3] *Constitution Fédérale*, art. 113.

Part I. the Federal Court are executed by the Government, it at once becomes clear that, according to any English standard, Swiss statesmanship has failed as distinctly as American statesmanship has succeeded in keeping the judicial apart from the executive department of government, and that this failure constitutes a serious flaw in the Swiss Constitution. That constitution, in the second place, does not in reality place the Federal Court on an absolute level with the Federal Assembly. That tribunal cannot question the constitutionality of laws or decrees passed by the Federal Parliament.[1] From this fact one might suppose that the Federal Assembly is (unlike Congress) a sovereign body, but this is not so. The reason why all Acts of the Assembly must be treated as constitutional by the Federal Tribunal is that the constitution itself almost precludes the possibility of encroachment upon its articles by the federal legislative body. No legal revision can take place without the assent both of a majority of Swiss citizens and of a majority of the Cantons, and an ordinary law duly passed by the Federal Assembly may be legally annulled by a popular veto. The authority of the Swiss Assembly nominally exceeds the authority of Congress, because in reality the Swiss legislative body is weaker than Congress. For while in each case there lies in the background a legislative sovereign capable of controlling the action of the ordinary legislature, the sovereign power is far more easily brought into play in Switzerland than in America.

[1] *Constitution Fédérale*, art. 113; and Dubs, *op. cit.*, ii (2nd ed.), pp. 92-95. The reason is that all such laws have the tacit consent of the majority. If not, a referendum would be demanded to change them.

When the sovereign power can easily enforce its will, it may trust to its own action for maintaining its rights; when, as in America, the same power acts but rarely and with difficulty, the courts naturally become the guardians of the sovereign's will expressed in the articles of the constitution.

Comparison between system of federalism and of parliamentary sovereignty.

Our survey from a legal point of view of the characteristics common to all federal governments forcibly suggests conclusions of more than merely legal interest, as to the comparative merits of federal government, and the system of Parliamentary sovereignty.

Weakness of federalism.

Federal government means weak government.[1]

The distribution of all the powers of the state among co-ordinate authorities necessarily leads to the

[1] This weakness springs from two different causes: first, the division of powers between the central Government and the States; secondly, the distribution of powers between the different members (*e.g.* the President and the Senate) of the national Government. The first cause of weakness is inherent in the federal system; the second cause of weakness is not (logically at least) inherent in federalism. Under a federal constitution the whole authority of the national Government might conceivably be lodged in one person or body, but we may feel almost certain that in practice the fears entertained by the separate States of encroachments by the central Government on their State rights will prohibit such a concentration of authority.

The statement that federal government means weak government should be qualified or balanced by the consideration that a federal system sometimes makes it possible for different communities to be united as one State when they otherwise could not be united at all. The bond of federal union may be weak, but it may be the strongest bond which circumstances allow.

The failure and the calamities of the Helvetic Republic are a warning against the attempt to force upon more or less independent states a greater degree of political unity than they will tolerate. [The view expressed in the last paragraph would appear to be true of the United States; it is not, according to Swiss lawyers, any longer true that in Switzerland federation means weak government.—Ed.]

result that no one authority can wield the same amount of power as under a unitarian constitution is possessed by the sovereign. A scheme again of checks and balances in which the strength of the common government is so to speak pitted against that of the state governments leads, on the face of it, to a certain waste of energy. A federation therefore will always be at a disadvantage in a contest with unitarian states of equal resources. Nor does the experience either of the United States or of the Swiss confederation invalidate this conclusion. The Union is threatened by no powerful neighbours and needs no foreign policy.[1] Circumstances unconnected with constitutional arrangements enable Switzerland to preserve her separate existence, though surrounded by powerful and at times hostile nations. The mutual jealousies moreover incident to federalism do visibly weaken the Swiss Republic. Thus, to take one example only, each member of the Executive must belong to a different canton.[2] But this rule may exclude from the government statesmen of high merit, and therefore diminish the resources of the state. A rule that each member of the Cabinet should be the native of a different county would appear to Englishmen palpably absurd. Yet this absurdity is forced upon Swiss politicians, and affords one among numerous instances in which the efficiency of the public service is sacrificed to the requirements of federal sentiment. Switzerland, moreover, is governed under a form of democratic federalism which tends towards

[1] The latter part of this statement was perhaps less true in 1908 than it was in 1885.

[2] *Constitution Fédérale*, art. 96.

unitarianism. Each revision increases the authority of the nation at the expense of cantonal independence. This is no doubt in part due to the desire to strengthen the nation against foreign attack. It is perhaps also due to another circumstance. Federalism, as it defines, and therefore limits, the powers of each department of the administration, is unfavourable to the interference or to the activity of government. Hence a federal government can hardly render services to the nation by undertaking for the national benefit functions which may be performed by individuals. This may be a merit of the federal system ; it is, however, a merit which does not commend itself to modern democrats, and no more curious instance can be found of the inconsistent currents of popular opinion which may at the same time pervade a nation or a generation than the coincidence in England of a vague admiration for federalism alongside with a far more decided feeling against the doctrines of so-called *laissez faire*. A system meant to maintain the *status quo* in politics is incompatible with schemes for wide social innovation.

Conservatism of federalism.

Federalism tends to produce conservatism.

This tendency is due to several causes. The constitution of a Federal state must, as we have seen, generally be not only a written but a rigid constitution, that is, a constitution which cannot be changed by any ordinary process of legislation. Now this essential rigidity of federal institutions is almost certain to impress on the minds of citizens the idea that any provision included in the constitution is immutable and, so to speak, sacred. The least observation of American politics shows how deeply the notion

Part I. that the constitution is something placed beyond the reach of amendment has impressed popular imagination. The difficulty of altering the constitution produces conservative sentiment, and national conservatism doubles the difficulty of altering the constitution. The House of Lords has lasted for centuries; the American Senate has now existed for more than one hundred years, yet to abolish or alter the House of Lords might turn out to be an easier matter than to modify the constitution of the Senate.[1] To this one must add that a federal constitution always lays down general principles which, from being placed in the constitution, gradually come to command a superstitious reverence, and thus are in fact, though not in theory, protected from change or criticism. The principle that legislation ought not to impair obligation of contracts has governed the whole course of American opinion. Of the conservative effect of such a maxim when forming an article of the constitution we may form some measure by the following reflection. If any principle of the like kind had been recognised in England as legally binding on the courts, the Irish Land Act would have been unconstitutional and void; the Irish Church Act, 1869, would, in great part at least, have been from a legal point of view so much waste paper, and there would have been great difficulty in legislating in the way in which the English Parliament has legislated for the reform of the Universities. One maxim only among those embodied in the Constitution of the United States would, that is to say, have been sufficient if adopted in England to have arrested the most vigorous efforts of recent Parliamentary legislation.

[1] See, however, note 2, p. 149, *ante*.

Chapter III.

Legal spirit of federalism.

Federalism, lastly, means legalism—the predominance of the judiciary in the constitution—the prevalence of a spirit of legality among the people.

That in a confederation like the United States the courts become the pivot on which the constitutional arrangements of the country turn is obvious. Sovereignty is lodged in a body which rarely exerts its authority and has (so to speak) only a potential existence; no legislature throughout the land is more than a subordinate law-making body capable in strictness of enacting nothing but by-laws; the powers of the executive are again limited by the constitution; the interpreters of the constitution are the judges. The Bench therefore can and must determine the limits to the authority both of the government and of the legislature; its decision is without appeal; the consequence follows that the Bench of judges is not only the guardian but also at a given moment the master of the constitution.[1] Nothing puts in a

[1] The expression "master of the constitution" has been criticised on the ground of exaggeration (Sidgwick, *Elements of Politics* (1897), p. 616). The expression, however, though undoubtedly strong, is, it is submitted, justifiable, if properly understood. It is true, as Sidgwick well pointed out, that the action of the Supreme Court is restrained, first, by the liability of the judges to impeachment for misconduct, and, secondly, by the fear of provoking disorder. And to these restraints a third and more efficient check must be added. The numbers of the court may be increased by Congress, and its decision in a given case has not even in theory that force as a decisive precedent which is attributable to a decision of the House of Lords; hence if the Supreme Court were to pronounce judgments which ran permanently counter to the opinion of the party which controlled the government of the Union, its action could be altered by adding to the Court lawyers who shared the convictions of the ruling party. (See Davis, *American Constitutions; the Relations of the Three Departments as adjusted by a Century* (1885), pp. 52-54). It would be idle therefore to maintain, what certainly cannot be asserted with truth, that the Supreme Court is the sovereign of the United States. It is, however, true that at any given moment the court may, on a case coming before it, pronounce a judgment which determines the working of the con-

Part I.

stronger light the inevitable connection between federalism and the prominent position of the judicial body than the history of modern Switzerland. The statesmen of 1848 desired to give the *Bundesgericht* a far less authoritative position than is possessed by the American Supreme Court. They in effect made the Federal Assembly for most, what it still is for some, purposes, a final Court of Appeal. But the necessities of the case were too strong for Swiss statesmanship; the revision of 1874 greatly increased the power of the Federal Tribunal.

Dangers arising from position of judiciary.

From the fact that the judicial Bench supports under federal institutions the whole stress of the constitution, a special danger arises lest the judiciary should be unequal to the burden laid upon them. In no country has greater skill been expended on constituting an august and impressive national tribunal than in the United States. Moreover, as already

stitution. The decision in the *Dred Scott Case* for example, and still more the judicial opinions delivered in deciding the case, had a distinct influence on the interpretation of the constitution both by slave-owners and by Abolitionists. In terming the court the "master of the constitution" it was not intended to suggest the exercise by it of irregular or revolutionary powers. No doubt, again, the Supreme Court may be influenced in delivering its judgments by fear of provoking violence. This apprehension is admittedly a limit to the full exercise of its theoretical powers by the most absolute of despots. It was never intended to assert that the Supreme Court, which is certainly not the sovereign of the United States, was in the exercise of its functions free from restraints which limit the authority of even a sovereign power. It must further be noted, in considering how far the Supreme Court could in fact exert all the authority theoretically vested in it, that it is hardly conceivable that the opinions of the court as to, say, the constitutional limits to the authority of Congress should not be shared by a large number of American citizens. Whenever in short the court differed in its view of the constitution from that adopted by the President or the Congress, the Court, it is probable, could rely on a large amount of popular support.

pointed out, the guardianship of the constitution is in America confided not only to the Supreme Court but to every judge throughout the land. Still it is manifest that even the Supreme Court can hardly support the duties imposed upon it. No one can doubt that the varying decisions given in the legal-tender cases, or in the line of recent judgments of which *Munn* v. *Illinois*[1] is a specimen, show that the most honest judges are after all only honest men, and when set to determine matters of policy and statesmanship will necessarily be swayed by political feeling and by reasons of state. But the moment that this bias becomes obvious a court loses its moral authority, and decisions which might be justified on grounds of policy excite natural indignation and suspicion when they are seen not to be fully justified on grounds of law. American critics indeed are to be found who allege that the Supreme Court not only is proving but always has proved too weak for the burden it is called upon to bear, and that it has from the first been powerless whenever it came into conflict with a State, or could not count upon the support of the Federal Executive. These allegations undoubtedly hit a weak spot in the constitution of the great tribunal. Its judgments are without force, at any rate as against a State if the President refuses the means of putting them into execution. "John Marshall," said President Jackson, according to a current story,[2] "has delivered his judgment; let him now enforce it, if he can"; and the judgment

[1] (1877) 4 Otto 113.

[2] See Sumner, *Andrew Jackson* (1882: American Statesmen Series), p. 182.

Part I. was never put into force. But the weight of criticisms repeated from the earliest days of the Union may easily be exaggerated.[1] Laymen are apt to mistake the growth of judicial caution for a sign of judicial weakness. Foreign observers, moreover, should notice that in a federation the causes which bring a body such as the Supreme Court into existence, also supply it with a source of ultimate power. The Supreme Court and institutions like it are the protectors of the federal compact, and the validity of that compact is, in the long run, the guarantee for the rights of the separate States. It is the interest of every man who wishes the federal constitution to be observed, that the judgments of the federal tribunals should be respected. It is therefore no bold assumption that, as long as the people of the United States wish to keep up the balanced system of federalism, they will ultimately compel the central government to support the authority of the federal court. Critics of the court are almost driven to assert that the American people are indifferent to State Rights. The assertion may or may not be true; it is a matter on which no English critic should speak with confidence. But censures on the working of a federal court tell very little against such an institution if they establish nothing more than the almost self-evident proposition that a federal tribunal will be ineffective and superfluous when the United States shall have ceased to be in reality a federation.

[1] See Davis, *American Constitutions; the Relations of the Three Departments as adjusted by a Century* (1885), pp. 55-57. Davis is distinctly of opinion that the power of the courts both of the United States and of the separate States has increased steadily since the foundation of the Union.

A federal court has no proper place in a unitarian Republic.

Judges, further, must be appointed by some authority which is not judicial, and where decisions of a court control the action of government there exists an irresistible temptation to appoint magistrates who agree (honestly it may be) with the views of the executive. A strong argument pressed against Mr. Blaine's election was, that he would have the opportunity as President of nominating four judges, and that a politician allied with railway companies was likely to pack the Supreme Court with men certain to wrest the law in favour of mercantile corporations. The accusation may have been baseless; the fact that it should have been made, and that even "Republicans" should declare that the time had come when "Democrats" should no longer be excluded from the Bench of the United States, tells plainly enough of the special evils which must be weighed against the undoubted benefits of making the courts rather than the legislature the arbiters of the constitution.

Federalism impossible where a legal spirit does not prevail.

That a federal system again can flourish only among communities imbued with a legal spirit and trained to reverence the law is as certain as can be any conclusion of political speculation. Federalism substitutes litigation for legislation, and none but a law-fearing people will be inclined to regard the decision of a suit as equivalent to the enactment of a law. The main reason why the United States has carried out the federal system with unequalled success is that the people of the Union are more thoroughly imbued with legal ideas than any other existing nation. Constitutional questions arising out of either the constitutions of the separate States or the articles of the federal constitution are of daily occurrence and constantly occupy the courts. Hence the citizens become a people of constitutionalists, and matters which excite the strongest popular feeling, as, for instance, the right of Chinese to settle in the country, are determined by the judicial Bench, and the decision of the Bench is acquiesced in by the people. This acquiescence or submission is due to the Americans inheriting the legal notions of the common law, *i.e.* of the "most legal system of law" (if the expression may be allowed) in the world. Tocqueville long ago remarked that the Swiss fell far short of the Americans in reverence for law and justice.[1] The events of the last sixty years suggest that he perhaps underrated Swiss submission to law. But the law to which Switzerland is accustomed recognises wide discretionary power on the part of the executive, and has never fully severed the functions of the judge from those of the government. Hence Swiss federalism fails, just where one would expect it to fail, in maintaining that complete authority of the courts which is necessary to the perfect federal system. But the Swiss, though they may not equal the Americans in reverence for judicial decisions, are a law-respecting nation. One may well doubt whether there are many states to be found where the mass of the people would leave so much political influence to the courts. Yet any nation who cannot acquiesce in the finality of possibly mistaken judgments is hardly fit to form part of a federal state.

[1] See passage cited, pp. 184-187, *post*.

PART II

THE RULE OF LAW

CHAPTER IV

THE RULE OF LAW: ITS NATURE AND GENERAL APPLICATIONS[1]

Chapter IV.

The Rule of Law.

Two features have at all times since the Norman Conquest characterised the political institutions of England.

The first of these features is the omnipotence or undisputed supremacy throughout the whole country of the central government. This authority of the state or the nation was during the earlier periods of our history represented by the power of the Crown. The King was the source of law and the maintainer of order. The maxim of the courts, *tout fuit in luy et vient de lui al commencement*,[2] was originally the expression of an actual and undoubted fact. This royal supremacy has now passed into that sovereignty of Parliament which has formed the main subject of the foregoing chapters.[3]

[1] Sir Ivor Jennings has been a most formidable critic of Dicey and in particular of this Part. See especially *The Law and the Constitution* (4th ed., 1952), ch. i, ii, vi, and App. ii, and the article, *In Praise of Dicey*, in *Public Administration*, vol. xi, No. 2 (April, 1935).—Ed.

[2] Year Books, xxiv Edward III, cited Gneist, *Englische Verwaltungsrecht* (1867), vol. i, p. 454.

[3] See Part i, *ante*.

Part II.

The second of these features, which is closely connected with the first, is the rule or supremacy of law. This peculiarity of our polity is well expressed in the old saw of the courts, "*La ley est le plus haute "inheritance, que le roy ad; car par la ley il même "et toutes ses sujets sont rulés, et si la ley ne fuit, "nul roi, et nul inheritance sera.*"[1]

This supremacy of the law, or the security given under the English constitution to the rights of individuals looked at from various points of view, forms the subject of this part of this treatise.

The rule of law in England noticed by foreign observers.

Foreign observers of English manners, such for example as Voltaire, De Lolme, de Tocqueville, or Gneist, have been far more struck than have Englishmen themselves with the fact that England is a country governed, as is scarcely any other part of Europe, under the rule of law; and admiration or astonishment at the legality of English habits and feeling is nowhere better expressed than in a curious passage from de Tocqueville's writings, which compares the Switzerland and the England of 1836 in respect of the spirit which pervades their laws and manners.

de Tocqueville on the want of respect for law in Switzerland and contrast with England.

"I am not about," he writes, "to compare Switzer-"land[2] with the United States, but with Great Britain. "When you examine the two countries, or even if you "only pass through them, you perceive, in my judg-"ment, the most astonishing differences between "them. Take it all in all, England seems to be "much more republican than the Helvetic Republic.

[1] Year Books, xix. Henry VI, cited Gneist, *op. cit.*, vol. i, p. 455.

[2] Many of de Tocqueville's remarks were not applicable to the Switzerland of 1908; they refer to a period before the creation in 1848 of the Swiss Federal Constitution.—Ed.

"The principal differences are found in the institu-
"tions of the two countries, and especially in their
"customs (*mœurs*).

"1. In almost all the Swiss Cantons liberty of the "press is a very recent thing.

"2. In almost all of them individual liberty is by "no means completely guaranteed, and a man may "be arrested administratively and detained in prison "without much formality.

"3. The courts have not, generally speaking, a "perfectly independent position.

"4. In all the Cantons trial by jury is unknown.

"5. In several Cantons the people were thirty-"eight years ago entirely without political rights. "Aargau, Thurgau, Tessin, Vaud, and parts of the "Cantons of Zurich and Berne were in this condition.

"The preceding observations apply even more "strongly to customs than to institutions.

"i. In many of the Swiss Cantons the majority of "the citizens are quite without taste or desire for *self-"government*, and have not acquired the habit of it. "In any crisis they interest themselves about their "affairs, but you never see in them the thirst for "political rights and the craving to take part in "public affairs which seem to torment Englishmen "throughout their lives.

"ii. The Swiss abuse the liberty of the press on "account of its being a recent form of liberty, and "Swiss newspapers are much more *revolutionary* and "much less *practical* than English newspapers.

"iii. The Swiss seem still to look upon associa-"tions from much the same point of view as the "French, that is to say, they consider them as a

Part II.

"means of revolution, and not as a slow and sure "method for obtaining redress of wrongs. The art of "associating and of making use of the right of asso- "ciation is but little understood in Switzerland.

"iv. The Swiss do not show the love of justice "which is such a strong characteristic of the English. "Their courts have no place in the political arrange- "ments of the country, and exert no influence on "public opinion. The love of justice, the peaceful "and legal introduction of the judge into the domain "of politics, are perhaps the most standing character- "istics of a free people.

"v. Finally, and this really embraces all the rest, "the Swiss do not show at bottom that respect for "justice, that love of law, that dislike of using force, "without which no free nation can exist, which strikes "strangers so forcibly in England.

"I sum up these impressions in a few words.

"Whoever travels in the United States is involun- "tarily and instinctively so impressed with the fact "that the spirit of liberty and the taste for it have "pervaded all the habits of the American people, that "he cannot conceive of them under any but a Repub- "lican government. In the same way it is impossible "to think of the English as living under any but a "free government. But if violence were to destroy the "Republican institutions in most of the Swiss Cantons, "it would be by no means certain that after rather a "short state of transition the people would not grow "accustomed to the loss of liberty. In the United "States and in England there seems to be more liberty "in the customs than in the laws of the people. In "Switzerland there seems to be more liberty in the "laws than in the customs of the country."[1]

Bearing of de Tocqueville's remarks on meaning of rule of law.

de Tocqueville's language has a twofold bearing on our present topic. His words point in the clearest manner to the rule, predominance, or supremacy of law as the distinguishing characteristic of English institutions. They further direct attention to the extreme vagueness of a trait of national character which is as noticeable as it is hard to portray. de Tocqueville, we see, is clearly perplexed how to define a feature of English manners of which he at once recognises the existence; he mingles or confuses together the habit of self-government, the love of order, the respect for justice and a legal turn of mind. All these sentiments are intimately allied, but they cannot without confusion be identified with each other. If, however, a critic as acute as de Tocqueville found a difficulty in describing one of the most marked peculiarities of English life, we may safely conclude that we ourselves, whenever we talk of Englishmen as loving the government of law, or of the supremacy of law as being a characteristic of the English constitution, are using words which, though they possess a real significance, are nevertheless to most persons who employ them full of vagueness and ambiguity. If therefore we are ever to appreciate the full import of the idea denoted by the term "rule, supremacy, or predominance of law," we must first determine precisely what we mean by such expressions when we apply them to the British constitution.

Three meanings of rule of law.

When we say that the supremacy or the rule of law is a characteristic of the English constitution, we

[1] See de Tocqueville, *Œuvres complètes* (14th ed., 1864), vol. viii (Mélanges historiques), pp. 455-457.

Part II.

generally include under one expression at least three distinct though kindred conceptions.

Absence of arbitrary power on part of the government.

We mean, in the first place, that no man is punishable or can be lawfully made to suffer in body or goods except for a distinct breach of law established in the ordinary legal manner before the ordinary courts of the land. In this sense the rule of law is contrasted with every system of government based on the exercise by persons in authority of wide, arbitrary, or discretionary powers of constraint.

Contrast between England and the Continent at present day.

Modern Englishmen may at first feel some surprise that the "rule of law" (in the sense in which we are now using the term) should be considered as in any way a peculiarity of English institutions, since, at the present day, it may seem to be not so much the property of any one nation as a trait common to every civilised and orderly state. Yet, even if we confine our observation to the existing condition of Europe, we shall soon be convinced that the "rule of law" even in this narrow sense is peculiar to England, or to those countries which, like the United States of America, have inherited English traditions. In almost every continental community the executive exercises far wider discretionary authority in the matter of arrest, of temporary imprisonment, of expulsion from its territory, and the like, than is either legally claimed or in fact exerted by the government in England; and a study of European politics now and again reminds English readers that wherever there is discretion there is room for arbitrariness, and that in a republic no less than under a monarchy discretionary authority on the part of the government must mean insecurity for legal freedom on the part of its subjects.

Chapter IV.

Contrast between England and Continent during eighteenth century.

If, however, we confined our observation to the Europe of to-day (1908), we might well say that in most European countries the rule of law is now nearly as well established as in England, and that private individuals at any rate who do not meddle in politics have little to fear, as long as they keep the law, either from the Government or from any one else; and we might therefore feel some difficulty in understanding how it ever happened that to foreigners the absence of arbitrary power on the part of the Crown, of the executive, and of every other authority in England, has always seemed a striking feature, we might almost say the essential characteristic, of the English constitution.[1]

Our perplexity is entirely removed by carrying back our minds to the time when the English constitution began to be criticised and admired by foreign thinkers. During the eighteenth century many of the continental governments were far from oppressive, but there was no continental country where men were secure from arbitrary power. The singularity of England was not so much the goodness or the leniency as the legality of the English system of government. When Voltaire came to England—and Voltaire represented the feeling of his age—his predominant sentiment clearly was that he had passed out of the realm of despotism to a land where the laws might be harsh, but where men were ruled by law and not by

[1] "La liberté est le droit de faire tout ce que les lois permettent; "et si un citoyen pouvoit faire ce qu'elles défendent, il n'auroit plus de "liberté, parce que les autres auroient tout de même ce pouvoir."—Montesquieu, *De l'esprit des lois* (1845), bk. xi, ch. iii.

"Il y a aussi une nation dans le monde qui a pour objet direct de "sa constitution la liberté politique."—*Ibid.* ch. v. The English are this nation.

Part II.

caprice.[1] He had good reason to know the difference. In 1717 Voltaire was sent to the Bastille for a poem which he had not written, of which he did not know the author, and with the sentiment of which he did not agree. What adds to the oddity, in English eyes, of the whole transaction is that the Regent treated the affair as a sort of joke, and, so to speak, "chaffed" the supposed author of the satire "*I have seen*" on being about to pay a visit to a prison which he "had not seen."[2] In 1725 Voltaire, then the literary hero of his country, was lured off from the table of a Duke, and was thrashed by lackeys in the presence of their noble master; he was unable to obtain either legal or honourable redress, and because he complained of this outrage, paid a second visit to the Bastille. This indeed was the last time in which he was lodged within the walls of a French gaol, but his whole life was a series of contests with arbitrary power, and nothing but his fame, his deftness, his infinite resource, and ultimately his wealth, saved him from penalties far more severe than temporary imprisonment. Moreover, the price at which Voltaire saved his property and his life was after all exile from France. Whoever wants to see how exceptional a phenomenon was that supremacy of law which existed in England during

[1] "Les circonstances qui contraignaient Voltaire à chercher un "refuge chez nos voisins devaient lui inspirer une grande sympathie "pour des institutions où il n'y avait nulle place à l'arbitraire. 'La "raison est libre ici et n'y connaît point de contrainte.' On y respire "un air plus généreux, l'on se sent au milieu de citoyens qui n'ont pas "tort de porter le front haut, de marcher fièrement, sûrs qu'on n'eût pu "toucher à un seul cheveu de leur tête, et n'ayant à redoubter ni lettres "de cachet, ni captivité immotivée."—Desnoiresterres, *Voltaire et la Société au XVIII*[ième] *Siècle* (2nd ed., vol. i, 1871), p. 365.

[2] Desnoiresterres, *Voltaire et la Société au XVIII*[ième] *Siècle* (2nd ed., vol. i), pp. 344-364.

the eighteenth century should read such a book as Morley's *Life of Diderot*. The effort lasting for twenty-two years to get the *Encyclopédie* published was a struggle on the part of all the distinguished literary men in France to obtain utterance for their thoughts. It is hard to say whether the difficulties or the success of the contest bear the strongest witness to the wayward arbitrariness of the French Government.

Royal lawlessness was not peculiar to specially detestable monarchs such as Louis the Fifteenth: it was inherent in the French system of administration. An idea prevails that Louis the Sixteenth at least was not an arbitrary, as he assuredly was not a cruel ruler. But it is an error to suppose that up to 1789 anything like the supremacy of law existed under the French monarchy. The folly, the grievances, and the mystery of the Chevalier D'Eon made as much noise little more than a century ago as the imposture of the Claimant in our own day. The memory of these things is not in itself worth reviving. What does deserve to be kept in remembrance is that in 1778, in the days of Johnson, of Adam Smith, of Gibbon, of Cowper, of Burke, and of Mansfield, during the continuance of the American war and within eleven years of the assembling of the States General, a brave officer and a distinguished diplomatist could for some offence still unknown, without trial and without conviction, be condemned to undergo a penance and disgrace which could hardly be rivalled by the fanciful caprice of the torments inflicted by Oriental despotism.[1]

[1] It is worth notice that even after the meeting of the States General the King was apparently reluctant to give up altogether the powers exercised by *lettres de cachet*. See "Déclaration des intentions du Roi," art. 15, Plouard, *Les Constitutions françaises* (1871–1876), p. 10.

Nor let it be imagined that during the latter part of the eighteenth century the government of France was more arbitrary than that of other countries. To entertain such a supposition is to misconceive utterly the condition of the continent. In France, law and public opinion counted for a great deal more than in Spain, in the petty States of Italy, or in the Principalities of Germany. All the evils of despotism which attracted the notice of the world in a great kingdom such as France existed under worse forms in countries where, just because the evil was so much greater, it attracted the less attention. The power of the French monarch was criticised more severely than the lawlessness of a score of petty tyrants, not because the French King ruled more despotically than other crowned heads, but because the French people appeared from the eminence of the nation to have a special claim to freedom, and because the ancient kingdom of France was the typical representative of despotism. This explains the thrill of enthusiasm with which all Europe greeted the fall of the Bastille. When the fortress was taken, there were not ten prisoners within its walls; at that very moment hundreds of debtors languished in English gaols. Yet all England hailed the triumph of the French populace with a fervour which to Englishmen of the twentieth century is at first sight hardly comprehensible. Reflection makes clear enough the cause of a feeling which spread through the length and breadth of the civilised world. The Bastille was the outward and visible sign of lawless power. Its fall was felt, and felt truly, to herald in for the rest of Europe that rule of law which already existed in England.[1]

Chapter IV.

Every man subject to ordinary law administered by ordinary tribunals.

We mean in the second place,[2] when we speak of the "rule of law" as a characteristic of our country, not only that with us no man is above the law, but (what is a different thing) that here every man, whatever be his rank or condition, is subject to the ordinary law of the realm and amenable to the jurisdiction of the ordinary tribunals.

In England the idea of legal equality, or of the universal subjection of all classes to one law administered by the ordinary courts, has been pushed to its utmost limit. With us every official, from the Prime Minister down to a constable or a collector of taxes, is under the same responsibility for every act done without legal justification as any other citizen. The Reports abound with cases in which officials have been brought before the courts, and made, in their personal capacity, liable to punishment, or to the payment of damages, for acts done in their official character but in excess of their lawful authority. A colonial governor,[3] a secretary of state,[4] a military

[1] For English sentiment with reference to the servitude of the French, see Goldsmith, *The Citizen of the World*, Letter iv; and see *ibid.*, Letter xxxviii, for a contrast between the execution of Lord Ferrers and the impunity with which a French nobleman was allowed to commit murder because of his relationship to the Royal family; and for the general state of feeling throughout Europe, de Tocqueville, *Œuvres complètes* (14th ed., 1864), vol. viii (Mélanges historiques), pp. 57-72. The idea of the rule of law in this sense implies, or is at any rate closely connected with, the absence of any dispensing power on the part either of the Crown or its servants. See Bill of Rights, Preamble 1 (Stubbs, *Select Charters* (8th ed., 1900), p. 523; cf. *Miller* v. *Knox* (1838) 6 Scott, 1; *Attorney-General* v. *Kissane* (1893) 32 L.R. Ir. 220.

[2] For first meaning see p. 188, *ante*.

[3] *Mostyn* v. *Fabrigas* (1774) 1 Cowp. 161; *Musgrave* v. *Pulido* (1879) 5 App. Cas. 102; *Governor Wall's Case* (1802) 28 St. Tr. 51.

[4] *Entick* v. *Carrington* (1765) 19 St. Tr. 1030; K. & L. 174.

Part II.

officer,[1] and all subordinates, though carrying out the commands of their official superiors, are as responsible for any act which the law does not authorise as is any private and unofficial person. Officials, such for example as soldiers [2] or clergyman of the Established Church, are, it is true, in England as elsewhere, subject to laws which do not affect the rest of the nation, and are in some instances amenable to tribunals which have no jurisdiction over their fellow-countrymen; officials, that is to say, are to a certain extent governed under what may be termed official law. But this fact is in no way inconsistent with the principle that all men are in England subject to the law of the realm; for though a soldier or a clergyman incurs from his position legal liabilities from which other men are exempt, he does not (speaking generally) escape thereby from the duties of an ordinary citizen.

Contrast in this respect between England and France.

An Englishman naturally imagines that the rule of law (in the sense in which we are now using the term) is a trait common to all civilised societies. But this supposition is erroneous. Most European nations had indeed, by the end of the eighteenth century, passed through that stage of development (from which England emerged before the end of the sixteenth century) when nobles, priests, and others could defy the law. But it is even now far from universally true that in continental countries all persons are subject to one and the same law, or that the courts are supreme throughout the state. If we take

[1] *Phillips* v. *Eyre* (1867) L.R. 4 Q.B. 225; K. & L. 492.

[2] As to the legal position of soldiers, see ch. viii and ix.

Chapter IV.

General rules of constitutional law are result of ordinary law of the land.

France as the type of a continental state, we may assert, with substantial accuracy, that officials—under which word should be included all persons employed in the service of the state—are, or have been,[1] in their official capacity, to some extent exempted from the ordinary law of the land, protected from the jurisdiction of the ordinary tribunals, and subject in certain respects only to official law administered by official bodies.[2]

There remains yet a third and a different sense in which the "rule of law" or the predominance of the legal spirit may be described as a special attribute of English institutions. We may say that the constitution is pervaded by the rule of law on the ground that the general principles of the constitution (as for example the right to personal liberty, or the right of public meeting) are with us the result of judicial decisions determining the rights of private persons in particular cases brought before the courts;[3] whereas under many foreign constitutions the security (such

[1] *The Law and the Constitution* (4th ed., 1952); see pp. 214 *et seq.* Sir Ivor Jennings points out that the words "or have been," did not appear in earlier editions. This is equally true of the qualification "to some extent." Cf. 6th ed., p. 190, with 7th ed., p. 190.—Ed.

[2] See ch. xii as to the contrast between the rule of law and foreign administrative law as understood by the author.

[3] Cf. *Calvin's Case* (1608) 7 Co. Rep. 1a; *Campbell* v. *Hall* (1774) Lofft. 655; K. & L. 487; *Wilkes* v. *Wood* (1763) 19 St. Tr. 1153; *Mostyn* v. *Fabrigas* (1774) 1 Cowp. 161. Parliamentary declarations of the law such as the Petition of Right and the Bill of Rights have a certain affinity to judicial decisions. [When the author refers to the general principles of the constitution in this context, it is clear from his examples that he is dealing with the means of protecting private rights. The origin of the sovereignty of Parliament cannot be traced to a judicial decision and the independence of the judges has rested on statute since the Act of Settlement, 1701.—Ed.]

Part II.

as it is) given to the rights of individuals results, or appears to result, from the general principles of the constitution.

This is one portion at least of the fact vaguely hinted at in the current but misguiding statement that "the constitution has not been made but has "grown." This dictum, if taken literally, is absurd. "Political institutions (however the proposition may "be at times ignored) are the work of men, owe their "origin and their whole existence to human will. "Men did not wake up on a summer morning and "find them sprung up. Neither do they resemble "trees, which, once planted, are 'aye growing' while "men 'are sleeping.' In every stage of their existence "they are made what they are by human voluntary "agency."[1]

Yet, though this is so, the dogma that the form of a government is a sort of spontaneous growth so closely bound up with the life of a people that we can hardly treat it as a product of human will and energy, does, though in a loose and inaccurate fashion, bring into view the fact that some polities, and among them the English constitution, have not been created at one stroke, and, far from being the result of legislation, in the ordinary sense of that term, are the fruit of contests carried on in the courts on behalf of the rights of individuals. Our constitution, in short, is a judge-made constitution, and it bears on its face all the features, good and bad, of judge-made law.

Contrast between the English constitution and Foreign constitutions.

Hence flow noteworthy distinctions between the constitution of England and the constitutions of most foreign countries.

[1] Mill, *Considerations on Representative Government* (3rd ed., 1865), p. 4.

There is in the English constitution an absence of those declarations or definitions of rights so dear to foreign constitutionalists. Such principles, moreover, as you can discover in the English constitution are, like all maxims established by judicial legislation, mere generalisations drawn either from the decisions or dicta of judges, or from statutes which, being passed to meet special grievances, bear a close resemblance to judicial decisions, and are in effect judgments pronounced by the High Court of Parliament. To put what is really the same thing in a somewhat different shape, the relation of the rights of individuals to the principles of the constitution is not quite the same in countries like Belgium, where the constitution is the result of a legislative act, as it is in England, where the constitution itself is based upon legal decisions. In Belgium, which may be taken as a type of countries possessing a constitution formed by a deliberate act of legislation, you may say with truth that the rights of individuals to personal liberty flow from or are secured by the constitution. In England the right to individual liberty is part of the constitution, because it is secured by the decisions of the courts, extended or confirmed as they are by the Habeas Corpus Acts. If it be allowable to apply the formulas of logic to questions of law, the difference in this matter between the constitution of Belgium and the English constitution may be described by the statement that in Belgium individual rights are deductions drawn from the principles of the constitution, whilst in England the so-called principles of the constitution are inductions or generalisations based upon particular decisions pronounced by the courts as to

Part II. the rights of given individuals.

This is of course a merely formal difference. Liberty is as well secured in Belgium as in England, and as long as this is so it matters nothing whether we say that individuals are free from all risk of arbitrary arrest, because liberty of person is guaranteed by the constitution, or that the right to personal freedom, or in other words to protection from arbitrary arrest, forms part of the constitution because it is secured by the ordinary law of the land. But though this merely formal distinction is in itself of no moment, provided always that the rights of individuals are really secure, the question whether the right to personal freedom or the right to freedom of worship is likely to be secure does depend a good deal upon the answer to the inquiry whether the persons who consciously or unconsciously build up the constitution of their country begin with definitions or declarations of rights, or with the contrivance of remedies by which rights may be enforced or secured. Now, most foreign constitution-makers have begun with declarations of rights. For this they have often been in nowise to blame. Their course of action has more often than not been forced upon them by the stress of circumstances, and by the consideration that to lay down general principles of law is the proper and natural function of legislators. But any knowledge of history suffices to show that foreign constitutionalists have, while occupied in defining rights, given insufficient attention to the absolute necessity for the provision of adequate remedies by which the rights they proclaimed might be enforced. The Constitution of 1791 proclaimed liberty of conscience, liberty of the press, the right of public meeting, the responsibility of government officials.[1] But there never was a period in the recorded annals of mankind when each and all of these rights were so insecure, one might almost say so completely non-existent, as at the height of the French Revolution. And an observer may well doubt whether a good number of these liberties or rights are even now so well protected under the French Republic as under the English Monarchy. On the other hand, there runs through the English constitution that inseparable connection between the means of enforcing a right and the right to be enforced which is the strength of judicial legislation. The saw, *ubi jus ibi remedium*, becomes from this point of view something much more important than a mere tautologous proposition. In its bearing upon constitutional law, it means that the Englishmen whose labours gradually framed the complicated set of laws and institutions which we call the Constitution, fixed their minds far more intently on providing remedies for the enforcement of particular rights or (what is merely the same thing looked at from the other side) for averting definite wrongs, than upon any declaration of the Rights of Man or of Englishmen. The Habeas Corpus Acts declare no principle and define no rights, but they are for practical purposes worth a hundred constitutional articles guaranteeing individual liberty. Nor let it be supposed that this connection between rights and remedies which depends upon the spirit of law pervading English

[1] See Plouard, *Les Constitutions françaises* (1871–1876), pp. 14-16; Duguit *et* Monnier, *Les Constitutions et les principales lois politiques de la France depuis 1789* (1898), pp. 4, 5.

Part II. institutions is inconsistent with the existence of a written constitution, or even with the existence of constitutional declarations of rights. The Constitution of the United States and the constitutions of the separate States are embodied in written or printed documents, and contain declarations of rights.[1] But the statesmen of America have shown unrivalled skill in providing means for giving legal security to the rights declared by American constitutions. The rule of law is as marked a feature of the United States as of England.

The fact, again, that in many foreign countries the rights of individuals, *e.g.* to personal freedom, depend upon the constitution, whilst in England the law of the constitution is little else than a generalisation of the rights which the courts secure to individuals, has this important result. The general rights guaranteed by the constitution may be, and in foreign countries constantly are, suspended. They are something extraneous to and independent of the ordinary course of

[1] The Petition of Right, and the Bill of Rights, as also the American Declarations of Rights, contain, it may be said, proclamations of general principles which resemble the declarations of rights known to foreign constitutionalists, and especially the celebrated Declaration of the Rights of Man of 1789. But the English and American Declarations on the one hand, and foreign declarations of rights on the other, though bearing an apparent resemblance to each other, are at bottom remarkable rather by way of contrast than of similarity. The Petition of Right and the Bill of Rights are not so much "declarations of rights" in the foreign sense of the term, as judicial condemnations of claims or practices on the part of the Crown, which are thereby pronounced illegal. It will be found that every, or nearly every, clause in the two celebrated documents negatives some distinct claim made and put into force on behalf of the prerogative. No doubt the Declarations contained in the American constitutions have a real similarity to the continental declarations of rights. They are the product of eighteenth-century ideas; they have, however, it is submitted, the distinct purpose of legally controlling the action of the legislature by the Articles of the Constitution.

Chapter IV.

the law. The declaration of the Belgian constitution, that individual liberty is "guaranteed," betrays a way of looking at the rights of individuals very different from the way in which such rights are regarded by English lawyers. We can hardly say that one right is more guaranteed than another. Freedom from arbitrary arrest, the right to express one's opinion on all matters subject to the liability to pay compensation for libellous or to suffer punishment for seditious or blasphemous statements, and the right to enjoy one's own property, seem to Englishmen all to rest upon the same basis, namely, on the law of the land. To say that the "constitution guaranteed" one class of rights more than the other would be to an Englishman an unnatural or a senseless form of speech. In the Belgian constitution the words have a definite meaning. They imply that no law invading personal freedom can be passed without a modification of the constitution made in the special way in which alone the constitution can be legally changed or amended. This, however, is not the point to which our immediate attention should be directed. The matter to be noted is, that where the right to individual freedom is a result deduced from the principles of the constitution, the idea readily occurs that the right is capable of being suspended or taken away. Where, on the other hand, the right to individual freedom is part of the constitution because it is inherent in the ordinary law of the land, the right is one which can hardly be destroyed without a thorough revolution in the institutions and manners of the nation. The so-called "suspension of the Habeas Corpus Act" bears, it is true, a certain similarity to what is called in foreign

Part II.

countries "suspending the constitutional guarantees." But, after all, a statute suspending the Habeas Corpus Act falls very far short of what its popular name seems to imply; and though a serious measure enough, is not, in reality, more than a suspension of one particular remedy for the protection of personal freedom. The Habeas Corpus Act may be suspended and yet Englishmen may enjoy almost all the rights of citizens. The constitution being based on the rule of law, the suspension of the constitution, as far as such a thing can be conceived possible, would mean with us nothing less than a revolution.[1]

Summary of meanings of Rule of Law.

That "rule of law," then, which forms a fundamental principle of the constitution, has three meanings, or may be regarded from three different points of view.

It means, in the first place, the absolute supremacy or predominance of regular law as opposed to the influence of arbitrary power, and excludes the existence of arbitrariness, of prerogative, or even of wide discretionary authority on the part of the government. Englishmen are ruled by the law, and by the law alone; a man may with us be punished for a breach of law, but he can be punished for nothing else.

It means, again, equality before the law, or the equal subjection of all classes to the ordinary law of the land administered by the ordinary law courts; the "rule of law" in this sense excludes the idea of any exemption of officials or others from the duty of

[1] For Habeas Corpus in war-time, see Wade and Phillips, *Constitutional Law* (5th ed., 1955), pp. 382-385.

obedience to the law which governs other citizens or from the jurisdiction of the ordinary tribunals; there can be with us nothing really corresponding to the "administrative law" (*droit administratif*) or the "administrative tribunals" (*tribunaux administratifs*) of France.[1] The notion which lies at the bottom of the "administrative law" known to foreign countries is, that affairs or disputes in which the government or its servants are concerned are beyond the sphere of the civil courts and must be dealt with by special and more or less official bodies. This idea is utterly unknown to the law of England, and indeed is fundamentally inconsistent with our traditions and customs.

The "rule of law," lastly, may be used as a formula for expressing the fact that with us the law of the constitution, the rules which in foreign countries naturally form part of a constitutional code, are not the source but the consequence of the rights of individuals, as defined and enforced by the courts; that, in short, the principles of private law have with us been by the action of the courts and Parliament so extended as to determine the position of the Crown and of its servants; thus the constitution is the result of the ordinary law of the land.

Influence of "Rule of Law" on leading provisions of constitution.

General propositions, however, as to the nature of the rule of law carry us but a very little way. If we want to understand what that principle in all its different aspects and developments really means, we must try to trace its influence throughout some of the main provisions of the constitution. The best

[1] See ch. xii and cf. pp. cxiii *et seq.*, App. 1, *post*, and Jennings, *The Law and the Constitution* (4th ed., 1952), App. ii.

Part II. mode of doing this is to examine with care the manner in which the law of England deals with the following topics, which are dealt with in succeeding chapters, namely, the right to personal freedom; the right to freedom of discussion; the right of public meeting; the use of martial law; the rights and duties of the army; the collection and expenditure of the public revenue; and the responsibility of Ministers. The true nature further of the rule of law as it exists in England will be illustrated by contrast with the idea of *droit administratif*, or administrative law, which prevails in many continental countries. These topics will each be treated of in their due order. The object, however, of this treatise, as the reader should remember, is not to provide minute and full information, *e.g.* as to the habeas corpus Acts, or other enactments protecting the liberty of the subject; but simply to show that these leading heads of constitutional law, which have been enumerated, these "articles," so to speak, of the constitution, are both governed by, and afford illustrations of, the supremacy throughout English institutions of the law of the land.[1] If at some future day the law of the constitution should be codified, each of the topics I have mentioned would be dealt with by the sections of the code. Many of these subjects

[1] The rule of equal law is in England now exposed to a new peril. "The Legislature has thought fit," wrote Sir F. Pollock, "by the Trade Disputes Act, 1906, to confer extraordinary immunities on combinations both of employers and of workmen, and to some extent on persons acting in their interests. Legal science has evidently nothing to do with this violent empirical operation on the body politic, and we can only look to jurisdictions beyond seas for the further judicial consideration of the problems which our courts were endeavouring (it is submitted, not without a reasonable measure of success) to work out on principles of legal justice."—Pollock, *Law of Torts* (8th ed., 1908), p. v.

are actually dealt with in the written constitutions of foreign countries, and notably in the articles of the Belgian constitution, which, as before noticed, makes an admirable summary of the leading maxims of English constitutionalism. It will therefore often be a convenient method of illustrating our topic to take the article of the Belgian, or it may be of some other constitution, which bears on the matter in hand, as for example the right to personal freedom, and to consider how far the principle therein embodied is recognised by the law of England; and if it be so recognised, what are the means by which it is maintained or enforced by our courts. One reason why the law of the constitution is imperfectly understood is, that we too rarely put it side by side with the constitutional provisions of other countries. Here, as elsewhere, comparison is essential to recognition.

CHAPTER V

THE RIGHT TO PERSONAL FREEDOM

Part II.

Security for personal freedom under Belgian constitution.

THE seventh article of the Belgian constitution establishes in that country principles which have long prevailed in England. The terms thereof so curiously illustrate by way of contrast some marked features of English constitutional law as to be worth quotation.

"*Art. 7. La liberté individuelle est garantie.*

"*Nul ne peut être poursuivi que dans les cas* "*prévus par la loi, et dans la forme qu'elle prescrit.*

"*Hors le cas de flagrant délit, nul ne peut être* "*arrêté qu'en vertu de l'ordonnance motivée du juge,* "*qui doit être signifiée au moment de l'arrestation, ou* "*au plus tard dans les vingt-quatre heures.*"[1]

How secured in England.

The security which an Englishman enjoys for personal freedom does not really depend upon or originate in any general proposition contained in any written document. The nearest approach which our statute-book presents to the statement contained in the seventh article of the Belgian constitution is the celebrated thirty-ninth article[2] of the Magna Charta:

[1] *Constitution de la Belgique*, art. 7.

[2] See Stubbs, *Select Charters* (8th ed., 1900), p. 301.

"*Nullus liber homo capiatur, vel imprisonetur, aut* "*dissaisiatur, aut utlagetur, aut exuletur, aut aliquo* "*modo destruatur, nec super eum ibimus, nec super* "*eum mittemus, nisi per legale judicium parium* "*suorum vel per legem terrae,*" which should be read in combination with the declarations of the Petition of Right. And these enactments (if such they can be called) are rather records of the existence of a right than statutes which confer it. The expression again, "guaranteed," is, as I have already pointed out, extremely significant; it suggests the notion that personal liberty is a special privilege insured to Belgians by some power above the ordinary law of the land. This is an idea utterly alien to English modes of thought, since with us freedom of person is not a special privilege but the outcome of the ordinary law of the land enforced by the courts.[1] Here, in short, we may observe the application to a particular case of the general principle that with us individual rights are the basis, not the result, of the law of the constitution.

The proclamation in a constitution or charter of the right to personal freedom, or indeed of any other right, gives of itself but slight security that the right has more than a nominal existence, and students who wish to know how far the right to freedom of person is in reality part of the law of the constitution must consider both what is the meaning of the right and, a matter of even more consequence, what are the legal methods by which its exercise is secured.

The right to personal liberty as understood in

[1] The Star Chamber Abolition Act, 1641, guaranteed to the subject that the writ of habeas corpus lay against the King and the Council.

Part II.

England means in substance a person's right not to be subjected to imprisonment, arrest, or other physical coercion in any manner that does not admit of legal justification.[1] That anybody should suffer physical restraint is in England *prima facie* illegal, and can be justified (speaking in very general terms) on two grounds only, that is to say, either because the prisoner or person suffering restraint is accused of some offence and must be brought before the courts to stand his trial, or because he has been duly convicted of some offence and must suffer punishment for it. Now personal freedom in this sense of the term is secured in England by the strict maintenance of the principle that no man can be arrested or imprisoned except in due course of law, *i.e.* (speaking again in very general terms indeed) under some legal warrant or authority, and, what is of far more consequence, it is secured by the provision of adequate legal means for the enforcement of this principle. These methods are twofold;[2] namely, redress for unlawful arrest or imprisonment by means of a prosecution or an action, and deliverance from unlawful imprisonment by means of the writ of habeas corpus. Let us examine the general character of each of these remedies.

Proceedings for wrongful arrest.

i. *Redress for Arrest.*—If we use the term redress in a wide sense, we may say that a person who has suffered a wrong obtains redress either when he gets

[1] For legal justification see Wade and Phillips, *Constitutional Law* (6th ed., 1960), pp. 466 ff., 674-676; Kenny, *Outlines of Criminal Law* (17th ed., 1958), pp. 535-540.—Ed.

[2] The author added in a footnote a third, namely, self-defence, or the assertion of legal rights by the use of a person's own force. —Ed.

the wrongdoer punished or when he obtains compensation for the damage inflicted upon him by the wrong.

Each of these forms of redress is in England open to every one whose personal freedom has been in any way unlawfully interfered with. Suppose, for example, that *X* without legal justification assaults *A*, by knocking him down, or deprives *A* of his freedom—as the technical expression goes, "imprisons" him—whether it be for a length of time, or only for five minutes; *A* has two courses open to him. He can have *X* convicted of an assault and thus cause him to be punished for his crime, or he can bring an action of trespass against *X* and obtain from *X* such compensation for the damage which *A* has sustained from *X*'s conduct as a jury think that *A* deserves. Suppose that in 1725 Voltaire had at the instigation of an English lord been treated in London as he was treated in Paris. He would not have needed to depend for redress upon the goodwill of his friends or upon the favour of the Ministry. He could have pursued one of two courses.[1] He could by taking the proper steps have caused all his assailants to be brought to trial as criminals. He could, if he had preferred it, have brought an action against each and all of them: he could have sued the nobleman who caused him to be thrashed, the footmen who thrashed him, the policemen who threw him into gaol, and the gaoler or lieutenant who kept him there. Notice particularly that the action for trespass, to which Voltaire would have had recourse, can be brought,

[1] The Crown could have granted a free pardon or have entered a *nolle prosequi*, *i.e.* declined to proceed with the prosecution. It could not have interfered with the civil actions.—ED.

Part II.

or, as the technical expression goes, "lies," against every person throughout the realm. It can and has been brought against governors of colonies, against secretaries of state, against officers who have tried by court-martial persons not subject to military law, against every kind of official high or low. Here then we come across another aspect of the "rule of law." No one of Voltaire's enemies would, if he had been injured in England, have been able to escape from responsibility on the plea of acting in an official character or in obedience to his official superiors.[1] Nor would any one of them have been able to say that the degree of his guilt could in any way whatever be determined by any more or less official court. Voltaire, to keep to our example, would have been able in England to have brought each and all of his assailants, including the officials who kept him in prison, before an ordinary court, and therefore before judges and jurymen who were not at all likely to think that official zeal or the orders of official superiors were either a legal or a moral excuse for breaking the law.

Before quitting the subject of the redress afforded by the courts for the damage caused by illegal interference with any one's personal freedom, we shall do well to notice the strict adherence of the judges in this as in other cases to two maxims or principles which underlie the whole law of the constitution, and the maintenance of which has gone a great way both to ensure the supremacy of the law of the land and ultimately to curb the arbitrariness of the Crown. The first of these maxims or principles is that every wrongdoer is individually responsible for every unlaw-

[1] Contrast the French *Code Pénal*, art. 114.

ful or wrongful act in which he takes part, and, what is really the same thing looked at from another point of view, cannot, if the act be unlawful, plead in his defence that he did it under the orders of a master or superior. Voltaire, had he been arrested in England, could have treated each and all of the persons engaged in the outrage as individually responsible for the wrong done to him. Now this doctrine of individual responsibility is the real foundation of the legal dogma that the orders of the Sovereign are no justification for the commission of a wrongful or illegal act. The ordinary rule, therefore, that every wrongdoer is individually liable for the wrong he has committed, is the foundation on which rests the great constitutional doctrine of ministerial responsibility. The second of these noteworthy maxims is, that the courts give a remedy for the infringement of a right whether the injury done be great or small. The assaults and imprisonment from which Voltaire suffered were serious wrongs; but it would be an error to fancy, as persons who have no experience in the practice of the courts are apt to do, that proceedings for trespass or for false imprisonment can be taken only where personal liberty is seriously interfered with. Ninety-nine out of every hundred actions for assault or false imprisonment have reference to injuries which in themselves are trifling. If one ruffian gives another a blow, if a policeman makes an arrest without lawful authority, if a schoolmaster keeps a scholar locked up at school for half an hour after he ought to have let the child go home,[1] if in short *X* interferes unlawfully to however slight a

[1] *Hunter* v. *Johnson* (1884) 13 Q.B.D. 225.

Part II. degree with the personal liberty of *A*, the offender exposes himself to proceedings in a court of law, and the sufferer, if he can enlist the sympathies of a jury, may recover heavy damages for the injury which he has or is supposed to have suffered. The law of England protects the right to personal liberty, as also every other legal right, against every kind of infringement, and gives the same kind of redress (I do not mean, of course, inflicts the same degree of punishment or penalty) for the pettiest as for the gravest invasions of personal freedom. This seems to us so much a matter of course as hardly to call for observation, but it may be suspected that few features in our legal system have done more to maintain the authority of the law than the fact that all offences great and small are dealt with on the same principles and by the same courts. The law of England now knows nothing of exceptional offences punished by extraordinary tribunals.[1]

The right of a person who has been wrongfully imprisoned on regaining his freedom to put his oppressor on trial as a criminal, or by means of an action to obtain pecuniary compensation for the wrong which he has endured, affords a most insufficient security for personal freedom. If *X* keeps *A* in confinement, it profits *A* little to know that if he could recover his freedom, which he cannot, he could punish and fine *X*. What *A* wants is to recover his liberty. Till this is done he cannot hope to punish the foe who has deprived him of it. It would have

[1] Contrast with this the extraordinary remedies adopted under the old French monarchy for the punishment of powerful criminals. As to which see Fléchier, *Mémoires de Fléchier sur les grands jours d'Auvergne, en 1665* (1856).

been little consolation for Voltaire to know that if he could have got out of the Bastille he could recover damages from his enemies. The possibility that he might when he got free have obtained redress for the wrong done him might, so far from being a benefit, have condemned him to lifelong incarceration. Liberty is not secure unless the law, in addition to punishing every kind of interference with a man's lawful freedom, provides adequate security that every one who without legal justification is placed in confinement shall be able to get free. This security is provided by the celebrated writ of habeas corpus and the Habeas Corpus Acts.

Writ of *habeas corpus.*

ii. *Writ of Habeas Corpus.*[1]—It is not within the scope of these lectures to give a history of the writ of habeas corpus or to provide the details of the legislation with regard to it. For minute information, both about the writ and about the Habeas Corpus Acts, you should consult the ordinary legal text-books. My object is solely to explain generally the mode in which the law of England secures the right to personal freedom. I shall therefore call attention to the following points: first, the nature of the writ; secondly, the effect of the so-called Habeas Corpus Acts; thirdly, the precise effect of what is called (not quite accurately) the Suspension of the Habeas Corpus Act; and, lastly, the relation of any Act suspending the operation of the Habeas Corpus Act to an Act of Indemnity. Each of these matters has a close bearing on the law of the constitution.

[1] See Star Chamber Abolition Act, 1641, s. 8; Habeas Corpus Acts, 1679, 1816, and 1862; Wade and Phillips, *Constitutional Law* (6th ed., 1960), pp. 474-481; Forsyth, *Cases and Opinions in Constitutional Law* (1869), ch. xvi.

Part II.

Nature of Writ.

Nature of Writ.—Legal documents constantly give the best explanation and illustration of legal principles. We shall do well therefore to examine with care the following copy of a writ of habeas corpus:—

"*Victoria, by the Grace of God, of the United*
"*Kingdom of Great Britain and Ireland Queen,*
"*Defender of the Faith,*

"*To J. K., Keeper of our Gaol of Jersey, in the*
"*Island of Jersey, and to J. C. Viscount of said*
"*Island, greeting. We command you that you have*
"*the body of C. C. W. detained in our prison under*
"*your custody, as it is said, together with the day*
"*and cause of his being taken and detained, by*
"*whatsoever name he may be called or known, in*
"*our Court before us, at Westminster, on the 18th*
"*day of January next, to undergo and receive all*
"*and singular such matters and things which our*
"*said Court shall then and there consider of him in*
"*this behalf; and have there then this Writ. Witness*
"THOMAS *Lord* DENMAN, *at Westminster, the 23rd*
"*day of December in the 8th year of our reign.*

"*By the Court,*

"*Robinson.*"[1]

"*At the instance of C. C. W.*

"*R. M. R.*"

"*W. A. L., 7 Gray's Inn Square, London,*
"*Attorney for the said C. C. W.*"

The character of the document is patent on its

1 *Carus Wilson's Case* (1845) 7 Q.B. 984, at p. 988. In this particular case the writ calls upon the gaoler of the prison to have the body of the prisoner before the court by a given day. It more ordinarily calls upon him to have the prisoner before the court "immediately after the receipt of this writ."

face. It is an order issued, in the particular instance, by the Court of Queen's Bench, calling upon a person by whom a prisoner is alleged to be kept in confinement to bring such prisoner—to "have his body" whence the name habeas corpus—before the court to let the court know on what ground the prisoner is confined, and thus give to the court the opportunity of dealing with the prisoner as the law may require. The essence of the whole transaction is that the court can by the writ of habeas corpus cause any person who is imprisoned to be actually brought before the court and obtain knowledge of the reason why he is imprisoned; and then having him before the court, either then and there set him free or else see that he is dealt with in whatever way the law requires, as, for example, brought speedily to trial.

The writ can be issued on the application either of the prisoner himself or of any person on his behalf, or (supposing the prisoner cannot act) then on the application of any person who believes him to be unlawfully imprisoned. It is issued by the High Court, or during vacation by any judge thereof; and the court or a judge should and will always cause it to be issued on being satisfied by affidavit that there is reason to suppose a prisoner to be wrongfully deprived of his liberty. You cannot say with strictness that the writ is issued "as a matter of course," for some ground must be shown for supposing that a case of illegal imprisonment exists. But the writ is granted "as a matter of right,"—that is to say, the court will always issue it if *prima facie* ground is shown for supposing that the person on whose behalf it is asked for is unlawfully deprived of his liberty.

Part II.

The writ or order of the court can be addressed to any person whatever, be he an official or a private individual, who has, or is supposed to have, another in his custody. Any disobedience to the writ exposes the offender to summary punishment for contempt of court,[1] and also in many cases to heavy penalties recoverable by the party aggrieved.[2] To put the matter, therefore, in the most general terms, the case stands thus. The High Court of Justice possesses, as the tribunals which make up the High Court used to possess, the power by means of the writ of habeas corpus to cause any person who is alleged to be kept in unlawful confinement to be brought before the court. The court can then inquire into the reason why he is confined, and can, should it see fit, set him then and there at liberty. This power moreover is one which the court always will exercise whenever ground is shown by any applicant whatever for the belief that any man in England is unlawfully deprived of his liberty.

Habeas Corpus Acts.

The Habeas Corpus Acts.—The right to the writ of habeas corpus existed at common law long before the passing in 1679 of the celebrated Habeas Corpus Act,[3] and you may wonder how it has happened that this and the Habeas Corpus Act, 1816, are treated, and (for practical purposes) rightly treated, as the basis on which rests an Englishman's security for the enjoyment of his personal freedom. The explana-

[1] *The King* v. *Winton* (1792) 5 T.R. 89; cf. Habeas Corpus Act, 1816, s. 2; see Corner, *Practice of the Crown Side of the Court of Queen's Bench* (1844).

[2] Habeas Corpus Act, 1679, s. 4.

[3] See also Star Chamber Abolition Act, 1641, s. 8.

tion is, that prior to 1679 the right to the writ was often under various pleas and excuses made of no effect. The aim of the Habeas Corpus Acts has been to meet all the devices by which the effect of the writ can be evaded, either on the part of the judges, who ought to issue the same, and if necessary discharge the prisoner, or on the part of the gaoler or other person who has the prisoner in custody. The earlier Act of Charles the Second applies to persons imprisoned on a charge of crime; the later Act of George the Third applies to persons deprived of their liberty otherwise than on a criminal accusation.

Take these two classes of persons separately.

Habeas Corpus Act, 1679.

A person is imprisoned on a charge of crime. If he is imprisoned without any legal warrant for his imprisonment, he has a right to be set at liberty. If, on the other hand, he is imprisoned under a legal warrant, the object of his detention is to ensure his being brought to trial. His position in this case differs according to the nature of the offence with which he is charged. In the case of the lighter offences known as misdemeanours he has, generally speaking,[1] the right to his liberty on giving security with proper sureties that he will in due course surrender himself to custody and appear and take his trial on such indictment as may be found against him in respect of the matter with which he is charged, or (to use technical expressions) he has the right to be admitted to bail. In the case, on the other hand, of the more serious offences, such as felonies or treasons,

[1] For Bail see Halsbury, *Laws of England* (3rd ed.), vol. x (1955), pp. 373-376, and Wade and Phillips, *Constitutional Law* (5th ed., 1955), p. 376.

a person who is once committed to prison is not entitled to be let out on bail. The right of the prisoner is in this case simply the right to a speedy trial. The effect of the writ of habeas corpus would be evaded either if the court did not examine into the validity of the warrant on which the prisoner was detained, and if the warrant were not valid release him, or if the court, on ascertaining that he was legally imprisoned, did not cause him according to circumstances either to go out on bail or to be speedily brought to trial.

The Act provides against all these possible failures of justice. The law as to persons imprisoned under accusations of crime stands through the combined effect of the rules of the common law and of the statute in substance as follows. The gaoler who has such person in custody is bound when called upon to have the prisoner before the court with the true cause of his commitment. If the cause is insufficient, the prisoner must of course be discharged; if the cause is sufficient, the prisoner, in case he is charged with a misdemeanour, can in general insist upon being bailed till trial; in case, on the other hand, the charge is one of treason or felony, he can insist upon being tried at the first sessions after his committal, or if he is not then tried, upon being bailed, unless the witnesses for the Crown cannot appear. If he is not tried at the second sessions after his commitment, he can insist upon his release without bail. The net result, therefore, appears to be that while the Habeas Corpus Act is in force no person committed to prison on a charge of crime can be kept long in confinement, for he has the legal means of insisting upon either being let out upon bail or else

Chapter V.

of being brought to a speedy trial.

Habeas Corpus Act, 1816.

A person, again, who is detained in confinement but not on a charge of crime needs for his protection the means of readily obtaining a legal decision on the lawfulness of his confinement, and also of getting an immediate release if he has by law a right to his liberty. This is exactly what the writ of habeas corpus affords. Whenever any Englishman or foreigner is alleged to be wrongfully deprived of liberty, the court will issue the writ, have the person aggrieved brought before the court, and if he has a right to liberty set him free. Thus if a child is forcibly kept apart from his parents,[1] if a man is wrongfully kept in confinement as a lunatic, if a nun is alleged to be prevented from leaving her convent, —if, in short, any man, woman, or child is, or is asserted on apparently good grounds to be, deprived of liberty, the court will always issue a writ of habeas corpus to any one who has the aggrieved person in his custody to have such person brought before the court, and if he is suffering restraint without lawful cause, set him free. Till, however, the year 1816 the machinery for obtaining the writ was less perfect[2] in the case of persons not accused of crime

[1] See *The Queen* v. *Nash* (1883) 10 Q.B.D. 454; and cf. *Re Agar-Ellis* (1883) 24 Ch.D. 317; *Barnardo* v. *Ford* [1892] A.C. 326; *Barnardo* v. *McHugh* [1891] A.C. 388; *The Queen* v. *Jackson* [1891] 1 Q.B. 671; *Cox* v. *Hakes* (1890) 15 App. Cas. 506; compare as to power of Court of Chancery for protection of children independently of Habeas Corpus Acts, *The Queen* v. *Gyngall* [1893] 2 Q.B. 232.

As to appeals to the Judicial Committee of the Privy Council, see *Eshugbayi Eleko* v. *Government of Nigeria* [1928] A.C. 459; and to the Court of Appeal, but not in a criminal cause; *Amand* v. *Home Secretary and Minister of Defence of Royal Netherlands Government* [1943] A.C. 147.

[2] The inconvenience ultimately remedied by the Habeas Corpus Act, 1816, was in practice small, for the judges extended to all cases

than in the case of those charged with criminal offences, and the effect of the Act of 1816 was in substance to apply to non-criminal cases the machinery of the great Habeas Corpus Act, 1679.

At the present day, therefore, the securities for personal freedom are in England as complete as laws can make them. The right to its enjoyment is absolutely acknowledged. Any invasion of the right entails either imprisonment or fine upon the wrongdoer; and any person, whether charged with crime or not, who is even suspected to be wrongfully imprisoned, has, if there exists a single individual willing to exert himself on the victim's behalf, the certainty of having his case duly investigated, and, if he has been wronged, of recovering his freedom. Let us return for a moment to a former illustration, and suppose that Voltaire has been treated in London as he was treated in Paris. He most certainly would very rapidly have recovered his freedom. The procedure would not, it is true, have been in 1726 quite as easy as it is now under the Act of George the Third. Still, even then it would have been within the power of any one of his friends to put the law in motion. It would have been at least as easy to release Voltaire in 1726 as it was in 1772 to obtain by means of habeas corpus the freedom of the slave James Sommersett when actually confined in irons on board a ship lying in the Thames and bound for Jamaica.[1]

The whole history of the writ of habeas corpus

of unlawful imprisonment the spirit of the Habeas Corpus Act, 1679, and enforced immediate obedience to the writ of habeas corpus, even when issued not under the statute, but under the common law authority of the courts, 3 Bl., *Comm.* 138.

[1] *Sommersett's Case* (1772) 20 St. Tr. 1.

illustrates the predominant attention paid under the English constitution to "remedies," that is, to modes of procedure by which to secure respect for a legal right, and by which to turn a merely nominal into an effective or real right. The Habeas Corpus Acts are essentially procedure Acts, and simply aim at improving the legal mechanism by means of which the acknowledged right to personal freedom may be enforced. They are intended, as is generally the case with legislation which proceeds under the influence of lawyers, simply to meet actual and experienced difficulties. Hence the Habeas Corpus Act of Charles the Second's reign was an imperfect or very restricted piece of legislative work, and Englishmen waited nearly a century and a half (1679-1816) before the procedure for securing the right to discharge from unlawful confinement was made complete. But this lawyer-like mode of dealing with a fundamental right had with all its defects the one great merit that legislation was directed to the right point. There is no difficulty, and there is often very little gain, in declaring the existence of a right to personal freedom. The true difficulty is to secure its enforcement. The Habeas Corpus Acts have achieved this end, and have therefore done for the liberty of Englishmen more than could have been achieved by any declaration of rights. One may even venture to say that these Acts are of really more importance not only than the general proclamations of the Rights of Man which have often been put forward in foreign countries, but even than such very lawyer-like documents as the Petition of Right or the Bill of Rights, though these celebrated enactments show almost equally with the

Part II.

Habeas Corpus Act that the law of the English constitution is at bottom judge-made law.[1]

Effect of writ of *habeas corpus* on authority of judges.

Every critic of the constitution has observed the effect of the Habeas Corpus Acts in securing the liberty of the subject; what has received less and deserves as much attention is the way in which the right to issue a writ of habeas corpus, strengthened as that right is by statute, determines the whole relation of the judicial body towards the executive. The authority to enforce obedience to the writ is nothing less than the power to release from imprisonment any person who in the opinion of the court is unlawfully deprived of his liberty, and hence in effect to put an end to or to prevent any punishment which the Crown or its servants may attempt to inflict in opposition to the rules of law as interpreted by the judges. The judges therefore are in truth, though not in name, invested with the means of hampering or supervising the whole administrative action of the government, and of at once putting a veto upon any proceeding not authorised by the letter of the law. Nor is this power one which has fallen into disuse by want of exercise. It has often been put forth, and this too in matters of the greatest consequence; the knowledge moreover of its existence governs the conduct of the administration. An example or two will best show the mode in which the "judiciary" (to use a convenient Americanism) can and do by means of the writ of habeas corpus keep a hold on the acts of the executive. In 1839 Canadian rebels, found

[1] Compare Imperial Constitution of 1804, ss. 60-63, under which a committee of the Senate was empowered to take steps for putting an end to illegal arrests by the Government. See Plouard, *Les Constitutions françaises* (1871–1876), p. 161.

guilty of treason in Canada and condemned to transportation, arrived in official custody at Liverpool on their way to Van Diemen's Land. The friends of the convicts questioned the validity of the sentence under which they were transported; the prisoners were thereupon taken from prison and brought upon a writ of habeas corpus before the Court of Exchequer. Their whole position having been considered by the court, it was ultimately held that the imprisonment was legal. But had the court taken a different view, the Canadians would at once have been released from confinement.[1] In 1859 an English officer serving in India was duly convicted of manslaughter and sentenced to four years' imprisonment: he was sent to England in military custody to complete there his term of punishment. The order under which he was brought to this country was technically irregular, and the convict having been brought on a writ of habeas corpus before the Queen's Bench, was on this purely technical ground set at liberty.[2] So, to take a very notorious instance of judicial authority in matters most nearly concerning the executive, the courts have again and again considered, in the case of persons brought before them by the writ of habeas corpus, questions as to the legality of impressment, and as to the limits within which the right of impressment may be exercised; and if, on the one hand, the judges have in this particular instance (which by the way is almost a singular one) supported the arbitrary powers of the prerogative, they have also strictly limited the exercise of this power within the bounds prescribed

[1] *The Case of the Canadian Prisoners* (1839) 5 M. & W. 32.

[2] *In re Allen* (1860) 30 L.J. (Q.B.) 38.

Part II. to it by custom or by statute.[1] Moreover, as already pointed out, the authority of the civil tribunals even when not actually put into force regulates the action of the government. In 1854 a body of Russian sailors were found wandering about the streets of Guildford, without any visible means of subsistence; they were identified by a Russian naval officer as deserters from a Russian man-of-war which had put into an English port; they were thereupon, under his instructions and with the assistance of the superintendent of police, conveyed to Portsmouth for the purpose of their being carried back to the Russian ship. Doubts arose as to the legality of the whole proceeding. The law officers were consulted, who thereupon gave it as their opinion that "the delivering-up of the Russian "sailors to the Lieutenant and the assistance offered "by the police for the purpose of their being con-"veyed back to the Russian ship were contrary to "law."[2] The sailors were presumably released; they no doubt would have been delivered by the Court had a writ of habeas corpus been applied for. Here then we see the judges in effect restraining the action of the executive in a matter which in most countries is considered one of administration or of policy lying beyond the range of judicial interference. The strongest examples, however, of interference by the judges with administrative proceedings are to be found in the decisions given under the Extradition Acts. Neither the Crown nor any servant of the

[1] See *The Case of Pressing Mariners* (1743) 18 St. Tr. 1323; Stephen, *Commentaries* (14th ed., 1903), vol. ii, pp. 574, 575; cf. Corner, *Forms of Writs and Other Proceedings on the Crown Side of the Court of Queen's Bench* (1844), p. 64, for form of habeas corpus for an impressed seaman.

[2] See Forsyth, *Cases and Opinions in Constitutional Law* (1869), p. 468.

Crown has any right to expel a foreign criminal from the country or to surrender him to his own government for trial.[1] A French forger, robber, or murderer who escapes from France to England cannot, independently of statutory enactments, be sent back to his native land for trial or punishment. The absence of any power on the part of the Crown to surrender foreign criminals to the authorities of their own state has been found so inconvenient, that the Extradition Acts, 1870-1906, have empowered the Crown to make treaties with foreign states for the mutual extradition of criminals or of persons charged with crime. The exercise of this authority is, however, hampered by restrictions which are imposed by the statute under which alone it exists. It therefore often happens that an offender arrested under the warrant of a Secretary of State and about to be

[1] See, however, *The King* v. *Lundy* (1690) 2 Ventris 314; *The King* v. *Kimberley* (1729) 2 Str. 848; *East India Company* v. *Campbell* (1749) 1 Ves. Senr. 246; *Mure* v. *Kaye* (1811) 4 Taunt. 34; and Chitty, *Criminal Law* (2nd ed., 1826), pp. 14-16, in support of the opinion that the Crown possessed a common law right of extradition as regards foreign criminals. This opinion may possibly once have been correct. (Compare, however, *The Queen* v. *Bernard* (1858) *Annual Register*, Appendix to Chronicle, 310, at p. 328, for opinion of Campbell, C.J., cited *In re Castioni* [1891] 1 Q.B. 149, at p. 153, by Sir C. Russell, *arguendo.*) It has, however, in any case (to use the words of a high authority) "ceased to be law now. If any magistrate were now to "arrest a person on this ground, the validity of the commitment "would certainly be tested, and, in the absence of special legislative "provisions, the prisoner as certainly discharged upon application to "one of the superior courts."—Clarke, *Extradition* (4th ed., 1903), p. 26. The case of *Musgrove* v. *Chun Teeong Toy* [1891] A.C. 272, which establishes that an alien has not a legal right enforceable by action, to enter British territory, suggests the possible existence of a common law right on the part of the Crown to expel an alien from British territory. [The admission and exclusion of aliens is now statutory. See Aliens Order, 1953, made under powers conferred by the Aliens Restriction Acts, 1914 and 1919.—Ed.]

Part II. handed over to the authorities of his own country conceives that, on some ground or other, his case does not fall within the precise terms of any Extradition Act. He applies for a writ of habeas corpus; he is brought up before the High Court; every technical plea he can raise obtains full consideration,[1] and if on any ground whatever it can be shown that the terms of the Extradition Act have not been complied with, or that they do not justify his arrest and surrender, he is as a matter of course at once set at liberty.[2] It is easy to perceive that the authority of the judges, exercised, as it invariably must be, in support of the strict rules of law, cuts down the discretionary powers of the Crown. It often prevents the English government from meeting public danger by measures of precaution which would as a matter of course be taken by the executive of any continental country. Suppose, for example, that a body of foreign anarchists come to England and are thought by the police on strong grounds of suspicion to be engaged in a plot, say for blowing up the Houses of Parliament. Suppose also that the existence of the conspiracy does not admit of absolute proof. An English Minister, if he is not prepared to put the conspirators on their trial, has no means of arresting them, or of expelling them from the country.[3] In case of arrest or imprisonment they would at once be brought before the High Court

[1] *In re Bellencontre* [1891] 2 Q.B. 122.

[2] *In re Coppin* (1866) L.R. 2 Ch. App. 47; *The Queen* v. *Wilson* (1877) 3 Q.B.D. 42.

[3] The Home Secretary now has power to order the deportation of any undesirable alien, if he considers that such action is in the public interest; Aliens Order, 1953, art. 20 (1) & (2); Wade and Phillips, *Constitutional Law* (6th ed., 1960), pp. 242-243.—Ed.

on a writ of habeas corpus, and unless some specific legal ground for their detention could be shown, they would be forthwith set at liberty. Of the political or, to use foreign expressions, of the "administrative" reasons which might make the arrest or expulsion of a foreign refugee highly expedient, the judges would hear nothing; that he was arrested by order of the Secretary of State, that his imprisonment was a simple administrative act, that the Prime Minister or the Home Secretary was prepared to make affidavit that the arrest was demanded by the most urgent considerations of public safety, or to assure the Court that the whole matter was one of high policy and concerned national interests, would be no answer whatever to the demand for freedom under a writ of habeas corpus. All that any judge could inquire into would be, whether there was any rule of common or of statute law which would authorise interference with a foreigner's personal freedom. If none such could be found, the applicants would assuredly obtain their liberty. The plain truth is that the power possessed by the judges of controlling the administrative conduct of the executive has been, of necessity, so exercised as to prevent the development with us of any system corresponding to the "administrative law" of continental states. It strikes at the root of those theories as to the nature of administrative acts, and as to the "separation of powers," on which, as will be shown in a later chapter,[1] the *droit administratif* of France depends, and it deprives the Crown, which now means the Ministry of the day, of all discretionary authority. The actual or possible

[1] See ch. xii.

intervention, in short, of the courts, exercisable for the most part by means of the writ of habeas corpus, confines the action of the government within the strict letter of the law; with us the state can punish, but it can hardly prevent the commission of crimes.

Contests of seventeenth century about position of judges.

We can now see why it was that the political conflicts of the seventeenth century often raged round the position of the judges, and why the battle might turn on a point so technical as the inquiry, what might be a proper return to a writ of habeas corpus.[1] Upon the degree of authority and independence to be conceded to the Bench depended the colour and working of our institutions. To supporters, on the one hand, of the prerogative who, like Bacon, were not unfrequently innovators or reformers, judicial independence appeared to mean the weakness of the executive, and the predominance throughout the state of the conservative legalism, which found a representative in Coke. The Parliamentary leaders, on the other hand, saw, more or less distinctly, that the independence of the Bench was the sole security for the maintenance of the common law, which was nothing else than the rule of established customs modified only by Acts of Parliament, and that Coke in battling for the power of the judges was asserting the rights of the nation; they possibly also saw, though this is uncertain, that the maintenance of rigid legality, inconvenient as it might sometimes prove, was the certain road to Parliamentary sovereignty.[2]

Suspension of the Habeas Corpus Act.—During

[1] *Darnel's Case* (1627) 3 St. Tr. 1; K. & L. 49.

[2] See Gardiner, *History of England*, vol. iii (1883), ch. xxii, for a statement of the different views entertained as to the position of judges.

Chapter V.

Suspension of Habeas Corpus Act.

periods of political excitement the power or duty of the courts to issue a writ of habeas corpus, and thereby compel the speedy trial or release of persons charged with crime, has been found an inconvenient or dangerous limitation on the authority of the executive government. Hence has arisen the occasion for statutes which are popularly called Habeas Corpus Suspension Acts. I say "popularly called," because if you take (as you may) the Act 34 Geo. III. c. 54[1] as a type of such enactments, you will see

[1] Of which s. 1 enacts "that every person or persons that are or "shall be in prison within the kingdom of Great Britain at or upon "the day on which this Act shall receive his Majesty's royal assent, "or after, by warrant of his said Majesty's most honorable Privy "Council, signed by six of the said Privy Council, for high treason, "suspicion of high treason, or treasonable practices, or by warrant, "signed by any of his Majesty's secretaries of state, for such causes "as aforesaid, may be detained in safe custody, without bail or main-"prize, until the first day of February one thousand seven hundred "and ninety-five; and that no judge or justice of the peace shall bail "or try any such person or persons so committed, without order from "his said Majesty's Privy Council, signed by six of the said Privy "Council, till the said first day of February one thousand seven "hundred and ninety-five; any law or statute to the contrary "notwithstanding."

The so-called suspension of the Habeas Corpus Act under a statute, such as that of 1794, produces both less and more effect than would the total repeal of the Habeas Corpus Acts. The suspension, while it lasts, makes it possible for the Government to arrest and keep in prison any persons declared in effect by the Government to be guilty or suspected of treasonable practices, and such persons have no means of obtaining either a discharge or a trial. But the suspension does not affect the position of persons not detained in custody under suspicion of treasonable practices. It does not therefore touch the ordinary liberty of ordinary citizens. The repeal of the Habeas Corpus Acts, on the other hand, would deprive every man in England of one security against wrongful imprisonment, but since it would leave alive the now unquestionable authority of the judges to issue and compel obedience to a writ of habeas corpus at common law, it would not, assuming the bench to do their duty, increase the power of the Government to imprison persons suspected of treasonable practices, nor materially diminish the freedom of any class of Englishmen. Cf. 3 Bl., *Comm.* 138; for modern practice see Wade and Phillips, *op. cit.*, pp. 670-674.

Part II.

that it hardly corresponds with its received name. The whole effect of the Act, which does not even mention the Habeas Corpus Act, is to make it impossible for any person imprisoned under a warrant signed by a Secretary of State on a charge of high treason, or on suspicion of high treason, to insist upon being either discharged or put on trial. No doubt this is a great diminution in the securities for personal freedom provided by the Habeas Corpus Acts; but it falls very far short of anything like a general suspension of the right to the writ of habeas corpus; it in no way affects the privileges of any person not imprisoned on a charge of high treason; it does not legalise any arrest, imprisonment, or punishment which was not lawful before the Suspension Act passed; it does not in any wise touch the claim to a writ of habeas corpus possessed by every one, man, woman, or child, who is held in confinement otherwise than on a charge of crime. The particular statute 34 Geo. III. c. 54 is, and (I believe) every other Habeas Corpus Suspension Act affecting England, has been an annual Act, and must, therefore, if it is to continue in force, be renewed year by year. The sole, immediate, and direct result, therefore, of suspending the Habeas Corpus Act is this: the Ministry may for the period during which the Suspension Act continues in force constantly defer the trial of persons imprisoned on the charge of treasonable practices. This increase in the power of the executive is no trifle, but it falls far short of the process known in some foreign countries as "suspending the constitutional guarantees," or in France as the "proclamation of a state of siege ";[1] it, indeed, extends the arbitrary powers of the government to a far less degree than many so-called Coercion Acts. That this is so may be seen by a mere enumeration of the chief of the extraordinary powers which were conferred by comparatively recent enactments on the Irish executive. Under the Act of 1881 the Irish executive obtained the absolute power of arbitrary and preventive arrest, and could without breach of law detain in prison any person arrested on suspicion for the whole period for which the Act continued in force. It is true that the Lord Lieutenant could arrest only persons suspected of treason or of the commission of some act tending to interfere with the maintenance of law and order. But as the warrant itself to be issued by the Lord Lieutenant was made under the Act conclusive evidence of all matters contained therein, and therefore (*inter alia*) of the truth of the assertion that the arrested person or " suspect " was reasonably suspected, *e.g.* of treasonable practices, and therefore liable to arrest, the result clearly followed that neither the Lord Lieutenant nor any official acting under him could by any possibility be made liable to any legal penalty for any arrest, however groundless or malicious, made in due form within the words of the Act. The Irish government, therefore, could arrest any person whom the Lord Lieutenant thought fit to imprison, provided only that the warrant was in the form and contained the allegations required

[1] See Duguit, *Manuel de Droit Public français, Droit Constitutionnel* (1907), para. 76, pp. 510-513, and article " Etat de Siège " in Chéruel, *Dictionnaire historique des Institutions de la France* (8th ed., 1910), vol. i, v° Etat de siège, p. 375.

Part II.

by the statute. Under the Prevention of Crime (Ireland) Act, 1882, the Irish executive was armed with the following (among other) extraordinary powers. The government could in the case of certain crimes [1] abolish the right to trial by jury,[2] could arrest strangers found out of doors at night under suspicious circumstances,[3] could seize any newspaper which, in the judgment of the Lord Lieutenant, contained matter inciting to treason or violence,[4] and could prohibit any public meeting which the Lord Lieutenant believed to be dangerous to the public peace or safety. Add to this that the Prevention of Crime Act, 1882, re-enacted (incidentally as it were) the Aliens Act of 1848, and thus empowered the British Ministry to expel from the United Kingdom any foreigner who had not before the passing of the Act been resident in the country for three years.[5] Not one of these extraordinary powers flows directly from a mere suspension of the Habeas Corpus Act; and, in truth, the best proof of the very limited legal effect of such so-called suspension is supplied by the fact that before a Habeas Corpus Suspension Act runs out its effect is, almost invariably, supplemented by legislation of a totally different character, namely, an Act of Indemnity.

Act of Indemnity.

An Act of Indemnity.[6]—Reference has already been made to Acts of Indemnity as the supreme instance of Parliamentary sovereignty. They are

[1] Viz. (*a*) treason or treason-felony; (*b*) murder or manslaughter; (*c*) attempt to murder; (*d*) aggravated crime of violence against the person; (*e*) arson, whether by common law or by statute; (*f*) attack on dwelling house.

[2] Section 1.

[3] Section 12.

[4] Section 13.

[5] Section 15.

[6] See Indemnity Act, 1920; Wade and Phillips, *op. cit.*, pp. 380-382.

retrospective statutes which free persons who have broken the law from responsibility for its breach, and thus make lawful acts which when they were committed were unlawful. It is easy enough to see the connection between a Habeas Corpus Suspension Act and an Act of Indemnity. The Suspension Act, as already pointed out, does not free any person from civil or criminal liability for a violation of the law. Suppose that a Secretary of State or his subordinates should, during the suspension of the Habeas Corpus Act, arrest and imprison a perfectly innocent man without any cause whatever, except (it may be) the belief that it is conducive to the public safety that the particular person—say, an influential party leader such as Wilkes, Fox, or O'Connell—should be at a particular crisis kept in prison, and thereby deprived of influence. Suppose, again, that an arrest should be made by orders of the Ministry under circumstances which involve the unlawful breaking into a private dwelling-house, the destruction of private property, or the like. In each of these instances, and in many others which might easily be imagined, the Secretary of State who orders the arrest and the officials who carry out his commands have broken the law. They may have acted under the *bona fide* belief that their conduct was justified by the necessity of providing for the maintenance of order. But this will not of itself, whether the Habeas Corpus Act be suspended or not, free the persons carrying out the arrests from criminal and civil liability for the wrong they have committed. The suspension, indeed, of the Habeas Corpus Act may prevent the person arrested from taking at the

Part II.

moment any proceedings against a Secretary of State or the officers who have acted under his orders. For the sufferer is of course imprisoned on the charge of high treason or suspicion of treason, and therefore will not, while the suspension lasts, be able to get himself discharged from prison. The moment, however, that the Suspension Act expires he can, of course, apply for a writ of habeas corpus, and ensure that, either by means of being put on his trial or otherwise, his arbitrary imprisonment shall be brought to an end. In the cases we have supposed the prisoner has been guilty of no legal offence. The offenders are in reality the Secretary of State and his subordinates. The result is that on the expiration of the Suspension Act they are liable to actions or indictments for their illegal conduct, and can derive no defence whatever from the mere fact that, at the time when the unlawful arrest took place, the Habeas Corpus Act was, partially at any rate, not in force. It is, however, almost certain that, when the suspension of the Habeas Corpus Act makes it possible for the government to keep suspected persons in prison for a length of time without bringing them to trial, a smaller or greater number of unlawful acts will be committed, if not by the members of the Ministry themselves, at any rate by their agents. We may even go farther than this, and say that the unavowed object of a Habeas Corpus Suspension Act is to enable the government to do acts which, though politically expedient, may not be strictly legal. The Parliament which destroys one of the main guarantees for individual freedom must hold, whether wisely or not, that a crisis has arisen when the rights of individuals must be postponed to considerations of state. A Suspension Act would, in fact, fail of its main object, unless officials felt assured that, as long as they *bona fide*, and uninfluenced by malice or by corrupt motives, carried out the policy of which the Act was the visible sign, they would be protected from penalties for conduct which, though it might be technically a breach of law, was nothing more than the free exertion for the public good of that discretionary power which the suspension of the Habeas Corpus Act was intended to confer upon the executive. This assurance is derived from the expectation that, before the Suspension Act ceases to be in force, Parliament will pass an Act of Indemnity, protecting all persons who have acted, or have intended to act, under the powers given to the government by the statute. This expectation has not been disappointed. An Act suspending the Habeas Corpus Act, which has been continued for any length of time, has constantly been followed by an Act of Indemnity. Thus the Act to which reference has already been made, 34 Geo. III. c. 54, was continued in force by successive annual re-enactments for seven years, from 1794 to 1801. In the latter year an Act was passed, 41 Geo. III. c. 66, "indemnifying such persons as since the first "day of February, 1793, have acted in the apprehend-"ing, imprisoning, or detaining in custody in Great "Britain of persons suspected of high treason or "treasonable practices." It cannot be disputed that the so-called suspension of the Habeas Corpus Act, which every one knows will probably be followed by an Act of Indemnity, is, in reality, a far greater interference with personal freedom than would appear

Part II.

from the very limited effect, in a merely legal point of view, of suspending the right of persons accused of treason to demand a speedy trial. The Suspension Act, coupled with the prospect of an Indemnity Act, does in truth arm the executive with arbitrary powers. Still, there are one or two considerations which limit the practical importance that can fairly be given to an expected Act of Indemnity. The relief to be obtained from it is prospective and uncertain. Any suspicion on the part of the public, that officials had grossly abused their powers, might make it difficult to obtain a Parliamentary indemnity for things done while the Habeas Corpus Act was suspended. As regards, again, the protection to be derived from the Act by men who have been guilty of irregular, illegal, oppressive, or cruel conduct, everything depends on the terms of the Act of Indemnity. These may be either narrow or wide. The Indemnity Act, for instance, of 1801, gives a very limited amount of protection to official wrongdoers. It provides, indeed, a defence against actions or prosecutions in respect of anything done, commanded, ordered, directed, or advised to be done in Great Britain for apprehending, imprisoning, or detaining in custody any person charged with high treason or treasonable practices. And no doubt such a defence would cover any irregularity or merely formal breach of the law, but there certainly could be imagined acts of spite or extortion, done under cover of the Suspension Act, which would expose the offender to actions or prosecutions, and could not be justified under the terms of the Indemnity Act. Reckless cruelty to a political prisoner, or, still more certainly, the arbitrary punishment or the execution of a political prisoner, between 1793 and 1801, would, in spite of the Indemnity Act, have left every man concerned in the crime liable to suffer punishment. Whoever wishes to appreciate the moderate character of an ordinary Act of Indemnity passed by the Imperial Parliament, should compare such an Act as the Act of Indemnity, 1801, with the enactment whereby the Jamaica House of Assembly attempted to cover Governor Eyre from all liability for unlawful deeds done in suppressing rebellion during 1865. An Act of Indemnity, again, though it is the legalisation of illegality, is also, it should be noted, itself a law. It is something in its essential character, therefore, very different from the proclamation of martial law, the establishment of a state of siege, or any other proceeding by which the executive government at its own will suspends the law of the land. It is no doubt an exercise of arbitrary sovereign power; but where the legal sovereign is a Parliamentary assembly, even acts of state assume the form of regular legislation, and this fact of itself maintains in no small degree the real no less than the apparent supremacy of law.

CHAPTER VI

THE RIGHT TO FREEDOM OF DISCUSSION[1]

Part II.

Freedom of discussion.

THE Declaration of the Rights of Man[2] and the French Constitution of 1791 proclaim freedom of discussion and the liberty of the press in terms which are still cited in text-books[3] as embodying maxims of French jurisprudence.

Principles laid down in foreign constitution.

"*La libre communication des pensées et des* "*opinions est un des droits les plus précieux de* "*l'homme; tout citoyen peut donc parler, écrire,* "*imprimer librement, sauf à répondre de l'abus de* "*cette liberté dans les cas déterminés par la loi.*"[4]

"*La constitution garantit, comme droit naturel et* "*civil . . . la liberté à tout homme de parler, d'écrire,* "*d'imprimer et publier ses pensées, sans que ses écrits* "*puissent être soumis à aucune censure ou inspection* "*avant leur publication.*"[5]

Belgian law, again, treats the liberty of the press as a fundamental article of the constitution.

"*Art.* 18. *La presse est libre; la censure ne* "*pourra jamais être établie; il ne peut être exigé*

[1] Wade and Phillips, *op. cit.*, Pt. viii, ch. 3.

[2] Duguit et Monnier, *Les Constitutions et les principales lois politiques de la France depuis 1789* (1898), Constitution du 3 Sept. 1791, p. 1.

[3] Bourguignon, *Eléments généraux de Législation française* (1873), p. 468.

[4] *Déclaration des droits*, art. 11, Plouard, *Les Constitutions françaises* (1871–1876), p. 16; Duguit et Monnier, *op. cit.*, p. 1.

[5] *Op. cit.*, p. 18; *op. cit.*, p. 4.

"*de cautionnement des écrivains, éditeurs ou im-* "*primeurs.*

Chapter VI.

"*Lorsque l'auteur est connu et domicilié en Bel-* "*gique, l'éditeur, l'imprimeur ou le distributeur ne* "*peut être poursuivi.*"[1]

No principle of freedom of discussion recognised by English law.

Both the revolutionists of France and the constitutionalists of Belgium borrowed their ideas about freedom of opinion and the liberty of the press from England, and most persons form such loose notions as to English law that the idea prevails in England itself that the right to the free expression of opinion, and especially that form of it which is known as the "liberty of the press," are fundamental doctrines of the law of England in the same sense in which they were part of the ephemeral constitution of 1791 and still are embodied in the articles of the existing Belgian constitution; and, further, that our courts recognise the right of every man to say and write what he pleases, especially on social, political, or religious topics, without fear of legal penalties. Yet this notion, justified though it be, to a certain extent, by the habits of modern English life, is essentially false, and conceals from students the real attitude of English law towards what is called "freedom of thought," and is more accurately described as the "right to the free expression of opinion." As every lawyer knows, the phrases "freedom of discussion" or "liberty of the press" are rarely found in any part of the statute-book nor among the maxims of the common law.[2] As terms of art they are indeed quite unknown to our courts. At no time has there in

[1] *Constitution de la Belgique*, art. 18.

[2] It appears, however, in the preamble to Lord Campbell's Libel Act, 1843.

Part II.

England been any proclamation of the right to liberty of thought or to freedom of speech. The true state of things cannot be better described than in these words from an excellent treatise on the law of libel:—

English law only secures that no one shall be punished except for statements proved to be breach of law.

"Our present law permits any one to say, write, "and publish what he pleases; but if he make a bad "use of this liberty he must be punished. If he "unjustly attack an individual, the person defamed "may sue for damages; if, on the other hand, the "words be written or printed, or if treason or im-"morality be thereby inculcated, the offender can be "tried for the misdemeanour either by information "or indictment."[1]

Any man may, therefore, say or write whatever he likes, subject to the risk of, it may be, severe punishment if he publishes any statement (either by word of mouth, in writing, or in print) which he is not legally entitled to make. Nor is the law of England specially favourable to free speech or to free writing in the rules which it maintains in theory and often enforces in fact as to the kind of statements which a man has a legal right to make. Above all, it recognises in general no special privilege on behalf of the "press," if by that term we mean, in conformity with ordinary language, periodical literature in general, and particularly the newspapers. In truth there is little in the statute-book which can be called a "press law."[2] The law

[1] Odgers, *Libel and Slander, Introduction* (3rd ed., 1896), p. 12.

[2] For exceptions to this, see *e.g.* Libel Act, 1843, and Newspaper Libel and Registration Act, 1881. It is, however, true, as pointed out by a critic (see Fisher & Strahan, *The Law of the Press* (2nd ed., 1898), p. iii), that "there is slowly growing up a distinct law of the Press."

of the press as it exists here is merely part of the law of libel, and it is well worth while to trace out with some care the restrictions imposed by the law of libel on the "freedom of the press," by which expression I mean a person's right to make any statement he likes in books or newspapers.

Libels on individuals.

There are many statements with regard to individuals which no man is entitled to publish in writing or print; it is a libel (speaking generally) thus to publish any untrue statement about another which is calculated to injure his interests, character, or reputation. Every man who directly or indirectly makes known or, as the technical expression goes, "publishes" such a statement, gives currency to a libel and is liable to an action for damages. The person who makes a defamatory statement and authorises its publication in writing, the person who writes, the publisher who brings out for sale, the printer who prints, the vendor who distributes a libel, are each guilty of publication, and may each severally be sued. The gist of the offence being the making public, not the writing of the libel, the person who having read a libel sends it on to a friend, is a libeller; and it would seem that a man who reads aloud a libel, knowing it to be such, may be sued. This separate liability of each person concerned in a wrongful act is, as already pointed out, a very noticeable

The tendency of recent press legislation is to a certain extent to free the proprietors of newspapers from the full amount of liability which attaches to other persons for the *bona fide* publication of defamatory statements made at public meetings and the like. [See especially the Defamation Act, 1952, ss. 4 and 7 and Schedule. In cases of unintentional defamation an offer of apology and amends may exclude the right to recover damages. Qualified privilege attaches to reports in newspapers and journals of a wide range of matters of general public interest.—Ed.]

Part II.

characteristic of our law. Honest belief, moreover, and good intentions on the part of a libeller, are no legal defence for his conduct. Nor will it avail him to show that he had good reason for thinking the false statement which he made to be true. Persons often must pay heavy damages for giving currency to statements which were not meant to be falsehoods, and which were reasonably believed to be true. Thus it is libellous to publish of a man who has been convicted of felony but has worked out his sentence that he "is a convicted felon." It is a libel on the part of *X* if *X* publishes that *B* has told him that *A*'s bank has stopped payment, if, though *B* in fact made the statement to *X*, and *X* believed the report to be true, it turns out to be false. Nor, again, are expressions of opinion when injurious to another at all certain not to expose the publisher of them to an action. A "fair" criticism, it is often said, is not libellous; but it would be a grave mistake to suppose that critics, either in the press or elsewhere, have a right to publish whatever criticisms they think true. Every one has a right to publish fair and candid criticism. But "a critic must confine himself to criticism, and "not make it the veil for personal censure, nor allow "himself to run into reckless and unfair attacks merely "from the love of exercising his power of denuncia-"tion."[1] A writer in the press and an artist or actor whose performances are criticised are apt to draw the line between "candid criticism" and "personal censure" at very different points. And when on this matter there is a difference of opinion between a critic and his victim, the delicate question what is meant by

[1] *Whistler* v. *Ruskin* (1878) The Times Newspaper, Nov. 27, p. 11, per Huddleston, B.

fairness has to be determined by a jury, and may be so answered as greatly to curtail the free expression of critical judgments. Nor let it be supposed that the mere "truth" of a statement is of itself sufficient to protect the person who publishes it from liability to punishment. For though the fact that an assertion is true is an answer to an action for libel, a person may be criminally punished for publishing statements which, though perfectly true, damage an individual without being of any benefit to the public. To write, for example, and with truth of *A* that he many years ago committed acts of immorality may very well expose the writer *X* to criminal proceedings, and *X* if put on his trial will be bound to prove not only that *A* was in fact guilty of the faults imputed to him, but also that the public had an interest in the knowledge of *A*'s misconduct. If *X* cannot show this, he will find that no supposed right of free discussion or respect for liberty of the press will before an English judge save him from being found guilty of a misdemeanour and sent to prison.

Libels on government.

So far in very general terms of the limits placed by the law of libel on freedom of discussion as regards the character of individuals. Let us now observe for a moment the way in which the law of libel restricts in theory, at least, the right to criticise the conduct of the government.

Every person commits a misdemeanour who publishes (orally or otherwise) any words or any document with a seditious intention. Now a seditious intention means an intention to bring into hatred or contempt, or to excite disaffection against the King or the government and constitution of the United

Part II.

Kingdom as by law established, or either House of Parliament, or the administration of justice, or to excite British subjects to attempt otherwise than by lawful means the alteration of any matter in Church or State by law established, or to promote feelings of illwill and hostility between different classes.[1] And if the matter published is contained in a written or printed document the publisher is guilty of publishing a seditious libel. The law, it is true, permits the publication of statements meant only to show that the Crown has been misled, or that the government has committed errors, or to point out defects in the government or the constitution with a view to their legal remedy, or with a view to recommend alterations in Church or State by legal means, and, in short, sanctions criticism on public affairs which is *bona fide* intended to recommend the reform of existing institutions by legal methods. But any one will see at once that the legal definition of a seditious libel might easily be so used as to check a great deal of what is ordinarily considered allowable discussion, and would if rigidly enforced be inconsistent with prevailing forms of political agitation.

Expression of opinion on religious or moral questions.

The case is pretty much the same as regards the free expression of opinion on religious or moral questions.[2] Of late years circumstances have recalled attention to the forgotten law of blasphemy. But it surprises most persons to learn that, on one view of the law, any one who publishes a denial of the truth of Christianity in general or of the existence of God,

[1] See Stephen, *Digest of the Criminal Law* (6th ed., 1904), arts. 96, 97, 98. [To secure a conviction a clear incitement to violence must be proved; *The King* v. *Aldred* (1909) 22 Cox 1; *The King* v. *Caunt* (1937) unreported.—Ed.]

[2] *Ibid.*, arts. 179-183.

Chapter VI.

whether the terms of such publication are decent or otherwise, commits the misdemeanour of publishing a blasphemous libel, and is liable to imprisonment; that, according to another view of the law, any one is guilty of publishing a blasphemous libel who publishes matter relating to God, Jesus Christ, or the Book of Common Prayer intended to wound the feelings of mankind, or to excite contempt against the Church by law established, or to promote immorality; and that it is at least open to grave doubt how far the publications which thus wound the feelings of mankind are exempt from the character of blasphemy because they are intended in good faith to propagate opinions which the person who publishes them regards as true.[1] Most persons, again, are astonished to find that the denial of the truth of Christianity or of the authority of the Scriptures, by "writing, printing, teaching, or advised speaking" on the part of any person who has been educated in or made profession of Christianity in England, is by statute a criminal offence entailing very severe penalties.[2] When once, however, the principles of the common law and the force of the enactments still contained in the statute-book are really appreciated, no one can maintain that the law of England recognises anything like that natural right to the free communication of thoughts and opinions which was pro-

[1] But see *The Queen* v. *Ramsay and Foote* (1883) 48 L.T. 733; and *Bowman* v. *Secular Society Ltd.* [1914] A.C. 406, where the House of Lords held that the propagation of anti-Christian doctrines, apart from scurrility or profanity, did not constitute the offence of blasphemy.—Ed.

[2] See 9 & 10 Will. III. c. 35, as amended by 53 Geo. III. c. 160, and Stephen, *op. cit.*, art. 181; cf. *Attorney-General* v. *Bradlaugh* (1885) 14 Q.B.D. 667, at p. 719, per Lindley, L.J.

Part II. claimed in France a little over a hundred years ago to be one of the most valuable Rights of Man. It is quite clear, further, that the effect of English law, whether as regards statements made about individuals, or the expression of opinion about public affairs, or speculative matters, depends wholly upon the answer to the question who are to determine whether a given publication is or is not a libel. The reply (as we all know) is, that in substance this matter is referred to the decision of a jury. Whether in any given case a particular individual is to be convicted of libel depends wholly upon their judgment, and they have to determine the questions of truth, fairness, intention, and the like, which affect the legal character of a published statement.[1]

Freedom of discussion is, then, in England little else than the right to write or say anything which a jury, consisting of twelve shopkeepers, think it expedient should be said or written. Such "liberty" may vary at different times and seasons from unrestricted license to very severe restraint, and the experience of English history during the last two centuries shows that under the law of libel the amount of latitude conceded to the expression of opinion has, in fact, differed greatly according to the condition of popular sentiment. Until very recent

[1] "The truth of the matter is very simple when stripped of all ornaments of speech, and a man of plain common sense may easily understand it. It is neither more nor less than this: that a man may publish anything which twelve of his countrymen think is not blamable, but that he ought to be punished if he publishes that which is blamable [*i.e.* that which twelve of his countrymen think is blamable]. This in plain common sense is the substance of all that has been said on the matter."—*The King* v. *Cuthell* (1799) 27 St. Tr. 642, at p. 675.

Chapter VI.

times the law, moreover, has not recognised any privilege on the part of the press. A statement which is defamatory or blasphemous, if made in a letter or upon a card, has exactly the same character if made in a book or a newspaper. The protection given by the Belgian constitution to the editor, printer, or seller of a newspaper involves a recognition of special rights on the part of persons connected with the press which is quite inconsistent with the general theory of English law. It is hardly an exaggeration to say, from this point of view, that liberty of the press is not recognised in England.

Why the liberty of the press has been thought peculiar to England.

Why then has the liberty of the press been long reputed as a special feature of English institutions?

The answer to this inquiry is, that for about two centuries the relation between the government and the press has in England been marked by all those characteristics which make up what we have termed the "rule" or "supremacy" of law, and that just because of this, and not because of any favour shown by the law of England towards freedom of discussion, the press, and especially the newspaper press, has practically enjoyed with us a freedom which till recent years was unknown in continental states. Any one will see that this is so who examines carefully the situation of the press in modern England, and then contrasts it either with the press law of France or with the legal condition of the press in England during the sixteenth and seventeenth centuries.

The present position of the English press is marked by two features.

First, " The liberty of the press," says Lord Mansfield, " consists in printing without any previous

Part II.

The position of the press in modern England. No censorship.

"license, subject to the consequences of law."[1] "The "law of England," says Lord Ellenborough, "is a "law of liberty, and consistently with this liberty "we have not what is called an *imprimatur*; there "is no such preliminary license necessary; but if "a man publish a paper, he is exposed to the penal "consequences, as he is in every other act, if it be "illegal."[2]

These dicta show us at once that the so-called liberty of the press is a mere application of the general principle, that no man is punishable except for a distinct breach of the law.[3] This principle is radically inconsistent with any scheme of licence or censorship by which a man is hindered from writing or printing anything which he thinks fit, and is hard to reconcile even with the right on the part of the courts to restrain the circulation of a libel, until at any rate the publisher has been convicted of publishing it. It is also opposed in spirit to any regulation requiring from the publisher of an intending newspaper a preliminary deposit of a certain sum of money, for the sake either of ensuring that newspapers should be published only by solvent persons, or that if a newspaper should contain libels there shall be a certainty of obtaining damages from the proprietor. No sensible person will argue that to demand a deposit from the owner of a newspaper, or to impose other limitations upon the right of publishing periodicals, is of necessity inexpedient or unjust. All that is here insisted upon is, that such

[1] *The King* v. *Dean of St. Asaph* (1784) 3 T.R. 428 (note).
[2] *The King* v. *Cobbett* (1804) 29 St. Tr. 1.
[3] See p. 188, *ante*.

checks and preventive measures are inconsistent with the pervading principle of English law, that men are to be interfered with or punished, not because they may or will break the law, but only when they have committed some definite assignable legal offence. Hence, with one exception,[1] which is a quaint survival from a different system, no such thing is known with us as a license to print, or a censorship either of the press or of political newspapers. Neither the government nor any other authority has the right to seize or destroy the stock of a publisher because it consists of books, pamphlets, or papers which in the opinion of the government contain seditious or libellous matter. Indeed, the courts themselves will, only under very special circumstances, even for the sake of protecting an individual from injury, prohibit the publication or republication of a libel, or restrain its sale until the matter has gone before a jury, and it has been established by their verdict that the words complained of are libellous.[2] Writers in the press are, in short, like every other person, subject to the law of the realm, and nothing else. Neither the government nor the courts have (speaking generally) any greater power to prevent or oversee the publication of a newspaper than the writing and sending of a letter. Indeed, the simplest way of setting forth broadly the position of writers in the press is to say that they stand in substantially the same position as letter-writers. A man who scribbles blasphemy on a gate[3]

[1] *I.e.* the licensing of the performance of stage plays by the Lord Chamberlain, see Theatres Act, 1843, s. 12.

[2] Compare Odgers, *Libel and Slander* (6th ed., 1929), ch. xiv, with 1st ed., 1881, pp. 13-16.

[3] *The Queen* v. *Pooley* (1857), cited Stephen, *Digest of the Criminal Law* (7th ed., 1926), p. 160, note 2.

Part II.

and a man who prints blasphemy in a paper or in a book commit exactly the same offence, and are dealt with in England on the same principles. Hence also writers in and owners of newspapers have, or rather had until very recently, no special privilege protecting them from liability.[1] Look at the matter which way you will, the main feature of liberty of the press as understood in England is that the press (which means, of course, the writers in it) is subject only to the ordinary law of the land.

Press offences dealt with by ordinary Courts.

Secondly, Press offences, in so far as the term can be used with reference to English law, are tried and punished only by the ordinary courts of the country, that is, by a judge and jury.[2]

Since the Restoration,[3] offences committed through the newspapers, or, in other words, the publication therein of libels whether defamatory, seditious, or blasphemous, have never been tried by any special tribunal. Nothing to Englishmen seems more a matter of course than this. Yet nothing has in reality contributed so much to free the periodical press from any control. If the criterion whether a publication be libellous is the opinion of the jury, and a man may

[1] This statement must be to a certain extent qualified in view of the Libel Act, 1843, the Newspaper Libel and Registration Act, 1881, and the Defamation Act, 1952, s. 7 (p. 240, note 2, *ante*).

[2] The existence, however, of process by criminal information, and the rule that truth was no justification, had the result that during the eighteenth century seditious libel rose almost to the rank of a press offence. Until Fox's Libel Act, 1792, the jury in a prosecution for seditious libel did not return a verdict on the general issue. It was for the judge alone to decide the issue of libel or no libel as a matter of law.

[3] See as to the state of the press under the Commonwealth, Masson, *Life of Milton* (1873), vol. iii, pp. 265-297. Substantially the possibility of trying press offences by special tribunals was put an end to by the abolition of the Star Chamber in 1641; Star Chamber Abolition Act, 1641.

publish anything which twelve of his countrymen think is not blamable, it is impossible that the Crown or the Ministry should exert any stringent control over writings in the press, unless (as indeed may sometimes happen) the majority of ordinary citizens are entirely opposed to attacks on the government. The times when persons in power wish to check the excesses of public writers are times at which a large body of opinion or sentiment is hostile to the executive. But under these circumstances it must, from the nature of things, be at least an even chance that the jury called upon to find a publisher guilty of printing seditious libels may sympathise with the language which the officers of the Crown deem worthy of punishment, and hence may hold censures which are prosecuted as libels to be fair and laudable criticism of official errors. Whether the control indirectly exercised over the expression of opinion by the verdict of twelve commonplace Englishmen is at the present day certain to be as great a protection to the free expression of opinion, even in political matters, as it proved a century ago, when the sentiment of the governing body was different from the prevalent feeling of the class from which jurymen were chosen, is an interesting speculation into which there is no need to enter. What is certain is, that the practical freedom of the English press arose in great measure from the trial with us of "press offences," like every other kind of libel, by a jury.

The liberty of the press, then, is in England simply one result of the universal predominance of the law of the land. The terms "liberty of the press," "press offences," "censorship of the press," and the like, are all but unknown to English lawyers, simply because

Part II. any offence which can be committed through the press is some form of libel, and is governed in substance by the ordinary law of defamation.

These things seem to us at the present day so natural as hardly to be noticeable; let us, however, glance as I have suggested at the press law of France both before and since the Revolution; and also at the condition of the press in England up to nearly the end of the seventeenth century. Such a survey will prove to us that the treatment in modern England of offences committed through the newspapers affords an example, as singular as it is striking, of the legal spirit which now pervades every part of the English constitution.

Comparison with the press law of France.

An Englishman who consults French authorities is struck with amazement at two facts: press law[1] has long constituted and still constitutes to a certain extent a special department of French legislation, and press offences have been, under every form of government which has existed in France, a more or less

[1] The press is governed in France by the *Loi sur la liberté de la presse*, 29-30 *Juill.* 1881. This law repealed all earlier edicts, decrees, laws and ordinances on the subject. Immediately before this law was passed there were in force more than thirty enactments regulating the position of the French press, and inflicting penalties on offences which could be committed by writers in the press; and the three hundred and odd closely printed pages of Dalloz, treating of laws on the press, show that the enactments then in vigour under the Republic were as nothing compared to the whole mass of regulations, ordinances, decrees, and laws which, since the earliest days of printing down to the year 1881, have been issued by French rulers with the object of controlling the literary expression of opinion and thought. See Dalloz, *Répertoire de Législation et de Jurisprudence*, vol. xxxvi (1856), v° presse, pp. 384-776, spécial; tit. i, ch. i, pp. 386-394, and tit. ii, ch. iv, pp. 445-491. Cf. *Supplément au Répertoire*, vol. xiii (1893), v° presse, pp. 247-262 and pp. 271-308; cf. vol. ii, 1929, v° presse, pp. 569, 571; *Additions au Répertoire*, 1938, v° presse, p. 651; Roger et Sorel, *Codes et Lois usuelles* (1882), v° presse, pp. 637-652; Duguit, *Manuel de Droit Public français; Droit Constitutionnel* (1907), para. 86, pp. 575-582.

special class of crimes. The Acts which have been passed in England with regard to the press since the days of Queen Elizabeth I do not in number equal one-tenth, or even one-twentieth, of the laws enacted during the same period on the same subject in France. The contrast becomes still more marked if we compare the state of things in the two countries since the beginning of the eighteenth century, and (for the sake of avoiding exaggeration) put the laws passed since that date, and which were till 1881 in force in France, against every Act which, whether repealed or unrepealed, has been passed in England since the year 1700. It will be found that the French press code consisted, till after the establishment of the present Republic, of over thirty enactments, whilst the English Acts about the press passed since the beginning of the last century do not exceed a dozen, and, moreover, have gone very little way towards touching the freedom of writers.

The ground of this difference lies in the opposite views taken in the two countries of the proper relation of the state to literature, or, more strictly, to the expression of opinion in print.

In England the doctrine has since 1700 in substance prevailed that the government has nothing to do with the guidance of opinion, and that the sole duty of the state is to punish libels of all kinds, whether they are expressed in writing or in print. Hence the government has (speaking generally) exercised no special control over literature, and the law of the press, in so far as it can be said to have existed, has been nothing else than a branch or an application of the law of libel.

Part II.

In France, literature has for centuries been considered as the particular concern of the state. The prevailing doctrine, as may be gathered from the current of French legislation, has been, and still to a certain extent is, that it is the function of the administration not only to punish defamation, slander, or blasphemy, but to guide the course of opinion, or, at any rate, to adopt preventive measures for guarding against the propagation in print of unsound or dangerous doctrines. Hence the huge amount and the special and repressive character of the press laws which have existed in France.

Up to the time of the Revolution the whole literature of the country was avowedly controlled by the state. The right to print or sell books and printed publications of any kind was treated as a special privilege or monopoly of certain libraries; the regulations (*réglements*) of 1723 (some part of which was till quite recently in force[1]) and of 1767 confined the right of sale and printing under the severest penalties to librarians who were duly licensed.[2] The right to publish, again, was submitted to the strictest censorship, exercised partly by the University (an entirely ecclesiastical body), partly by the Parliaments, partly by the Crown. The penalties of death, of the galleys, of the pillory, were from time to time imposed upon the printing or sale of forbidden works. These punishments were often evaded; but they after all retained practical force till the very eve of the Revolution. The most celebrated literary works of France

[1] See Dalloz, *Répertoire de Législation*, vol. xxxvi (1856), v° presse, tit. i, ch. i. Cf. Roger et Sorel, *Codes et Lois usuelles* (1882), v° presse, pp. 637-652.

[2] *Ibid.*

were published abroad. Montesquieu's *Esprit des Lois* appeared at Geneva. Voltaire's *Henriade* was printed in England; the most remarkable of his and of Rousseau's writings were published in London, in Geneva, or in Amsterdam. In 1775 a work entitled *Philosophie de la Nature* was destroyed by the order of the Parliament of Paris, the author was decreed guilty of treason against God and man, and would have been burnt if he could have been arrested. In 1781, eight years before the meeting of the States General, Raynal was pronounced by the Parliament guilty of blasphemy on account of his *Histoire des Indes.*[1] The point, however, to remark is, not so much the severity of the punishments which under the *Ancien Régime* were intended to suppress the expression of heterodox or false beliefs, as the strict maintenance down to 1789 of the right and duty of the state to guide the literature of the country. It should further be noted that down to that date the government made no marked distinction between periodical and other literature. When the *Lettres Philosophiques* could be burnt by the hangman, when the publication of the *Henriade* and the *Encyclopédie* depended on the goodwill of the King, there was no need for establishing special restrictions on newspapers. The daily or weekly press, moreover, hardly existed in France till the opening of the States General.[2]

[1] See Dalloz, *Répertoire de Législation,* vol. xxxvi (1856), v° presse, tit. i, ch. i, p. 386. Cf. Roger et Sorel, *Codes et Lois usuelles* (1882), v° presse, pp. 637-652.

[2] See Rocquain, *L'Esprit révolutionnaire avant la Révolution* (1878), for a complete list of "*Livres Condamnés*" from 1715 to 1789. Rocquain's book is full of information on the arbitrariness of the French Government during the reigns of Louis XV and Louis XVI.

Part II.

The Revolution (it may be fancied) put an end to restraints upon the press. The Declaration of the Rights of Man proclaimed the right of every citizen to publish and print his opinions, and the language has been cited[1] in which the Constitution of 1791 guaranteed to every man the natural right of speaking, printing, and publishing his thoughts without having his writings submitted to any censorship or inspection prior to publication. But the Declaration of Rights and this guarantee were practically worthless. They enounced a theory which for many years was utterly opposed to the practice of every French government.

The Convention did not establish a censorship, but under the plea of preventing the circulation of seditious works it passed the law of 29th March 1793, which silenced all free expression of opinion. The Directory imitated the Convention. Under the First Empire the newspaper press became the property of the government, and the sale, printing, and publication of books was wholly submitted to imperial control and censorship.[2]

The years which elapsed from 1789 to 1815 were, it may be suggested, a revolutionary era which provoked or excused exceptional measures of state interference. Any one, however, who wants to see how consonant to the ideas which have permanently governed French law and French habits is the notion that the administration should by some means keep its hand on the national literature of the country, ought to note with care the course of legislation from

[1] See p. 238, *ante*.

[2] Dalloz, *Répertoire de Législation*, vol. xxxvi (1856), v° presse, tit. i, ch. i, p. 386.

the Restoration to the present day. The attempt, indeed, to control the publication of books has been by slow degrees given up; but one government after another has, with curious uniformity, proclaimed the freedom and ensured the subjection of the newspaper press. From 1814 to 1830 the censorship was practically established (21st Oct. 1814), was partially abolished, was abolished (1819), was re-established and extended (1820), and was re-abolished (1828).[1] The Revolution of July 1830 was occasioned by an attempt to destroy the liberty of the press. The Charter made the abolition of the censorship part of the constitution, and since that date no system of censorship has been in name re-established. But as regards newspapers, the celebrated decree of 17th February 1852 enacted restrictions more rigid than anything imposed under the name of *la censure* by any government since the fall of Napoleon I. The government took to itself under this law, in addition to other discretionary powers, the right to suppress any newspaper without the necessity of proving the commission of any crime or offence by the owner of the paper or by any writer in its columns.[2] No one, further, could under this decree set up a paper without official authorisation. Nor have different forms of the censorship been the sole restrictions imposed in France on the liberty of the press. The combined operations of enactments passed during the existence of the Republic of 1848, and under the Empire, was (among other things) to make the signature of newspaper articles by their

[1] See Duguit, *Traité de Droit constitutionnel* (2nd ed., vol. v, 1925), ch. iii, para. 35, pp. 414, 415.

[2] Décret, 17 Février, 1852, sec. 32; Roger et Sorel, *Codes et Lois usuelles* (1882), v° presse, p. 646.

authors compulsory,[1] to require a large deposit from any person who wished to establish a paper,[2] to withdraw all press offences whatever from the cognisance of a jury,[3] to re-establish or reaffirm the provision contained in the *réglement* of 1723 by which no one could carry on the trade of a librarian or printer (*commerce de la librairie*) without a license. It may, in fact, be said with substantial truth that between 1852 and 1870 the newspapers of France were as much controlled by the government as was every kind of literature before 1789, and that the Second Empire exhibited a retrogression towards the despotic principles of the *Ancien Régime.* The Republic,[4] it is true, has abolished the restraints on the liberty of the press which grew up both before and under the

[1] Roger et Sorel, *op. cit.* (1882), v° etat de siège, p. 436, loi du 16 Juillet, 1850.

[2] Roger et Sorel, *op. cit.* (1882), v° presse, p. 646, loi du 16 Juillet, 1850.

[3] Lois, 31 Dec., 1851.

[4] One thing was perfectly clear and deserved notice. The legislation of the existing Republic was not till 1881, any more than that of the Restoration or the Empire, based on the view of the press which pervaded the modern law of England. "Press law" still formed a special department of the law of France. "Press offences" were a particular class of crimes, and there were at least two provisions, and probably several more, to be found in French laws which conflicted with the doctrine of the liberty of the press as understood in England. A law passed under the Republic (6th July, 1871. Roger et Sorel, *op. cit.*, p. 652) reimposed on the proprietors of newspapers the necessity of making a large deposit, with the proper authorities, as a security for the payment of fines or damages incurred in the course of the management of the paper. A still later law (29th December, 1875, s. 5. Roger et Sorel, *op. cit.*, p. 652), while it submitted some press offences to the judgment of a jury, subjected others to the cognisance of courts of which a jury formed no part. The law of 29th July, 1881, established the freedom of the press. Later French legislation exhibited, no doubt, a violent reaction against all attempts to check the freedom of the press, but in its very effort to secure this freedom betrayed the existence of the notion that offences committed through the press required in some sort exceptional treatment.

Chapter VI.

Empire. But though for the last twenty-seven years the ruling powers in France have favoured the liberty or licence of the press, nothing is more plain than that until quite recently the idea that press offences were a peculiar class of offences to be dealt with in a special way and punished by special courts was accepted by every party in France. This is a matter of extreme theoretical importance. It shows how foreign to French notions is the idea that every breach of law ought to be dealt with by the ordinary law of the land. Even a cursory survey—and no other is possible in these lectures—of French legislation with regard to literature proves, then, that from the time when the press came into existence up to almost the present date the idea has held ground that the state, as represented by the executive, ought to direct or control the expression of opinion, and that this control has been exercised by an official censorship—by restrictions on the right to print or sell books—and by the subjection of press offences to special laws administered by special tribunals. The occasional relaxation of these restrictions is of importance. But their recurring revival is of far more significance than their temporary abolition.[1]

Contrast with position of press in England during seventeenth century.

Let us now turn to the position of the English press during the sixteenth and seventeenth centuries.

[1] Note the several laws passed since 1881 to repress the abuse of freedom in one form or another by the press, *e.g.* the law of 2nd August, 1882, modified and completed by the law of 16th March, 1898, for the suppression of violations of moral principles (*outrages aux bonnes mœurs*) by the press, the law of 28th July, 1894, to suppress the advocacy of anarchical principles by the press, and the law of 16th March, 1893, giving the French government special powers with regard to foreign newspapers, or newspapers published in a foreign language. Cf. Duguit, *Manuel de Droit Public français ; Droit Constitutionnel* (1907), para. 86, p. 582.

Part II.

The Crown originally held all presses in its own hands, allowed no one to print except under special license, and kept all presses subject to regulations put forward by the Star Chamber in virtue of the royal prerogative: the exclusive privilege of printing was thus given to ninety-seven London stationers and their successors, who, as the Stationers' Company, constituted a guild with power to seize all publications issued by outsiders; the printing-presses ultimately conceded to the Universities existed only by a decree of the Star Chamber.

Side by side with the restrictions on printing—which appear to have more or less broken down—there grew up a system of licensing which constituted a true censorship.[1]

Press offences constituted a special class of crimes cognisable by a special tribunal—the Star Chamber—which sat without a jury and administered severe punishments.[2] The Star Chamber indeed fell in 1641, never to be revived, but the censorship survived the Commonwealth, and was under the Restoration (1662) given a strictly legal foundation by the Licensing Act of 1662, which by subsequent enactments was kept in force till 1695.[3]

Original likeness and subsequent unlikeness between press law of England and of France.

There existed, in short, in England during the sixteenth and seventeenth centuries every method of curbing the press which was then practised in France,

[1] See for the control exercised over the press down to 1695, Odgers, *Libel and Slander* (6th ed., 1929), pp. 10-12; Holdsworth, *History of English Law*, vol. vi (1924), pp. 360-379, and vol. x (1938), pp. 28, 29.

[2] Gardiner, *History of England*, vol. vii (1884), pp. 51, 130; *ibid.*, vol. viii (1884), pp. 225, 234; Holdsworth, *op. cit.*, vol. vi (1924), pp. 367-370.

[3] See Macaulay, *History of England*, vol. iv (1858), ch. xix, xxi.

and which has prevailed there almost up to the present day. In England, as on the Continent, the book trade was a monopoly, the censorship was in full vigour, the offences of authors and printers were treated as special crimes and severely punished by special tribunals. This similarity or identity of the principles with regard to the treatment of literature originally upheld by the government of England and by the government of France is striking. It is rendered still more startling by the contrast between the subsequent history of legislation in the two countries. In France (as we have already seen) the censorship, though frequently abolished, has almost as frequently been restored. In England the system of licensing, which was the censorship under another name, was terminated rather than abolished in 1695. The House of Commons, which refused to continue the Licensing Act, was certainly not imbued with any settled enthusiasm for liberty of thought. The English statesmen of 1695 neither avowed nor entertained the belief that the "free communication of "thoughts and opinions was one of the most valuable "of the rights of man."[1] They refused to renew the Licensing Act, and thus established freedom of the press without any knowledge of the importance of what they were doing. This can be asserted with confidence, for the Commons delivered to the Lords a document which contains the reasons for their refusing to renew the Act.

"This paper completely vindicates the resolution "to which the Commons had come. But it proves "at the same time that they knew not what they

[1] See *Declaration of the Rights of Man*, art. 11, p. 234, *ante*.

Part II.

"were doing, what a revolution they were making, "what a power they were calling into existence. "They pointed out concisely, clearly, forcibly, and "sometimes with a grave irony which is not un- "becoming, the absurdities and iniquities of the "statute which was about to expire. But all their "objections will be found to relate to matters of "detail. On the great question of principle, on the "question whether the liberty of unlicensed printing "be, on the whole, a blessing or a curse to society, "not a word is said. The Licensing Act is con- "demned, not as a thing essentially evil, but on "account of the petty grievances, the exactions, the "jobs, the commercial restrictions, the domiciliary "visits, which were incidental to it. It is pronounced "mischievous because it enables the Company of "Stationers to extort money from publishers, because "it empowers the agents of the government to search "houses under the authority of general warrants, "because it confines the foreign book trade to the "port of London; because it detains valuable "packages of books at the Custom House till the "pages are mildewed. The Commons complain that "the amount of the fee which the licenser may "demand is not fixed. They complain that it is "made penal in an officer of the Customs to open a "box of books from abroad, except in the presence "of one of the censors of the press. How, it is "very sensibly asked, is the officer to know that "there are books in the box till he has opened it? "Such were the arguments which did what Milton's "*Areopagitica* had failed to do." [1]

[1] Macaulay, *op. cit.*, vol. iv (1858), p. 543.

Chapter VI.

How slight was the hold of the principle of the liberty of the press on the statesmen who abolished the censorship is proved by their entertaining, two years later, a bill (which, however, never passed) to prohibit the unlicensed publication of news.[1] Yet while the solemn declaration by the National Assembly of 1789 of the right to the free expression of thought remained a dead letter, or at best a speculative maxim of French jurisprudence which, though not without influence, was constantly broken in upon by the actual law of France, the refusal of the English Parliament in 1695 to renew the Licensing Act did permanently establish the freedom of the press in England. The fifty years which followed were a period of revolutionary disquiet fairly comparable with the era of the Restoration in France. But the censorship once abolished in England was never revived, and all idea of restrictions on the liberty of the press other than those contained in the law of libel have been so long unknown to Englishmen, that the rare survivals in our law of the notion that literature ought to be controlled by the state appear to most persons inexplicable anomalies, and are tolerated only because they produce so little inconvenience that their existence is forgotten.

Questions suggested by original similarity and final difference between press law of France and of England.

To a student who surveys the history of the liberty of the press in France and in England two questions suggest themselves. How does it happen that down to the end of the seventeenth century the principles upheld by the Crown in each country were in substance the same? What, again, is the explanation of the fact that from the beginning of the eighteenth

[1] Macaulay, *op. cit.*, pp. 774, 775.

Part II.

century the principles governing the law of the press in the two countries have been, as they still continue to be, essentially different? The similarity and the difference each seems at first sight equally perplexing. Yet both one and the other admit of explanation, and the solution of an apparent paradox is worth giving because of its close bearing on the subject of this lecture, namely, the predominance of the spirit of legality which distinguishes the law of the constitution.

Reasons for original similarity.

The ground of the similarity between the press law of England and of France from the beginning of the sixteenth till the beginning of the eighteenth century, is that the governments, if not the people, of each country were during that period influenced by very similar administrative notions and by similar ideas as to the relation between the state and individuals. In England, again, as in every European country, the belief prevailed that a King was responsible for the religious belief of his subjects. This responsibility involves the necessity for regulating the utterance and formation of opinion. But this direction or control cannot be exercised without governmental interference with that liberty of the press which is at bottom the right of every man to print any opinion which he chooses to propagate, subject only to risk of punishment if his expressions contravene some distinct legal maxim. During the sixteenth and seventeenth centuries, in short, the Crown was in England, as in France, extending its administrative powers; the Crown was in England, as in France, entitled, or rather required by public opinion, to treat the control of literature as an affair

Chapter VI.

of state. Similar circumstances produced similar results; in each country the same principles prevailed; in each country the treatment of the press assumed, therefore, a similar character.

Reasons for later dissimilarity.

The reason, again, why, for nearly two centuries, the press has been treated in France on principles utterly different from those which have been accepted in England, lies deep in the difference of the spirit which has governed the customs and laws of the two countries.

In France the idea has always flourished that the government, whether Royal, Imperial, or Republican, possesses, as representing the state, rights and powers as against individuals superior to and independent of the ordinary law of the land. This is the real basis of that whole theory of a *droit administratif*,[1] which it is so hard for Englishmen fully to understand. The increase, moreover, in the authority of the central government has at most periods both before and since the Revolution been, or appeared to most Frenchmen to be, the means of removing evils which oppressed the mass of the people. The nation has in general looked upon the authority of the state with the same favour with which Englishmen during the sixteenth century regarded the prerogative of the Crown. The control exercised in different forms by the executive over literature has, therefore, in the main fully harmonised with the other institutions of France. The existence, moreover, of an elaborate administrative system, the action of which has never been subject to the control of the ordinary tribunals, has always placed in the hands of whatever power was supreme

[1] See Appendix I.

in France the means of enforcing official surveillance of literature. Hence the censorship (to speak of no other modes of checking the liberty of the press) has been on the whole in keeping with the general action of French governments and with the average sentiment of the nation, whilst there has never been wanting appropriate machinery by which to carry the censorship into effect.

No doubt there were heard throughout the eighteenth century, and have been heard ever since, vigorous protests against the censorship, as against other forms of administrative arbitrariness; and at the beginning of the Great Revolution, as at other periods since, efforts were made in favour of free discussion. Hence flowed the abolition of the censorship, but this attempt to limit the powers of the government in one particular direction was quite out of harmony with the general reverence for the authority of the state. As long, moreover, as the whole scheme of French administration was left in force, the government, in whatever hands it was placed, always retained the means of resuming its control over the press, whenever popular feeling should for a moment favour the repression of free speech. Hence arose the constantly recurring restoration of the abolished censorship or of restraints which, though not called by the unpopular name of *la censure*, were more stringent than has ever been any Licensing Act. Restrictions, in short, on what Englishmen understand by the liberty of the press have continued to exist in France and are hardly now abolished, because the exercise of preventive and discretionary authority on the part of the executive harmonises with the general spirit of

French law, and because the administrative machinery, which is the creation of that spirit, has always placed (as it still places) in the hands of the executive the proper means for enforcing discretionary authority.

In England, on the other hand, the attempt made by the Crown during the sixteenth and seventeenth centuries to form a strong central administration, though it was for a time attended with success, because it met some of the needs of the age, was at bottom repugnant to the manners and traditions of the country; and even at a time when the people wished the Crown to be strong, they hardly liked the means by which the Crown exerted its strength.

Hundreds of Englishmen who hated toleration and cared little for freedom of speech, entertained a keen jealousy of arbitrary power, and a fixed determination to be ruled in accordance with the law of the land.[1] These sentiments abolished the Star Chamber in 1641, and made the re-establishment of the hated Court impossible even for the frantic loyalty of 1660. But the destruction of the Star Chamber meant much more than the abolition of an unpopular tribunal; it meant the rooting up from its foundations of the whole of the administrative system which had been erected by the Tudors and extended by the Stuarts. This overthrow of a form of administration which contradicted the legal habits of Englishmen had no direct connection with any desire for the uncontrolled expression of opinion. The Parliament which would not restore the Star Chamber or the Court of High

[1] See Selden's remarks on the illegality of the decrees of the Star Chamber, cited Gardiner, *History of England*, vol. vii (1884), p. 51.

Part II.

Commission passed the Licensing Act, and this statute, which in fact establishes the censorship, was, as we have seen, continued in force for some years after the Revolution. The passing, however, of the statute, though not a triumph of toleration, was a triumph of legality. The power of licensing depended henceforward, not on any idea of inherent executive authority, but on the statute law. The right of licensing was left in the hands of the government, but this power was regulated by the words of a statute; and, what was of more consequence, breaches of the Act could be punished only by proceedings in the ordinary courts. The fall of the Star Chamber deprived the executive of the means for exercising arbitrary power.[1] Hence the refusal of the House of Commons in 1695 to continue the Licensing Act was something very different from the proclamation of freedom of thought contained in the French Declaration of Rights, or from any of the laws which have abolished the censorship in France. To abolish the right of the government to control the press, was, in England, simply to do away with an exceptional authority, which was opposed to the general tendency of the law, and the abolition was final, because the executive had already lost the means by which the control of opinion could be effectively enforced.

To sum the whole matter up, the censorship though constantly abolished has been constantly revived in France, because the exertion of discretionary powers by the government has been and still is in

[1] But the Council after the Restoration exercised considerable administrative power and in it are to be found the beginnings of the modern Government Departments.—Ed.

harmony with French laws and institutions. The abolition of the censorship was final in England, because the exercise of discretionary power by the Crown was inconsistent with our system of administration and with the ideas of English law.[1] The contrast is made the more striking by the paradoxical fact, that the statesmen who tried with little success to establish the liberty of the press in France really intended to proclaim freedom of opinion, whilst the statesmen who would not pass the Licensing Act, and thereby founded the liberty of the press in England, held theories of toleration which fell far short of favouring unrestricted liberty of discussion. This contrast is not only striking in itself, but also affords the strongest illustration that can be found of English conceptions of the rule of law.

[1] The Bill of Rights did not destroy the discretionary powers of the Crown; it severely curtailed the more extravagant claims advanced under pretence of prerogative during the seventeenth century.—Ed.

CHAPTER VII

THE RIGHT OF PUBLIC MEETING[1]

Part II.

Right of public meeting.

THE law of Belgium[2] with regard to public meetings is contained in the nineteenth article of the constitution, which is probably intended in the main to reproduce the law of England, and runs as follows:—

Rules of Belgian constitution.

"*Art.* 19. *Les Belges ont le droit de s'assembler* "*paisiblement et sans armes, en se conformant aux* "*lois, qui peuvent régler l'exercice de ce droit,* "*sans néanmoins le soumettre à une autorisation* "*préalable.*

"*Cette disposition ne s'applique point aux ras*"*semblements en plein air, qui restent entièrement* "*soumis aux lois de police.*"[3]

Principles of English law as to right of public meeting.

The restrictions on the practice of public meeting appear to be more stringent in Belgium than in England, for the police have with us no special authority to control open-air assemblies. Yet just as it cannot with strict accuracy be asserted that

[1] The author referred to Stephen, *Commentaries* (14th ed., 1903), vol. iv, pp. 174-178, and Kenny, *Outlines of Criminal Law* (3rd ed., 1907), pp. 280-286, on this subject. See Wade and Phillips, *op. cit.*, pp. 396-401.—ED.

[2] See *Law Quarterly Review*, vol. iv (1888), p. 159. See also as to right of public meeting in Italy, *ibid.* p. 78; in France, *ibid.* p. 165; in Switzerland, *ibid.* p. 169; in United States, *ibid.* p. 257. See as to history of law of public meeting in France, Duguit, *Manuel de Droit Public français; Droit Constitutionnel* (1907), para. 83, pp. 554-559.

[3] *Constitution de la Belgique*, art. 19.

English law recognises the liberty of the press, so it can hardly be said that our constitution knows of such a thing as any specific right of public meeting. No better instance can indeed be found of the way in which in England the constitution is built up upon individual rights than our rules as to public assemblies. The right of assembling is nothing more than a result of the view taken by the courts as to individual liberty of person and individual liberty of speech. There is no special law allowing *A*, *B*, and *C* to meet together either in the open air or elsewhere for a lawful purpose, but the right of *A* to go where he pleases so that he does not commit a trespass, and to say what he likes to *B* so that his talk is not libellous or seditious, the right of *B* to do the like, and the existence of the same rights of *C*, *D*, *E*, and *F*, and so on *ad infinitum*, lead to the consequence that *A*, *B*, *C*, *D*, and a thousand or ten thousand other persons, may (as a general rule)[1] meet together in any place where otherwise they each have a right to be for a lawful purpose and in a lawful manner. *A* has a right to walk down the High Street or to go on to a common. *B* has the same right. *C*, *D*, and all their friends have the same right to go there also. In other words, *A*, *B*, *C*, and *D*, and ten thousand such, have a right to hold a public meeting; and as *A* may say to *B* that he thinks an Act ought to be passed abolishing the House of Lords, or that the House of Lords are bound to reject any bill modifying the constitution

[1] No opinion is expressed here on the point whether an agreement on the part of *A*, *B*, and *C* to meet together may not under exceptional circumstances be a conspiracy.

of their House, and as *B* may make the same remark to any of his friends, the result ensues that *A* and ten thousand more may hold a public meeting either to support the government or to encourage the resistance of the Peers. Here then you have in substance that right of public meeting for political and other purposes which is constantly treated in foreign countries as a special privilege, to be exercised only subject to careful restrictions. The assertion, however, that *A*, *B*, *C*, and *D*, and a hundred thousand more persons, just because they may each go where they like, and each say what they please, have a right to hold meetings for the discussion of political and other topics, does not of course mean that it is impossible for persons so to exercise the right of meeting as to break the law. The object of a meeting may be to commit a crime by open force, or in some way or other to break the peace, in which case the meeting itself becomes an unlawful assembly. The mode in which a meeting is held may threaten a breach of the peace on the part of those holding the meeting, and therefore inspire peaceable citizens with reasonable fear; in which case, again, the meeting will be unlawful. In either instance the meeting may lawfully be broken up, and the members of it expose themselves to all the consequences, in the way of arrest, prosecution, and punishment, which attend the doing of unlawful acts, or, in other words, the commission of crimes.[1]

[1] The offence of unlawful assembly nowadays plays only a small part in the control of public expression of opinion, *e.g.* to prevent clashes between Fascists and Communists. See Public Order Act, 1936.

Chapter VII.

Meeting not unlawful because it will excite unlawful opposition.

A public meeting which, from the conduct of those engaged in it, as, for example, through their marching together in arms, or through their intention to excite a breach of the peace on the part of opponents,[1] fills peaceable citizens with reasonable fear that the peace will be broken, is an unlawful assembly. But a meeting which is not otherwise illegal does not[2] become an unlawful assembly solely because it will excite violent and unlawful opposition, and thus may indirectly lead to a breach of the peace. Suppose, for example, that the members of the Salvation Army propose to hold a meeting at Oxford, suppose that a so-called Skeleton Army announce that they will attack the Salvationists and disperse them by force, suppose, lastly, that thereupon peaceable citizens who do not like the quiet of the town to be disturbed and who dread riots, urge the magistrates to stop the meeting of the Salvationists. This may seem at first sight a reasonable request, but the magistrates cannot, it is submitted,[3] legally take the course suggested to them. That under the present state of the law this must be so is on reflection pretty clear. The right of *A* to walk down the High Street is not, as a rule,[4] taken away by the threat of *X* to knock *A* down if *A*

[1] Cf. *O'Kelly* v. *Harvey* (1883) 14 L.R. Ir. 105; *Humphries* v. *Connor* (1864) 17 Ir. C.L.R. 1, at pp. 8, 9, per Fitzgerald, J.

[2] This statement must be read subject to the limitations stated, pp. 277, 278, *post*.

[3] It is assumed that the Salvationists meet together, as they certainly do, for a lawful purpose, and meet quite peaceably, and without any intent either themselves to break the peace or to incite others to a breach thereof. The magistrates, however, could require the members of the Skeleton Army, or perhaps even the members of the Salvation Army, to find sureties for good behaviour or to keep the peace. Cf. Kenny, *Outlines of Criminal Law* (3rd ed., 1907), pp. 282, 486; *Wise* v. *Dunning* [1902] 1 K.B. 167; K. & L. 409.

[4] See p. 282, *post*, and cf. *Humphries* v. *Connor*, *ante*.

Part II.

takes his proposed walk. It is true, that *A*'s going into the High Street may lead to a breach of the peace, but *A* no more causes the breach of the peace than a man whose pocket is picked causes the theft by wearing a watch. *A* is the victim, not the author of a breach of the law. Now, if the right of *A* to walk down the High Street is not affected by the threats of *X*, the right of *A*, *B*, and *C* to march down the High Street together is not diminished by the proclamation of *X*, *Y*, and *Z* that they will not suffer *A*, *B*, and *C* to take their walk. Nor does it make any difference that *A*, *B*, and *C* call themselves the Salvation Army, or that *X*, *Y*, and *Z* call themselves the Skeleton Army. The plain principle is that *A*'s right to do a lawful act, namely, walk down the High Street, cannot be diminished by *X*'s threat to do an unlawful act, namely, to knock *A* down. This is the principle established, or rather illustrated, by the case of *Beatty* v. *Gillbanks*.[1] The Salvation Army met together at Weston-super-Mare with the knowledge that they would be opposed by the Skeleton Army. The magistrates had put out a notice intended to forbid the meeting. The Salvationists, however, assembled, were met by the police, and told to obey the notice. *X*, one of the members, declined to obey and was arrested. He was subsequently, with others, convicted by the magistrates on a summary charge of unlawfully assembling in breach of the peace in a public thoroughfare and bound over

[1] (1882) 9 Q.B.D. 308; K. & L. 406. Cf. *Duncan* v. *Jones* [1936] 1 K.B. 218; K. & L. 411, which shows that it is an offence for anybody to resist the order of a constable to move on from the place of a meeting, if in the opinion of the constable, based on reasonable grounds, such an order is necessary to prevent a breach of the peace.—Ed.

to keep the peace. It was an undoubted fact that the meeting of the Salvation Army was likely to lead to an attack by the Skeleton Army, and in this sense cause a breach of the peace. The conviction, however, of *X* by the magistrates was quashed on appeal to the Queen's Bench Division.

"What has happened here," says Field, J., "is "that an unlawful organisation [the Skeleton Army] "has assumed to itself the right to prevent the appel-"lants and others from lawfully assembling together, "and the finding of the justices amounts to this, that "a man may be convicted for doing a lawful act if "he knows that his doing it may cause another to do "an unlawful act. There is no authority for such a "proposition."[1]

The principle here laid down is thus expressed by an Irish judge in a case which has itself received the approval of the English King's Bench Division.[2]

"Much has been said on both sides in the course of "the argument about the case of *Beatty* v. *Gillbanks*. "I am not sure that I would have taken the same view "of the facts of that case as was adopted by the court "that decided it; but I agree with both the law as laid "down by the judges, and their application of it to the

[1] *Beatty* v. *Gillbanks, ante*, at p. 314; *Beaty* v. *Glenister* (1884) W.N. 93; *The Queen* v. *Justices of Londonderry* (1891) 28 L.R. Ir. 440; with which contrast *Wise* v. *Dunning* [1902] 1 K.B. 167; K. & L. 409; and the Irish cases, *Humphries* v. *Connor* (1864) 17 Ir. C.L.R. 1; *The Queen* v. *M'Naughten* (1881) 14 Cox C.C. 576; *O'Kelly* v. *Harvey* (1883) 14 L.R. Ir. 105.

It is to be noted that the King's Bench Division in deciding *Wise* v. *Dunning* did not mean to overrule *Beatty* v. *Gillbanks*, and apparently conceived that they were following *The Queen* v. *Justices of Londonderry*.

[2] See *The Queen* v. *Justices of Londonderry, ante*, and *Wise* v. *Dunning, ante*, at p. 179, per Darling, J.

"facts as they understood them. The principle underlying the decision seems to me to be that an act innocent in itself, done with innocent intent, and reasonably incidental to the performance of a duty, to the carrying on of business, to the enjoyment of legitimate recreation, or generally to the exercise of a legal right, does not become criminal because it may provoke persons to break the peace, or otherwise to conduct themselves in an illegal way."[1]

Nor is it in general an answer to the claim of, *e.g.* the Salvationists, to exercise their right of meeting, that whilst such exercise may excite wrongdoers to break the peace, the easiest way of keeping it is to prevent the meeting, for "if danger arises from the exercise of lawful rights resulting in a breach of the peace, the remedy is the presence of sufficient force to prevent that result, not the legal condemnation of those who exercise those rights."[2]

The principle, then, that a meeting otherwise in every respect lawful and peaceable is not rendered unlawful merely by the possible or probable misconduct of wrongdoers, who to prevent the meeting are determined to break the peace, is, it is submitted,[3]

[1] *The Queen* v. *Justices of Londonderry, ante,* at p. 461, per Holmes, J.

[2] *Ibid.,* at p. 450, per O'Brien, J.

[3] *Wise* v. *Dunning, ante,* or rather some expressions used in the judgments in that case, may undoubtedly be cited as laying down the broader rule, that a public meeting in itself lawful, and carried on, so far as the promoters and the members of it are concerned, perfectly peaceably, may become unlawful solely because the natural consequence of the meeting will be to produce an unlawful act, viz. a breach of the peace on the part of opponents (see pp. 175, 176, per Alverstone, C.J.; p. 178, per Darling, J.; pp. 179, 180, per Channell, J.). It should be noted, however, that *Wise* v. *Dunning* has reference, not to the circumstances under which a meeting becomes an unlawful assembly, but to the different question, what are the circumstances under which a

well established, whence it follows that in general an otherwise lawful public meeting cannot be forbidden or broken up by the magistrates simply because the meeting may probably or naturally lead to a breach of the peace on the part of wrongdoers.

To the application of this principle there exist certain limitations or exceptions. They are grounded on the absolute necessity for preserving the Queen's peace.

(1) Where illegality in meeting provokes breach of peace.

First limitation.—If there is anything unlawful in the conduct of the persons convening or addressing a meeting, and the illegality is of a kind which naturally provokes opponents to a breach of the peace, the speakers at and the members of the meeting may be held to cause the breach of the peace, and the meeting itself may thus become an unlawful meeting. If, for example, a Protestant controversialist surrounded by his friends uses in some public place where there is a large Roman Catholic population, abusive language which is in fact slanderous of Roman Catholics, or which he is by a local by-law forbidden to use in the streets, and thereby provokes a mob of Roman Catholics to break the peace, the meeting may become an unlawful assembly. And the same result may ensue where, though there is nothing in the mode in which the meeting is carried on which provokes a breach of the peace, yet the object of the meeting is in itself not strictly lawful, and may therefore excite opponents to a breach of the peace.[1]

person may be required to find sureties for good behaviour? The magistrate had held that Wise's language had been provocative and that it was likely to occur again. Large crowds had assembled and a serious riot was only prevented by police interference; p. 178.

[1] Cf. *Wise* v. *Dunning*, *ante*, and *O'Kelly* v. *Harvey*, *ante*.

(2) Where meeting lawful but peace can only be kept by dispersing it.

Second limitation.—Where a public meeting, though the object of the meeting and the conduct of the members thereof are strictly lawful, provokes a breach of the peace, and it is impossible to preserve or restore the peace by any other means than by dispersing the meeting, then magistrates, constables, and other persons in authority may call upon the meeting to disperse, and, if the meeting does not disperse, it becomes an unlawful assembly.[1] Let us suppose, for example, that the Salvation Army hold a meeting at Oxford, that a so-called Skeleton Army come together with a view to preventing the Salvationists from assembling, and that it is in strictness impossible for the peace to be preserved by any other means than by requiring the Salvationists to disperse. Under these circumstances, though the meeting of the Salvation Army is in itself perfectly lawful, and though the wrongdoers are the members of the Skeleton Army, yet the magistrates may, it would seem, if they can in no other way preserve the peace, require the Salvationists to disperse, and if the Salvationists do not do so, the meeting becomes an unlawful assembly; and it is possible that, if the magistrates have no other means of preserving the peace, *i.e.* cannot protect the Salvationists from attack by the Skeleton Army, they may lawfully prevent the Salvationists from holding the meeting.[2] But the only justification for prevent-

[1] See especially *O'Kelly* v. *Harvey*, *ante*.

[2] It is particularly to be noted that in *O'Kelly* v. *Harvey*, *ante*, the case in which is carried furthest the right of magistrates to preserve the peace by dispersing a lawful meeting, *X*, the magistrate against whom an action for assault was brought, believed that there would be a breach of the peace if the meeting broken up continued assembled, and that there was no other way by which the breach of the peace could be avoided but by stopping and dispersing the meeting. *Ibid.*, at p. 109, per Law, L.C.

ing the Salvationists from exercising their legal rights is the *necessity of the case.* If the peace can be preserved, not by breaking up an otherwise lawful meeting, but by arresting the wrongdoers—in this case the Skeleton Army—the magistrates or constables are bound, it is submitted, to arrest the wrongdoers and to protect the Salvationists in the exercise of their lawful rights.[1]

One point, however, deserves special notice since it is apt to be overlooked.

Limitations on right of public meeting are really limitations on individual freedom.

The limitations or restrictions which arise from the paramount necessity for preserving the Queen's peace are, whatever their extent,—and as to their exact extent some fair doubt exists,—in reality nothing else than restraints, which, for the sake of preserving the peace, are imposed upon the ordinary freedom of individuals.

Thus if *A*, a religious controversialist, acting alone and unaccompanied by friends and supporters, addresses the public in, say, the streets of Liverpool, and uses language which is defamatory or abusive, or, without being guilty of defamation, uses terms of abuse which he is by a local by-law forbidden to use in the streets, and thereby, as a natural result of his oratory, excites his opponents to a breach of the peace, he may be held liable for the wrongful acts of which his language is the cause though not the legal justification, and this though he does not himself break the peace, nor intend to cause others to violate it. He may, certainly, be called upon to find sureties for his good behaviour, and he may, probably, be prevented by the police from continuing addresses which

[1] This is particularly well brought out in *O'Kelly* v. *Harvey, ante.*

 are exciting a breach of the peace, for "the cases with "respect to apprehended breaches of the peace show "that the law does regard the infirmity of human "temper to the extent of considering that a breach of "the peace, although an illegal act, may be the natural "consequence of insulting or abusive language or "conduct."[1]

So again it may, where the public peace cannot otherwise be preserved, be lawful to interfere with the legal rights of an individual and to prevent him from pursuing a course which in itself is perfectly legal. Thus *A*, a zealous Protestant lady, walks through a crowd of Roman Catholics wearing a party emblem, namely, an orange lily, which under the circumstances of the case is certain to excite, and does excite, the anger of the mob. She has no intention of provoking a breach of the peace, she is doing nothing which is in itself unlawful; she exposes herself, however, to insult, and to pressing danger of public attack. A riot has begun; *X*, a constable who has no other means of protecting *A*, or of restoring the peace, requests her to remove the lily. She refuses to do so. He then, without use of any needless force, removes the flower and thereby restores the peace. The conduct of *X* is apparently legal, and *A* has no ground of action for what would otherwise have been an assault. The legal vindication of *X*'s conduct is not that *A* was a wrongdoer, or that the rioters were within their rights, but that the Queen's peace could not be restored without compelling *A* to remove the lily.[2]

[1] *Wise* v. *Dunning* [1902] 1 K.B. 167, at pp. 179, 180, per Channell, J.

[2] *Humphries* v. *Connor* (1864) 17 Ir. C.L.R. 1. The case is very noticeable; it carries the right of magistrates or constables to interfere with the legal conduct of *A*, for the sake of preventing or terminat-

Chapter VII.

Meeting not made unlawful by official proclamation of its illegality.

No public meeting, further, which would not otherwise be illegal, becomes so (unless in virtue of some special Act of Parliament) in consequence of any proclamation or notice by a Secretary of State, by a magistrate, or by any other official. Suppose, for example, that the Salvationists advertise throughout the town that they intend holding a meeting in a field which they have hired near Oxford, that they intend to assemble in St. Giles's and march thence with banners flying and bands playing to their proposed place of worship. Suppose that the Home Secretary thinks that, for one reason or another, it is undesirable that the meeting should take place, and serves formal notice upon every member of the army, or on the officers who are going to conduct the so-called "campaign" at Oxford, that the gathering must not take place. This notice does not alter the character of the meeting, though, if the meeting be illegal, the notice makes any one who reads it aware of the character of the assembly, and thus affects his responsibility for attending it.[1] Assume that the

ing a breach of the peace by *X*, to its very furthest extent. The interference, if justifiable at all, can be justified only by necessity, and an eminent Irish judge (Fitzgerald, J., 17 Ir. C.L.R., at pp. 8, 9) doubted whether it was not in this case carried too far. "I do not see where "we are to draw the line. If [*X*] is at liberty to take a lily from one "person [*A*] because the wearing of it is displeasing to others, who may "make it an excuse for a breach of the peace, where are we to stop? "It seems to me that we are making, not the law of the land, but the "law of the mob supreme, and recognising in constables a power of "interference with the rights of the Queen's subjects, which, if carried "into effect to the full extent of the principle, might be accompanied "by constitutional danger. If it had been alleged that the lady wore "the emblem with an intent to provoke a breach of the peace, it "would render her a wrongdoer; and she might be chargeable as a "person creating a breach of the peace," but compare *Duncan* v. *Jones* [1936] 1 K.B. 218; K. & L. 411 and E. C. S. Wade in *Cambridge Law Journal* (1937), vol. vi, *Police Powers and Public Meetings*, at pp. 175 *et seq.*

[1] *The King* v. *Fursey* (1833) 6 Car. & P. 81.

Part II.

meeting would have been lawful if the notice had not been issued, and it certainly will not become unlawful because a Secretary of State has forbidden it to take place. The proclamation has under these circumstances as little legal effect as would have a proclamation from the Home Office forbidding me or any other person to walk down the High Street. It follows, therefore, that the government has little or no power of preventing meetings which to all appearance are lawful, even though they may in fact turn out when actually convened to be unlawful because of the mode in which they are conducted. This is certainly a singular instance of the way in which adherence to the principle that the proper function of the state is the punishment, not the prevention, of crimes, deprives the executive of discretionary authority.

Meeting may be lawful though its holding contrary to public interest.

A meeting, lastly, may be lawful which, nevertheless, any wise or public-spirited person would hesitate to convene. For *A*, *B*, and *C* may have a right to hold a meeting, although their doing so will as a matter of fact probably excite opponents to deeds of violence, and possibly produce bloodshed. Suppose a Protestant zealot were to convene a meeting for the purpose of denouncing the evils of the confessional, and were to choose as the scene of the open-air gathering some public place where meetings were usually held in the midst of a large town filled with a population of Roman Catholic poor. The meeting would, it is conceived, be lawful, but no one can doubt that it might provoke violence on the part of opponents. Neither the government, however, nor the magistrates could (it is submitted), as a rule, at any rate, prohibit and prevent the meeting from taking place. They might, it would seem, prevent the meeting if the Protestant controversialist and his friends intended to pursue a course of conduct, *e.g.* to give utterance to libellous abuse, which would be both illegal and might naturally produce a breach of the peace, or if the circumstances were such that the peace could not be preserved otherwise than by preventing the meeting.[1] But neither the government nor the magistrates can, it is submitted, solely on the ground that a public meeting may provoke wrongdoers to a breach of the peace, prevent loyal citizens from meeting together peaceably and for a lawful purpose. Of the policy or of the impolicy of denying to the highest authority in the state very wide power to take in their discretion precautionary measures against the evils which may flow from the injudicious exercise of legal rights, it is unnecessary here to say anything. The matter which is worth notice is the way in which the rules as to the right of public meeting illustrate both the legal spirit of our institutions and the process by which the decisions of the courts as to the rights of individuals have in effect made the right of public meeting a part of the law of the constitution.

[1] See p. 273, *ante*, and compare *O'Kelly* v. *Harvey* (1883) 14 L.R. Ir. 105, with *The Queen* v. *Justices of Londonderry* (1891) 28 L.R. Ir. 440, and *Wise* v. *Dunning* [1902] 1 K.B. 167; K. & L. 409, with *Beatty* v. *Gillbanks* (1882) 9 Q.B.D. 308; K. & L. 406. And the magistrates might probably bind over the conveners of the meeting to find sureties for their good behaviour. Magistrates have a wide power to order any person to enter into an undertaking (recognisance) with or without sureties to keep the peace or to be of good behaviour, either in general or to a particular person. A person may be bound over whenever it is apprehended that he is likely to commit a breach of the peace or do something contrary to law: *Lansbury* v. *Riley* [1914] 3 K.B. 229; Wade & Phillips, *op. cit.*, pp. 398-399.

CHAPTER VIII

MARTIAL LAW[1]

Part II.

No sharp line can be drawn between rules of private law or of criminal law and constitutional law.

THE rights already treated of in the foregoing chapter, as for example the right to personal freedom or the right to free expression of opinion, do not, it may be suggested, properly belong to the province of constitutional law at all, but form part either of private law strictly so called, or of the ordinary criminal law. Thus *A*'s right to personal freedom is, it may be said, only the right of *A* not to be assaulted, or imprisoned, by *X*, or (to look at the same thing from another point of view) is nothing else than the right of *A*, if assaulted by *X*, to bring an action against *X*, or to have *X* punished as a criminal for the assault. Now in this suggestion there lies an element of important truth, yet it is also undoubted that the right to personal freedom, the right to free discussion, and the like, appear in the forefront of many written constitutions, and are in fact the chief advantages which

[1] See Forsyth, *Cases and Opinions in Constitutional Law* (1869), ch. vi, and Appendix; Stephen, *History of the Criminal Law* (1883), vol. i, pp. 201-216; *The King* v. *Pinney* (1832) 5 Car. & P. 254; K. & L. 418; *The Queen* v. *Vincent* (1839) 9 Car. & P. 91; *The Queen* v. *Neale* (1839) 9 Car. & P. 431; Keir and Lawson, *Cases in Constitutional Law* (4th ed., 1954), pp. 421-434, especially for later Irish cases; *Law Quarterly Review*, vol. xviii (1902), pp. 117-151, for four articles on the subject.

citizens hope to gain by the change from a despotic to a constitutional form of government.

The truth is that these rights may be looked upon from two points of view. They may be considered simply parts of private or, it may be, of criminal law; thus the right to personal freedom may, as already pointed out, be looked at as the right of *A* not to have the control of his body interfered with by *X*. But in so far as these rights hold good against the governing body in the state, or in other words, in so far as these rights determine the relation of individual citizens towards the executive, they are part, and a most important part, of the law of the constitution.

Now the noticeable point is that in England the rights of citizens as against each other are (speaking generally) the same as the rights of citizens against any servant of the Crown. This is the significance of the assertion that in this country the law of the constitution is part of the ordinary law of the land. The fact that a Secretary of State cannot at his discretion and for reasons of state arrest, imprison, or punish any man, except, of course, where special powers are conferred upon him by statute, as by an Aliens Act or by an Extradition Act, is simply a result of the principle that a Secretary of State is governed in his official as in his private conduct by the ordinary law of the realm. Were the Home Secretary to assault the leader of the Opposition in a fit of anger, or were the Home Secretary to arrest him because he thought his political opponent's freedom dangerous to the state, the Secretary of State would in either case be liable to an action, and all other penalties to which a person exposes himself by committing an assault.

Part II. The fact that the arrest of an influential politican whose speeches might excite disturbance was a strictly administrative act would afford no defence to the Minister or to the constables who obeyed his orders.

The subjects treated of in this chapter and in the next three chapters clearly belong to the field of constitutional law, and no one would think of objecting to their treatment in a work on the law of the constitution that they are really part of private law. Yet, if the matter be looked at carefully, it will be found that, just as rules which at first sight seem to belong to the domain of private law are in reality the foundation of constitutional principles, so topics which appear to belong manifestly to the law of constitution depend with us at bottom on the principles of private or of criminal law. Thus the position of a soldier is in England governed, as we shall see, by the principle, that though a soldier is subject to special liabilities in his military capacity, he remains while in the ranks, as he was when out of them, subject to all the liabilities of an ordinary citizen. So, from a legal point of view, ministerial responsibility is simply one application of the doctrine which pervades English law,[1] that no one can plead the command of a superior, were it the order of the Crown itself, in defence of conduct otherwise not justified by law.

Turn the matter which way you will, you come back to the all-important consideration on which we have already dwelt, that whereas under many foreign constitutions the rights of individuals flow, or appear to flow, from the articles of the constitution, in England the law of the constitution is the result, not the

[1] Mommsen, *Abriss des römischen Staatsrecht* (1893), p. 672.

source of the rights of individuals.[1] It becomes, too, more and more apparent that the means by which the courts have maintained the law of the constitution have been the strict insistence upon the two principles, first of "equality before the law," which negatives exemption from the liabilities of ordinary citizens or from the jurisdiction of the ordinary courts, and, secondly, of "personal responsibility of wrongdoers," which excludes the notion that any breach of law on the part of a subordinate can be justified by the orders of his superiors; the legal dogma, as old at least as the time of Edward the Fourth, that, if any man arrest another without lawful warrant, even by the King's command, he shall not be excused, but shall be liable to an action for false imprisonment, is not a special limitation imposed upon the royal prerogative, but the application to acts done under royal orders of that principle of individual responsibility which runs through the whole law of torts.[2]

Martial Law.

"Martial law," in the proper sense of that term, in which it means the suspension of ordinary law and the temporary government of a country or parts of it by military tribunals, is unknown to the law of England. We have nothing equivalent to what is called in France the "Declaration of the State of Siege,"[3] under which the authority ordinarily

[1] Cf. Jennings, *The Law and the Constitution* (4th ed., 1952), pp. 297-298.

[2] See Hearn, *Government of England* (2nd ed., 1887), ch. iv; cf. Gardiner, *History of England*, vol. x (1884), pp. 144, 145.

[3] See *Loi sur l'état de siège, 9 Août, 1849*, Roger et Sorel, *Codes et Lois* (1882), p. 436; *Loi 3 Avril, 1878*, art. 1, and generally Duguit, *Manuel de Droit Public français; Droit Constitutionnel* (1907), para. 76, pp. 510-513; and para. 130, p. 926. See p. 292, *post*.

Part II.

vested in the civil power for the maintenance of order and police passes entirely to the army (*autorité militaire*). This is an unmistakable proof of the permanent supremacy of the law under our constitution.

The assertion, however, that no such thing as martial law exists under our system of government, though perfectly true, will mislead any one who does not attend carefully to the distinction between two utterly different senses in which the term "martial law" is used by English writers.

In what sense martial law recognised by English law.

Martial law is sometimes employed as a name for the common law right of the Crown and its servants to repel force by force in the case of invasion, insurrection, riot, or generally of any violent resistance to the law. This right, or power, is essential to the very existence of orderly government, and is most assuredly recognised in the most ample manner by the law of England. It is a power which has in itself no special connection with the existence of an armed force. The Crown has the right to put down breaches of the peace. Every subject, whether a civilian or a soldier, whether what is called a "servant of the government," such for example as a policeman, or a person in no way connected with the administration, not only has the right, but is, as a matter of legal duty,[1] bound to assist in putting down breaches of the peace. No doubt policemen or soldiers are the persons who, as being specially employed in the maintenance of order, are most generally called upon to suppress a riot, but it is clear that all loyal subjects are bound to take their part in the suppression of riots.

[1] Cf. *Miller* v. *Knox* (1838) 6 Scott 1. See *Report of the Committee* (including Bowen, L.J., and R. B. Haldane, Q.C.), *appointed to inquire into the Disturbances at Featherstone in 1893* [C. 7234].

It is also clear that a soldier has, as such, no exemption from liability to the law for his conduct in restoring order. Officers, magistrates, soldiers, policemen, ordinary citizens, all occupy in the eye of the law the same position; they are, each and all of them, bound to withstand and put down breaches of the peace, such as riots and other disturbances; they are, each and all of them, authorised to employ so much force, even to the taking of life, as may be necessary for that purpose, and they are none of them entitled to use more; they are, each and all of them, liable to be called to account before a jury for the use of excessive, that is, of unnecessary force; they are each, it must be added—for this is often forgotten—liable, in theory at least, to be called to account before the courts for non-performance of their duty as citizens in putting down riots, though of course the degree and kind of energy which each is reasonably bound to exert in the maintenance of order may depend upon and differ with his position as officer, magistrate, soldier, or ordinary civilian. Whoever doubts these propositions should study the leading case of *The King* v. *Pinney*,[1] in which was fully considered the duty of the Mayor of Bristol in reference to the Reform Riots of 1831.

So accustomed have people become to fancy that the maintenance of the peace is the duty solely of soldiers or policemen, that many students will probably feel surprise on discovering, from the doctrine laid down in *The King* v. *Pinney*, how stringent are the obligations of a magistrate in time of tumult, and how unlimited is the amount of force which he is bound to

[1] (1832) 5 Car. & P. 254; K. & L. 418.

employ in support of the law. A student, further, must be on his guard against being misled, as he well might be, by the language of the Riot Act, 1714. That statute provides, in substance, that if twelve rioters continue together for an hour after a magistrate has made a proclamation to them in the terms of the Act (which proclamation is absurdly enough called reading the Riot Act) ordering them to disperse, he may command the troops to fire upon the rioters or charge them sword in hand.[1] This, of course, is not the language, but it is the effect of the enactment. Now the error into which an uninstructed reader is likely to fall, and into which magistrates and officers have from time to time (and notably during the Gordon riots of 1780) in fact fallen, is to suppose that the effect of the Riot Act is negative as well as positive, and that, therefore, the military cannot be employed without the fulfilment of the conditions imposed by the statute. This notion is now known to be erroneous; the occasion on which force can be employed, and the kind and degree of force which it is lawful to use in order to put down a riot, is determined by nothing else than the necessity of the case.

If, then, by martial law be meant the power of the government or of loyal citizens to maintain public order, at whatever cost of blood or property may be necessary, martial law is assuredly part of the law of England. Even, however, as to this kind of martial law one should always bear in mind that the question whether the force employed was necessary or excessive will, especially where death has ensued, be ultimately

[1] See Stephen, *History of the Criminal Law* (1883), vol. i, pp. 202-205.

determined by a judge and jury,[1] and that the estimate of what constitutes necessary force formed by a judge and jury, sitting in quiet and safety after the suppression of a riot, may differ considerably from the judgment formed by a general or magistrate, who is surrounded by armed rioters, and knows that at any moment a riot may become a formidable rebellion, and the rebellion if unchecked become a successful revolution.

Chapter VIII.

In what sense martial law not recognised by English law.

Martial law is, however, more often used as the name for the government of a country or a district by military tribunals, which more or less supersede the jurisdiction of the courts. The proclamation of martial law in this sense of the term is, as has been already pointed out,[2] nearly equivalent to the state of things which in France and many other foreign countries is known as the declaration of a "state of siege," and is in effect the temporary and recognised government of a country by military force. The legal aspect of this condition of affairs in states which recognise the existence of this kind of martial law can hardly be better given than by citing some of the

[1] This statement does not contradict anything decided by *Marais* v. *General Officer Commanding* [1902] A.C. 109; K. & L. 446, nor is it inconsistent with the language used in the judgment of the Privy Council, if that language be strictly construed, as it ought to be, in accordance with the important principles that, first, a case is only an authority for what it actually decides, and, secondly, every judgment must be read as applicable to the particular facts proved, or assumed to be proved, since the generality of the expressions which may be found there are not intended to be expositions of the whole law, but governed and qualified by the particular facts of the case in which such expressions are to be found. Moreover the courts reserve for themselves the right to decide whether the situation calls for such an exercise of military force as to justify the existence of a state of war; *The King* (*Garde*) v. *Strickland* [1921] 2 I.R. 317, at p. 329.

[2] See p. 287, *ante*.

Part II.

French Law as to state of siege.

provisions of the law which at the present day regulates the state of siege in France:—

"7. *Aussitôt l'état de siège déclaré, les pouvoirs "dont l'autorité civile était revêtue pour le maintien "de l'ordre et de la police passent tout entiers à "l'autorité militaire.—L'autorité civile continue "néanmoins à exercer ceux de ces pouvoirs dont "l'autorité militaire ne l'a pas dessaisie.*

"8. *Les tribunaux militaires peuvent être saisis "de la connaissance des crimes et délits contre la "sûreté de la République, contre la constitution, "contre l'ordre et la paix publique, quelle que soit "la qualité des auteurs principaux et des complices.*

"9. *L'autorité militaire a le droit,—1° De faire "des perquisitions, de jour et de nuit, dans le domicile "des citoyens;—2° D'éloigner les repris de justice et "les individus qui n'ont pas leur domicile dans les "lieux, soumis à l'état de siège;—3° D'ordonner la "remise des armes et munitions, et de procéder à leur "recherche et à leur enlèvement;—4° D'interdire les "publications et les réunions qu'elle juge de nature "à exciter ou à entretenir le désordre."* [1]

We may reasonably, however, conjecture that the terms of the law give but a faint conception of the real condition of affairs when, in consequence of tumult or insurrection, Paris, or some other part of France, is declared in a state of siege, and, to use a significant expression known to some continental countries, "the constitutional guarantees are suspended." We shall hardly go far wrong if we assume that, during this suspension of ordinary law, any man whatever is liable

[1] Roger et Sorel, *Codes et Lois usuelles* (1882), v° *état de siège*, pp. 435, 436.

to arrest, imprisonment, or execution at the will of a military tribunal consisting of a few officers who are excited by the passions natural to civil war. However this may be, it is clear that in France, even under the present Republican government, the suspension of law involved in the proclamation of a state of siege is a thing fully recognised by the constitution, and (strange though the fact may appear) the authority of military courts during a state of siege is greater under the Republic than it was under the monarchy of Louis Philippe.[1]

Now, this kind of martial law is in England utterly unknown to the constitution. Soldiers may suppress a riot as they may resist an invasion, they may fight rebels just as they may fight foreign enemies, but they have no right under the law to inflict punishment for riot or rebellion. During the effort to restore peace, rebels may be lawfully killed just as enemies may be lawfully slaughtered in battle, or prisoners may be shot to prevent their escape, but any execution (independently of military law) inflicted by a court-martial is illegal, and technically murder. Nothing better illustrates the noble energy with which judges have maintained the rule of regular law, even at periods of revolutionary violence, than *Wolfe Tone's Case*.[2] In 1798, Wolfe Tone, an Irish rebel, took part in a French invasion of Ireland. The man-of-war in which he sailed was

[1] See *Geoffroy's Case* (1832) 24 *Journal du Palais*, 1218, cited Forsyth, *op. cit.*, p. 483. Cf. for a statement of limits imposed by French law on action of military authorities during state of siege, Duguit, *Manuel de Droit Public français; Droit Constitutionnel* (1907), para. 76, pp. 512, 513.

[2] (1798) 27 St. Tr. 614.

Part II.

captured, and Wolfe Tone was brought to trial before a court-martial in Dublin. He was thereupon sentenced to be hanged. He held, however, no commission as an English officer, his only commission being one from the French Republic. On the morning when his execution was about to take place application was made to the Irish King's Bench for a writ of habeas corpus. The ground taken was that Wolfe Tone, not being a military person, was not subject to punishment by a court-martial, or, in effect, that the officers who tried him were attempting illegally to enforce martial law. The Court of King's Bench at once granted the writ. When it is remembered that Wolfe Tone's substantial guilt was admitted, that the court was made up of judges who detested the rebels, and that in 1798 Ireland was in the midst of a revolutionary crisis, it will be admitted that no more splendid assertion of the supremacy of the law can be found than the protection of Wolfe Tone by the Irish Bench.

CHAPTER IX

THE ARMY [1]

THE British army may for the purposes of this treatise be treated as consisting of the Standing Army or, in technical language, the Regular Forces [2] and of the Territorial Army,[3] which, like the Militia,[4] is a

Chapter IX.

The Army.

[1] See *Manual of Military Law* (1958, pt. II, s. i, and 1929, ch. lix), especially ch. i, ii and ix; and Wade and Phillips, *Constitutional Law*, 5th ed., 1955, pt. i, chs. 27-29. The keeping of a standing army within the realm in time of peace without the consent of Parliament was declared to be against the law by the Bill of Rights, 1689. The Petition of Right, 1628, had declared commissions of martial law to be illegal. The Crown thus could neither maintain nor discipline the army at home except by consent of Parliament. As the text shows, these two objections were overcome by a succession of Mutiny Acts. These Acts served the double purpose of authorising the keeping of permanent land forces for a fixed period which by convention was for one year only and of providing a code of military rules for enforcing discipline. Military law was codified by the Army Discipline and Regulation Act, 1879, which was subsequently replaced by the Army Act, 1881. This code of military law was until 1957 continued in force from year to year by an Annual Act, known originally as the Army (Annual) Act and, after the constitution of a separate Air Force in 1917, as the Army and Air Force (Annual) Act. In 1955 Parliament enacted separate disciplinary measures for these two forces, the Army Act, 1955, and the Air Force Act, 1955. But there is no longer any need for an annual Act in order to remove the prohibition in the Bill of Rights, as this is achieved by the Annual Appropriation Act, which sanctions the votes for Army and Air Force pay, and therefore by implication allows these forces to be maintained. The Acts of 1955 require renewal by annual Order in Council and

Part II. territorial army for the defence of the United Kingdom.

Each of these forces has been rendered subordinate to the law of the land. My object is not to give even an outline of the enactments affecting the army, but simply to explain the legal principles on which this supremacy of the law throughout the army has been secured.

It will be convenient in considering this matter to reverse the order pursued in the common text-books; these contain a great deal about the militia, the territorial force of its day, and comparatively little about the regular forces, or what we now call the "army." The reason of this is that historically the militia is an older institution than the permanent army, and the existence of a standing army is historically, and according to constitutional theories, an anomaly. Hence the standing army has often been treated by writers of authority as a sort of exceptional or subordinate topic, a kind of excrescence, so to speak, on the national and constitutional force known as the

expire at the end of five years, unless Parliament shall otherwise determine.

[2] "The expression 'regular forces' is defined by the Army Act, 1955, s. 225, as follows: 'Regular forces' means any of Her Majesty's military forces other than the army reserve, the Territorial Army and the Home Guard, and other than forces raised under the law of a colony, so however that an officer of any reserve of officers, or an officer who is retired within the meaning of any Royal Warrant, shall not be treated for the purposes of this Act as a member of the regular forces save in so far as is expressly provided by this Act."

[3] The Territorial Army was created by the Territorial and Reserve Forces Act, 1907; see now the Auxiliary Forces Act, 1953, a consolidating measure.

[4] The Militia.—The old County force which was disbanded in 1908. The term, Militia, was applied between 1921 and 1939 to a special branch of the Army Reserve.

militia.[1] As a matter of fact, of course, the standing army is now the real national force, and the territorial force is a body of secondary importance.

Chapter IX.

Standing Army. Its existence reconciled with Parliamentary government by annual Mutiny Acts.

As to the Standing Army.—A permanent army of paid soldiers, whose main duty is one of absolute obedience to commands, appears at first sight to be an institution inconsistent with that rule of law or submission to the civil authorities, and especially to the judges, which is essential to popular or Parliamentary government; and in truth the existence of permanent paid forces has often in most countries and at times in England—notably under the Commonwealth—been found inconsistent with the existence of what, by a lax though intelligible mode of speech, is called a free government.[2] The belief, indeed, of our statesmen down to a time considerably later than the Revolution of 1689 was that a standing army must be fatal to English freedom, yet very soon after the Revolution it became apparent that the existence of a body of paid soldiers was necessary to the safety of the nation. Englishmen, therefore, at the end of the seventeenth and the beginning of the eighteenth centuries, found themselves placed in this dilemma.

[1] In the seventeenth century Parliament apparently meant to rely for the defence of England upon this national army raised from the counties and placed under the guidance of country gentlemen. See Militia Act, 1662.

[2] Macaulay, *History of England*, vol. iii (1858), pp. 42-47. "Throughout the period [of the Civil War and the Interregnum] the "military authorities maintained with great strictness their exclusive "jurisdiction over offences committed both by officers and soldiers. "More than once conflicts took place between the civil magistrates "and the commanders of the army over this question."—Firth, *Cromwell's Army* (1902), p. 310. The author gives several examples (pp. 310-312) of the assertion or attempted assertion of the authority of the civil power, even during a period of military predominance.

Part II.

With a standing army the country could not, they feared, escape from despotism; without a standing army the country could not, they were sure, avert invasion; the maintenance of national liberty appeared to involve the sacrifice of national independence. Yet English statesmanship found almost by accident a practical escape from this theoretical dilemma, and the Mutiny Act, though an enactment passed in a hurry to meet an immediate peril, contains the solution of an apparently insolvable problem.

In this instance, as in others, of success achieved by what is called the practical good sense, the political instinct, or the statesmanlike tact of Englishmen, we ought to be on our guard against two errors.

We ought not, on the one hand, to fancy that English statesmen acted with some profound sagacity or foresight peculiar to themselves, and not to be found among the politicians of other countries. Still less ought we, on the other, to imagine that luck or chance helps Englishmen out of difficulties with which the inhabitants of other countries cannot cope. Political common sense, or political instinct, means little more than habitual training in the conduct of affairs; this practical acquaintance with public business was enjoyed by educated Englishmen a century or two earlier than by educated Frenchmen or Germans; hence the early prevalence in England of sounder principles of government than have till recently prevailed in other lands. The statesmen of the Revolution succeeded in dealing with difficult problems, not because they struck out new and brilliant ideas, or because of luck, but because the notions of law and government which had grown up in England were in many points sound, and because the statesmen of 1689 applied to the difficulties of their time the notions which were habitual to the more thoughtful Englishmen of the day. The position of the army, in fact, was determined by an adherence on the part of the authors of the first Mutiny Act to the fundamental principle of English law, that a soldier may, like a clergyman, incur special obligations in his official character, but is not thereby exempted from the ordinary liabilities of citizenship.

The object and principles of the first Mutiny Act of 1689 are exactly the same as the object and principles of the Army Act,[1] under which the English army is in substance now governed. A comparison of the two statutes shows at a glance what are the means by which the maintenance of military discipline has been reconciled with the maintenance of freedom, or, to use a more accurate expression, with the supremacy of the law of the land.

The preamble to the first Mutiny Act has reappeared with slight alterations in every subsequent Mutiny Act, and recites that "Whereas no man may "be forejudged of life or limb, or subjected to any "kind of punishment by martial law, or in any other "manner than by the judgment of his peers, and "according to the known and established laws of "this realm; yet, nevertheless, it" [is] "requisite for "retaining such forces as are, or shall be, raised "during this exigence of affairs, in their duty an

[1] Applied to the Air Force with certain amendments since 1917; Air Force (Constitution) Act, 1917, s. 12; see now Air Force Act, 1955.

Part II. "exact discipline be observed; and that soldiers who "shall mutiny or stir up sedition, or shall desert "their majesties' service, be brought to a more ex-"emplary and speedy punishment than the usual "forms of law will allow."[1]

This recital states the precise difficulty which perplexed the statesmen of 1689. Now let us observe the way in which it has been met.

A soldier, whether an officer or a private, in a standing army, or (to use the wider expression of modern Acts) "a person subject to military law,"[2] stands in a two-fold relation: the one is his relation towards his fellow-citizens outside the army; the other is his relation towards the members of the army, and especially towards his military superiors; any man, in short, subject to military law has duties and rights as a citizen as well as duties and rights as a soldier. His position in each respect is under English law governed by definite principles.

Soldier's position as citizen.

A soldier's position as a citizen.—The fixed doctrine of English law is that a soldier, though a member of a standing army, is in England subject to all the duties and liabilities of an ordinary citizen.

[1] See p. 295, n. 1, *ante*, for the reason why annual Acts were formerly required.

[2] The Army Act, 1955, and the Air Force Act, 1955, ss. 205-213, define persons who are subject to military law. Such persons are liable to be tried by court-martial for military and in some circumstances for civil offences under the provisions of the Acts. These Acts for the first time extend a modified application of the military code of discipline to certain categories of civilians employed with the Forces (s. 209 in both Acts). These include the families of servicemen and servicewomen when outside the United Kingdom and not on active service. The Army Act applies to the Royal Marines, though this force is also subject to the Naval Discipline Act, 1957, when carried on the books of ships of the Royal Navy (s. 210).

Chapter IX.

"Nothing in this Act contained" (so runs the first Mutiny Act) "shall extend or be construed to exempt "any officer or soldier whatsoever from the ordinary "process of law."[1] These words contain the clue to all our legislation with regard to the standing army whilst employed in the United Kingdom. A soldier by his contract of enlistment undertakes many obligations in addition to the duties incumbent upon a civilian. But he does not escape from any of the duties of an ordinary British subject.

The results of this principle are traceable throughout the Mutiny Acts.

Criminal liability.

A soldier is subject to the same criminal liability as a civilian.[2] He may when in the British dominions be put on trial before any competent "civil" (*i.e.* non-military) court for any offence for which he would be triable if he were not subject to military law, and there are certain offences, such as murder, for which he must in general be tried by a civil tribunal.[3] Thus, if a soldier murders a companion or robs a traveller whilst quartered in England or in Van Diemen's Land, his military character will not save him from standing in the dock on the charge of murder or theft.

Civil liability.

A soldier cannot escape from civil liabilities, as, for example, responsibility for debts; the only exemption which he can claim is that he cannot be taken out of the service of the Crown by order of any court of law or be compelled to appear in person before such

[1] See Clode, *Military Forces of the Crown* (1869), vol. i, p. 500.

[2] Cf. Army Act, 1955, ss. 70, 133, 134, 146; and see Allied Forces Act, 1952.

[3] Cf. Jurisdiction in Homicides Act, 1862, and Clode, *op. cit.*, vol. i, pp. 206, 207.

Part II.

court on a civil claim against him which does not exceed £30.[1]

No one who has entered into the spirit of continental legislation can believe that (say in France or Prussia) the rights of a private individual would thus have been allowed to override the claims of the public service.

In all conflicts of jurisdiction between a military and a civil court the authority of the civil court prevails. Thus, if a soldier is acquitted or convicted of an offence by a competent civil court, he cannot be tried for the same offence by a court-martial;[2] but an acquittal or conviction by a court-martial, say for manslaughter or robbery, is no plea to an indictment for the same offence at the Assizes.[3]

Order of superiors no defence to charge of crime.

When a soldier is put on trial on a charge of crime, obedience to superior orders is not of itself a defence.[4]

[1] See Army Act, 1881, s. 144; cf. Army Act, 1955, s. 185, for present exemption, which is limited to taking in execution property used for military purposes.

[2] Army Act, cf. 1955, s. 134.

[3] *Ibid.* Contrast the position of the army in relation to the law of the land in France. The fundamental principle of French law is, as it apparently always has been, that every kind of crime or offence committed by a soldier or person subject to military law must be tried by a military tribunal. See *Code de Justice Militaire*, arts. 55, 56, 76, 77, and Le Faure, *Les Lois militaires de la France* (1876), pp. 167, 173.

[4] Stephen, *History of the Criminal Law* (1883), vol. i, pp. 204-206; cf. Clode, *op. cit.*, vol. ii, pp. 125-155. The position of a soldier is curiously illustrated by the following case. *X* was a sentinel on board a ship in the Royal Navy when she was paying off. "The orders to him from the preceding sentinel were, to keep off all boats, unless they had officers with uniforms in them, or unless the officer on deck allowed them to approach; and he received a musket, three blank cartridges, and three balls. The boats pressed; upon which he called repeatedly to them to keep off; but one of them persisted and came close under the ship; and he then fired at a man who was in the boat, and killed him. The jury found that the sentinel fired under the mistaken impression that it was his duty. On a case reserved, the judges were unanimous that the killing was nevertheless murder;

This is a matter which requires explanation.

A soldier is bound to obey any lawful order which he receives from his military superior. But a soldier cannot any more than a civilian avoid responsibility for breach of the law by pleading that he broke the law in *bona fide* obedience to the orders (say) of the commander-in-chief. Hence the position of a soldier is in theory and may be in practice a difficult one. He may, as it has been well said, be liable to be shot by a court-martial if he disobeys an order, and to be hanged by a judge and jury if he obeys it. His situation and the line of his duty may be seen by considering how soldiers ought to act in the following cases.

During a riot an officer orders his soldiers to fire upon rioters. The command to fire is justified by the fact that no less energetic course of action would be sufficient to put down the disturbance. The soldiers are, under these circumstances, clearly bound from a legal, as well as from a military, point of view to obey the command of their officer. It is a lawful

but were of opinion, that if the act had been necessary for the preservation of the ship, as if the deceased had been stirring up a mutiny, the sentinel would have been justified."—Russell, *Crime* (9th ed., 1936), vol. i, p. 510, citing *The King* v. *Thomas* (1816) MS., Bayley, J. The date of the decision is worth noticing; no one can suppose that the judges of 1816 were disposed to underrate the rights of the Crown and its servants. The judgment of the court rests upon and illustrates the incontrovertible principle of the common law that the fact of a person being a soldier and of his acting strictly under orders, does not of itself exempt him from criminal liability for acts which would be crimes if done by a civilian, but compare *Keighley* v. *Bell* (1866) 4 F. & F. 763, at p. 790, cited in *The Queen* v. *Smith* (1900) 17 Cape S.C. Reports 561; K. & L. 396. In the opinion of Willes, J., obedience to an order of a superior officer which is not necessarily or manifestly illegal may be a good defence to a criminal charge against a person subject to military law; see Wade and Phillips, *op. cit.*, pp. 420, 421.

order, and the men who carry it out are performing their duty both as soldiers and as citizens.

An officer orders his soldiers in a time of political excitement then and there to arrest and shoot without trial a popular leader against whom no crime has been proved, but who is suspected of treasonable designs. In such a case there is (it is conceived) no doubt that the soldiers who obey, no less than the officer who gives the command, are guilty of murder, and liable to be hanged for it when convicted in due course of law. In such an extreme instance as this the duty of soldiers is, even at the risk of disobeying their superior, to obey the law of the land.

An officer orders his men to fire on a crowd who he thinks could not be dispersed without the use of firearms. As a matter of fact the amount of force which he wishes to employ is excessive, and order could be kept by the mere threat that force would be used. The order, therefore, to fire is not in itself a lawful order, that is, the colonel, or other officer, who gives it is not legally justified in giving it, and will himself be held criminally responsible for the death of any person killed by the discharge of firearms. What is, from a legal point of view, the duty of the soldiers? The matter is one which has never been absolutely decided; the following answer, given by Mr. Justice Stephen, is, it may fairly be assumed, as nearly correct a reply as the state of the authorities makes it possible to provide:—

"I do not think, however, that the question how "far superior orders would justify soldiers or sailors "in making an attack upon civilians has ever been "brought before the courts of law in such a manner "as to be fully considered and determined. Probably "upon such an argument it would be found that the "order of a military superior would justify his in-"feriors in executing any orders for giving which they "might fairly suppose their superior officer to have "good reasons. Soldiers might reasonably think "that their officer had good grounds for ordering "them to fire into a disorderly crowd which to them "might not appear to be at that moment engaged in "acts of dangerous violence, but soldiers could hardly "suppose that their officer could have any good "grounds for ordering them to fire a volley down a "crowded street when no disturbance of any kind "was either in progress or apprehended. The doc-"trine that a soldier is bound under all circumstances "whatever to obey his superior officer would be fatal "to military discipline itself, for it would justify the "private in shooting the colonel by the orders of the "captain, or in deserting to the enemy on the field of "battle on the order of his immediate superior. I "think it is not less monstrous to suppose that "superior orders would justify a soldier in the "massacre of unoffending civilians in time of peace, "or in the exercise of inhuman cruelties, such as the "slaughter of women and children, during a rebellion. "The only line that presents itself to my mind is "that a soldier should be protected by orders for "which he might reasonably believe his officer to "have good grounds. The inconvenience of being "subject to two jurisdictions, the sympathies of which "are not unlikely to be opposed to each other, is an "inevitable consequence of the double necessity of "preserving on the one hand the supremacy of the

Part II.

"law, and on the other the discipline of the "army." [1]

The hardship of a soldier's position resulting from this inconvenience is much diminished by the power of the Crown to nullify the effect of an unjust conviction by means of a pardon.[2] While, however, a soldier runs no substantial risk of punishment for obedience to orders which a man of common sense may honestly believe to involve no breach of law, he can under no circumstances escape the chance of his military conduct becoming the subject of inquiry before a civil tribunal, and cannot avoid liability on the ground of obedience to superior orders for any act which a man of ordinary sense must have known to be a crime.[3]

Soldier's position as member of army.

A soldier's position as a member of the army.—A citizen on entering the army becomes liable to special duties as being "a person subject to military law." Hence acts which if done by a civilian would be either no offence at all or only slight misdemeanours.

[1] Stephen, *op. cit.*, vol. i, pp. 205, 206; cf. Report of Committee on Featherstone Riots, 1893 [C. 7234].

[2] As also by the right of the Attorney-General as representing the Crown to enter a *nolle prosequi*. See Stephen, *op. cit.*, vol. i, p. 496, and Archbold, *Pleading, Evidence and Practice in Criminal Cases* (33rd ed., 1954), p. 110.

[3] *Buron* v. *Denman* (1848) 2 Ex. 167, K. & L. 102; is sometimes cited as showing that obedience to the orders of the Crown is a legal justification to an officer for committing a breach of law, but the decision in that case does not, in any way, support the doctrine erroneously grounded upon it. What the judgment in *Buron* v. *Denman* shows is that an act done by an English military or naval officer in a foreign country to a foreigner, previously authorised or subsequently ratified by the Crown, is an act of state, but does not constitute any breach of law for which an action can be brought against the officer in an English court; cf. *Feather* v. *The Queen* (1865) 6 B. & S. 257, at p. 295.

e.g. an insult or a blow offered to an officer, may when done by a soldier become serious crimes and expose the person guilty of them to grave punishment. A soldier's offences, moreover, can be tried and punished by a court-martial. He therefore in his military character of a soldier occupies a position totally different from that of a civilian; he has not the same freedom, and in addition to his duties as a citizen is subject to all the liabilities imposed by military law; but though this is so, it is not to be supposed that, even as regards a soldier's own position as a military man, the rule of the ordinary law is, at any rate in time of peace, excluded from the army.

The general principle on this subject is that the courts of law have jurisdiction to determine who are the persons subject to military law, and whether a given proceeding, alleged to depend upon military law, is really justified by the rules of law which govern the army.

Hence flow the following (among other) consequences.

The civil courts determine[1] whether a given person is or is not "a person subject to military law."[2]

Enlistment, which constitutes the contract[3] by

[1] See *Wolfe Tone's Case* (1798) 27 St. Tr. 614; *Frye* v. *Ogle* (1743), cited *Manual of Military Law* (7th ed., 1929), ch. viii, sec. 35.

[2] See Army Act, 1955, ss. 205-213.

[3] The enlistment of a regular soldier is a species of contract between the Sovereign and the soldier, and under the ordinary law cannot be altered without the consent of both parties. The result is that the conditions laid down in the Act under which a man is enlisted cannot be varied without his consent; but his service is liable to be determined at the pleasure of the Crown and there is no remedy for dismissal or recovery of pay; *Leaman* v. *The King* [1920] 3 K.B. 663; *Kynaston* v. *Attorney-General* (1933) 49 T.L.R. 300.

which a person becomes subject to military law, is a civil proceeding, and a civil court may sometimes have to inquire whether a man has been duly enlisted, or whether he is or is not entitled to his discharge.[1]

If a court-martial exceeds its jurisdiction, or an officer, whether acting as a member of a court-martial or not, does any act not authorised by law, the action of the court, or of the officer, is subject to the supervision of the courts. "The proceedings by which "the courts of law supervise the acts of courts-"martial and of officers may be criminal or civil. "Criminal proceedings take the form of an indict-"ment for assault, false imprisonment, manslaughter, "or even murder. Civil proceedings may either "be preventive, *i.e.* to restrain the commission "or continuance of an injury; or remedial, *i.e.* to "afford a remedy for injury actually suffered. Broadly "speaking, the civil jurisdiction of the courts of law "is exercised as against the tribunal of a court-"martial by writs of prohibition or certiorari; and as "against individual officers by actions for damages. "A writ of habeas corpus also may be directed to "any officer, governor of a prison, or other, who has

[1] See Army Act, 1881, s. 96, which was not re-enacted in Army Act, 1955, for special provisions as to the delivering to a master of an apprentice who, being under twenty-one, had enlisted as a soldier. Under the present law, at any rate, it can very rarely happen that a court should be called upon to consider whether a person is improperly detained in military custody as a soldier. See Army Act, 1955, s. 18, for validity of attestation and enlistment. The courts used to interfere, when soldiers were impressed, in cases of improper impressment. See Clode, *Military Forces of the Crown* (1869), vol. ii, pp. 8, 587.

A civil court may also be called upon to determine whether a person subject to military law has, or has not, a right to resign his commission; *Hearson* v. *Churchill* [1892] 2 Q.B. 144.

"in his custody any person alleged to be improperly "detained under colour of military law."[1]

Chapter IX.

Lastly, the whole existence and discipline of the standing army, at any rate in time of peace, depends upon the passing of what is known as an annual Mutiny Act,[2] or in strict correctness of the Army (Annual) Act. If this Act were not in force a soldier would not be bound by military law. Desertion would be at most only a breach of contract, and striking an officer would be no more than an assault.

Territorial Army.

As to the Territorial Army.—This force in many respects represents the militia and the volunteers. It is, as was in fact the militia in later times, raised by voluntary enlistment. All members of the Territorial Army are required, not by military law, but by the actual terms of their engagement, to accept liability to serve overseas, provided that an Act of Parliament has been passed authorising the dispatch overseas of the Territorial Army. It is from its nature, in this too like the militia, a body hardly capable of being used for the overthrow of Parliamentary government. But even with regard to this territorial force, care has been taken to ensure that it shall be subject to the rule of law. The members of this local army are (speaking in general terms)

[1] *Manual of Military Law* (6th ed., 1914), ch. viii, sec. 8, substantially reproduced in the 7th ed. (1929), ch. viii, sec. 2. It should, however, be noted that the courts of law will not, in general at any rate, deal with rights dependent on military status and military regulations.

[2] See p. 295, note 1, for a short account of the past and present methods of sanctioning military law by Parliament. The present Acts—Army Act, 1955, and Air Force Act, 1955—came into force on 1st January 1957; they expire at the end of five years, but provision is made for annual review of particular provisions if necessary.

Part II. subject to military law only when in training or when the force is embodied.[1] Embodiment indeed converts the territorial force into a territorial army, an army which previously could not be required to serve abroad.

But the embodiment can lawfully take place only in case of imminent national danger or great emergency, or unless the emergency requires it, until Parliament has had an opportunity of presenting an address against the embodiment of the Territorial Army. The general effect of the enactments on the subject is that, at any rate when there is a Parliament in existence, the embodiment of this territorial force cannot, except under the pressure of urgent necessity, be carried out without the sanction of Parliament.[2] Add to this, that the maintenance of discipline among the members of the Territorial Army when it is embodied depends on the continuance in force of the Army Act and of the Army (Annual) Act.[3]

[1] But in one case at least, *i.e.* failure to attend on embodiment, a man of the Territorial Army may be liable to be tried by court-martial, though not otherwise subject to military law. (Auxiliary Forces Act, 1953, s. 27 ; see also as to cases of concurrent jurisdiction of a court-martial and a court of summary jurisdiction, *ibid.*, ss. 31, 33.)

[2] Cf. Auxiliary Forces Act, 1953, s. 23 (2), and see note 4, p. 295, *ante*.

[3] There exists an instructive analogy between the position of persons subject to military law, and the position of the clergy of the Established Church.

A clergyman of the National Church, like a soldier of the National Army, is subject to duties and to courts to which other Englishmen are not subject. He is bound by restrictions, as he enjoys privileges peculiar to his class, but the clergy are no more than soldiers exempt from the law of the land. Any deed which would be a crime when done by a layman, is a crime when done by a clergyman, and is in either case dealt with by the ordinary tribunals.

Moreover, as the common law courts determine the legal limits to the jurisdiction of courts-martial, so the same courts in reality determine (subject, of course, to Acts of Parliament) what are the limits to the jurisdiction of ecclesiastical courts.

The original difficulty, again, of putting the clergy on the same footing as laymen, was at least as great as that of establishing the supremacy of the civil power in all matters regarding the army. Each of these difficulties was met at an earlier date and has been overcome with more completeness in England than in some other countries. We may plausibly conjecture that this triumph of law was due to the acknowledged supremacy of the King in Parliament, which itself was due to the mode in which the King, acting together with the two Houses, manifestly represented the nation, and therefore was able to wield the whole moral authority of the state.

CHAPTER X

THE REVENUE[1]

Part II. Revenue.

As in treating of the army my aim was simply to point out what were the principles determining the relation of the armed forces of the country to the law of the land, so in treating of the revenue my aim is not to give even a sketch of the matters connected with the raising, the collection, and the expenditure of the national income, but simply to show that the collection and expenditure of the revenue, and all things appertaining thereto, are governed by strict rules of law. Attention should be fixed upon three points,—the *source* of the public revenue—the *authority* for expending the public revenue—and the *securities* provided by law for the due appropriation of the public revenue, that is, for its being expended in the exact manner which the law directs.

Source.

Source of public revenue.—It is laid down by Blackstone and other authorities that the revenue consists of the hereditary or "ordinary" revenue of the Crown and of the "extraordinary" revenue depending upon taxes imposed by Parliament.

[1] See Hills and Fellowes, *Finance of Government* (2nd ed., 1932), and May, *Parliamentary Practice* (16th ed., 1957), ch. xxiv and xxviii.

Historically this distinction is of interest. But for our purpose we need hardly trouble ourselves at all with the hereditary revenue of the Crown, arising from Crown lands, droits of admiralty, and the like. It forms an insignificant portion of the national resources, amounting to not much more than £500,000 a year. It does not, moreover, at the present moment belong specially to the Crown, for it was commuted at the beginning of the reign of King Edward VII.,[1] as it was at the beginning of the reign of William IV. and of the reign of Queen Victoria, for a fixed "civil list,"[2] or sum payable yearly for the support of the dignity of the Crown. The whole then of the hereditary revenue is now paid into the national exchequer and forms part of the income of the nation. We may, therefore, putting the hereditary revenue out of our minds, direct our whole attention to what is oddly enough called the "extraordinary," but is in reality the ordinary, or Parliamentary, revenue of the nation.

The whole of the national revenue had come to amount in a normal year to somewhere about £144,000,000.[3] It is (if we put out of sight the small hereditary revenue of the Crown) raised wholly by taxes imposed by law. The national revenue, therefore, depends wholly upon law and upon statute law; it is the creation of Acts of Parliament.

While no one can nowadays fancy that taxes

[1] Civil List Acts, 1910, 1936, 1937, 1953.

[2] See as to Civil List, May, *Constitutional History* (1912 ed.), vol. i, ch. iv.

[3] In 1907 the total revenue for the year (Exchequer receipts) 1906-7 was £144,814,000. The figure, which excludes borrowings on long and short term loans, had risen by 1958 to over £5,000,000,000.

Part II. can be raised otherwise than in virtue of an Act of Parliament, there prevails, it may be suspected, with many of us a good deal of confusion of mind as to the exact relation between the raising of the revenue and the sitting of Parliament. People often talk as though, if Parliament did not meet, no taxes would be legally payable, and the assembling of Parliament were therefore secured by the necessity of filling the national exchequer. This idea is encouraged by the study of periods, such as the reign of Charles I., during which the Crown could not legally obtain necessary supplies without the constant intervention of Parliament. But the notion that at the present day no money could legally be levied if Parliament ceased to meet is unfounded. Millions of money would come into the Exchequer even though Parliament did not sit at all. For though all taxation depends upon Act of Parliament, it is far from being the case that all taxation now depends upon annual or temporary Acts.

Taxes are made payable in two different ways, *i.e.* either by annual enactment in the Finance Act or by Acts which impose the tax until repeal or amendment or for a fixed period exceeding one year.[1]

Taxes, the proceeds of which amounted in the year 1906-7 to at least three-fourths of the whole yearly revenue, are imposed by permanent Acts; such taxes are the land tax, the excise, the stamp duties, and by far the greater number of existing taxes. These taxes would continue to be payable even though Parliament should not be convened

[1] And also since 1932 by statutory orders under the Import Duties Acts, 1932 and 1958, in the case of customs duties.—Ed.

for years. We should all, to take an example which comes home to every one, be legally compellable to buy the stamps for our letters even though Parliament did not meet again for several years.

Chapter X.

Other taxes—and notably the income tax—the proceeds of which make up the remainder of the national income, are imposed by yearly Acts.[1] If by any chance Parliament should not be convened for a year, no one would be under any legal obligation to pay income tax.

This distinction between revenue depending upon permanent Acts and revenue depending upon temporary Acts is worth attention, but the main point, of course, to be borne in mind is that all taxes are imposed by statute, and that no one can be forced to pay a single shilling by way of taxation which cannot be shown to the satisfaction of the judges to be due from him under Act of Parliament.

Authority for expenditure.

Authority for expending revenue.—At one time revenue once raised by taxation was in truth and in reality a grant or gift by the Houses of Parliament to the Crown. Such grants as were made to Charles the First or James the First were moneys truly given to the King. He was, as a matter of moral duty, bound, out of the grants made to him, as out of the hereditary revenue, to defray the expenses of government; and the gifts made to the King by Parliament were never intended to be "money to put into his own pocket," as the expression goes. Still it was in truth money of which the King or his Ministers could and did regulate the distribution. One of the

[1] The greater part of the sum raised annually by taxation is nowadays imposed by provisions in the Finance Acts which do not require annual renewal. The rate of income tax is, however, fixed every year.

singularities which mark the English constitution is the survival of mediæval notions, which more or less identified the King's property with the national revenue, after the passing away of the state of society to which such ideas naturally belonged; in the time of George the Third many public expenses, as, for example, the salaries of the judges, were charged upon the civil list, and thus were mixed up with the King's private expenditure. At the present day, however, the whole public revenue is treated, not as the property of the Sovereign, but as public income; and as to this two matters deserve special observation.

First, The whole revenue of the nation is paid into the Bank of England[1] to the "account of her Majesty's Exchequer,"[2] mainly through the Inland Revenue, the Customs and Excise and the Post Office. That office is a mere place for the receipt of taxes; it is a huge money-box into which day by day moneys paid as taxes are dropped, and whence such moneys are taken daily to the Bank. What, I am told, takes place is this. Each day large amounts are received at the Inland Revenue Office; two gentlemen come there each afternoon in a cab from the Bank; they go through the accounts for the day with the proper officials; they do not leave

[1] See Exchequer and Audit Departments Act, 1866, s. 10.

[2] *Ibid.* and *Control and Audit of Public Receipts and Expenditure*, pp. 7, 8. By a system of appropriations in aid moneys which formerly were treated as extra receipts, and paid into the Exchequer, are now shown in the Estimates separately from the money which Parliament is asked to vote and are applied by the Departments to reduce the total of the Supply Vote. Appropriations in aid must receive parliamentary sanction in the annual Appropriation Act and surplus receipts under this head are surrendered to the Exchequer.

till every item is made perfectly clear; they then take all the money received, and drive off with it and pay it into the Bank of England.

Secondly, Not a penny of revenue can be legally expended except under the authority of some Act of Parliament.

This authority may be given by a permanent Act, as, for example, by the Civil List Act, 1837, or by the National Debt and Local Loans Act, 1887; or it may be given by the Appropriation Act, that is, the annual Act by which Parliament "appropriates" or fixes the sums payable to objects (the chief of which is the support of the army and navy) which are not provided for, as is the payment of the National Debt, by permanent Acts of Parliament.

The whole thing, to express it in general terms, stands thus.

There is paid into the Bank of England in a normal year a national income raised by different taxes amounting to nearly £144,000,000 per annum, This £144,000,000 constitutes the revenue or "consolidated fund."

Every penny of it is, unless the law is broken, paid away in accordance with Act of Parliament. The authority to make payments from it is given in many cases by permanent Acts; thus the whole of the interest on the National Debt is payable out of the Consolidated Fund under the National Debt and Local Loans Act, 1887. The order or authority to make payments out of it is in other cases given by a yearly Act, namely, the Appropriation Act, which determines the mode in which the supplies granted by Parliament

Part II.

(and not otherwise appropriated by permanent Acts) are to be spent. In either case, and this is the point to bear in mind, payments made out of the national revenue are made by and under the authority of the law, namely, under the directions of some special Act of Parliament.

The details of the method according to which supplies are annually voted and appropriated by Parliament are amply treated of in works which deal with Parliamentary practice.[1] The matter which requires our attention is the fact that each item of expenditure (such, for example, as the total sum of wages paid to the army and navy) which is not directed and authorised by some permanent Act is ultimately authorised by the Appropriation Act for the year, or by special Acts which for convenience are passed prior to the Appropriation Act and are enumerated therein. The expenditure, therefore, no less than the raising of taxation, depends wholly and solely upon Parliamentary enactment.

Security for proper expenditure.

Security for the proper appropriation of the revenue.—What, it may be asked, is the real security that moneys paid by the taxpayers are expended by the government in accordance with the intention of Parliament?

The answer is that this security is provided by an elaborate scheme of control and audit. Under this system not a penny of public money can be obtained by the government without the authority or sanction of persons (quite independent, be it remarked, of the Cabinet) whose duty it is to see that no money is paid out of the Exchequer except

[1] See especially May, *Parliamentary Practice* (16th ed., 1957), ch. xxvi.

under legal authority. To the same officials ultimately comes the knowledge of the way in which money thus paid out is actually expended, and they are bound to report to Parliament upon any expenditure which is or may appear to be not authorised by law.

The centre of this system of Parliamentary control is the Comptroller and Auditor General.[1]

He is a high official, absolutely independent of the Cabinet; he can take no part in politics, for he cannot be either a member of the House of Commons, or a peer of Parliament. He in common with his subordinate—the Assistant Comptroller and Auditor General—is appointed by a patent under the Great Seal, holds his office during good behaviour, and can be removed only on an address from both Houses of Parliament.[2] He is head of the Exchequer and Audit Department. He thus combines in his own person two characters which formerly belonged to different officials. He is controller of the issue of public money; he is auditor of public accounts. He is called upon, therefore, to perform two different functions, which the reader ought, in his own mind, to keep carefully distinct from each other.

In exercise of his duty of control the Comptroller General is bound, with the aid of the officials under him, to see that the whole of the national revenue, which, it will be remembered, is lodged in the Bank of England to the account of the Exchequer, is paid out under legal authority, that is, under the provisions of some Act of Parliament.

[1] See Hills and Fellowes, *op. cit.*, pp. 79-85, 107-113.

[2] Exchequer and Audit Departments Act, 1886, s. 3.

Part II.

The Comptroller General is enabled to do this because, whenever the Treasury (through which office alone the public moneys are drawn out from the Bank) needs to draw out money for the public service, the Treasury must make a requisition to the Comptroller General authorising the payment from the public moneys at the Bank of the definite sum required.

The payments made by the Treasury are, as already pointed out, made either under some permanent Act, for what are technically called "Consolidated Fund services," as, for example, to meet the interest on the National Debt, or under the yearly Appropriation Act, for what are technically called "supply services," as, for example, to meet the expenses of the army or the navy.

In either case the Comptroller General must, before granting the necessary credit, satisfy himself that he is authorised in doing so by the terms of the Act under which it is demanded. He must also satisfy himself that every legal formality, necessary for obtaining public money from the Bank, has been duly complied with. Unless, and until, he is satisfied he ought not to grant, and will not grant, a credit for the amount required; and until this credit is obtained, the money required cannot be drawn out of the Bank.

The obtaining from the Comptroller General of a grant of credit may appear to many readers a mere formality, and we may suppose that it is in most cases given as a matter of course. It is, however, a formality which gives an opportunity to an official, who has no interest in deviating from the law, for preventing the least irregularity on the part of the government in the drawing out of public money.

The Comptroller's power of putting a check on government expenditure has, oddly enough, been pushed to its extreme length in comparatively modern times. In 1811 England was in the midst of the great war with France; the King was a lunatic, a Regency Bill was not yet passed, and a million pounds were required for the payment of the navy. Lord Grenville, the then Auditor of the Exchequer, whose office corresponded to a certain extent with that of the present Comptroller and Auditor General, refused to draw the necessary order on the Bank, and thus prevented the million, though granted by Parliament, from being drawn out. The ground of his lordship's refusal was that he had received no authority under the Great Seal or the Privy Seal, and the reason why there was no authority under the Privy Seal was that the King was incapable of affixing the Sign Manual, and that the Sign Manual not being affixed, the clerks of the Privy Seal felt, or said they felt, that they could not consistently with their oaths allow the issue of letters of Privy Seal upon which the warrant under the Privy Seal was then prepared. All the world knew the true state of the case. The money was granted by Parliament, and the irregularity in the issue of the warrants was purely technical, yet the law officers—members themselves of the Ministry—advised that Lord Grenville and the clerks of the Privy Seal were in the right. This inconvenient and, as it seems to modern readers,

Part II. unreasonable display of legal scrupulosity masked, it may be suspected, a good deal of political by-play. If Lord Grenville and his friends had not been anxious that the Ministry should press on the Regency Bill, the officials of the Exchequer would perhaps have seen their way through the technical difficulties which, as it was, appeared insurmountable, and it is impossible not to suspect that Lord Grenville acted rather as a party leader than as Auditor of the Exchequer. But be this as it may, the debates of 1811[1] prove to demonstration that a Comptroller General can, if he chooses, put an immediate check on any irregular dealings with public moneys.

In exercise of his duty as Auditor the Comptroller General audits all the public accounts;[2] he reports annually to Parliament upon the accounts of the past year. Accounts of the expenditure under the Appropriation Act are submitted by him at the beginning of every session to the Public Accounts Committee of the House of Commons—a Committee appointed for the examination of the accounts—showing the appropriation of the sums granted by Parliament to meet the public expenditure. This examination is no mere formal or perfunctory supervision; a glance at the reports of the Committee shows that the smallest expenses which bear the least appearance of irregularity, even if amounting only to a pound or two, are gone into and discussed

[1] Cobbett's *Parliamentary Debates*, vol. xviii (1812), columns 678, 734, 787.

[2] In auditing the accounts he directs attention to any excess of authorised expenditure as well as to irregular payments and extravagant items in the accounts of a Department, and in his report to Parliament calls attention to any expenditure of doubtful legality or extravagance.

by the Committee. The results of their discussions are published in reports submitted to Parliament.

The general result of this system of control and audit is, that in England we possess accounts of the national expenditure of an accuracy which cannot be rivalled by the public accounts of other countries, and that every penny of the national income is expended under the authority and in accordance with the provisions of some Act of Parliament.[1]

How, a foreign critic might ask, is the authority of the Comptroller General compatible with the orderly transaction of public business; how, in short, does it happen that difficulties like those which arose in 1811 are not of constant recurrence?

The general answer of course is, that high English officials, and especially officials removed from the

[1] The main features of the system for the control and audit of national expenditure have been authoritatively summarised as follows:—

"The gross revenue collected is paid into the Exchequer.

"Issues from the Exchequer can only be made to meet expenditure "which has been sanctioned by Parliament, and to an amount not "exceeding the sums authorised.

"The issues from the Exchequer and the audit of Accounts are "under the control of the Comptroller and Auditor General, who is "an independent officer responsible to the House of Commons, and "who can only be removed by vote of both Houses of Parliament.

"Such payments only can be charged against the vote of a year as "actually came in course of payment within the year.

"The correct appropriation of each item of Receipt and Expendi-"ture is ensured.

"All unexpended balances of the grants of a year are surrendered "to the Exchequer, as also are all extra Receipts and the amount of "Appropriations-in-Aid received in excess of the sum estimated to be "taken in aid of the vote.

"The accounts of each year are finally reviewed by the House of "Commons, through the Committee of Public Accounts, and any "excess of expenditure over the amount voted by Parliament for any "service must receive legislative sanction."—*Control and Audit of Public Receipts and Expenditure* (1885), pp. 24, 25.

Part II.

sphere of politics, have no wish or temptation to hinder the progress of public business; the Auditor of the Exchequer was in 1811, be it noted, a peer and a statesman. The more technical reply is, that the law provides two means of overcoming the perversity or factiousness of any Comptroller who should without due reason refuse his sanction to the issue of public money. He can be removed from office on an address of the two Houses, and he probably might, it has been suggested, be coerced into the proper fulfilment of his duties by a mandamus[1] from the High Court of Justice. The worth of this suggestion, made by a competent lawyer, has never been, and probably never will be tested. But the possibility that the executive might have to seek the aid of the courts in order to get hold of moneys granted by Parliament, is itself a curious proof of the extent to which the expenditure of the revenue is governed by law, or, what is the same thing, may become dependent on the decision of the judges upon the meaning of an Act of Parliament.[2]

[1] Hearn, *Government of England* (2nd ed., 1887), p. 375.

[2] This chapter deals only with the Revenue from the point of view of the rules of law governing the collection and expenditure of money raised by taxation by the Central Government. The full account of Public Revenue would of course include loan expenditure and rates levied by, and other sources of income of, local authorities.

The rule which requires all proposals for expenditure by the Central Government to receive the recommendation of the Crown is one of the most fundamental rules of ministerial responsibility. But with this aspect of the subject the author was not concerned here.—Ed.

CHAPTER XI

THE RESPONSIBILITY OF MINISTERS

Chapter XI.

Ministerial responsibility.

MINISTERIAL responsibility means two utterly different things.

It means in ordinary parlance the responsibility of Ministers to Parliament, or, the liability of Ministers to lose their offices if they cannot retain the confidence of the House of Commons.

This is a matter depending on the conventions of the constitution with which law has no direct concern.

It means, when used in its strict sense, the legal responsibility of every Minister for every act of the Crown in which he takes part.

This responsibility, which is a matter of law, rests on the following foundation. There is not to be found in the law of England, as there is found in most foreign constitutions, an explicit statement that the acts of the monarch must always be done through a Minister, and that all orders given by the Crown must, when expressed in writing, as they generally are, be countersigned by a Minister. Practically, however, the rule exists.[1]

In order that an act of the Crown may be recognised as an expression of the Royal will and have any legal effect whatever, it must in general be done with the assent of, or through some Minister or Ministers who will be held responsible for it. For the Royal will can, speaking generally, be expressed

[1] In the case of some of the independent statutory authorities, such as the National Assistance Board, the functions of the body and of its officers and servants are by statute deemed to be exercised on behalf of the Crown. The functions are such that they could not be exercised by the Crown or the body without statutory authority.—ED.

Part II. only in one of three different ways, viz. (1) by Order in Council; (2) by order, commission, or warrant under the sign-manual; (3) by proclamations, writs, patents, letters, or other documents under the Great Seal.

An Order in Council is made by the Queen "by and with the advice of his Privy Council"; and those persons who are present at the meeting of the Council at which the order was made, bear the responsibility for what was there done. The sign-manual warrant, or other document to which the sign-manual is affixed, bears in general the countersignature of one responsible Minister or of more than one; though it is not unfrequently authenticated by some one of the seals for the use of which a Secretary of State is responsible. The Great Seal is affixed to a document on the responsibility of the Chancellor, and there may be other persons also, who, as well as the Chancellor, are made responsible for its being affixed. The result is that at least one Minister and often more must take part in, and therefore be responsible for, any act of the Crown which has any legal effect, *e.g.* the making of a grant, the giving of an order, or the signing of a treaty.[1]

The Minister or servant of the Crown who thus takes part in giving expression to the Royal will is legally responsible for the act in which he is concerned, and he cannot get rid of his liability by pleading that he acted in obedience to royal orders. Now supposing that the act done is illegal, the Minister

[1] On the whole of this subject the reader should consult Anson, *Law and Custom of the Constitution*, vol. ii (4th ed., 1935), part i, pp. 62-72, 170, 171. Anson gives a full account of the forms for the expression of the Royal pleasure and of the effect of these forms in enforcing the legal responsibility of Ministers. See also Clode, *Military Forces of the Crown* (1869), vol. ii, pp. 320, 321; *Buron* v. *Denman* (1848) 2 Ex. 167; K. & L. 102, at p. 189; Great Seal Act, 1884; Wade and Phillips, *op. cit.*, App. B.

concerned in it becomes at once liable to criminal or civil proceedings in a court of law. In some instances, it is true, the only legal mode in which his offence could be reached may be an impeachment. But an impeachment itself is a regular though unusual mode of legal procedure before a recognised tribunal, namely, the High Court of Parliament. Impeachments indeed may, though one took place as late as 1805, be thought now obsolete, but the cause why this mode of enforcing Ministerial responsibility is almost out of date is partly that Ministers are now rarely in a position where there is even a temptation to commit the sort of crimes for which impeachment is an appropriate remedy, and partly that the result aimed at by impeachment could now in many cases be better obtained by proceedings before an ordinary court. The point, however, which should never be forgotten is this: it is now well-established law that the Crown can act only through Ministers and according to certain prescribed forms which absolutely require the co-operation of some Minister, such as a Secretary of State or the Lord Chancellor, who thereby becomes not only morally but legally responsible for the legality of the act in which he takes part. Hence, indirectly but surely, the action of every servant of the Crown, and therefore in effect of the Crown itself, is brought under the supremacy of the law of the land. Behind parliamentary responsibility lies legal liability, and the acts of Ministers no less than the acts of subordinate officials are made subject to the rule of law.[1]

[1] See Intro. pp. clxxix *et seq.*, *ante*, for the sanctions which ensure obedience to the conventions relating to ministerial responsibility. It is only since the Crown Proceedings Act, 1947, that the Crown may be held liable in tort for the acts of its servants and agents, with certain exceptions, especially ss. 9, 10.—Ed.

CHAPTER XII[1]

RULE OF LAW COMPARED WITH *DROIT ADMINISTRATIF*[2]

Part II.

Introduction.

IN many continental countries, and notably in France, there exists a scheme of administrative law[3]—known

[1] As in other chapters no attempt has been made to bring up to date the text or the references to authorities cited by the author. There will be found in Appendix 1 a short account of modern French administrative law, together with a bibliography contributed by Professor P. M. Gaudemet.—ED.

[2] On *droit administratif* the author cited Aucoc, *Conférences sur l'Administration et sur le Droit administratif* (3rd ed., 1885); Berthélemy, *Traité élémentaire de Droit administratif* (5th ed., 1908); Chardon, *L'Administration de la France; Les fonctionnaires* (1908), pp. 79-105; Duguit, *Traité de Droit constitutionnel* (1st ed., 1911); Duguit, *L'Etat, les gouvernants et les agents* (1903); Duguit, *Manuel de Droit Public français; Droit Constitutionnel* (1907); Esmein, *Eléments de Droit constitutionnel français* (1st ed., 1896), Hauriou, *Précis de Droit administratif* (3rd ed., 1897); Jacquelin, *La Juridiction administrative* (1891); Jacquelin, *Les Principes Dominants du Contentieux Administratif* (1899); Jèze, *Les principes généraux du Droit administratif* (1st ed., 1904); Laferrière, *Traité de la Juridiction administrative et des recours contentieux*, 2 vols. (2nd ed., 1896); Teissier, *La responsabilité de la puissance publique* (1906).

Dicey's note read as follows:—

"It is not my aim in this chapter to give a general account of *droit administratif.* My object is to treat of *droit administratif* in so far as its fundamental principles conflict with modern English ideas of the rule of law, and especially to show how it always has given, and still does give, special protection or privileges to the servants of the State. I cannot, however, avoid mentioning some other aspects of a noteworthy legal system or omit some notice of the mode in which the administrative law of France, based as it originally was on the prerogatives of the Crown under the *ancien régime*, has of recent years, by the genius of French legists, been more or less judicialised —if so I may render the French term *juridictionnaliser*—and incorporated with the law of the land."

[3] Known in different countries by different names, *e.g.* in Germany

to Frenchmen as *droit administratif*—which rests on ideas foreign to the fundamental assumptions of our English common law, and especially to what we have termed the rule of law. This opposition is specially apparent in the protection given in foreign countries to servants of the State, or, as we say in England, of the Crown, who, whilst acting in pursuance of official orders, or in the *bona fide* attempt to discharge official duties, are guilty of acts which in themselves are wrongful or unlawful. The extent of this protection has in France—with which country we are for the most part concerned—varied from time to time. It was once all but complete; it is now far less extensive than it was thirty-six years ago.[1] It forms only one portion of the whole system of *droit administratif*,[2] but it is the part of French law to which in this chapter I wish to direct particularly the attention of students. I must, however, impress upon them that the whole body of *droit administratif* is well worth their study. It has been imitated in most of the countries of continental Europe. It

as *Verwaltungsrecht*. The administrative law of France comes nearer than does the *Verwaltungsrecht* of Germany (cf. Otto Mayer, *Le Droit administratif allemand* (1903-1906) (vol. i, 1903), para. 17, pp. 293-315, to the rule of law as understood by Englishmen. Here, as elsewhere, it is the similarity as much as the dissimilarity between France and England which prompts comparison. The historical glories of French arms conceal the important fact that among the great States of Europe, France and England have the most constantly attempted, though with unequal success, to maintain the supremacy of the civil power against any class which defies the legitimate sovereignty of the nation.

[1] Or than it was throughout the German Empire. See Duguit, *L'Etat, les gouvernants et les agents* (1903), ch. v, para. 10, note 1, p. 624.

[2] This recognition that *contentieux administratif* forms only a part of *droit administratif* was first made in the seventh edition (1908).—Ed.

Part II.

illustrates, by way of contrast, the full meaning of that absolute supremacy of the ordinary law of the land—a foreign critic might say of that intense legalism—which we have found to be a salient feature of English institutions. It also illustrates, by way of analogy rather than of contrast, some phases in the constitutional history of England. For *droit administratif* has, of recent years, been so developed as to meet the requirements of a modern and a democratic society, and thus throws light upon one stage at least in the growth of English constitutional law.[1]

Our subject falls under two main heads. The one head embraces the nature and the historical growth of *droit administratif*, and especially of that part thereof with which we are chiefly concerned. The other head covers a comparison between the English rule of law and the *droit administratif* of France.

(A) *Droit Administratif.*

For the term *droit administratif* English legal phraseology supplies no proper equivalent. The words "administrative law," which are its most natural rendering, are unknown to English judges and counsel, and are in themselves hardly intelligible without further explanation.

This absence from our language of any satisfactory equivalent for the expression *droit administratif* is significant; the want of a name arises at bottom from our non-recognition of the thing itself. In England, and in countries which, like the United States, derive their civilisation from English sources, the system of administrative law and the very principles on which it rests are in truth unknown.

[1] See pp. 375-383, *post*.

This absence from the institutions of the American Commonwealth of anything answering to *droit administratif* arrested the observation of de Tocqueville from the first moment when he began his investigations into the characteristics of American democracy. In 1831 he writes to an experienced French judge (*magistrat*), Monsieur De Blosseville, to ask both for an explanation of the contrast in this matter between French and American institutions, and also for an authoritative explanation of the general ideas (*notions générales*) governing the *droit administratif* of his country.[1] He grounds his request for information on his own ignorance [2] about this special branch of French jurisprudence, and clearly implies that this want of knowledge is not uncommon among French lawyers.

When we know that a legist of de Tocqueville's genius found it necessary to ask for instruction in the "general ideas" of administrative law, we may safely assume that the topic was one which, even in

[1] de Tocqueville's language is so remarkable and bears so closely on our topic that it deserves quotation: "*Ce qui m'empêche le plus, je* "*vous avoue, de savoir ce qui se fait sur ces différents points en Amérique,* "*c'est d'ignorer, à peu près complètement, ce qui existe en France.* "*Vous savez que, chez nous, le droit administratif et le droit civil forment* "*comme deux mondes séparés, qui ne vivent point toujours en paix, mais* "*qui ne sont ni assez amis ni assez ennemis pour se bien connaître. J'ai* "*toujours vécu dans l'un et suis fort ignorant de ce qui se passe dans* "*l'autre. En même temps que j'ai senti le besoin d'acquérir les notions* "*générales qui me manquent à cet égard, j'ai pensé que je ne pouvais* "*mieux faire que de m'adresser à vous.*"—de Tocqueville, *Œuvres complètes* (14th ed., 1864), vol. vii (Correspondance), pp. 67, 68.

[2] This want of knowledge is explainable, if not justifiable. In 1831 de Tocqueville was a youth of not more than twenty-six years of age. There were at that date already to be found books on *droit administratif* written to meet the wants of legal practitioners. But the mass of interesting constitutional literature represented by the writings of Laferrière, Hauriou, Duguit, Jèze, or Berthélemy which now elucidates the theory, and traces the history of a particular and most curious branch of French law, had not come into existence.

Part II. the eyes of a French lawyer, bore an exceptional character, and need not wonder that Englishmen find it difficult to appreciate the nature of rules which are, admittedly, foreign to the spirit and traditions of our institutions. It is, however, this very contrast between administrative law as it exists in France, and still more as it existed during by far the greater part of the nineteenth century, and the notions of equality before the law of the land which are firmly established in modern England, that mainly makes it worth while to study, not of course the details, but what de Tocqueville calls the *notions générales* of French *droit administratif.* Our aim should be to seize the general nature of administrative law and the principles on which the whole system of *droit administratif* depends, to note the salient characteristics by which this system is marked, and, lastly, to make clear to ourselves how it is that the existence of a scheme of administrative law makes the legal situation of every government official in France different from the legal situation of servants of the State in England, and in fact establishes a condition of things fundamentally inconsistent with what Englishmen regard as the due supremacy of the ordinary law of the land.

(1) Nature of *droit administratif.*

Droit administratif, or "administrative law," has been defined by French authorities in general terms as "the body of rules which regulate the relations "of the administration or of the administrative "authority towards private citizens";[1] and Aucoc in his work on *droit administratif* describes his topic

[1] "*On le définit ordinairement l'ensemble des règles qui régissent les* "*rapports de l'administration ou de l'autorité administrative avec les* "*citoyens.*"—Aucoc, *Conférences sur l'Administration et sur le Droit administratif* (3rd ed., 1885), vol. i, Intro., N° 6, p. 15.

in this very general language:[1] "Administrative law "determines (1) the constitution and the relations of "those organs of society which are charged with the "care of those social interests (*intérêts collectifs*) which "are the object of public administration, by which "term is meant the different representatives of society "among which the State is the most important, and "(2) the relation of the administrative authorities "towards the citizens of the State."

These definitions are wanting in precision, and their vagueness is not without significance. As far, however, as an Englishman may venture to deduce the meaning of *droit administratif* from foreign treatises, it may, for our present purpose, be best described as that portion of French law which determines, (i.) the position and liabilities of all State officials, (ii.) the civil rights and liabilities of private individuals in their dealings with officials as representatives of the State, and (iii.) the procedure by which these rights and liabilities are enforced.

An English student will never, it should particularly be noticed, understand this branch of French law unless he keeps his eye firmly fixed upon its historical aspect, and carefully notes the changes, almost amounting to the transformation, which *droit administratif* has undergone between 1800 and 1908, and above all during the last thirty or forty years. The fundamental ideas which underlie this department

[1] "*Nous préférerions dire, pour notre part: Le droit administratif "détermine: 1°· la constitution et les rapports des organes de la société "chargés du soin des intérêts collectifs qui font l'objet de l'administration "publique, c'est-à-dire des différentes personnifications de la société, dont "l'Etat est la plus importante; 2°· les rapports des autorités administra- "tives avec les citoyens."—Ibid.*

Part II.

of French law are, as he will discover, permanent, but they have at various times been developed in different degrees and in different directions. Hence any attempt to compare the administrative law of France with our English rule of law will be deceptive unless we note carefully what are the stages in the law of each country which we bring into comparison. If, for instance, we compare the law of England and the law of France as they stand in 1908, we are likely to fancy (in my judgment erroneously) that, *e.g.* in regard to the position or privileges of the State and its servants when dealing with private citizens, there may be little essential difference between the laws of the two countries. It is only when we examine the administrative law of France at some earlier date, say between 1800 and 1815, or between the accession to the throne of Louis Philippe (1830) and the fall of the Second Empire (1870), that we can rightly appreciate the essential opposition between our existing English rule of law and the fundamental ideas which lie at the basis of administrative law not only in France but in any country where this scheme of State or official law has obtained recognition.

(2) Historical development.

The modern administrative law of France has grown up, or at any rate taken its existing form, during the nineteenth century; it is the outcome of more than a hundred years of revolutionary and constitutional conflict.[1] Its development may conveniently be divided into three periods, marked by the

[1] The author's source of the history of *droit administratif* was in particular: Laferrière, *Traité de la Juridiction administrative et des recours contentieux* (2nd ed., 1896), vol. i, bk. 1, ch. i-iv, pp. 137-301.

Chapter XII.

names of the Napoleonic Empire and the Restoration (1800-1830), the Orleanist Monarchy and the Second Empire (1830-1870), the Third Republic (1870-1908).

Napoleon and the Restoration.

First Period.—Napoleon and the Restoration, 1800-1830. In the opinion of Frenchmen true *droit administratif* owes its origin to the consular constitution of the Year VIII. (1800) created by Bonaparte after the *coup d'état* of the 18th of Brumaire. But legists,[1] no less than historians, admit that the ideas on which *droit administratif* rests, may be rightly traced back, as they have been by de Tocqueville,[2] to the *ancien régime*; every feature of Bonaparte's governmental fabric recalls some characteristic of the ancient monarchy; his *Conseil d'Etat* revives the *Conseil du Roi*, his Prefects are copies of the royal Intendants. Yet in this instance public opinion

[1] "*Aussi haut que l'on remonte dans notre histoire, depuis que des "juridictions régulières ont été instituées, on ne trouve pas d'époque où les "corps judiciaires chargés d'appliquer les lois civiles et criminelles aient "été en même temps appelés à statuer sur les difficultés en matière d'adminis- "tration publique.*"—Laferrière, *Traité de la Juridiction administrative et des recours contentieux* (2nd ed., 1896), vol. i, bk. i, p. 139; cf. bk. 3, ch. vii, p. 640.

[2] "*Ce qui apparaît . . . quand on étudie les paperasses administra- "tives, c'est l'intervention continuelle du pouvoir administratif dans la "sphère judiciaire. Les légistes administratifs nous disent sans cesse, "que le plus grand vice du gouvernement intérieur de l'ancien régime était "que les juges administraient. On pourrait se plaindre avec autant de "raison de ce que les administrateurs jugeaient. La seule différence est "que nous avons corrigé l'ancien régime sur le premier point, et l'avons "imité sur le second. J'avais eu jusqu'à présent la simplicité de croire "que ce que nous appelons la justice administrative était une création de "Napoléon. C'est du* pur ancien régime conservé; *et le principe que "lors même qu'il s'agit de* contrat, *c'est-à-dire d'un engagement formel et "régulièrement pris entre un particulier et l'Etat, c'est à l'Etat à juger la "cause, cet axiome, inconnu chez la plupart des nations modernes, était "tenu pour aussi sacré par un intendant de l'ancien régime, qu'il pourrait "l'être de nos jours par le personnage qui ressemble le plus à celui-là, je "veux dire un préfet.*"—de Tocqueville, *op. cit.*, vol. vi (Correspondance), pp. 221, 222.

Part II.

has come to a right conclusion. It was from Bonaparte that modern *droit administratif* received its form. If he was the restorer of the *ancien régime*, he was also the preserver of the Revolution. Whatever he borrowed from the traditions of old France he adapted to the changed conditions of the new France of 1800. At his touch ancient ideas received a new character and a new life. He fused together what was strongest in the despotic traditions of the monarchy with what was strongest in the equally despotic creed of Jacobinism. Nowhere is this fusion more clearly visible than in the methods by which Bonaparte's legislation and policy gave full expression to the ideas or conceptions of royal prerogative underlying the administrative practice of the *ancien régime*, and emphasised the jealousy felt in 1800 by every Frenchman of the least interference by the law courts with the free action of the government. This jealousy itself, though theoretically justified by revolutionary dogma, was inherited by the Revolution from the statecraft of the monarchy.

Droit administratif—its two leading principles.

Any one who considers with care the nature of the *droit administratif* of France, or the topics to which it applies, will soon discover that it rests, and always has rested, at bottom on two leading ideas alien to the conceptions of modern Englishmen.

Privileges of the State.

The first of these ideas is that the government, and every servant of the government, possesses, as representative of the nation, a whole body of special rights, privileges, or prerogatives as against private citizens, and that the extent of these rights, privileges, or prerogatives is to be determined on principles different from the considerations which fix the legal

Separation of powers.

rights and duties of one citizen towards another. An individual in his dealings with the State does not, according to French ideas, stand on anything like the same footing as that on which he stands in dealings with his neighbour.[1]

The second of these general ideas is the necessity of maintaining the so-called "separation of powers" (*séparation des pouvoirs*), or, in other words, of preventing the government, the legislature, and the courts from encroaching upon one another's province. The expression, however, separation of powers, as applied by Frenchmen to the relations of the executive and the courts, with which alone we are here concerned, may easily mislead. It means, in the mouth of a French statesman or lawyer, something different from what we mean in England by the "independence of the judges," or the like expressions. As interpreted by French history, by French legislation, and by the decisions of French tribunals, it means neither more nor less than the maintenance of the

[1] "*Un particulier qui n'exécute pas un marché doit à l'entrepreneur* "*une indemnité proportionnée au gain dont il le prive; le Code civil l'établit* "*ainsi. L'administration qui rompt un tel marché ne doit d'indemnité* "*qu'en raison de la perte éprouvée. C'est la règle de la jurisprudence* "*administrative. A moins que le droit ne s'y oppose, elle tient que l'Etat,* "*c'est-à-dire la collection de tous les citoyens, et le trésor public, c'est-à-dire* "*l'ensemble de tous les contribuables, doivent passer avant le citoyen ou le* "*contribuable isolés, défendant un intérêt individuel.*"—Vivien, *Etudes administratives* (2nd ed., 1852), pp. 140, 141. This was the language of a French lawyer of high authority writing in 1853. The particular doctrine which it contains is now repudiated by French lawyers. Vivien's teaching, however, even though it be no longer upheld, illustrates the general view taken in France of the relation between the individual and the State. That Vivien's application of this view is now repudiated, illustrates the change which French *droit administratif* and the opinion of Frenchmen has undergone during the last fifty-five years.

principle that while the ordinary judges ought to be irremovable and thus independent of the executive, the government and its officials ought (whilst acting officially) to be independent of and to a great extent free from the jurisdiction of the ordinary courts.[1] It were curious to follow out the historical growth of the whole theory as to the "separation of powers." It rests apparently upon Montesquieu's *Esprit des Lois*, Book XI. c. 6, and is in some sort the offspring of a double misconception; Montesquieu misunderstood on this point the principles and practice of the English constitution, and his doctrine was in turn, if not misunderstood, exaggerated, and misapplied by the French statesmen of the Revolution. Their judgment was biassed, at once by knowledge of the inconveniences and indeed the gross evils which had resulted from the interference of the French "parliaments" in matters of State and by the belief that these courts would offer opposition, as they had done before, to fundamental and urgently needed reforms. Nor were the leaders of French opinion uninfluenced by the traditional desire, felt as strongly by despotic democrats as by despotic kings, to increase the power of the central government by curbing the authority of the law courts. The investigation, however, into the varying fate of a dogma which has undergone a different development on each side of the Atlantic would lead us too far from our immediate topic. All that we need note is the extraordinary influence exerted in France, and in all countries which have followed French examples, by this part of Montesquieu's

[1] See Aucoc, *Conférences sur l'Administration et sur le Droit administratif* (3rd ed., 1885), vol. i, part i, bk. i, ch. i, N°s 20-24, pp. 47-60.

teaching, and the extent to which it still underlies the political and legal institutions of the French Republic.

Chapter XII.

Characteristics.

To the combination of these two general ideas may be traced four distinguishing characteristics of French administrative law.

(1) Rights of State determined by special rules.

The first of these characteristics is, as the reader will at once perceive, that the relation of the government and its officials towards private citizens must be regulated by a body of rules which are in reality laws, but which may differ considerably from the laws which govern the relation of one private person to another. This distinction between ordinary law and administrative law is one which since 1800 has been fully recognised in France, and forms an essential part of French public law, as it must form a part of the public law of any country where administrative law in the true sense exists.[1]

(2) Law Courts without jurisdiction in matters concerning the State and administrative litigation to be determined by administrative courts.

The second of these characteristics is that the ordinary judicial tribunals which determine ordinary questions, whether they be civil or criminal, between man and man, must, speaking generally, have no concern whatever with matters at issue between a private person and the State, *i.e.* with questions of administrative law, but that such questions, in so far as they form at all matter of litigation (*contentieux administratif*), must be determined by administrative courts in some way connected with the government or the administration.

No part of revolutionary policy or sentiment was

[1] Of course it is possible that rules of administrative law may exist in a country, *e.g.* in Belgium, where these rules are enforced only by the ordinary courts.

Part II. more heartily accepted by Napoleon than the conviction that the judges must never be allowed to hamper the action of the government. He gave effect to this conviction in two different ways.

In the first place, he constituted, or reconstituted, two classes of courts. The one class consisted of "judicial" or, as we should say, "common law" courts. They performed, speaking generally, but two functions. The one function was the decision of disputes in strictness between private persons; this duty was discharged by such courts as the courts of First Instance and the courts of appeal. The other function was the trial of all criminal cases; this duty was discharged by such courts as the Correctional Courts (*Tribunaux Correctionnels*) or the Courts of Assize[1] (*Cours d'Assises*). At the head of all these judicial tribunals was placed, and still stands, the Court of Cassation (*Cour de Cassation*), whereof it is the duty to correct the errors in law of the inferior judicial courts.[2] The other class of so-called courts were and are the administrative courts, such as the Courts of the Prefects (*Conseil de Préfecture*) and the *Conseil d'Etat*. The function of these bodies, in so far as they acted judicially (for they fulfilled many duties that were not judicial), was to determine questions of administrative law. The two kinds of courts stood opposed to one another. The judicial courts had, speaking generally,[3] no

[1] The *Cours d'Assises* are the only courts in France where there is trial by jury.

[2] The *Cour de Cassation* is not in strictness a Court of Appeal.

[3] There existed even under Napoleon exceptional instances, and their number has been increased, in which, mainly from motives of

concern with questions of administrative law, or, in other words, with cases in which the interest of the State or its servants was at issue; to entrust any judicial court with the decision of any administrative suit would have been deemed in 1800, as indeed it is still deemed by most Frenchmen, a violation of the doctrine of the separation of powers, and would have allowed the interference by mere judges with cases in which the interest of the State or its servants was at issue. The administrative courts, on the other hand, had, speaking generally, no direct concern with matters which fell within the jurisdiction of the judicial tribunals, but when we come to examine the nature of the *Conseil d'Etat* we shall find that this restriction on the authority of a body which in Napoleon's time formed part of the government itself was far less real than the strict limitations imposed on the sphere of action conceded to the common law courts.

Napoleon, in the second place, displayed towards the ordinary judges the sentiment of contemptuous suspicion embodied in revolutionary legislation. The law of 16-24 August, 1790,[1] is one among a score of examples which betray the true spirit of the Revolution. The judicial tribunals are thereby forbidden to interfere in any way whatever with any

immediate convenience, legislation has given to judicial courts the decision of matters which from their nature should fall within the sphere of the administrative tribunals, just as legislation has exceptionally given to administrative tribunals matters which would naturally fall within the jurisdiction of the judicial courts. These exceptional instances cannot be brought within any one clear principle, and may for our purpose be dismissed from consideration.

[1] Hélie, *Les Constitutions de la France* (1879), ch. i, p. 147 (Loi des 16-24 Août, 1790) tit. ii, art. 11-13.

Part II. acts of legislation. Judicial functions, it is laid down, must remain separate from administrative functions. The judges must not, under penalty of forfeiture, disturb or in any way interfere with the operations of administrative bodies, or summon before them administrative officials on account of anything done by reason of their administrative duties. Napoleon had imbibed to the utmost the spirit of these enactments. He held, as even at a much later date did all persons connected with the executive government, that "the "judges are the *enemies* of the servants of the State, "and that there is always reason to fear their attempts "to compromise the public interests by their male-"volent, or at best rash, interference in the usual "course of government business."[1] This fear was during the Empire, at any rate, assuredly groundless. Administrative officials met with no resistance from the courts. After the Revolution the judges exhibited boundless humility and servile submission, they trembled before the power and obeyed the orders, often insolent enough, of the government.[2] It is difficult, however, to see how in the days of Napoleon the ordinary judges could, whatever their courage or boldness, have interfered with the conduct of the govern-

[1] "*On a subi l'influence de ce préjugé dominant chez les gouvernants,* "*dans l'administration et même chez la plupart des jurisconsultes, que les* "*agents judiciaires sont les* ennemis *nés des agents administratifs, qu'il y* "*a toujours à craindre leurs tentatives de compromettre la chose publique* "*par leur intervention—malveillante ou tout au moins inconsidérée—dans* "*la marche normale de l'administration.*"—Jèze, *Les principes généraux du Droit administratif* (1st ed., 1904), p. 139.

[2] "*Les agents administratifs, dans leur arbitraire véritablement inouï,* "*ne recontrèrent aucune résistance chez les agents judiciaires. Ceux-ci.* "*après la Révolution, ont montré une humilité sans limite et une soumis-*"*sion servile. C'est en tremblant qu'ils ont toujours obéi aux ordres* "*parfois insolents du Gouvernement.*"—Jèze, *op. cit.*, p. 128.

ment or its agents. They are even now, as a rule, without jurisdiction in matters which concern the State. They have no right to determine, for instance, the meaning and legal effect in case it be seriously disputed of official documents, as, for example, of a letter addressed by a Minister of State to a subordinate, or by a general to a person under his command. They are even now in certain cases without jurisdiction as to questions arising between a private person and a department of the government. In Napoleon's time [1] they could not, without the consent of the government, have entertained criminal or civil proceedings against an official for a wrong done or a crime committed by such official in respect of private individuals when acting in discharge of his official duties. The incompetence, however, of the judicial courts did not mean, even under Napoleon, that a person injured by an agent of the government was without a remedy. He might bring his grievance before, and obtain redress from, the administrative tribunals, *i.e.* in substance the *Conseil d'Etat*, or proceedings might, where a crime or a wrong was complained of, be, with the permission of the government, taken before the ordinary courts.

(3) Conflicts of jurisdiction.

The co-existence of judicial courts and of administrative courts results of necessity in raising questions of jurisdiction. *A*, for example, in some judicial court claims damages against *X* for a breach of contract, or it may be for what we should term an assault or false imprisonment. *X*'s defence in substance is that he acted merely as a servant of the

[1] Hélie, *Les Constitutions de la France* (1879), ch. iv, p. 583 (Constitution du 22 Frimaire, An VIII.), tit. vi, art. 75.

State, and that the case raises a point of administrative law determinable only by an administrative tribunal, or, speaking broadly, by the *Conseil d'Etat*. The objection, in short, is that the judicial court has no jurisdiction. How is this dispute to be decided? The natural idea of an Englishman is that the conflict must be determined by the judicial courts, *i.e.* the ordinary judges, for that the judges of the land are the proper authorities to define the limits of their own jurisdiction. This view, which is so natural to an English lawyer, is radically opposed to the French conception of the separation of powers, since it must, if systematically carried out, enable the courts to encroach on the province of the administration. It contradicts the principle still recognised as valid by French law that administrative bodies must never be troubled in the exercise of their functions by any act whatever of the judicial power;[1] nor can an Englishman, who recollects the cases on general warrants, deny that our judges have often interfered with the action of the administration. The worth of Montesquieu's doctrine is open to question, but if his theory be sound, it is clear that judicial bodies ought not to be allowed to pronounce a final judgment upon the limits of their own authority.

Under the legislation of Napoleon the right to determine such questions of jurisdiction was in theory reserved to the head of the State, but was

[1] See Aucoc, *Conférences sur l'Administration et sur le Droit administratif* (3rd ed., 1885), vol. i, part i, bk. i, ch. i, N° 24, pp. 54-60.

in effect given to the *Conseil d'Etat*, that is, to the highest of administrative courts. Its authority in this matter was, as it still is, preserved in two different ways. If a case before an ordinary or judicial court clearly raised a question of administrative law, the court was bound to see that the inquiry was referred to the *Conseil d'Etat* for decision. Suppose, however, the court exceeded, or the government thought that it exceeded, its jurisdiction and trenched upon the authority of the administrative court, a prefect, who, be it remarked, is a mere government official, could raise a conflict, that is to say, could, by taking the proper steps, insist upon the question of jurisdiction being referred for decision to the *Conseil d'Etat*. We can hardly exaggerate the extent of the authority thus conferred upon the *Conseil*. It had the right to fix the limits of its own power, it could in effect take out of the hands of a judicial court a case of which the court was already seised.[1]

(4) Protection of officials.

The fourth and most despotic characteristic of *droit administratif* lies in its tendency to protect[2] from the supervision or control of the ordinary law courts any servant of the State who is guilty of an act, however illegal, whilst acting in *bona fide* obedi-

[1] Up to 1828 it was possible "élever un conflit" in any criminal no less than in any civil case. Nor is it undeserving of notice that, whilst a conflict could be raised in order to prevent a judicial court from encroaching on the sphere of an administrative court, there was in Napoleon's time no legal means for raising a conflict with a view to prevent an administrative court from encroaching on the sphere of a judicial court.

[2] This protection of officials may be displayed in parts of French law (*e.g.* French Code Pénal, art. 114) which do not technically belong to *droit administratif*, but it is in reality connected with the whole system of administrative law.

Part II.

ence to the orders of his superiors and, as far as intention goes, in the mere discharge of his official duties.

Such an official enjoyed from 1800 till 1872 a triple protection (*garantie des fonctionnaires*).

Act of State.

In the first place, he could not be made responsible before any court, whether judicial or administrative, for the performance of any act of State (*acte de gouvernement*).

The law of France has always recognised an indefinite class of acts, *i.e.* acts of State, which, as they concern matters of high policy or of public security, or touch upon foreign policy or the execution of treaties, or concern dealings with foreigners, must be left to the uncontrolled discretion of the government, and lie quite outside the jurisdiction of any court whatever. What may be the exact definition of an act of State is even now, it would appear in France, a moot point on which high authorities are not entirely agreed. It is therefore impossible for any one but a French lawyer to determine what are the precise qualities which turn conduct otherwise illegal into an act of State of which no French court could take cognisance. Of recent years the tendency of French lawyers has certainly been to narrow down the sense of an ambiguous term which lends itself easily to the justification of tyranny. We may feel sure, however, that during the Napoleonic era and for long afterwards any transaction on the part of the government or its servants was deemed to be an act of State which was carried out *bona fide* with the object of furthering the interest or the security of the country.

Chapter XII.

Obedience to orders.

In the second place, the French Penal Code, Art. 114,[1] protected, as it still protects, an official from the penal consequences of any interference with the personal liberty of fellow citizens when the act complained of is done under the orders of his official superior.[2]

In the third place, under the celebrated Article 75[3]

[1] *French Code Pénal*, art. 114 : " *Lorsqu'un fonctionnaire public, un " agent ou un préposé du Gouvernement, aura ordonné ou fait quelque acte " arbitraire ou attentatoire soit à la liberté individuelle, soit aux droits " civiques d'un ou de plusieurs citoyens, soit à la Charte, il sera condamné " à la peine de la dégradation civique.*

" *Si néanmoins il justifie qu'il a agi par ordre de ses supérieurs pour " des objets du ressort de ceux-ci, sur lesquels il leur était dû l'obéissance " hiérarchique il sera exempté de la peine, laquelle sera, dans ce cas, " appliquée seulement aux supérieurs qui auront donné l'ordre.*"—With this read Garçon, *Code pénal annoté* (1901-1906), p. 245, and art. 34, p. 87 ; compare *Code d'Instruction criminelle*, Art. 10 ; Duguit, *Manuel de Droit Public français ; Droit Constitutionnel* (1907), para. 76, 77, pp. 524-527, and generally Duguit, *L'Etat, les gouvernants et les agents* (1903), ch. v, para. 10, pp. 615-634.

[2] None but a French criminalist can pronounce with anything like certainty on the full effect of Art. 114, but Garçon's comment thereon (Garçon, *Code pénal annoté* (1901-1906), pp. 245-255) suggests to an English lawyer that an offender who brings himself within the exemption mentioned in the second clause of the Article, though he may be found guilty of the offence charged, cannot be punished for it under Art. 114, or any other Article of the Penal Code, and that Art. 114 protects a very wide class of public servants. (See Garçon, comment under heads D and E, pp. 249-252, and under G, p. 253, and para. 100, p. 254. Read also Duguit, *Manuel de Droit Public français ; Droit Constitutionnel* (1907), para. 75-77, spécial, pp. 504-527 ; Duguit, *L'Etat, les gouvernants et les agents* (1903), ch. v, para. 10, pp. 615, 634.)

It is difficult for an Englishman to understand how under the *Code Pénal* a prefect, a policeman, or any other servant of the State, acting *bona fide* under the orders of his proper official superior, can be in danger of punishment for crimes such as assault, unlawful imprisonment, and the like.

[3] " *Les agents du Gouvernement, autres que les ministres, ne peuvent être " poursuivis pour des faits relatifs à leurs fonctions, qu'en vertu d'une " décision du conseil d'état : en ce cas, la poursuite a lieu devant les " tribunaux ordinaires.*"—Duguit et Monnier, *Les Constitutions et les principales lois politiques de la France depuis 1789* (1898), Constitution du 22 Frimaire, An. VIII, p. 127.

of the Constitution of the Year VIII., *i.e.* of 1800, no official could, without the permission of the *Conseil d'Etat*, be prosecuted, or otherwise be proceeded against, for any act done in relation to his official duties.

The protection given was ample. Article 75 reads indeed as if it applied only to prosecutions, but was construed by the courts so as to embrace actions for damages.[1] Under the Napoleonic Constitution no servant of the State, whether a prefect, a mayor, or a policeman, whose conduct, however unlawful, met with the approval of the government, ran any real risk of incurring punishment or of paying damages for any act which purported to be done in discharge of his official duties.

The effect practically produced by the four characteristics of *droit administratif*, and especially the amount of the protection provided for officials acting in obedience to the orders of their superiors, depends in the main on the answer to one question: What at a given time is found to be the constitution and the character of the *Conseil d'Etat*? Was it then under Napoleon a law court administering judicially a particular branch of French law, or was it a department of the executive government? The answer is plain. The *Conseil*, as constituted or revived by Bonaparte, was the very centre of his whole governmental fabric. It consisted of the most eminent administrators whom Napoleon could gather round him. The members of the *Conseil* were entitled and were bound to give the supreme ruler

[1] See Jacquelin, *Les principes dominants du Contentieux administratif* (1899), part i, tit. ii, ch. iv, p. 127.

advice The *Conseil*, or some of the Councillors, took part in affairs of all descriptions. It is hardly an exaggeration to say that, subject to the absolute will of Napoleon, the members of the *Conseil* constituted the government. They held office at his pleasure. The Councillors dealt with policy, with questions of administration, with questions of administrative law. In 1800 it is probable that administrative suits were not very clearly separated from governmental business. The *Conseil*, moreover, even when acting judicially, was more of a Ministry than of a court, and when the *Conseil*, acting as a court, had given its decision, or tendered its advice, it possessed no means for compelling the executive to give effect to its decisions. As a matter of fact, years have sometimes elapsed before the executive of the day has thought fit to put the judgments of the *Conseil* into force, and it was not till 1872 that its decisions acquired by law the character of real judgments. It was, moreover, as we have already pointed out, originally the final *Tribunal des Conflits*. It had a right to determine whether a given case did or did not concern administrative law, and therefore whether it fell within its own jurisdiction or within the jurisdiction of the ordinary courts. Thus the state of things which existed in France at the beginning of the nineteenth century bore some likeness to what would be the condition of affairs in England if there were no, or little, distinction between the Cabinet as part of the Privy Council and the Judicial Committee of the Privy Council, and if the Cabinet, in its character of a Judicial Committee, determined all questions arising between the government on the

Part II.

one side, and private individuals on the other, and determined them with an admitted reference to considerations of public interest or of political expediency. Nor was any material change produced by the fall of Napoleon. The restored monarchy eagerly grasped the prerogatives created by the Empire. There was even a sort of return to the unrestrained arbitrariness of the Directory. It was not until 1828, that is, within two years of the expulsion of Charles X., that public opinion enforced some restriction on the methods by which the administrative authorities, *i.e.* the government, invaded the sphere of the judicial courts.

There are two reasons why it is worth while to study with care the *droit administratif* of our first period. The administrative law of to-day has been built up on the foundations laid by Napoleon. The courts created by him still exist; their jurisdiction is still defined in accordance, in the main, with the lines which he laid down. True it is that machinery invented to support a scheme of rational absolutism has in later times been used by legists and reformers for the promotion of legal liberty. But it is a fact never to be forgotten that the administrative law of France originated in ideas which favour the prerogatives of the government as the proper defence for the interest of the nation.

Monarchical period.

Second Period.—The Orleans Monarchy and the Second Empire 1830-1870.[1]

This period deserves the special attention of

[1] Little account need be taken of the Second Republic, 1848-1851. Its legislative reforms in administrative law did not outlive its brief and troubled duration.

English students. Napoleonic Imperialism was absolutism; the Restoration was reaction; neither admits of satisfactory comparison with any governmental system known to modern England. The forty years, on the other hand, which intervened between the expulsion of Charles X. and the fall of Napoleon III., though marked by three violent changes — the Revolution of 1848, the *coup d'état* of 1851, the overthrow of the Second Empire in 1870 —form, as a whole, a time of civil order. During these forty years France was, with the exception of not more than six months, governed under the established law of the land. An age of peaceful progress gives an opening for illuminative comparison between the public law of France and the public law of England. This remark is particularly applicable to the reign of Louis Philippe. He was, in the eyes of Englishmen, above all things, a constitutional king.[1] His Parliamentary ministries, his House of peers, and his House of deputies, the whole framework and the very spirit of his government, seemed to be modelled upon the constitution of England; under his rule the supremacy of the ordinary law of the land, administered by the ordinary law courts, was, as Englishmen supposed, as securely established in France as in England. They learn with surprise, that during the whole of these forty years few, if

[1] His accession to the throne was aided by an obvious, but utterly superficial, analogy between the course of the English Revolution in the seventeenth century and of the great French Revolution in the eighteenth and nineteenth centuries. Louis Philippe, it was supposed, was exactly the man to perform in France the part which William III. had played in England, and close the era of revolution.

Part II.

any, legislative or Parliamentary reforms[1] touched the essential characteristics of *droit administratif* as established by Napoleon. It remained, as it still does, a separate body of law, dealt with by administrative courts. With this law the judicial courts continued to have, as they still have, no concern. The introduction of Parliamentary government took from the *Conseil d'Etat*, during the reign of Louis Philippe, many of its political functions. It remained, however, as it does to-day, the great administrative court. It preserved what it does not now retain,[2] the right to define the jurisdiction of the judicial courts. Servants of the State remained in possession of every prerogative or privilege ensured to them by custom or by Napoleonic legislation. *Droit administratif*, in short, retained till 1870 all its essential features. That this was so is apparent from two considerations:—

The *Conseil* not an absolutely judicial body.

First. The *Conseil d'Etat* never, during the period with which we are concerned, became a thoroughly judicial body.

This indeed is a point on which an English critic must speak with some hesitation. He will remember how easily a Frenchman, even though well acquainted with England, might at the present moment misinterpret the working of English institutions, and imagine, for instance, from the relation of the Lord Chancellor to the Ministry, that the Cabinet, of which the Chancellor is always

[1] It was, however, gradually reformed to a great extent by a process of judicial legislation, *i.e.* by the *Conseil d'Etat* acting in the spirit of a law court.

[2] This function since 1872 has been performed by the *Tribunal des Conflits*. See pp. 365-366, *post*, and App. 1, p. 485, *post*.—Ed.

a member, could influence the judgment given in an action entered in the Chancery Division of the High Court, whereas, as every Englishman knows, centuries have passed since the Lord Chancellor, when acting as a judge in Chancery, was in the slightest degree guided by the interest or the wishes of the Cabinet. An English critic will also remember that at the present day the *Conseil d'Etat* commands as profound respect as any court in France, and stands in popular estimation on a level with the *Cour de Cassation*—the highest of judicial tribunals—and further, that the repute of the *Conseil* has risen during every year since 1830. Yet, subject to the hesitation which becomes any one who comments on the working of institutions which are not those of his own country, an English lawyer must conclude that between 1830 and 1870 the *Conseil*, while acting as an administrative tribunal, though tending every year to become more and more judicialised, was to a considerable extent an official or governmental body, the members of which, when acting in the discharge of quasi-judicial functions, were likely to be swayed by ministerial or official sentiment. This assertion does not imply that the *Conseil*, consisting of persons of the highest eminence and character, did not aim at doing or did not constantly do justice. What is meant is that the *Conseil's* idea of justice was not likely to be exactly the same as that entertained by judicial or common law courts.

No diminution in protection of officials.

Secondly. The legal protection of officials suffered no diminution.

No man could be made liable before any court whatever for carrying out an act of State (*acte*

Part II.

de gouvernement).[1] And under the rule of Louis Philippe, as under the Second Empire, wide was the extension given, both in theory and in practice, to this indefinite and undefined expression.

In 1832 the Duchesse de Berry attempted to raise a civil war in La Vendée. She was arrested. The king dared not let her leave the country. He would not put on trial the niece of his wife. Republicans and Legitimists alike wished her to be brought before a law court. The one class desired that Caroline Berry should be treated as an ordinary criminal, the other hoped to turn the Duchess into a popular heroine. The case was debated in Parliament again and again. Petitions demanded that she should either be set at liberty or brought before a jury. The government refused to take either course. She was detained in prison until private circumstances deprived her both of credit and of popularity. She was then quietly shipped off to Sicily. The conduct of the government, or in fact of the king, was illegal from beginning to end. The Ministry confessed, through the mouth of Monsieur Thiers, that the law had been violated. A vote of the Chamber of Deputies—not be it noted an act of legislation—supplied, it was held, full justification for a breach of the law.[2] This was the kind of authority ascribed in 1832 by the constitutional Ministers of a constitutional monarch to an act of

[1] See p. 345, *ante*.

[2] "*M. Thiers, dans la séance du 20 juin, avoua hautement tout ce "qu'il y avait eu d'illégal dans l'arrestation, la détention, la mise en "liberté de la duchesse; c'était à la Chambre à decider si l'on avait agi "dans l'intérêt bien entendu du salut public. La Chambre passa à "l'ordre du jour.*"—Grégoire, *Histoire de France et notions d'histoire générale* (1904), vol. i, p. 364. See also *ibid.*, pp. 292-308, 356-364.

State. This most elastic of pleas was, it would seem, the excuse or the defence for the dealings of Napoleon III. with the property of the Orleans family; nor is it easy to believe that even as late as 1880 some of the proceedings against the unauthorised congregations were not examples of the spirit which places an act of State above the law of the land.

The Penal Code, Article **114**,[1] protecting from punishment, though not from legal condemnation, an agent of the government who though he committed a crime acted in obedience to the commands of his official superiors, remained, as it still remains, in full force.

The celebrated Article 75 of the Constitution of the Year VIII.,[2] which made it impossible to take legal proceedings for a crime or a wrong against any official without the permission of the *Conseil d'Etat*, which surely in this case must have acted in accordance with the government of the day, still stood unrepealed.

Public opinion refused to regard the *Conseil* as a judicial tribunal, and condemned the protection extended to official wrongdoers. Hear on this point the language of Alexis de Tocqueville:

"In the Year VIII. of the French Republic a "constitution was drawn up in which the following "clause was introduced: 'Art. 75. All the agents "of the government below the rank of ministers can "only be prosecuted[3] for offences relating to their

[1] See p. 346, note 1, *ante*.

[2] See p. 350, *ante*.

[3] This term was extended by legal decisions so as to cover actions for damages. See Jacquelin, *Les principes dominants du Contentieux administratif* (1899), part i, tit. ii, ch. iv, p. 127.

Part II.

"several functions by virtue of a decree of the *Con-*"*seil d'Etat*; in which case the prosecution takes "place before the ordinary tribunals.' This clause "survived the 'Constitution de l'An VIII.,' and it is "still maintained in spite of the just complaints of "the nation. I have always found the utmost diffi-"culty in explaining its meaning to Englishmen or "Americans. They were at once led to conclude "that the *Conseil d'Etat* in France was a great "tribunal, established in the centre of the king-"dom, which exercised a preliminary and somewhat "tyrannical jurisdiction in all political causes. But "when I told them that the *Conseil d'Etat* was not "a judicial body, in the common sense of the term, "but an administrative council composed of men "dependent on the Crown, so that the King, after "having ordered one of his servants, called a Prefect, "to commit an injustice, has the power of command-"ing another of his servants, called a Councillor of "State, to prevent the former from being punished; "when I demonstrated to them that the citizen who "has been injured by the order of the sovereign is "obliged to solicit from the sovereign permission to "obtain redress, they refused to credit so flagrant an "abuse, and were tempted to accuse me of falsehood "or of ignorance. It frequently happened before "the Revolution that a Parliament issued a warrant "against a public officer who had committed an "offence, and sometimes the proceedings were stopped "by the authority of the Crown, which enforced "compliance with its absolute and despotic will. It "is painful to perceive how much lower we are sunk "than our forefathers, since we allow things to pass "under the colour of justice and the sanction of the "law which violence alone could impose upon them."[1]

This classical passage from de Tocqueville's *Democracy in America* was published in 1835, when, at the age of 30, he had obtained a fame which his friends compared to that of Montesquieu. His estimate of *droit administratif* assuredly had not changed when towards the end of his life he published *L'Ancien Régime et la Révolution*, by far the most powerful and the most mature of his works.

"We have, it is true," he writes, "expelled the "judicial power from the sphere of government into "which the *ancien régime* had most unhappily allowed "its introduction, but at the very same time, as any "one can see, the authority of the government has "gradually been introducing itself into the natural "sphere of the courts, and there we have suffered "it to remain as if the confusion of powers was not "as dangerous if it came from the side of the govern-"ment as if it came from the side of the courts, or "even worse. For the intervention of the courts of "Justice into the sphere of government only impedes "the management of business, whilst the intervention "of government in the administration of justice "depraves citizens and turns them at the same time "both into revolutionists and slaves."[2]

[1] de Tocqueville, *Democracy in America* (translation by H. Reeve, 1875), vol. i, p. 101; *Œuvres complètes* (14th ed., 1864), vol. i (Démocratie en Amérique), pp. 174, 175.

[2] "*Nous avons, il est vrai, chassé la justice de la sphère administrative* "*où l'ancien régime l'avait laissée s'introduire fort indûment; mais dans* "*le même temps, comme on le voit, le gouvernement s'introduisait sans* "*cesse dans la sphère naturelle de la justice, et nous l'y avons laissé:* "*comme si la confusion des pouvoirs n'était pas aussi dangereuse de ce* "*côté que de l'autre, et même pire; car l'intervention de la justice dans* "*l'administration ne nuit qu'aux affaires, tandis que l'intervention de*

Part II.

These are the words of a man of extraordinary genius who well knew French history, who was well acquainted with the France of his day, who had for years sat in Parliament, who at least once had been a member of the Cabinet, and to whom the public life of his own country was as well known as the public life of England to Macaulay. de Tocqueville's language may bear marks of an exaggeration, explainable partly by his turn of mind, and partly by the line of thought which made him assiduously study and possibly overrate the closeness of the connection between the weaknesses of modern democracy and the vices of the old monarchy. Be this as it may, he assuredly expressed the educated opinion of his time. A writer who has admirably brought into view the many merits of the *Conseil d'Etat* and the methods by which it has in matters of administrative litigation acquired for itself more and more of a judicial character, acutely notes that till the later part of the nineteenth century the language of everyday life, which is the best expression of popular feeling, applied the terms "courts of justice" or "justice" itself only to the judicial or common law courts.[1] What stronger confirmation can be found of the justice of de Tocqueville's judgment for the time at least in which he lived?

Effect of *droit administratif* on position of French officials.

We can now understand the way in which from 1830 to 1870 the existence of a *droit administratif* affected the whole legal position of French public

"*l'administration dans la justice déprave les hommes et tend à les rendre* "*tout à la fois révolutionnaires et serviles.*"—de Tocqueville, *op. cit.*, vol. iv (Ancien Régime et Révolution), p. 103.

[1] Jèze, *Les principes généraux du Droit administratif* (1st ed., 1904), p. 138, note 1.

servants, and rendered it quite different from that of English officials. Chapter XII.

Persons in the employment of the government, who formed, be it observed, a more important part of the community than do the whole body of English civil servants, occupied in France a situation in some respects resembling that of soldiers in England. For the breach of official discipline they were, we may safely assume, readily punishable in one form or another. But if like English soldiers they were subject to official discipline, they enjoyed what even soldiers in England do not possess, a very large amount of protection against proceedings before the judicial courts for wrongs done to private citizens. The position, for instance, of say a prefect or a policeman, who in the over-zealous discharge of his duties had broken the law by committing an assault or a trespass, was practically unassailable. He might plead that the wrong done was an act of State. If this defence would not avail him he might shelter himself behind Article 114 of the Penal Code, and thus escape not indeed an adverse verdict but the possibility of punishment. But after all, if the Ministry approved of his conduct, he had no need for legal defences. He could not, without the assent of the *Conseil d'Etat*, be called upon to answer for his conduct before any court of law. Article 75 was the palladium of official privilege or irresponsibility. Nor let any one think that this arm of defence had grown rusty with time and could not in practice be used. Between 1852 and 1864 there were 264 applications for authorisations under Article 75 to take proceedings against officials. Only 34 were

Part II. granted, or, in other words, 230 were refused.[1] The manifest injustice of the celebrated Article had been long felt. Even in 1815 Napoleon had promised its modification.

Third Period.—The Third Republic—1870-1908.

Within two years from the fall of the Second Empire public opinion insisted upon three drastic reforms in the administrative or official law of France.

Repeal of Art. 75.

On the 19th of September, 1870, Article 75 was repealed. It had survived the Empire, the Restoration, the Orleans Monarchy, the Republic of 1848, and the Second Empire. The one thing which astonishes an English critic even more than the length of time during which the celebrated Article had withstood every assault, is the date, combined with the method of its abolition. It was abolished on the 19th of September 1870, when the German armies were pressing on to Paris. It was abolished by a Government which had come into office through an insurrection, and which had no claim to actual power or to moral authority except the absolute necessity for protecting France against invasion. It is passing strange that a provisional government, occupied with the defence of Paris, should have repealed a fundamental principle of French law. Of the motives which led men placed in temporary authority by the accidents of a revolution to carry through a legal innovation which, in appearance at least, alters the whole position of French officials, no foreign observer can form a certain opinion.

[1] See Jacquelin, *Les principes dominants du Contentieux administratif* (1899), part i, tit. ii, ch. iv, p. 128.

It is worth notice that the principle of Article 75 was recognised in more than one State of the old German Empire.

It is, however, a plausible conjecture, confirmed by subsequent events, that the repeal of Article 75 was lightly enacted and easily tolerated, because, as many lawyers may have suspected, it effected a change more important in appearance than in reality, and did not after all gravely touch the position of French functionaries or the course of French administration.[1]

A circumstance which fills an English lawyer with further amazement is that the repeal of Article 75 became, and still without any direct confirmation by any legislative assembly remains, part of the law of the land. Here we come across an accepted principle of French constitutional law which betrays the immense authority conceded both by the law and by the public opinion of France to any *de facto* and generally accepted government. Such a body, even if like the provisional government of 1848 it is called to office one hardly knows how, by the shouts of a mob consisting of individuals whose names for the most part no one now knows at all, is deemed to possess whilst it continues in power the fullest legislative authority. It is, to use French terms, not only a legislative but a constituent authority. It can issue decrees, known by the technical name of decree

[1] For some confirmation of this view, see Aucoc, *Conférences sur l'Administration et sur le Droit administratif* (3rd ed., 1885), vol. i, bk. v, ch. ii, N°s 419-426, pp. 740-768; Jacquelin, *La Juridiction administrative* (1891), p. 427; Laferrière, *Traité de la Juridiction administrative et des recours contentieux* (2nd ed., 1896), vol. i, bk. iii, ch. vii, pp. 637-654.

The admission, however, involved in the repeal of Article 75 of the general principle that officials are at any rate *prima facie* liable for illegal acts, in the same way as private persons, marks, it is said by competent authorities, an important change in the public opinion of France, and is one among other signs of a tendency to look with jealousy on the power of the State.

laws (*decréts lois*),[1] which, until regularly repealed by some person or body with acknowledged legislative authority, are often as much law of the land as any Act passed with the utmost formality by the present French National Assembly. Contrast with this ready acceptance of governmental authority the view taken by English Courts and Parliaments of every law passed from 1642 to 1660 which did not receive the Royal assent. Some of them were enacted by Parliaments of a ruler acknowledged both in England and in many foreign countries as the head of the English State; the Protector, moreover, died in peace, and was succeeded without disturbance by his son Richard. Yet not a single law passed between the outbreak of the Rebellion and the Restoration is to be found in the English Statute Book. The scrupulous legalism of English lawyers acknowledged in 1660 no Parliamentary authority but that Long Parliament which, under a law regularly passed and assented to by Charles I., could not be dissolved without its own consent. A student is puzzled whether most to admire or to condemn the sensible but, it may be, too easy acquiescence of Frenchmen in the actual authority of any *de facto* government,

[1] See for the legal doctrine and for examples of such decree laws, Duguit, *Manuel de Droit Public français ; Droit Constitutionnel* (1907), para. 141, pp. 1037, 1038 ; Moreau, *Le règlement administratif* (1902), para. 66, pp. 103, 104. Such decree laws were passed by the provisional government between the 24th of February and the 4th of May, 1848 ; by Louis Napoleon between the *coup d'état* of 2nd December, 1851, and 29th March, 1852, that is, a ruler who, having by a breach both of the law of the land and of his oaths usurped supreme power, had not as yet received any recognition by a national vote ; and lastly, by the Government of National Defence between 4th September, 1870, and 12th February, 1871, that is, by an executive which might in strictness be called a government of necessity.

or the legalism carried to pedantic absurdity of Englishmen, who in matters of statesmanship placed technical legality above those rules of obvious expediency which are nearly equivalent to principles of justice. This apparent digression is in reality germane to our subject. It exhibits the different light in which, even in periods of revolution, Frenchmen and Englishmen have looked upon the rule of law.

The strange story of Article 75 needs a few words more for its completion. The decree law of 19th September, 1870, reads as if it absolutely subjected officials accused of any breach of the law to the jurisdiction of the judicial courts. This, moreover, was in fact the view taken by both the judicial and the administrative courts between 1870 and 1872.[1] But judicial decisions can in France, as elsewhere, frustrate the operation of laws which they cannot repeal. After 1870 proceedings against officials, and officials of all ranks, became frequent. This fact is noteworthy. The government wished to protect its own servants. It brought before the newly constituted *Tribunal des Conflits*[2] a case raising for reconsideration the effect of the decree law of 19th September, 1870. The court held that, though proceedings against officials might be taken without the leave of the *Conseil d'Etat*, yet that the dogma of the separation of powers must still be respected, and that it was for the *Tribunal des Conflits* to determine whether any particular case fell within the jurisdiction of the judicial courts or of the administrative courts, that is in effect of the *Conseil*

[1] See in support of this view, Jacquelin, *Les principes dominants du Contentieux administratif* (1899), part i, tit. ii, ch. iv, pp. 127-144.

[2] See p. 365, *post*.

Part II.

d'Etat.[1] The principle of this decision has now obtained general acceptance. Thus a judgment grounded on that doctrine of the separation of powers which embodies traditional jealousy of interference by ordinary judges in affairs of State has, according at any rate to one high authority, reduced the effect of the repeal of Article 75 almost to nothing. "To sum the matter up," writes Duguit, "the only difference between the actual system and that which existed under the Constitution of the Year VIII. is that before 1870 the prosecution of State officials was subject to the authorisation of the *Conseil d'Etat*, whilst to-day it is subject to the authorisation of the *Tribunal des Conflits.*"[2]

(2) Decisions of *Conseil d'Etat* become judgments.

Under the law of 24th May, 1872,[3] the decisions of the *Conseil d'Etat* concerning cases of administrative law received for the first time the obligatory force of judgments. They had hitherto been in theory, and from some points of view even in practice, as already pointed out,[4] nothing but advice given to the head of the State.

(3) Creation of independent Conflict-Court.

The same law[5] which enhanced the authority of the *Conseil's* decisions diminished its jurisdiction.

[1] See *Pelletier's Case*, decided 26th July, 1873; and in support of an interpretation of the law which has now received general approval, Laferrière, i, pp. 637-654; Berthélemy, *Traité élémentaire de Droit administratif* (5th ed., 1908), p. 65; Duguit, *Manuel de Droit Public français; Droit Constitutionnel* (1907), para. 67, pp. 463, 464; Jèze, *Les principes généraux du Droit administratif* (1st ed., 1904), pp. 133-135.

[2] "*Finalement la seule différence entre le système actuel et celui de la* "*constitution de l'an VIII., c'est qu'avant 1870 la poursuite contre les* "*fonctionnaires était subordonnée à l'autorisation du Conseil d'Etat, et* "*qu'aujourd'hui elle est subordonnée à l'autorisation du tribunal des* "*conflits.*"—Duguit, *op. cit.* (1907), para. 67, p. 464.

[3] Sect. 9.

[4] See p. 349, *ante*.

[5] Law of 24th May, 1872, Tit. iv, art. 25-28.

The *Conseil* had, since 1800, decided whether a given case, or a point that might arise in a given case, fell within the jurisdiction of the judicial courts or of the administrative courts, *i.e.* in substance of the *Conseil* itself. This authority or power was, in 1872, transferred to a separate and newly constituted *Tribunal des Conflits*.[1]

This *Tribunal des Conflits* has been carefully constituted so as to represent equally the authority of the *Cour de Cassation*—the highest judicial court in France—and the authority of the *Conseil d'Etat*—the highest administrative court in France. It consists of nine members:—three members of the *Cour de Cassation* elected by their colleagues; three members of the *Conseil d'Etat*, also elected by their colleagues; two other persons elected by the above six judges of the *Tribunal des Conflits*. All these eight members of the court hold office for three years. They are re-eligible, and are almost invariably re-elected. The Minister of Justice (*garde des sceaux*) for the time being, who is a member of the Ministry, is *ex officio* President of the court. He rarely attends. The court elects from its own members a Vice-President who generally presides.[2] The *Tribunal des Conflits* comes near to an absolutely judicial body; it commands, according to the best authorities, general confidence. But its connection with the Government of the day through the Minister of Justice (who is

[1] Such a separate *Tribunal des Conflits* had been created under the Second Republic, 1848-1851. It fell to the ground on the fall of the Republic itself in consequence of the *coup d'état* of 1851.

[2] See Berthélemy, *Traité élémentaire de Droit administratif* (10th ed., 1930), p. 1077. For this Tribunal, see App. 1, p. 485, *post*.—Ed.

Part II.

not necessarily a lawyer) being its President, and the absence on the part of its members of that permanent tenure of office,[1] which is the best security for perfect judicial independence, are defects, which, in the opinion of the fairest among French jurists, ought to be removed,[2] and which, as long as they exist, detract from the judicial character of the *Tribunal des Conflits*. An Englishman, indeed, can hardly fail to surmise that the court must still remain a partly official body which may occasionally be swayed by the policy of a Ministry, and still more often be influenced by official or governmental ideas. Nor is this suspicion diminished by the knowledge that a Minister of Justice has within the year 1908 defended his position as President of the Court on the ground that it ought to contain some one who represents the interests of the government.[3]

The reforms the result of evolution of *droit administratif.*

These three thorough-going reforms were carried out by legislative action. They obviously met the requirements of the time.[4] They were rapid; they appeared to be sudden. This appearance is delusive. They were in reality the outcome of a slow but continuous revolution in French public opinion and also

[1] A member of the *Conseil d'Etat* does not hold his position as Councillor for life. He may be removed from the *Conseil* by the Government. But no Councillor has been removed since 1875.

[2] Laferrière, *Traité de la Juridiction administrative et des recours contentieux* (2nd ed., 1896), vol. i, bk. prélim., ch. i, p. 24; Chardon, *L'Administration de la France—les fonctionnaires* (1908), p. 4, note 2; Jèze, *Les principes généraux du Droit administratif* (1st ed., 1904), pp. 133, 134.

[3] See Jèze, *Revue de Droit public*, vol. xxv (1908), p. 257.

[4] They were either tacitly sanctioned (decree law of 19th September, 1870) or enacted (law of 24th May, 1872) even before the formal establishment of the Republic (1875) by a National Assembly of which the majority were so far from being revolutionists, or even reformers, that they desired the restoration of the monarchy.

of the perseverance with which the legists of the *Conseil d'Etat*, under the guidance of French jurisprudence and logic, developed out of the arbitrariness of administrative practice a fixed system of true administrative law. To understand this evolution of *droit administratif* during the lapse of more than a century (1800-1908) we must cast a glance over the whole development of this branch of French law and regard it in the light in which it presents itself, not so much to an historian of France as to a lawyer who looks upon the growth of French public law from an historical point of view. We shall then see that the years under consideration fall into three periods or divisions.[1] They are:—

(i.) The period of unnoticed growth, 1800-18 (*Période d'élaboration secrète*). During these years the *Conseil*, by means of judicial precedents, created a body of maxims, in accordance with which the *Conseil* in fact acted when deciding administrative disputes.

(ii.) The period of publication, 1818-60 (*Période de divulgation*). During these forty-two years various reforms were carried out, partly by legislation, but, to a far greater extent, by judge-made law. The judicial became more or less separated off from the administrative functions of the *Conseil*. Litigious business (*le contentieux administratif*) was in practice assigned to and decided by a special committee (*section*), and, what is of equal consequence, such business was

[1] See Hauriou, *Précis de Droit administratif* (3rd ed., 1897), pp. 245-268. These periods do not precisely correspond with the three eras marked by political changes in the annals of France under which have already been considered (see p. 334, *ante*) the history of *droit administratif*.

decided by a body which acted after the manner of a court which was addressed by advocates, heard arguments, and after public debate delivered judicial decisions. These decisions were reported, became the object of much public interest, and were, after a manner with which English lawyers are well acquainted, moulded into a system of law. The judgments, in short, of the *Conseil* acquired the force of precedent. The political revolutions of France, which have excited far too much notice, whilst the uninterrupted growth of French institutions has received too little attention, sometimes retarded or threw back, but never arrested the continuous evolution of *droit administratif*; even under the Second Empire this branch of French jurisprudence became less and less arbitrary and developed more and more into a system of fixed and subtle legal rules.

(iii.) The period of organisation, 1860-1908 (*Période d'organisation*). During the last forty-eight years, marked as they have been in France by the change from the Empire to a Republic, by the German invasion, and by civil war, the development of *droit administratif* has exhibited a singular and tranquil regularity. Sudden innovations have been rare and have produced little effect. The reforms introduced by the decree law of 19th September, 1870, and by the law of 24th May, 1872, are, taken together, considerable; but they in reality give effect to ideas which had since 1800 more or less guided the judicial legislation and practice both of the *Conseil d'Etat* and of the *Cour de Cassation*. If the legal history of France since 1800 be looked at as a whole, an Englishman may reasonably conclude that the arbitrary authority of the executive as it existed in the time of Napoleon, and even as it was exercised under the reign of Louis Philippe or of Louis Napoleon, has gradually, as far as the jurisdiction of the administrative courts is concerned, been immensely curtailed, if not absolutely brought to an end. *Droit administratif*, though administered by bodies which are perhaps not in strictness courts, and though containing provisions not reconcilable with the modern English conception of the rule of law, comes very near to law, and is utterly different from the capricious prerogatives of despotic power.

(B) Comparison between *droit administratif* and rule of law.

A comparison between the administrative law of France and our English rule of law, if taken from the right point of view, suggests some interesting points of likeness, no less than of unlikeness.

I. Likeness.

1st Point. *Droit administratif* not opposed to English ideas current in sixteenth and seventeenth centuries.

It will be observed that it is "modern" English notions which we have contrasted with the ideas of administrative law prevalent in France and other continental states. The reason why the opposition between the two is drawn in this form deserves notice. At a period which historically is not very remote from us, the ideas as to the position of the Crown which were current, if not predominant in England, bore a very close analogy to the doctrines which have given rise to the *droit administratif* of France.[1] Similar beliefs moreover necessarily produced similar results, and there was a time when it must have seemed possible that what we now call administrative law should become a permanent part of

[1] This is illustrated by the similarity between the views at one time prevailing both in England and on the continent as to the relation between the Government and the press. See pp. 259-264, *ante*.

Part II. English institutions. For from the accession of the Tudors till the final expulsion of the Stuarts the Crown and its servants maintained and put into practice, with more or less success and with varying degrees of popular approval, views of government essentially similar to the theories which under different forms have been accepted by the French people. The personal failings of the Stuarts and the confusion caused by the combination of a religious with a political movement have tended to mask the true character of the legal and constitutional issues raised by the political contests of the seventeenth century. A lawyer, who regards the matter from an exclusively legal point of view, is tempted to assert that the real subject in dispute between statesmen such as Bacon and Wentworth on the one hand, and Coke or Eliot on the other, was whether a strong administration of the continental type should, or should not, be permanently established in England. Bacon and men like him no doubt underrated the risk that an increase in the power of the Crown should lead to the establishment of despotism. But advocates of the prerogative did not (it may be supposed) intend to sacrifice the liberties or invade the ordinary private rights of citizens; they were struck with the evils flowing from the conservative legalism of Coke, and with the necessity for enabling the Crown as head of the nation to cope with the selfishness of powerful individuals and classes. They wished, in short, to give the government the sort of rights conferred on a foreign executive by the principles of administrative law. Hence for each feature of French *droit administratif* one may find some curious analogy either in the claims put forward or in the institutions favoured by the Crown lawyers of the seventeenth century.

The doctrine, propounded under various metaphors by Bacon, that the prerogative was something beyond and above the ordinary law is like the foreign doctrine that in matters of high policy (*acte de gouvernement*) the administration has a discretionary authority which cannot be controlled by any court. The celebrated dictum that the judges, though they be "lions," yet should be "lions under "the throne, being circumspect that they do not "check or oppose any points of sovereignty,"[1] is a curious anticipation of the maxim formulated by French revolutionary statesmanship that the judges are under no circumstances to disturb the action of the administration, and would, if logically worked out, have led to the exemption of every administrative act, or, to use English terms, of every act alleged to be done in virtue of the prerogative, from judicial cognisance. The constantly increasing power of the Star Chamber and of the Council gave practical expression to prevalent theories as to the Royal prerogative, and it is hardly fanciful to compare these courts, which were in reality portions of the executive government, with the *Conseil d'Etat* and other *Tribunaux administratifs* of France. Nor is a parallel wanting to the celebrated Article 75 of the Constitution of the Year VIII.[2] This parallel is to be found in Bacon's attempt to prevent the judges by means of the writ *De non procedendo Rege inconsulto*

[1] Gardiner, *History of England*, vol. iii (1883), p. 2.

[2] See pp. 347, 348, *ante*.

from proceeding with any case in which the interests of the Crown were concerned. "The working of this "writ," observes Mr. Gardiner, "if Bacon had "obtained his object, would have been, to some "extent, analogous to that provision which has been "found in so many French constitutions, according "to which no agent of the Government can be sum-"moned before a tribunal, for acts done in the exercise "of his office, without a preliminary authorisation by "the *Conseil d'Etat*. The effect of the English writ "being confined to cases where the King was him-"self supposed to be injured, would have been of less "universal application, but the principle on which it "rested would have been equally bad."[1] The principle moreover admitted of unlimited extension, and this, we may add, was perceived by Bacon. "The "writ," he writes to the King, "is a mean provided "by the ancient law of England to bring any case "that may *concern your Majesty in profit or power* "*from the ordinary Benches, to be tried and judged* "*before the Chancellor of England*, by the ordinary "and legal part of this power. And your Majesty "knoweth *your Chancellor is ever a principal* "*counsellor and instrument of monarchy, of im-*"*mediate dependence on the king; and therefore* "*like to be a safe and tender guardian of the* "*regal rights*."[2] Bacon's innovation would, if successful, have formally established the fundamental dogma of administrative law, that administrative questions must be determined by administrative bodies.

The analogy between the administrative ideas

[1] Gardiner, *op. cit.*, vol. iii (1883), p. 7, note 2.

[2] Abbott, *Francis Bacon* (1885), p. 234.

Chapter XII.

which still prevail on the Continent[1] and the conception of the prerogative which was maintained by the English crown in the seventeenth century has considerable speculative interest. That the administrative ideas supposed by many French writers to have been originated by the statesmanship of the great Revolution or of the first Empire are to a great extent developments of the traditions and habits of the French monarchy is past a doubt, and it is a curious inquiry how far the efforts made by the Tudors or Stuarts to establish a strong government were influenced by foreign examples. This, however, is a problem for historians. A lawyer may content himself with noting that French history throws light on the causes both of the partial success and of the ultimate failure of the attempt to establish in England a strong administrative system. The endeavour had a partial success, because circumstances, similar to those which made French monarchs ultimately despotic, tended in England during the sixteenth and part of the seventeenth century to augment the authority of the Crown. The attempt ended in failure, partly because of the personal deficiencies of the Stuarts, but chiefly because the whole scheme of administrative law was opposed to those habits of equality before the law which had long been essential characteristics of English institutions.

2nd Point. *Droit administratif* is case-law.

Droit administratif is in its contents utterly unlike any branch of modern English law, but in the method of its formation it resembles English law

[1] It is worth noting that the system of "administrative law," though more fully judicialised in France than elsewhere, exists in one form or another in most of the Continental States.

far more closely than does the codified civil law of France. For *droit administratif* is, like the greater part of English law, "case-law," or "judge-made law."[1] The precepts thereof are not to be found in any code; they are based upon precedent: French lawyers cling to the belief that *droit administratif* cannot be codified, just as English and American lawyers maintain, for some reason or other which they are never able to make very clear, that English law, and especially the common law, does not admit of codification. The true meaning of a creed which seems to be illogical because its apologists cannot, or will not, give the true grounds for their faith, is that the devotees of *droit administratif* in France, in common with the devotees of the common law in England, know that the system which they each admire is the product of judicial legislation, and dread that codification might limit, as it probably would, the essentially legislative authority of the *tribunaux administratifs* in France, or of the judges in England. The prominence further given throughout every treatise on *droit administratif* to the *contentieux administratif* recalls the importance in English law-books given to matters of procedure. The cause is in each case the same, namely, that French jurists and English lawyers are each dealing with a system of law based on precedent.

Nor is it irrelevant to remark that the *droit administratif* of France, just because it is case-law based on precedents created or sanctioned by

[1] See Dicey, *Law and Opinion in England* (2nd ed., 1914), Lecture XI. (p. 361), and App. 1 at pp. 486-488, *post*. Dicey suspected that English lawyers underrated the influence at the present day exerted by precedent (jurisprudence) in French courts.—Ed.

tribunals, has, like the law of England, been profoundly influenced by the writers of text-books and commentaries. There are various branches of English law which have been reduced to a few logical principles by the books of well-known writers. Stephen transformed pleading from a set of rules derived mainly from the experience of practitioners into a coherent logical system. Private international law, as understood in England at the present day, has been developed under the influence first of Story's *Commentaries on the Conflict of Laws*, and next, at a later date, of Mr. Westlake's *Private International Law*. And the authority exercised in every field of English law by these and other eminent writers has in France been exerted, in the field of administrative law, by authors or teachers such as Cormenin, Macarel, Vivien, Laferrière, and Hauriou. This is no accident. Wherever courts have power to form the law, there writers of text-books will also have influence. Remark too that, from the very nature of judge-made law, Reports have in the sphere of *droit administratif* an importance equal to the importance which they possess in every branch of English law, except in the rare instances in which a portion of our law has undergone codification.

3rd point. Evolution of *droit administratif.*

But in the comparison between French *droit administratif* and the law of England a critic ought not to stop at the points of likeness arising from their each of them being the creation of judicial decisions. There exists a further and very curious analogy between the process of their historical development. The *Conseil d'Etat* has been converted from an executive into a judicial or quasi-judicial body by the gradual separation of its judicial from its executive functions through the transference of the former to committees (*sections*), which have assumed more and more distinctly the duties of courts. These "judicial committees" (to use an English expression) at first only advised the *Conseil d'Etat* or the whole executive body, though it was soon understood that the Council would, as a general rule, follow or ratify the decision of its judicial committees. This recalls to a student of English law the fact that the growth of our whole judicial system may historically be treated as the transference to parts of the King's Council of judicial powers originally exercised by the King in Council; and it is reasonable to suppose that the rather ill-defined relations between the *Conseil d'Etat* as a whole, and the *Comité du contentieux*,[1] may explain to a student the exertion, during the earlier periods of English history, by the King's Council, of hardly distinguishable judicial and executive powers; it explains also how, by a natural process which may have excited very little observation, the judicial functions of the Council became separated from its executive powers, and how this differentiation of functions gave birth at last to courts whose connection with the political executive was merely historical. This process, moreover, of differentiation assisted at times, in France no less than in England, by legislation, has of quite recent years changed the *Conseil d'Etat* into a real tribunal of *droit administratif*, as it created in England the Judicial Committee of the Privy Council for the regular and judicial decision of

[1] See Laferrière, *Traité de la Juridiction administrative et des recours contentieux* (2nd ed., 1896), vol. i, bk. i, ch. iii, p. 236.

appeals from the colonies to the Crown in Council. Nor, though the point is a minor one, is it irrelevant to note that, as the so-called judgments of the *Conseil d'Etat* were, till 1872, not strictly "judgments," but in reality advice on questions of *droit administratif* given by the *Conseil d'Etat* to the head of the Executive, and advice which he was not absolutely bound to follow, so the "judgments" of the Privy Council, even when acting through its judicial committee, though in reality judgments, are in form merely humble advice tendered by the Privy Council to the Crown. This form, which is now a mere survival, carries us back to an earlier period of English constitutional history, when the interference by the Council, *i.e.* by the executive, with judicial functions, was a real menace to that supremacy of the law which has been the guarantee of English freedom, and this era in the history of England again is curiously illustrated by the annals of *droit administratif* after the restoration of the Bourbons, 1815-30.

At that date the members of the *Conseil d'Etat*, as we have seen,[1] held, as they still hold, office at the pleasure of the Executive; they were to a great extent a political body; there existed further no Conflict-Court; or rather the *Conseil d'Etat* was itself the *Tribunal des Conflits*, or the body which determined the reciprocal jurisdiction of the ordinary law courts and of the administrative courts, *i.e.* speaking broadly, the extent of the Council's own jurisdiction. The result was that the *Conseil d'Etat* used its powers to withdraw cases from the decision of the law courts, and this at a time when government functionaries

[1] See p. 348, *ante*.

Part II.

were fully protected by Article 75 of the Constitution of the Year VIII. from being made responsible before the courts for official acts done in excess of their legal powers. Nevertheless, the *Conseil d'Etat*, just because it was to a great extent influenced by legal ideas, resisted, and with success, exertions of arbitrary power inspired by the spirit of Royalist reaction. It upheld the sales of the national domain made between 1789 and 1814; it withstood every attempt to invalidate decisions given by administrative authorities during the period of the Revolution or under the Empire. The King, owing, it may be assumed, to the judicial independence displayed by the *Conseil d'Etat*, took steps which were intended to transfer the decision of administrative disputes from the Council or its committees, acting as courts, to Councillors, acting as part of the executive. Ordinances of 1814 and of 1817 empowered the King to withdraw any administrative dispute which was connected with principles of public interest (*toutes les affaires du contentieux de l'administration qui se lieraient à des vues d'intérêt général*) from the jurisdiction of the *Conseil d'Etat* and bring it before the Council of Ministers or, as it was called, the *Conseil d'en haut*, and the general effect of this power and of other arrangements, which we need not follow out into detail, was that questions of *droit administratif*, in the decision of which the government were interested, were ultimately decided, not even by a quasi-judicial body, but by the King and his Ministers, acting avowedly under the bias of political considerations.[1] In 1828 France insisted upon and obtained

[1] See Laferrière, *Traité de la Juridiction administrative et des recours*

from Charles X. changes in procedure which diminished the arbitrary power of the Council.[1] But no one can wonder that Frenchmen feared the increase of arbitrary power, or that French liberals demanded, after the Revolution of 1830, the abolition of administrative law and of administrative courts. They felt towards the jurisdiction of the *Conseil d'Etat* the dread entertained by Englishmen of the sixteenth and seventeenth centuries with regard to the jurisdiction of the Privy Council, whether exercised by the Privy Council itself, by the Star Chamber, or even by the Court of Chancery. In each country there existed an appreciable danger lest the rule of the prerogative should supersede the supremacy of the law.

The comparison is in many ways instructive; it impresses upon us how nearly it came to pass that something very like administrative law at one time grew up in England. It ought, too, to make us perceive that such law, if it be administered in a judicial spirit, has in itself some advantages. It shows us also the inherent danger of its not becoming in strictness law at all, but remaining, from its close connection with the executive, a form of arbitrary power above or even opposed to the regular law of the land. It is certain that in the sixteenth and seventeenth centuries the jurisdiction of the Privy Council and even of the Star Chamber, odious as its name has remained, did confer some benefits on the public. It should always be remembered that the patriots who resisted the tyranny of the Stuarts were fanatics for

contentieux (2nd ed., 1896), vol. i, bk. i, ch. iii, pp. 226-234, and Cornemin, *Le Conseil d'Etat envisagé comme Conseil et comme Juridiction dans notre Monarchie constitutionnelle* (1818).

[1] Ordinance of 1st June, 1828, Laferrière, *op. cit.*, vol. i, p. 232.

the common law, and could they have seen their way to do so would have abolished the Court of Chancery no less than the Star Chamber. The Chancellor, after all, was a servant of the Crown holding his office at the pleasure of the King, and certainly capable, under the plea that he was promoting justice or equity, of destroying the certainty no less than the formalism of the common law. The parallel therefore between the position of the English puritans, or whigs, who, during the seventeenth century, opposed the arbitrary authority of the Council, and the position of the French liberals who, under the Restoration (1815-30), resisted the arbitrary authority of the *Conseil d'Etat* and the extension of *droit administratif*, is a close one. In each case, it may be added, the friends of freedom triumphed.

The result, however, of this triumph was, it will be said, as regards the matter we are considering, markedly different. Parliament destroyed, and destroyed for ever, the arbitrary authority of the Star Chamber and of the Council, and did not suffer any system of administrative courts or of administrative law to be revived or developed in England. The French liberals, on the expulsion of the Bourbons, neither destroyed the *tribunaux administratifs* nor made a clean sweep of *droit administratif*.

The difference is remarkable, yet any student who looks beyond names at things will find that even here an obvious difference conceals a curious element of fundamental resemblance. The Star Chamber was abolished; the arbitrary jurisdiction of the Council disappeared, but the judicial authority of the Chancellor was touched neither by the Long Parliament nor by any of the Parliaments which met yearly after the Revolution of 1688. The reasons for this difference are not hard to discover. The law administered by the Lord Chancellor, or, in other words, Equity, had in it originally an arbitrary or discretionary element, but it in fact conferred real benefits upon the nation and was felt to be in many respects superior to the common law administered by the common-law Judges. Even before 1660 acute observers might note that Equity was growing into a system of fixed law. Equity, which originally meant the discretionary, not to say arbitrary interference of the Chancellor, for the avowed and often real purpose of securing substantial justice between the parties in a given case, might, no doubt, have been so developed as to shelter and extend the despotic prerogative of the Crown. But this was not the course of development which Equity actually followed; at any rate from the time of Lord Nottingham (1673) it was obvious that Equity was developing into a judicial system for the application of principles which, though different from those of the common law, were not less fixed. The danger of Equity turning into the servant of despotism had passed away, and English statesmen, many of them lawyers, were little likely to destroy a body of law which, if in one sense an anomaly, was productive of beneficial reforms. The treatment of *droit administratif* in the nineteenth century by Frenchmen bears a marked resemblance to the treatment of Equity in the seventeenth century by Englishmen. *Droit administratif* has been the subject of much attack. More than one publicist of high reputation has

Part II. advocated its abolition, or has wished to transfer to the ordinary or civil courts (*tribunaux judiciaires*) the authority exercised by the administrative tribunals, but the assaults upon *droit administratif* have been repulsed, and the division between the spheres of the judicial and the spheres of the administrative tribunals has been maintained. Nor, again, is there much difficulty in seeing why this has happened. *Droit administratif* with all its peculiarities, and administrative tribunals with all their defects, have been suffered to exist because the system as a whole is felt by Frenchmen to be beneficial. Its severest critics concede that it has some great practical merits, and is suited to the spirit of French institutions. Meanwhile *droit administratif* has developed under the influence rather of lawyers than of politicians; it has during the last half-century and more to a great extent divested itself of its arbitrary character, and is passing into a system of more or less fixed law administered by real tribunals; administrative tribunals indeed still lack some of the qualities, such as complete independence of the Government, which Englishmen and many Frenchmen also think ought to belong to all courts, but these tribunals are certainly very far indeed from being mere departments of the executive government. To any person versed in the judicial history of England, it would therefore appear to be possible, or even probable, that *droit administratif* may ultimately, under the guidance of lawyers, become, through a course of evolution, as completely a branch of the law of France (even if we use the word "law" in its very strictest sense) as Equity has for more than two centuries become an acknowledged branch of the law of England.

Chapter XII.

4th Point. Rapid growth of case-law.

The annals of *droit administratif* during the nineteenth century elucidate again a point in the earlier history of English law which excites some perplexity in the mind of a student, namely, the rapidity with which the mere existence and working of law courts may create or extend a system of law. Any reader of the *History of English Law* by Pollock and Maitland may well be surprised at the rapidity with which the law of the King's Court became the general or common law of the land. This legal revolution seems to have been the natural result of the vigorous exertion of judicial functions by a court of great authority. Nor can we feel certain that the end attained was deliberately aimed at. It may, in the main, have been the almost undesigned effect of two causes: the first is the disposition always exhibited by capable judges to refer the decision of particular cases to general principles, and to be guided by precedent; the second is the tendency of inferior tribunals to follow the lead given by any court of great power and high dignity. Here, in short, we have one of the thousand illustrations of the principle developed in M. Tarde's *Lois de l'imitation*, that the innate imitativeness of mankind explains the spread, first, throughout one country, and, lastly, throughout the civilised world, of any institution or habit on which success or any other circumstance has conferred prestige. It may still, however, be urged that the creation under judicial influence of a system of law is an achievement which requires for its performance a consider-

Part II.

able length of time, and that the influence of the King's Court in England in moulding the whole law of the country worked with incredible rapidity. It is certainly true that from the Norman Conquest to the accession of Edward I. (1066-1272) is a period of not much over two centuries, and that by 1272 the foundations of English law were firmly laid; whilst if we date the organisation of our judicial system from the accession of Henry II. (1154), we might say that a great legal revolution was carried through in not much more than a century. It is at this point that the history of *droit administratif* helps the student of comparative law.

One need not, however, be greatly astonished at rapidity in the development of legal principles and of legal procedure at a period when the moral influence or the imaginative impressiveness of powerful tribunals was much greater than during the later stages of human progress. In any case it is certain—and the fact is a most instructive one—that under the conditions of modern civilisation a whole body of legal rules and maxims, and a whole system of quasi-judicial procedure, have in France grown up within not much more than a century. The expression "grown up" is here deliberately used; the development of *droit administratif* between 1800 and 1908 resembles a natural process. It is as true of this branch of French law as of the English constitution that it "has not been made but has grown."

II. Unlikeness. 1st Point. *Droit administratif* not to be identified with any part of law of England.

An intelligent student soon finds that *droit administratif* contains rules as to the status, the privileges, and the duties of government officials. He therefore thinks he can identify it with the laws, regulations, or customs which in England determine the position of the servants of the Crown, or (leaving the army out of consideration) of the Civil Service. Such "official law" exists, though only to a limited extent, in England no less than in France, and it is of course possible to identify and compare this official law of the one country with the official law of the other. But further investigation shows that official law thus understood, though it may form part of, is a very different thing from *droit administratif*. The law, by whatever name we term it, which regulates the privileges or disabilities of civil servants is the law of a class, just as military law is the law of a class, namely, the army. But *droit administratif* is not the law of a class, but—a very different thing—a body of law which, under given circumstances, may affect the rights of any French citizen, as for example, where an action is brought by *A* against *X* in the ordinary courts (*tribunaux judiciaires*), and the rights of the parties are found to depend on an administrative act (*acte administratif*), which must be interpreted by an administrative tribunal (*tribunal administratif*). In truth, *droit administratif* is not the law of the Civil Service, but is that part of French public law which affects every Frenchman in relation to the acts of the public administration as the representative of the State. The relation indeed of *droit administratif* to the ordinary law of France may be best compared not with the relation of the law governing a particular class (*e.g.* military law) to the general law of England, but with the relation of Equity to the common law of England. The point of likeness.

slight though in other respects it be, is that *droit administratif* in France and Equity in England each constitute a body of law which differs from the ordinary law of the land, and under certain circumstances modifies the ordinary civil rights of every citizen.

When our student finds that *droit administratif* cannot be identified with the law of the Civil Service, he naturally enough imagines that it may be treated as the sum of all the laws which confer special powers and impose special duties upon the administration, or, in other words, which regulate the functions of the Government. Such laws, though they must exist in every country, have till recently been few in England, simply because in England the sphere of the State's activity has, till within the last fifty or sixty years, been extremely limited. But even in England laws imposing special functions upon government officials have always existed, and the number thereof has of late vastly increased; to take one example among a score, the Factory legislation, which has grown up mainly during the latter half of the nineteenth century, has, with regard to the inspection and regulation of manufactories and workshops, given to the Government and its officials wide rights, and imposed upon them wide duties. If, then, *droit administratif* meant nothing more than the sum of all the laws which determine the functions of civil servants, *droit administratif* might be identified in its general character with the governmental law of England. The idea that such an identification is possible is encouraged by the wide definitions of *droit administratif* to be gathered from French works of authority,[1] and by the vagueness with which English writers occasionally use the term "administrative law." But here, again, the attempted identification breaks down. *Droit administratif*, as it exists in France, is not the sum of the powers possessed or of the functions discharged by the administration; it is rather the sum of the principles which govern the relation between French citizens, as individuals, and the administration as the representative of the State. Here we touch upon the fundamental difference between English and French ideas. In England the powers of the Crown and its servants may from time to time be increased as they may also be diminished. But these powers, whatever they are, must be exercised in accordance with the ordinary common law principles which govern the relation of one Englishman to another. A factory inspector, for example, is possessed of peculiar powers conferred upon him by Act of Parliament; but if in virtue of the orders of his superior officials he exceeds the authority given him by law, he becomes at once responsible for the wrong done, and cannot plead in his defence strict obedience to official orders, and, further, for the tort he has committed he becomes amenable to the ordinary courts. In France, on the other hand, whilst the powers placed in the hands of the administration might be diminished, it is always assumed that the relation of individual citizens to the State is regu-

[1] See Aucoc, *Conférences sur l'Administration et sur le Droit administratif* (3rd ed., 1885), Intro., N° 6, p. 15; Hauriou, *Précis de Droit administratif* (3rd ed., 1897), p. 242; (10th ed., 1921), p. 10; Laferrière, *Traité de la Juridiction administrative et des recours contentieux* (2nd ed., 1896), vol. i, bk. prélim., ch. i, pp. 1-8.

Part II.

lated by principles different from those which govern the relation of one French citizen to another. *Droit administratif*, in short, rests upon ideas absolutely foreign to English law: the one, as I have already explained,[1] is that the relation of individuals to the State is governed by principles essentially different from those rules of private law which govern the rights of private persons towards their neighbours; the other is that questions as to the application of these principles do not lie within the jurisdiction of the ordinary courts. This essential difference renders the identification of *droit administratif* with any branch of English law an impossibility. Hence inquiries which rightly occupy French jurists, such, for example, as what is the proper definition of the *contentieux administratif*; what is the precise difference between *actes de gestion* and *actes de puissance publique*, and generally, what are the boundaries between the jurisdiction of the ordinary courts (*tribunaux judiciaires*) and the jurisdiction of the administrative courts (*tribunaux administratifs*) have under English law no meaning.

2nd Point. *Droit administratif* not in reality introduced into law of England.

Has *droit administratif* been of recent years introduced in any sense into the law of England?

This is an inquiry which has been raised by writers of eminence,[2] and which has caused some

[1] See p. 336, *ante*.

[2] See Laferrière, *Traité de la Juridiction administrative et des recours contentieux* (2nd ed., 1896), vol. i, bk. prélim., ch. iv, pp. 97-106. To cite such enactments as the Public Authorities Protection Act, 1893, which did little more than generalise provisions to be found in many Acts extending from 1601 to 1900, as an example of the existence of administrative law in England, seemed to the author little more than playing with words. The Act assumed that every person might legally do the act which by law he was ordered to do. It also gave a person who acted in pursuance of his legal duty, *e.g.* under an Act of Parliament,

perplexity. We may give thereto a decided and negative reply.[1]

The powers of the English Government have, during the last sixty years or so, been largely increased; the State has undertaken many new functions, such, for example, as the regulation of labour under the Factory Acts, and the supervision of public education under the Education Acts. Nor is the importance of this extension of the activity of the State lessened by the consideration that its powers are in many cases exercised by local bodies, such, for example, as County Councils. But though the powers conferred on persons or bodies who directly or indirectly represent the State have been greatly increased in many directions, there has been no intentional introduction into the law of England of the essential principles of *droit administratif.* Any official who exceeds the authority given him by the law incurs the common law responsibility for his wrongful act; he is amenable to the authority of the ordinary courts, and the ordinary courts have themselves jurisdiction to determine what is the extent of his legal power, and whether the orders under which he has acted were legal and valid. Hence the courts do in effect limit and interfere with the action of the "administration," using that word in its widest sense.

special privileges as to the time within which an action must be brought against him for any wrong committed by him in the course of carrying out his duty, but it did not to the least extent provide that an order from a superior official should protect for any wrong done by him. This Act was repealed by the Law Reform (Limitation of Actions) Act, 1954, which abolished the special time limit for bringing actions against public servants, and put all defendants, whether private citizens or public authorities, on the same footing.

[1] Cf. Intro. pp. cxiii, *et seq.*

Part II. The London School Board, for example, has claimed and exercised the right to tax the ratepayers for the support of a kind of education superior to the elementary teaching generally provided by School Boards; the High Court of Justice has decided that such right does not exist. A year or two ago some officials, acting under the distinct orders of the Lords of the Admiralty, occupied some land alleged to belong to the Crown; the title of the Crown being disputed, a court of law gave judgment against the officials as wrong-doers. In each of these cases nice and disputable points of law were raised, but no English lawyer, whatever his opinion of the judgments given by the court, has ever doubted that the High Court had jurisdiction to determine what were the rights of the School Board or of the Crown.

Droit administratif, therefore, has obtained no foothold in England, but, as has been pointed out by some foreign critics, recent legislation has occasionally, and for particular purposes, given to officials something like judicial authority. It is possible in such instances, which are rare, to see a slight approximation to *droit administratif*, but the innovations, such as they are, have been suggested merely by considerations of practical convenience, and do not betray the least intention on the part of English statesmen to modify the essential principles of English law. There exists in England no true *droit administratif.*

An English lawyer, however, who has ascertained that no branch of English law corresponds with the administrative law of foreign countries must be on his guard against falling into the error that the *droit administratif* of modern France is not "law" at all, in the sense in which that term is used in England, but is a mere name for maxims which guide the executive in the exercise if not of arbitrary yet of discretionary power. That this notion is erroneous will, I hope, be now clear to all my readers. But for its existence there is some excuse and even a certain amount of justification.

The French Government does in fact exercise, especially as regards foreigners, a wide discretionary authority which is not under the control of any court whatever. For an act of State the Executive or its servants cannot be made amenable to the jurisdiction of any tribunal, whether judicial or administrative. Writers of high authority have differed[1] indeed profoundly as to the definition of an act of State (*acte de gouvernement*).[2] Where on a question of French law French jurists disagree, an English lawyer can form no opinion; he may be allowed, however, to conjecture that at times of disturbance a French Government can exercise discretionary powers without the dread of interference on the part of the ordinary courts, and that administrative tribunals, when they can intervene, are likely to favour that interpretation of the term act of State which supports the authority of the Executive. However this may be, the possession by the French Executive of large prerogatives is apt, in the mind of

[1] See p. 346, *ante*.

[2] Compare Laferrière, *op. cit.* (2nd ed., 1896), vol. ii, bk. iv, ch. ii, p. 32, and Hauriou, *Précis de Droit administratif* (3rd ed., 1897), pp. 282-287, (10th ed., 1921), pp. 431-436, with Jacquelin, *Les principes dominants du Contentieux administratif* (1899), part ii, tit. ii, ch. iii, pp. 297-326.

an Englishman, to be confused with the character of the administrative law enforced by courts composed, in part at any rate, of officials.

The restrictions, again, placed by French law on the jurisdiction of the ordinary courts (*tribunaux judiciaires*) whereby they are prevented from interfering with the action of the Executive and its servants, seem to an Englishman accustomed to a system under which the courts of law determine the limits of their own jurisdiction, to be much the same thing as the relegating of all matters in which the authority of the State is concerned to the discretion of the Executive. This notion is erroneous, but it has been fostered by a circumstance which may be termed accidental. The nature and the very existence of *droit administratif* has been first revealed to many Englishmen, as certainly to the present writer, through the writings of Alexis de Tocqueville, whose works have exerted, in the England of the nineteenth century, an influence equal to the authority exerted by the works of Montesquieu in the England of the eighteenth century. Now de Tocqueville by his own admission knew little or nothing of the actual working of *droit administratif* in his own day.[1] He no doubt in his later years increased his knowledge, but to the end of his life he looked upon *droit administratif*, not as a practising lawyer but as the historian of the *ancien régime*, and even as an historian he studied the subject from a very peculiar point of view, for the aim of *L'Ancien Régime et la Révolution* is to establish the doctrine that the institutions of modern France are in many respects

[1] de Tocqueville, *Œuvres complètes* (14th ed., 1864), vol. vii (Correspondance), p. 66.

in spirit the same as the institutions of the ancient monarchy; and de Tocqueville, moved by the desire to maintain a theory of history which in his time sounded like a paradox, but, owing greatly to his labours, has now become a generally accepted truth, was inclined to exaggerate the similarity between the France of the Revolution, the Empire, or the Republic, and the France of the *ancien régime.* Nowhere is this tendency more obvious than in his treatment of *droit administratif.* He demonstrates that the ideas on which *droit administratif* is based had been accepted by French lawyers and statesmen long before 1789; he notes the arbitrariness of *droit administratif* under the monarchy; he not only insists upon but deplores the connection under the *ancien régime* between the action of the Executive and the administration of justice, and he certainly suggests that the *droit administratif* of the nineteenth century was all but as closely connected with the exercise of arbitrary power as was the *droit administratif* of the seventeenth or the eighteenth century.

He did not recognise the change in the character of *droit administratif* which was quietly taking place in his own day. He could not by any possibility anticipate the reforms which have occurred during the lapse of well-nigh half a century since his death. What wonder that English lawyers who first gained their knowledge of French institutions from de Tocqueville should fail to take full account of that judicialisation (*juridictionnalisation*) of administrative law which is one of the most surprising and noteworthy phenomena in the legal history of France.

Part II.

III. Merits and demerits.

Rule of law—its merits.

It is not uninstructive to compare the merits and defects, on the one hand, of our English rule of law, and, on the other, of French *droit administratif*.[1]

Our rigid rule of law has immense and undeniable merits. Individual freedom is thereby more thoroughly protected in England against oppression by the government than in any other European country; the Habeas Corpus Acts[2] protect the liberty no less of foreigners than of British subjects; martial law[3] itself is reduced within the narrowest limits, and subjected to the supervision of the courts; an extension of judicial power which sets at nought the dogma of the separation of powers, happily combined with judicial independence, has begotten reverence for the bench of judges. They, rather than the government, represent the august dignity of the State, or, in accordance with the terminology of English law, of the Crown. Trial by jury is open to much criticism; a distinguished French thinker may be right in holding that the habit of submitting difficult problems of fact to the decision of twelve men of not more than average education and intelligence will in the near future be considered an absurdity as patent as ordeal by battle. Its success in England is wholly due to, and is the most extraordinary sign of, popular confidence in the judicial bench. A judge is the colleague and the readily accepted guide of the jurors. The House of Commons shows the feeling of the electors, and has handed over to the High Court of Justice the

[1] See especially Jennings, *The Law and the Constitution* (4th ed., 1952), pp. 214 *et seq.*

[2] See p. 216, *ante*. [3] See p. 284, *ante*.

trial of election petitions. When rare occasions arise, as at Sheffield in 1866, which demand inquiries of an exceptional character which can hardly be effected by the regular procedure of the courts, it is to selected members of the bench that the nation turns for aid. In the bitter disputes which occur in the conflicts between capital and labour, employers and workmen alike will often submit their differences to the arbitration of men who have been judges of the High Court. Reverence, in short, for the supremacy of the law is seen in its very best aspect when we recognise it as being in England at once the cause and the effect of reverence for our judges.

Defects.

The blessings, however, conferred upon the nation by the rule of law are balanced by undeniable, though less obvious, evils. Courts cannot without considerable danger be turned into instruments of government. It is not the end for which they are created; it is a purpose for which they are ill suited at any period or in any country where history has not produced veneration for the law and for the law courts.[1] Respect for law, moreover, easily degenerates into legalism which from its very rigidity may work considerable injury to the nation. Thus the refusal to look upon an agent or servant of the State as standing, from a legal point of view, in a different position from the servant of any other employer, or as placed under obligations or entitled to immunities different from those imposed upon or granted to an ordinary citizen, has certainly saved England from the development of

[1] In times of revolutionary passion trial by jury cannot secure respect for justice. The worst iniquities committed by Jeffreys at the Bloody Assize would have been impossible, had he not found willing accomplices in the jurors and freeholders of the western counties.

the arbitrary prerogatives of the Crown, but it has also in more ways than one been injurious to the public service.

The law, for instance, has assuredly been slow to recognise the fact that violations of duty by public officials may have an importance and deserve a punishment far greater than the same conduct on the part of an agent of an ordinary employer. Some years ago a copyist in a public office betrayed to the newspapers a diplomatic document of the highest importance. Imagination can hardly picture a more flagrant breach of duty, but there then apparently existed no available means for punishing the culprit. If it could have been proved that he had taken from the office the paper on which the communication of state was written, he might conceivably have been put on trial for larceny.[1] But a prisoner put on trial for a crime of which he was in fact morally innocent, because the gross moral offence of which he was really guilty was not a crime, might have counted on an acquittal. The Official Secrets Act, 1889,[2] now, it is true, renders the particular offence, which could not be punished in 1878, a misdemeanour, but the Act, after the manner of English legislation, does not establish the general principle that an official breach of trust is a crime. It is therefore more than possible that derelictions of duty on the part of public servants which in some foreign countries would be severely punished may still in England expose the wrong-doer to no legal punishment.

[1] See *Annual Register*, 1878, Chronicle, pp. 71, 72.

[2] See now Official Secrets Acts, 1911, 1920 and 1939. See especially s. 2 of the former Act, which imposes a prohibition on the unauthorised disclosure of information acquired in the public service.

Nor is it at all wholly a benefit to the public that *bona fide* obedience to the orders of superiors is not a defence available to a subordinate who, in the discharge of his functions as a government officer, has invaded the legal rights of the humblest individual, or that officials are, like everybody else, accountable for their conduct to an ordinary court of law, and to a court, be it noted, where the verdict is given by a jury.

In this point of view few things are more instructive than an examination of the actions which have been brought against officers of the Board of Trade for detaining ships about to proceed to sea. Under the Merchant Shipping Acts since 1876 the Board have been and are bound to detain any ship which from its unsafe and unseaworthy condition cannot proceed to sea without serious danger to human life.[1] Most persons would suppose that the officials of the Board, as long as they, *bona fide*, and without malice or corrupt motive, endeavoured to carry out the provisions of the statute, would be safe from an action at the hands of a shipowner. This, however, is not so. The Board and its officers have more than once been sued with success.[2] They have never been accused of either malice or negligence, but the mere fact that the Board act in an administrative capacity is not a protection to the Board, nor is mere obedience to the orders of the Board an answer to an action against its servants. Any deviation, moreover, from the exact terms of the Acts—the omission of the most unmeaning formality—may make every person, high

[1] Merchant Shipping Act, 1894, s. 459.

[2] See *ibid.*, s. 460, and *Thompson* v. *Farrer* (1882) 9 Q.B.D. 372; cf. *Marshall Shipping Co.* v. *Board of Trade* [1923] 2 K.B. 343.

Part II.

and low, concerned in the detention of the ship, a wrong-doer. The question, on the answer to which the decision in each instance at bottom depends, is whether there was reasonable cause for detaining the vessel, and this inquiry is determined by jurymen who sympathise more keenly with the losses of a ship-owner, whose ship may have been unjustly detained, than with the zeal of an inspector anxious to perform his duty and to prevent loss of life. The result has (it is said) been to render the provisions of the Merchant Shipping Acts, with regard to the detention of unseaworthy ships, nugatory. Juries are often biassed against the Government. A technical question is referred for decision, from persons who know something about the subject, and are impartial, to persons who are both ignorant and prejudiced. The government, moreover, which has no concern but the public interest, is placed in the false position of a litigant fighting for his own advantage. These things ought to be noticed, for they explain, if they do not justify, the tenacity with which statesmen, as partial as de Tocqueville to English ideas of government, have clung to the conviction that administrative questions ought to be referred to administrative courts.

Droit administratif—merits.

The merits of administrative law as represented by modern French *droit administratif*, that is, when seen at its very best, escape the attention, and do not receive the due appreciation of English constitutionalists.[1] No jurist can fail to admire the skill with which the *Conseil d'Etat*, the authority and the jurisdiction whereof as an administrative court year by year receives extension, has worked out new

[1] One, and not the least of them, is that access to the *Conseil d'Etat* as an administrative court is both easy and inexpensive. Decisions may, however, be subject to very long delay.—Ed.

remedies for various abuses which would appear to be hardly touched by the ordinary law of the land. The *Conseil*, for instance, has created and extended the power of almost any individual to attack, and cause to be annulled, any act done by any administrative authority (using the term in a very wide sense) which is in excess of the legal power given to the person or body from whom the act emanates. Thus an order issued by a prefect or a by-law made by a corporation which is in excess of the legal power of the prefect or of the corporate body may, on the application of a plaintiff who has any interest in the matter whatever, be absolutely set aside or annulled for the benefit not only of the plaintiff, but of all the world, and this even though he has not himself suffered, from the act complained of, any pecuniary loss or damage. The ingenious distinction[1] again, which has been more and

[1] French law draws an important distinction between an injury caused to a private individual by act of the administration or government which is in excess of its powers (*faute de service*), though duly carried out, or at any rate, carried out without any gross fault on the part of a subordinate functionary, *e.g.* a policeman acting in pursuance of official orders, and injury caused to a private individual by the negligent or malicious manner (*faute personnelle*) in which such subordinate functionary carries out official orders which may be perfectly lawful. In the first case the policeman incurs no liability at all, and the party aggrieved must proceed in some form or other against the State in the *tribunaux administratifs*; in the second case the policeman is personally liable, and the party aggrieved must proceed against him in the *tribunaux civils* (see Hauriou, *Précis de Droit administratif* (3rd ed., 1897), pp. 170, 171; (10th ed., 1921), pp. 366-380; Laferrière, *Traité de la Juridiction administrative et des recours contentieux* (2nd ed., 1896), vol. i, bk. iii, ch. vii, p. 652), and apparently cannot proceed against the State.

French authorities differ as to what is the precise criterion by which to distinguish a *faute personnelle* from a *faute de service*, and show a tendency to hold that there is no *faute personnelle* on the part, *e.g.*, of a policeman, when he has *bona fide* attempted to carry out his official duty. See Duguit, *L'Etat, les gouvernants et les agents* (1903), ch. v, para. 11, pp. 638-640; *Traité de Droit constitutionnel* (2nd ed., vol. iii, 1923), ch. iv, para. 72, pp. 262-295; cf. App. sec. i (4), p. 500.

 more carefully elaborated by the *Conseil d'Etat*, between damage resulting from the personal fault (*faute personnelle*), *e.g.* spite, violence, or negligence of an official, *e.g.* a prefect or a mayor, in the carrying out of official orders, and the damage resulting, without any fault on the part of the official, from the carrying out of official orders, illegal or wrongful in themselves (*faute de service*), has of recent years afforded a valuable remedy to persons who have suffered from the misuse of official power, and has also, from one point of view, extended or secured the responsibility of officials—a responsibility enforceable in the ordinary courts—for wrongful conduct, which is in strictness attributable to their personal action. And in no respect does this judge-made law of the *Conseil* appear to more advantage than in cases, mostly I conceive of comparatively recent date, in which individuals have obtained compensation for governmental action, which might possibly be considered of technical legality, but which involves in reality the illegitimate use of power conferred upon the government or some governmental body for one object, but in truth used for some end different from that contemplated by the law. One example explains my meaning. The State in 1872 had, as it still has, a monopoly of matches. To the government was given by law the power of acquiring existing match factories under some form of compulsory purchase. It occurred to some ingenious minister that the fewer factories there were left open for sale, the less would be the purchase-money which the State would need to pay. A prefect, the direct servant of the government, had power to close factories on sanitary grounds.

Under the orders of the minister he closed a factory belonging to *A*, nominally on sanitary grounds, but in reality to lessen the number of match factories which the State, in the maintenance of its monopoly, would require to purchase. There was no personal fault on the part of the prefect. No action could with success be maintained against him in the judicial courts,[1] nor, we may add, in the administrative courts.[2] *A*, however, attacked the act itself before the *Conseil d'Etat*, and got the order of the prefect annulled,[2] and ultimately obtained, through the *Conseil d'Etat*, damages from the State of over £2000 for the illegal closing of the factory, and this in addition to the purchase-money received from the State for taking possession of the factory.[3]

Defects.

No Englishman can wonder that the jurisdiction of the *Conseil d'Etat*, as the greatest of administrative courts, grows apace; the extension of its power removes, as did at one time the growth of Equity in England, real grievances, and meets the need of the ordinary citizen. Yet to an Englishman imbued with an unshakeable faith in the importance of maintaining the supremacy of the ordinary law of the land enforced by the ordinary law courts, the *droit administratif* of modern France is open to some grave criticism.

The high and increasing authority of the *Conseil d'Etat* must detract, he surmises, from the dignity and respect of the judicial courts. "The more there is of the more, the less there is of the less" is a Spanish proverb of profound wisdom and wide appli-

[1] Dalloz, *Recueil périodique et critique de Jurisprudence, de Législation et de Doctrine, Cass. Crim.*, 6 Mars, 1875; D. 1875.1.495.

[2] Dalloz, *op. cit.*, *Trib. de Conflits*, 5 Mai, 1877; D. 1878.3.13.

[3] Dalloz, *op. cit.*, *Conseil d'Etat*, 4 Décembre, 1879; D. 1880.3.41.

cation. There was a time in the history of England when the judicial power of the Chancellor, bound up as it was with the prerogative of the Crown, might have overshadowed the courts of law, which have protected the hereditary liberties of England and the personal freedom of Englishmen. It is difficult not to suppose that the extension of the *Conseil's* jurisdiction, beneficial as may be its direct effects, may depress the authority of the judicial tribunals. More than one writer, who ought to represent the ideas of educated Frenchmen, makes the suggestion that if the members of the *Conseil d'Etat* lack that absolute security of tenure which is universally acknowledged to be the best guarantee of judicial independence, yet irremovable judges, who, though they may defy dismissal, are tormented by the constant longing for advancement,[1] are not more independent of the Government at whose hands they expect promotion than are members of the *Conseil d'Etat* who, if legally removable, are by force of custom hardly ever removed from their high position.

Trial by jury, we are told, is a joke, and, as far as the interests of the public are concerned, a very bad joke.[2] Prosecutors and criminals alike prefer the *Tribunaux Correctionnels,* where a jury is unknown, to the *Cours d'Assises,* where a judge presides and a jury gives a verdict. The prosecutor knows that in the *Tribunaux Correctionnels* proved guilt will lead to condemnation. The criminal knows that though in the inferior court he may lose the chance of acquittal by good-natured or sentimental jurymen, he also

[1] See Chardon, *L'Administration de la France—Les fonctionnaires* (1908), pp. 326-328. [2] *Ibid.*

avoids the possibility of undergoing severe punishment. Two facts are certain. In 1881 the judges were deprived of the right of charging the jury. Year by year the number of causes tried in the *Cours d'Assises* decreases. Add to this that the procedure of the judicial courts, whether civil or criminal, is antiquated and cumbrous. The procedure in the great administrative court is modelled on modern ideas, is simple, cheap, and effective. The *Cour de Cassation* still commands respect. The other judicial courts, one can hardly doubt, have sunk in popular estimation. Their members neither exercise the power nor enjoy the moral authority of the judges of the High Court.

It is difficult, further, for an Englishman to believe that, at any rate where politics are concerned, the administrative courts can from their very nature give that amount of protection to individual freedom which is secured to every English citizen, and indeed to every foreigner residing in England. However this may be, it is certain that the distinction between ordinary law and administrative law (taken together with the doctrine of the separation of powers, at any rate as hitherto interpreted by French jurists), implies the general belief that the agents of the government need, when acting in *bona fide* discharge of their official duties, protection from the control of the ordinary law courts. That this is so is proved by more than one fact. The desire to protect servants of the State has dictated the enactment of the *Code Pénal*, Article 114. This desire kept alive for seventy years Article 75 of the Constitution of the Year VIII. It influenced even the men by whom that Article was repealed, for the repeal itself is expressed

Part II.

in words which imply the intention of providing some special protection for the agents of the government. It influenced the decisions which more or less nullified the effect of the law of 19th December, 1870, which was at first supposed to make the judicial courts the sole judges of the liability of civil servants to suffer punishment or make compensation for acts of dubious legality done in the performance of their official duties. Oddly enough, the success with which administrative courts have extended the right of private persons to obtain damages from the State itself for illegal or injurious acts done by its servants, seems, as an English critic must think, to supply a new form of protection for the agents of the government when acting in obedience to orders. There surely can be little inducement to take proceedings against a subordinate, whose guilt consists merely in carrying out a wrongful or illegal order, given him by his official superior, if the person damaged can obtain compensation from the government, or, in other words, from the State itself.[1] But turn the matter which way you will, the personal immunities of officials who take part, though without other fault of their own, in any breach of the law, though consistent even with the modern *droit administratif* of France, are inconsistent with the ideas which

[1] Compare the extended protection offered to every servant of the State by the doctrine, suggested by at least one good authority, that he cannot be held personally responsible for any wrong (*faute*) committed whilst he is acting in the spirit of his official duty. "*Si, en effet, le* "*fonctionnaire a agi dans l'esprit de sa fonction, c'est-à-dire en poursuivant* "*effectivement le but qu'avait l'Etat en établissant cette fonction, il ne peut* "*être responsable ni vis-à-vis de l'Etat, ni vis-à-vis des particuliers, alors* "*même qu'il ait commis une faute.*"—Duguit, *L'Etat, les gouvernants et les agents* (1903), ch. v, para. 11. p. 638.

underlie the common law of England. This essential opposition has been admirably expressed by a French jurist of eminence.

"Under every legal system," writes Hauriou, "the right to proceed against a servant of the government for wrongs done to individuals in his official capacity exists in some form or other; the right corresponds to the instinctive impulse felt by every victim of a legal wrong to seek compensation from the immediately visible wrong-doer. But on this point the laws of different countries obey utterly different tendencies. There are countries [such, for example, as England or the United States] where every effort is made to shelter the liability of the State behind the personal responsibility of its servant. There are other countries where every effort is made to cover the responsibility of the servant of the State behind the liability of the State itself, to protect him against, and to save him from, the painful consequences of faults committed in the service of the State. The laws of centralised countries, and notably the law of France, are of this type. There you will find what is called the protection of officials" (*garantie des fonctionnaires*).[1]

[1] "*Ce principe est admis par toutes les législations, la poursuite du fonctionnaire existe partout, d'autant qu'elle répond à un mouvement instinctif qui est, pour la victime d'un méfait, de s'en prendre à l'auteur immédiatement visible. Mais les législations obéissent à deux tendances bien opposées : il en est qui s'efforcent d'abriter l'Etat derrière le fonctionnaire, il en est d'autres, au contraire, qui s'efforcent de faire couvrir le fonctionnaire par l'Etat, de le protéger, de le rassurer contre les conséquences fâcheuses de ses erreurs. Les législations des pays centralisés et notamment celle de la France sont de ce dernier type ; il y a ce que l'on appelle une* garantie des fonctionnaires."—Hauriou, *Précis de Droit administratif* (3rd ed., 1897), pp. 170, 171 ; (10th ed., 1921), pp. 366-380.

CHAPTER XIII

RELATION BETWEEN PARLIAMENTARY SOVEREIGNTY AND THE RULE OF LAW

Part II.

The sovereignty of Parliament and the supremacy of the law of the land—the two principles which pervade the whole of the English constitution—may appear to stand in opposition to each other, or to be at best only counterbalancing forces. But this appearance is delusive; the sovereignty of Parliament, as contrasted with other forms of sovereign power, favours the supremacy of the law, whilst the predominance of rigid legality throughout our institutions evokes the exercise, and thus increases the authority, of Parliamentary sovereignty.

Parliamentary sovereignty favours rule of law.

The sovereignty of Parliament favours the supremacy of the law of the land.[1]

That this should be so arises in the main from two

[1] Sir Ivor Jennings in *The Law and the Constitution* (4th ed., 1952), pp. 56 *et seq.*, suggests that legislation need not be deliberate, *e.g.* Defence of the Realm Acts. The provisions of the Parliament Act, 1911, as to Money Bills, reduce the function of the House of Lords to that of a rubber stamp. See too the Provisional Collection of Taxes Act, 1913. The difficulty in accepting Dicey's argument lies in the fact that parliamentary supremacy is a legal rule. How then can the law limit it? Cases where it does appear to be limited are governed by convention, not law recognised by courts, *e.g.* s. 4 of Statute of Westminster, 1931. See Intro. pp. xlix, lxxxvii *et seq.*, *ante*.—Ed.

characteristics or peculiarities which distinguish the English Parliament from other sovereign powers.

Chapter XIII.

The first of these characteristics is that the commands of Parliament (consisting as it does of the Queen, the House of Lords, and the House of Commons) can be uttered only through the combined action of its three constituent parts, and must, therefore always take the shape of formal and deliberate legislation. The will of Parliament[1] can be expressed only through an Act of Parliament.

This is no mere matter of form; it has most important practical effects. It prevents those inroads upon the law of the land which a despotic monarch, such as Louis XIV., Napoleon I., or Napoleon III., might effect by ordinances or decrees, or which the different constituent assemblies of France, and above all the famous Convention, carried out by sudden resolutions. The principle that Parliament speaks only through an Act of Parliament greatly increases the authority of the judges. A Bill which has passed into a statute immediately becomes subject to judicial interpretation, and the English Bench have always refused, in principle at least, to interpret an Act of Parliament otherwise than by reference to the words of the enactment. An English judge will take no notice of the resolutions of either House, of anything which may have passed in debate (a matter of which

[1] In the author's opinion a strong, if not the strongest, argument in favour of the so-called "bi-cameral" system, was to be found in the consideration that the co-existence of two legislative chambers prevented the confusion of resolutions passed by either House with laws, and thus checked the substitution of the arbitrary will of an assembly for the supremacy of the ordinary law of the land. To appreciate the force of this argument the history, not only of the French Convention but also of the English Long Parliament, had to be considered.

officially he has no cognisance), or even of the changes which a Bill may have undergone between the moment of its first introduction to Parliament and of its receiving the Royal assent. All this, which seems natural enough to an English lawyer, would greatly surprise many foreign legists, and no doubt often does give a certain narrowness to the judicial construction of statutes. It contributes greatly, however, both (as I have already pointed out) to the authority of the judges and to the fixity of the law.[1]

The second of these characteristics is that the English Parliament as such has never, except at periods of revolution, exercised direct executive power or appointed the officials of the executive government.[2]

No doubt in modern times the House of Commons has in substance obtained the right to designate for appointment the Prime Minister and the other members of the Cabinet. But this right is, historically speaking, of recent acquisition, and is exercised in a very roundabout manner; its existence does not affect the truth of the assertion that the Houses of Parlia-

[1] The principle that the sovereign legislature can express its commands only in the particular form of an Act of Parliament originates in historical causes; it is due to the fact that an Act of Parliament was once in reality, as it still is in form, a law enacted by the King by and with the advice and consent of the Lords and Commons in Parliament assembled.

[2] But it may be questioned whether any legislature could conduct administration. The feature of British parliamentary democracy is that the legislature is guided by the same Ministers as are controlling the administration. This does not depend upon the rule of law, but it produces the result that Ministers can be reasonably sure of Parliament enacting any changes in the law which they propose, while at the same time Ministers answer for the acts of themselves and the officials of their Departments. It is the electorate which forces a change of Ministers by its verdict at the polls.—Ed.

ment do not directly appoint or dismiss the servants of the State; neither the House of Lords nor the House of Commons, nor both Houses combined, could even now issue a direct order to a military officer, a constable, or a tax-collector; the servants of the State are still in name what they once were in reality—"servants of the Crown"; and, what is worth careful notice, the attitude of Parliament towards government officials was determined originally, and is still regulated, by considerations and feelings belonging to a time when the "servants of the Crown" were dependent upon the King, that is, upon a power which naturally excited the jealousy and vigilance of Parliament.

Hence several results all indirectly tending to support the supremacy of the law. Parliament, though sovereign, unlike a sovereign monarch who is not only a legislator but a ruler, that is, head of the executive government, has never hitherto been able to use the powers of the government as a means of interfering with the regular course of law;[1] and what is even more important, Parliament has looked with disfavour and jealousy on all exemptions of officials from the ordinary liabilities of citizens or from the jurisdiction of the ordinary courts; Parliamentary sovereignty has been fatal to the growth of "administrative law."[2] The action, lastly, of Parliament has tended as naturally to protect the independence

[1] Contrast with this the way in which, even towards the end of the eighteenth century, French Kings interfered with the action of the courts.

[2] Administrative law is now recognised as the creation of Parliament. The inverted commas show that the author is referring here, as always, to his own conception of *droit administratif* as applied to conditions in England.—Ed.

of the judges, as that of other sovereigns to protect the conduct of officials. It is worth notice that Parliamentary care for judicial independence has, in fact, stopped just at that point where on *a priori* grounds it might be expected to end. The judges are not in strictness irremovable; they can be removed from office on an address of the two Houses; they have been made by Parliament independent of every power in the State except the Houses of Parliament.

Tendency to support rule of law often not found in foreign representative assemblies.

The idea may suggest itself to a reader that the characteristics or peculiarities of the English Parliament on which I have just dwelt must now be common to most of the representative assemblies which exist in continental Europe. The French Parliament (Chamber and Senate) bears a considerable external resemblance to our own Parliament. It is influenced, however, by a different spirit; it is the heir, in more ways than one, of the Bourbon Monarchy and the Napoleonic Empire. It is apparently, though on this point a foreigner must speak with hesitation, inclined to interfere in the details of administration. It does not look with special favour on the independence or authority of the ordinary judges. It shows no disapprobation of the system of *droit administratif* which Frenchmen—very likely with truth—regard as an institution suited to their country, and it certainly leaves in the hands of the government wider executive and even legislative powers than the English Parliament has ever conceded either to the Crown or to its servants. What is true of France is true under a different form of many other continental states, such, for example, as Switzerland or Prussia. The sovereignty of Parliament as developed in England supports the supremacy of the law. But this is certainly not true of all the countries which enjoy representative or Parliamentary government.

Rule of law favours Parliamentary sovereignty.

The supremacy of the law necessitates the exercise of Parliamentary sovereignty.

The rigidity of the law constantly hampers (and sometimes with great injury to the public) the action of the executive, and from the hard-and-fast rules of strict law, as interpreted by the judges, the government can escape only by obtaining from Parliament the discretionary authority which is denied to the Crown by the law of the land. Note with care the way in which the necessity for discretionary powers brings about the recourse to exceptional legislation. Under the complex conditions of modern life no government can in times of disorder, or of war, keep the peace at home, or perform its duties towards foreign powers, without occasional use of arbitrary authority. During periods, for instance, of social disturbance you need not only to punish conspirators, but also to arrest men who are reasonably suspected of conspiracy; foreign revolutionists are known to be spreading sedition throughout the land; order can hardly be maintained unless the executive can expel aliens. When two foreign nations are at war, or when civil contests divide a friendly country into two hostile camps, it is impossible for England to perform her duties as a neutral unless the Crown has legal authority to put a summary check to the attempts of English sympathisers to help one or other of the belligerents. Foreign nations, again, feel aggrieved if

Part II.

they are prevented from punishing theft and homicide, —if, in short, their whole criminal law is weakened because every scoundrel can ensure impunity for his crimes by an escape to England. But this result must inevitably ensue if the English executive has no authority to surrender French or German offenders to the government of France or of Germany. The English executive needs therefore the right to exercise discretionary powers, but the Courts must prevent, and will prevent at any rate where personal liberty is concerned, the exercise by the government of any sort of discretionary power. The Crown cannot, except under statute, expel from England any alien[1] whatever, even though he were a murderer who, after slaughtering a whole family at Boulogne, had on the very day crossed red-handed to Dover. The executive therefore must ask for, and always obtains, aid from Parliament. An Aliens Act enables the Ministry to expel any foreigner from the country; a Foreign Enlistment Act makes it possible for the Ministry to check intervention in foreign contests or the supply of arms to foreign belligerents. Extradition Acts empower the government at the same time to prevent England from becoming a city of refuge for foreign criminals, and to co-operate with foreign states in that general repression of crime in which the whole civilised world has an interest. Nor have we yet exhausted the instances in which the rigidity of the law necessitates the intervention of Parliament. There are times of tumult or invasion when for the sake of legality itself the rules of law must be broken. The course which

[1] See, however, p. 225, note 1, *ante*.

the government must then take is clear. The Ministry must break the law and trust for protection to an Act of Indemnity. A statute of this kind is (as already pointed out[1]) the last and supreme exercise of Parliamentary sovereignty. It legalises illegality; it affords the practical solution of the problem which perplexed the statesmanship of the sixteenth and seventeenth centuries, how to combine the maintenance of law and the authority of the Houses of Parliament with the free exercise of that kind of discretionary power or prerogative which, under some shape or other, must at critical junctures be wielded by the executive government of every civilised country.

This solution may be thought by some critics a merely formal one, or at best only a substitution of the despotism of Parliament for the prerogative of the Crown. But this idea is erroneous. The fact that the most arbitrary powers of the English executive must always be exercised under Act of Parliament places the government, even when armed with the widest authority, under the supervision, so to speak, of the courts. Powers, however extraordinary, which are conferred or sanctioned by statute, are never really unlimited, for they are confined by the words of the Act itself, and, what is more, by the interpretation put upon the statute by the judges. Parliament is supreme legislator, but from the moment Parliament has uttered its will as lawgiver, that will becomes subject to the interpretation put upon it by the judges of the land, and the judges, who are influenced by the feelings of magistrates no less than by the general spirit of the common law, are disposed to

[1] See pp. 49, 50, 232-237, *ante*.

Part II.

construe statutory exceptions to common law principles in a mode which would not commend itself either to a body of officials, or to the Houses of Parliament, if the Houses were called upon to interpret their own enactments. In foreign countries, and especially in France, administrative ideas—notions derived from the traditions of a despotic monarchy—have restricted the authority and to a certain extent influenced the ideas of the judges. In England judicial notions have modified the action and influenced the ideas of the executive government. By every path we come round to the same conclusion, that Parliamentary sovereignty has favoured the rule of law, and that the supremacy of the law of the land both calls forth the exertion of Parliamentary sovereignty, and leads to its being exercised in a spirit of legality.

PART III

THE CONNECTION BETWEEN THE LAW OF THE CONSTITUTION AND THE CONVENTIONS OF THE CONSTITUTION

CHAPTER XIV

NATURE OF CONVENTIONS OF CONSTITUTION

Chapter XIV.

Questions remaining to be answered.

In an earlier part of this work[1] stress was laid upon the essential distinction between the "law of the constitution," which, consisting (as it does) of rules enforced or recognised by the courts, makes up a body of "laws" in the proper sense of that term, and the "conventions of the constitution," which consisting (as they do) of customs, practices, maxims, or precepts which are not enforced or recognised by the courts, make up a body not of laws, but of constitutional or political ethics; and it was further urged that the law, not the morality of the constitution, forms the proper subject of legal study.[2] In accordance with this view, the reader's attention has been hitherto exclusively directed to the meaning and applications of two principles which pervade the law of the constitution, namely, the Sovereignty of Parliament[3] and the Rule of Law.[4]

But a lawyer cannot master even the legal side of the English constitution without paying some attention to the nature of those constitutional understandings which necessarily engross the attention of

[1] See pp. 23-30, *ante*.
[2] See pp. 30-32, *ante*.
[3] See Part i.
[4] See Part ii.

historians or of statesmen. He ought to ascertain, at any rate, how, if at all, the law of the constitution is connected with the conventions of the constitution; and a lawyer who undertakes this task will soon find that in so doing he is only following one stage farther the path on which we have already entered, and is on the road to discover the last and most striking instance of that supremacy of the law which gives to the English polity the whole of its peculiar colour.

My aim therefore throughout the remainder of this book is to define, or ascertain, the relation or connection between the legal and the conventional elements in the constitution, and to point out the way in which a just appreciation of this connection throws light upon several subordinate questions or problems of constitutional law.

This end will be attained if an answer is found to each of two questions: What is the nature of the conventions or understandings of the constitution? What is the force or (in the language of jurisprudence) the "sanction" by which is enforced obedience to the conventions of the constitution? These answers will themselves throw light on the subordinate matters to which I have made reference.

Nature of constitutional understandings.

The salient characteristics, the outward aspects so to speak, of the understandings which make up the constitutional morality of modern England, can hardly be better described than in the words of Mr. Freeman:—

"We now have a whole system of political "morality, a whole code of precepts for the guidance of "public men, which will not be found in any page "of either the statute or the common law, but which "are in practice held hardly less sacred than any

Chapter XIV.

"principle embodied in the Great Charter or in the "Petition of Right. In short, by the side of our "written Law, there has grown up an unwritten or "conventional constitution. When an Englishman "speaks of the conduct of a public man being consti-"tutional or unconstitutional, he means something "wholly different from what he means by conduct "being legal or illegal. A famous vote of the House "of Commons, passed on the motion of a great states-"man, once declared that the then Ministers of the "Crown did not possess the confidence of the House "of Commons, and that their continuance in office "was therefore at variance with the spirit of the con-"stitution. The truth of such a position, accord-"ing to the traditional principles on which public men "have acted for some generations, cannot be disputed; "but it would be in vain to seek for any trace of such "doctrines in any page of our written Law. The "proposer of that motion did not mean to charge the "existing Ministry with any illegal act, with any act "which could be made the subject either of a prose-"cution in a lower court or of impeachment in the "High Court of Parliament itself. He did not mean "that they, Ministers of the Crown, appointed "during the pleasure of the Crown, committed "any breach of the Law of which the Law could "take cognisance, by retaining possession of their "offices till such time as the Crown should think "good to dismiss them from those offices. What he "meant was that the general course of their policy "was one which to a majority of the House of Com-"mons did not seem to be wise or beneficial to the "nation, and that therefore, according to a conven-

Part III.

"tional code as well understood and as effectual as "the written Law itself, they were bound to resign "offices of which the House of Commons no longer "held them to be worthy."[1]

The one exception which can be taken to this picture of our conventional constitution is the contrast drawn in it between the "written law" and the "unwritten constitution"; the true opposition, as already pointed out, is between laws properly so called, whether written or unwritten, and understandings, or practices, which, though commonly observed, are not laws in any true sense of that word at all. But this inaccuracy is hardly more than verbal, and we may gladly accept Mr. Freeman's words as a starting-point whence to inquire into the nature or common quality of the maxims which make up our body of constitutional morality.

Examples of constitutional understandings.

The following are examples[2] of the precepts to which Mr. Freeman refers, and belong to the code by which public life in England is (or is supposed to be) governed. "A Ministry which is outvoted in the House of Commons is in many cases bound to retire from office." "A Cabinet, when outvoted on any vital question, may appeal once to the country by means of a dissolution." "If an appeal to the electors goes against the Ministry they are bound to retire from office, and have no right to dissolve Parliament a second time." "The Cabinet are responsible to Parliament as a body, for the general conduct of affairs." "They are further

[1] Freeman, *Growth of the English Constitution* (1st ed., 1872), pp. 109, 110.

[2] See, for further examples, p. 26, *ante*.

responsible to an extent, not however very definitely fixed, for the appointments made by any of their number, or to speak in more accurate language, made by the Crown under the advice of any member of the Cabinet." "The party who for the time being command a majority in the House of Commons, have (in general) a right to have their leaders placed in office." "The most influential of these leaders ought (generally speaking) to be the Premier, or head of the Cabinet." These are precepts referring to the position and formation of the Cabinet. It is, however, easy to find constitutional maxims dealing with other topics. "Treaties can be made without the necessity for any Act of Parliament; but the Crown, or in reality the Ministry representing the Crown, ought not to make any treaty which will not command the approbation of Parliament." "The foreign policy of the country, the proclamation of war, and the making of peace ought to be left in the hands of the Crown, or in truth of the Crown's servants. But in foreign as in domestic affairs, the wish of the two Houses of Parliament or (when they differ) of the House of Commons ought to be followed." "The action of any Ministry would be highly unconstitutional if it should involve the proclamation of war, or the making of peace, in defiance of the wishes of the House." "If there is a difference of opinion between the House of Lords and the House of Commons, the House of Lords ought, at some point, not definitely fixed, to give way, and should the Peers not yield, and the House of Commons continue to enjoy the confidence of the country, it becomes the duty of the Crown, or of

Part III.

its responsible advisers, to create or to threaten to create enough new Peers to override the opposition of the House of Lords, and thus restore harmony between the two branches of the legislature."[1] "Parliament ought to be summoned for the despatch of business at least once in every year." "If a sudden emergency arise, *e.g.* through the outbreak of an insurrection, or an invasion by a foreign power, the Ministry ought, if they require additional authority, at once to have Parliament convened and obtain any powers which they may need for the protection of the country. Meanwhile Ministers ought to take every step, even at the peril of breaking the law, which is necessary either for restoring order or for repelling attack, and (if the law of the land is violated) must rely for protection on Parliament passing an Act of Indemnity."

Common characteristic of constitutional understandings.

These rules (which I have purposely expressed in a lax and popular manner), and a lot more of the same kind, make up the constitutional morality of the day. They are all constantly acted upon, and, since they cannot be enforced by any court of law, have no claim to be considered laws. They are multifarious, differing, as it might at first sight appear, from each other not only in importance but in general character and scope. They will be found however, on careful examination, to possess one common quality or property; they are all, or at any rate most of them, rules for determining the mode in which the discretionary powers of the Crown (or of the Ministers as servants of the Crown)

[1] It is doubtful if this convention has survived the Parliament Acts, 1911 and 1949, and the Life Peerages Act, 1958; see Intro. p. clxxiii, *ante*.

Chapter XIV.

ought to be exercised;[1] and this characteristic will be found on examination to be the trait common not only to all the rules already enumerated, but to by far the greater part (though not quite to the whole) of the conventions of the constitution. This matter, however, requires for its proper understanding some further explanation.

Constitutional conventions are mainly rules for governing exercise of prerogative.

The discretionary powers of the government mean every kind of action which can legally be taken by the Crown, or by its servants, without the necessity for applying to Parliament for new statutory authority. Thus no statute is required to enable the Crown to dissolve or to convoke Parliament, to make peace or war, to create new Peers, to dismiss a Minister from office or to appoint his successor. The doing of all these things lies legally at any rate within the discretion of the Crown; they belong therefore to the discretionary authority of the government. This authority may no doubt originate in Parliamentary enactments, and, in a limited number of cases, actually does so originate.[2] Thus the British Nationality and Status of Aliens Act, 1914, gives to a Secretary of State the right under certain circumstances to convert an alien into a naturalised British subject; and the Extradition Act, 1870, enables a

[1] They go further and provide for the whole working of the complicated government machine. Nowadays the majority of Ministers are concerned with statutory functions; the exceptions include, however, the Prime Minister, the Secretaries of State, and the First Lord of the Admiralty. But much of the work of the Home Secretary and the Secretary of State for Scotland is statutory. See Jennings, *The Law and the Constitution* (4th ed., 1952), pp. 86-88.—Ed.

[2] In 1958 the greater part of this authority is statutory. See Intro. p. cxvii, *ante*.—Ed.

Part III.

Secretary of State (under conditions provided by the Act) to override the ordinary law of the land and hand over a foreigner to his own government for trial. With the exercise, however, of such discretion as is conferred on the Crown or its servants by Parliamentary enactments we need hardly concern ourselves. The mode in which such discretion is to be exercised is, or may be, more or less clearly defined by the Act itself, and is often so closely limited as in reality to become the subject of legal decision, and thus pass from the domain of constitutional morality into that of law properly so called. The discretionary authority of the Crown originates generally, not in Act of Parliament, but in the prerogative—a term which has caused more perplexity to students than any other expression referring to the constitution. The prerogative appears to be both historically and as a matter of actual fact nothing else than the residue of discretionary or arbitrary authority, which at any given time is legally left in the hands of the Crown.[1] The King was originally in truth what he still is in name, the sovereign, or, if not strictly the sovereign in the sense in which jurists use that word, at any rate by far the most powerful part of the sovereign power. In 1791 the House of Commons compelled the government of the day, a good deal against the will of Ministers, to put on trial Mr. Reeves, the learned author of the *History of English Law*, for the expression of opinions meant to exalt the prerogative of the Crown at the expense of the authority of the House of

[1] Cited by Lord Dunedin in *Attorney-General* v. *De Keyser's Royal Hotel Ltd.* [1920] A.C. 508, at p. 526; K. & L. 86.

Commons. Among other statements for the publication of which he was indicted, was a lengthy comparison of the Crown to the trunk, and the other parts of the constitution to the branches and leaves of a great tree. This comparison was made with the object of drawing from it the conclusion that the Crown was the source of all legal power, and that while to destroy the authority of the Crown was to cut down the noble oak under the cover of which Englishmen sought refuge from the storms of Jacobinism, the House of Commons and other institutions were but branches and leaves which might be lopped off without serious damage to the tree.[1] The publication of Mr. Reeves's theories during a period of popular excitement may have been injudicious. But a jury, one is happy to know, found that it was not seditious; for his views undoubtedly rested on a sound basis of historical fact.

The power of the Crown was in truth anterior to that of the House of Commons. From the time of the Norman Conquest down to the Revolution of 1688, the Crown possessed in reality many of the attributes of sovereignty. The prerogative is the name for the remaining portion of the Crown's original authority, and is therefore, as already pointed out, the name for the residue of discretionary power left at any moment in the hands of the Crown, whether such power be in fact exercised by the Queen herself or by her Ministers. Every act which the executive government can lawfully do without the authority of the Act of Parliament is done in virtue of this prerogative. If therefore we omit from view (as

[1] See (1796) 29 St. Tr., at pp. 530-534.

Part III. we conveniently may do) powers conferred on the Crown or its servants by Parliamentary enactments, as for example under an Aliens Act, we may use the term "prerogative" as equivalent to the discretionary authority of the executive, and then lay down that the conventions of the constitution are in the main precepts for determining the mode and spirit in which the prerogative is to be exercised, or (what is really the same thing) for fixing the manner in which any transaction which can legally be done in virtue of the Royal prerogative (such as the making of war or the declaration of peace) ought to be carried out. This statement holds good, it should be noted, of all the discretionary powers exercised by the executive, otherwise than under statutory authority; it applies to acts really done by the Queen herself in accordance with her personal wishes, to transactions (which are of more frequent occurrence than modern constitutionalists are disposed to admit) in which both the Queen and her Ministers take a real part, and also to that large and constantly increasing number of proceedings which, though carried out in the Queen's name, are in truth wholly the acts of the Ministry. The conventions of the constitution are in short rules intended to regulate the exercise of the whole of the remaining discretionary powers of the Crown, whether these powers are exercised by the Queen herself or by the Ministry. That this is so may be seen by the ease and the technical correctness with which such conventions may be expressed in the form of regulations in reference to the exercise of the prerogative. Thus, to say that a Cabinet when outvoted on any vital question are bound in general to retire from office, is equivalent to the assertion, that the prerogative of the Crown to dismiss its servants at the will of the Queen must be exercised in accordance with the wish of the Houses of Parliament; the statement that Ministers ought not to make any treaty which will not command the approbation of the Houses of Parliament,[1] means that the prerogative of the Crown in regard to the making of treaties—what the Americans call the "treaty-making power"—ought not to be exercised in opposition to the will of Parliament. So, again, the rule that Parliament must meet at least once a year, is in fact the rule that the Crown's legal right or prerogative to call Parliament together at the Queen's pleasure must be so exercised that Parliament meet once a year.

Some constitutional conventions refer to exercise of Parliamentary privilege.

This analysis of constitutional understandings is open to the one valid criticism, that, though true as far as it goes, it is obviously incomplete; for there are some few constitutional customs or habits which have no reference to the exercise of the royal power. Such, for example, is the understanding—a very vague one at best—that in case of a permanent conflict between the will of the House of Commons and the will of the House of Lords the Peers must at some point give way to the Lower House.[2] Such, again, is, or at any rate was, the practice by which the judicial functions of the House of Lords are discharged solely by the Law Lords, or the understanding under which Divorce Acts were treated as judicial and not as legislative proceedings.[3] Habits such as

[1] In practice it is perhaps the House of Commons only. This was the view first taken by the Labour Government, 1929–31.—Ed.

[2] See now Parliament Acts, 1911 and 1949. Intro. pp. clxix *et seq.*, *ante*.

[3] Divorce Bills are now unnecessary; before the establishment of

Part III.

these are at bottom customs or rules meant to determine the mode in which one or other or both of the Houses of Parliament shall exercise their discretionary powers, or, to use the historical term, their privileges.[1] The very use of the word privilege is almost enough to show us how to embrace all the conventions of the constitution under one general head. Between prerogative and privilege there exists a close analogy: the one is the historical name for the discretionary authority of the Crown; the other is the historical name for the discretionary authority of each House of Parliament. Understandings then which regulate the exercise of the prerogative determine, or are meant to determine, the way in which one member of the sovereign body, namely the Crown, should exercise its discretionary authority; understandings which regulate the exercise of privilege determine, or are meant to determine, the way in which the other members of the sovereign body should each exercise their discretionary authority. The result follows, that the conventions of the constitution, looked at as a whole, are customs, or understandings, as to the mode in which the several members of the sovereign legislative body, which, as it will be remembered, is the "Queen in Parliament,"[2] should each exercise their discretionary authority, whether

the Irish Free State in 1922 they were used by persons domiciled in Ireland who were thus excluded from the jurisdiction of the English High Court in matrimonial causes.—Ed.

[1] There are many other rules to be included in the law and custom of Parliament. The privileges, for example, are enforced by each House of the High Court of Parliament, as by a court of law.—Ed.

[2] See p. 39, *ante*.

it be termed the prerogative of the Crown or the privileges of Parliament. Since, however, by far the most numerous and important of our constitutional understandings refer at bottom to the exercise of the prerogative, it will conduce to brevity and clearness if we treat the conventions of the constitution, as rules or customs determining the mode in which the discretionary power of the executive, or in technical language the prerogative, ought (*i.e.* is expected by the nation) to be employed.

Aim of constitutional understandings.

Having ascertained that the conventions of the constitution are (in the main) rules for determining the exercise of the prerogative, we may carry our analysis of their character a step farther. They have all one ultimate object. Their end is to secure that Parliament, or the Cabinet which is indirectly appointed by Parliament, shall in the long run give effect to the will of that power which in modern England is the true political sovereign of the State—the majority of the electors or (to use popular though not quite accurate language) the nation.

At this point comes into view the full importance of the distinction already insisted upon [1] between legal sovereignty and political sovereignty. Parliament is, from a merely legal point of view, the absolute sovereign of the British Empire, since every Act of Parliament is binding on every court throughout the British dominions, and no rule, whether of morality or of law, which contravenes an Act of Parliament, binds any court throughout the realm.[2] But if Parliament be in the eye of the law a supreme legislature, the essence of representative government

[1] See pp. 70-76, *ante*. [2] See Intro. pp. lxxxiii *et seq.*, *ante*.

is, that the legislature should represent or give effect to the will of the political sovereign, *i.e.* of the electoral body, or of the nation. That the conduct of the different parts of the legislature should be determined by rules meant to secure harmony between the action of the legislative sovereign and the wishes of the political sovereign, must appear probable from general considerations. If the true ruler or political sovereign of England were, as was once the case, the King, legislation might be carried out in accordance with the King's will by one of two methods. The Crown might itself legislate, by royal proclamations, or decrees; or some other body, such as a *Conseil d'Etat* or Parliament itself, might be allowed to legislate as long as this body conformed to the will of the Crown. If the first plan were adopted, there would be no room or need for constitutional conventions. If the second plan were adopted, the proceedings of the legislative body must inevitably be governed by some rules meant to make certain that the Acts of the legislature should not contravene the will of the Crown. The electorate is in fact the sovereign of England. It is a body which does not, and from its nature hardly can, itself legislate, and which, owing chiefly to historical causes, has left in existence a theoretically supreme legislature. The result of this state of things would naturally be that the conduct of the legislature, which (*ex hypothesi*) cannot be governed by laws, should be regulated by understandings of which the object is to secure the conformity of Parliament to the will of the nation. And this is what has actually occurred. The conventions of the constitution now consist of customs which (whatever their historical origin) are at the present day maintained for the sake of ensuring the supremacy of the House of Commons, and ultimately, through the elective House of Commons, of the nation. Our modern code of constitutional morality secures, though in a roundabout way, what is called abroad the "sovereignty of the people."

That this is so becomes apparent if we examine into the effect of one or two among the leading articles of this code. The rule that the powers of the Crown must be exercised through Ministers who are members of one or other House of Parliament and who "command the confidence of the House of Commons," really means, that the elective portion of the legislature in effect, though by an indirect process, appoints the executive government; and, further, that the Crown, or the Ministry, must ultimately carry out, or at any rate not contravene, the wishes of the House of Commons. But as the process of representation is nothing else than a mode by which the will of the representative body or House of Commons is made to coincide with the will of the nation, it follows that a rule which gives the appointment and control of the government mainly to the House of Commons is at bottom a rule which gives the election and ultimate control of the executive to the nation. The same thing holds good of the understanding, or habit, in accordance with which the House of Lords are expected in every serious political controversy to give way at some point or other to the will of the House of Commons as expressing the deliberate resolve of the nation, or of that further custom which, though of comparatively recent growth, forms an essential article of modern constitutional

Part III.

ethics, by which, in case the Peers should finally refuse to acquiesce in the decision of the Lower House, the Crown is expected to nullify the resistance of the Lords by the creation of new peerages.[1] How, it may be said, is the point to be fixed at which, in case of a conflict between the two Houses, the Lords must give way, or the Crown ought to use its prerogative in the creation of new Peers? The question is worth raising, because the answer throws great light upon the nature and aim of the articles which make up our conventional code. This reply is, that the point at which the Lords must yield or the Crown intervene is properly determined by anything which conclusively shows that the House of Commons represents on the matter in dispute the deliberate decision of the nation. The truth of this reply will hardly be questioned, but to admit that the deliberate decision of the electorate is decisive, is in fact to concede that the understandings as to the action of the House of Lords and of the Crown are, what we have found them to be, rules meant to ensure the ultimate supremacy of the true political sovereign, or, in other words, of the electoral body.[2]

Rules as to dissolution of Parliament.

By far the most striking example of the real sense attaching to a whole mass of constitutional conventions is found in a particular instance, which appears at first sight to present a marked exception to the general principles of constitutional morality. A Ministry placed in a minority by a vote of the Commons have, in accordance with received doctrines,

[1] Hearn denied, on inadequate grounds as it seemed to the author, the existence of this rule or understanding. See Hearn, *op. cit.*, p. 178.

[2] Cf. Bagehot, *English Constitution* (1872 ed.), pp. 25-27.

a right to demand a dissolution of Parliament. On the other hand, there are certainly combinations of circumstances under which the Crown has a right to dismiss a Ministry who command a Parliamentary majority, and to dissolve the Parliament by which the Ministry are supported.[1] The prerogative, in short, of dissolution may constitutionally be so employed as to override the will of the representative body, or, as it is popularly called, "The People's House of Parliament." This looks at first sight like saying that in certain cases the prerogative can be so used as to set at nought the will of the nation. But in reality it is far otherwise. The discretionary power of the Crown occasionally may be, and according to constitutional precedents sometimes ought to be, used to strip an existing House of Commons of its authority. But the reason why the House can in accordance with the constitution be deprived of power and of existence is that an occasion has arisen on which there is fair reason to suppose that the opinion of the House is not the opinion of the electors. A dissolution is in its essence an appeal from the legal to the political sovereign. A dissolution is allowable, or necessary, whenever the wishes of the legislature are, or may fairly be presumed to be, different from the wishes of the nation.

Chapter XIV.

The dissolutions of 1784 and 1834.

This is the doctrine established by the celebrated contests of 1784 and of 1834. In each instance the King dismissed a Ministry which commanded the confidence of the House of Commons. In each case there was an appeal to the country by means of a

[1] See Jennings, *Cabinet Government* (3rd ed., 1959), pp. 412-428; Evatt, *The King and his Dominion Governors* (1936), ch. ix-xii, xx.

Part III. dissolution. In 1784 the appeal resulted in a decisive verdict in favour of Pitt and his colleagues, who had been brought into office by the King against the will of the House of Commons. In 1834 the appeal led to a verdict equally decisive against Peel and Wellington, who also had been called to office by the Crown against the wishes of the House. The essential point to notice is that these contests each in effect admit the principle that it is the verdict of the political sovereign which ultimately determines the right or (what in politics is much the same thing) the power of a Cabinet to retain office, namely, the nation.

Much discussion, oratorical and literary, has been expended on the question whether the dissolution of 1784 or the dissolution of 1834 was constitutional.[1] To a certain extent the dispute is verbal, and depends upon the meaning of the word "constitutional." If we mean by it "legal," no human being can dispute that George the Third and his son could without any breach of law dissolve Parliament. If we mean "usual," no one can deny that each monarch took a very unusual step in dismissing a Ministry which commanded a majority in the House of Commons. If by "constitutional" we mean "in conformity with the fundamental principles of the constitution," we must without hesitation pronounce the conduct of George the Third constitutional, *i.e.* in conformity with the principles of the constitution as they are now understood. He believed that the nation did not approve of the policy pursued by the House of Com-

[1] See Emden, *The People and the Constitution* (2nd ed., 1956), pp. 194-196, 197-201.—Ed.

mons. He was right in this belief. No modern constitutionalist will dispute that the authority of the House of Commons is derived from its representing the will of the nation, and that the chief object of a dissolution is to ascertain that the will of Parliament coincides with the will of the nation. George the Third then made use of the prerogative of dissolution for the very purpose for which it exists. His conduct, therefore, on the modern theory of the constitution, was, as far as the dissolution went, in the strictest sense constitutional. But it is doubtful whether in 1784 the King's conduct was not in reality an innovation, though a salutary one, on the then prevailing doctrine. Any one who studies the questions connected with the name of John Wilkes, or the disputes between England and the American colonies, will see that George the Third and the great majority of George the Third's statesmen maintained up to 1784 a view of Parliamentary sovereignty which made Parliament in the strictest sense the sovereign power. To this theory Fox clung, both in his youth as a Tory and in his later life as a Whig. The greatness of Chatham and of his son lay in their perceiving that behind the Crown, behind the Revolution Families, behind Parliament itself, lay what Chatham calls the "great public," and what we should call the nation, and that on the will of the nation depended the authority of Parliament. In 1784 George the Third was led by the exigencies of the moment to adopt the attitude of Chatham and Pitt. He appealed (oddly enough) from the sovereignty of Parliament, of which he had always been the ardent champion, to that sovereignty of the people which he never ceased to hold in abhorrence. Whether this appeal be termed constitutional or revolutionary is now of little moment; it affirmed decisively the fundamental principle of our existing constitution that not Parliament but the nation is, politically speaking, the supreme power in the State. On this very ground the so-called "penal" dissolution was consistently enough denounced by Burke, who at all periods of his career was opposed to democratic innovation, and far less consistently by Fox, who blended in his political creed doctrines of absolute Parliamentary sovereignty with the essentially inconsistent dogma of the sovereignty of the people.

Of William the Fourth's action it is hard to speak with decision. The dissolution of 1834 was, from a constitutional point of view, a mistake; it was justified (if at all) by the King's belief that the House of Commons did not represent the will of the nation. The belief itself turned out erroneous, but the large minority obtained by Peel, and the rapid decline in the influence of the Whigs, proved that, though the King had formed a wrong estimate of public sentiment, he was not without reasonable ground for believing that Parliament had ceased to represent the opinion of the nation. Now if it be constitutionally right for the Crown to appeal from Parliament to the electors when the House of Commons has in reality ceased to represent its constituents, there is great difficulty in maintaining that a dissolution is unconstitutional simply because the electors do, when appealed to, support the opinions of their representatives. Admit that the electors are the political sovereign of the State, and the result appears naturally to follow, that an appeal to them by means of a dissolution is constitutional, whenever there is valid and reasonable ground for supposing that their Parliamentary representatives have ceased to represent their wishes. The constitutionality therefore of the dissolution in 1834 turns at bottom upon the still disputable question of fact, whether the King and his advisers had reasonable ground for supposing that the reformed House of Commons had lost the confidence of the nation. Whatever may be the answer given by historians to this inquiry, the precedents of 1784 and 1834 are decisive; they determine the principle on which the prerogative of dissolution ought to be exercised, and show that in modern times the rules as to the dissolution of Parliament are, like other conventions of the constitution, intended to secure the ultimate supremacy of the electorate as the true political sovereign of the State; that, in short, the validity of constitutional maxims is subordinate and subservient to the fundamental principle of popular sovereignty.[1]

Relation of right of dissolution to Parliamentary sovereignty.

The necessity for dissolutions stands in close connection with the existence of Parliamentary sovereignty. Where, as in the United States, no legislative assembly is a sovereign power, the right of dissolution may be dispensed with; the constitution provides security that no change of vital importance can be effected without an appeal to the people; and the change in the character of a legislative body by the re-election of the whole or of part thereof at stated periods makes it certain that in

[1] Cf. Jennings, *Cabinet Government* (3rd ed., 1959), pp. 412-428.

Part III.

the long run the sentiment of the legislature will harmonise with the feeling of the public. Where Parliament is supreme, some further security for such harmony is necessary, and this security is given by the right of dissolution, which enables the Crown or the Ministry to appeal from the legislature to the nation. The security indeed is not absolutely complete. Crown, Cabinet, and Parliament may conceivably favour constitutional innovations which do not approve themselves to the electors. The Septennial Act could hardly have been passed in England, the Act of Union with Ireland would not, it is often asserted, have been passed by the Irish Parliament, if, in either instance, a legal revolution had been necessarily preceded by an appeal to the electorate. Here, as elsewhere, the constitutionalism of America proves of a more rigid type than the constitutionalism of England. Still, under the conditions of modern political life, the understandings which exist with us as to the right of dissolution afford nearly, if not quite, as much security for sympathy between the action of the legislature and the will of the people, as do the limitations placed on legislative power by the constitutions of American States. In this instance, as in others, the principles explicitly stated in the various constitutions of the States, and in the Federal Constitution itself, are impliedly involved in the working of English political institutions. The right of dissolution is the right of appeal to the people, and thus underlies all those constitutional conventions which, in one way or another, are intended to produce harmony between the legal and the political sovereign power.

CHAPTER XV

THE SANCTION BY WHICH THE CONVENTIONS OF THE CONSTITUTION ARE ENFORCED

Chapter XV.

WHAT is the sanction by which obedience to the conventions of the constitution is at bottom enforced?

The problem to be solved.

This is by far the most perplexing of the speculative questions suggested by a study of constitutional law. Let us bear in mind the dictum of Paley, that it is often far harder to make men see the existence of a difficulty, than to make them, when once the difficulty is perceived, understand its explanation, and in the first place try to make clear to ourselves what is the precise nature of a puzzle of which most students dimly recognise the existence.

Constitutional understandings are admittedly not laws; they are not (that is to say) rules which will be enforced by the courts. If a Premier were to retain office after a vote of censure passed by the House of Commons, if he were (as did Lord Palmerston under like circumstances) to dissolve, or strictly speaking to get the Crown to dissolve, Parliament, but, unlike Lord Palmerston, were to be again censured by the newly elected House of Commons, and then, after all this had taken place, were still to remain at the head of the government,—no one could deny that such a Prime Minister had acted unconstitutionally. Yet no court of law would take notice of his conduct. Suppose, again, that on the passing by both Houses of an important bill, the Queen should refuse her assent to the measure, or (in popular language) put her "veto" on it. Here there would be a gross violation of usage, but the matter could not by any proceeding known to English law be brought before the judges. Take another instance. Suppose that Parliament were for more than a year not summoned for the despatch of business. This would be a course of proceeding of the most unconstitutional character. Yet there is no court in the land before which one could go with the complaint that Parliament had not been assembled.[1] Still the conventional rules of the constitution, though not laws, are, as it is constantly asserted, nearly if not quite as binding as laws. They are, or appear to be, respected quite as much as most statutory enactments, and more than many. The puzzle is to see what is the force which habitually compels obedience to rules which have not behind them the coercive power of the courts.

Partial answer, that constitutional understandings often disobeyed.

The difficulty of the problem before us cannot indeed be got rid of, but may be shifted and a good deal lessened, by observing that the invariableness of the obedience to constitutional understandings is itself more or less fictitious. The special articles of the conventional code are in fact often

[1] See 4 Edward III. c. 14; 16 Car. II. c. 1; and the Bill of Rights, 1689; cf. the repealed 16 Car. I. c. 1, which would have made the assembling of Parliament a matter of law.

disobeyed. A Minister sometimes refuses to retire when, as his opponents allege, he ought constitutionally to resign office; not many years have passed since the Opposition of the day argued, if not convincingly yet with a good deal of plausibility, that the Ministry had violated a rule embodied in the Bill of Rights; in 1784 the House of Commons maintained, not only by argument but by repeated votes, that Pitt had deliberately defied more than one constitutional precept, and the Whigs of 1834 brought a like charge against Wellington and Peel. Nor is it doubtful that any one who searches through the pages of Hansard will find other instances in which constitutional maxims of long standing and high repute have been set at nought. The uncertain character of the deference paid to the conventions of the constitution is concealed under the current phraseology, which treats the successful violation of a constitutional rule as a proof that the maxim was not in reality part of the constitution. If a habit or precept which can be set at nought is thereby shown not to be a portion of constitutional morality, it naturally follows that no true constitutional rule is ever disobeyed.[1]

Chapter XV.

But principle of conformity to will of the nation always obeyed.

Yet, though the obedience supposed to be rendered to the separate understandings or maxims of public life is to a certain extent fictitious, the assertion that they have nearly the force of law is not without meaning. Some few of the conventions of the constitution are rigorously obeyed. Parliament, for example, is summoned year by year with as much regularity as though its annual meeting were provided for by a law of nature; and (what is of more con-

[1] See Intro. pp. clxxix *et seq.*, *ante*.

sequence) though particular understandings are of uncertain obligation, neither the Crown nor any servant of the Crown ever refuses obedience to the grand principle which, as we have seen, underlies all the conventional precepts of the constitution, namely, that government must be carried on in accordance with the will of the House of Commons, and ultimately with the will of the nation as expressed through that House. This principle is not a law; it is not to be found in the statute-book, nor is it a maxim of the common law; it will not be enforced by any ordinary judicial body. Why then has the principle itself, as also have certain conventions or understandings which are closely connected with it, the force of law? This, when the matter is reduced to its simplest form, is the puzzle with which we have to deal. It sorely needs a solution. Many writers, however, of authority, chiefly because they do not approach the constitution from its legal side, hardly recognise the full force of the difficulty which requires to be disposed of. They either pass it by, or else apparently acquiesce in one of two answers, each of which contains an element of truth, but neither of which fully removes the perplexities of any inquirer who is determined not to be put off with mere words.

Insufficient answers. Impeachment.

A reply more often suggested than formulated in so many words, is that obedience to the conventions of the constitution is ultimately enforced by the fear of impeachment.

If this view were tenable, these conventions, it should be remarked, would not be "understandings" at all, but "laws" in the truest sense of that term, and their sole peculiarity would lie in their being laws the breach of which could be punished only by one extraordinary tribunal, namely, the High Court of Parliament. But though it may well be conceded —and the fact is one of great importance—that the habit of obedience to the constitution was originally generated and confirmed by impeachments, yet there are insuperable difficulties to entertaining the belief that the dread of the Tower and the block exerts any appreciable influence over the conduct of modern statesmen, nor even the fear of civil proceedings or criminal prosecutions. No impeachment for violations of the constitution (since for the present purpose we may leave out of account such proceedings as those taken against Lord Macclesfield, Warren Hastings, and Lord Melville) has occurred for more than a century and a half. The process, which is supposed to ensure the retirement from office of a modern Prime Minister, when placed in a hopeless minority, is, and has long been, obsolete. The arm by which attacks on freedom were once repelled has grown rusty by disuse; it is laid aside among the antiquities of the constitution, nor will it ever, we may anticipate, be drawn again from its scabbard. For, in truth, impeachment, as a means for enforcing the observance of constitutional morality, always laboured under one grave defect. The possibility of its use suggested, if it did not stimulate, one most important violation of political usage; a Minister who dreaded impeachment would, since Parliament was the only court before which he could be impeached, naturally advise the Crown not to convene Parliament. There is something like a contradiction in terms in saying that a Minister is compelled to advise the meeting of Parliament by the dread of impeachment

Part III.

if Parliament should assemble. If the fear of Parliamentary punishment were the only difficulty in the way of violating the constitution, we may be sure that a bold party leader would, at the present day, as has been done in former centuries, sometimes suggest that Parliament should not meet.

Power of public opinion.

A second and current answer to the question under consideration is, that obedience to the conventional precepts of the constitution is ensured by the force of public opinion.

Now that this assertion is in one sense true, stands past dispute. The nation expects that Parliament shall be convened annually; the nation expects that a Minister who cannot retain the confidence of the House of Commons, shall give up his place, and no Premier even dreams of disappointing these expectations. The assertion, therefore, that public opinion gives validity to the received precepts for the conduct of public life is true. Its defect is that, if taken without further explanation, it amounts to little else than a re-statement of the very problem which it is meant to solve. For the question to be answered is, at bottom, Why is it that public opinion is, apparently at least, a sufficient sanction to compel obedience to the conventions of the constitution? and it is no answer to this inquiry to say that these conventions are enforced by public opinion. Let it also be noted that many rules of conduct which are fully supported by the opinion of the public are violated every day of the year. Public opinion enjoins the performance of promises and condemns the commission of crimes, but the settled conviction of the nation that promises ought to be kept does not hinder merchants from going into the *Gazette*, nor does the universal execration of the villain who sheds man's blood prevent the commission of murders. That public opinion does to a certain extent check extravagance and criminality is of course true, but the operation of opinion is in this case assisted by the law, or in the last resort by the physical power at the disposal of the state. The limited effect of public opinion when aided by the police hardly explains the immense effect of opinion in enforcing rules which may be violated without any risk of the offender being brought before the courts. To contend that the understandings of the constitution derive their coercive power solely from the approval of the public, is very like maintaining the kindred doctrine that the conventions of international law are kept alive solely by moral force. Every one, except a few dreamers, perceives that the respect paid to international morality is due in great measure, not to moral force, but to the physical force in the shape of armies and navies, by which the commands of general opinion are in many cases supported; and it is difficult not to suspect that, in England at least, the conventions of the constitution are supported and enforced by something beyond or in addition to the public approval.

True answer,—Obedience to conventions enforced by power of law.

What then is this "something"? My answer is, that it is nothing else than the force of the law. The dread of impeachment may have established, and public opinion certainly adds influence to, the prevailing dogmas of political ethics. But the sanction which constrains the boldest political adventurer to obey the fundamental principles of the constitution and the conventions in which these principles are

Part III.

expressed, is the fact that the breach of these principles and of these conventions will almost immediately bring the offender into conflict with the courts and the law of the land.

This is the true answer to the inquiry which I have raised, but it is an answer which undoubtedly requires both explanation and defence.

Explanation.

The meaning of the statement that the received precepts of the constitution are supported by the law of the land, and the grounds on which that statement is based, can be most easily made apparent by considering what would be the legal results which would inevitably ensue from the violation of some indisputable constitutional maxim.

Yearly meeting of Parliament.

No rule is better established than that Parliament must assemble at least once a year. This maxim, as before pointed out, is certainly not derived from the common law, and is not based upon any statutory enactment. Now suppose that Parliament were prorogued once and again for more than a year, so that for two years no Parliament sat at Westminster. Here we have a distinct breach of a constitutional practice or understanding, but we have no violation of law. What, however, would be the consequences which would ensue? They would be, speaking generally, that any Ministry who at the present day sanctioned or tolerated this violation of the constitution, and every person connected with the government, would immediately come into conflict with the law of the land.

A moment's reflection shows that this would be so. The Army (Annual) Act[1] would in the first place

[1] This Act is no longer required; see p. 295, n. 1, *ante*.

expire. Hence the Army Act,[1] on which the discipline of the army depends, would cease to be in force.[2] But thereupon all means of controlling the army without a breach of law would cease to exist. Either the army must be discharged, in which case the means of maintaining law and order would come to an end, or the army must be kept up and discipline must be maintained without legal authority for its maintenance. If this alternative were adopted, every person, from the Commander-in-Chief downwards, who took part in the control of the army, and indeed every soldier who carried out the commands of his superiors, would find that not a day passed without his committing or sanctioning acts which would render him liable to stand as a criminal in the dock. Then, again, though most of the taxes would still come into the Exchequer, large portions of the revenue would cease to be legally due and could not be legally collected, whilst every official, who acted as collector, would expose himself to actions or prosecutions.[3] The part, moreover, of the revenue which came in, could not be legally applied to the purposes of the government. If the Ministry laid hold of the revenue they would find it difficult to avoid breaches of definite laws which would compel them to appear before the courts. Suppose however that the Cabinet were willing to defy the law. Their criminal daring would not suffice for its purpose; they could not get

[1] Extended to the Air Force by the Air Force (Constitution) Act, 1917, s. 12; see now Air Force Act, 1955.

[2] See p. 295, n. 1, *ante*.

[3] See p. 315, n. 1, *ante*.

hold of the revenue without the connivance or aid of a large number of persons, some of them indeed officials, but some of them, such as the Comptroller General, the Governors of the Bank of England, and the like, unconnected with the administration. None of these officials, it should be noted, could receive from the government or the Crown any protection against legal liability; and any person, *e.g.* the Commander-in-Chief, or the colonel of a regiment, who employed force to carry out the policy of the government would be exposed to resistance supported by the courts. For the law (it should always be borne in mind) operates in two different ways. It inflicts penalties and punishment upon law-breakers, and (what is of equal consequence) it enables law-respecting citizens to refuse obedience to illegal commands. It legalises passive resistance. The efficacy of such legal opposition is immensely increased by the non-existence in England of anything resembling the *droit administratif* of France,[1] or of that wide discretionary authority which is possessed by every continental government. The result is, that an administration which attempted to dispense with the annual meeting of Parliament could not ensure the obedience even of its own officials, and, unless prepared distinctly to violate the undoubted law of the land, would find itself not only opposed but helpless.

The rule, therefore, that Parliament must meet once a year, though in strictness a constitutional convention which is not a law and will not be enforced by the courts, turns out nevertheless to be

[1] See ch. xii, *ante*; cf. App. 1.

an understanding which cannot be neglected without involving hundreds of persons, many of whom are by no means specially amenable to government influence, in distinct acts of illegality cognisable by the tribunals of the country. This convention therefore of the constitution is in reality based upon, and secured by, the law of the land.

This no doubt is a particularly plain case. I have examined it fully, both because it is a particularly plain instance, and because the full understanding of it affords the clue which guides us to the principle on which really rests such coercive force as is possessed by the conventions of the constitution.

Resignation of Ministry which has lost confidence of the House of Commons.

To see that this is so let us consider for a moment the effect of disobedience by the government to one of the most purely conventional among the maxims of constitutional morality,—the rule, that is to say, that a Ministry ought to retire on a vote that they no longer possess the confidence of the House of Commons. Suppose that a Ministry, after the passing of such a vote, were to act at the present day as Pitt acted in 1783, and hold office in the face of the censure passed by the House. There would clearly be a *prima facie* breach of constitutional ethics. What must ensue is clear. If the Ministry wished to keep within the constitution they would announce their intention of appealing to the constituencies, and the House would probably assist in hurrying on a dissolution. All breach of law would be avoided, but the reason of this would be that the conduct of the Cabinet would not be a breach of constitutional morality; for the true rule of the constitution admittedly is, not that a Ministry cannot keep office when censured by the House of Commons, but that under such circumstances a Ministry ought not to remain in office unless they can by an appeal to the country obtain the election of a House which will support the government.[1] Suppose then that, under the circumstances I have imagined, the Ministry either would not recommend a dissolution of Parliament, or, having dissolved Parliament and being again censured by the newly elected House of Commons, would not resign office. It would, under this state of things, be as clear as day that the understandings of the constitution had been violated. It is however equally clear that the House would have in their own hands the means of ultimately forcing the Ministry either to respect the constitution or to violate the law. Sooner or later the moment would come for passing the Army (Annual) Act or the Appropriation Act, and the House by refusing to pass either of these enactments would involve the Ministry in all the inextricable embarrassments which (as I have already pointed out) immediately follow upon the omission to convene Parliament for more than a year.[2] The breach, therefore, of a purely conventional rule, of a maxim utterly unknown and indeed opposed to the theory of English law, ultimately entails upon those who break it direct conflict with the undoubted law of the land. We have then a right to assert that the force which in

[1] See Jennings, *Cabinet Government* (3rd ed., 1959), p. 420.

[2] Until the Annual Act became unnecessary (p. 295, n. 1, *ante*), it was passed in April and the Appropriation Act, as now, at the end of July. Therefore a Ministry could remain in office from August to April without breaking the law in this respect, if it suffered defeat during the period.

the last resort compels obedience to constitutional morality is nothing else than the power of the law itself. The conventions of the constitution are not laws, but, in so far as they really possess binding force, derive their sanction from the fact that whoever breaks them must finally break the law and incur the penalties of a law-breaker.

Objections.

It is worth while to consider one or two objections which may be urged with more or less plausibility against the doctrine that the obligatory force of constitutional morality is derived from the law itself.

Law may be overpowered by force.

The government, it is sometimes suggested, may by the use of actual force carry through a *coup d'état* and defy the law of the land.

This suggestion is true, but is quite irrelevant. No constitution can be absolutely safe from revolution or from a *coup d'état;* but to show that the laws may be defied by violence does not touch or invalidate the statement that the understandings of the constitution are based upon the law. They have certainly no more force than the law itself. A Minister who, like the French President in 1851, could override the law could of course overthrow the constitution. The theory propounded aims only at proving that when constitutional understandings have nearly the force of law they derive their power from the fact that they cannot be broken without a breach of law. No one is concerned to show, what indeed never can be shown, that the law can never be defied, or the constitution never be overthrown.

It should further be observed that the admitted sovereignty of Parliament tends to prevent violent attacks on the constitution. Revolutionists or conspirators generally believe themselves to be supported by the majority of the nation, and, when they succeed, this belief is in general well founded. But in modern England, a party, however violent, who count on the sympathy of the people, can accomplish by obtaining a Parliamentary majority all that could be gained by the success of a revolution. When a spirit of reaction or of innovation prevails throughout the country, a reactionary or revolutionary policy is enforced by Parliament without any party needing to make use of violence. The oppressive legislation of the Restoration in the seventeenth century, and the anti-revolutionary legislation of the Tories from the outbreak of the Revolution till the end of George the Third's reign, saved the constitution from attack. A change of spirit averted a change of form; the flexibility of the constitution proved its strength.

Parliament has never refused to pass Mutiny Act.

If the maintenance of political morality, it may with some plausibility be asked, really depends on the right of Parliament to refuse to pass laws such as the Army (Annual) Act, which are necessary for the maintenance of order, and indeed for the very existence of society, how does it happen that no English Parliament has ever employed this extreme method of enforcing obedience to the constitution?

The true answer to the objection thus raised appears to be that the observance of the main and the most essential of all constitutional rules, the rule, that is to say, requiring the annual meeting of Parliament, is ensured, without any necessity for Parliamentary action, by the temporary character of the Mutiny Act, and that the power of Parliament to compel obedience to its wishes by refusing to pass the Act is so complete that the mere existence of the power has made its use unnecessary. In matter of fact, no Ministry has since the Revolution of 1689 ever defied the House of Commons, unless the Cabinet could confide in the support of the country, or, in other words, could count on the election of a House which would support the policy of the government. To this we must add, that in the rare instances in which a Minister has defied the House, the refusal to pass the Mutiny Act has been threatened or contemplated. Pitt's victory over the Coalition is constantly cited as a proof that Parliament cannot refuse to grant supplies or to pass an Act necessary for the discipline of the army. Yet any one who studies with care the great "Case of the Coalition" will see that it does not support the dogma for which it is quoted. Fox and his friends did threaten and did intend to press to the very utmost all the legal powers of the House of Commons. They failed to carry out their intention solely because they at last perceived that the majority of the House did not represent the will of the country. What the "leading case" shows is, that the Cabinet, when supported by the Crown, and therefore possessing the power of dissolution, can defy the will of a House of Commons if the House is not supported by the electors. Here we come round to the fundamental dogma of modern constitutionalism; the legal sovereignty of Parliament is subordinate to the political sovereignty of the nation. This the conclusion in reality established by the events of 1784. Pitt over-

Part III.

rode the customs, because he adhered to the principles, of the constitution. He broke through the received constitutional understandings without damage to his power or reputation; he might in all probability have in case of necessity broken the law itself with impunity. For had the Coalition pressed their legal rights to an extreme length, the new Parliament of 1784 would in all likelihood have passed an Act of Indemnity for illegalities necessitated, or excused, by the attempt of an unpopular faction to drive from power a Minister supported by the Crown, by the Peers, and by the nation. However this may be, the celebrated conflict between Pitt and Fox lends no countenance to the idea that a House of Commons supported by the country would not enforce the morality of the constitution by placing before any Minister who defied its precepts the alternative of resignation or revolution.[1]

Subordinate inquiries.

A clear perception of the true relation between the conventions of the constitution and the law of the land supplies an answer to more than one subordinate question which has perplexed students and commentators.

Why has impeachment gone out of use?

How is it that the ancient methods of enforcing Parliamentary authority, such as impeachment, the formal refusal of supplies, and the like, have fallen into disuse?

The answer is, that they are disused because ultimate obedience to the underlying principle of all

[1] It is further not the case that the idea of refusing supplies is unknown to modern statesmen. In 1868 such refusal was threatened in order to force an early dissolution of Parliament; in 1886 the dissolution took place before the supplies were fully granted, and the supplies granted were granted for only a limited period.

modern constitutionalism, which is nothing else than the principle of obedience to the will of the nation as expressed through Parliament, is so closely bound up with the law of the land that it can hardly be violated without a breach of the ordinary law. Hence the extraordinary remedies, which were once necessary for enforcing the deliberate will of the nation, having become unnecessary, have fallen into desuetude. If they are not altogether abolished, the cause lies partly in the conservatism of the English people, and partly in the valid consideration that crimes may still be occasionally committed for which the ordinary law of the land hardly affords due punishment, and which therefore may well be dealt with by the High Court of Parliament.

Why are constitutional understandings variable?

Why is it that the understandings of the constitution have about them a singular element of vagueness and variability?

Why is it, to take definite instances of this uncertainty and changeableness, that no one can define with absolute precision the circumstances under which a Prime Minister ought to retire from office? Why is it that no one can fix the exact point at which resistance of the House of Lords to the will of the House of Commons becomes unconstitutional? and how does it happen that the Peers could at one time arrest legislation in a way which now would be generally held to involve a distinct breach of constitutional morality? What is the reason why no one can describe with precision the limits to the influence on the conduct of public affairs which may rightly be exerted by the reigning monarch? and how does it happen that George the Third and even George the

Part III. Fourth each made his personal will or caprice tell on the policy of the nation in a very different way and degree from that in which Queen Victoria ever attempted to exercise personal influence over matters of State?

The answer in general terms to these and the like inquiries is, that the one essential principle of the constitution is obedience by all persons to the deliberately expressed will of the House of Commons in the first instance, and ultimately to the will of the nation as expressed through Parliament. The conventional code of political morality is, as already pointed out, merely a body of maxims meant to secure respect for this principle. Of these maxims some indeed—such, for example, as the rule that Parliament must be convoked at least once a year—are so closely connected with the respect due to Parliamentary or national authority, that they will never be neglected by any one who is not prepared to play the part of a revolutionist; such rules have received the undoubted stamp of national approval, and their observance is secured by the fact that whoever breaks or aids in breaking them will almost immediately find himself involved in a breach of law. Other constitutional maxims stand in a very different position. Their maintenance up to a certain point tends to secure the supremacy of Parliament, but they are themselves vague, and no one can say to what extent the will of Parliament or the nation requires their rigid observance; they therefore obtain only a varying and indefinite amount of obedience.

Thus the rule that a Ministry who have lost the confidence of the House of Commons should retire

Chapter XV.

With-drawal of confidence by House of Commons.

from office is plain enough, and any permanent neglect of the spirit of this rule would be absolutely inconsistent with Parliamentary government, and would finally involve the Minister who broke the rule in acts of undoubted illegality. But when you come to inquire what are the signs by which you are to know that the House has withdrawn its confidence from a Ministry,—whether, for example, the defeat of an important Ministerial measure or the smallness of a Ministerial majority is a certain proof that a Ministry ought to retire,—you ask a question which admits of no absolute reply.[1] All that can be said is, that a Cabinet ought not to continue in power (subject, of course, to the one exception on which I have before dwelt [2]) after the expression by the House of Commons of a wish for the Cabinet's retirement. Of course, therefore, a Minister or a Ministry must resign if the House passes a vote of want of confidence. There are, however, a hundred signs of Parliamentary disapproval which, according to circumstances, either may or may not be a sufficient notice that a Minister ought to give up office. The essential thing is that the Ministry should obey the House as representing the nation. But the question whether the House of Commons has or has not indirectly intimated its will that a Cabinet should give up office is not a matter as to which any definite principle can be

[1] See Hearn, *Government of England* (2nd ed., 1887), ch. ix, for an attempt to determine the circumstances under which a Ministry ought or ought not to keep office. See debate in House of Commons of 24th July, 1905, for consideration of, and reference to, precedents with regard to the duty of a Ministry to retire from office when they have lost the confidence of the House of Commons.—*Parl. Deb., H. of C.*, 4th ser., vol. 150, col. 50.

[2] See pp. 432-438, *ante*.

Part III.

laid down. The difficulty which now exists, in settling the point at which a Premier and his colleagues are bound to hold that they have lost the confidence of the House, is exactly analogous to the difficulty which often perplexed statesmen of the 18th century, of determining the point at which a Minister was bound to hold he had lost the then essential confidence of the King. The ridiculous efforts of the Duke of Newcastle to remain at the head of the Treasury, in spite of the broadest hints from Lord Bute that the time had come for resignation, are exactly analogous to the undignified persistency with which later Cabinets have occasionally clung to office in the face of intimations that the House desired a change of government. As long as a master does not directly dismiss a servant, the question whether the employer's conduct betrays a wish that the servant should give notice must be an inquiry giving rise to doubt and discussion. And if there be sometimes a difficulty in determining what is the will of Parliament, it must often of necessity be still more difficult to determine what is the will of the nation, or, in other words, of the majority of the electors.

When House of Lords should give way to Commons.

The general rule that the House of Lords must in matters of legislation ultimately give way to the House of Commons is one of the best-established maxims of modern constitutional ethics. But if any inquirer asks how the point at which the Peers are to give way is to be determined, no answer which even approximates to the truth can be given, except the very vague reply that the Upper House must give way whenever it is clearly proved that the will of the House of Commons represents the deliberate will of the nation. The nature of the proof differs under different circumstances.[1]

When once the true state of the case is perceived, it is easy to understand a matter which, on any cut-and-dried theory of the constitution, can only with difficulty be explained, namely, the relation occupied by modern Cabinets towards the House of Lords. It is certain that for more than half a century Ministries have constantly existed which did not command the confidence of the Upper House, and that such Ministries have, without meeting much opposition on the part of the Peers, in the main carried out a policy of which the Peers did not approve.[2] It is also certain that while the Peers have been forced to pass many bills which they disliked, they have often exercised large though very varying control over the course of legislation. Between 1834 and 1840 the Upper House, under the guidance of Lord Lyndhurst, repeatedly and with success opposed Ministerial measures which had passed the House of Commons. For many years Jews were kept out of Parliament simply because the Lords were not prepared to admit them. If you search for the real cause of this state of things, you will find that it was nothing else than the fact, constantly concealed under the misleading rhetoric of party warfare, that on the matters in question the electors were not prepared to support the Cabinet in taking the steps necessary to compel the submission of the House of Lords. On any matter upon which the electors are firmly resolved, a Premier, who is in

[1] See Intro. pp. clxix, *et seq.*, *ante*.

[2] And also from 1906 to 1914, in 1924, from 1929–31 and from 1945–51.

Part III. effect the representative of the House of Commons, has the means of coercion, namely, by the creation of Peers. In a country indeed like England, things are rarely carried to this extreme length. The knowledge that a power can be exercised constantly prevents its being actually put in force. This is so even in private life; most men pay their debts without being driven into court, but it were absurd to suppose that the possible compulsion of the courts and the sheriff has not a good deal to do with regularity in the payment of debts. The acquiescence of the Peers in measures which the Peers do not approve arises at bottom from the fact that the nation, under the present constitution, possesses the power of enforcing, through very cumbersome machinery, the submission of the Peers to the conventional rule that the wishes of the House of Lords must finally give way to the decisions of the House of Commons. But the rule itself is vague, and the degree of obedience which it obtains is varying, because the will of the nation is often not clearly expressed, and further, in this as in other matters, is itself liable to variation. If the smoothness with which the constitutional arrangements of modern England work should, as it often does, conceal from us the force by which the machinery of the constitution is kept working, we may with advantage consult the experience of English colonies. No better example can be given of the methods by which a Representative Chamber attempts in the last resort to compel the obedience of an Upper House than is afforded by the varying phases of the conflict which raged in Victoria during 1878 and 1879 between the two Houses of the Legislature. There the Lower House attempted to enforce upon the Council the passing of measures which the Upper House did not approve, by, in effect, inserting the substance of a rejected bill in the Appropriation Bill. The Council in turn threw out the Appropriation Bill. The Ministry thereupon dismissed officials, magistrates, county court judges, and others, whom they had no longer the means to pay, and attempted to obtain payments out of the Treasury on the strength of resolutions passed solely by the Lower House. At this point, however, the Ministry came into conflict with an Act of Parliament, that is, with the law of the land. The contest continued under different forms until a change in public opinion finally led to the election of a Lower House which could act with the Council. With the result of the contest we are not concerned. Three points, however, should be noticed. The conflict was ultimately terminated in accordance with the expressed will of the electors; each party during its course put in force constitutional powers hardly ever in practice exerted in England; as the Council was elective, the Ministry did not possess any means of producing harmony between the two Houses by increasing the number of the Upper House. It is certain that if the Governor could have nominated members of the Council, the Upper House would have yielded to the will of the Lower, in the same way in which the Peers always in the last resort bow to the will of the House of Commons.

Why is the personal influence of the Crown uncertain?

How is it, again, that all the understandings which are supposed to regulate the personal relation of the Crown to the actual work of government are marked by the utmost vagueness and uncertainty?

The matter is, to a certain extent at any rate, explained by the same train of thought as that which we have followed out in regard to the relation between the House of Lords and the Ministry. The revelations of political memoirs and the observation of modern public life make quite clear two points, both of which are curiously concealed under the mass of antiquated formulas which hide from view the real working of our institutions. The first is, that while every act of State is done in the name of the Crown, the real executive government of England is the Cabinet. The second is, that though the Crown has no real concern in a vast number of the transactions which take place under the Royal name, no one of the Queen's predecessors, nor, it may be presumed, the Queen herself, has ever acted upon or affected to act upon the maxim originated by Thiers, that "the King reigns but does not govern." George the Third took a leading part in the work of administration; his two sons, each in different degrees and in different ways, made their personal will and predilections tell on the government of the country. No one really supposes that there is not a sphere, though a vaguely defined sphere, in which the personal will of the Queen has under the constitution very considerable influence. The strangeness of this state of things is, or rather would be to any one who had not been accustomed from his youth to the mystery and formalism of English constitutionalism, that the rules or customs which regulate the personal action of the Crown are utterly vague and undefined. The reason of this will, however, be obvious to any one who has followed these chapters. The personal influence of the Crown exists, not because acts of State are done formally in the Crown's name, but because neither the legal sovereign power, namely Parliament, nor the political sovereign, namely the nation, wishes that the reigning monarch should be without personal weight in the government of the country. The customs or understandings which regulate or control the exercise of the Queen's personal influence are vague and indefinite, both because statesmen feel that the matter is one hardly to be dealt with by precise rules, and because no human being knows how far and to what extent the nation wishes that the voice of the reigning monarch should command attention.[1] All that can be asserted with certainty is, that on this matter the practice of the Crown and the wishes of the nation have from time to time varied. George the Third made no use of the so-called veto which had been used by William the Third; but he more than once insisted upon his will being obeyed in matters of the highest importance. None of his successors have after the manner of George the Third made their personal will decisive as to general measures of policy. In small things as much as in great one can discern a tendency to transfer to the Cabinet powers once actually exercised by the King. The scene between Jeanie Deans and Queen Caroline is a true picture of a scene which might have taken place under George the Second; George the Third's firmness secured the execution of Dr. Dodd. At the present day the right of pardon belongs in fact

[1] See Evatt, *The King and his Dominion Governors* (1936), for a plea for the formulation of conventional rules which determine the Sovereign's exercise of his powers.

Part III.

to the Home Secretary. A modern Jeanie Deans would be referred to the Home Office; the question whether a popular preacher should pay the penalty of his crimes would now, with no great advantage to the country, be answered, not by the Sovereign, but by the Cabinet.

The effect of surviving prerogatives of Crown.

What, again, is the real effect produced by the survival of prerogative powers?

Here we must distinguish two different things, namely, the way in which the existence of the prerogative affects the personal influence of the Sovereign, and the way in which it affects the power of the executive government.

The fact that all important acts of State are done in the name of the Sovereign[1] and in most cases with the cognisance of the Sovereign, and that many of these acts, such, for example, as the appointment of judges or the creation of bishops, or the conduct of negotiations with foreign powers and the like, are exempt from the direct control or supervision of Parliament, gives the reigning monarch an opportunity for exercising great influence on the conduct of affairs; and Bagehot has marked out, with his usual subtlety, the mode in which the mere necessity under which Ministers are placed of consulting with and giving information to the Sovereign secures a wide sphere for the exercise of legitimate influence by a constitutional ruler.

But though it were a great error to underrate the extent to which the formal authority of the Crown confers real power upon the Queen, the far more

[1] In the case of most modern Departments, the Minister is empowered to act in his own name by and on behalf of the Crown.

important matter is to notice the way in which the survival of the prerogative affects the position of the Cabinet. It leaves in the hands of the Premier and his colleagues, large powers which can be exercised, and constantly are exercised, free from Parliamentary control. This is especially the case in all foreign affairs. Parliament may censure a Ministry for misconduct in regard to the foreign policy of the country. But a treaty made by the Crown, or in fact by the Cabinet, is valid without the authority or sanction of Parliament; and it is even open to question whether the treaty-making power of the executive might not in some cases override the law of the land.[1] However this may be, it is not Parliament, but the Ministry, who direct the diplomacy of the nation, and virtually decide all questions of peace or war. The founders of the American Union showed their full appreciation of the latitude left to the executive government under the English constitution by one of the most remarkable of their innovations upon it. They lodged the treaty-making power in the hands, not of the President, but of the President and the Senate; and further gave to the Senate a right of veto on Presidential appointments to office. These arrangements supply a valuable illustration of the way in which restrictions on the prerogative become re-

[1] The *Parlement Belge* (1879) 4 P.D. 129; on appeal (1880) 5 P.D. 197. "Whether the power [of the Crown to compel its subjects "to obey the provisions of a treaty] does exist in the case of treaties of "peace, and whether if so it exists equally in the case of treaties akin "to a treaty of peace, or whether in both or either of these cases interference with private rights can be authorised otherwise than by the "legislature, are grave questions upon which their Lordships do not "find it necessary to express an opinion."—*Walker* v. *Baird* [1892] A.C. 491, at p. 497; K. & L. 115-117.

Part III. strictions on the discretionary authority of the executive. Were the House of Lords to have conferred upon it by statute the rights of the Senate, the change in our institutions would be described with technical correctness as the limitation of the prerogative of the Crown as regards the making of treaties and of official appointments. But the true effect of the constitutional innovation would be to place a legal check on the discretionary powers of the Cabinet.

The survival of the prerogative, conferring as it does wide discretionary authority upon the Cabinet, involves a consequence which constantly escapes attention. It immensely increases the authority of the House of Commons, and ultimately of the constituencies by which that House is returned. Ministers must in the exercise of all discretionary powers inevitably obey the predominant authority in the State. When the King was the chief member of the sovereign body, Ministers were in fact no less than in name the King's servants. At periods of our history when the Peers were the most influential body in the country, the conduct of the Ministry represented with more or less fidelity the wishes of the Peerage. Now that the House of Commons has become by far the most important part of the sovereign body, the Ministry in all matters of discretion carry out, or tend to carry out, the will of the House. When however the Cabinet cannot act except by means of legislation, other considerations come into play. A law requires the sanction of the House of Lords. No government can increase its statutory authority without obtaining the sanction of the Upper

Chamber. Thus an Act of Parliament when passed represents, not the absolute wishes of the House of Commons, but these wishes as modified by the influence of the House of Lords. The Peers no doubt will in the long run conform to the wishes of the electorate. But the Peers may think that the electors will disapprove of, or at any rate be indifferent to, a bill which meets with the approval of the House of Commons. Hence while every action of the Cabinet which is done in virtue of the prerogative is in fact though not in name under the direct control of the representative chamber, all powers which can be exercised only in virtue of a statute are more or less controlled in their creation by the will of the House of Lords; they are further controlled in their exercise by the interference of the courts. One example, taken from the history of recent years, illustrates the practical effect of this difference.[1] In 1872 the Ministry of the day carried a bill through the House of Commons abolishing the system of purchase in the army. The bill was rejected by the Lords: the Cabinet then discovered that purchase could be abolished by Royal warrant, *i.e.* by something very like the exercise of the prerogative.[2] The system was then and there abolished. The change, it will probably be conceded, met with the approval, not only of the Commons, but of the electors. But it will equally be conceded that had the alteration required

[1] On this subject there are remarks worth noting in Stephen, *Life of Fawcett* (1885), pp. 271, 272.

[2] Purchase was not abolished by the prerogative in the ordinary legal sense of the term. A statute prohibited the sale of offices except in so far as might be authorised in the case of the army by Royal warrant. When therefore the warrant authorising the sale was cancelled, the statute took effect.

statutory authority the system of purchase might have continued in force up to the present day. The existence of the prerogative enabled the Ministry in this particular instance to give immediate effect to the wishes of the electors, and this is the result which, under the circumstances of modern politics, the survival of the prerogative will in every instance produce. The prerogatives of the Crown have become the privileges of the people, and any one who wants to see how widely these privileges may conceivably be stretched as the House of Commons becomes more and more the direct representative of the true sovereign, should weigh well the words in which Bagehot describes the powers which can still legally be exercised by the Crown without consulting Parliament; and should remember that these powers can now be exercised by a Cabinet who are really servants, not of the Crown, but of a representative chamber which in its turn obeys the behests of the electors.

"I said in this book that it would very much sur-"prise people if they were only told how many things "the Queen could do without consulting Parliament, "and it certainly has so proved, for when the Queen "abolished purchase in the army by an act of pre-"rogative (after the Lords had rejected the bill for "doing so), there was a great and general astonishment.

"But this is nothing to what the Queen can by law "do without consulting Parliament. Not to mention "other things, she could disband the army (by law "she cannot engage more than a certain number of "men, but she is not obliged to engage any men); "she could dismiss all the officers, from the General "commanding-in-chief downwards; she could dis-

Chapter XV.

"miss all the sailors too; she could sell off all our "ships-of-war and all our naval stores; she could "make a peace by the sacrifice of Cornwall, and begin "a war for the conquest of Brittany. She could make "every citizen in the United Kingdom, male or "female, a peer; she could make every parish in "the United Kingdom a 'university'; she could "dismiss most of the civil servants; she could pardon "all offenders. In a word, the Queen could by "prerogative upset all the action of civil govern- "ment within the government, could disgrace the "nation by a bad war or peace, and could, by dis- "banding our forces, whether land or sea, leave us "defenceless against foreign nations."[1]

If government by Parliament is ever transformed into government by the House of Commons, the transformation will, it may be conjectured, be effected by use of the prerogatives of the Crown.[2]

Conclusion

Let us cast back a glance for a moment at the results which we have obtained by surveying the English constitution from its legal side.

The constitution when thus looked at ceases to appear a "sort of maze"; it is seen to consist of two different parts; the one part is made up of understandings, customs, or conventions which, not being enforced by the courts, are in no true sense of the word laws; the other part is made up of rules which are

[1] Bagehot, *English Constitution* (1872 ed.), Intro. pp. xxxv, xxxvi.

[2] Or, as in 1832 and 1911, by the threat of its use, *e.g.* to create peers. See Jennings, *Cabinet Government* (3rd ed., 1959), pp. 428-448, esp. 445.

Dicey, by modern standards, over-emphasises in these pages the importance of the prerogative. Modern government is a matter largely of statutory power.—ED.

Part III. enforced by the courts, and which, whether embodied in statutes or not, are laws in the strictest sense of the term, and make up the true law of the constitution.

This law of the constitution is, we have further found, in spite of all appearances to the contrary, the true foundation on which the English polity rests, and it gives in truth even to the conventional element of constitutional law such force as it really possesses.[1]

The law of the constitution, again, is in all its branches the result of two guiding principles, which have been gradually worked out by the more or less conscious efforts of generations of English statesmen and lawyers.

The first of these principles is the sovereignty of Parliament, which means in effect the gradual transfer of power from the Crown to a body which has come more and more to represent the nation.[2] This curious

[1] See pp. 439-454, *ante*.

[2] A few words may be in place as to the method by which this transfer was accomplished. The leaders of the English people in their contests with Royal power never attempted, except in periods of revolutionary violence, to destroy or dissipate the authority of the Crown as head of the State. Their policy, continued through centuries, was to leave the power of the King untouched, but to bind down the action of the Crown to recognised modes of procedure which, if observed, would secure first the supremacy of the law, and ultimately the sovereignty of the nation. The King was acknowledged to be supreme judge, but it was early established that he could act judicially only in and through his courts; the King was recognised as the only legislator, but he could enact no valid law except as King in Parliament; the King held in his hands all the prerogatives of the executive government, but, as was after long struggles determined, he could legally exercise these prerogatives only through Ministers who were members of his Council, and incurred responsibility for his acts. Thus the personal will of the King was gradually identified with and transformed into the lawful and legally expressed will of the Crown. This transformation was based upon the constant use of fictions. It bears on its face that it was the invention of lawyers. If proof of this

process, by which the personal authority of the King has been turned into the sovereignty of the King in Parliament, has had two effects: it has put an end to the arbitrary powers of the monarch; it has preserved intact and undiminished the supreme authority of the State.

The second of these principles is what I have called the "rule of law," or the supremacy throughout all our institutions of the ordinary law of the land. This rule of law, which means at bottom the right of the courts to punish any illegal act by whomsoever committed, is of the very essence of English institutions. If the sovereignty of Parliament gives the form, the supremacy of the law of the land determines the substance of our constitution. The English constitution in short, which appears when looked at from one point of view to be a mere collection of practices or customs, turns out, when examined in its legal aspect, to be more truly than any other polity in the world, except the Constitution of the United States,[1] based on the law of the land.

When we see what are the principles which truly

were wanted, the author found it in the fact that the "Parliaments" of France towards the end of the eighteenth century tried to use against the fully-developed despotism of the French monarchy, fictions recalling the arts by which, at a far earlier period, English constitutionalists had nominally checked the encroachments, while really diminishing the sphere, of the royal prerogative. Legal statesmanship bears everywhere the same character. See Rocquain, *L'esprit révolutionnaire avant la Révolution* (1878).

[1] The constitution of the United States, as it actually exists, rests to a considerable extent on case law.

Marshall, C.J., as the "expounder of the constitution," may almost be reckoned among the builders, if not the founders, of the American policy. See for a collection of his judgments on constitutional questions, *The Writings of John Marshall on the Federal Constitution* (1839).

underlie the English polity, we also perceive how rarely they have been followed by foreign statesmen who more or less intended to copy the constitution of England. The sovereignty of Parliament is an idea fundamentally inconsistent with the notions which govern the inflexible or rigid constitutions existing in by far the most important of the countries which have adopted any scheme of representative government. The "rule of law" is a conception which in the United States indeed has received a development beyond that which it has reached in England; but it is an idea not so much unknown to as deliberately rejected by the constitution-makers of France, and of other continental countries which have followed French guidance. For the supremacy of the law of the land means in the last resort the right of the judges to control the executive government, whilst the *séparation des pouvoirs* means, as construed by Frenchmen, the right of the government to control the judges. The authority of the Courts of Law as understood in England can therefore hardly coexist with the system of *droit administratif* as it prevails in France. We may perhaps even go so far as to say that English legalism is hardly consistent with the existence of an official body which bears any true resemblance to what foreigners call "the administration." To say this is not to assert that foreign forms of government are necessarily inferior to the English constitution, or unsuited for a civilised and free people. All that necessarily results from an analysis of our institutions, and a comparison of them with the institutions of foreign countries, is, that the English constitution is still marked, far more deeply than is generally supposed, by peculiar features, and that these peculiar characteristics may be summed up in the combination of Parliamentary Sovereignty with the Rule of Law.[1]

[1] Compare Intro. pp. clxxix *et seq.*, *ante*; Jennings, *Cabinet Government* (3rd ed., 1959); *The Law and the Constitution* (4th ed., 1952), pp. 126 *et seq.* The objections to the contentions advanced in this chapter are that many conventions are unsupported by law, that it is a fallacy to assume that law can be enforced against a Government, that it is difficult to determine in many cases what is the line between law and convention. Jennings concluded that a Government obeys a rule, whether law or convention, because it is concerned with the attitude of the House of Commons to its proposed action.—Ed.

APPENDIX 1

DROIT ADMINISTRATIF IN FRANCE

BY

P. M. GAUDEMET

Professor in the Faculty of Law, University of Nancy

THE expression, *droit administratif*, has three different meanings. It is desirable to define these before giving the principal characteristics of French *droit administratif*.

(I) DEFINITION OF *DROIT ADMINISTRATIF*

Like the other branches of law, *droit administratif* is firstly a matter of scientific study, second, a body of specific legal provisions, and there is also a third conception of *droit administratif*, when Dicey compares the French *droit administratif* with the English rule of law ; here *droit administratif* means organisation of public administration within the French legal system, the organisation called by Hauriou the *régime administratif*. These three conceptions of *droit administratif* must be analysed one after the other.

(A) *The Science of Droit Administratif*

In this respect *droit administratif* is the part of internal public law concerning the organisation of the administrative authorities and the relations of public administration with the citizens. Thus, in his treatise on *droit administratif*, Professor A. de Laubadère gives the following definition of *droit administratif* : " *la branche du droit public interne qui comprend l'organisation et l'activité de ce que l'on appelle couramment l'administration, c'est à dire l'ensemble des autorités, agents et organismes, chargés, sous l'impulsion des pouvoirs politiques, d'assurer les multiples interventions de l'Etat moderne.*" Here, *droit administratif* is opposed to the other part of internal public law, *droit constitutionnel*; one is the law of public administration, the other the law of government.

The field of *droit administratif* is very large, and to-day is increasingly so, as the public authorities have had their functions extended in the economic life of the nation. The best evidence of this development is in the fact that the teaching of *droit administratif* in the law faculties was formerly organised for one year only, whereas since the reform of legal studies in 1954 two years are devoted to this study. The first, which is compulsory for all legal students, is devoted to *droit administratif général*, the second, which is reserved for students specialising in public law and political science, is devoted to the law of *les grands services publics*.

Many subjects are studied in *droit administratif général* and one can distinguish three principal divisions in this science.

(1) The first is devoted to the organic structure of public administration. Here the textbooks on *droit administratif* explain the management of the central administrative authorities, such as the ministries and the great advisory councils. They state the principles of the local government of the *départements* and the *communes* and the structure of the public corporations managing industrial services. The treatises on *droit administratif* classify the categories of status of State officials and administrative authorities who are employed to manage these services, describe how they are appointed or dismissed, enumerate their duties and their rights, and explain how the civil service is organised. The organic structure of public administration also involves the study of the legal status of public property, in particular the rules concerning compulsory purchase for the public utilities and those concerning the *domaine public*, such as roads, rivers and fortifications.

(2) The second part of *droit administratif général* is devoted to the operation of public administration. It is a function of *droit administratif* to determine how the public services

operate to meet the needs of the citizens. Here the writers formulate the theory of the so-called *actes administratifs* and analyse the rules concerning contracts and torts between the public authorities and the private citizens. They study the relations between public officials and public corporations and citizens. Thus they are concerned with the rights and duties of those who make use of a public service, with the obligations of a contractor for public works as well as with the remedies which are available to an individual who has suffered injury at the hands of an official. This last topic, however, is on the borderline of the third division of *droit administratif*.

(3) The third division of *droit administratif* is the *contentieux administratif*, *i.e.* the study of the control of the administrative authorities by the administrative courts. And it is this which is the most original part of French *droit administratif*. In all countries there are special agencies which are entrusted with the satisfaction of collective needs and in all countries their management and their activities can be studied, but the control of the administrative agencies by administrative courts is specially developed in France and for many people *contentieux administratif* is the whole of *droit administratif*. In fact, as we have seen, it is only a part, but the most interesting one.

In *contentieux administratif* the legal writers expound the organic structure of the administrative tribunals and their proceedings. They define the jurisdiction of the administrative courts. They specify the powers of these tribunals with regard to administrative authorities, the civil servants and the citizens. And generally they determine what legal rules are applied by these courts.

Hitherto most of the works on *droit administratif* have been devoted to these three principal divisions. But with the growth of specialised public services and of the State intervention in economics this *droit administratif général* has become insufficient and a new branch of *droit administratif* has been created, *le droit des grands services publics*. This branch is very young and there are not yet many works about these topics. The first lectures on *le droit des grands services publics* were given in the French faculties of law in November, 1958. This *droit administratif spécial* will be more descriptive than *droit administratif général.* It will deal with the management and the structure of the various public services, such as Education, Army, Health and Transport. It will also explain the status of the nationalised corporations, such as *Electricité de France* and *Charbonnages de France*, and describe the various private, semi-public or public corporations created to satisfy the collective needs of the citizens. Here *droit administratif* comes close to administrative science, which has also considerably developed in France of recent years.

(B) *The Rules of Droit Administratif*

The second notion of *droit administratif* is a body of juridical rules. There are two possible definitions of these rules.

The first is a comprehensive definition where *droit administratif* includes all the legal rules governing the organisation and the activities of the administrative authorities, in particular their relations with private persons. Two kinds of rules are applied to civil servants and to the administrative authorities. Some are the same rules as in private law, *i.e.* the rules of family, company or property law, which are applied by the ordinary courts ; others are special legal rules completely different from those of private law, which are applied by special courts, the administrative courts. When, for instance, an officer buys some vegetables from a farmer to provide his soldiers with food during manœuvres, the contract is governed by the rules of private law, and the ordinary courts are competent in case of litigation. On the contrary, if a privately owned lorry falls in a river because a bridge has fallen into a state of disrepair, the liability of the State for the accident is governed by special rules applied by special courts. In both cases the rules can be called rules of *droit administratif lato sensu,* because in both cases these rules are applied to public authorities.

In this first comprehensive conception *droit administratif* then can be defined as the law applied by and to public administration. There is also a second conception which is more limited but which is in fact much more important. In this limited conception *droit administratif* includes only those legal rules governing the administrative activity which are different from the rules of private law and which are applied by the administrative courts. These rules form an autonomous province in French law and French legal writers can really talk of *l'autonomie du droit administratif*. This principle of *autonomie du droit administratif* must be clearly understood, though its realisation is not very easy for an English lawyer familiar with the universality of the common law. The meaning of the principle is clearly stated by Professor A. de Laubadère in his treatise, when he writes that it implies that "*les règles spéciales de celui-ci* (*le droit administratif*) *ne font pas figure de dérogations à un droit commun*." Thus, when the administrative judge brings out a rule applicable to a case, he is wholly free from private law and applies the rule of *droit administratif* following the special needs of administration. As the *commissaire du gouvernement*, Rivet told the *Conseil d'Etat* in his *conclusions* in the *Olive* case (C.E. 25 Nov., 1921), "*Vous êtes maîtres de votre jurisprudence. A vous de la créer . . . en ne retenant les règles du Code Civil que dans la mesure où l'application en est compatible avec les nécessités de la vie collective. . . .*" Thus the rules of *droit administratif* are not an exception to the rules of private law; they compose a body of rules wholly independent of them. This *autonomie du droit administratif* is fairly new in France. In the nineteenth century the civil law was held to be the common law in France and was set aside only when a special Act laid down a rule diverging from the civil law. It is the merit of the *Conseil d'Etat* and of the textbook writers, especially of Edouard Laferrière, to have freed *droit administratif* from its subjection to civil law. The principle of this *autonomie du droit administratif* was vigorously stated in the *Blanco* case (T.C. 8 Feb., 1873) in which the *Tribunal des Conflits* asserted that the liability of the administrative bodies "*ne peut être régie par les principes qui sont établis dans le Code Civil . . . elle a ses règles spéciales.*"

Although the principle of *autonomie du droit administratif* is now firmly laid down, we must not overrate its implications. For instance, although the *autonomie* means that the body of the rules of *droit administratif* is independent of the body of the rules of the civil law, it does not imply that what is laid down in administrative rules is always totally different from the civil equivalent. On the contrary, since Governments have been called upon to govern more extensively and to take a more active part in the economy of the nation and since individual citizens have been called upon to co-operate more closely with the administrative bodies, there is a trend towards lessening the distance between what is laid down in private and in public law. Nevertheless, each body remains wholly independent.

This independence of the rules of *droit administratif* and the rules of civil law creates the problem of the limits between the two kinds of rules and leads us to ask what is the criterion of administrative law. There has been much controversy over this question and opinions have varied greatly. Even now, the matter is still under discussion. In the nineteenth century, with Laferrière and afterwards with Berthélemy, the doctrine distinguished two kinds of State activity: *l'activité de puissance publique*, when the State makes use of the public power, and *l'activité de gestion*, when it runs a service in the same way as an individual citizen would. In the first case the rules applied are those of *droit administratif*; in the second they are the rules of private law. When, for instance, the mayor orders the destruction of a building on the point of collapse it is an activity of *puissance publique*, and *droit administratif* is applied. When, however, the mayor sells the wood felled in the *commune*, it is an activity of *gestion* and the rules of private law are applied.

But this criterion was abandoned because the province of *droit administratif* was then too limited. A new criterion, that of *service public*, was applied at the beginning of the twentieth century. According to this criterion, when the administrative activity is not organised as a *service public*, private law is applied and the ordinary courts are competent; but when it is organised as a *service public* the rules of *droit administratif* are applied and litigation is decided by the administrative courts. Nevertheless the whole activity of the *service public* is not governed by *droit administratif*. In the *service public* the administrative body can voluntarily and exceptionally choose the machinery of private law, in which case private law is applied and the ordinary courts are competent. When, for instance, a *commune* leases a vicarage to the vicar, there is no *service public* and the lease is governed by private law. On the other hand, when the fire brigade of the city extinguishes a fire, it is a *service public* and its activity is governed by *droit administratif*; nevertheless when the captain buys some helmets for his firemen, he can choose the machinery of private law (*i.e.* purchase) and not the public procedure of requisition, and the contract is governed by the principles of civil law.

This criterion of *service public* was specially applied in the first half of the twentieth century by Duguit and Jèze. To-day, however, the notion of *service public* is very vague, especially since the increase in number of administrative bodies entrusted with industrial and commercial services and the improvement of the co-operation of the individual for the satisfaction of collective needs. And for many *services publics*, in particular for the industrial and commercial services, and for all *services publics qu'aucune particularité ne distingue des organisations similaires relevant des personnes ou des institutions de droit privé* (*Naliato*. T.C. 22 Jan. 1955), the application of private law is no longer exceptional, but normal.

So we are led to look for a new criterion of *droit administratif*. Some writers, amongst whom is Professor de Laubadère, suggest the criterion of *gestion publique*. Here, *droit administratif* governs the activity of the administrative bodies when they run the *service public* according to the procedure of *gestion publique*, but private law is applied for the activity of *gestion privée*. The test of the *gestion publique* is not necessarily the use of the privileges of *puissance publique*, but more generally the unusual nature, *caractère exorbitant*, of the administrative activity. This criterion of *gestion publique* is fairly vague. So the borderline between private law and *droit administratif* is still uncertain and there is no absolutely sure criterion of *droit administratif*.

(C) *Le Régime Administratif*

When Dicey compares the English principle of rule of law with the French *droit administratif* he is not thinking of the *science du droit administratif*, because the rule of law is not a science ; neither is he thinking of the body of rules of *droit administratif*, because the rule of law is not a body of rules. What he means by the French words, *droit administratif*, is the peculiar juridical system governing French public administration as opposed to the legal system implied by the rule of law. In this instance French authors generally do not use the expression, *droit administratif*, as Dicey did, but they employ, as does Hauriou, the words *régime administratif*. This *régime administratif* is typical of the French legal system and we must describe its contents and give its justification.

Two features characterise the French *régime administratif* and oppose it to the English rule of law. The first is that the administrative bodies in France are not supervised by the ordinary courts. The second is the establishment of special administrative courts.

(1) The notion of the independence of the administrative bodies of the ordinary courts is a fundamental principle of French law. On the one hand it means that the ordinary courts cannot interfere with the life of the administration ; they are not competent for litigation involving the application of rules of *droit administratif* ; they are forbidden to exercise jurisdiction over administrative bodies whether by way of injunction or the award of damages against them. On the other hand it means that the administrative authorities are able without the co-operation of the courts to take decisions binding the citizens and are able to compel them to carry them out ; *i.e.* the administrative bodies possess the so-called *pouvoir d'action d'office*.

This separation of the administrative bodies and the courts is regarded in France as a consequence of the principle of the separation of powers ; this separation was ordered by the famous Act of 16-24 August 1790, which forbids the courts to interfere in any way in the working of the administrative bodies. In fact, this Act was less an application of the principle of the separation of powers than the result of the distrust prevailing in France towards the courts since the abuses committed by the *Parlements* before the French Revolution.

The independence of the administrative bodies from the control of the ordinary courts could jeopardise the right of the individual and the liberty of the administration means some risk of leading to despotism. Nevertheless the *régime administratif* is not despotic ; this is due to the second principle governing the organisation of French administration.

(2) Although the administrative bodies are not supervised by the ordinary courts, they are not free from all control. The second feature characterising the *régime administratif* is the supervision of the administrative bodies by special administrative tribunals.

There are many administrative tribunals in France. Some, such as the *Cour des Comptes*, *Conseil des Prises*, *Cour de Discipline Budgétaire*, *Conseils de Revision*, *Conseil Supérieur de l'Education Nationale*, and a few special tribunals for war pensions or war damages, have jurisdiction in specialised matters ; others are competent for the whole of *droit administratif*. These are the *Tribunaux Administratifs* (twenty-three in number) of Metropolitan France, which have been the ordinary tribunals for administrative matters since the decree of 30 September 1953, and the *Conseil d'Etat*.

The *Conseil d'Etat* is the most important institution of the *régime administratif*. Created by Bonaparte in the Constitution of the Year VIII (1800), it is now governed by the Ordinance of 31 July 1945. It is composed for the most part of civil servants recruited by the competitive examination of the *Ecole d'Administration*, but the Government can also appoint a quarter of the *maîtres des requêtes* and a third of the *conseillers* from " outsiders " without competitive examination. The members of the *Conseil d'Etat* are not irremovable, as are the judges in the ordinary courts. The *conseillers* can be dismissed by *décret en Conseil des Ministres*. The Presidency of the *Conseil d'Etat* is vested in the Prime Minister, but he delegates this function to the Minister of Justice. On the face of it, the *Conseil d'Etat* is not an independent institution like a court. But as a matter of fact it is very independent. For though theoretically the members of the *Conseil d'Etat* can be dismissed by the political authorities, they have the same security of tenure as the judges in the ordinary courts. Nor would public opinion allow nowadays that a member should be removed merely on the grounds of his activity in a judicial capacity in the *Conseil.* The promotion of the members of the *Conseil* is governed by precise rules guaranteeing their independence. The Minister of Justice does not interfere in the judicial activities. He presides only over purely formal sittings, and as a matter of fact the real presidency is assumed by an independent vice-president. Thus the independence of the members of the *Conseil d'Etat* is complete, and nobody would dare to challenge it.

This independence is very important because the *Conseil d'Etat* is not only a purely administrative body giving advice to the Government in administrative matters, but it is also a tribunal and hence impartiality must be its first characteristic.

The function of the *Conseil d'Etat* as an administrative tribunal is extremely important. Although it is no longer the ordinary tribunal for administrative matters, it is nevertheless still the tribunal of first and last instance for many cases, especially for the *recours pour excès de pouvoir* against the *décrets* and for litigation concerning the individual status of civil servants appointed by *décrets.* It is also a Court of Appeal (*Cour de Cassation*) for all the other administrative tribunals, including the *Cour des Comptes.* Thus all the administrative tribunals, whether specialised or not, are subordinated to the *Conseil d'Etat.* This superior position of the *Conseil d'Etat* is very important. It secures the unity of *droit administratif*, because all decisions of administrative tribunals are subject to review by the *Conseil d'Etat* on points of law. It secures also *l'autonomie du droit administratif* because no decision of the *Conseil d'Etat* or of another administrative tribunal can be reviewed by the ordinary courts.

Thanks to the *Conseil d'Etat* the administrative tribunals in France possess a cohesion and an autonomy unknown in countries where, as for instance in England, there are many administrative tribunals, but no general administrative appeal tribunal such as was proposed by Professor Robson to the Committee on Tribunals and Inquiries.

This body of administrative tribunals must be protected against the possible interference of the ordinary courts. To prevent the competence of the administrative tribunals being reduced by the ordinary courts, the latter cannot decide whether a given case falls within the jurisdiction of the judicial courts or of the administrative tribunals. This power is given to a separate *Tribunal des Conflits* created by the Act of 24 May 1872. The decisions of this tribunal, whose structure is still that as stated by Professor Dicey, endeavour to define the province of competence of the judicial courts and administrative tribunals. From these decisions the doctrine has tried to bring out the criterion of *droit administratif*, as we have seen. Though the *Tribunal des Conflits* is presided over by the Minister of Justice in order to maintain the balance between the judicial courts, *i.e. Cour de Cassation*, and the administrative courts, *i.e. Conseil d'Etat*, it is really an independent court. The Minister of Justice seldom presides in person, in fact only six times between 1872 and 1950. He intervenes only when the voices of the ordinary members of the tribunal are equally divided, and he then has a casting vote.

Thus the organisation of the administrative tribunals in the French *régime administratif* meets the requirements of an administrative jurisdiction, such as that recommended in the Report of the Committee on Tribunals and Inquiries for the United Kingdom.

(*a*) Openness. Although generally the procedure is written, all the documents must be communicated to the opponent (*Leven*, C.E. 14 May 1937). (*b*) Fairness. Although the procedure is *inquisitoire*, *i.e.* directed by the judge, it is very cheap and many facilities are given to the plaintiff to state his case before an administrative tribunal. (*c*) Impartiality. Although the members of the administrative tribunals, in particular those of the *Conseil d'Etat*, are not legally irremovable, they are in fact neutral, and their impartiality in relation to the policy of the Government is practically secured.

The *régime administratif*, contrary to an old belief, is not machinery directed " to support a scheme of rational absolutism." On the contrary, it guarantees the improvement of *droit administratif* in France which is, as we shall see, especially liberal.

(II) CHARACTERISTICS OF *DROIT ADMINISTRATIF*

Two principal characteristics particularise the French *droit administratif*. One is that it is "judge-made law"; the other is that *droit administratif* establishes a very harmonious " balance between private right and public advantage, between fair play for the individual and efficiency of administration." These two characteristics must be explained.

(A) A judge-made law. As Dicey stated very clearly, the French *droit administratif* is essentially judge-made law, case law, and " it resembles English law far more closely than does the codified civil law of France." Certainly there are some written laws and regulations in *droit administratif*. But these texts are not the most important parts. Generally these laws and regulations govern a very specific matter, for instance the Press Law of 1881 or the *Décrets* of 8 August and 30 October 1935 concerning compulsory purchase, or the law of 5 April 1937 concerning the liability of teachers. Generally, however, the fundamental principles of *droit administratif* are not enacted; they flow from the decisions of the *Conseil d'Etat*. Thus the structure of *droit administratif* is opposed to that of *droit civil*; for in *droit civil* the principles are written in the *code civil* and it is only concerning detail of application that solutions are sought in the decisions of the courts. For instance, the fundamental principles of civil liability are stated by Articles 1382 ff. of the *Code Civil*, but the rules of liability in case of car accidents are fixed by decisions of the ordinary courts. By contrast the fundamental rules of *droit administratif* are stated in leading cases by the *Conseil d'Etat*, with certain particular subjects being regulated by enacted law or *décrets*. The general principle of the liability of the State and of civil servants, for instance, is stated in decisions of the *Conseil d'Etat* or the *Tribunal des Conflits*, such as the cases of *Blanco* (T.C. 8 February 1873), *Pelletier* (T.C. 30 July 1873), *Lemonnier* (C.E. 26 July 1918), *Laruelle* (C.E. 28 July 1951), but the liability in a few particular circumstances is fixed by enacted law such as the Acts of 5 April 1884 and 16 April 1915 concerning the liability of municipal corporations in case of riot or the Act of 5 April 1937 concerning the liability of teachers.

This special structure of the *droit administratif*, which is very unusual in the framework of an habitually codified French law, is easily explained. In *droit administratif* the rejection of the rules of private law which resulted from *autonomie du droit administratif* caused a *vacuum juris*. It was impossible for the legislator to enact new laws which could take the place of the rules of private law. So, for want of written rules, the administrative judges, *i.e.* the *Conseil d'Etat*, were compelled to state the fundamental principles of the new *droit administratif* in their decisions. Thus the rules of administrative liability, of administrative contracts, of nullification of administrative decisions and of public property, are all judge-made rules.

Although *droit administratif* is case law, there is a written *code administratif*. Moreover, there is now a trend towards the codification of *droit administratif*. But these codifications are quite different from Napoleonic codifications of private law. They are not the enactment of customs and general principles applied by the courts, but merely either the grouping of the principal administrative laws and regulations or the methodical editing of the laws and regulations in force at the date of publication and governing some very definite subject matter, such as public health, mines and town planning. Thus the fundamental principles of *droit administratif* are, and remain, stated by the decisions of the *Conseil d'Etat*. It is still essentially judge-made law.

This characteristic of *droit administratif* leads to a second, namely, flexibility. As the rules of *droit administratif* are not written, they have a flexibility which permits constant adaptation to changes in the administrative life. It is true that the *Conseil d'Etat* seldom reverses the principles of its decisions. And there are very few *revirements de jurispru-*

dence, even though the *Conseil d'Etat* is not bound as the English courts are by the *stare decisis* principle. But the *Conseil* is very cautious ; it gives the grounds of its decisions very shortly ; it avoids employing formulae which bind it for the future. A continual evolution of *droit administratif* ensures an almost immediate adaptation of its solutions to new problems and the new requirements of the juridical conscience. Thus the rules concerning the liability of the State have evolved without any action on the part of the legislature from a position of non-liability to one far more binding than for individual citizens.

In this way the flexibility of *droit administratif* facilitates the improvement of its liberalism, which is now one of its most important characteristics.

(B) The balance between private rights and public benefit. The *autonomie du droit administratif* allows a very special balance between private rights and public benefit. The possibility of the administrative tribunals creating new and specific legal rules explains how the problems concerning public administration have received solutions adapted to their specific needs. The organic structure of the administration and the special needs of the public corporations, combined with the necessity of safeguarding the rights of individual citizens, requires specific rules for the organisation of the administration. Thus the best justification of the *régime administratif* is no longer the former French conception of the separation of powers and the law of 16-24 August 1790, but the increasingly technical character of administrative problems. When in fact the *Conseil d'Etat* formulates *droit administratif*, it considers the technical needs of public corporations without neglecting private rights. Thus two characteristics are conspicuous in the balance fixed by *droit administratif* between public and private needs. The first is the maintenance of the prerogatives of the public corporations. The second is the defence of individuals' rights and liberties by the administrative tribunals.

(1) The prerogatives of public corporations. As Dicey explained so clearly, the *régime administratif* was marked by its Napoleonic origin. The attempt pursued with marked

continuity by the ancient monarchy, the Revolution and Napoleon to establish an hierarchical and centralised State in France endowed it with a strong administration. This strong administration requires extensive special powers which are not given to individual citizens. So *droit administratif* granted and still grants special rights to public corporations, the so-called *privilèges de l'administration* which are typical of the *régime administratif*.

We have already mentioned the *privilège d'action d'office* which empowers civil servants to enforce their decisions without having recourse to the courts. In like manner, there is *privilège du Trésor*, which permits the State to be paid before all the other creditors. The rights of requisition and expropriation empower public corporations to acquire property without the consent of the owner. There is also a privilege of public authorities whereby they have the monopoly of compulsory measures towards individuals and are secure from any coercion on the part of private citizens. One can quote too the privilege of civil servants who are specially protected against attack by a system of penalties established by law.

With all these privileges the French administration might well appear as not only strong but also dictatorial and France might be taken for a police State. However, she is not so, for as Professor Waline wrote, " *c'est inconcevable du pays de la déclaration des droits de l'homme, très individualiste, sinon autant que les pays anglo-saxons.*" And although the *Conseil d'Etat* has maintained the traditional privileges of public corporations, it has developed a very special system for the protection of individual rights and civil liberties against the possible attacks of the public authorities. This trend was already perceived by Dicey, but has been considerably increased since the time when he wrote. In spite of its Napoleonic origin the *Conseil d'Etat* is the bulwark of civil liberties in France to-day. Thus the defence of individual rights is one of the most typical features of French *droit administratif*.

(2) The defence of individual rights. Although the prerogatives of public authorities are very extensive, they are not absolute. In order to defend private citizens against the

public corporations, the administrative courts have established two principal limitations on their activities : viz. they must not act against the law and they must pay damages when they cause injuries.

The supervision of the legality of administrative activity has enabled the *Conseil d'Etat* to take decisions protecting individual rights. So the *recours pour excès de pouvoir* enables private citizens whose interests are injured by an *acte administratif* to obtain its nullification by the administrative courts when this *acte* is *ultra vires.*

This procedure is one of the best means given to individuals to protect them against the abuses of public corporations. It is much cheaper than proceedings in the ordinary courts and does not require the assistance of a barrister. It is very wide. For instance, the taxpayer of a *commune* or *département* is entitled to claim the nullification of a decision increasing the liabilities of the corporation. (*Hivet,* C.E. 25 March 1955.) In the overseas territories, where most of the taxes are purchase taxes, all the purchasers, *i.e.* practically all the inhabitants, can bring an action for the nullification of decisions increasing the liabilities or the taxes of the territory. (*Galandou Diouf,* C.E. 24 June 1932.) This *recours pour excès de pouvoir* empowers the *Conseil d'Etat* to supervise the form and content of administrative decisions ; it can also supervise the grounds, notably in case of nullification for *détournement de pouvoir.* So the *Conseil d'Etat* can be called *le gardien de la moralité administrative.*

The other very important proceedings protecting individuals against the wrongs of public corporations are the actions for damages. When the *régime administratif* was established, there was in theory no liability of the State or of public corporations. Now this principle is wholly reversed. The liability of the State has been progressively admitted. At first when the State caused wrongs through fault it was possible for the plaintiff to obtain damages. Now the *Conseil d'Etat* even grants damages for injuries caused without fault by State or public corporations. Since the case *La Fleurette* (C.E. 14 January 1938) the *Conseil d'Etat* even grants damages for injuries caused to individual citizens by Acts of

Parliament. Also to-day it is frequently easier to obtain damages from the State through the *Conseil d'Etat* than from private persons through the ordinary courts. For a long time the damages granted by the administrative courts were not very high. The *Conseil d'Etat*, sparing of public money, did not always grant sufficient damages and the injured citizen was not wholly compensated. But for some years now the *Conseil d'Etat*, deferring to the criticisms of legal writers, has increased its measure of damages. The decisions of the administrative tribunals also are more and more favourable to the individual persons injured by the public corporations or by civil servants.

In conclusion, we can maintain that in spite of its origins *droit administratif* is one of the best protections of the French citizen against the " new despotism " of public administration. The *Conseil d'Etat* has succeeded in establishing a *droit administratif* which is the bulwark of civil liberties. Here, like common law in England, judge-made law gives to the private citizen the best security against the abuse of power.

SHORT MODERN BIBLIOGRAPHY

Textbooks :

Duez et Debeyre : *Traité de droit administratif*, 1952 (*mise à jour* 1955).

de Laubadère : *Traité élémentaire de droit administratif* (2nd ed.), 1957.

Rolland : *Précis de droit administratif* (11th ed.), 1957.

Vedel : *Manuel de droit administratif* (tome 1), 1957.

Waline : *Traité de droit administratif* (8th ed.), 1959.

Summaries :

Jurisclasseur administratif (5 vol.), *sous la direction de MM. Mihura et Liet Veaux.*

Long, Weil, Braibant : *Les Grand Arrêts de la jurisprudence administrative* (2nd ed.), 1958.

Special Works :

Chapus : *Responsabilité publique et responsabilité privée*, 1954 (*mise à jour* 1957).

de Corail : *La Crise de la notion juridique de service public en droit administratif français*, 1954.

Jeanneau : *Les Principes généraux du droit dans la jurisprudence administrative*, 1954.

de Laubadère : *Traité théorique et pratique des contrats administratifs* (3 vol.), 1956.

Letourneur et Meric : *Conseil d'Etat et juridiction administrative*, 1955.

Plantey : *Traité pratique de la fonction publique*, 1956.

Vedel : *Les Bases constitutionnelles du droit administratif* (*in* Conseil d'Etat : *Etudes et documents*, 1954).

Reviews :

Actualité juridique—Droit administratif.

Conseil d'Etat. *Etudes et documents* (publication annuelle).

Revue administrative.

Revue du droit public et de la science politique.

Revue pratique de droit administratif.

APPENDIX 2

THE DEVELOPMENT OF ADMINISTRATIVE LAW IN ENGLAND[1]

By A. V. Dicey

The Board of Education v. *Rice* [1911] A.C. 179, 80 L.J.K.B. 796, and *Local Government Board* v. *Arlidge* [1915] A.C. 120, 84 L.J.K.B. 72, ought to be read together. They each deserve the most careful attention of all students interested in the development of the English system of government or in the growth of the legislative opinion which in effect governs parliamentary legislation. Each case finally lays down, as far as the courts of England are concerned, a clear and distinct principle by which any department of the Government, such for example as the Board of Education, must be guarded in the exercise of powers conferred upon it by statute. The *Board of Education* v. *Rice* establishes, or rather illustrates, in its application to particular circumstances, the principle that any power conferred upon a Government department by a statute must be exercised in strict conformity with the terms of the statute, and that any action by such department which is not so exercised should be treated by a court of law as invalid. This is all that the judgment of the House of Lords in reality decides. This should be noted, for *Board of Educa-*

[1] This article is reproduced from Vol. 31 (1915) by kind permission of Professor A. L. Goodhart, the Editor of the *Law Quarterly Review*. To him, and to the publishers, Messrs. Stevens & Sons Ltd., the editor of the present book wishes to express his indebtedness.

tion v. *Rice* suggests, and in a sense raises, a question of more popular interest, namely, whether under the Education Act, 1902, s. 7, a local authority is bound to treat every elementary school subject to its control with strict equality, or whether it may lawfully, whilst duly and efficiently maintaining each school under its control, give advantages to one class of school not bestowed upon another class. To this inquiry the judgment of the House of Lords gives no answer. The *Local Government Board* v. *Arlidge* in strictness establishes the principle, which is open to considerable doubt (as appears from the reversal by the House of Lords of the judgment delivered in this case by the Court of Appeal[1]), that when a statute confers upon a Government department judicial or quasi-judicial jurisdiction (in the matters with which the department is concerned) and does not lay down any rule how this jurisdiction is to be exercised, the department is not bound to adopt the rules of procedure followed by English courts, but is certainly at liberty, and probably is intended by Parliament, to exercise this jurisdiction in accordance with the rules adhered to by the department in the conduct of its usual business. This principle may be stated in a slightly different form: a Government department when it exercises judicial or quasi-judicial jurisdiction under a statute is bound to act with judicial fairness and equity, but is not in any way bound to follow the rules of procedure which prevail in English courts.[2]

The principles enunciated in these two judgments of the House of Lords are in themselves of high importance; they undoubtedly are now part of the law of the land which can be modified only by Act of Parliament. They also raise the following general question: Has recent legislation, as now interpreted by English courts, introduced or tended to introduce into the law of England a body of administrative law resembling in spirit, though certainly by no means identical with, the administrative law (*droit administratif*) which has for centuries been known to, and during the last hundred years been carefully developed by, the jurists and legislators of

[1] See [1914] 1 K.B. 160; 83 L.J.K.B. 86.

[2] See judgment of Lord Haldane, etc. [1915] A.C., at pp. 132, 133.

France? This is an inquiry which does not admit of an off-hand answer. The right reply is not directly given, but yet is suggested by the following considerations:

First. During the last fifty years, and notably since the beginning of the twentieth century, the nation as represented in Parliament has undertaken to perform the large number of duties with which before the Reform Act of 1832 no English Government had any concern whatever. This assertion is so obviously and admittedly true that it is hardly necessary to produce evidence in its support. If any critic doubts its substantial accuracy he should study the long line of Elementary Education Acts dating from 1870, the Old Age Pensions Acts, 1908 and 1911, and the National Insurance Acts, 1911 and 1913. Even the cursory examination of these three statutes alone will certainly remove scepticism.

Secondly. The imposition upon the Government of new duties inevitably necessitates the acquisition by the Government of extended authority. But this extension of authority almost implies, and certainly has in fact promoted, the transference to departments of the central government (*e.g.* to the Board of Education or the Local Government Board) of judicial or quasi-judicial functions. Of course, it is conceivable that in a country such as England where a strict rule of law [1] had been for generations accepted by the people, a great number of administrative questions might, in the nineteenth or even in the twentieth century, have been wholly left for their determination to the law courts. Something of this kind is in reality the method pursued by the Workmen's Compensation Act, 1906, which in effect enacts that claims for compensation under the Act shall be settled by arbitration as therein provided or, if either party objects, by a county court judge. But it is obvious enough that there is great convenience in leaving to a Government department, which deals with any business in which large numbers of persons are interested (such, for example, as the payment of old age pensions, national health insurance or unemployment insurance), power to decide questions which are more or less of a judicial character. In other words, it becomes almost

[1] See *Law of the Constitution*, pt. ii, ch. iv.

inevitable that jurisdiction should be given to a department of the Government or to officials very closely connected with such department. The objection to bestowing upon the Government of the day, or upon servants of the Crown who come within the control or the influence of the Cabinet functions which in their nature belong to the law courts, is obvious. Such transference of authority saps the foundation of that rule of law which has been for generations a leading feature of the English constitution. But we must remember that when the State undertakes the management of business properly so called, and business which hitherto has been carried on by each individual citizen simply with a view to his own interest, the Government, or, in the language of English law, the servants of the Crown, will be found to need that freedom of action necessarily possessed by every private person in the management of his own personal concerns. If a man of business were to try to conduct his own affairs in accordance with the rules which, quite properly, guide our judges in the administration of justice, he would discover at the end of the year he had realised no profit and had come near to bankruptcy. How could any trade prosper if it were in the hands of a man who could not dismiss a clerk until the employer had obtained conclusive proof of fraud or misconduct by the servant, or if no evidence were allowed to tell against the alleged delinquent unless it were what lawyers consider the very "best evidence"? The management of business, in short, is not the same thing as the conduct of a trial. The two things must in many respects be governed by totally different rules.

Thirdly. When judicial functions, which involve jurisdiction, are transferred by statute from a law court to a Government department (*e.g.* to the Local Government Board) it is possible to entertain one or two different and opposed views as to the effects of this transfer. The Local Government Board, it may be said on the one hand, is called upon to exercise judicial functions, or in other words jurisdiction; and hence it follows that the Local Government Board must, when acting as a judge, comply with the rules of judicial procedure. This in the case of *Local Government Board* v. *Arlidge* was the conclusion arrived at by the Court of Appeal. On the other hand, it may be said that the transference of jurisdiction from a court to the Local Government Board is in itself prima facie evidence that Parliament intended that such jurisdiction should be exercised in accordance, not with the rules which govern judicial procedure, but with the rules which govern the fair transaction of business by the Local Government Board. This is the conclusion arrived at by the King's Bench Division and by the House of Lords. There is a great deal to be said in favour of each view. The conjecture may be hazarded that if under any Act of Parliament the question decided by *Local Government Board* v. *Arlidge* could in 1860 have been brought before the House of Lords, their lordships would probably have adopted the same view as has been maintained by the Court of Appeal. It may also, however, be suggested that the conclusion arrived at by the House of Lords is in harmony with the legislative opinion dominant in 1915. The cautious observer can, however, not shut his eyes to the fact that the decision of the House of Lords in *Local Government Board* v. *Arlidge* may have far-reaching consequences. It may lead to the result that any Government department which is authorised by statute to exercise judicial or quasi-judicial authority may, or rather must, exercise it in accordance, not with the procedure of the law courts, but with the rules which are found to be fair and convenient in the transaction of the business with which the department is officially concerned.

Fourthly. There remain two checks upon the abuse of judicial or quasi-judicial powers by a Government department. In the first place, every department in the exercise of any power possessed by it must conform precisely to the language of any statute by which the power is given to the department, and if the department fails to observe this rule the courts of justice may treat its action as a nullity. This is the effect of *Board of Education* v. *Rice*. In the second place, a Government department must exercise any power which it possesses, and above all any judicial power, in the spirit of judicial fairness and equity, though it is not bound to adopt the rules appropriate to the procedure of the law courts. This duty of compliance with the rules of fair dealing is insisted upon by the House of Lords in *Local Government Board* v. *Arlidge*, and it is probable that in some form or other the English courts will always find the means for correcting the injustice, if demonstrated, of any exercise by a Government department of judicial or quasi-judicial authority.

The Lord Chancellor, be it observed, when delivering judgment in *Local Government Board* v. *Arlidge*, refers to the fact that the "Minister at the head of the Board is directly responsible to Parliament like other Ministers," and lays down that "provided the work is done judicially and fairly . . . the only authority that can review what has been done in Parliament to which the Minister in charge is responsible." This reference to so-called ministerial responsibility is somewhat unfortunate. It is calculated to promote the belief that such ministerial responsibility is a real check upon the action of a Minister or a Cabinet when tempted to evade or override the law of the land. But any man who will look plain facts in the face will see in a moment that ministerial liability to the censure not in fact by Parliament, nor even by the House of Commons, but by the party majority who keep the Government in office, is a very feeble guarantee indeed against the action which evades the authority of the law courts. A Cabinet is rarely indeed tempted to defy the wishes of the majority of the House of Commons since it is the support of that majority which keeps the Cabinet in office. If a Minister or the Government is tempted to evade in some form or other the authority of the law, the temptation must arise from the fact that his action is desired, or at lowest will not be censured, by the majority of the House of Commons. It were [*sic*] an exaggeration to say that ministerial responsibility is an unmeaning term. It does mean the necessity of conforming to the wishes of the party which forms a majority of the House of Commons and keeps a Ministry in power, but it is no security whatever that a Cabinet will scrupulously obey that rule of law which has been created, and must be enforced, if at all, by the power of the law courts.

If anyone will weigh the above consideration he will, it is submitted, be able to answer, though still with some hesitation, the inquiry raised in this article. Modern legislation and that dominant legislative opinion which in reality controls the action of Parliament have undoubtedly conferred upon the Cabinet, or upon the servants of the Crown who may be influenced or guided by the Cabinet, a considerable amount of judicial or quasi-judicial authority. This is a considerable step towards the introduction among us of something like the *droit administratif* of France, but the fact that the ordinary law courts can deal with any actual and provable breach of the law committed by any servant of the Crown still preserves that rule of law which is fatal to the existence of true *droit administratif*. Nor, in a period of rapid and revolutionary change, though generally unaccompanied by violence, is it useless to bear in mind that impeachment is still part of the law of England, and that impeachment is the legal action of the High Court of Parliament.

APPENDIX 3

SHORT BIBLIOGRAPHY OF MODERN AUTHORITIES

BOOKS

ALLEN, SIR CARLETON. *Law and Orders* (2nd ed., 1956).
Administrative Jurisdiction (1956).

AMERY, L. S. *Thoughts on the Constitution* (1953).

DAWSON, R. M. *The Government of Canada* (2nd ed., 1956).

DENNING, LORD. *Freedom under the Law*, Hamlyn Lecture (1949).

DICEY, A. V. *Law and Opinion in England during the Nineteenth Century* (2nd ed., 1914).

DICEY, A. V., and Rait, R. S. *Thoughts on the Union between England and Scotland.*

EMDEN, C. S. *The People and the Constitution* (2nd ed., 1956).

FRIEDMANN, W. *Principles of Australian Administrative Law* (1950).
Law and Social Change in Contemporary Britain (1951).
Legal Theory (3rd ed., 1953).

GRIFFITH, J. A. C., and STREET, H. *The Principles of Administrative Law* (2nd ed., 1957).

HAMSON, C. J. *Executive Discretion and Judicial Control*, Hamlyn Lecture (1954).

HANBURY, H. G. *Vinerian Chair and Legal Education* (1958).

HILLS, J. W., and FELLOWES, E. A. *Finance of Government* (2nd ed., 1932).

HUGHES, C. *The Federal Constitution of Switzerland* (1954).

JENNINGS, SIR IVOR. *Cabinet Government* (3rd ed., 1959).
Parliament (2nd ed., 1957).
The Law and the Constitution (4th ed., 1952).

KEIR, SIR DAVID, and LAWSON, F. H. *Cases in Constitutional Law* (4th ed., 1954).

MacDermott, Lord. *Protection from Power under English Law*, Hamlyn Lecture (1957).

McWhinney, E. *Judicial Review in the English Speaking World* (1956).

Marshall, G. *Parliamentary Sovereignty and the Commonwealth* (1957).

May, H. J. *The South African Constitution* (3rd ed., 1955).

Rait, R. S. (Editor). *Memorials of A. V. Dicey* (1925).

Robson, W. A. *Justice and Administrative Law* (3rd ed., 1951).

Schwartz, B. *Law and the Executive in Britain. A Comparative Study* (1949).

French Administrative Law and the Common Law World (1954).

American Constitutional Law (1955).

American Administrative Law (2nd ed., 1958).

Sieghart, M. A. *Government by Decree: A Comparative Study of the Ordinance in English and French Law* (1950).

Street, H. *Governmental Liability: A Comparative Study* (1953).

Vernon, R. V., and Mansergh, N. *Advisory Bodies: A Study of their uses in relation to Central Government 1919–1939* (1940).

Wheare, K. C. *The Statute of Westminster and Dominion Status* (5th ed., 1953).

Federal Government (3rd ed., 1953).

Government by Committee: An Essay on the British Constitution (1955).

Willis, J. *The Parliamentary Powers of English Government Departments* (1933).

Articles

Allen, Sir Carleton. " Parliament and Ultra Vires " (1956), 72 *L.Q.R.* 29.

Beinart, B. " Sovereignty and the Law," *Tydskrif vir Hedendaagse Romeins Hollandse Reg* (1952), 101.

Centlivres, A. van de S. " The South African Constitution and the Rule of Law," *Butterworth's S.A. Law Rev.* (1956), 3.

Cowen, D. V. " The Constitutional Crisis in South Africa," *Journal of the Society of Clerks-at-the-Table* (1951), 149, and (1952), 91.

" Legislature and Judiciary " (1952), 15 *M.L.R.* 282, and (1953), 16 *M.L.R.* 273.

" The Entrenched Sections of the South Africa Act: Two Great Legal Battles " (1953), 70 *S.A.L.J.* 238.

Cowen, Zelman. " The Injunction and Parliamentary Process " (1955), 71 *L.Q.R.* 336.

de Smith, S. A. " The Limits of Judicial Review: Statutory Discretion and the Doctrine of Ultra Vires " (1948), 11 *M.L.R.* 309.

Friedmann, W. " Trethowan's Case, Parliamentary Sovereignty and the Limits of Legal Changes " (1950), 24 *Australian L.J.* 104.

Gray, H. R. " The Sovereignty of Parliament Today " (1953), 10 *University of Toronto Law Journal*, 54.

Griswold, E. N. " The Coloured Vote Case in South Africa " (1952), 66 *Harvard Law Review* 1361.

" The Demise of the High Court of Parliament in South Africa " (1953), 66 *Harvard Law Review* 864.

Hamson, C. J. " Executive Discretion and Judicial Control " (Hamlyn Lecture, 1954).

Jennings, Sir Ivor. " The Makings of a Dominion Constitution " (1949), 65 *L.Q.R.* 456.

McWhinney, E. " The Union Parliament, The Supreme Court and the Entrenched Clauses of the South Africa Act " (1952), 30 *C.B.R.* 692.

" The New High Court of Parliament " (1952), 30 *C.B.R.* 734.

" Sovereignty in the United Kingdom and the Commonwealth Countries at the Present Day " (1953), 68 *Pol. Sci. Qu.* 511.

Sawer, G. " Injunction, Parliamentary Process, and the Restriction of Parliamentary Competence " (1944), 60 *L.Q.R.* 83.

Smith, T. B. " The Union of 1707 as Fundamental Law " (1957), *Public Law*, 99.

Wade, E. C. S. " Administration under the Law " (1957), 73 *L.Q.R.* 470.

Wade, H. W. R. " The Twilight of Natural Justice ? " (1951), 67 *L.Q.R.* 103.

" The Basis of Legal Sovereignty " (1955), *C.L.J.* 172.

" The Senate Act Case and the Entrenched Sections of the South Africa Act " (1957), 74 *S.A.L.J.* 160.

Official Publications

Report of the Committee on Ministers' Powers. Cmd. 4060 (1932).

Report of the Committee on Administrative Tribunals and Public Inquiries. Cmd. 218 (1957).

Parliament Bill, 1947: Agreed Statement of Party Leaders. Cmd. 7380 (1948).

TABLE OF STATUTES

A

B

C

I

J

L

M

N

O

U

V

W

TABLE OF CASES[1]

A

B

[1] Decisions of the *Conseil d'Etat* (*see* App. 1) are not included.

C

D

E

F

G

H

N

O

P

Q

GENERAL INDEX

A

G

I

J

K

L

M

S

T

U

V

W

PRINTED BY R. & R. CLARK, LTD., EDINBURGH